SHORT LOAN

THIS ITEM MAY BE BORROWED UP TO
THE DATE/TIME INDICATED BELOW

PLEASE NOTE,
ITEMS MAY *NOT* BE RENEWED BY TELEPHONE OR ON-LINE

FINES ARE IN OPERATION

1 5 NOV 2010

BY 2PM

1 8 NOV 2010

BY 2PM

Global Cases
on Hospitality Industry

Vinnie Jauhari
Editor

Routledge
Taylor & Francis Group

NEW YORK AND LONDON

First Published by

The Haworth Press, Taylor & Francis Group, 270 Madison Avenue, New York, NY 10016.

Transferred to Digital Printing 2010 by Routledge
270 Madison Ave, New York NY 10016
2 Park Square, Milton Park, Abingdon, Oxon, OX14 4RN

For more information on this book or to order, visit
http://www.haworthpress.com/store/product.asp?sku=5923

or call 1-800-HAWORTH (800-429-6784) in the United States and Canada
or (607) 722-5857 outside the United States and Canada

or contact orders@HaworthPress.com

Cover design by Jennifer M. Gaska.

Library of Congress Cataloging-in-Publication Data

Global cases on hospitality industry / Vinnie Jauhari, editor.
    p. cm.
  ISBN: 978-0-7890-3415-1 (hard : alk. paper)
  ISBN: 978-0-7890-3416-8 (soft : alk. paper)
  1. Hospitality industry. I. Jauhari, Vinnie.

  TX907.G54 2008
  338.4'791—dc22   2007046208

Dedicated to my family for continued
support in all my endeavors

CONTENTS

ABOUT THE EDITOR

Vinnie Jauhari, PhD, is Professor and the Head of the School of Management and Entrepreneurship at IIMT, and founding editor of the *Journal of Services Research.* She has over seventy publications in national and international journals and has also authored several books. Her area of expertise is corporate entrepreneurship, strategic management, and technology issues. Dr. Jauhari is on the editorial board of the *International Journal of Contemporary Hospitality Management,* and is a guest editor for a special issue of the journal.

Contributors

Aldrin Abdullah, PhD, is faculty of the School of Housing, Building and Planning, Universiti Sains Malaysia, Minden, Penang, Malaysia.

Sajith K. Augustine is pursuing a master's degree in human resource management at Rajagiri College of Social Sciences, Rajagiri Post, Kochi, Kerala, India.

Azizi Bahauddin, PhD, is lecturer/specialist in Interior/Exhibition Design School of Housing, Building and Planning, Universiti Sains Malaysia, Minden, Penang, Malaysia.

Johannes Bauer, PhD, is faculty of rural management, the University of Sydney and Charles Sturt University, Leeds PDF, Orange, Australia.

Tom Baum, PhD, is professor of international tourism and hospitality management, The Scottish Hotel School, The University of Strathclyde, Glasgow, Scotland, UK.

Wayne Binney is lecturer in the School of Hospitality, Tourism and Marketing, Victoria University, Melbourne, Australia.

Jiaolan Bowden, PhD, is research fellow, Scottish Centre of Tourism, Aberdeen Business School, Robert Gordon University, Garthdee, Garthdee Road, Aberdeen, UK.

Sue Broad, PhD, is postdoctoral research fellow and research coordinator, Newcastle. Tourism Research Unit, Monash University, Australia.

R.W. Carter, PhD, is associate professor, University of the Sunshine Coast, Maroochydore, Queensland, Australia.

Global Cases on Hospitality Industry
© 2008 by The Haworth Press, Taylor & Francis Group. All rights reserved.
doi:10.1300/5923_b

xix

Prakash K. Chathoth, PhD, is currently an assistant professor in the School of Hotel and Tourism Management at the Hong Kong Polytechnic University.

Vincent Cho is assistant professor in the Department of Management and Marketing, The Hong Kong Polytechnic University, Hong Kong.

Kam-Ho Manson Chung is chief instructor, Vocational Training Council, Hong Kong Institute of Vocational Education, Wan Chai, Hong Kong.

T. De Lacy, PhD, is chief executive, Cooperative Research Centre for Sustainable Tourism; professor of environmental policy, University of Queensland; chair of management board, Green Globe Asia Pacific Pty Ltd., Australia.

Danielle Felix, BBus, BTourism, BBusEco, is faculty of the Tourism Research Unit, Monash University, Australia.

Vinayshil Gautam, PhD, is founder director of Indian Institute of Management Kozhikode and Dalmia chair professor of Management Department, Indian Institute of Technology–Delhi, New Delhi, India.

Maureen Griffiths is lecturer of BBus (hospitality), MBus (tourism), Department of Marketing, Monash University, Australia.

John Hall, PhD, is associate professor and associate director, Business Research Centre, Deakin Business School, Deakin University, Melbourne, Australia.

Hsin-Hui "Sunny" Hu is assistant professor, The Department of Hospitality Management, Ming-Chuan University, Taipei, Taiwan.

Hadyn Ingram, PhD, is chairman of Clovelly Hotel Limited Consultancy; professor and associate dean at Revans University, The University of Action Learning, Salisbury, Wiltshire; and a lecturer in hotel management at the University of Surrey.

Sanjay K. Jain, PhD, is professor of marketing and international business, Department of Commerce, Delhi School of Economics, University of Delhi, Delhi.

Binoy Joseph is faculty of human resources management, Rajagiri School of Social Sciences, Rajagiri Post, Kochi, Kerala, India.

Mahmood A. Khan, PhD, is professor of hospitality and tourism management, Pamplin College of Business, Virginia Tech University, Blacksburg, VA.

Maryam Khan, PhD, is director and assistant professor, Hospitality Management Program, School of Business, Howard University, Washington, DC.

Terry Lam, PhD, was associate professor, School of Hotel and Tourism Management, Hong Kong Polytechnic University, Hung Hom, Kowloon. Hong Kong. Dr. Lam passed away in May 2006.

Kyuho Lee, PhD, is assistant professor of hospitality management, School of Business, Western Carolina University, Cullowhee, North Carolina.

Sofia Lourenço is lecturer of finance and accounting, ISEG School of Economics and Management, Technical University of Lisbon, Lisbon, Portugal.

Andrew Martin is director, Scottish Centre of Tourism, Aberdeen Business School, The Robert Gordon University, Aberdeen, UK.

Badaruddin Mohamed, PhD, is associate professor in Design School of Housing, Building and Planning, Universiti Sains Malaysia, Minden, Penang, Malaysia.

Vishnuprasad Nagadevara, PhD, is professor, quantitative methods and information systems, Indian Institute of Management, Bangalore, India.

João C. Neves, PhD, is professor of finance and control, ISEG School of Economics and Management, Technical University of Lisbon, Lisbon, Portugal; visiting professor of accounting and control, HEC School of Management, Paris, France.

Michael D. Olsen, PhD, is professor in the Department of Hospitality and Tourism Management, Pamplin College of Business, Virginia Tech University, Blacksburg, VA.

G. Barry O' Mahony, PhD, is director of Centre for Hospitality and Tourism Research, Victoria University, Melbourne City MC, Victoria, Australia.

H.G. Parsa, PhD, FMP, is associate professor and graduate coordinator of hospitality management, Department of Consumer Sciences, The Ohio State University, Columbus, OH.

Ray Pine, PhD, is professor, School of Hotel and Tourism Management, The Hong Kong Polytechnic University, Kowloon, Hong Kong.

Pingshu Qi is executive officer and researcher, Department of Policy and Legal, China National Tourism Administration, Beijing, China.

Henk Roest, PhD, is associate professor of marketing, Department of Marketing, Tilburg University, LE Tilburg, the Netherlands.

Angela Roper, PhD, Savoy Educational Trust; senior lecturer in hospitality management, School of Management, University of Surrey, Surrey, UK.

Shveta Singh is faculty of business administration and information technology, Indian Institute for Information Technology–Allahabad, Deoghat-Jhalwa Allahabad, India.

Stephen R. Sizer, PhD, is vicar of Christ Church, Virginia Water, Surrey; chairman of the International Bible Society (UK).

Nadine Sulkowski MSc (Hospitality), is lecturer, Department of Leisure, Tourism and Hospitality, University of Gloucestershire, Cheltenham, UK.

Vijayshri Tewari is faculty of business administration and information technology, Indian Institute for Information Technology–Allahabad, Deoghat-Jhalwa Allahabad, India.

Randall S. Upchurch, PhD, is associate professor of timeshare development, Rosen School of Hospitality Management, University of Florida, Orlando, FL; lecturer with American Resort Development Association.

Umashankar Venkatesh, PhD, is professor and dean, Institute for International Management and Technology, Udyog Vihar, Gurgaon, Haryana, India.

Chak-Keung Simon Wong, PhD, is senior lecturer, School of Hotel and Tourism Management, The Hong Kong Polytechnic University, Hong Kong.

B. Zeng, PhD, is Scientific Officer, Biodiversity Conservation (South) at Department of Natural resources, Environment and the Arts, Northern Territory Government, Northern Territory, Australia.

Preface

Travel and tourism is one of the world's largest industries. The World Travel and Tourism Council's latest projection for the industry is that a quarter of a billion people will work in travel and tourism worldwide by the end of the decade, with the prospect of sustainable growth into the future. World Tourism Organization's *Tourism 2020 Vision* (World Tourism Organization, 2007) forecasts that international arrivals will reach more than 1.56 billion by the year 2020. Of these worldwide arrivals in 2020, 1.2 billion will be intraregional, and 0.4 billion will be long-haul travelers. As per the World Tourism Organization (WTO), about 808 million tourists traveled internationally—a growth of 5.6 percent over 2004—and spent about $680 billion (U.S. dollars) (World Tourism Organization, 2007). Furthermore, according to the World Travel and Tourism Council (WTTC), tourism accounted for 10.6 percent of global gross domestic product, 12.0 percent of the total world exports, and 8.3 percent of global employment in the year 2005 (Ministry of Finance, 2007).

Of the total tourist arrivals by region by 2020, according to WTO, the top three receiving regions will be Europe (717 million tourists), East Asia and the Pacific (397 million), and Americas (282 million), followed by Africa, the Middle East, and South Asia (World Tourism Organization, 2007).

The world is rapidly changing. The closed economies are opening their doors to foreign investment. Technology has reduced the geographical distances and has had an impact on service delivery and access modes for consumers the world over. Convenience and flawless solutions are the demands of the modern consumer. Competition is increasing. Pressure has been placed on sustainable practices with resources being finite and energy costs rising. The consumer is becoming value conscious, and firms must be cost-effective. Brands from economies such as India and China are looking at international markets. Asian brands are looking at global expansion. Markets in India

Global Cases on Hospitality Industry
© 2008 by The Haworth Press, Taylor & Francis Group. All rights reserved.
doi:10.1300/5923_c

and China are growing as never before. The global giants are striving to customize their strategies to meet the local aspirations.

In light of the broader macroeconomic changes that are being witnessed, it is pertinent that the mega trends are documented and the strategies and dynamics across various countries are captured to understand the new rules of the game. This book has been conceptualized with the objective of capturing global dynamics in the hospitality industry across various strategic and functional areas.

The amount of case studies in the area of hospitality and tourism is lacking. These sectors provide employment to large number of people, and they are emerging as major growth areas in India and Asian region. A need exists to develop cases that become a useful aid in understanding the conceptual underpinnings as well.

This book is an attempt to capture some of the critical areas in management of hospitality industry, which spans across the travel and tour firms, hotels, restaurants, and tourism associations among hosts of other firms such as technology and equipment providers. It is a complex web of service providers and forward and the backward linkage firms.

This book gives a global perspective on a range of issues such as marketing, strategy, human resources, finance, entrepreneurship, and ethics. Some eminent authors from a wide spectrum of countries, such as China, India, Hong Kong, Australia, France, Malaysia, Taiwan, UK, United States, and Portugal, have contributed to this book. The book adopts a multidisciplinary approach, and it is research-based, giving credibility to the findings. The book follows the prescriptive approach and hence offers implications for the practitioners and policymakers both.

The book has been a painstaking effort with contributions from numerous authors all across the globe. I hope that reading this book will be enriching experience.

REFERENCES

Ministry of Finance (2007). Union budget and economic survey: Economic survey 2006-2007. Government of India. Available at: http://indiabudget.nic.in/es 2006-07/esmain.htm.

World Tourism Organization (2007). Facts and figures: Tourism 2020 vision. Available at: http://www.unwto.org/facts/eng/vision.htm.

Acknowledgments

This book is an outcome of contributions from many researchers, consultants, trainers, and academics from across the globe. I extend my heartfelt thanks to the contributors to this book. I thank them for their immense patience and support throughout the project.

My gratitude to Dr. Richard Teare for his very special support to this project. I especially thank the *International Journal of Contemporary Hospitality Management* for letting us use some of their published papers.

I would like to express my thanks to the team at University Relations at Hewlett Packard for supporting my academic endeavors. My very special thanks to Robert Bouzon and P. Ravindranath.

I express a deep gratitude to Mr. K.B. Kachru for his inspiration and for always paving a way for me to strive toward excellence. My special thanks to Dr. R. Kapur, Dr. K. Misra, and Dr. U. Venkatesh, for their continued support for my academic pursuits. My special thanks to all at IIMT.

I also express my gratitude to Amit, who has worked for long hours in putting the book together. He has been a tremendous help, and his continued support has helped in completing this work. My special thanks to Ashok Sahu, librarian, IIMT, and Manjit for helping me with my work at various stages.

I acknowledge immense support from my family—my husband Sunil, son Shaurya, in-laws, parents, and my brother Shallen, who have always been there for me.

Chapter 1

Culture and Its Impact on International Service Management: Exploring Global Consumers' Different Service Perceptions and Preferences in the International Hospitality Industry

Kyuho Lee
Maryam Khan

Today's global economy has expanded at an unprecedented rate in a borderless world (Ohmae, 1990). Ohmae (1995) contended that nationality or national border does not have significant meaning in the globalization era because the globalizing economy has driven global consumers to access competitive global products and services easily and in an inexpensive way. Furthermore, the rapid development of technology such as high-speed Internet, and global media such as MTV and CNN have connected global consumers in a way that they can share multinational products and brands (Fraser and Oppenheim, 1997; Ohmae, 1995).

Among all industry segments, the hospitality industry is a forerunner in developing a global market. The hospitality industry is the fastest growing service sector in the dynamic global environment. For example, Starbucks, the global coffee chain giant, currently operates its outlets in more than 100 countries, and they plan to open more than 15,000 outlets in the near future. McDonald's operates more than 16,600 outlets throughout 119 countries, and the revenue and profit from its international markets accounts for about 58 percent and 54 percent of company's total revenue and profit ("Boss talk,"

Global Cases on Hospitality Industry
© 2008 by The Haworth Press, Taylor & Francis Group. All rights reserved.
doi:10.1300/5923_01

1

2003). The U.S. fast-food chains have been able to succeed in the global markets because of a number of key attributes such as convenience, competitive prices, and the standardized operational system, which have appealed to global consumers (Miller, 2003). Furthermore, enhancing urbanization, developing transportation systems, a growing middle class, the deregulation of the service industry, and the preference of a modern urban lifestyle among developing countries provide huge opportunities for multinational hospitality operators to expand potential global markets (Merwe, 1987; Price, 1996). Also, since many national barriers related to international business, such as foreign exchange control and ownership restriction, have been eased in many developing countries, the prospect to explore global markets will likely continue (Incandela et al., 1999; Ohmae, 1995).

In order to capture these emerging opportunities, multinational hospitality operators must develop competitive global operational strategies to survive in the fierce global markets (Carman and Verbeke, 1994; Geller 1998). One of the critical challenges that the hospitality operators have often faced in developing foreign markets is to understand local cultures and tailor products and service standards accordingly (Ghemawat and Shukla, 2000; Krishna, 1987). Unlike the manufacturing industry, the nature of service requires a high degree of interaction between customers and service providers because of the inseparability of production and consumption (Carman and Verbeke, 1994; Malhotra et al., 1994). Culture plays a significant role in the interaction process between customers and service providers in many different ways, such as through customers' specific service preferences (de Mooji, 1998; Malhotra et al., 1994). Therefore, global service operators need to understand each local culture and reflect cultural impacts when developing global service operational strategies.

PROBLEM SETTINGS

The multinational service operators often rely on their domestic operation strategies and experiences in the global market rather than on developing competitive global service strategies that are designed to accommodate a specific market. Therefore, quite a few service firms failed in the foreign markets due to the lack of competitive service strategies based on the understanding of each foreign market's culture (Ghemawat and Shukla, 2000; Krishna, 1987; McLauglin and Fitzsimmons, 1996). Understanding cultural impacts in developing international service management is a growing need. Even though a substantial body of literature on domestic service management exists, to date international service management, especially in the hospitality industry, has not received much academic attention (Gronroos, 1999). In particular, a large void exists in the theoretical understanding of whether and/or how culture impacts a firm's international service management. This research attempts to fill that void by building a conceptual model of cultural roles in the establishment of the international service management.

The significant growth of the international service industry is likely to continue since all service sectors are still at the premature stage of development in the globalizing economy (Fraser and Oppenheim, 1997). On the brink of noteworthy growth in the international service sector, this study provides global hospitality operators a better understanding of cultural impacts and of how to establish international service strategies.

PURPOSE OF THE STUDY

This research is designed to answer the following questions:

- How does culture influence consumers' service perception, preferences, and expectations in the international service industry?
- What are key cultural dimensions that influence consumers' service preferences, perceptions, and expectations?

RESEARCH METHOD

A qualitative study approach was chosen in order to develop a conceptual model showing the impact of cultural roles in the development of competitive international service management. Multiple secondary data, such as document analysis and secondary literature from scholarly journals, were used in an effort to develop a conceptual model.

THE RELATIONSHIP BETWEEN CULTURE
AND INTERNATIONAL SERVICE MANAGEMENT

Cultural typologies developed by Hofstede (2001) and Hall and Hall (1990) have been employed by several researchers in an attempt to understand cultural roles on the multinational service management (Donthu and Yoo, 1998; Liu et al., 2001; Mattila, 1999a,b). Hall and Hall (1990) analyzed the underlying dimensions of culture and provided detailed definitions of culture. They developed a concept of cultural context and related it to consumers' communication patterns. The cultural context is about information flow surrounding occasions and events among people. People in a high-context culture often exchange information and share personal stories with one another (Hall and Hall, 1990). Most Asian countries belong to a high-context culture. On the other hand, people in a low-context culture are more likely to be hesitant in sharing personal information and stories with others, because people in a low-context culture value more privacy (Hall and Hall, 1990). Most Western countries belong to a low-context culture. Interestingly, most countries in high-context culture are likely to belong to collectivistic countries. At the same time, most countries in low-context culture tend to belong to individualistic countries.

Understanding the cultural context concept is critical in identifying global consumers' purchasing behaviors and in developing multinational marketing strategies. For example, the cultural context impacts consumers' word-of-mouth intents significantly (Lee et al., 2004). More specifically, consumers in a high-context culture are more likely to spread personal experiences of services and products with their friends or relatives since people in a high-context culture like to share and discuss their personal experiences with their acquaintances. Also, the information acquired through word of mouth is considered to be the most reliable information source in the high-context culture (Lee et al., 2004). On the other hand, consumers in a low-context culture are less likely to share personal stories with their friends and relatives about product and service experiences. They do not value sharing personal experiences and tend to have distance between "I" and "others" (Lee et al., 2004).

Furthermore, people in a low-context culture are more likely to rely on product and service information through objective information sources such as product brochures, books, and company homepages, whereas consumers in a high-context culture tend to depend on subjective information sources such as informal personal routes from friends or relatives (Hall and Hall, 1990). According to Hall and Hall (1990), people in high-context culture involve one another closely and keep intimate relationships, which are important to maintain a social life. Therefore, people in high-context cultures have extensive information networks from family, friends, and colleagues. These personal information networks play an important role in motivating consumers' purchases of products and services (Kim et al., 1998).

On the other hand, people in the low-context culture are likely to have relatively weak social bonds among people compared to people belonging to a high-context culture, and members in a low-context society are not involved as closely. People in low-context culture are less likely to share information. Therefore, they prefer to acquire information in an explicit way without ambiguity (de Mooji, 1998). Liu et al. (2001) found that consumers in a high-context culture have more channels through which they can share their service experiences compared to consumers in low-context culture. Therefore, the impacts of word of mouth in the high-context culture are much more powerful compared to those of word of mouth in low-context culture.

The cultural context also influences the effectiveness of service advertising (de Mooji, 1998). According to de Mooji (1998), people in high-context cultures are less likely to obtain products and services information through advertising since people in high-context culture tend to collect a great amount of information through their personal networks such as family, friends, colleagues, and clients. However, people in low-context culture consider advertising a valuable information source to gain information related to products and services (de Mooji, 1998). Therefore, people in low-context culture are more likely to prefer advertising focused on facts and data of products and services rather than advertising focusing on emotional aspects (Bradley and Thorson, 1994).

GLOBAL CASES ON HOSPITALITY INDUSTRY

Hofstede (2001) attempted to investigate the nature of culture based on data collected from about 70,000 employees across 66 different foreign subsidiaries of the IBM Corporation. Based on the data, he developed a substantial conceptual framework of culture and identified four major cultural dimensions, which can be used to distinguish cultures. The four cultural dimensions include (1) power distance, (2) uncertainty avoidance, (3) individualism versus collectivism, and (4) masculinity versus femininity. Hofstede's cultural typology has been adopted widely by a variety of researchers in many areas, such as international marketing, cross-cultural studies, and international business. Table 1.1 summarizes each dimension of culture developed by Hofstede (2001).

TABLE 1.1. Major Cultural Dimensions

Cultural Dimension		Characteristics	Countries
Power distance	Small power distance	Trend in society to minimize inequality; decentralization preferred and flatter organization	Western countries
	Larger power distance	Institutionalized hierarchies in which low and high have their place; centralization preferred	Asia and Arab
Avoidance	Weak uncertainty avoidance	Ease in the face of uncertainty; as few rules as possible	Western countries
	Strong uncertainty avoidance	Nothing should be unexpected; high tension and anxiety and strong need for formal rules to go by	Asia and Arab
Individualism	Collectivistic or low-individualistic	Individual interests should be sacrificed to the group in exchange for protection; social norms and policies valued more than individual desire	Asia and Arab
	Individualistic	"I" thinking; people are supposed to take care of their immediate families only; privacy is valued	Western countries
	Feminine	Overlapping roles of men and women; men should be modest and yielding and not more assertive than women; general sympathy for the small, slow, and weak	Western countries
	Masculine	Strict separation between sexes; men should be more assertive and aggressive; women should serve; general sympathy for the big, the fast, and the strong	Arab and Asia

Source: Adopted from Hofstede (2001).

As seen in Table 1.1, people possess different behaviors, logical thinking, work ethic, and communication based on their culture. In general, Asian countries belong to collectivistic, masculine, high risk avoidance, and high power distance culture. On the other hand, most Western countries belong to an individualistic, low risk avoidance, low masculinity, and low power distance culture. The understanding of Hofstede's four cultural typologies is crucial in analyzing global consumers' behaviors and characteristics. For example, Donthu and Yoo (1998) investigated how culture influences consumers' service expectations and preferences based on Hofstede's cultural typologies. According to the results of the study, people in high risk avoidance culture, such as Asians, are more likely to show higher service expectations in comparison to people in low risk avoidance culture. Because the desire that people in a high risk avoidance culture do not want to confront any unexpected and uncomfortable situations is much higher compared to people in low risk avoidance culture, consumers' service expectations in a high risk avoidance culture might be much stronger than that of people in low risk avoidance culture (Donthu and Yoo, 1998).

Subsequently, consumers in a high risk avoidance culture try to minimize any risk-associated service and products. As a result, consumers in a high risk avoidance culture tend to prefer purchasing well-known brand products having reputation and prestige, thereby securing high degrees of assurances related to products and services. In addition, Donthu and Yoo (1998) claimed that people in highly individualistic culture are more likely to place an importance on assurance and empathy service dimensions compared to people in a less individualistic culture. Because people in a highly individualistic society value individual attentions and personal care, certain service dimensions such as empathy have become important.

Even though Donthu and Yoo's study (1998) explains the relationships between culture and consumers' service expectation, the authors fail to reflect certain factors that might influence consumer service expectations and preferences. For instance, service firms in Asian countries are likely to focus on personalized service even though most Asian countries are a low individualistic culture. The inexpensive labor costs in many Asian countries allow service firms in the region to provide more personalized services (Gee, 1994). Consequently, Asian service firms are able to provide high personalized service, and consumers are accustomed to receive the personalized service. This is one of the probable reasons why a number of service firms in the region, such as Singapore Airlines and Mandarin Oriental Hotel chains, have established good reputations due to their high service standards.

According to Aaker (1990), typical Japanese hotels have twice the number of service staff per room compared to those of the U.S. hotels. For instance, Hotel Okura in Tokyo employs 1,600 full-time service staffers for its 880 rooms, whereas The New York Palace Hotel, which has the same level of service standards, employs only 1,000 service staff for 1,008 guest rooms. In addition to the inexpensive labor costs, many Asian hotels could provide a high employee ratio per guest room due to their strong desire for establishing high service standards (Aaker, 1990). Furthermore, the significant emphases on hiring appropriate service staff and ongoing training plays a key role in maintaining high service standards for many Asian service firms. On the other hand, Western service operators tend to place more focus on operational efficiency and saving labor costs (Gee, 1994; Schmitt and Pan, 1994).

Liu et al. (2001) discussed relationships between culture and consumers' complaining patterns. Consumers in highly individualistic cultures are more likely to complain directly to service operators if customers confront service or product problems, because people in highly individualistic cultures place a significant value on expressing their opinion freely rather than hiding their emotions. On the other hand, consumers in a highly collectivistic culture tend to avoid complaining to service providers directly regarding service problems or service dissatisfaction because consumers in a highly collectivistic culture are not comfortable in expressing their emotions to others in public (Liu et al., 2001). In addition, complaining any service failures to service providers directly in public can be considered humiliation, which might not be appropriate in a collectivistic culture in which the philosophy of living with others or forming society harmony is critical to maintain the society (Hofstede, 2001).

Huang et al. (1996) also examined the relationship between culture and consumers' complaint patterns. They compared the complaining patterns between Japanese and American consumers. According to the results of the study, American consumers are more likely to complain about any service problems to service providers, whereas Japa-

nese customers tended to avoid complaining service f
vice providers directly. Instead of solving service or product pro
lems, Japanese consumers tend instead not to return to the restaurants
that provide inappropriate services and products.

Even though Liu et al. (2001) and Huang et al. (1996) found interesting results about the relationships between consumers' complaining patterns and culture, the researchers failed to reflect certain social
variables such as age and educational levels that might affect the results of the study. For example, growing young generations in Asian
countries who have been influenced by Western culture and educational experiences might possess more individualized and Western-
ized attitudes in comparison with older generations in Asian countries. Indeed, today's young Asians are likely to express their
opinions and thought more freely in public. Therefore, it might not be
appropriate to generalize the findings of the Liu et al. (2001) and
Huang et al. (1996). Future study should be developed considering
certain factors such as demographic variables to further explore the
cross-cultural studies relevant to consumers' complaint patterns.

THE RELATIONSHIP BETWEEN SERVICE
PREFERENCES AND CULTURE

Mattila (1999a) examined how culture influences consumers' service preferences and expectations. She compared Western business
travelers' service preferences with those of Asian business travelers
on luxury hotel services. According to the results of the study, Western travelers tend to value concrete attributes on hotel services and
products. For example, Western business travelers considered hotel
room price and location as important criteria in their hotel selection,
whereas Asian consumers placed high importance on abstract hotel
service attributes such as room quietness, the speed of service, and
hotel image in their selection of a hotel. One possible reason that
Asian consumers place a high importance on abstract aspects of hotel
services and products is that Asians are accustomed to be emotional
in thinking compared to Westerners who tend to think in a logical
way (Chung, 1991). Subsequently, the results of Mattila's (1999a)
study do make sense since Westerners, placing an importance on logical thought in their decision making process, tend to consider tangi-

ble attributes of hotel services seriously, whereas Asians valuing emotional aspects emphasize the intangible attributes of hotel service and products.

Stauss and Mang (1999) examined the impacts of cultural differences on service encounters. According to them, consumers could have different evaluations and appreciations on the same service encounters. The desired service, adequate service, perceived service, and the zone of tolerance differ based on consumers' culture affiliation (Stauss and Mang, 1999). The results of the study indicated that international consumers could confront high degrees of service gaps. The characteristics of these service gaps include:

- Customer's physical environment gap: if foreign customers are not able to execute their tasks effectively because they are hindered by an unusual layout of the facilities, e.g., buffet style service
- A service customer's personnel gap: if foreign customers violate expectations regarding consumer behavior in personal interactions
- A service customer's system gap: this gap results when foreign customers are not familiar with the service systems of the service provider, e.g., unfamiliar reservation systems and queuing procedures.

Therefore, global service providers need to reflect the customer gaps in their service setting and develop competitive service design to minimize the service gaps between service providers and consumers. Pullman et al. (2001) suggested that establishing balanced combinations between standardization and customization is important in designing international service management. According to Pullman et al. (2001), global service operators call for thorough understanding of consumers' cultural norms and tailor products and services according to those norms to achieve competitive advantages in the global service industry. For example, Japanese customers like to see the pictures of entrees on menus when they choose a restaurant because of their custom in Japan (Lee and Zhao, 2003; Pullman et al., 2001). Most Japanese restaurants display either actual menu items or their pictures at the entrance of a restaurant in order to assure the quality and portion sizes of their menu items. However, very few restaurants in the United States display photos of their menu items in their restaurants.

Pullman et al. (2001) stressed that the food service operators attracting a high number of Japanese, such as restaurants in major international airports, might need to exhibit pictures of menu items to accommodate these customers' needs and preferences. Lee and Zhao (2003) also contended that the major U.S. chains in certain cities such as Hawaii, which has a high number of Japanese tourists, should focus on including products and services with Japanese traveler's needs and preferences in order to secure a competitive advantage.

Mattila (1999b) argued that service standards designed by Westerners might not reflect Asian consumers' needs and preferences properly. Western culture based on equality might ignore differences of status between service providers and consumers, which might be an important issue to Asian consumers (Mattila, 1999b). In most Asian cultures based on the high power distance, the equality between service providers and customers might not be established, and thus the relationship between customers and service providers is more likely to be hierarchic. Therefore, customers in Asia might not appreciate friendly service from servers because of high power distance between customers and service operators, unlike Western countries.

Dace (1995) suggested that customers are more valued in Japan than in Western countries. He argued that the difference in service expectation between Japanese and Westerners could be found in their definition of customer status. According to the Japanese definition, a guest is considered a god, whereas a guest is considered a king in Western civilizations. This demonstrates that a high degree of status difference exists between service operators and customers in Asian countries. In conclusion, Figure 1.1 presents the relationship between culture and its impact on international service management.

As shown in Figure 1.1, culture influences international service management in many different ways. Four major areas that become distinctly evident include service preferences, customers' complaint types, customers' service recovery preferences, and word-of-mouth intent. Based on thorough understanding of the cultural impacts on the four major areas, competitive international service strategies should be developed taking into consideration all cultural differences.

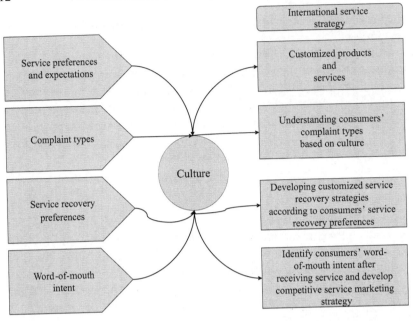

FIGURE 1.1. The Effect of Discount Format and Service Level Consumer Perception

CONCLUSION AND DISCUSSION

The objective of this study was to critically evaluate cross-cultural service literature and to understand cultural impacts on consumers' service preferences, expectations, complaint patterns, and word-of-mouth intents. The results of this study illustrate that consumers' service preferences, expectations, complaint patterns, and word-of-mouth intents differ based on consumers' culture. Subsequently, global service operators are required to reflect the cultural differences in formulating international service strategies. In particular, since service involves high degrees of human interactions, the chance of cultural incongruity or conflict between service operators and customers might be much greater than that of manufacturing industry (Gronroos, 1999; Samiee, 1999). Therefore, comprehending the cultural differences has become a critical issue in expanding global markets and succeeding in the competitive global markets (Samiee, 1999).

With growing significance of international markets in the globalizing world, more and more multinational service operators are expected to develop global markets (Gronroos, 1999). However, the development of the global market entails competitive strategic planning. A number of the U.S. restaurant chains tend to fail in international markets because of lack of strategic planning and of misunderstanding of local cultures and business environments (Kim and Chon, 2003). In particular, one of the significant reasons that many U.S. service operators have trembled and have faced high financial risks in foreign markets is because the U.S. service firms are more likely to depend on the same domestic service experiences and tactics in international markets without developing new competitive international service strategies based on the understanding of local cultures and consumers (Becker et al., 1999).

The international service industry has been changing dynamically with rapid development of globalization (Vandermerwe and Chadwick, 1989). Multinational service operators have great potential to expand foreign markets in the future. However, a real opportunity exists only for those service firms that understand cultural differences and develop sustainable competitive strategies based on the awareness of cultural differences among global consumers.

REFERENCES

Aaker, D. A. (1990). How will the Japanese compete in retail services? *California Management Review, 33*(1): 54-67.

Becker, C., Murrmann, S. K., Murrmann, K. F., and Cheung, G.W. (1999). A pancultural study of restaurant service expectations in the United States and Hong Kong. *Journal of Hospitality and Tourism Research, 23*(4): 235-255.

Boss talk: It's grande-latte world; Starbucks's CEO serves tales of global Frappuccino: green tea, or strawberries? (2003, Dec 15). *Wall Street Journal,* B1.

Carman, J. M. and Langeard. (1979). Growth strategies for service firms. *Strategic Management Journal, 1:* 7-22.

Chung, T.Z. (1991). Culture: A key to management communication between the Asian-Pacific area and Europe. *European Management Journal, 9*(4): 419-424.

de Mooji, M. (1998). *Global Marketing and Advertising: Understanding Cultural Paradoxes.* London: Sage Publications.

Donthu, N. and Yoo, B. (1998). Cultural influences on service quality expectations. *Journal of Service Research, 1*(2): 178-186.

Fraser, J. and Oppenheim. (1997). What's new about globalization? *The McKinsey Quarterly, 2:* 168-179.

Gee, C. Y. (1994). *International Hotels: Development and Management.* Lansing, MI: Educational Institute of America Hotel and Motel Association.

Geller, L. (1998). The demands of globalization on the lodging industry. *FIU Hospitality Review, 16*(1): 1-6.

Ghemawat, P. and Shukla, R. (2000). Tricon restaurants international: Globalization re-examined. *Harvard Business School Case Study,* 9-700-030.

Gronroos, C. (1999). Internationalization strategies for services. *Journal of Service Marketing, 13*(4/5): 290-297.

Hall, E. and Hall, M. (1990). *Understanding Cultural Differences.* New York: Anchor Press.

Hofstede, G. (2001). *Culture's Consequences: Comparing Values, Behaviors, Institutions and Organizations across Nations.* Thousand Oaks, CA: Sage Publications.

Huang, J., Huang, C. T., and Wu, S. (1996). National character and response unsatisfactory hotel service. *International Journal of Hospitality Management, 15*(3): 229-243.

Incandela, D., McLaughlin, K. L., and Shi, C. S. (1999). Retailers to the world. *The McKinsey Quarterly, 3:* 84-97.

Kim, D., Pan, Y., and Park, H. (1998). High versus low context culture: A comparison of Chinese, Korean, and American cultures. *Psychology and Marketing, 15*(6): 507-521.

Kim, W. G. and Chon, K. (2003). Survivorship in international chain restaurants in Korea. *FIU Hospitality Review, 21*(1): 22-32.

Krishna, E. M. (1987). Understanding the foreign market entry mode choice in service firm: An exploratory study, Unpublished doctoral dissertation, University of Arkansas, Fayetteville, Arkansas.

Lee, K., Khan, M., and Ko, J. (2004). A cross-cultural comparison of consumer perceptions: The impact of service recovery over loyalty, word-of-mouth, and future patronage intent. Presentation at the International Council on Hotel, Restaurant and Institutional Education (CHRIE) Conference, Philadelphia, PA, July 28-31.

Lee, K., and Zhao, J. (2003). Japanese travelers' service preferences in U.S. hotels. *Journal of Travel and Tourism Marketing, 14*(2): 67-85.

Liu, B. S., Furrer, O., and Sudharshan. (2001). The relationships between culture and behavioral intentions towards services. *Journal of Service Research, 4*(2): 118-129.

Malhotra, N. K., Ulgado, F. M., Agarwal, J., and Baalbaki, I. B. (1994). International service marketing. *International Marketing Review, 11*(2): 5-15.

Mattila, A. (1999a). An analysis of means-hierarchies in cross-cultural context: What motivate asian and western business travelers to stay at luxury hotels? *Journal of Hospitality & Leisure Marketing, 6*(2): 19-28.

Mattila, A. (1999b). The role of culture and purchase motivation in service encounter evaluations. *Journal of Service Marketing, 13*(4/5): 376-389.

Merwe, S. V. D. (1987). Deregulation in services and the marketing challenge. *The Service Industries Journal, 7*(1): 24-34.

Miller, L. (2003). Restaurants: We're recommending a steady diet of fast food. Prudential Equity Group Report, September 11. Newark, NJ: Prudential Equity Group.

Ohmae, G. (1990). *The Borderless World: Power and Strategy in the Interlinked Economy.* New York: Harper Business.

Ohmae, G. (1995). *The End of the Nation State: The Rise of Regional Economies.* New York The Free Press.

Price, C. C. (1996). The U.S. foodservice industry looks abroad. *Food Review, 19*(2): 13-17.

Pullman, M. E., Verma, R., and Goodale, J. C. (2001). Service design and operations strategy formulation in multicultural markets. *Journal of Operations Management, 19*: 239-254.

Samiee, S. (1999). The internationalization of services: Trends, obstacles and issues. *Journal of Service Marketing, 13*(4/5): 319-328.

Schmitt, B. H. and Pan, Y. (1994). Managing corporate and brand identities in the Asia-Pacific region. *California Management Review, 36*: 32-48.

Stauss, B. and Mang, P. (1999). Culture shocks in inter-cultural service encounters. *Journal of Service Marketing, 13*(4/5): 329-346.

Vandermerwe, S. and Chadwick, M. (1989). The internationalization of services. *The Service Industries Journal, 9*: 9-93.

Chapter 2

Effectiveness of Price Discount Levels and Formats in Service Industries

Hsin-Hui "Sunny" Hu
H. G. Parsa
Maryam Khan

Services play a major role in the world economy. In the United States, services were estimated to account for 70 percent of the gross domestic product (GDP) in 2003 (Messinger, 2003). However, the unique characteristics of services cause difficulties in pricing and promotion. Because services are intangible, consumers have difficulty accessing exactly what they are paying for. In the absence of available cues, consumers often use price as key to expect the quality of products and make purchase decisions (Kurtz and Clow, 1998). Hence, the way service providers set up the prices and promotions of the services affects consumers' purchase decisions.

Price promotions can be more readily used in services than in goods. Since the service provider is not actually losing the ownership of the service to the buyer, price cutting can be practiced more readily. The provider does lose time and effort during service delivery, but these can be offered again. In contrast, a goods manufacturer actually loses a physical object, which might be difficult to replace (Kandampully, 2002). For this reason, a service seller might feel more comfortable about offering price promotions and convincing consumers to use its services. Several studies have been done in price promotions in the retail industry (e.g. Kalwani and Yim, 1992; Raju and Hastak, 1983; Shoemaker, 1979). However, limited efforts have been exerted in determining the perceptions of consumers' responding to price promotions for services. Thus, the need exists to expand

Global Cases on Hospitality Industry
© 2008 by The Haworth Press, Taylor & Francis Group. All rights reserved.
doi:10.1300/5923_02

our knowledge and conceptualization of price promotions to include consumer responses to services price promotions.

While making price promotion decisions, service providers must consider two problems: how much the price reduction should be, and how to frame the promotion and communicate the information of price reduction (Della Bitta et al., 1981). In order to have better understanding of consumers' responses to price promotions in the service sector, the current study concentrates on (1) whether different discount formats for describing the same price promotion will influence consumers' perceptions any differently, and (2) the role of various discount levels in formation of consumer price perceptions depending on the level of services expected.

PRICE PROMOTIONS

In previous studies, the issues of price promotion and its impact on price perceptions and purchase intention in the retail industry have been widely examined (Kalwani and Yim, 1992; Raju and Hastak, 1983; Shoemaker, 1979). Price perception theories study the relationship between objective price and consumers' judgments of the price (Sawyer and Dickson, 1984). Folkes and Wheat (1995) found that framing via various types of promotions significantly affects consumers' price perceptions. Kalwani and Yim (1992) explored the field of consumers' price expectations. Their study proposed that consumers form expectations of prices and use them in formulating their response to retail pricing. Their findings reveal that consumer reaction depends not only on retail prices, but also on the comparison they make with the reservation prices. In other words, consumers use the price they expect to pay for a brand on a given purchase occasion as reference in forming price judgments. Therefore, even if different processes have been hypothesized, a cognitive process exists. This process can be described as a cognitive evaluation, made by the consumers, of the benefits of a price promotion.

Moreover, price promotions also have a significant impact on purchase behavior. Shoemaker (1979) showed that purchase acceleration was due to price promotions. His findings suggested that promotions were more apt to be associated with increased quantity than with shorter interpurchase time. Blattberg and colleagues (1981) then tried to explain the dealing of storable products based on the idea of transferring inventory-carrying costs from the retailer to the consumer. For four product classes, they found statistically significant evidence of purchase acceleration in terms of both larger quantities and shorter interpurchase times. Raju and Hastak (1983), who examined the effect of the deal's magnitude on the purchase behavior due to promotions, confirmed these results. At the individual level, however, price promotions seemed to act as a disturbing element, which inhibits negative thoughts that might arise about the brand. In summary, a good amount of empirical support exists for the impact on price perception and purchase intension due to price promotions in the context of consumer packaged goods. Also, as suggested by Lichtenstein and colleagues (1998), deal-prone consumers tend to develop links between their liking of specific price promotions and their inclination to buy products using these promotions. Indeed, the notion of transaction utility dictates the behavior of the consumer. It allows a particular psychological inducement (i.e., feeling good about using the promotion) to play the major role in directing the behavior.

SERVICE PRICE PROMOTIONS

Price remains one of the least researched aspects of marketing. Research and expertise pertaining to the pricing of services are particularly lacking (Guiltinan, 1988). In addition, limited efforts have been exerted in determining the perceptions of consumers' responding to price promotions for services. Service organizations are shifting more promotional dollars toward price promotion techniques since they tend to yield quicker and more measurable results. A summary report by Kindel (1993) indicated that some business organizations are allocating up to 75 percent of their marketing budgets to price promotions. However, price promotions for services may be evaluated in a manner different from price promotions for products. Consumer search and evaluation of services occurs prior to entering the service environment (Monroe and Guiltinan, 1975), and therefore consumers must evaluate the value of price promotions relative to search and experience qualities (Nelson, 1970). Unless consumers are aware of available price promotions before entering the service facility, the only likely function of the price promotion is to reinforce the patronage decision. Thus, the relevant information processing (exposure, attention, comprehension, acceptance, and retention) of services price promotions often occurs outside of the service environment.

In addition, effective price promotions for products could smooth demand immediately; however, for services, it may not change consumers' buying behaviors instantly. Price promotions may smooth demand directly in certain services markets, such as restaurants, but it may be difficult to do the same with other services. This is partly because the perishability of services and the inability to inventory services become "most troublesome" in demand fluctuations for services marketing (Zeithaml, 1981). Nevertheless, price promotions may affect attention and awareness. For example, when service firms include price discounts in advertisements, consumers' attention, awareness, and recall for those advertisements increase (Bearden et al., 1984). Since consumers are apt to pay attention to information that interests them and to information that is congruent with their current beliefs (Klapper, 1960), by offering price promotions business and professional organizations may generate additional awareness for their services. During their next buying situation, consumers may still be positively influenced to purchase the specific brand because of prior exposure to information (Bawa and Shoemaker, 1989). Moreover, consumers may perceive price promotion differently in high-end services and low-end services.

Consumers tend to invest more cognitive resources in high-risk situations, and higher prices are associated with greater risk (Bearden and Shimp, 1982). In addition, as stated, the price-quality literature has found that price is interpreted as an indicator of quality. Consumers tend to equate higher prices with higher quality, and relatively low prices generally are interpreted as indicators of inferior quality (Rao and Monroe, 1988; Olson, 1977). Furthermore, high-price products or services tend to be more complicated than the low-price products and/or services. For these reasons, consumers may invest more cognitive recourses in evaluating and making purchase decisions for high-end products or services than low-end products/services. Hence, consumers treat high- and low-end services differently with reference to price discounts. The current study examines the role of price discount formats and discount levels in the service context. Thus, the following hypotheses:

- H1a: Consumers' perceptions of discount formats differ depending on service levels.
- H1b: Consumers' perceptions of discount levels differ depending on service levels.

PRICE PROMOTION FRAMES

Framing effect refers to the finding that consumers respond differently to different descriptions of the same decision question (Frisch, 1993). Framing of decision problems can affect consumers' judgments and, therefore, preferences (Kahneman and Tversky, 1979). Communicating a price promotion in different formats is similar to the framing of purchase decision (Monroe, 1990). Different message formats, e.g., "dollar off," "percentage off," "2 for 1," or "Buy 1, get 1 at 1/2 price" illustrate direct reference to the price differences (Raghubir, 1992). Consumers often possibly favor one particular presentation frame over the other. Numerous studies revealed that framing price promotion in different formats affects consumer's purchase perceptions (e.g., Chen et al., 1998; Della Bitta et al., 1981; Lichtenstein et al., 1991; Raghubir, 1992).

Della Bitta and colleagues (1981) conducted an experiment to access consumer perceptions of comparative price advertisements. Their study was designed to explore the effects of different ways of presenting comparative price offers. Della Bitta and colleagues focused on the comparative information to describe a sale, such as describing a sale by dollar amount off or percent off. The findings of their study indicated that presenting a percent-off format produced a significantly lower perception of value for the money than did presenting a dollar-amount-off format. Promotions presented in dollar amount off were more positively evaluated than the percentage-off formats. Lichtensteien and colleagues (1991) examined the differential effects of two types of semantic cues, comparative prices (see elsewhere $\_\_$, our price $\_\_$) and past prices (was $\_\_$, now only $\_\_$), on consumer perceptions. By using an actual newspaper advertisement modified for the study, they learned that comparative prices influenced consumer's purchase intention more favorably than past prices. Raghubir (1992) investigated the effects of semantic cues on consumer evaluations of promotional deals, and found that "2 for $"

and "Buy 1, get 1 at 1/2 price" frames were most effective across price levels. Moreover, "save $__" frame is particularly effective at high price level, but not low price levels. Harlam and colleagues (1995) demonstrated that discounts presenting in "together" format (e.g., buy X and Y together at $__) produce highest purchase intent and "separate" (e.g., buy X at $__ and Y at $__ if buy the bundle) format produce the lowest intent. In addition, Chen and colleagues (1998) investigated how the framing of price promotions influences consumers' perceptions of these promotions and consumers' purchase intentions. An experiment was conducted to test the effects of price-discount frames by manipulating product-price level (high price versus low price), promotion types (coupon versus discount), and the presentation forms (dollar versus percentage). The results suggested that consumers evaluated a price reduction framed in dollar terms and percentage terms differently for high-end and low-end products. For high-price products, consumers perceive a price reduction framed in dollar terms as more significant than the same price reduction framed in percentage terms. Oppositely for low-price products, consumers evaluate the price reduction framed in percentage terms more positively than in dollar terms. The current study focuses only on the effect of dollar and percentage discount formats on consumer's perception in the context of services. Thus the following hypotheses:

- H2a: In case of high-end services, a difference in consumer preferences exists between dollar-off format and percentage-off format while evaluating price discounts.
- H2b: In case of low-end services, a difference in consumer preferences exists between dollar-off format and percentage-off format while evaluating price discounts

DEPTH OF PRICE REDUCTION

The effectiveness of price discounts is not only influenced by discount formats but also discount levels. A promotion threshold is the minimum value of price promotion required to change consumers' purchase intentions (Gupta and Cooper, 1992). The amount of a price reduction is a relative indicator of the depth of the reduction bounded by 0 percent and 100 percent at low and high ends. Consumers can use the amount of a price reduction to compare the relative attractiveness of price promotions and the actual monetary savings on products sold. Some of the studies have demonstrated that consumer purchase intention is indeed more sensitive to price increases than to price decreases. Changes in purchase intention due to a price increase are larger than changes in purchase intention due to a price decrease. Several studies have shown that the amount of a price reduction and the depth of price discount affect consumer's price perceptions (e.g. Della Bitta et al., 1981; Gupta and Cooper, 1992; Harlam et al., 1995; Kalwani and Yim, 1992).

Uhl and Brown (1971) postulated that the perception of a retail price change depends on the magnitude of the price change. The results of their study indicated that 5 percent deviations were identified correctly 64 percent of the time, whereas 15 percent deviations were identified correctly 84 percent of the time. Della Bitta and Monroe (1980) reported that price reductions of about 15 percent are needed to attract consumers to purchase an item. Della Bitta et al. (1981) found that consumer's perception of savings for price discount do not differ significantly between 30 percent, 40 percent, and 50 percent discounts. However, significant differences exist between the 10 percent and the 30 percent, 40 percent, and 50 percent level, and between 20 percent and 50 percent discount levels. Kalwani and Yim (1992) confirmed that a concave relationship exists between the expected price and the depth of price discounts. The results of their study revealed that significant differences exist between 30 percent and 40 percent discount levels and 10 percent and 30 percent price discounts. Gupta and Cooper (1992) investigated the existence of discount threshold level. Their study showed that consumers do not change their intentions to buy the product used in the study unless the advertisement discount meets or exceeds the 20 percent point. Moreover, promotions reach a saturation level at which the effect on consumers' purchase intentions is minimal beyond this level. Harlam et al. (1995) also confirmed that 20 percent price decreases have significant impact on consumer purchase intentions. In addition, Chen et al. (1998) postulated that for high discount levels on high-end products, emphasis should be on the relative savings, describing the deal in percentage format. On the other hand, for high discount levels on low-end products, emphasis should be on the absolute savings, describing the deal in dollar format. Thus the following hypotheses:

- H3a: In the case of high-end services, a relationship exists between consumer preferences of discount formats and discount levels.
- H3b: In case of low-end services, a relationship exists between consumer preferences of discount formats and discount levels.

METHODOLOGY

Experimental Design

To explore the role of discount formats and levels for service industry, a $2 \times 4 \times 2 \times 4$ mixed design experiment was conducted. The factors in this experiment included 2 price promotion frames (dollar off and percentage off), 4 discount levels (5 percent, 20 percent, 40 percent, and 50 percent), 2 levels of price (high end and low end) and 4 types of services (restaurants, beauty care, automotive, and hotels) requiring 8 treatment groups. Each of the four services at the two price levels received one of the two promotional frames. Different groups rated the given services on the different promotional frames with different discount levels. The eight groups received different service-frame combinations. In order to avoid the effect of the brand, no brand names were included in the price promotions. Price levels and service types were manipulated both between and across subjects. Promotion frames and discount levels were manipulated within subjects. Subjects were randomly assigned to groups and groups were randomly assigned to treatments. Order of promotion statement in the questionnaire were randomized and controlled across subjects.

Selection of Services, Price, and Discount Levels

Criteria for choice of services included services likely to be purchased by the student population and independent of gender. The services chosen were restaurants, beauty care, automotives, and hotels. The two price levels were chosen so that they were significantly different. Four services at the two price levels were pretested on a student sample. Four discount levels, 5 percent, 20 percent, 40 percent, and 50 percent were chosen. The literature in retail goods showed that price reductions of about 15 percent are needed to attract consumers to purchase an item (e.g., Della Bitta and Monroe, 1980; Harlam et al., 1995); however, the depth of price reduction may also affect consumers' perceptions of the qualities of the services. In addition, the literature reported inconsistent results for different discount levels. In the context of service, the low discount level (5 percent) was chosen to examine the quality perception of price reduction.

Procedure and Dependent Variables

Respondents were randomly assigned to the eight treatment groups. Each respondent received a short booklet that contained the instructions and survey questions about the price promotions. All booklets looked exactly the same, and subjects were unaware of manipulations of key information in the price promotions. In a regular classroom setting, the introduction was projected to a screen and subjects were told that the study would investigate how consumers evaluate and respond to price promotions. Three main dependent measures were used to evaluate a subject's perception of the promotions: value perception, quality perception, and purchase intentions. These measures were recorded by using a seven-point Likert-type scale. The scales for value perceptions were measured by statements such as "trivial saving" or "significant saving," "attractive or unattractive," and "good or bad" (Raghubir, 1992). Quality perceptions measured by "very high quality" or "very low quality." Finally, purchase intentions were measured by "definitely will buy" or "definitely will not buy."

RESULTS AND DISCUSSIONS

Discount Format

The obtained data were analyzed using ANOVA with SPSS. High- and low-end services were analyzed for the effect of discount frames, dollar off, and percentage off. Results indicated that a significant interaction occurs between the service level and discount format (F_1, $344 = 14.19$, $p < .001$) (Figure 2.1). The results were supported by value perception (F_1, $344 = 14.40$, $p < .001$), quality perception (F_1, $344 = 6.98$, $p < .01$), and purchase intention (F_1, $344 = 11.50$, $p < .001$). Thus, we supported the hypothesis H1a, and concluded that a

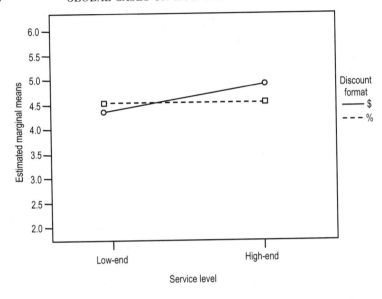

FIGURE 2.1. The Effect of Discount Format and Service Level on Consumer Perception

significant main effect of discount format exists across all measures. The effects of different discount formats on consumers' perception significantly differ depending on services levels.

Then high- and low-end services were compared for differences in price discounts both in dollar and percentage formats. An interaction effect existed between the service levels and the discount formats on subjects' perceptions of the significance of the price reduction. In case of high-end services, subjects have higher overall perception ($F1, 344 = 11.17, p < .01$), value perception ($F1, 344 = 12.40, p < .01$), quality perception ($F1, 344 = 5.19, p < .03$), and purchase intention ($F1, 344 = 7.58, p < .02$) for dollar format. Thus the hypothesis H2a was supported.

In case of high-end services, subjects perceived the price discount presented in dollar format as more significant than the same price discount presented in percentage format. On the other hand, results for low-end services indicated that subjects prefer percentage format on overall perception ($F1, 344 = 7.94, p < .02$), value perception ($F1, 344 = 7.92, p < .02$), and purchase intention ($F1, 344 = 7.04, p < .02$), but not for perceive quality (F1, 344 = 3.05, p < .10). Therefore, hypothesis H2b was also supported. For low-end services, subjects tend to have higher perceptions for percentage discount format than dollar format.

Discount Level

According to Table 2.1, the differences in mean values of quality perception, value perception, and purchase intention at the 5 percent price discount level were significantly less than the mean values for the 20 percent, 40 percent, and 50 percent discount levels. Although for a low discount level (5 percent) subjects have relatively higher mean values for quality perceptions, their purchase intentions are still lower than that of higher discount levels. On the other hand, subjects' quality perception have not increased much when the discount levels changed from 40 percent price reductions to 50 percent price reductions; however, their purchase intentions increase significantly (Figure 2.2). Consequently, the depth of price reduction may affect subjects' quality intentions; however, their purchase intentions increase dramatically as the depth of the price reductions increase.

Analysis continued with discount levels in high- and low-end service levels. The obtained results demonstrated that consumers perceived discount levels differently than the service levels (F3, 2,744 = 5.69, p < .001). The results were supported by value perceptions (F3, 2,744 = 4.32, p < .006), quality perceptions (F3, 2,744 = 7.38, p < .001), and purchase intentions (F3, 2,744 = 3.17, p < .03). Therefore, hypothesis H1b was supported.

Subjects tend to have higher perceptions for price discounts in high-end services than in low-end services within different discount

TABLE 2.1. Means for Consumer Perceptions

Discount Level	N	Quality Mean	Value Mean	PI Mean
5%	687	3.11	2.90	2.63
20%	688	4.18	4.46	4.27
40%	689	4.83	5.15	5.02
50%	688	5.07	5.57	5.45

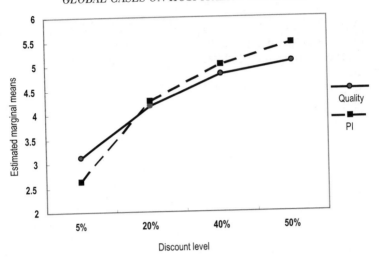

FIGURE 2.2. The Effect of Discount Level on Consumer Quality Perception and Purchase Intention

levels. This finding implies that price discounts on the high-end services were evaluated as more significant than those on the low-end services. High- and low-end services were then compared for differences in price discount levels. According to Figures 2.3 and 2.4, when evaluating the price reductions for high-end services, subjects' quality perceptions (X = 4.87 and X = 4.51) and purchase intentions (X = 5.04 and X = 5.69) continuously increase as price reductions increase from 40 percent to 50 percent. In contrast, when evaluating the price reductions of low-end services, subjects' quality perceptions dropped (X = 4.80 and X = 4.63) and purchase intentions increase only slightly (X = 5.00 and X = 5.22) as price reductions increase from 40 percent to 50 percent. Interestingly, for low-end services, subjects perceive quality significantly lower $(F1, 2,744 = 47.24, p < .001)$ in high discount level (50 percent) compared to the high-end services. These findings imply that in the case of low-end services, high discount level (50 percent) may lower consumers' quality perceptions and may not motivate their purchase intentions.

When discount formats were introduced into the equation, a significant interaction occurred between the service level, discount format, and discount level on overall subjects' perceptions $(F3, 2,736 =$

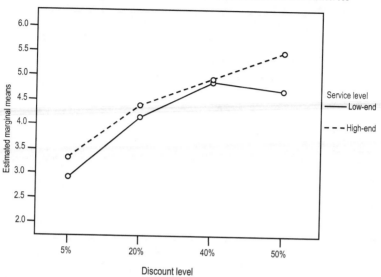

FIGURE 2.3. The Effect of Discount Level and Service Level on Consumer Quality Perceptions

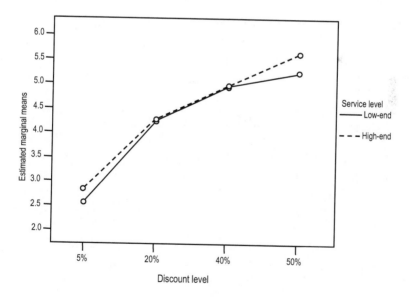

FIGURE 2.4. The Effect of Discount Level and Service Level on Consumer Purchase Intentions

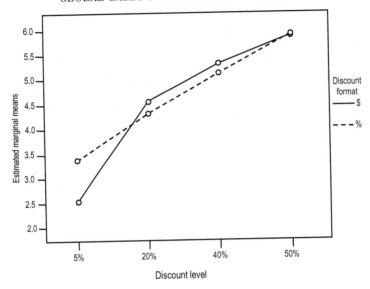

FIGURE 2.5. The Effect of Discount Level and Discount Format at High-End Services

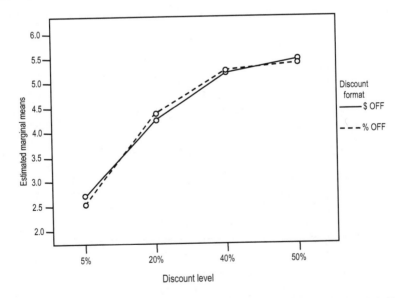

FIGURE 2.6. The Effect of Discount Level and Discount Format at High-End Services

11.10, p < .001), value perceptions (F3, 2,736 = 10.76, p < .001), quality perceptions (F3, 2,736 = 3.96, p < .01), and purchase intentions (F3, 2,736 = 13.75, p < .001). In case of high-end services (Figure 2.5), percentage format were more preferable for a low discount level (5 percent) (F1, 1,368 = 33.32, p < .001). No significant difference existed between dollar format and percentage format in high discount levels (50 percent). Thus, the results support the hypotheses H3a. However, in low-end services (Figure 2.6), the difference between dollar format and percentage format across four different discount levels was not significant. Thus, H3b was rejected.

HOSPITALITY INDUSTRY VERSUS NONHOSPITALITY INDUSTRY

Interestingly, subjects perceive discount formats differently (F1, 2,748 = 6.66, p < .01) depending on different industries. The results indicated that subjects prefer dollar format for hospitality industries (hotel and restaurant industry) and prefer percentage format for nonhospitality industries (beauty care and automotive) (Figure 2.7).

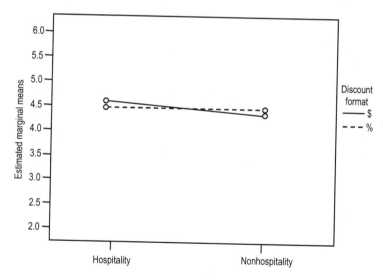

FIGURE 2.7. The Effect of Discount Format and Industries on Consumer Perception

For hospitality industries, subjects have higher perceptions for price reductions in dollar format consistently for both high- and low-end services (Figure 2.8). However, in case of nonhospitality industries, price reductions on high-end services framed in dollar format were considered more significantly than those framed in percentage format. On the other hand, price reductions expressed in percentage format were evaluated more significantly higher than those expressed in dollar format for low-end nonhospitality services (Figure 2.9).

CONCLUSIONS

Price promotions are an integral and essential part of marketing in the service industries. Most services depend on price discounts as "pull" strategies. Unfortunately, effectiveness of type of frames and levels of discounts while using service price discounts is least understood. Results from the current study indicated that in service industries, high- and low-end services are significantly different from each other in preference for type of discount formats. This study provides

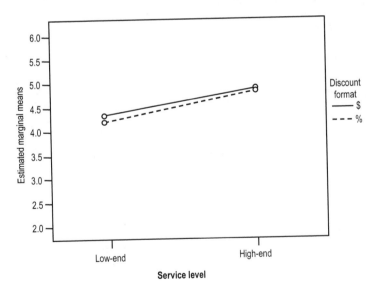

FIGURE 2.8. The Effect of Discount Format and Discount Level for Hospitality Industry

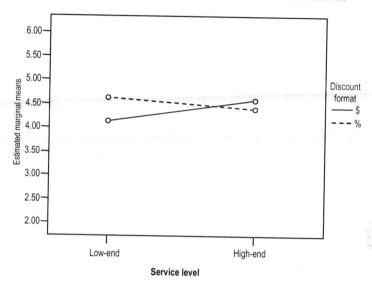

FIGURE 2.9. The Effect of Discount Format and Discount Level for Hospitality Industry

empirical evidence to support that price reductions should be stated in dollar format for high-end services, whereas price reductions should be framed in percentage format for low-end services.

Moreover, consumers perceived discount levels differently depending on high- and low-end services. Consumers perceive price reductions more significantly in high-end services than in low-end services. In addition, consumers perceive quality attributes significantly lower in high discount levels (50 percent) for low-end services compared to high-end services. For low-end services, high discount levels (50 percent) may lower consumers' quality perceptions and may not motivate their purchase intentions. Firms specializing in low-end services should not emphasize large price reductions (50 percent) in order to avoid discounting consumers' perceptions of quality and further affect their purchase intentions. Furthermore, in high-end services, at low discount levels (5 percent) consumers prefer price reductions in percentage format than in dollar format. Therefore, firms that provide high-end services should consider small price reductions and offer price reductions in percentage format. Finally, industry effects are significant across the types of discount formats. In the hospitality industry, consumers prefer dollar format over percentage format. Percentage format is preferable for nonhospitality industry.

LIMITATIONS

The limitations of this study include that the findings were generated from the laboratory experiment. These findings may need to be tested in field study. In addition, the nature of the service act can be tangible, intangible, or a combination of both. Hence, different categories of services need to be included in order to have better understanding in service price promotions. Moreover, different price-reduction levels with the same discount ranges may be considered to provide better analysis of consumers' responses to price reductions. Furthermore, consumer knowledge of service prices may not be as efficient as for goods. Many providers who are unable to estimate price in advance may cause customer's lack of accurate reference price for services. Also, individual customers' needs may vary. Future research could consider the effect of price discount without referencing price on consumers' pricing decisions.

REFERENCES

Bawa, K. and Shoemaker, R.W. (1989). Analyzing incremental sales from a direct mail coupon promotion. *Journal of Marketing Research, 24*(November): 370-376.

Bearden, W.O., Liechtenstein, D.R., and Teel, J.E. (1984). Comparison price, coupon and brand effects on consumer reactions to retail newspaper advertisements. *Journal of Retailing, 60*(Summer): 11-34.

Bearden, W.O. and Shimp, T.A. (1982). The use of extrinsic cues to facilitate product adoption. *Journal of Marketing Research,* May, 229-239.

Blattberg, R.C., Eppen, G.D., and Lieberman, J. (1981). A theoretical and empirical evaluation of price deals for consumer nondurables. *Journal of Marketing,* 45: 116-129.

Chen, S.F., Monroe, K., and Lou, Y.C. (1998). The effects of framing price promotion messages on consumers' perception and purchase intentions. *Journal of Retailing, 73*(3): 353-372.

Della Bitta, A. and Monroe, K. (1980). A multivariate analysis of the perception of value from retail price advertisements, in advances in consumer research. In

Monroe, K. (ed.), *Advances in Consumer Research,* Vol. 8 (pp. 161-165). Ann Arbor, MI: Association of Consumer Research.

Della Bitta, A., Monroe, K., and McGinnis, J. (1981). Consumer perception of comparative price advertisements. *Journal of Marketing Research,* November: 416-427.

Folkes, V. and Wheat, R.D. (1995). Consumer's price perceptions of promoted products. *Journal of Retailing, 71*(3): 317-328.

Frisch, D. (1993). Reasons for framing effects. *Organizational Behavior and Human Decision Processes, 54*(April): 399-429.

Guiltinan, J.P. (1988). A conceptual framework for pricing consumer services. In Bitner M.J. and Crosby L.A. (eds.), *Designing a Winning Service Strategy* (pp. 11-15). Chicago, IL: American Marketing.

Gupta, S. and Cooper, L.G. (1992). The discounting of discount and promotion thresholds. *Journal of Consumer Research, 19*(December): 401-411.

Harlam, B., Krishna, A., Lehman, D., and Mela, C. (1995). Impact of bundle type, price framing and familiarity on purchase intention for the bundle. *Journal of Business Research, 33:* 57-66.

Kahneman, D. and Tversky, A. (1979). Prospect theory: An analysis of decision under risk. *Econometrica, XLVII:* 263-291.

Kalwani, M. and Yim, C.K. (1992). Consumer price and promotion expectations: An experimental study. *Journal of Marketing Research,* February: 90-100.

Kandampully, J. (2002). *Service Management: The New Paradigm in Hospitality.* New South Wales: Pearson Education Australia.

Kindel, S. (1993). Cutting through the clutter. *Financial World, 163* (April): 36-38.

Klapper, J. (1960). *The Effects of Mass Communication.* New York: The Free Press.

Kurtz, D.I. and Clow, K.E. (1998). *Services Marketing.* New York: John Wiley and Sons.

Lichtenstein, D.R, Burton, S., and Karson, E.J. (1991). The effect of semantic cues on consumer perceptions of reference price ads. *Journal of Consumer Research, 18:* 380-391.

Lichtenstein, D.R, Burton, S., and Netemeyer, R.G. (1998). A scale for measuring attitude toward private label products and an examination of its psychological and behavioral correlates. *Academy of Marketing Science, 26:* 293-306.

Messinger, H. (2003). Monthly GDP for service producing industries. Organization for Economic Co-operation and Development Short-Term Economic Statistics Expert Group Presentation. Available at http://www.oecd.org/dataoecd/59/56/1. Statistics Canada. June 26.

Monroe, K.B. (1990). *Pricing: Making Profitable Decisions.* New York: McGraw-Hill.

Monroe, K.B. and Guiltinan, J.P. (1975). A path-analytic exploration of retail patronage influences. *Journal of Consumer Research, 2*(June): 19-28.

Nelson, P. (1970). Information and consumer behavior. *Journal of Political Economy, 78*(March/April): 311-29.

Olson, J.C. (1977). Price as an informational cue effects on product evaluation, in consumer and industrial buying behavior. In Woodside, A.G., Sheth, J.N., and Bennett, P.D. (eds.) *Consumer and Industrial Buying Behavior* (pp. 267-286). New York: Elsevier.

Raghubir, P. (1992). Semantic cues and buyer evaluation of promotional communication. *American Marketing Association,* Summer: 12-17.

Raju, P.S. and Hastak, M. (1983). Pre-trial cognitive effects of cents-off coupons. *Journal of Advertising, 12*(2): 24-32.

Rao, A.R. and Monroe, K.B. (1988). The moderating effect of prior knowledge on cue utilization in product evaluations. *Journal of Consumer Research, 15*(2): 253-264.

Sawyer, A.G. and Dickson, P.H. (1984). Psychological perspectives on consumer response to sales promotion. In Jocz, K.E. (ed.), *Research on Sales Promotion: Collected Papers* (pp. 1-21). Cambridge, MA: Marketing Science Institute.

Shoemaker, R. (1979). An analysis of consumer reactions to product promotions. In *Educators' Conference Proceedings* (pp. 244-248). Chicago, IL: American Marketing Association.

Uhl, J. N. and H. L. Brown (1971). Consumer perception of experimental retail food price changes. *Journal of Consumer Affairs, 5*(2): 174-185.

Zeithaml, V. (1981). How consumer evaluation processes differ between goods and services. In Donnelly, J.H. and George, W.R. (eds.), *Marketing of Services* (pp. 186-190). Chicago, IL: American Marketing Association.

Chapter 3

Leisure: Meaning and Impact on Travel Behavior

Umashankar Venkatesh

INTRODUCTION

Leisure as a part of human existence today has acquired a significant meaning and impact as the human race tries to grapple with the growing complexities of balancing work, social, and personal or family lives. Leisure is advised to be integrated in work life as a means of enhancement of the quality of life. On the other hand, the workplace is invading private lives with such practices as flextime, working from home, and technology that enables individuals to be "at work" anywhere and anytime. Therefore, most working people undergo a constant tussle trying to resolve this conundrum, which usually translates into managing time, expenditure, relationships, personal desires, and social commitments. The pressure that the workplace and earning a livelihood exerts on average individuals and families today can be well gauged from the Wellner (2000) report that in the United States an average married couple labors for a staggering 717 hours (or 26 percent) more each year than a working couple did in 1969. This pressure on time, and the effort needed to be "at leisure," must be considered in the context of the importance of leisure in our lives. Bright (2000) lists the benefits of leisure as constituting all aspects of human existence, including psychological (e.g., improved self-concept, reflection of personal values, peak experiences); psychophysiological (e.g., cardiovascular health, disease control, mental and physical restoration); sociological (e.g., community stability, family solidarity, cultural identity); economic (e.g., employment, income,

Global Cases on Hospitality Industry
© 2008 by The Haworth Press, Taylor & Francis Group. All rights reserved.
doi:10.1300/5923_03

health care costs); and environmental (e.g., preservation, conservation). A study of the impact of the expectation of a holiday on an individual's sense of well-being conducted by Gilbert and Junaida (2002) offers an investigation into what effect the expectation of a holiday has on the sense of well-being of would-be tourists. They report significant differences between the holiday-taking group and the non-holiday-taking group in terms of current effect, well-being, and in three specific life domains: family, economic situation, and health. It appears that those who are waiting to go on holiday are much happier with their life as a whole, experience less negative or unpleasant feelings, and thus enjoy an overall net positive effect or pleasant feelings. The holiday-taking groups were also happier with their family, economic situation, and health domains compared to the non-holiday-taking-group. Apart from the sociological and psychological interest in the concept, leisure has serious connotations for any economy, and could be seen within the following (corporate and economic) perspectives:

1. Demands for increased productivity from employees as a financial, human resource, and operations management objective.
2. The ability of organizations to create (flexible) work schedules revolving around the daily lives of their employees, such that employee effectiveness and efficiency increase.
3. The ability of organizations to continue to remain as preferred employers and retain employees.
4. The ability to design and deliver relevant and profitable leisure products and services, based on the understanding of leisure and related consumption behavior encompassing the needs, wants, and aspirations of target groups.
5. The capacity of the leisure sector in any economy to provide employment and generate wealth for the society.

Leisure as a business is huge today and exploding further. Consumption in this area is directly proportional to the development and discretionary income that a society experiences. Developing countries such as India are good examples of this explosive growth in leisure (and lifestyle) related consumption, with new development of malls and amusement parks and increasing personal outbound and domestic travel are clear indicators of not only an increase in the capacity to spend but also of the willingness to partake of the good things of life and display varying degrees of hedonism. This chapter focuses on the latter two items listed previously, in the specific context of leisure and leisure tourism customers. Within this the focus is on the underpinnings of consumer behavior and how it translates for marketers of such products and services. The determinants of leisure, as having eventual consequences for tourism, are attempted to be identified such that a better understanding of the way consumers conceptualize leisure and manifest leisure travel behavior can be reached.

TRAVEL AS AN EXPRESSION OF LEISURE BEHAVIOR

The consumption of leisure products and services in developed as well as developing societies is seemingly increasing at an escalating rate, and the pace (as well as nature) is getting frenetic if not already so. Linder (1970) was perhaps the first economist to understand and predict the frantic pace of modern life and leisure. He proposed that consumption had to be measured in temporal as well as economic terms. Consumption takes time, and as specialized work leads to higher rates of productivity, increased level of products and services are consumed. Hence, he argued that the process must be sped up by consuming more rapidly, by consuming higher quality versions of a product or service, or by simultaneous consumption in which more than one product or service is consumed at a time. Such an acceleration of consumption leads to an acceleration of the pace of life, and it converts the populace into what he calls the "harried leisure-class."

Travel as an expression of what leisure means to people is a popular choice, and relevant across strata in all types of societies. The human desire to see the unseen and know the unknown drives us to new places and destinations, with motives varying from wanting to understand different cultures, to experience (or get respite from) cooler or warmer climes, to indulge in pure adventure, or to experience intense rest and rejuvenation. Personal values have been used to predict a number of leisure behaviors, including choice of recreation activities (Beatty et al., 1985; Boote, 1981), and choice of leisure activities engaged in while on vacation (Madrigal and Kahle, 1994). Likewise, personality has also been related to leisure activity (Allen, 1982;

Driver and Knopf, 1977) and travel decisions (Nickerson and Ellis, 1991; Plog, 1974). Haywood and colleagues (1995) also confirm that leisure is translated and manifested frequently in the form of travel and tourism, and they indicate that tourism represents a significant and often prolonged leisure activity. In their opinion, leisure-related tourism has grown in importance as household real incomes have increased, and it constitutes one of the largest elements of household leisure spending.

THE ECONOMIC IMPACT OF LEISURE TOURISM

The impact of tourism on the economy can be studied by measuring the effect on such indicators as employment, capital investment, GDP, etc. These impacts are being taken as a given and as having strategic importance for most economies. This chapter focuses on leisure-related travel, hence personal travel and tourism (PT & T) as a component of overall tourism is being considered as an indicator of leisure travel. As per estimates of the World Travel and Tourism Council (2004b), es3., 3.B, and 3.C, the world PT & T alone is estimated at $2,537.8 billion (U.S.) or 10.2 percent of total personal consumption, constituting 46.2 percent of total travel and tourism (T & T) demand in 2004. By 2014, this is estimated to reach $4,206.5 billion (U.S.) or 10.9 percent of total consumption and 44 percent of global T & T demand.

If we look at India's example as a developing economy, the PT & T component is estimated at 927.3 billion (rupee, Rs), $19.5 billion (U.S.) or 5 percent of total personal consumption in year 2004. This constitutes about 50.2 percent of the total Indian T & T demand. By 2014, this is predicted to reach 3,612.9 billion (Rs), $46.5 billion (U.S.) or 6.1 percent of total consumption and 51.4 percent of total T & T demand. India business travel is estimated at 114.5 billion (Rs), $2.4 billion (U.S.) in 2004. By 2014, this should reach 387.4 billion (Rs) or $5 billion (U.S.) (WTTC, 2004b). India therefore compares favorably with the world average in the context of the percentage share of PT & T in total T & T. PT & T demand, which includes leisure travel, contributes to almost half of the total T & T in India compared to 46 percent worldwide, and this is predicted to increase further. Thus, the importance of the PT & T segment (hence leisure travel) cannot be ignored. Aspects that may differentiate PT & T demand in India from the Occident is the religious and rituals related travel, socializing related travel, and leisure. A study conducted by Dave (2003) puts the size of domestic travel market of India at 320 million trips (in 2000) of which 109 million visits were in the urban segment. Profiling the characteristics of domestic travel, the study says globally, on average, 35 percent of visitors leave home to meet friends and relations (VFR), and around 50 percent seek holidays. This segment is showing the greatest growth. In India, however, VFR travel dominates; leisure is still limited, and, this is surprising, pilgrimages are not that high. Only 6.9 percent go to religious places. Business constitutes 10.4 percent. Leisure is a little more, at 13.8 percent. Social functions attract 30.3 percent, while the rest, 31.5 percent, come in the category of "other," which could be largely VFR.

The estimated T & T economy employment for India is estimated by the WTTC (2004b) at 24,456,600 jobs in 2004, 5.6 percent of total employment, or 1 in every 17.8 jobs. By 2014, this is predicted to go up to 27,790,000 jobs, or 5.7 percent of total employment. This converts to about 4.9 percent of the GDP in 2004 rising up to 5.2 percent by 2014.

MEANING OF LEISURE AND ITS IMPACT ON CONSUMER BEHAVIOR

Rapoport and Rapoport (1974) in their work on the sociology of leisure record that in exploring the context and meaning of leisure, many generations of researchers and thinkers have approached the field in varied ways and sometimes in such dissimilar fashion that it actually confuses the whole picture rather than clarifies it. They go on to state that the earlier sociologists thought they knew what the definition of leisure was; their concern was with its diffusion. Later generations watched it diffuse—vertically and laterally—and have been concerned with how it combined with other elements of life to form lifestyles. More recently, with an appreciation of the diversification of lifestyles and no longer certain that a single definition of leisure is possible, sociologists are concerning themselves with the issues of social integration and the relationship between the individuals and their society.

Leisure has been traditionally defined in terms related to work—or rather the absence of work. Indeed, the understanding that leisure occurs in time free from work is rife, as evident from the definition provided by the Countryside Recreation and Research Advisory Group (1970), which indicates that leisure is the leftover periods of time that an individual has after taking out the time spent at work, in sleep, and for other basic needs. As Rapoport and Rapoport (1974) posit, the chief problem in defining leisure in contradistinction to the time spent in employment is apparent as the subjective experience of work and leisure is considered. The psychological experience of a sense of freedom from constraint, enjoyment of current activity, and personal control, which are for many investigators the essence of leisure, is available to many people as all or part of their paid employment. The judgment of what is "work" and what "leisure" on this criterion is in any case highly individual. Therefore, definitions of leisure that are based on a single criterion (time, pleasure, etc.) are of limited value because of the difficulties involved in comparing research results.

Kaplan (1961), who developed a multicriteria-based definition of leisure, has classified leisure to be integral and manifest in aspects such as (1) an antithesis to "work" as an economic function, (2) a pleasant expectation and recollection, (3) a minimum of involuntary social-role obligations, (4) a psychological perception of freedom, (5) a close relation to the values of the culture, (6) the inclusion of an entire range from inconsequence and insignificance to weightiness and importance, and (7) often, but not necessarily, an activity characterized by the element of play. Leisure is none of these by itself, but is all together in one emphasis or another. Parker (1971) has presented a life-space analysis to overcome the cumbersomeness of multicriteria-based definitions of leisure on one hand and the constraints of single criterion definitions on the other. "Life space" is explained as the total of activities or ways of spending time that people have. The researcher avers that in considering the various definitions of work and leisure it is obvious that assigning all parts of life space to work or leisure would be a gross oversimplification. It is because of the temporal overlap of many work and nonwork/leisure activities that less global categories are required.

Foley and colleagues (1999) report leisure having at least three distinct meanings. These include the following:

1. Leisure as "time-off": this refers to the usage of the of the word *leisure* as a residual time concept, usually indicating to a "time off" after routine workplace and domestic chores, together with other unavoidable obligations such as personal hygiene or commuting, have been completed.
2. Leisure as recreation: this indicates the usage of the term as a generic descriptor to indicate certain activities broadly functioning to recreate or entertain individuals or groups wherein "leisure" is associated with the idea of recreations (activities that recreate through relaxation, and challenge or foster social, cultural, intellectual, or creative development). These activities are voluntary, having an element of choice on the part of those who participate, and, therefore, represent active use of free time within an individual's lifestyle.
3. Leisure as a state of mind: leisure in this definition is perceived as a state of mind, with individuals feeling that they are "at leisure" in any particular set of circumstances.

Thus we see that leisure as a part of the lives of individuals is inextricably linked with the concept of work. Defining leisure by default, that is, the "absence" of work, rather than on its own is seemingly the rule rather than an exception. The important parameters that are however common in most definitions could be summarized as the absence of obligation either related to work or involuntary discharge of social roles, a sense of freedom, and discretionary time. Thus, when we conceive of travel for leisure purposes these aspects should be inherent in the activity, and these factors must be used as the basic motivational foundations.

DETERMINANTS OF LEISURE AND CONSEQUENCES FOR TOURISM

The following variables will be discussed as having bearing on the choice of tourism as a manifestation of leisure behavior, namely, personality, motivation, attitude, and situational and environmental factors.

Personality

Personality as a psychological factor affecting consumer behavior in general is a known entity. Hawkins and colleagues (2001) indicate that the personality of consumers guides and directs their behavior chosen to accomplish goals in different situations. To demonstrate how personality and leisure travel behavior may be connected, Plog (1974, 1990) delineates personality types along a continuum ranging from allocentrism to psychocentrism. The psychocentric personality type tends toward territory boundedness, insecurity, and powerlessness, and these individuals also tend to have inactive lifestyles and are unadventurous. In contrast, allocentric individuals tend to be self-confident, intellectually curious, and feel in control of their lives. According to Plog (1991), psychocentrics tend to prefer a high degree of familiarity in their travel, and, as a result, enjoy group or "packaged" tours. In contrast, allocentrics enjoy vacations to exotic and unique destinations, and prefer to travel independently (i.e., not as part of group tours). Nickerson and Ellis (1991) have furthered the conception of allocentrism and psychocentrism proposed by Plog (1974, 1990) by trying to identify the source of energy for these two dispositions. They tried to differentiate between the energy sources as a result of stable personality characteristics of the individual on one hand and of a learned response on the other. Their refinement helps further explain travelers personalities and enhances Plog's (1991) theory. The "energy" that learned responses are supposed to generate clearly indicates toward one of the determinants of the conceptualization (and choice of alternative modes) of leisure on the part of consumers, namely the situation or the environment (as it forms, conditions, and shapes the motivations). MacCannell (2002) in his essay exploring the noneconomic relation at the heart of tourism avers that the dominant way commercially successful destinations have organized tourist experiences has been to model them as closely as possible on the ego. He argues that commercially successful tourist attractions are those that are modeled on the structure of the ego, those that stage a narcissistic relation between ego and attraction. He goes on to say that the collective behavior that fuels the global tourist economy is grounded in symbolic and psychic structures (rather than on any economic motives) that remain mainly unexamined, urging him to state that the factors that motivate tourist desire are mysterious and illusive, even to the tourists themselves.

Motivation

Given the previous discussion, leisure travel motivations need to be understood in terms of its meaning and limits. McIntosh (1977) categorized motivation for travel into the following four categories:

1. Physical motivators consisting of rest and relaxation, sports participation, beach recreation, etc.
2. Cultural motivators indicating the desire for knowledge of other countries and cultures, including music, art, religion, etc.
3. Interpersonal motivators consisting of the need to meet new people, friends, and relatives, to escape from the routine, family, or neighbors, etc.
4. Status and prestige motivators indicating the desire for recognition and attention.

Cohen (1979) proposes a typology emphasizing the manner in which tourists relate to environments and thus explaining their motivations to travel. The main assumption is that tourists travel because they believe that they will find valuable experience by doing so.

He categorizes tourists as those who are on a quest for a new spiritual center or on a quest for pleasure. In the context of pleasure the motives are (1) recreational: for those who fully identify with their own culture, values, and society, it is for entertainment and relaxation, undertaken to recreate the body and mind (as they have little attraction for other "cultures"); and (2) diversionary: the tourist is alienated from home society but does not wish to gain a new spiritual center, and thus the holiday is a diversion or escape from the boredom of the mundane and routine. For both the diversionary and recreational tourist, pleasure is the experience being sought.

Specifically in the context of leisure, Crompton (1979) investigated the motivations for pleasure vacations and tried identifying the motives of pleasure vacationers that influence the selection of a destination. He also sought to develop a conceptual framework capable of encompassing such motives. Empirically nine motives were identified as the following:

1. Escape from a perceived mundane environment
2. Exploration and evaluation of self
3. Relaxation
4. Prestige
5. Regression
6. Enhancement of kinship relationships
7. Facilitation of social interaction
8. Novelty
9. Education

Items 1 through 7 are classified under sociopsychological motives, whereas items 8 and 9 form the motivations under the alternate cultural category. The latter were, noted to be at least, partially aroused by the particular qualities that a destination offered. By contrast, sociopsychological motives were found to be unrelated to destination attributes. Here the emphasis shifted from the destination itself to its function as a medium through which sociopsychological needs could be satisfied. The research data suggested that the tourist industry may usefully pay greater attention to sociopsychological motives in developing product and promotion strategies.

If we compare the previous conceptualizations, distinct overlaps and similarities are apparent. As far as motives for leisure tourism go, McIntosh's (1977) "physical motivators" (item 1) compares with Crompton's (1979) motives of escaping from the mundane, relaxation, and perhaps novelty (items 1, 3, and 8). This also is similar to Cohen's (1979) diversionary and recreational motives. These therefore could be said to form the core of what leisure travelers seek. Second, these are the aspects that can be used to design marketing strategies without getting fixated on the destination characteristics alone.

Attitude

Reflects an individual's learned predisposition to respond to an object or a class of objects in a consistently favorable or unfavorable manner (Allport, 1935). Attitude consists of three components: cognitive, affective, and conative or behavioral component. The cognitive aspect refers to the perceptions and beliefs about the object; the affective component relates to evaluation or affect pertaining to the object and includes emotions or feelings about specific attributes of the object or the overall object; and the conative component refers to the behavioral intentions with respect to the specific attributes or the overall object.

Sussmann and Unel (1999) indicate that attitudes tend to form eclectically, with respect to past and present individual needs, and they arise from four main sources: information exposure, group membership, environment, and need satisfaction. They go on to say that "attitudes serve people's needs by simplifying their responses to complex information stimuli or decision making including decision making related to (say) a holiday destination."

As far as leisure tourism is concerned, obviously the study of attitudes may be taken up with two distinct perspectives of the tourist: what the individual attitude is toward travel as a manifestation of leisure, and if the individual is positively predisposed toward travel as a leisure manifestation, then the derivative attitude toward the destination, mode of travel available, how convenient or inconvenient the purchase (ticketing, reservations, and other logistical arrangements) process itself is, etc.

Finally, the cognitive, affective, and conative components tend to be consistent, implying that a change in any one of the components usually changes the other two remaining components (Dabholkar 1994). This has clear connotations for marketing strategy and promotion planning, as bringing about attitudinal change is something that destination or event (attitudinal object) managers and travel managers (as do most marketing managers of products and services) commonly need to bring about to attract more tourists. For instance, providing information along with images and/or stories of guest satisfaction is supposed to build a positive attitude toward the object, by having addressed the cognitive and affective components respectively. It may not, however, necessarily convert to a behavior (conducive to what the marketer wishes for), but is a way for indirectly influencing the beliefs and feelings of the customer and consequently his or her behavior.

Situational or Environmental Factors

For the purposes of this chapter, environmental and situational factors are being taken as nonpsychological stimuli (akin to what has been conceptualized by Hawkins et al. 2001) that exist in the environment other than the focal stimulus (namely travel as a manifest form of leisure and the destination), and as temporary characteristics that are induced by environmental factors such as time pressure, unavailability of preferred travel mode, group or travel party composition, family life cycle stage, etc. Belk (1974) defines situational influences as those arising from factors that are particular to a specific time and place and that are relatively independent of consumer and product characteristics. Examples include physical surroundings, social settings, time, task (type of decision to be made), and antecedent states such as moods and physical conditions (Belk 1975).

Information sources existing in the environment are also being considered as an important constituent that shapes and determines the personality, attitude, and perceptions of leisure travelers. Fodness and Murray (1999) in their study examined the correlates of tourist information search behavior. They have specified and tested a model in which tourist search strategies are related to search contingencies, individual (tourist) characteristics, and behavioral search outcomes. Using survey data from a large sample of leisure travelers, they propose that in any given purchase situation, at least three distinct strategies for information search exist: spatial, temporal, and operational. They define the spatial dimension as reflecting the locus of search activity: internal (accessing the contents of memory) or external (acquiring information from the environment). The temporal dimension represents the timing of search activity. Search can be either ongoing, building up a knowledge base for unspecified future purchase decisions, or prepurchase, in response to a current purchase problem. The third dimension is operational, reflecting the conduct of search and focusing on the particular sources used and their relative effectiveness for problem solving and decision-making. Literature indicates that consumers usually have either internal or external sources of information that they try to access during their search process. Also, that they access these two sources in that order or sequence (Bettman, 1975; Leigh and Rethans, 1984). Basically, internal search involves customers accessing their memory to find decision-relevant information or inputs usually based on prior purchase experience (Engel et al., 1994) by self or even by vicariously learned inputs based on hearsay. External search results from a motivated consumer's decision to seek information outside personal experience (Kotler and Armstrong, 1994; Murray, 1991). Thus, the spatial as well as operational aspects of information search in the context of leisure travelers is affected and shaped by environmental or situational forces, and as a consequence the entire purchase behavior also gets determined by the same. Fodness and Murray (1999) have also included situational influences and product characteristics as contingencies that have a deterministic effect on the information search strategies of tourists. Nickerson and Ellis (1991) have also referred to the energy that learned responses (based on situational or environmental factors) generate, determining the individual dispositions toward allocentrism or psychocentrism.

TOURIST BUYING DECISION PROCESS

The tourist buying decision process is a long, drawn out one, and is often prepared and planned over a considerable period of time. The consumer buying decision is said to consist of stages such as problem recognition, information search, alternative evaluation, purchase decision, and postpurchase behavior (see Hawkins et al., 2001).

Schmoll (1977) proposed a four-stage buying decision process, specifically in the context of pleasure travelers, consisting of need formulation, information gathering and deliberation, decision, and travel preparation. The previous model obviously focuses on stages that lead up to the purchase decision on part of a consumer. This does not address the postpurchase scenario, which becomes crucial in the context of repeat purchase, as past experience is one of the crucial factors that affects service purchase behavior. Second, word of mouth is also a manifestation of postpurchase behavior and is also a determinant of service purchase.

Moutinho (1987) in his model of tourist purchase behavior takes care of these inadequacies and indicates that the tourist decision process involves the tourists' motives and intentions as well as the stimuli that turn intention into choice of product or destination. A large part of the motives significant to choice may not be conscious. Of course, more is involved in a travel decision than in purchasing some specific items.

He indicates that a range of subdecisions are considered in relation to destination transportation, accommodation, activities, budget, reservations, etc. In the decision-making process, external search occurs in order to reduce perceived risk to tolerable levels. The buying decision is taken with some caution, the degree of caution being proportionate to the risk perceived (or the inability to estimate risk through ignorance), and to the importance of the amount committed in relation to the tourist's total resources. When travelers use extensive decision making, they spend considerable time and effort seeking information and evaluating the alternatives available. The final act is seen as emerging from a "funneling" process that portrays how the experience of a problem triggers search activities that gradually narrow the area of possible solutions until a "final" solution is found. In this contention travel behavior gets influenced from forces outside the individual, including the influence of other people or social influences. These societal forces can be grouped into (1) role and family influences, (2) reference groups, (3) social classes, and (4) culture and subculture.

The vacation tourist behavior model proposed by Moutinho (1987) consists of three phases: (1) predecision and decision process, (2) postpurchase evaluation, and (3) future decision making. Each part is composed of fields and subfields, linked by other concepts related to the tourist's behavioral processes. The predecision and decision processes are concerned with the flow of events from the tourist stimuli to purchase decision. The fields that are included are preference structure (as a major process in the predecision phase), decision, and purchase. Since the two last phases are outcomes of predecision, the model is more detailed in respect to predecision, and its analysis includes the following subfields: stimulus filtration, attention and learning processes, and choice criteria. The postpurchase evaluation phase consists of postchoice evaluative feedback and is posited to have a significant impact on the decision maker's attitude set and/or subsequent behavior. One of the key elements noted as affecting a tourist's expectations is the satisfaction with postpurchase. Postpurchase evaluation has been described to have three major purposes. First, it adds to the tourist's store of experiences, and it is through postpurchase assessment that experience is taken into the tourist's frame of reference. Hence, it broadens personal needs, ambitions, drives, perceptions, and understanding. Second, postpurchase assessment provides a check on market-related decisions. Third, it provides feedback to serve as a basis for adjusting future purchase behavior. Finally, the future decision-making phase is concerned with reasoning out the probabilities of repeat purchase or otherwise.

CONCLUSION

In Moutinho's (1987) model the factors considered in this study, namely personality, motives, attitude, and internalized environmental (situational) influences, are all evident in forming the so-called "preference structure" and "intention" on which the individual formulates the choice criteria for purchase. As a conclusion to this study, the previous determinants and the manner in which they are related to the conceptualization of travel as a manifestation of leisure behavior is presented in a schematic diagram in Figure 3.1.

It is proposed that personality is an enveloping variable that shapes consumer motivations and attitudes as far as the definition and visualization of leisure by the individual is concerned. The environment to an extent shapes the personality, but only over the long term, and has comparatively a more direct or immediate impact on the motives and attitudes of the individual. The way in which the individual visualizes

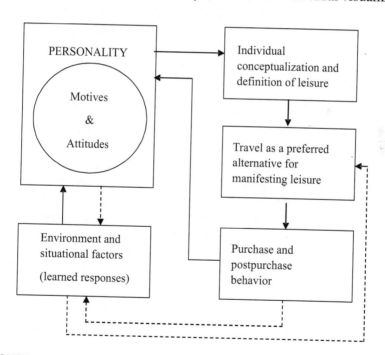

FIGURE 3.1. Leisure As a Function of Personality, Motives, Attitude, and Environment

and defines leisure would therefore be highly individualistic, either arrived at consciously or subconsciously. The environment does have an impact on the attitude and motives as it also contains the learned responses of the individual based on past experiences or through vicarious learning. The choice of travel as a manifestation of leisure behavior is a decision that is arrived at by the individual once the details of leisure in terms of its limits and resource requirements has been worked out. This is also seen as affected by the environment, as the environment consists of external information sources and situational factors that may help or determine the comparison of two travel alternatives in terms of destinations or timing or other such operating details. For the sake of brevity, the purchase and postpurchase stages have been shown combined in the schematic diagram, but they obviously can be exploded into the detailed flow of decisions as depicted in various consumer behavior models pertaining to vacation travel. In the context of this chapter, they have been considered as a given and focus is only on the conceptualization of leisure by the individual. Finally, personality is also connected to environment in a way that suggests that, albeit weak, a deterministic aspect of the personality of the individual may exists that helps shape the immediate environment around him or her. This could obviously be real or perceptual (selective exposure, selective retention, and selective distortion).

Marketers of travel products and services therefore need to first help, directly or indirectly, the completion of the definition and visualization of leisure, and second in facilitating the choice making on part of the individual for selecting travel as a means of "achieving" or operationalizing leisure. This would require not only provision of relevant information and messages, but, more important, the design and timing of release of such information from credible sources that is believable and realistically addresses consumer motivations.

REFERENCES

Allen, L.R. (1982). The relationship between Murray's personality needs and leisure interests. *Journal of Leisure Research, 14*(1): 63-76.

Allport, G.W. (1935). Attitudes. In C.A. Murchinson (ed.), *A Handbook of Social Psychology* (pp. 798-844). Worcester, MA: Clark University Press.

Beatty, S.E., Kahle, L.R., Homer, P.M,. and Mirsa, S. (1985). Alternative measurement approaches to consumer values: The list of values and the rokeach value survey. *Psychology and Marketing, 2*(5): 181-200.

Belk, R.W. (1974). An exploratory assessment of situational effects in buyer behavior. *Journal of Marketing Research, 11*(May): 156-163.

Belk, R.W. (1975). Situational variables and consumer behavior. *Journal of Consumer Research, 2*(4): 157-164.

Bettman, J.R. (1975). Issues in designing consumer information environments. *Journal of Consumer Research, 2*(4): 69-177.

Boote, A.S. (1981). Market segmentation by personal values and salient product attributes. *Journal of Advertising Research, 21*(February): 29-35.

Bright, A.D. (2000). The role of social marketing in leisure and recreation management. *Journal of Leisure Research, 32*(1): 12-17.

Cohen, E. (1979). Phenomenology of tourist experiences. *Sociology, 13*(2): 179-202.

Countryside Recreation and Research Advisory Group (1970). *Countryside Recreation Glossary.* London, UK: CRRAG.

Crompton, J.L. (1979). Motivations for pleasure vacations. *Annals of Tourism Research, 6*(4): 408-424.

Dabholkar, P.A. (1994). Incorporating choice in attitudinal framework. *Journal of Consumer Research, 21*(1): 100-118.

Dave, U. (2003). It's time to go for domestic tourism. *Express Hotelier and Caterer,* January 6. Available at: http://www.expresshospitality.com/20030106/perspective 1.shtml.

Driver, B.L. and Knopf, R.C. (1977). Personality, outdoor recreation, and expected consequences. *Environment and Behavior, 9*(2): 169-193.

Engel, J.F., Blackwell, R.D., and Miniard, P.W. (1994). *Consumer Behavior,* 8th edition. Fort Worth, Texas: Dryden.

Fodness, D. and Murray, B. (1999). A model of tourist information search behavior. *Journal of Travel Research, 37*(3): 220-230.

Foley, M., Maxwell, G., and McGillivray, D. (1999). Women at leisure and in work—unequal opportunities? *Equal Opportunities International, 18*(1): 8-18.

Gilbert, D. and Junaida, A. (2002). A study of the impact of the expectation of a holiday on an individual's sense of well-being. *Journal of Vacation Marketing, 8*(4): 352-361.

Hawkins, D.I., Best, R.J., and Coney, K.A. (2001). *Consumer Behavior-Building Marketing Strategy.* New York: Irwin McGraw-Hill.

Haywood, L.J., Kew, F.C., Branham, P., Spink, J., Capenerhurst, J., and Henry, I. (1995). *Understanding Leisure,* 2nd edition. Cheltenham, UK: Stanley Thornes (Publishers) Ltd.

Kaplan, M. (1961). *Leisure in America: A Social Enquiry.* New York: Wiley.

Kotler, P. and Armstrong, G. (1994). *Principles of Marketing,* 6th edition. Englewood Cliffs, NJ: Prentice Hall.

Leigh, T.W. and Rethans, A.J. (1984). A script-theoretic analysis of industrial purchasing behavior. *Journal of Marketing, 48*(Fall): 22-32.

Linder, S. (1970). *The Harried Leisure Class.* New York: Columbia University Press.

MacCannell, D. (2002). The ego factor in tourism. *Journal of Consumer Research, 29*(1): 146-151.

Madrigal, R. and Kahle, L.R. (1994). Predicting vacation activity preferences on the basis of value-system segmentation. *Journal of Travel Research, 32*(3): 22-28.

McIntosh, R.W. (1977). *Tourism—Principles, Practices, Philosophies.* New York: Wiley.

Moutinho, L. (1987). Consumer behavior in tourism. *European Journal of Marketing, 21*(10): 5-44.

Murray, K.B. (1991). A test of services marketing theory: Consumer information acquisition activities. *Journal of Marketing, 55*(January): 10-25.

Nickerson, N.P. and Ellis, G.D. (1991). Traveler types and activation theory: A comparison of two models. *Journal of Travel Research, 29*(3): 26-31.

Parker, S.R. (1971). *The Future of Work and Leisure.* London, UK: Granada.

Plog, S.C. (1974). Why destination areas rise and fall in popularity. *Cornell Hotel and Restaurant Administration Quarterly, 14*(4): 55-58.

Plog, S.C. (1990). A carpenter's tools: An answer to Stephen L.J. Smith's review of psychocentrism/allocentrism. *Journal of Travel Research, 28*(4): 43-45.

Plog, S.C. (1991). *Leisure Travel: Making it a Growth Market Again!* New York: Wiley.

Rapoport, R. and Rapoport, R.N. (1974). Four themes in the sociology of leisure. *British Journal of Sociology, 25*(3): 215-229.

Schmoll, G.A. (1977). *Tourism Promotion.* London, UK: Tourism International Press.

Sussmann, U. and Ünel, A. (1999). Destination image and its modification after travel: An empirical study on Turkey. In A. Pizam and Y. Mansfeld (eds.), *Consumer Behavior in Travel and Tourism* (pp. 207-225). Binghamton NY: The Haworth Press.

Wellner, A.S. (2000). The end of leisure? *American Demographics, 22*(7): 50-55.

World Travel and Tourism Council (2004a). Executive summary: Travel and tourism forging ahead. In *The 2004 Travel and Tourism Economic Research.* London, UK: WTTC.

World Travel and Tourism Council (2004b). India: Travel and tourism forging ahead. In *The 2004 Travel and Tourism Economic Research.* London, UK: WTTC.

Chapter 4

The Bed-and-Breakfast Experience:
An Analysis of Hosts'
and Guests' Expectations

Danielle Felix
Sue Broad
Maureen Griffiths

INTRODUCTION

The tourism industry consists of a variety of businesses that serve the needs of tourists. One of the main components of the tourism industry is the accommodation sector, which offers a range of services and facilities for tourists when traveling (Middleton and Clarke, 2001). Many types of accommodation exist, such as hotels, motels, resorts, apartments, holiday houses, backpacker hostels, caravan parks, and camping grounds. Many "nontraditional" forms of accommodation also provide guests with personal service and a high level of host-guest interaction in a rural setting where the establishment is owner-operated (Morrison et al., 1996). This type of accommodation includes bed-and-breakfasts (B & Bs).

Two groups of people are primarily involved in this style of accommodation: hosts and guests. Research has indicated that the host-guest relationship directly affects small accommodation establishments such as B & Bs (Oppermann, 1995; Tucker, 2003). This is perhaps because B & Bs are primarily run by hosts who offer personalized service in a homely environment, which often facilitates the interaction between hosts and guests. It has been suggested that further research is required to understand the interactions between hosts

Global Cases on Hospitality Industry
© 2008 by The Haworth Press, Taylor & Francis Group. All rights reserved.
doi:10.1300/5923_04

and guests in the B & B experience due to its implications to the tourism industry (Oppermann, 1995; Tucker, 2003). Therefore, in this chapter a case study is presented examining hosts' and guests' expectations in terms of service quality attributes at selected B & Bs in the Mornington Peninsula region of Victoria, Australia.

LITERATURE REVIEW

The literature was reviewed in order to understand issues relating to hosts' and guests' expectations of the B & B experience in terms of service quality attributes. In particular, empirical and conceptual research studies were examined in reference to B & Bs, the host-guest relationship, expectations, and service quality.

Defining B & Bs

The B & B sector has experienced phenomenal growth worldwide, including in Victoria, Australia (Davidson and Spearritt, 2000). The definition of the term *B & B* may appear to be simple; however, several contrasting definitions of B & Bs are apparent in the both the literature and the industry. Specifically, much debate exists regarding the number of rooms and the meals provided at a B & B (Lanier and Berman, 1993; Zane, 1997; Lubetkin, 1999). These variations have referred to traditional B & B homestays, farm-stay accommodations, self-contained cottages, guesthouses, retreats, and inns, which have different characteristics and provide different services.

The various definitions and characteristics of a B & B contribute to the difficulty in defining the term B & B, which has significant implications to research in this area. Many Australians have visions of a B & B from their holiday experiences in the United Kingdom and Europe, however Australian B & Bs are often quite different from overseas B & Bs in terms of the host-guest interaction, property characteristics, and facilities (Dickman and Maddock, 2000).

Australian B & B guests tend to travel as couples for romantic getaways, are most likely between the ages of twenty-five and fifty-four, and are likely to work full time (Market and Communications Research, 2001). Australian B & B hosts are generally middle-aged couples who operate a B & B due to lifestyle and family reasons as a form of socializing and entertaining people (Getz and Carlsen, 2000; Getz et al., 2004). As noted by Dickman and Maddock (2000), Australian B & B hosts and guests tend to interact during the B & B experience, most studies of B & Bs focus either on the host or the guest. Much of the literature pertaining to B & B hosts provides practical guides of how to be successful in terms of marketing and advertising (Kaufman et al., 1996; Lubetkin, 1999; Lee et al., 2003), whereas other studies focus on the demographic profiles of B & B guests to understand their motivations, expenditures, and perceptions of quality (Vallen and Rande, 1997; Zane, 1997; Hill and Busby, 2002).

Host-Guest Relationship

It has been argued that one of the key functions for tourism businesses is managing the host-guest relationship (Morrison, 2002). The host-guest relationship has been examined in studies of farm tourism. Such studies found that guests had the desire to meet and be among the local people and to have an authentic experience, as the hosts were often perceived as the key attraction (Pearce, 1990; Tucker, 2003). It was also revealed that cross-cultural difficulties existed between hosts and guests, particularly in terms of the social roles and rules (Stringer, 1981; Pearce, 1990).

Although these studies provide valuable findings, researchers have noted that the host-guest relationship has still received little attention theoretically and empirically (Stringer, 1981; Pearce, 1990; Tucker, 2003). In particular, Oppermann (1995) recognizes the absence of comparative studies relating to hosts' and guests' perceptions, which could be vital to understanding the host-guest relationship. It is also noted that the host-guest relationship directly affects the B & B experience, particularly in rural communities, therefore further research is required in understanding these interactions (Oppermann, 1995; Tucker, 2003). This study addresses the issues relating to the host-guest relationship in terms of hosts' and guests' expectations of the B & B experience.

Service Quality Expectations

The construct of expectation is an important area of study since understanding what consumers expect is essential to practitioners and academicians alike. Although this area of research has been widely documented and reported, no accepted definition of the term *expectation* exists (Coye, 2004). In particular, variations are apparent between consumer-satisfaction literature and service-quality literature regarding the definition of expectations. This is because consumer-satisfaction literature defines expectations as predictions based on the likelihood of an occurrence of a future event (Oliver, 1980; Zeithaml et al., 1993). Alternatively, service-quality literature views expectations as desires in terms of what should be offered by a service provider (Boulding et al., 1993).

Several researchers have attempted to define expectations to determine the nature, types, and determinants of expectations that exist in a service encounter (Boulding et al., 1993; Zeithaml et al., 1993; Walker and Baker, 2000). This has been particularly applied to literature relating to service quality in which a range of products and services have been examined. Expectations have typically been considered to be an element in the process of satisfaction based on the development of several models of consumer satisfaction (Oliver, 1980; Cadotte et al., 1987; Spreng et al., 1996). Several studies have proposed that consumer expectations play a crucial role in developing satisfaction and that service-quality judgements are often a fundamental factor in the evaluation of services (Zeithaml et al., 1993; Walker and Baker, 2000).

Service industries have become a dominant sector in industrialized world economies since the 1970s, which has contributed to the interest in the research domain of service quality (Johns et al., 1997). The study of service quality has stimulated great interest, particularly in terms of understanding consumers' expectations (Clow et al., 1997; Johnson and Mathews, 1997; Bebko, 2000). Several models have been developed to explain the determinants, influences, and attributes of service quality (Parasuraman et al., 1985; Boulding et al., 1993; Bebko, 2000). Accordingly, managing service quality has also been the focus of research, which has important implications for service providers (Mersha and Adlakha, 1992; Coye, 2004).

A commonly accepted framework for measuring service quality was developed by Parasuraman et al. (1985). The framework summarizes the nature and determinants of service quality from the perspective of consumers. The model explains the gaps between the perceptions of both the consumer and the service provider that directly impact the consumers' evaluation of service quality. In particular, the model asserts that a gap exists between consumers' expectations of service and management's perceptions of consumers' expectations. (Parasuraman et al., 1985). Based on this notion, many research studies have examined service quality expectations to identify whether a discrepancy exists between consumers' expectations and management's perceptions of consumers' expectations in a variety of service industries in which considerable differences have been reported (Bebko, 2000; Tsang and Qu, 2000; Douglas and Connor, 2003; Juwaheer and Lee-Ross, 2003).

It has also been noted that consumers often evaluate service quality based on the importance and presence of certain attributes that have the potential to determine satisfaction (Kivela et al., 1999). This illustrates the direct connection between consumers' expectations and the attributes present in a service encounter. Such attributes in service industries include location, facilities, price, atmosphere, level of service, and quality of food. These types of attributes are commonly measured in studies throughout services marketing in the form of questionnaires using a five-point Likert-type rating scale (Lewis, 1987; Kivela et al., 1999).

Although research in consumer expectations has been examined in numerous service industries, few studies have been applied to small businesses, which tend to dominate the service industry in Australia (Lee-Ross, 1998). This highlights the need to explore consumer expectations in the service industry, particularly in the tourism sector, in which many small businesses operate. From a review of the literature, it is clear that little is known about the expectations of hosts and guests despite the growth of the B & B sector. This calls for an examination of expectations and the attributes that impact service quality in order to gain a better understanding of the B & B experience. Therefore, this study explores the areas of research in which gaps in the literature exist in order to determine both hosts' and guests' expectations of service quality attributes and to identify whether discrepancies exist between them in the B & B experience.

METHODOLOGY

The chosen geographical location for this study is the Mornington Peninsula, which is situated in Australia, approximately one hour's drive from Melbourne, Victoria's capital city. The region is a popular holiday destination, ideal for a short break, a romantic escape, a family holiday, or a weekend touring the wineries (Peninsula Pages, 2004). A variety of accommodations are offered in the Mornington Peninsula including hotels, motels, resorts, B & Bs, vineyard retreats, caravan parks, and camping grounds.

The study was conducted in the B & B accommodation sector in which both qualitative and quantitative approaches were combined in two stages. Initially, semistructured interviews were conducted to explore hosts' and guests' expectations of the B & B experience relating to service-quality attributes. The findings were then utilized to develop self-completed questionnaires, which were applied to a larger sample of respondents.

Since little is known about hosts' and guests' expectations specific to the B & B accommodation sector, a qualitative, exploratory approach was considered most appropriate to identify a list of service quality attributes for further examination in stage two. Two groups of respondents were used in stage one, consisting of guests who had previously stayed at a B & B in Victoria during the previous two years, and hosts of a B & B establishment located in the Mornington Peninsula. Purposive sampling was used to select participants in stage one, which required the researcher to decide who would be potentially involved in a study (Jennings, 2001). Semistructured interviews, with five open-ended questions, were chosen to be the most appropriate method of data collection. The face-to-face interviews were conducted during winter 2004 and were tape recorded by the interviewer during the discussion.

For the purpose of data analysis, pseudonyms were given to respondents to ensure that they could not be identified throughout the study. The qualitative data were analyzed using categorization. The interview transcripts were examined, and certain words or phrases were compiled to create a list of attributes that were then sorted into categories (Miles and Huberman, 1994). The transcripts showed some conflicting perceptions between hosts' and guests' expectations of certain service quality attributes, thus these issues were explored further in the questionnaires.

Two groups of respondents were used in stage two, consisting of B & B guests who were adult members (eighteen years or older) staying at a B & B at the time of data collection and who completed a questionnaire. The sample of B & B hosts in stage two consisted of B & B establishments in the Mornington Peninsula who were members of either the local tourism association or the local B & B association who agreed to participate in the study themselves and to distribute questionnaires to their guests. Convenience sampling was used in stage two to obtain the sample of hosts and guests.

Self-completed questionnaires, with a larger sample of hosts and guests, were the most suitable method of determining whether a discrepancy existed between hosts' and guests' expectations in stage two. Two self-completed questionnaires were designed, one for hosts and one for guests, which contained the same questions but were worded differently to apply to the two samples. The questionnaires were based on the literature review and the results from the stage one semistructured interviews. The questionnaires were divided into two sections. The first section measured respondents' expectations of the service-quality attributes in a B & B experience on a five-point scale that ranged from 1 (low expectation) to 5 (extremely high expectation). The second section requested respondents' demographic information, as Douglas and Connor (2003) suggest be done, since obtaining a demographic profile of visitors provides more valuable findings.

The questionnaires were distributed to B & B hosts along with a brief explanation of the procedures involved when handing out the guest questionnaires. B & B hosts were requested to ask each of their guests whether they would be willing to participate, and if they agreed the hosts handed them a questionnaire and asked them to fill it out on arrival at their B & B property. Guests were then asked to deposit their completed questionnaires in a sealed box that was provided at each B & B property by the researcher. From the 25 B & B properties that participated in the study, a total of 28 host questionnaires were collected, as more than one host completed a questionnaire at the properties. In addition, from the guests who stayed at the B & B properties, 75 usable guest questionnaires were collected for analysis. The total number of guests who stayed at the B & Bs in the sample was 260; this represents a 28.8 percent response rate.

The quantitative data were analyzed using descriptive statistics in order to summarize the data and to provide a profile of hosts and guests. Frequency distributions were used in terms of means and standard deviations for continuous data, and percentages were used to describe categorical data. Inferential statistics were also used to determine whether a discrepancy existed between hosts' and guests' expectations of service quality attributes in the form of independent t-tests and chi-square tests (George and Mallery, 2003; Saunders et al., 2003). To further test whether hosts' and guests' expectations were significantly different, the effect size statistical technique was used. This is also known as "strength of association" or "eta squared," which indicates the magnitude of the difference between means (Pallant, 2001).

RESULTS AND DISCUSSION

The results of this study have been examined in two parts: the interview results followed by the questionnaire results.

Interview Results

The first three questions of the semistructured interviews were designed to identify hosts' and guests' expectations' of the service-quality attributes in the B & B experience in terms of facilities, the service encounter, and atmosphere. Other questions were asked during the semistructured interviews to address the issues relating to the definition of a B & B, however this aspect is not discussed in this chapter. A qualitative data analysis approach was used to interpret the results, as mentioned earlier. The responses from both hosts and guests were combined for the purpose of analysis to examine both perspectives simultaneously, given that stage one was exploratory in nature and designed only to identify attributes or issues for further investigation.

The first question asked during the semistructured interviews related to the facilities that would generally be expected to be provided in a B & B experience. The most frequent responses included a bathroom, bed, privacy, television, digital video disc (DVD) player, kitchen, breakfast, double spa, and fireplace. These responses were classified into categories, which assisted the design of a question in stage two's questionnaires relating to the facilities in a B & B experience. Utilizing the most frequent responses from stage one, respondents were asked to rate the following on a five-point scale, as previously discussed, to indicate their level of expectation:

- Private bathroom
- Private entrance
- Television
- Private kitchen
- Double spa
- Fireplace
- DVD player

Note: These items would be available to guests for their exclusive use in their room.

The issue of privacy was also frequently mentioned, suggesting that it was highly important in a B & B experience. For instance, Melanie (guest) noted, ". . . respecting my privacy is probably the biggest service they can provide. . . ." In the same way, Tracey (host) believed that guests should expect ". . . some degree of privacy, obviously private bedroom and I would imagine private bathroom facilities, just to make it comfortable." Therefore, a question was included in stage two's questionnaires to examine the degree of privacy expected in a B & B experience, which was specifically related to the characteristics and the design of the B & B property. Respondents were asked to rate the following items on a five-point scale to indicate their level of expectation:

- A traditional homestead where guests stay in the hosts' house
- A self-contained cottage separate to the hosts' house
- Accommodation that has a unique theme
- A shared dining room or lounge area
- Facilities for children

Another question asked during the semistructured interviews related to the services that were expected to be provided in a B & B experience. The most frequent responses included breakfast, local knowledge and information, cleanliness, extra meals, service (accommodation) every day, and cooked meals. The responses were classified into categories, and it was apparent that they varied substantially for this question; therefore it was deemed appropriate for stage two's questionnaires to examine specific services that are provided in a B & B experience separately.

Further examination of hosts' and guests' expectations in relation to breakfast was undertaken, as it was evident from the interview responses that differences existed between what hosts perceived that guests expected for breakfast. For example, Bob (host) said, ". . . type of breakfast is not so critical . . . some B & Bs provide a fully cooked breakfast with all the bells and whistles whereas we provide a gourmet breakfast . . . and leave it in a utility room where they can go and pick it up when they're ready to eat. . . ." However, Melanie (guest) indicated, "I'd like them to either provide breakfast for me to cook or cook it for me. . . ." Similarly, Thomas (guest) stated, ". . . I always expect it to be cooked, otherwise to me it's not really a bed-and-breakfast." Therefore, stage two's questionnaires asked respondents about the type of breakfast expected in a B & B experience. Respondents were requested to indicate their expectation on a categorical scale relating to the following statements:

- Guests expect a fully cooked breakfast, prepared by the host that is served at their door
- Guests expect a fully cooked breakfast prepared by the host to be eaten in a dining area that is shared by the hosts and other guests
- Guests expect to be provided with a gourmet hamper for breakfast that they prepare for themselves
- Guests expect to be provided with a gourmet hamper of food that does not require cooking, which may include fruit and bakery items

Furthermore, an analysis of the interviews revealed that various responses were made relating to the host-guest relationship in the B & B experience. For example, Tracey (host) said, ". . . I think the hosting and the interaction of the host, if it is required by the guest, is a primary importance." In contrast, Rachel (host) suggested that guests ". . . particularly want friendly hosts but they don't want to be overhosted. . . . They haven't come here with their partner for a romantic weekend away to be harassed by hosts." Therefore, it seemed appropriate to include a question in stage two's questionnaires to examine what was expected from the hosts of a B & B establishment. Respondents were asked to indicate their level of expectation on a five-point scale for the following items:

- Friendly and welcoming
- Provide local knowledge and information
- Interact and converse with guests
- Provide a hospitable and comfortable environment
- Be nonintrusive and respect guests' privacy

Another interview question asked respondents about the atmosphere in a B & B experience. The most frequent responses were country setting, comfortable, warm, cozy, romantic, peaceful, inviting, relaxing, and privacy. The responses were classified into categories, which were utilized to make descriptive statements that were included in stage two's questionnaires. Respondents were asked to indicate their level of expectation on a categorical scale in terms of the atmosphere in a B & B experience. The following options were provided:

- A view of the country with attractive natural surroundings
- A peaceful and inviting setting that allows guests to relax
- A romantic setting that is intimate and private
- A comfortable, warm, and cozy setting with a personal touch
- A sociable atmosphere in which to meet and converse with other guests

Questionnaire Results

Demographic Profile of B & B Hosts and Guests

Demographic information was collected in stage two's questionnaires to gain an understanding of both hosts and guests in the Mornington Peninsula. A demographic profile of hosts (Table 4.1) and guests (Table 4.2) who participated in stage two is provided.

The majority of hosts sampled were females and almost half of the B & B hosts were between 51 and 64 years old. A number of the hosts who were also between 36 and 50 years of age and who were over 65 years old. This supports Getz et al.'s (2004) claim that B & B hosts generally consist of middle-aged couples or families. The majority of B & B hosts had been operating their B & B between one to five years, similar to Stokes' (1998) study, which stated that the average B & B has been in operation for less than five years.

TABLE 4.1. Host Demographic Profile

Hosts	Total	Percent
Gender (N=28)		
Male	8	28.6
Female	20	71.4
Age (N=28)		
Under 35	1	3.6
36-50	7	25.0
51-64	13	46.4
65+	7	25.0
Years in operation (N=27)		
1-5	19	70.4
6-10	5	18.5
11+	3	11.1

Note: Respondents were selective in providing answers to demographic questions, hence the differences in N.

The sample of B & B guests revealed that they were generally between the ages of 35 and 44 years old, and a substantial number of guests were aged between 55 and 64. A higher proportion of guests were female than were male, and the guests sampled were primarily domestic visitors from Victoria. This is consistent with previous B & B studies in which similar demographic profiles were obtained (Market and Communications Research, 2001).

EXPECTATIONS

As the study sought to explore hosts' and guests' expectations and to identify whether discrepancies between them in the B & B experience exist, the results are examined accordingly. The findings are presented in terms of the specific service-quality attributes that were identified in stage one, which included breakfast, facilities, property characteristics, atmosphere, and the B & B host characteristics. The quantitative results are analyzed using descriptive, inferential, and eta-squared statistics. In particular, to determine whether significant

TABLE 4.2. Guest Demographic Profile

Guests	Total	%
Gender (N=74)		
Male	28	37.8
Female	46	62.2
Age (N=75)		
18-25	6	8.0
26-34	12	16.0
35-44	23	30.7
45-54	10	13.3
55-64	19	25.3
65+	5	6.7
Type of visitor (N=72)		
Domestic	68	94.5
International	4	5.5
State of origin (N=67)		
Victoria	50	74.6
Other states	17	25.4

Note: Respondents were selective in providing answers to demographic questions, hence the differences in N.

differences existed, independent t-tests were conducted at the 95 percent confidence level, which is commonly used in services marketing literature; however, variations at 90 percent and 99 percent are also included (Walker and Baker, 2000).

The interviews in stage one revealed particular differences between what guests expect for breakfast compared to what hosts think guests expect. As a result, stage two's questionnaires addressed the issue of breakfast, which was examined in terms of a fully cooked breakfast or a gourmet hamper. The results are presented in Table 4.3.

The results indicate that although "a gourmet hamper that guests prepare themselves" was the most frequent response, the majority of respondents reported that guests expect to be provided with a fully cooked breakfast (H: −60.7 percent, G: −53.3 percent). This was ex-

TABLE 4.3. Hosts' and Guests' Expectations of Breakfast

Breakfast	Host expectation (N = 28) Percent	Guest expectation (N = 75) Percent
A fully cooked breakfast, prepared by the host that is served at the door	35.7	28.0
A fully cooked breakfast prepared by the host to be eaten in a dining area that is shared by the hosts and other guests	25.0	25.3
A gourmet hamper for breakfast that guests pre-pare themselves	35.7	32.0
A gourmet hamper of food that does not require cook-ing, which may include fruit and bakery items	3.6	14.7
Total	100	100

Note: This question was rated categorically

pected to either be "prepared by the host that is served at the door" or "prepared by the host to be eaten in a dining area that is shared by the hosts and other guests." A small proportion of respondents indicated that they preferred "a gourmet hamper of food that does not require cooking." Further analysis utilizing chi-square revealed that no significant differences existed between hosts' and guests' expectations relating to breakfast in a B & B experience.

The findings from stage one identified several facilities that required further examination. Respondents were asked to indicate their expectations for each of these seven facilities, shown in Table 4.4.

Respondents indicated that a private bathroom was highly expected in a B & B experience. Little variation existed in the responses to this question, as indicated by the relatively low standard deviations. These results are consistent with the literature, in which it has been reported that guests are concerned about whether personal bathroom facilities would be available to them (Market and Communications Research, 2001). It was also identified that guests expect to be

TABLE 4.4. Hosts' and Guests' Expectations of Facilities

Facilities	Host expectation (N = 28)		Guest expectation (N = 75)	
	Mean	Standard deviation	Mean	Standard deviation
Private bathroom	4.89	0.41	4.79	0.53
Television	4.36	0.83	3.79	1.19
Private entrance	3.86	1.32	3.13	1.32
Fireplace	3.57	1.10	3.08	1.14
Double spa	3.14	1.51	2.70	1.44
Kitchen	2.86	1.45	2.71	1.34
DVD player	2.32	1.33	2.35	1.26

Note: Questions were rated on a five-point scale where 1 = low expectation and 5 = extremely high expectation.

provided with a television while staying at a B & B. The facilities that were least expected were a kitchen, double spa, and a DVD player.

The results from the independent t-tests suggested a statistically significant difference between hosts' and guests' expectations of a private entrance [t (103) = −2.48, p < 0.05]. This suggests that hosts tended to rate guests' expectations higher than guests regarding a private entrance. It was found that the magnitude of difference in the means had a large effect (eta squared = 0.57). In addition, it was revealed that a statistically significant difference existed between hosts' and guests' expectations of a television [t (103) = 3.31, p < 0.01]. Therefore, hosts perceived guests to have a higher level of expectation regarding a television than guests actually did. From the results, the magnitude of the difference in the means also had a considerable large effect (eta squared = 0.98).

It was also found that a statistically significant difference existed in hosts' and guests' expectations of a kitchen [t (103) = −6.07, p < 0.001]. This suggests that hosts placed greater expectations on a kitchen compared to what guests actually expected. The magnitude of the differences had a large effect (eta squared = 0.26). Similarly, a statistically significant difference existed between hosts' and guests' expectations of a fireplace [t (103) = -1.95, p < 0.05]. This indicates that hosts perceived guests to have a higher level of expectation relating to a fireplace than what guests reported. It was also found that the magnitude of the differences was quite high (eta squared = 0.36).

In order to address the issue of privacy, respondents were asked to respond to a question in stage two's questionnaires regarding the characteristics and the design of the B & B property, as presented in Table 4.5.

"A self-contained cottage separate to the hosts' house" generated the highest mean score in terms hosts' and guests' expectations. The lowest mean score obtained was "facilities for children," reflecting that respondents perhaps consider a B & B a form of accommodation in which guests generally stay without children.

It was revealed a statistically significant difference between the means of hosts and guests in relation to "accommodation that has a unique theme" [t (103) = -2.96, p < 0.01]. This illustrates that hosts tended to rate guests' expectations higher than guests regarding a B & B as a form of accommodation with a unique theme. The magnitude

TABLE 4.5. Hosts' and Guests' Expectations of B&B Property Characteristics

Property characteristics	Host expectation (N = 28)		Guest expectation (N = 74)	
	Mean	Standard deviation	Mean	Standard deviation
A self-contained cottage separate to the hosts' house	3.82	1.33	3.60	1.03
Accommodation that has a unique theme	3.57	1.13	2.72	1.35
A traditional homestead where guests stay in the hosts' house	3.25	1.29	2.97	1.29
A shared dining room or lounge area	2.68	0.94	2.41	1.14
Facilities for children	2.18	1.15	1.70	1.10

Note: Questions were rated on a five-point scale where 1 = low expectation and 5 = extremely high expectation. Respondents were selective in providing answers to property characteristics, hence the difference in N.

of the difference in the means also had a considerable large effect (eta squared = 0.79).

Another aspect of the B&B experience that was examined in stage two's questionnaires was the atmosphere. The results are illustrated in Table 4.6. The analysis of Table 4.6 highlights that respondents indicated that guests expect to be provided with "a peaceful and inviting setting that allows guests to relax." In addition, the results reveal that "a comfortable, warm, and cozy setting with a personal touch" was the second most expected atmosphere for guests. Certainly, "a sociable atmosphere to meet and converse with other guests" appeared to be the least expected type of atmosphere in a B & B experience. This suggests that guests prefer a more private setting rather than a sociable atmosphere. These findings support previous studies that have examined B & Bs and farm stays in which it was found that guests were motivated to stay at a B & B because of the peaceful atmosphere (Pearce, 1990; Tucker, 2003). Further analysis utilizing chi-square revealed that no significant differences existed between hosts' and guests' expectations relating to the atmosphere in a B & B experience.

TABLE 4.6. Hosts' and Guests' Expectations of the Atmosphere at a B&B

Atmosphere	Host expectation (N = 28) Percent	Guest expectation (N = 75) Percent
A peaceful and inviting setting that allows guests to relax	46.4	34.7
A comfortable, warm, and cosy setting with a personal touch	21.4	29.3
A romantic setting that is intimate and private	14.3	18.7
A view of country with attractive natural surroundings	10.7	16.0
A sociable atmosphere to meet and converse with other guests	7.2	1.3
Total	100	100

Note: This question was rated categorically.

TABLE 4.7. Hosts' and Guests' Expectations of B&B Host Characteristics

Hosts	Host expectation (N = 28)		Guest expectation (N = 75)	
	Mean	Standard deviation	Mean	Standard deviation
Friendly and welcoming	4.82	0.47	4.61	0.63
Provide a hospitable environment	4.82	0.47	4.52	0.55
Be nonintrusive	4.57	0.99	4.43	0.84
Provide local knowledge	4.50	0.64	4.37	0.67
Interact and converse with guests	2.89	1.13	3.35	1.13

Note: Questions were rated on a five-point scale where 1 = low expectation and 5 = extremely high expectation.

The results from stage one indicated that various views existed relating to what was expected by the hosts of a B & B establishment, therefore this required further analysis. Stage two's questionnaires asked respondents to indicate their expectations based on the statements shown in Table 4.7.

Both hosts and guests placed high expectations on the majority of the five B & B host characteristics in Table 4.7 (with the mean scores above the average of 3.0). The results revealed that it is highly expected for hosts to be "friendly and welcoming"; these findings are also noted in Stokes (1998) study of B & Bs in Queensland in which the friendliness of the host was considered to be the most important feature for guests when choosing to stay at a B & B. The other host characteristics that were highly expected were for hosts to "provide a hospitable and comfortable environment," "be nonintrusive and respect guests' privacy," and to "provide local knowledge and information."

It appeared that both hosts and guests had similar expectations regarding B & B host characteristics. However, the results showed a statistically significant difference between hosts' and guests' expectations of what is expected of hosts regarding the "provision of a hospitable environment" [t (103) = -2.73, p < 0.01]. Therefore, it can be assumed that hosts tended to rate guests' expectations higher than guests in terms of the provision of a hospitable environment. The magnitude of the difference in the means had a moderate effect (eta squared = 0.06).

CONCLUSIONS AND RECOMMENDATIONS

The results revealed that the majority of hosts had a relatively accurate idea of guests' expectations, similar to Tsang and Qu's (2000) study in which managers appeared to have a reasonably good understanding of consumers' expectations. The majority of hosts and guests indicated that guests expected to be provided with a fully cooked breakfast, a private bathroom, and a self-contained cottage separate to the hosts' house when staying at a B & B. Both hosts and guests rated a peaceful and inviting setting that allows guests to relax as the most expected type of atmosphere, and expectations were high for B & B hosts to be friendly and welcoming.

However, the findings indicated statistically significant differences between hosts' and guests' expectations relating to specific facilities, property characteristics, and characteristics of B & B hosts. In addition, in many cases B & B hosts tended to rate guests' expectations of the service quality attributes higher than the guests did. These findings support the model developed by Parasuraman et al. (1985) suggesting that a gap exists between consumers' expectations and management's perceptions of consumer expectations.

It is recommended that future research identify how guests' expectations are influenced by factors such as prior experience, word-of-mouth communication, and a firm's image in the B & B experience (Clow et al., 1997). These findings could be compared between the demographic profiles of guests to identify how guests' expectations differ according to their age and gender, their country and state of origin, the number of times they have stayed at a B & B, and whether they are traveling with children. In addition, future research could examine how hosts' expectations are influenced by factors such as age, gender, and the number of years in operation.

It is likely that all research studies are subject to limitations, thus the limitations in this study are considered. First, the findings are geographically limited to B & Bs in the Mornington Peninsula, given the case study approach adopted, and thus are not reflective of the entire B & B sector. Second, the time period in which the study took place was during low season (July and August), which contributed to the low response rate. Third, a degree of sampling bias exists due to the convenience and purposive sampling techniques used.

This study has attempted to provide B & B hosts with greater insights into understanding guests' expectations. In particular, hosts may choose to revise the type of breakfast offered at their B & B based on the findings, which suggest the majority of guests expect a fully cooked breakfast. This study has also contributed to the growing body of literature by comparing hosts' and guests' expectations to gain a better understanding of the host-guest relationship. Since little is known about the expectations of hosts and guests despite the growth of the B & B sector, this study has attempted to set a benchmark against which subsequent studies can be compared.

REFERENCES

Bebko, C. (2000). Service intangibility and its impact on consumer expectation's of service quality. *Journal of Services Marketing, 14*(1): 9-26.

Boulding, W., Kalra, A., Staelin, R., and Zeithaml, V. (1993). A dynamic process model of service quality: From expectations to behavioral intentions. *Journal of Marketing Research, 30*(1): 7-27.

Cadotte, E., Woodruff, R. and Jenkins, R. (1987). Expectations and norms in models of consumer satisfaction. *Journal of Marketing Research, 24*(3): 305-314.

Clow, K., Kurtz, D., Ozment, J., and Beng, S. (1997). The antecedents of consumer expectations of services: An empirical study across four industries. *Journal of Services Marketing, 11*(4): 230-248.

Coye, R. (2004). Managing customer expectation's in the service encounter. *International Journal of Service Industry Management, 15*(1): 54-71.

Davidson, J. and Spearritt, P. (2000). *Holiday Business: Tourism in Australia Since 1870.* Melbourne, Australia: University Press.

Dickman, S. and Maddock, M. (2000). *The Business of Bed and Breakfasts.* Melbourne, Australia: Hospitality Press.

Douglas, L. and Connor, R. (2003). Attitudes to service quality: The expectation gap. *Nutrition & Food Science, 33*(4): 165-172.

George, D. and Mallery, P. (2003). *SPSS for Windows Step By Step: A Simple Guide and Reference 11.0 Update,* 4th edition. Boston, MA: Pearson Education.

Getz, D. and Carlsen, J. (2000). Characteristics and goals of family and owner-operated businesses in the rural tourism and hospitality sectors. *Tourism Management, 21*(6): 547-560.

Getz, D., Carlsen, J., and Morrison, A. (2004). *The Family Business in Tourism and Hospitality.* Oxfordshire, UK: CABI Publishing.

Hill, R. and Busby, G. (2002). An inspector calls: Farm accommodation providers' attitudes to quality assurance schemes in the county of Devon. *International Journal of Tourism Research, 4*: 459-478.

Jennings, G. (2001). *Tourism Research.* Queensland, Australia: John Wiley and Sons Australia.

Johns, N., Lee-Ross, D., and Ingram, H. (1997). A study of service quality in small hotel's and guesthouses. *Progress in Tourism and Hospitality Research, 3*(4): 351-363.

Johnson, C. and Mathews, B. (1997). Influence of experience on service expectation's. *International Journal of Service Industry Management, 8*(4): 290-305.

Juwaheer, T. and Lee-Ross, D. (2003). A study of hotel guest perception's in Mauritius. *International Journal of Contemporary Hospitality Management, 15*(2): 105-115.

Kaufman, T., Weaver, P., and Poynter, J. (1996). Success attributes of B&B operators. *Cornell Hotel and Restaurant Administration Quarterly, 37*(4): 29-34.

Kivela, J., Inbakaran, R., and Reece, J. (1999). Consumer research in the restaurant environment, part 1: A conceptual model of dining satisfaction and return patronage. *International Journal of Contemporary Hospitality Management, 11* (5): 205-222.

Lanier, P. and Berman, J. (1993). Bed and breakfasts come of age. *Cornell Hotel and Restaurant Administration Quarterly, 34*(4): 5-23.

Lee, S., Reynolds, J., and Kennon, L. (2003). Bed and breakfast industries: Successful marketing strategies. *Journal of Travel & Tourism Marketing, 14*(1): 37-53.

Lee-Ross, D. (1998). Comment: Australia and the small to medium-sized hotel sector. *International Journal of Contemporary Hospitality Management, 10*(5): 177-179.

Lewis, R. (1987). The measurement of gaps in the quality of hotel services. *International Journal of Hospitality Management, 6*(2): 83-88.

Lubetkin, M. (1999). Bed-and-breakfasts: Advertising and promotion. *Cornell Hotel and Restaurant Administration Quarterly, 40*(4): 84-90.

Market and Communications Research (MCR) (2001). *Domestic Consumer Research: Bed and Breakfast/Farm Stays Research Report.* Brisbane, Australia: Tourism Queensland.

Mersha, T. and Adlakha, V. (1992). Attribute's of service quality: The consumers' perspective. *International Journal of Service Industry Management, 3*(3): 34-45.

Middleton, V. and Clarke, J. (2001). *Marketing in Travel and Tourism,* 3rd edition. Oxford, UK: Butterworth-Heinemann.

Miles, M.B. and Huberman, A.M. (1994). *An Expanded Sourcebook, Qualitative Data Analysis,* 2nd edition. Thousand Oaks: Sage Publications.

Morrison, A.M. (2002). *Hospitality and Travel Marketing,* 3rd edition. New York: Delmar.

Morrison, A., Pearce, P., Moscardo, G., Nadkarni, N., and O'Leary, J. (1996). Specialist accommodation: Definition, markets served and roles in tourism development. *Journal of Travel Research, 6*(1): 18-26.

Oliver, R. (1980). A cognitive model of the antecedents and consequence's of satisfaction decisions. *Journal of Marketing Research, 17*(4): 460-469.

Oppermann, M. (1995). Holidays on the farm: A case study of German hosts and guests. *Journal of Travel Research, 34*(1): 63-67.

Pallant, J. (2001). *SPSS Survival Manual: A Step by Step Guide to Data Analysis Using SPSS.* New South Wales, Australia: Allen and Unwin.

Parasuraman, A., Zeithaml, V., and Berry, L. (1985). A conceptual model of service quality and its' implication's for future research. *Journal of Marketing, 49*(4): 41-50.

Pearce, P. (1990). Farm tourism in New Zealand: A social situation analysis. *Annals of Tourism Research, 17:* 337-352.

Peninsula Pages (2004). Melbourne's Peninsula Accommodation Guide. (2004). Available at: http://www.peninsulapages.com

Saunders, M., Lewis, P., and Thornhill, A. (2003). *Research Methods for Business Students,* 3rd edition. Essex, UK: Pearson Education Ltd.

Spreng, R., MacKenzie, S., and Olshavsky, R. (1996). A reexamination of the determinant's of consumer satisfaction. *Journal of Marketing, 60*(3): 15-32.

Stokes, R. (1998). *Queensland Bed and Breakfast and Farm Tourism Research Report.* Queensland, Australia: Queensland University of Technology.

Stringer, P.F. (1981). Hosts and guests the bed-and-breakfast phenomenon. *Annals of Tourism Research, 8*(3): 357-376.

Tsang, N. and Qu, H. (2000). Service quality in China's hotel industry: A perspective from tourists and hotel managers. *International Journal of Contemporary Hospitality Management, 12*(5): 316-326.

Tucker, H. (2003). The host-guest relationship and its implications for rural tourism. In Hall, D., Roberts, L., and Mitchell, M. (eds.), *New Directions in Rural Tourism* (pp.80-89). Aldershot, UK: Ashgate Publishing.

Vallen, G. and Rande, W. (1997). Bed and breakfasts in Arizona. *Cornell Hotel and Restaurant Administration Quarterly, 38*(4): 62-68.

Walker, J. and Baker, J. (2000). An exploratory study of a multi-expectation framework for services. *Journal of Services Marketing, 14*(5): 411-431.

Zane, B. (1997). The B&B guest: A comprehensive view. *Cornell Hotel and Restaurant Administration Quarterly, 38*(4): 69-75.

Zeithaml, V., Leonard, B., and Parasuraman, A. (1993). The nature and determinant's of customer expectations of service. *Journal of the Academy of Marketing Science, 21*(1): 1-12.

FURTHER READING

Lanier, P., Caples, D., and Cook, C. (2000). How big is small? *Cornell Hotel and Restaurant Administration Quarterly, 41*(5): 90-95.

Lynch, P. (1994). Demand for training by bed and breakfast operators. *International Journal of Hospitality Management, 6*(4): 25-31.

Nuntsu, N., Tassiopoulos, D., and Haydam, N. (2004). The bed and breakfast market of Buffalo City (BC) South Africa: Present status, constraints and success factors. *Tourism Management, 25*(4): 515-522.

Warnick, R. and Lawrence, R. (1991). The bed and breakfast and small inn industry of the commonwealth of Massachusetts: An exploratory survey. *Journal of Travel Research, 29*: 17-25.

Chapter 5

Searching for Critical Success Factors: A Dimension-Specific Assessment of Service Quality and Its Relationship with Customer Satisfaction and Behavioral Intentions in Fast-Food Restaurants

Sanjay K. Jain

Service quality has come to be recognized as a strategic tool for surviving and thriving in the present day fiercely competitive markets. Higher quality leads to higher customer satisfaction, and also results in higher repeat purchases, cross-selling, and positive word-of-mouth communications—all of which help the business firms achieve higher sales revenues, profits, and market shares (e.g., Aaker and Jacobson, 1994; Anderson and Sullivan, 1993; Bolton, 1998; Boulding et al., 1993; Danaher, 1997; Headley and Miller, 1993; Gilbert et al., 2004; Jones and Sasser, 1995; Magi and Julander, 1996; McColl-Kennedy and Schneider, 2000; Rucci et al., 1998; Yavas et al., 2001; Zeithaml et al., 1996). In the hypercompetitive markets, service firms can use superior quality even as a positioning plank for differentiating their service products from other look-alike competitive offers (Parasuraman et al., 1991). In view of its strategic importance, it's of little wonder that service quality has drawn considerable attention of the researchers in the past. Several studies have been conducted to develop and validate the scales used to measure service quality and to establish its linkage with customer satisfaction and purchase intentions.

Global Cases on Hospitality Industry
© 2008 by The Haworth Press, Taylor & Francis Group. All rights reserved.
doi:10.1300/5923_05

Such studies, however, conspicuously lack in India, especially in context of fast-food restaurants, which have undergone significant metamorphosis during the past decade or so. The fast-food restaurant services sector has grown rapidly in the past and is fast catching up to the fancies of customers in metropolitan cities and towns. Competition in the market has considerably shot up in the recent years, and customers today have a variety of fast-food restaurants to choose from. Entry of multinational fast-food restaurant chains such as McDonald's and Pizza Hut have changed the whole scenario. Coupled with increased sophistication and a rise in expectations, future customers are likely to become more selective in their patronization of fast-food restaurants. Local confectionary shops, eating jaunts, and home-delivery caterers have fast mushroomed and are becoming customers' favorites. In such a changed market place, it is natural for the management of the fast-food restaurants to be concerned about consolidating their market position and doing something to increase their market shares.

Management of the fast-food restaurants do recognize the importance of delivering high-quality services, but they are seldom aware of the attributes that constitute core components of customer service quality perceptions. Unless the management knows which of the several service attributes are important and influence customer satisfaction and future intentions, they can do little to achieve success at this front. Findings of the studies undertaken in other countries are likely to be of little help since the food business is largely region and culture specific and does not permit any direct transference of knowledge from operations in one country to another (Gilbert et al., 2004; Zhou, 2004). Recognition of service quality importance notwithstanding, service firms are unlikely to provide more than lip service to the cause of quality improvement efforts unless and until the empirical evidence builds up to show linkages between service quality and customer satisfaction and the consequent payoffs to the firms in terms of greater customer franchise and positive word of mouth communications (for a similar emphasis, see Zeithaml et al., 1996).

The present study aims at filling this void in literature. The study primarily aims at measuring service quality and establishing its linkage with customer satisfaction and behavioral intentions in the context of fast-food restaurant services in India. In the process, the study also evaluates the validity and reliability of the SERVPERF instrument, which is one of the two most widely used and recommended scales in the service literature. The study makes use of the data that were collected in connection with consumer survey of fast-food restaurants in Delhi.[1] Besides exploring service-quality linkages with customer satisfaction and behavioral intentions at the aggregative level, as has been done in the past research, the present study also delves into a dimension-specific analysis of the impact of service quality on such consequences. Dimension-specific analysis of service quality impact is a relatively new phenomenon in the service-quality research stream (e.g., Zhou, 2004) and is likely to gain the status as a research area in the coming years.

This chapter is organized into five sections. With an introduction to the study provided in this section, the next section delves into a discussion of a service-quality concept and its measurement. Relationship of service quality with customer satisfaction and behavioral intentions is described in the succeeding section. Research methodology used in the study and the results are discussed next. The final section sums up the discussion and provides managerial implications and directions for future research.

SERVICE QUALITY, CUSTOMER SATISFACTION, AND BEHAVIORAL CONSEQUENCES: THE CONCEPTUAL FRAMEWORK

Concept of Service Quality and Its Operation

Notwithstanding considerable work done in the area, no clear meaning of the term *service quality* exists. Garvin (1987) rightly observes in this connection that quality is a slippery concept that is easy to visualize but difficult to define. The service-quality literature is replete with a diverse set of quality concepts, ranging from "innate excellence," "quantity of some ingredient or attribute possessed by a product," "consumer's preferences," "conformance to specifications," and "performance or conformance at an acceptable price or cost" (Garvin, 1987). A major reason for the lack of conceptual clarity is that the term *service quality* has been defined and examined in past research from different perspectives.

Attempts made by Parasuraman and colleagues (1985, 1988) constitute a pioneering effort in the direction of conceptualizing and implementing the service-quality concept. An extensive review of literature and focus-group discussions led them to define perceived service quality as "a global judgment, or attitude, relating to the superiority of the service" (Parasuraman et al., 1988). Based on this conceptualization, they implemented service quality as a difference between consumer expectations of "what they want" and their perceptions of "what they get" (i.e., a performance-minus-expectation score). An empirically validated SERVQUAL (*service quality*) scale was put forward by them for measuring service quality (Parasuraman et al., 1985, 1988), which has since then been extensively applied in different service settings.

In view of certain conceptual and methodological flaws with SERVQUAL scale, Cronin and Taylor (1992) proposed an alternate scale—referred to as SERVPERF scale.[2] More specifically, Cronin and Taylor (1992) opined that the expectation component of SERVQUAL be discarded and instead a performance component alone be used. The SERVPERF (*service performance*) scale has also been applied in a number of past studies. Which one of these two scales is a superior measure of service quality has for a long time been a matter of debate. The majority opinion, however, now seems to be in favor of the SERVPERF scale (Babakus and Boller, 1992; Boulding et al., 1993; Brady et al., 2002; Brown et al., 1993; Buttle, 1996; Lee et al., 2000; Page and Spreng, 2002; Teas, 1993, 1994; Zhou, 2004). Even Parasuraman and colleagues (1994) suggested that only the perceptions and not the expectations be measured in assessing the influence of service quality on other constructs.

In view of the psychometric and methodological superiority of SERVPERF over SERVQUAL scale, the present study too makes use of the twenty-two item, performance-only SERVPERF scale. It is hoped that use of this scale in the context of fast-food restaurants in India would also be able to throw some light on the ongoing contentious issue whether this scale in its present form can be applied to different service industries across countries (Furrer et al,. 2000; Smith and Reynolds, 2001; Winsted, 1997; Zhou, 2004).

Service Quality: Functional versus Outcome Quality

Irrespective of which of the two scales is used, a problem common to both these scales is their preoccupation with *functional aspect* of service quality. *Outcome* (i.e., technical) quality, as emphasized in the European school of thought, is altogether missing from these scales. Whereas the functional quality is related to process or "how" part of the service delivery, outcome quality refers to the result of service transaction and is concerned with what is delivered to the customer (Gronroos, 1982, 1990; Lehtinen and Lehtinen, 1982; Mangold and Babakus, 1991; Richard and Allaway, 1993). Though the developers of SERVQUAL initially suggested that service quality consists of functional (process) and technical (outcome) dimensions, the SERVQUAL instrument developed by them incidentally does not contain any measure of technical quality dimension (Kang and James, 2004). Too much focus on the functional aspect of service quality is highly misplaced, especially in the case of services such as fast-food restaurants, for which a tangible part is also dominant, and outcome aspect cannot be simply brushed aside.

In order to overcome this limitation, the present study also includes "quality of food served" as one of the components of customer service-quality evaluations. Incorporation of the outcome component in the service-quality framework is in line with the recommendations made by several researchers for using industry or context specific rather than a generic scale across various service industries and contexts. (e.g., Babakus and Boller, 1992; Buttle, 1996; Carman, 1990; Cronin and Taylor, 1992; Dabholkar et al., 2000; Lewis, 1987; Powpaka, 1996; Voss et al., 1985). Since not many studies have empirically tested the European perspective of including the outcome component (Kang and James, 2004), incorporation of this component into the service quality analysis in the present work can very well serve the purpose of assessing its relevance in adding to the predictive and diagnostic ability of service-quality scale.

Service Quality: Dimensionality and Need for Dimension-Specific Analysis

A contentious issue in service-quality literature has been whether service quality is a unidimensional or multidimensional construct.

Though consumers view the concept of quality holistically, it is now widely recognized that the consumers base their quality judgment and purchase decisions on certain characteristics related either to the service provider or to other elements associated with the service offering, such as appearance and reliability (Bitner, 1990; Le Blanc and Nguyen, 1988). A considerable body of research has emerged that suggests that customers' assessments of quality include perceptions of multiple factors, and that it is not a unidimensional phenomenon. Though the majority opinion now seems to be that the customer perceptions of service quality are based on multiple dimensions, no agreement exists on the nature or number of such dimensions. Two to ten dimensions have been proposed and used in past studies (Garvin, 1987; Gronroos, 1982; Lehtinen and Lehtinen, 1982; Mels et al., 1997; Parasuraman et al., 1985, 1988; Rust and Oliver, 1994). Recent research further complicates the matter by asserting that service-quality perceptions are not only multidimensional, but are also multi-level (e.g., Brady and Cronin, 2001). However, a consensus now exists among the researchers that the five-factor structure as proposed by Parasuraman and colleagues (1988) is not a sacrosanct one. Depending on the service industries and contexts, one can arrive at different factor structures and dimensions.

This debate aside, what is ironic is that the researchers, despite having used service quality as a multidimensional construct and having identified various service quality dimensions, have preferred using only the summed index (as derived by averaging the distinctive dimensions of service quality) for linking it to customer satisfaction and behavioral intentions. This has resulted in a substantial loss of information that otherwise could have been used to provide strategic insights to the service firms by telling them which of the several dimensions are more important in determining customer satisfaction and behavioral outcomes.

Not only theoretically, but empirically too, dimension-specific analysis appears to be a superior approach. Conceptually, this kind of analysis more closely reflects consumers' mental representations of consumption experiences and evaluations (Mittal et al., 1999; Oliver, 1993). Empirically, such an attribute-specific analysis in the area of physical products has found significant variations in customer satisfaction (LaTour and Peat, 1979; Mittal et al., 1999). Though conceptualization of direct links between service attributes and customer satisfaction is a relatively new phenomenon (Johns and Howard, 1998; Johnston, 1995; Mersha and Adlakha, 1992; Oliver, 1993; Winsted, 1997; Zhou, 2004), select few studies undertaken so far do point to different service quality dimensions differently affecting customer satisfaction and behavioral outcomes. As compared to SERVPERF, SERVQUAL has for long been considered a better scale in view of its superior diagnostic power (e.g., Jain and Gupta, 2004; Kassim and Bojei, 2002; Newman, 2001). A dimension-specific analysis, however, can substantially add to the diagnostic value of the SERVPERF scale (Zhou, 2004), thus making it both psychometrically and diagnostically a superior scale.

In view of the strategic relevance of such an analysis in managing service quality, the present study attempts a dimension-specific analysis of service-quality linkage with customer satisfaction and behavioral intentions.

SERVICE QUALITY, CUSTOMER SATISFACTION, AND BEHAVIORAL INTENTIONS: THE LINKAGE

Though most researchers subscribe to the view that customer satisfaction is "an evaluative, affective or emotional response" (Oliver, 1980, p. 460), the debate continues as to what customer satisfaction exactly is and how it differs from service quality. Measurement of customer satisfaction has also been an equally debatable issue, and it remains mired with divergence of approaches (Gilbert et al., 2004). Although some researchers in the past have been of the opinion that service quality and satisfaction are similar terms (e.g., Dabholkar 1993; Spreng and Singh, 1993), others have held the view that these two are distinct constructs (Bitner and Hubbert, 1994; Iacobucci et al., 1994; Oliver, 1993; Taylor and Baker, 1994; Zeithaml et al., 1993). Especially the service-quality researchers have argued that the two concepts differ according to the level at which they are measured: customer satisfaction is a transaction-specific assessment, whereas service quality is comprised of global assessment (e.g., Carman 1990; Parasuraman et al., 1988). Of late, however, a few researchers have started opining that both service quality and customer satisfaction can be examined meaningfully from transaction-specific as well as global perspectives (e.g., Teas, 1993; Dabholkar, 1993; Cronin and Taylor, 1992; Parasuraman et al., 1994).

Those who subscribe to the school that customer satisfaction and service quality are different constructs point out a few more distinctions. Oliver (1993), for instance, opined that the dimensions underlying quality judgments are rather specific, whether they are cues or attributes. Satisfaction judgment, however, can result from any dimensions that may or may not be quality related. A belief also exists among the researcher that whereas quality expectations are based on "ideals" or "excellence" perceptions, satisfaction judgment is formed by a large number of nonquality issues, including needs and equity or "fairness" perceptions (Oliver and Swan, 1989). Furthermore, it has been held that consumers can form quality perceptions without having any actual experience with the service or its provider. Satisfaction, on the other hand, is purely experimental in nature. Though efforts have been made to conceptually differentiate the two terms, empirically the researchers have not always been able to separate service quality from satisfaction (Bansal and Taylor, 1997; Dabholkar, 1995). Notwithstanding different viewpoints held in the past, consensus now seems to be emerging that the two constructs are different. Whereas service quality is considered primarily a cognitive construct, satisfaction is viewed more as a complex concept comprising both the cognitive and affective components (Dhabolkar, 1995; Yavas et al., 2001).

Considerable debate has occurred over the issue of causal relationships between customer satisfaction and service quality and the consequent linkages of these two constructs with behavioral outcomes. Some researchers have held the view that service quality results from customer satisfaction (Bitner, 1990; Bolton and Drew, 1991a,b; Oliver, 1980; Mohr and Bitner, 1995), but others have opined that service quality is an antecedent of customer satisfaction (e.g., Anderson and Sullivan, 1993; Cronin and Taylor, 1992; Gotlieb et al., 1994; Parasuraman et al., 1985, 1988; Rust and Oliver, 1994). However, views seem to be converging that favorable service-quality perceptions lead to improved satisfaction (e.g., Cronin et al., 2000; Kang and James, 2004; Ting, 2004; Yavas et al., 2001; Zhou, 2004), and that satisfaction has a significant effect on behavioral intentions (Taylor and Baker, 1994; Fullerton and Taylor, 2002; Zhou, 2004). So far as the linkage between service quality and behavior is concerned, though some researchers have tried to relate service quality to behavioral intentions directly (e.g., Yavas et al., 2001; Zeithaml et al., 1996), others have examined the relationship between the two indirectly through the mediating effect of customer satisfaction (e.g., Zhou, 2004), or even directly as well as interactively along with customer satisfaction (e.g., Taylor, 1997; Wang et al., 2004[3]).

Keeping in view the current thinking and emerging evidence, the present study too endeavors to examine the relationship of service quality with customer satisfaction and behavioral intentions in a two-phased process: first, how service-quality affects customer satisfaction, and second, how service quality impacts behavioral consequences both directly and interactively with customer satisfaction. Figure 5.1 provides a diagrammatic view of the two-phased process through which service quality affects customer satisfaction and behavioral outcomes.

METHODOLOGY

The Sample

The present study makes use of the data that were collected in connection with a survey of fast-food restaurants in Delhi. A pilot study was conducted to identify fast-food restaurants that are most popular and patronized by the people living in Delhi. A total of eight fast-food restaurants, Nirula's, Wimpy, Domino's, McDonald's, Pizza Hut, Haldiram's, Bikanervala, and Rameshwar's, were identified, and these were used as the focal restaurants for undertaking empirical analysis in the study. Students and lecturers of different colleges and

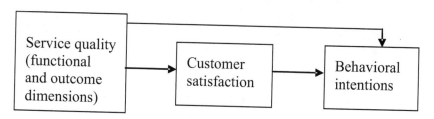

FIGURE 5.1. Research Model Used in the Study Examining Relationships between Service Quality, Customer Satisfaction, and Behavioral Intentions

departments of the University of Delhi constituted the sampling frame used in the study. The reasons underlying the selection of these two types of respondents were their high familiarity with and patronization of fast-food restaurants, and also their easy access to them. Using convenience sampling, respondents from these two subsets of the population were personally approached and requested to fill in a undisguised questionnaire prepared for this purpose. A total of two hundred duly filled-in questionnaires were received, with each respondent providing information about two restaurants—one the most frequently visited, and the other the least frequently visited, and a pooling of their responses at the data-analysis stage resulted in a total of four hundred sample observations.

A majority of the respondents were in the age group 18 to 24 (52 percent). Regarding gender and occupation (i.e., male versus female, and students versus lecturers), the respondents were almost in same proportion. Only about 14 percent of the respondents had monthly family income below 15,000 (Rs). The rest of the respondents in equal proportion had monthly income either between 15,000 and 25,000 (Rs) or 25,000 (Rs) and above. No doubt the sample is comprised of relatively educated, high income, and young people, but from the marketing point of view this should not be much of a problem as it is rather the young, educated, and high-income people who constitute a promising market segment for the fast-food restaurants.

Research Instrument

The data on service-quality perceptions were obtained using a twenty-two-item SERVPERF scale as developed by Cronin and Taylor (1992). These items are the same as used in the SERVQUAL scale developed by Parasuraman and colleagues (1988). As previously mentioned, the only difference between the two scales is that whereas SERVQUAL scale requires data on both the customers' expectations and perceptions of services, the SERVPERF scale entails measurement of only the perception data. An exploratory analysis of these items (discussed in detail in the next section) resulted in four factors. These four factors were used as the four distinct dimensions of SQF22 construct. Table 5.1 lists the four factors and their constituent items along with their reliability coefficients. Although the first two factors have nonstandardized Cronbach alpha values of more than

TABLE 5.1. Scales, Scale-Items Used in Study and Reliability Coefficients

Scale and Scale Items	Reliability (Cronbach alpha)
Service Quality – Functional (SQF13)	
A. Tangibility (TAN)	0.76
1. Visually appealing physical facilities	
2. Up-to-date equipment and technology	
3. Well dressed and neat employees	
4. Appearance of physical facilities as per the type of service provided	
B. Empathy/Responsiveness (EMP)	0.67
1. Employees not giving personal attention (reverse coded)	
2. Giving individual attention (reverse coded)	
3. Employees knowing customer needs (reverse coded)	
4. Employees too busy to respond to customer needs promptly (reverse coded)	
C. Dependability/Assurance (DEP)	0.57
1. Dependable restaurant	
2. Sympathetic and reassuring restaurant in case customers have problems	
3. Not getting prompt service from employees (reverse coded)	
D. Support (SUP)	0.51
1. Employees getting support from restaurant to do their jobs well	
2. Keeping records accurately	
Service Quality – Outcome (SQO)	0.64
1. Quality of food	
2. Fresh and delicious food	
3. Presentation of food	
4. Flavor, topping, spiciness of food not being as per individual customer taste (reverse coded)	
5. Choice and range of food	
Overall Service Quality (OSQ)	—
1. Restaurant's overall service quality excellence	

TABLE 5.1 *(continued)*

Scale and Scale Items	Reliability (Cronbach alpha)
Customer Satisfaction (CS)	0.79
1. Enjoyable experience with the restaurant	
2. Services better than expected	
3. Overall satisfaction with the services at the restaurant	
Price Equity (PE)	—
1. Reasonableness of the price charged at the restaurant	
Behavioral Intentions	
Patronization Intentions (PI)	0.85
1. Probability of using their facilities again	
2. Chance of making the same choice again	
Recommendation Intentions (RI)	
1. Likelihood of recommending restaurant to a friend	—

0.65, the reliability of the latter two factors is quite low, being only marginally above the 0.50 threshold level as suggested by Nunnally (1978) for use in the exploratory analysis.

Scale items tapping the outcome (i.e., technical) component of the service-quality construct were generated through focus-group discussions and in-depth interviews held with select customers at the time of questionnaire preparation. The exercise resulted in generation of five items. In view of their high face validity, all of the five items were retained as constituting the outcome quality scale (SQO). Responses to these items were obtained on a five-point Likert scale, with anchors 1 (strongly disagree) and 5 (strongly agree). A Cronbach alpha value of 0.64 shows that the scale is only somewhat reliable and needs to be improved in the future.

One additional single-item scale for assessing the convergent validity of SERVPERF scale was added to the questionnaire. This variable was named as OSQ (overall service quality). Customer perception of price equity was measured in terms of the reasonableness of the price charged at the restaurant through a single-item scale. Customer satisfaction (CS) with the fast-food restaurant was measured using a three-item scale. Responses to all the scale items were obtained on a five-point Likert scale, anchored on strongly disagree (1) to strongly agree (5). The scale was found highly reliable, with Cronbach alpha value being 0.79 (see Table 5.1).

Though a wide variety of behavioral measures have been used in the past (see, for instance, Yavas et al., 2001; Zeithaml et al., 1996; Zhou, 2004), the present study focuses on two major behavioral intentions: customer restaurant patronization intentions and restaurant recommendation intentions. A two-item scale was used for measuring customer restaurant patronization intentions (PI). Customer intentions to recommend a given restaurant to others (RI) were assessed through a single-item scale. The items for both scales came from previous studies (Brady and Robertson, 2001; Brady et al., 2002; Zeithaml et al., 1996) and were adapted to suit the requirements of the present study. A five-point Likert scale ranging from 1 (very low) to 5 (very high) was used for soliciting the responses. A nonstandardized Cronbach alpha value of 0.85 for the two-item patronization intentions scale points to its high reliability.

A variety of statistical techniques have been used in the study to analyze the collected data. Besides computing descriptive statistics such as mean scores and median ranks, factor analysis has been performed on a twenty-two-item SERVPERF scale to discover underlying service-quality dimensions. The antecedent-criterion variable relationships in the study have been assessed through regression analyses. With a view to identify critical service attributes, dimension-specific regression equations were also run. A one-way ANOVA technique has been used to assess the statistical significance of differences in mean scores relating to service-quality perceptions, customer satisfaction, and behavioral intentions across the surveyed fast-food restaurants.

STUDY FINDINGS AND DISCUSSIONS

The major findings of the study are discussed in the following paragraphs.

Usefulness of SERVPERF in Measuring Customers' Service Quality Perceptions in Fast-Food Restaurants in India: Dimensionality, Validity, and Reliability Analyses

Exploratory factor analysis using principal component method with varimax rotation was employed to assess the dimensionality of the twenty-two item SERVPERF scale. All factors having an eigen value of more than one were retained. Nine items that were found to be loading either lowly (less than 0.50) or loading simultaneously on other factors were deleted, and the factor analysis was rerun. The process continued until all items were found loading appropriately on a single factor. In total, three rounds of factor analysis were performed, and the final round produced four factors that together explained 58.59 percent of the variance present in the data (see Table 5.2). Based on the item configurations, the four factors were named as "tangibility," "empathy," "dependability/assurance," and "support and accounting accuracy" dimensions. Since both the twenty-two items SERVPERF scale and its thirteen-item counterpart focus only on a functional-service aspect, these have been coded as SQF22 and SQF13 respectively, with the letter F signifying their functional focus.

The factor-analysis results suggested retention of only 13 out of a total of 22 items contained in the SERPERF scale. The 9 items not found appropriate in the study include: not telling customers when services will be performed, not getting prompt service, restaurant providing service by the promised time, restaurants providing service by the time they promise, restaurants not having convenient operating hours, employees being polite, employees not *always willing to help* (emphasis added), unrealistic to expect employees of these restaurants to have customers' *best interest* in mind (emphasis added), and feeling *safe* in transactions with employees (emphasis added). A closer look at these excluded items reveals that most of these items do not seem either relevant to the fast-food restaurant service context or are poorly worded. The first five excluded items, for instance, relate to the timeliness of service. Timeliness may be a more relevant issue in services such as banking, travel, or conventional restaurants, but this seems to be of little relevance in the fast-food restaurant business which by nature is built around the core theme of providing speedy services. It is not clear as to why the item "politeness" was not prop-

TABLE 5.2. Service Quality (Functional): Factor Analysis Results and Reliability Coefficients

Scale and scale items	Factor loadings	Variance explained	Reliability (Cronbach alpha)
Service Quality – Functional (SQF13)			
A. Tangibility (TAN)		19.07	0.76
1. Visually appealing physical facilities	0.823		
2. Up-to-date equipment and technology	0.753		
3. Well dressed and neat employees	0.740		
4. Appearance of physical facilities as per the type of service provided	0.644		
B. Empathy/Responsiveness (EMP)		16.46	0.67
1. Employees not giving personal attention (reverse coded)	0.798		
2. Giving individual attention (reverse coded)	0.681		
3. Employees knowing customer needs (reverse coded)	0.648		
4. Employees too busy to respond to customer needs promptly (reverse coded)	0.621		
C. Dependability/Assurance (DEP)		11.88	0.57
1. Dependable restaurant 10	0.790		
2. Sympathetic and reassuring restaurant in case customers have problems	0.607		
3. Not getting prompt service from employees (reverse coded)	0.578		
D. Support (SUP)		11.18	0.51
1. Employees getting support from restaurant to do their jobs well	0.800		
2. Keeping records accurately	0.730		
Total variance explained		**58.59**	

erly loaded in the factor analysis, and hence it has to be dropped from the scale. The last three items were excluded perhaps due to their poor wordings, marked in italics. The phrases such as "always willing to help," "best interest," and "safe" are quite ambiguous and lack specificity. These items, moreover, do not appear relevant in the context of fast-food restaurant business, which has no or little scope for service customization. Even in a few past studies, some of these items have been dropped at the analysis stage (e.g., Kang and James, 2004; Zhou, 2004).

A comparison of the retained items and their factor structure with the one proposed by Parasuraman and colleagues (1988) in respect of their SERVQUAL scale reveals a close similarity between the two. The item composition of the tangibility dimension in the present study is exactly the same as the one postulated in the SERVQUAL scale. The items belonging to reliability, responsiveness, and empathy dimensions of SERVQUAL scale, however, have been merged into one single dimension, christened as the empathy/responsiveness dimension in the present study. In previous studies too, items belonging to these three dimensions have been found converging into one or two dimensions (e.g., Zhou, 2004). The dependability/assurance dimension in the present study closely corresponds to Parasuraman and colleague's (1988) reliability dimension. Support/accuracy is the only dimension in the present study that is problematic, because it contains items belonging to two different dimensions (reliability and assurance) of SERVQUAL scale. Due to meaningless item composition, it's little wonder that this dimension is having a very low Cronbach alpha value (see Table 5.1).

In order to assess the *convergent validity* of the thirteen-item scale, the summed mean SQF13 scores were computed and correlated with overall service quality (OSQ) perception scores measured directly with a single-item scale. A Karl Pearson coefficient of 0.48 ($p \leq 0.00$) shows convergent validity of the thirteen-item service quality scale (i.e., SQF13) derived at our end. Though the thirteen-item scale is little less convergent valid than the twenty-two item SERVPERF scale (the correlation coefficient between SERVPERF and OSQ being $r = 0.54$, $p \leq 0.00$), the thirteen-item scale appears a better measure of service quality perceptions for being more parsimonious (requiring collection of data for only thirteen rather than twenty-two items) and also having a relatively better factor structure.

For assessing the predictive ability of thirteen-item scale (SQF13), customers' overall service-quality perceptions (OSQ) were regressed on the former. The results are presented in Table 5.3. A rather low adjusted R^2 value of 0.230 implies that the thirteen-item service quality scale (SQF13) is able to explain only 23 percent of the variations present in the customers' OSQ. This lower explanatory power of SQF13, however, has not resulted due to exclusion of nine items from the SERVPERF scale in our study. A rather modest and similar adjusted R^2 value of 0.290 obtained in respect of regression of OSQ on SERVPERF scale (i.e., SQF22) points to the SERVPERF scale in its original form is being only partly able to capture the customers' overall service-quality perceptions.

The previous discussion thus brings us to two important conclusions. First, the five-dimension structure as proposed by the developers of SERVQUAL scale (on which SERVPERF scale is based) is not valid across service industries and countries. This finding is in conformity with the results obtained by several other researchers in the past (e.g., Babakus and Boller, 1992; Carman, 1990; Zhou, 2004). The obvious inference is that the dimensionality of the service-quality scale is both context and country specific, and, hence, is not directly transferable across industries and countries. Second, the thirteen items retained in the present study for measuring service quality (functional aspect) are not adequate enough to capture customers' overall service-quality perceptions. This finding points to a pressing need for adding additional items/dimensions to Cronin and Taylor's (1992) SERVPERF scale.

Role of "Outcome" Component and Dimension-Specific Analysis in Predicting Customers' Overall Service-Quality Perceptions

Since the literature suggests that outcome quality (SQO) is an important determinant of perceived service quality, it was included as another independent variable in the regression equation. The results presented in Tables 5.3 and 5.4 show an improvement in the adjusted R^2 value from 0. 230 (when SQF13 alone is used as independent variable) to 0.278 when both SQF13 and SQO are used as independent variables. Both the predictor variables are statistically significant, with outcome component emerging as an equally important determi-

TABLE 5.3. Overall Service Quality (OSQ) Perceptions, Thirteen-Item Service Quality (SQF13) and SERVPERF (SQF22) Scales: Regression Results and Correlation Coefficients

Eq. No.	Variable	B coefficient	Adj. R^2	F value
1.	Dependent variable = OSQ			
	Constant	0.41		
	Service quality – functional (SQF13)	0.97*	0.230*	119.23
2.	Dependent variable = OSQ			
	Constant	0.14		
	Service quality – functional (SQF22, i.e., SERVPERF)	1.13*	0.294*	165.83
	Correlation Coefficients:			
	SQF13* OSQ = 0.48* ; SQF22* OSQ = 0.54*			

Note: Significance levels are: * p < 0.01; ** P < 0.05.

nant. Almost similar standardized regression coefficient's of 0.32 and 0.28 bear testimony to the equal importance of this variable. A significant improvement in adjusted R^2 value with the addition of OSQ variable suggests that the outcome component is an important determinant of service quality and needs to be taken into account while measuring consumer perceptions of service quality in the case of fast-food restaurants. Notwithstanding improvements in the results, even these two factors taken together are not able to adequately explain variations present in the customers' overall service quality perceptions, adjusted R^2 value being just 0.278. This once again implies that efforts be made in the future to identify additional items/dimensions in respect of both the functional and outcome service-quality components so as to be able to improve the predictive capabilities of two multi-item service quality scales.

As suggested in the literature, a dimension-specific analysis of service quality scale (SQF13) was undertaken along with the outcome service quality component as another explanatory variable. Results corresponding to equation 3 are quite revealing (see Table 5.4). Of the four functional service-quality dimensions, empathy and support are not significant explanatory variables. In terms of standardized beta

TABLE 5.4. Overall Service Quality OSQ) and Its Relationship with Functional (SQF13) and Outcome Service Quality (SQO) - Regression Results

Eq. No.	Variable	B	Stand-ardised B	Adj. R²	F value	ΔR²	F value of ΔR²	TOI[b]	VIF[c]
				Coefficients[a]					
1.	Dependent variable = OSQ								
	Constant	0.22							
	Functional quality (SQF13)	0.64*	0.32*					0.65	1.55
	Outcome quality (SQO)	0.38*	0.28*	0.278*	77.07	0.049*	27.03	0.65	1.55
2.	Dependent variable = OSQ								
	Constant	0.12	—						
	Tangibility (TAN)	0.43*	0.29*					0.73	1.37
	Empathy (EMP)	0.06	0.04					0.73	1.38
	Dependence (DEP)	0.14**	0.10**					0.71	1.42
	Support (SUP)	−0.00	−0.03					0.81	1.23
	Outcome quality SQO)	0.42*	0.30*	0.305*	35.66	—	—	0.62	1.59
3.	Dependent variable = OSQ								
	Constant	0.12	—						
	Tangibility (TAN)	0.42*	0.28*					0.80	1.25
	Dependence (DEP)	0.15**	0.11**					0.74	1.36
	Outcome quality SQO)	0.45*	0.32*	0.306*	59.19	—	—	0.78	1.29

[a]Significance levels are: * p<0.01 and ** P<0.05.

[b]TOI refers to tolerance score for the independent variable.

[c]VIF refers to variance inflated factor.

coefficients, tangibility (TAN) emerges as the most important determinant of service quality, closely followed by outcome quality (SQO). The variable empathy (EMP) is also a significant variable, but it trails far behind the tangibility and outcome components. The two collinear statistics—TOI and VIF—being greater than 0.10 and less than 10 respectively imply an absence of multicollinearity among the independent variables (Hair et al., 1995), thus adding to our confidence in the results.

Empathy and support dimensions have not only low beta values, but are also not statistically significant. This probably has happened due to nature of the service industry under consideration. As already mentioned, fast-food restaurants offer highly standardized service, thus leaving no or little scope for customization. Hence, empathy has not emerged as a significant determinant. The other variable, "support" (capturing the influence of availability of support to the employees from management and accuracy of records), is not only psychometrically unsound for being less valid and reliable, but it also does not seem to hold much relevance. Availability of support to employees is an internal matter and is of no direct relevance to the customers in forming their service-quality perceptions. Even the item accuracy of records seems of little importance in the case of fast-food restaurants because all of them currently make use of cash registers and hand out printed receipts with all of the necessary details to enable the customers to check the accuracy of bills, thus leaving no scope for the accuracy to vary across the restaurants.

Since empathy and support are not found to be significant explanatory variables, these were dropped from further analysis in the study. A regression analysis performed on the remaining variables (equation 4) produced results that are more or less similar to those obtained in equation 3.

Service Quality As an Antecedent of Customer Satisfaction: Aggregative and Dimension-Specific Analysis

Customer satisfaction (CS) was regressed on various variants of service-quality measure to assess the role of service quality as an antecedent of customer satisfaction perceptions. The results reported in Table 5.5 show that overall service quality (OSQ) is a major and significant determinant of customer satisfaction in the fast-food restaurants. An adjusted R^2 value of 0.551 shows that the overall service-quality perceptions are able to explain 55.10 percent of the variations present in the customer satisfaction. Since the customers form their satisfaction judgments on the basis of service quality and price perceptions, the variable price equity (PE) was also introduced in the regression equation. The results reveal a marginal but significant rise in the adjusted R^2 value. Both the explanatory variables are statistically significant, with OSQ remaining as the major determinant. Price turns out to be as a considerably less important factor.

TABLE 5.5. Service Quality as Antecedent of Customer Satisfaction (CS) – Regression Results

Eq. No.	Variable	Coefficients[a]							
		B	Standardized B	Adj. R^2	F value	ΔR^2	F value of ΔR^2	TOI[b]	VIF[c]
1.	Dependent variable = CS								
	Constant	0.97	—						
	Overall SQ (OSQ)	0.67*	0.74*	0.552*	486.37	—	—	—	—
2.	Dependent variable = CS								
	Constant	0.77							
	Overall SQ (OSQ)	0.64*	0.71*					0.94	1.06
	Price equity (PE)	0.09*	0.13*	0.567*	258.62	0.017*	15.03	0.94	1.06
3.	Dependent variable = CS								
	Constant	−0.49	—						
	Functional quality (SQF22, i.e., SERVPERF)	0.78*	0.42*					0.55	1.80
	Outcome quality (SQO)	0.31*	0.25*					0.60	1.68
	Price equity (PE)	0.05*	0.07*	0.404*	90.37	—	—	0.85	1.18
4.	Dependent variable = CS								
	Constant	−0.16	—						
	Functional quality (SQF13)	0.59*	0.33*					0.60	1.67
	Outcome quality (SQO)	0.39*	0.31*					0.64	1.57
	Price equity (PE)	0.07**	0.09**	0.376*	78.87			0.85	1.17
5.	Dependent variable = CS								
	Constant	−0.24*	—						
	Tangibility (TAN)	0.35*	0.26*					0.80	1.25
	Dependence (DEP)	0.18*	0.14*					0.69	1.44
	Outcome quality SQO)	0.44*	0.35*					0.76	1.32
	Price equity (PE)	0.07**	0.10**	0.404*	66.20	—	—	0.84	1.19

[a]Significance levels are: *p<0.01 and **P<0.05.

[b]TOI refers to tolerance score for the independent variable.

[c]VIF refers to variance inflated factor.

In order to assess the usefulness of using multi-item service-quality scales in place of OSQ scale, customer satisfaction was regressed on SQF22 and SQF13 alternately along with service outcome (SQO) component. Results corresponding to equation 2 in Table 5.5 show a rather poor fit of SQF22 to customer-satisfaction perceptions. Even the use of variable SQF13 causes a further (though marginal) decline in adjusted R^2 value. Price equity in both equations remains a significant but marginal determinant. The lower adjusted R^2 values in respect of both the SQF13 and SQF22 scales imply need for improving these two scales in the future.

A dimension-specific analysis (substituting SQF13 by its two major dimensions, TAN and DEP) does help improve the adjusted R^2 value to a level that was attained earlier (equation 3). Taken together, the four antecedents, TAN, DEP, SQO, and PE, are able to explain 40.4 percent of variations present in the customer-satisfaction perceptions. Furthermore, all of the antecedents are significant. Service outcome quality (SQO) turns out to the most important determinant, closely followed by tangibility dimension (TAN). The other two variables, DEP and PE, are individually about half as strong as the other two variables (SQO and TAN) are individually in their impact on customer satisfaction.

The previous analysis thus shows that service quality does affect customer satisfaction, with service outcome playing a major role in the case of fast-food restaurants. The results further show that a dimension-specific analysis is a better alternative to link service quality to customer satisfaction by pointing out which of the several service-quality dimensions have stronger impact on customer satisfaction than does the aggregative analysis using only the summed service quality (SQF13) score. The variable price equity, however, is found to play a significant but marginal role in influencing the customer satisfaction with fast-food restaurants.

Service Quality and Customer Satisfaction as Predictors of Behavioral Intentions: Aggregative and Dimension-Specific Analyses

Higher service quality has been empirically linked to higher satisfaction and favorable behavioral intentions both directly as well as interactively with customer satisfaction in the past studies reviewed earlier. Two subconstructs used for tapping the behavioral intentions in the present study include restaurant patronization intentions (PI) and recommendation intentions (RI). In order to assess whether service quality and customer satisfaction affect behavioral intentions in a curvilinear and interactive manner, higher order regression equations with provision for interactions between service quality and customer satisfaction were run. However, all of the quadratic regression equations, as well as those with interaction terms, did not produce satisfactory fits due to high collinearity present among the higher order and cross products of direct measures of independent variables. Hence, it was decided to use only the first order basic regression equations.

The results corresponding to equation 1 in Table 5.6 show a significant and strong influence of customers' overall service quality (OSQ) perceptions on their restaurant patronization intentions. However, with the inclusion of customer satisfaction as another independent variable, adjusted R^2 value significantly increases, to 0.330, and both the OSQ and CS emerge as significant predictors. However, when OSQ is replaced by SQF22—its twenty-two multi-item counterpart—the results turn out to be poorer. Not does the value of adjusted R^2 fall, the variable SQF22 also becomes insignificant, suggesting, albeit erroneously, that functional service quality (i.e., SERVPERF) is not a determinant of customers' patronization intentions. This probably is occurring due to poor validity of the scale pointed out earlier in connection with the factor analysis undertaken in the study. The results, however, show an improvement when the variable SQF13 is used instead of SQF22.

A dimension-specific analysis of functional service quality as undertaken in equation 5 brings the results closer to those obtained earlier in equation 3, where OSQ has been used as a measure of functional service quality. A value of 0.342 of adjusted R^2 suggests that the four variables taken together (TAN, DEP, SQO, and CS) are able to explain 34.2 percent of variations in customer patronization intentions, with customer satisfaction being the most important and significant determinant. The three service-quality-related variables—TAN, DEP, and SQO—are also significant, but these are individually almost half as important as the customer-satisfaction variable alone (see Table 5.6). A lack of multicollinearity among the independent variables, as evident from the TOI value being higher than 0.10 and

TABLE 5.6. Service Quality and Customer Satisfaction (CS) as Predictors of Restaurant Patronization Intentions (PI) - Regression Results

Eq. No.	Variable	B	Stand-ardized B	Adj. R^2	F value	ΔR^2	F value of ΔR^2	TOI[b]	VIF[c]
1.	Dependent variable = PI								
	Constant	0.78							
	Overall service quality (OSQ)	0.66*	0.55*	0.302*	169.49	—	—	—	—
2.	Dependent variable = PI								
	Constant	0.44							
	OSQ	0.42*	0.36*					0.45	2.23
	CS	0.35*	0.268	0.330*	97.47	0.031*	97.47	0.45	2.23
3.	Dependent variable = PI								
	Constant	−0.33							
	Functional quality (SQF22, i.e., SERVPERF)	0.19	0.8					0.50	1.99
	Outcome quality (SQO)	0.34*	0.21*					0.51	1.57
	CS	0.49*	0.37*	0.319*	62.42	—	—	0.60	1.57
4.	Dependent variable = PI								
	Constant	−0.46							
	Functional quality (SQF13)	0.25***	0.11					0.57	1.75
	SQO	0.32*	0.20*					0.58	1.71
	CS	0.49*	0.37*	0.322*	63.41	—	—	0.63	1.58
5.	Dependent variable = PI								
	Constant	−0.87							
	Tangibility (TAN)	0.24*	0.14*					0.73	1.37
	Dependence (DEP)	0.17**	0.11**					0.72	1.39
	Outcome quality (SQO)	0.32*	0.19*					0.66	1.51
	CS	0.42*	0.32*	0.342*	52.23	—	—	0.61	1.65

[a]Significance levels are: *p < 0.01, **P < 0.05 and ***p < 0.10.

[b]TOI refers to tolerance score for the independent variable.

[c]VIF refers to variance inflated factor.

the VIF value being less than 10, further adds to the reliability of regression results arrived at our end.

Results relating to customer restaurant recommendation intentions appear almost similar to those obtained in regard to customer patronization intentions patter (see Table 5.7). Overall service-quality perceptions constitute an important determinant of the recommendation intentions, but the fit is significantly improved with the inclusion of customer satisfaction as another independent variable. Between the two multi-item functional service quality scales, SQF13 is providing better results than SQF22. Outcome service quality is a significant and major determinant of the recommendation intentions. A dimension-specific analysis of functional service quality shows that that all four variables present in equation 5 are significant, with CS being the most important determinant, followed by SQO and TAN in that order. DEP (dependence) turns out to be the least important determinant.

SQ, CS, and BI Sores: A Restaurant Analysis

Having identified the determinants of customers' restaurant patronization and recommendation intentions, let us look at the performance scoreboard of each of the eight fast-food restaurants under investigation. Table 5.8 contains the results relating to various service-quality, customer-satisfaction, and behavioral-intention measures as well as those relating to customers' preference ranking for the restaurants and their perceptions about the price equity of the services provided by these restaurants. For the sake of better diagnosis, even the results relating to service-quality dimensions that were not found significant in the earlier analysis are reported in Table 5.8. A correspondence between mean scores of service quality, customer satisfaction, and behavioral intentions reinforces the earlier findings of the study that the former is positively related to the latter.

Based on both the overall service-quality perceptions (OSQ) and the thirteen-item summed functional service quality scores (SQF13), McDonald's emerges as a real winner, with Nirula's and Pizza Hut being close challengers. Haldiram's, Bikanervala, Domino's, and Wimpy constitute the next rung of players and in that order. Rameshwar's is the laggard and trails far behind all other competitors on the fast-food track.

TABLE 5.7. Service Quality and Customer Satisfaction (CS) as Predictors of Restaurant Recommendation Intentions (RI) - Regression Results

Eq. No.	Variable	Coefficients[a]							
		B	Stand-ardized B	Adj. R^2	F value	ΔR^2	F value of ΔR^2	TOI[b]	VIF[c]
1.	Dependent variable = RI								
	Constant	0.61							
	Overall service quality (OSQ)	0.71*	0.55*	0.295*	164.82	—		—	—
2.	Dependent variable = RI								
	Constant	0.29							
	OSQ	0.49*	0.38*					0.45	2.23
	CS	0.33*	0.23*	0.316*	91.55	0.023*	13.16	0.45	2.23
3.	Dependent variable = RI								
	Constant	-0.36							
	Functional quality (SQF22, i.e., SERVPERF)	0.20	0.08					0.50	1.99
	Outcome quality (SQO)	0.30*	0.17*					0.56	1.77
	CS	0.54*	0.37*	0.284*	53.22	—		0.60	1.58
4.	Dependent variable = RI								
	Constant	-0.33							
	Functional quality (SQF13)	0.18	0.07					0.57	1.75
	SQO	0.30*	0.17*					0.58	1.71
	CS	0.55*	0.38*	0.284*	53.17	—		0.63	1.58
5.	Dependent variable = RI								
	Constant	-0.71							
	Tangibility (TAN)	0.23**	0.12**					0.73	1.37
	Dependence (DEP)	0.09	0.05					0.72	1.39
	Outcome quality SQO)	0.30**	0.17**					0.66	1.51
	CS	0.49*	0.34*	0.296*	42.37	—		0.61	1.65

[a]Significance levels are: *p < 0.01 and **P < 0.05.

[b]TOI refers to tolerance score for the independent variable.

[c]VIF refers to variance inflated factor.

TABLE 5.8. Service Quality, Customer Satisfaction, Preference Perceptions, and Behavioral Intentions: Restaurant Analysis and ANOVA Results

| Restaurant | Overall service quality perceptions (OSQ) | Service quality–functional (SQF13) | Service quality dimensions | | | | | Price equity (PE) | Preference ranking (median score) | Customer satisfaction (CS) | Patronization intentions (PI) | Recommendation intentions (RI) |
			Empathy (EMP)	Support (SUP)	Depend-ability (DEP)	Tangibi-lity (TAN)	Outcome service quality (SQO)					
McDonald's	4.23	3.72	3.25	3.65	3.68	4.26	3.67	3.52	1	3.85	3.72	3.82
Nirula's	4.04	3.65	3.25	3.54	3.74	4.03	3.75	3.18	1	3.76	3.80	3.65
Pizza Hut	4.00	3.67	3.34	3.59	3.67	4.05	3.62	3.08	2	3.62	3.45	3.54
Haldiram's	3.72	3.54	3.09	3.68	3.60	3.88	3.66	3.18	2	3.49	3.32	3.24
Bikanervala	3.65	3.36	3.08	3.38	3.38	3.60	3.65	3.09	4	3.48	2.97	3.09
Domino's	3.52	3.43	3.12	3.47	3.45	3.73	3.25	3.13	3	3.27	2.69	2.84
Wimpy	3.46	3.37	3.05	3.39	3.37	3.67	3.30	2.96	2	3.09	2.63	2.78
Rameshwar's	3.19	3.18	3.00	3.19	3.19	3.36	3.17	2.62	2	2.78	2.43	2.43
Overall mean scores	3.86	3.56	3.18	3.53	3.58	3.93	3.57	3.18	—	3.55	3.33	3.36
F-value (ANOVA)	6.77*	7.28*	1.07	2.09**	3.40*	10.628*	4.64*	2.17**	—	8.39*	12.40*	7.96*

Note: Significance levels are: $^*p < 0.01$; $^{**}p < 0.05$

Dimension-specific analysis brings to the fore interesting insights. So far as the *empathy/responsiveness* and *support/accuracy of records* dimensions are concerned, the restaurants under investigation do not significantly differ from one another. As found earlier in connection with the regression analysis, these two dimensions do not turn out to be major differentiators among the surveyed restaurants. A significant difference is observable in respect to support dimensions, but it has probably happened due to utterly poor performance of Rameshwar's on this front.

In respect of *dependability/assurance,* the performance of the first four restaurants including Haldiram's is more or less similar. Bikanervala, Domino's, and Wimpy constitute the next rung. Once again, Rameshwar's is found to be a very poor performer on this count. Customers' perceptions of *tangibility* show significant differences among the surveyed restaurants. McDonald's holds the place of pride, with Nirula's and Pizza Hot trailing behind it. Haldiram's, Bikanervala, Domino's, and Wimpy are yet to catch up with the two front-runners. Rameshwar's lags tangibly behind all others in this category as well.

Scores in regard to *outcome quality* present a different picture. Though it may sound surprising, it is a reality (and reality is what customers perceive) that customers perceive McDonald's to be lagging somewhat behind its arch rival Nirula's. However, when asked about the reasonableness of price charged at these two restaurants, customers opine McDonald's to be stealing the show. Leaving aside these skirmishes, and of customers having greater intentions to visit Nirula's in future, we find that the two leaders are quite ahead of their counterparts. Be it customer satisfaction levels or patronization and recommendation inclinations, other players in the market must substantially improve their performance before they can think of seeing eye to eye to their market leaders.

MANAGERIAL IMPLICATIONS, STUDY LIMITATIONS, AND DIRECTIONS FOR FUTURE RESEARCH

Service quality has been posited in the literature as a key determinant of a firm's success in the marketplace. Though a number of studies have been undertaken in other countries to establish an empirical link between service quality, customer satisfaction, and behavioral intentions, hardly any published academic study exists in respect to fast-food restaurants in the Indian context to show that it does pay to invest in service-quality-improvement efforts. The present study has been an attempt in this direction. The data used in the study have come from a consumer survey of eight fast-food restaurants in Delhi during December 2001 to March 2002. In view of the alleged superiority of the twenty-two item SERVPERF over SERVQUAL scale, the former was employed to measure customer perceptions of service quality. The following paragraphs summarize findings of the study and discuss their managerial and research implications.

The analysis in the present study fails to find all twenty-two items being relevant to measurement of service quality in the context of fast-food restaurants in India. Only thirteen items are found pertinent. In particular, items relating to *empathy* and *timeliness* aspects of service quality are found having no significant relationship with customers' service-quality perceptions in the fast-food business. Even the factor structure as proposed by the developers of SERVQUAL scale on which the SERVPERF is based does not get supported. The factor analysis in the present study rather produces a four-factor structure with tangibility, dependability/assurance, empathy/responsiveness, and support/accuracy of records as being the four service quality dimensions. The tangibility items have a clear loading on the postulated factor, but the other items due to their overlapping nature resulted in somewhat a hybrid factor item structure. Even several past several studies replicating and testing SERVQUAL have not found the scale to be converging to the proposed five-factor structure (e.g., Babakus and Mangold, 1989; Spreng and Singh, 1993).

On regressing overall service-quality perceptions (OSQ) on the twenty-two item SERVPERF (i.e., SQF22) scale and the thirteen-item (SQF13) scale derived at our end, we find both scales powerful enough to capture variations present in customers' overall service-quality perceptions. However, until the time a better measure of service quality develops, the fast-food restaurants can rely on the thirteen-item SQF13 rather than the SERVPERF scale. The reason underlying this recommendation is that SQF13 is a more parsimonious scale and lacks only slightly in terms its predictive power.

Since the SERVPERF scale and its pruned version (SQF13) focus only on the functional aspect of service quality, a service outcome component (SQO) was added to the analysis, and it did lead to some improvement in the predictive ability of service-quality scales. The results imply that especially in the case of services such as fast-food restaurants outcome quality is an important ingredient and needs be included in future analyses. Similar views have been echoed in past works (Gronroos, 1982, 1990; Kang and James, 2004; Lehtinen and Lehtinen, 1982; Mangold and Babakus, 1991; Richard and Allaway, 1993).

However, the fact remains that even inclusion of an outcome component is not able to sufficiently account for variations present in customers' overall service-quality perceptions. This is evident from relatively lower adjusted R^2 values in our analysis. The results thus point to the need for identifying additional items/dimensions as specific to the formation of customer quality perceptions in the fast-food restaurant services. The previous finding is in consonance with the suggestions made in previous studies for inclusion of industry-specific items in the service-quality scale (Cronin and Taylor, 1992; Dabholkar et al., 2000; Le Blanc and Nguyen, 1988; Lehtinen and Lehtinen, 1982; Lewis, 1987). As mentioned, even Parasuraman and colleagues (1994) suggested modifications in their scale to make it more fitting to a specific service context.

An important finding of the study is that service quality is a much more important determinant of customer satisfaction than is price equity (PE). The obvious implication of this inference is that the management of the fast-food restaurants needs to place more emphasis on building service quality than on trying to compete on the price front to lure customers. It, however, should not be construed to imply that the fast-food restaurants can charge any price they wish for selling their high-quality products. The prices charged by them must be well within a reasonable band around the prices charged by their competitors.

A dimension-specific analysis of service quality does add to the predictive and diagnostic ability of the service-quality scale. Such an analysis in the present study is a pointer to the dimensions not being equally important in forming customer quality and satisfaction perceptions and in influencing behavioral intentions. The present study identifies service-outcome quality, tangibility, and dependability/assurance as being more important determinants than the empathy/responsiveness and support/accuracy of record dimensions.

A restaurant-oriented analysis of customer perceptions finds McDonald's as being the market leader, with Nirula's closely occupying the second slot. Although McDonald's is ahead of Nirula's in terms of tangibility dimension, it lags behind Nirula's in respect of both the dependability and outcome-quality aspects. The management of McDonald's should try to find specific reasons for being deficient in these service attributes and take corrective measures lest it loses the market hegemony to its rival. On the other hand, Nirula's too needs to look into the tangibility aspect of its service setup in which it lags behind McDonald's. It should try revamping its physical facilities, layout, and décor to be at par with McDonald's. The other restaurants are quite far behind their leaders and need to initiate measures to revamp quality in respect of tangibility as well as dependability and outcome dimensions. Rameshwar's is truly a laggard in respect to all dimensions and needs to go all the way both at the functional and outcome-quality fronts to improve its quality perceptions.

Every study has its own limitations, and this study is no exception. The present study has been based on a survey of students and lecturers from the University of Delhi. No doubt it is relatively the younger and more educated people from the higher income groups who constitute a prime market segment of the fast-food restaurant services, but they by no means exhaust the list. People owning their own business, professionals, and those working in private and public sector organizations are equally important fast-food restaurant customers and as such need be surveyed in future. Since the food habits and preferences generally tend to be region and culture specific, findings of the study do not seem directly applicable to customers from other regions and cultures. Larger samples of customers from different regions and different walks of life are, therefore, called for to arrive at more valid and reliable inferences about the country's restaurant-going population.

Since the thirteen-item service-equality scale is not found capable of sufficiently explaining variations in customers' overall service-quality perceptions, and because some of the service-quality dimensions have been found less valid and reliable, attempts should be made by the researchers in the future to develop psychometrically more valid and reliable scales. As found by Bonner and Nelson (1985) in their research on food products, aspects such as rich flavor, natural taste, fresh taste, good aroma, and appetizing looks can serve as potential scale items in future studies.

The present study has made use of only two behavioral dimensions. It will be desirable if the researchers in future attempt to study additional behavioral consequences, such as those relating to customers' complaining and switching intentions. Recent use of structural equation method (SEM) in some studies (e.g., Kang and James, 2004; Zhou, 2004) can also be of great help in fully capturing the intricate relationships present among the three variables.

A growing realization exists among the service-quality theoreticians and researchers that corporate image be considered an important determinant of service-quality perceptions (Groonroos, 1982, 1990; Lehtinen and Lehtinen, 1982). Kang and James (2004) argue in this connection that

> a favorable and well-known image is an asset for any firm because image has an impact on customer perceptions of the communication and operations of the firm in many respects. . . . If a service provider has a positive image in the minds of customers, minor mistakes will be forgiven. If a provider's image is negative, the impact of any mistake will often be magnified in the customer's mind. In a word, image can be viewed as a filter in terms of a consumer's perception of quality. (p. 267)

It would be a worthwhile endeavor on the part of the future researchers to delve into this aspect and assess the extent to which inclusion of image component in service-quality analysis is conceptually tenable and can add to the predictive ability of service quality scale.

Notwithstanding these limitations and need for further research in the area, findings of the present study do suggest that service quality is an important determinant of customer satisfaction and behavioral intentions. It is therefore worth investing in quality-improvement efforts to win customer applaud and their patronage. The study demonstrates that not all the all of the service-quality dimensions are equally important to customers. The management of the fast-food restaurants can immensely gain by taking up such studies from time to time for identifying and prioritizing the areas customers' deem deserve utmost attention. A focused quality-building approach can go a long way in enabling the management of fast-food restaurants to make optimal use of their resources and building side by side maximum possible customer satisfaction and franchise.

NOTES

1. The author is grateful to Ms. Garima Gupta for carrying out the fieldwork and for other help provided in preparation of this chapter.

2. Although SERVQUAL was posited as multidimensional scale by Parasuraman and colleagues (1988), Cronin and Taylor (1992) implemented SERVPERF as a unidimensional scale and accordingly used it as a summed index derived by averaging the distinctive dimension of service quality. Even in a replication study later, Brady and colleagues (2002) used SERVPERF as a unidimensional summed index.

3. Although the study by Wang and colleagues (2004) did not examine the impact of service quality on behavioral intentions in an explicit manner; these two constructs were indirectly tested by way of being part of functional value and customer-relationship-management performance measures. One of the components of value used in the study was functional value, which to a great extent is a measure of perceived quality. Similarly, though they preferred to call their outcome variable a customer-relationship-management performance, it was nothing but a three-item customer-behavioral-intentions scale.

BIBLIOGRAPHY

Aaker, D. A. and Jacobson, R. (1994). The financial information content of perceived quality. *Journal of Marketing Research, 31*(2): 191-201.

Anderson, E.W. and Sullivan, M. (1993). The antecedents and consequences of customer satisfaction for firms. *Marketing Science, 12*(2): 125-143.

Babakus, E. and Boller, G.W. (1992). An empirical assessment of the servqual scale. *Journal of Business Research, 24:* 253-268.

Babakus, E. and Mangold, W.G. (1989). Adapting the servqual scale to hospital services: An empirical investigation. *Health Service Research, 26*(6): 767-780.

Bansal, H.S. and Taylor, S. (1997). Investigating the relationship between service quality, satisfaction and switching intentions. In Wilson, E.J. and Hair, J.C. (eds.), *Developments in Marketing Science* (pp. 304-313). Coral Gables, FL: Academy of Marketing Science.

Bitner, M.J. (1990). Evaluating service encounters: The effects of physical surroundings and employee response. *Journal of Marketing, 2:* 69-82.

Bitner, M.J. and Hubbert, A.R. (1994). *Encounter Satisfaction versus Overall Satisfaction versus Quality.* In Rust, R.T. and Oliver, R.L. (eds.), *Service Quality: New Directions in Theory and Practice* (pp. 72-94). Thousands Oaks, CA: Sage Publications.

Bolton, R.N. (1998). A dynamic model of the duration of the customer's relationship with a continuous service provider: The role of customer satisfaction. *Marketing Science, 17*(1): 45-65.

Bolton, R.N. and Drew, J.H. (1991a). A longitudinal analysis of the impact of service changes on customer attitudes. *Journal of Marketing, 55*(January): 1-9.

Bolton, R.N. and Drew, J.H. (1991b). A multistage model of customer's assessment of service quality and value. *Journal of Consumer Research, 17*(March): 375-385.

Bonner, P. and Nelson, R. (1985). Product attributes and perceived quality: Foods. In Jacoby, J. (ed.), *Perceived Quality* (pp. 64-79). Lanham, MD: Lexington Books.

Boulding, W., Kalra, A., Staelin R., and Zeithaml, V.A. (1993). A dynamic process model of service quality: From expectations to behavioral intentions. *Journal of Marketing Research, 30*(February): 7-27.

Brady, M.K. and Cronin, J. (2001). Some new thoughts on conceptualizing perceived service quality: A hierarchical approach. *Journal of Marketing, 65*(July): 34-49.

Brady, M.K., Cronin, J., and Brand, R.R. (2002). Performance-only measurement of service quality: A replication and extension. *Journal of Business Research, 55:* 17-31.

Brady, M.K. and Robertson, C.J. (2001). Searching for a consensus on the antecedent role of service quality and satisfaction: An exploratory cross-national study. *Journal of Business Research, 51:* 53-60.

Brown, T.J., Churchill, G.A., and Peter, J.P. (1993). Improving the measurement of service quality. *Journal of Retailing, 69*(1): 127-139.

Buttle, F. (1996). SERVQUAL: Review, critique, research agenda. *European Journal of Marketing, 30*(1): 8-32.

Carman, J.M. (1990). Consumer perceptions of service quality: An assessment of the SERVQUAL dimensions. *Journal of Retailing, 66*(1): 33-35.

Cronin, J., Brady, M.K., and Hult, T.M. (2000). Assessing the effects of quality, value and customer satisfaction on consumer behavioral intentions in service environments. *Journal of Retailing, 76*(2): 193-218.

Cronin, J. and Taylor, S.A. (1992). Measuring service quality: A reexamination and extension. *Journal of Marketing, 56* (July): 55-67.

Dabholkar, P.A. (1993). Customer satisfaction and service quality: Two constructs or one? In Cravens, D.W. and Dickson, P.R. (eds.), *Enhancing Knowledge Development in Marketing* (pp. 10-18). Chicago, IL: American Marketing Association.

Dabholkar, P.A. (1995). Contingency framework for predicting causality between customer satisfaction and service quality. *Advances in Consumer Research, 202:* 21-31.

Dabholkar, P.A., Shepherd, D.C., and Torpe, D.I. (2000). A comprehensive framework for service quality: An investigation of critical conceptual and measurement issues through a longitudinal study. *Journal of Retailing, 76*(2): 139-173.

Danaher, P.J. (1997). Using conjoint analysis to determine the relative importance of service attributes measured in customer satisfaction surveys. *Journal of Retailing, 2:* 235-260.

Fullerton, G. and Taylor, S. (2002). Mediating, interactive, and non-linear effects in service quality and satisfaction with services research. *Canadian Journal of Administrative Sciences, 19*(2): 124-135.

Furrer, O., Liu, S.C., and Sudharshan, D. (2000). The relationship between culture and service quality perceptions: Basis for cross-cultural market segmentation and resource allocation. *Journal of Service Research, 2*(4): 355-371.

Garvin, D.A. (1987). Competing on the eight dimension's of quality. *Harvard Business Review, 65*(November/December): 101-109.

Gilbert, G.R., Veloutsou, C., Goode, M. M. H., and Moutinho, L. (2004). Measuring customer satisfaction in the fast food industry: A cross-national approach. *Journal of Services Marketing, 18*(5): 371-382.

Gotlieb, J.B., Grewal, D., and Brown, S.W. (1994). Consumer satisfaction and perceived quality: Complementary or divergent constructs, *Journal of Applied Psychology, 79*(6): 875-885.

Gronroos, C. (1982). *Strategic Management and Marketing in the Service Sector.* Helsinki, Finland: Swedish School of Economics and Business Administration.

Gronroos, C. (1990). *Service Management and Marketing: Managing the Moments of Truth in Service Competition.* Lanham, MD: Lexington Books.

Hair, J.F., Jr., Anderson, R.E., Tatham, R.L., and Black, W.C. (1995). *Multivariate Data Analysis with Readings,* 4th edition. Englewood Cliffs, NJ: Prentice Hall.

Headley, D.E. and Miller, S.J. (1993). Measuring service quality and its relationship to future consumer behavior. *Journal of Health Care Marketing, 4*: 32-41.

Iacobucci, D., Grayson, K.A., and Ostrom, A.L. (1994). The calculus of service quality and customer satisfaction: Theoretical and empirical differentiation and integration. In Swartz, T A., Bowen, D. H. and Brown, S.W. (eds.), *Advances in Services Marketing and Management (pp. 1-67).* Greenwich, CT: JAI Press.

Jain, S.K. and Gupta, G. (2004). Measuring service quality: SERVQUAL vs. SERVPERF scales. *Vikalpa: The Journal for Decision Makers, 29*(1) (April-June): 25-38.

Johns, N. and Howard, A. (1998). Customer expectations versus perceptions of service performance in the food service industry. *International Journal of Service Industry Management, 9*(3): 248-265.

Johnston, R. (1995). The determinants of service quality satisfiers and dissatisfiers. *International Journal of Service Industry Management, 6*(5): 53-71.

Jones, T.O. and Sasser, W.E. Jr (1995). Why satisfied customers defect. *Harvard Business Review, 73*(6): 88-99.

Kang, Gi-Du and James, J. (2004). Service quality dimensions: An examination of gronroos's service quality model. *Managing Service Quality, 14*(4): 267-277.

Kassim, N.M. and Bojei, J. (2002). Service quality: Gaps in the telemarketing industry. *Journal of Business Research, 55*: 845-852.

LaTour, S.A. and Peat, N.C. (1979). Cultural and methodological issues in consumer satisfaction research. In Wilkie, W.F. (ed.), *Advances in Consumer Re-*

search, Volume 6 (pp. 431-437). Ann Arbor, MI: Association for Consumer Research.

Le Blanc, G. and Nguyen, N. (1988). Customer's perceptions of service quality in financial institutions. *International Journal of Bank Marketing, 6*(4): 7-18.

Lee, H., Lee, Y., and Yoo, D. (2000). The determinants of perceived service quality and its relationship with satisfaction. *Journal of Services Marketing, 14*(3): 217-231.

Lehtinen, U. and Lehtinen, J.R. (1982). Service Quality: A Study of Quality Dimensions. Working Paper. Helsinki, Finland: Service Management Institute.

Lewis, R.C. (1987). The measurement of gaps in the quality of hotel service. *International Journal of Hospitality Management, 6*(2): 83-88.

Magi, A. and Julander, C.R. (1996). Perceived service quality and customer satisfaction in a store performance framework. *Journal of Retailing and Consumer Services, 1:* 33-41.

Mangold, G.W. and Babakus, E. (1991). Service quality: The front-stage perspective vs. the back-stage perspective. *Journal of Services Marketing, 5*(4): 59-70.

McColl-Kennedy, J. and Schneider, U. (2000). Measuring customer satisfaction: Why, what, and how. *Total Quality Management, 11*(7): 883-896.

Mels, G., Boshoff, C., and Nel, D. (1997). The dimensions of service quality: The original European perspective revisited. *Service Industries Journal, 17*(1): 173-189.

Mersha, T. and Adlakha, V. (1992). Attributes of service quality: The consumer's perspective. *International Journal of Service Industry Management, 3*(3): 34-45.

Mittal, V., Kumar, P., and Tsiros, M. (1999). Attribute-level performance, satisfaction and behavioral intentions over time: A consumption-system approach. *Journal of Marketing, 63* (April): 88-101.

Mohr, L.A. and Bitner, M.J. (1995). The role of employee effort in satisfaction with service transactions, *Journal of Business Research, 32*(3): 239-252.

Newman, K. (2001). Interrogating SERVQUAL: A critical assessment of service quality measurement in a high street retail bank. *International Journal of Bank Marketing, 19*(3): 126-139.

Nunnally, J. C. (1978). *Psychometric Theory.* New York: McGraw-Hill.

Oliver, R.L. (1980). A conceptual model of the antecedents and consequences of satisfaction decisions. *Journal of Marketing Research, 17:* 460-469.

Oliver, R.L. (1993). A conceptual model of service quality and service satisfaction: Compatible goals, different concepts. In Swartz, T.A., Bowen, D.E. and Brown, S.W. (eds), *Advances in Services Marketing and Management: Research and Practice,* Volume 2 (pp. 65-85). Greenwich, CT: JAI Press.

Oliver, R.L. and Swan, L.E. (1989). Consumer perceptions of interpersonal equity and satisfaction in transaction: A fields survey approach. *Journal of Marketing, 53:* 21-35.

Page, T.J., Jr and Spreng, R.A. (2002). Difference scores versus direct effects in service quality measurement. *Journal of Service Research, 4*(February): 184-192.

Parasuraman, A., Berry, L.L., and Zeithaml, V.A. (1991). Refinement and reassessment of the SERVQUAL- scale. *Journal of Retailing, 67*(4): 420-50.

Parasuraman, A., Zeithaml, V.A., and Berry, L.L. (1985). A conceptual model of service quality and its implications for future research. *Journal of Marketing, 49*(Fall): 41-50.

Parasuraman, A., Zeithaml, V.A., and Berry, L.L. (1988). SERVQUAL: A multiple item scale for measuring consumer perceptions of service quality,.*Journal of Retailing, 64*(1): 12-40.

Parasuraman, A., Zeithaml, V.A., and Berry L.L. (1994). Reassessment of expectations as a comparison standard in measuring service quality: Implications for further research. *Journal of Marketing, 58*(January): 111-124.

Powpaka, S. (1996). The role of outcome quality as a determinant of overall service quality in different categories of services industries: An empirical investigation. *Journal of Services Marketing, 10*(2): 5-25.

Richard, M.D. and Allaway, A.W. (1993). Service quality attributes and choice behavior. *Journal of Services Marketing, 7*(1): 59-68.

Rucci, A.I., Kirn, S.P. and Quinn, T.T. (1998). The employee-customer-profit chain at sears. *Harvard Business Review, 76*(1): 82-97.

Rust, R.T. and Oliver, R.L. (1994). *Service Quality:New Directions in Theory and Practice.* Thousand Oak, CA: Sage Publications.

Smith, A.M. and Reynolds, N.L. (2001). Measuring cross cultural service quality: A framework for assessment. *International Marketing Review, 19*(5): 450-481.

Spreng, R.A. and Singh, A.K. (1993). An empirical assessment of the SERVQUAL scale, and the relationship between service quality and satisfaction. In Peter, D.W., Cravens, R., and Dickson P. (eds.), *Enhancing Knowledge Development in Marketing* (pp. 1-6). Chicago, IL: American Marketing Association.

Taylor, S.A. (1997). Assessing regression-based importance weights for quality perceptions and satisfaction judgments in the presence of higher order and/or interaction effects. *Journal of Retailing, 73*(1): 135-159.

Taylor S.A. and Baker T.L. (1994). An assessment of the relationship between service quality and customer satisfaction in the formation of consumers' purchase intentions. *Journal of Retailing, 70*(2): 163-178.

Teas, K.R. (1993). Expectations, performance evaluation, and consumer's perceptions of quality. *Journal of Marketing, 57*(October): 18-34.

Teas, K.R. (1994). Expectations as a comparison standard in measuring service quality: An assessment of reassessment. *Journal of Marketing, 58*(January): 132-139.

Ting, D.H. (2004). Service quality and satisfaction perceptions: Curvilinear and interaction effect. *The International Journal of Bank Marketing, 22*(6): 407-420.

Voss, C.A., Armistead, C.G., Johnston, R., and Morris, B. (1985). *Operations Management in Service Industries and the Public Sector.* Chichester, UK: Wiley.

Wang, Y., Lo, H.P., Chi, R., and Yang, Y. (2004). An integrated framework for customer value and customer-relationship-management performance: A customer-based perspective from China. *Managing Service Quality, 14*(2/3): 169-182.

Winsted K.F. (1997). The service experience in two cultures: A behavioral perspective. *Journal of Retailing, 73*(3): 337-360.

Yavas, U., Benkenstein, M., and Stuhldrerier, U. (2001). Relationships between service quality and behavioral outcomes: A study of private bank customers in Germany. *The International Journal of Bank Marketing, 22*(2): 144-157.

Zeithaml, V.A., Berry, L.L., and Parasuraman, A. (1993). The nature and determinants of customer expectation of service. *Journal of Academy of Marketing Science, 21*(1): 1-12.

Zeithaml, V.A., Berry, L.L., and Parasuraman, A. (1996). The behavioral consequences of service quality. *Journal of Marketing, 60*(April): 31-46.

Zhou, L. (2004). A dimension-specific analysis of performance-only measurement of service quality and satisfaction in China's retail banking. *Journal of Services Marketing, 18*(7): 534-546.

Chapter 6

Experience-Based Category Expectations in Service Quality Research and Management

Henk Roest

Based on the premise that consumers buy products whose benefits conform best to their specific needs, product attributes play a pivotal role in purchase decision making as they may offer the benefits valued and searched for by the consumer. Many studies have focused on determining these attributes (Olson and Jacoby, 1972; Jun and Jolibert, 1983; Steenkamp, 1989), especially in services and on service quality (Parasuraman et al., 1985, 1988; Carman, 1990; Lapierre et al., 1996). Within this area, service quality has been defined as the difference between the perceived performances on a set of salient quality attributes and the consumer's expectations on these attributes. Originally, Parasuraman and colleagues (1988) advocated the use of ideal expectations; later they proposed the use of desired and adequate expectations in service-quality research since they were more achievable than the ideal service (Zeithaml et al., 1991).

Although consumers assess different expectations, and multiple determinants will have an effect on whether a service will be satisfactory, focusing on desired and adequate expectations may not be the best choice for service-quality research and service-quality management. Consumers, on the one hand, may find it difficult to interpret what is actually being measured when they are asked about desired or adequate service quality. Teas (1993), for example, argued that "... a considerable portion of variance in the response to the Servqual expectation-scale is because of variance in respondents' interpretation

Global Cases on Hospitality Industry
© 2008 by The Haworth Press, Taylor & Francis Group. All rights reserved.
doi:10.1300/5923_06

of the question being asked" (p. 21). Managers, on the other hand, may find it hard to control for them because these expectations will be different from consumer to consumer; in fact, what is good enough for one consumer may still not be acceptable for another. Although Zeithaml and Bitner (1996) have proposed a large number of determinants of desired and adequate expectations, including differences in personal needs, transitory service intensifiers, situational factors, and word-of-mouth communication, very little empirical evidence is available that supports these suggestions and that can help service managers.[1] Moreover, since quality is regarded as a degree of excellence (Zeithaml, 1988), perhaps consumers' personal needs should not be criteria, but instead the performance level of competitors should have our focal attention when we set the comparison standard.

In this chapter a different type of expectation is introduced in service-quality research: experience-based expectations. Whereas the concept of experience-based expectations has been developed in the customer-satisfaction literature (Cadotte et al., 1987), experience-based expectations are valuable in quality research as well, for at least three reasons: First, experience-based expectations are based on comparative and competitive perceived performances. As such, these expectations may be treated as the standards for quality in the marketplace (benchmark). Second, these expectations are based on multiple experiences, and they are stored in memory as category exemplars or prototypes (Sujan, 1985; Ozanne et al., 1992). Being readily available, their use requires less cognitive effort than, for example, desired or adequate expectations, which require piecemeal inference processes. Given that consumers are not always able or willing to make such inferences (Iacobucci et al., 1996), they often choose prototypical products (Nedungadi and Hutchinson, 1985; Ward and Loken, 1988). Third, since exemplars and prototypes represent product and service categories, and consumers frequently distinguish between the categories (Rosch, 1978), experience-based expectations may be to a large extent equivalent for many consumers. Such robustness in expectations would make experience-based expectations more appealing to target by managers.

In this chapter, the literature on different types of expectations is reviewed first. Using a conceptual framework, these expectations are compared to the perceived service-quality construct. Next, the literature on service categorization is examined, to explore how categories and experience-based expectations are associated. Finally, an empirical study in the restaurant business shows how experience-based expectations can be measured, and how they are related to one another.

CONSUMER EXPECTATIONS

Consumers form expectations for different reasons (Hunt, 1977). First, expectations facilitate decision making since they are forecasts of the future and, to some degree, uncertain events. Second, expectations are thought to create a frame of reference that facilitates judgmental processes, and with which one makes a finite comparative judgment (Helson, 1964; Kahneman and Tversky, 1979). The expectations used in these instances can be distinguished as either "will" expectations or "should" expectations (Boulding et al., 1993).

WILL EXPECTATIONS

Consumers usually purchase a product to obtain the benefits offered by the attributes of the product. Consumers, however, may not have complete information about these benefits or attributes, or may not be able to acquire this information, especially in services. Therefore, purchase decisions are usually based on estimations of the relevant product benefits and attributes (Olson and Dover, 1979; Oliver and Winer, 1987; Tse and Wilton, 1988; Miller and Grush, 1988). In this manner, future states of being are consciously anticipated and elaborated by the consumer as pretrial beliefs about a focal brand or its attribute's performances (Oliver, 1977; Olson and Dover, 1979; Cadotte et al., 1987). *Will* expectations therefore are cognitive (Oliver and Winer, 1987) and active; they are held in an active memory state (Kahneman and Tversky, 1982). Will expectations may be based on memory about past purchase experiences (Bettman, 1979; Burnkrant, 1978; Surprenant and Solomon, 1987; Alba and Hutchinson, 1987; Ozanne et al., 1992), information obtained from the product itself (e.g., testing, brand, price), the context in which it is found (e.g., retail environment), the people who use it (e.g., other customers, word of mouth) (Fishbein and Ajzen, 1975; Meyer, 1981; Duncan and Olshavsky, 1982; Furse et al., 1984; Goering, 1985; Cohen and Basu,

1987; Murray, 1991), and learned inferential mechanisms, as often no direct information is provided on the product benefits (for an overview of these mechanisms, see Lee and Olshavsky, 1994).

Because will expectations are estimations of the focal product's performance, they involve an objective calculation of the benefit level and an objective calculation of the probability that this level will be attained (Miller, 1977). They therefore involve uncertainty (Ozga, 1965). Some of this uncertainty may be caused by factors outside the individual (e.g., the weather conditions, or the mood of a service employee) and is called exogenous uncertainty (Pesaran, 1987). Endogenous uncertainty, on the other hand, may arise because consumers (1) know little of their own needs and purchase goals (Deering and Jacoby, 1972), (2) are incapable of perfectly anticipating the behavior and actions of others in the marketplace (Pesaran, 1987), and (3) usually have to anticipate purchase results and consequences on the basis of the few attributes they can determine in advance (Helson, 1964; Deering and Jacoby, 1972; Darby and Karni, 1973; Einhorn and Hogarth, 1985). This uncertainty may be affected over time as new experiences are gathered and as the future to which the estimates refer becomes less distant (Ozga, 1965). On the one hand, new evidence may sometimes support will expectations since it is consistent information or clarify them if the new evidence provides an answer to a question that could not have been answered before. On the other hand, additional information can make it necessary for the consumer to revise his or her will expectations. Will expectations, therefore, are also dynamic, as they are being updated on a continuous basis.

SHOULD EXPECTATIONS

Research provides some evidence that, over time, fulfilled estimates become standards or norms (Boulding et al., 1993). In this case, expectations are thought to be service norms that organizations should fulfill (Grönroos, 1983; Woodruff et al., 1983; Parasuraman et al., 1985, 1988; Brown and Swartz, 1989). Unlike will expectations, *should* expectations generally exist as passive assumptions about objects and events (Oliver and Winer, 1987), and are usually not processed until disconfirmed (Bolton and Drew, 1991). Should expectations reflect what should be performed or should have been performed instead of what the customer believes (i.e., thinks or predicts) will be performed. Next, four different should expectations are considered: ideal expectations, desired expectations, adequate expectations, and experience-based expectations.

The consumer's ideal expectations are what a consumer wants in an ideal sense (Parasuraman et al., 1988). That is, the optimal product performance a consumer ideally would hope for, or as Miller (1977, p. 76) put it ". . . the best wished-for level of performance." This reflection of what performance potential is (Levitt, 1980) or "can be" (Tse and Wilton, 1988) represents enduring customer wants, needs, and values, which remain rather unaffected by the full range of marketing and competitive factors postulated to affect the other types of should expectations (Prakash, 1984). As such, ideal expectations are believed to be much more stable over time (Boulding et al., 1993). Ideals as expectations can be viewed as perfect states of nature that are perhaps unattainable, unrealistic, and unrelated to what the service provider tells the customer to expect (Oliver, 1993).

Desired expectations primarily deal with what the consumer desires or thinks he or she deserves (Prakash, 1984). They can be defined as the level at which the customer essentially wants the product or organization to perform (Swan and Trawick, 1981; Parasuraman et al., 1991a; Boulding et al., 1993). What "ought to happen" (Tse and Wilton, 1988) is not only influenced by the customer's own experiences, but also by what he or she views as reasonable and equitable (Parasuraman et al., 1991b). As such, it is a blend of what the customer needs and believes should be and can be attained (Zeithaml et al., 1991). Although these expectations seem to be more attainable and realistic than ideal expectations, Johnson and Mathews (1997) found that desired expectations are closely related to ideal norms in the eyes of the consumer.

Parasuraman et al.'s (1991a) adequate expectations reflect the minimum performance level required by customers after they have considered a variety of individual and situational factors. Adequate expectations are related to Miller's (1977) minimum tolerable expectations, defined as the poorest performance level acceptable to the customers, including the consumers' subjective evaluation of their own product investment. In effect, adequate expectations are the minimal acceptable levels of the desired expectations. According to Parasuraman et al. (1991a), the adequate service level is considerably more variable and flexible than the desired service.

Experience-based expectations are primarily based on comparative and competitive perceived performances of services (Prakash, 1984), such as the normal (average) or excellent (superior) performance (Woodruff et al., 1983). Experiences with real brands set limits on the performance a consumer believes the focal brand is supposed to offer. Consumers may establish these expectations in at least two different ways (Sujan, 1985; Alba and Hutchinson, 1987; Cohen and Basu, 1987; Cadotte et al., 1987; Ward et al., 1992). First, the experience-based expectations may be represented by the typical performance of a particular brand, for example, the consumer's most preferred brand, a popular brand, or the last-purchased brand (Kahneman and Miller, 1986). Such brand-based expectations may be used when one single brand dominates a consumer's set of brand experiences. Second, the set of experience-based expectations might also be an averaged performance a consumer considers as typical for a group of similar brands in a particular product or service category competing for the same consumer benefits (e.g., fast-food service). Such product-based expectations may be operative when a consumer has had experience with several brands within a product class and does not perceive any dominance by one particular brand.

CONCEPTUALIZATION ON CONSUMER EXPECTATIONS

Using a conceptual framework that has been used to distinguish perceived service quality from related constructs such as customer satisfaction and product attitude, perceived service quality has been defined as a relativistic (not absolute), cognitive (not affective), product-related (not consumer-related), post-purchase (not pre-purchase) evaluation of "get" components (not sacrifices) (Roest and Pieters, 1997). This same conceptual framework will be used now to specify the theoretically most suitable type of expectations for perceived service-quality assessment and management. The results of this conceptualization are presented in Table 6.1, showing that on a theoretical basis experience-based expectations fit the dimensional structure of perceived service quality best.

1. *Time.* The aspect of time has to do with whether the expectations are prospective or retrospective. Because will expectations are focused on the unknown and future performance of a focal

brand, they are prepurchase directed. Should expectations, on the other hand, are less time restricted since they are known references in pre- and postpurchase evaluation processes.

2. *Basis.* The aspect of basis deals with what the expectation comprises: "give" components, "get" components, or their trade-off. Will expectations, experience-based expectations, and perhaps also ideal expectations are concerned with either give or get components. Desired and adequate expectations, however, seem to be an instant trade-off between give and get components since what is "good enough" to receive from the service organization will be based on what is offered by the consumer (i.e., equity).

3. *Object.* The aspect of object deals with whether the expectations are informative of the product (e.g., "the product performs well") or the consumer (e.g., ". . . and that satisfies me"). Whereas ideal, desired, and adequate expectations express subjective preferences, will expectations and experience-based expectations are expressions of predicted and averaged product performances respectively. In other words, whereas the ideal, desired, and adequate expectations reflect information about the consumer, will expectations and experience-based expectations reflect information about the brand's performance or the product category.

4. *Content.* The aspect of content deals with the cognitive, affective, and conative aspects involved. In this respect, will expectations and experience-based expectations may be considered as cognitive measures, whereas ideal, desired, and adequate expectations (also) involve affective aspects.

5. *Context.* The aspect of context deals with whether or not the measure is relativistic. Whereas will expectations and ideal expectations appear to be absolute measures, desired, adequate, and experience-based expectations appear more relativistic since they are based on comparative offerings, and are sometimes also affected by personal and situational influences.

6. *Aggregation.* The aspect of aggregation deals with whether the measure is assessed for a single transaction or fits multiple transactions. Because will expectations involve predictions about one particular brand and one particular encounter, they must be treated as a transaction measure. Should expectations, on the other hand, are more robust across different transactions.

They are generally based on many experiences with different brands and may be treated and used as a relationship measure, although specific personal circumstances can make desired and adequate expectations exclusive for this particular encounter.

SERVICE CATEGORIZATION
AND EXPERIENCE-BASED EXPECTATIONS

Consumers are continuously confronted with an almost endless number of apparently different object stimuli and experiences. As a reaction to this, consumers form categories in memory enabling an efficient understanding and processing of the environment (Fiske, 1982; Sujan, 1985). Consumers use these categories to attend to information, interpret and infer meanings, solve problems, set goals, or select a behavior (Kahneman and Miller, 1986; Cohen and Basu, 1987; Ward and Loken, 1986; Loken and Ward, 1990; Folkes, 1994). Categories are based on the degree of equivalence, which is determined by the extent to which objects share a set of characteristics, such as features and attributes. As consumers store information in memory simultaneously at different levels of abstraction (Tolman, 1932; Olson and Reynolds, 1983), equivalence may be determined at different levels of comprehensiveness (Rosch et al., 1976; Nedungadi

TABLE 6.1. A Typology of Consumer Expectations

| Dimensions | Will expectations | Should expectations | | |
		Experience-Based	Ideal	Desired and Adequate
Time	Prepurchase	Pre- and post-purchase	Pre- and post-purchase	Pre- and post-purchase
Basis	Give or get	Give or get	Give or get	Give and get
Object	Product	Product	Consumer	Consumer
Content	Cognitive	Cognitive	Cognitive and affective	Cognitive and affective
Context	Absolute	Relative	Absolute	Relative
Aggregation	Transaction	Relationship	Relationship	Transaction or relationship

Source: Roest (1998)

and Hutchinson, 1985). The basic level is the level at which a number of attributes are shared by all or most members of the category and are most differentiated from other categories (e.g., birds have feathered wings to fly whereas mammals do not) (Rosch, 1978; Alba and Hutchinson, 1987). Superordinate categories are more comprehensive than this basic-level category, and they generally share only a few attributes among one another (e.g., not all animals have wings, but those that do are not necessarily birds). Subordinate categories are less comprehensive and enclose many attributes that overlap with other categories but are different on the levels or values of these attributes (e.g., both birds of prey and poultry birds have wings, but those of the bird of prey are much larger) (Jones, 1983). From a linguistic perspective, Rosch and colleagues (1976) suggest that, on the basic level, people generally use a single sign as a label for identification (birds), whereas on the subordinate level multiple sign sequences are used (birds of prey).

Within the categorization literature, a distinction has been made between common or taxonomic categories and ad-hoc or goal-directed categories (Barsalou, 1983, 1985). Taxonomic categories are those commonly used by members of a culture to classify phenomena such as "animals," "birds," "fruits," and "vegetables." Goal-directed categories are occasionally created as, for example, in "things to take from one's home during a fire." In those categories, the items are related to goal achievement and may be physically dissimilar (Loken and Ward, 1990). Although theory would suggest that consumers have well-established category representations in memory for taxonomic categories only (Hoffman, 1986), Ratneshwar and Shocker (1991) showed that consumers are able to define category representations in goal-directed instances as well. Such representations may especially be observed when products and goals are processed frequently by consumers, or when their category structures are actively created on the basis of their judgments of product substitutability across different usage contexts (Barsalou, 1983).

Categories may be represented as either concrete or abstract in memory. Representation as an abstract set of rules for identifying instances of the concept, category, or class generally include necessary and sufficiency conditions, defining and characteristic features, and simple frequency of occurrence information for attributes across known exemplars in the category (Alba and Hasher, 1983). Alternatively, people may have a concrete and specific image of the "exemplar" or "prototypical" concept instance (Sujan, 1985). Exemplars are known, good examples of the category, whereas prototypes are images embodying dimensions or attributes most commonly associated with members of the category but probably not possessed by any particular exemplar in conjunction.

In general, it may be argued that categories include hypotheses about the usual values, their importance, and the variability across brands on the attributes and benefits that they have in common (Sujan and Bettman, 1989; Ozanne et al, 1992). Apparently, they deal with coherent clusters of "experience-based expectations" on salient attributes stored in memory, i.e., their level, salience, and relationships (Woodruff et al., 1983; Cadotte et al., 1987; Kahneman, 1992).

MEASURING EXPERIENCE-BASED CATEGORY EXPECTATIONS

In order to explore how experience-based expectations can be measured and to verify our proposition that most consumers have a high consensus on the attribute expectations within distinguished categories, an empirical study was conducted in the restaurant business.

Service Selection

Restaurants were selected as the service industry. Since we are interested in differences in expectations on a fixed set of salient attributes, a service was needed in which most consumers have at least some experience, within service categories, and across service categories. Some across-category experience is needed in order to facilitate the comparison of performances between categories (subordinate: e.g., fast-food versus atmosphere restaurants), within a more general product class (basic-level: restaurants). Some within-category experience (different fast-food restaurants) is desirable, as we are interested in experience-based category expectations. The existence of a wide variety of restaurants and the popularity of dining out almost ensures that consumers have stored distinct and specific categories in memory, capturing their experience-based norms (Ozanne et al., 1992; Kahneman, 1992).

To specify the restaurant categories that consumers actually distinguish and use, sixteen videotaped consumer interviews were conducted. Each respondent was asked to categorize photographs randomly taken from a wide variety of (1) restaurant interiors, (2) restaurant exteriors, (3) menu cards, and (4) quality marks. In this "natural grouping" task, the respondents were allowed to make as many categories as they thought were necessary (cf. Walker et al., 1987). After allocating all the pictures they were asked to label the categories they had distinguished (cf. Urban et al., 1993). In general (93 percent of the cases), five restaurant categories were labeled: atmosphere restaurants, bistros, roadside restaurants, lunchrooms, and fast-food restaurants.

Sample

A consumer panel of visitors of fifteen different restaurants in two midsize cities in the Netherlands was recruited. The restaurants selected were distributed equally over the five categories. All of the restaurants were located close to or inside a shopping mall with competition across and within its own category at a close distance. This selection procedure makes it reasonable to assume that the restaurant actually chosen by the respondent was expected to perform (at least) in accordance with the expectations sought.

Data were collected using a self-administered questionnaire that visitors leaving the restaurant were asked to complete at home and return in a freepost envelope to a post-office box address within seven days. In the accompanying letter, respondents were told that for every fourth completed and returned questionnaire a gift voucher of ten euros would be remitted to them. The net response was 40 percent, which resulted in 480 respondents.[2] Their age averaged 44 years, 48 percent were male. On average, 1.7 persons accompanied respondents on their visit.

Measures

Before the respondents were asked to respond to questions concerning categories and expectations, they were asked about the name of the particular restaurant they had visited and two local restaurants in the same category, the respondent's company, and the food items ordered. These questions were asked to create a situation in which respondents were reminded of the dinner occasion in order to elicit more realistic answers and to circumvent the overall-first versus attribute-first measurement bias (see Moorthy, 1991).

Building on previous research in the restaurant industry (e.g., Miller and Ginter, 1979; Bridges, 1993) and the results of the 16 videotaped consumer interviews, respondents were asked to reply to 26 items concerning the quality of restaurants (see Table 6.2). Per item, the respondents assessed: (1) the experience-based score, i.e., how

TABLE 6.2. Validity and Reliability of Restaurant Service Quality Attributes

Measures	Items	Factor loadings	Corrected item-total correlation	Alpha if item deleted
Service quality attributes variance explained = 61.5 percent				
Empathy (coefficient alpha = .81)	Personal attention	.77	.72	.71
	Time spent on you	.75	.63	.74
	Friendliness of personnel	.69	.60	.75
	Concerned personnel	.64	.44	.81
	Free and easy personnel	.51	.54	.77
Ambiance (coefficient alpha = .80)	Attractive furnishings	.69	.52	.77
	Comfortable ambiance	.68	.62	.74
	Pleasant interior	.67	.58	.75
	Attractive food served	.53	.57	.76
	Taste of food served	.50	.58	.76
Professionalism (coefficient alpha = .76)	Explanation	.76	.59	.68
	Personal advice	.61	.65	.67
	Food choice	.59	.41	.75
	Competence of personnel	.53	.59	.68
	Nutrition of food served	.44	.37	.76
Reliability (coefficient alpha = .83)	Correct service	.84	.69	.70
	Correct food processing	.80	.72	.66
	Flexibility	.57	.56	.83
Service Scapes (coefficient alpha = .56)	Attractive environment	.69	.44	.43
	Attractiveness facade	.68	.37	.56
	Immaculately dressed	.55	.40	.49
Privacy (coefficient alpha = .63)	Quietness	.82	.49	.45
	Peaceful	.78	.47	.48
	Privacy	.60	.38	.61
Access (coefficient alpha = .74)	Easy access	.87	.56	.
	Fast access	.86	.56	.

restaurants in that specific category typically performed on that item; and (2) the disconfirmation score, i.e., to what extent this particular restaurant's performance deviated from the experience-based score. Since research shows that attribute salience differs between different services (Carman, 1990), the item disconfirmation scores (Oliver, 1981) were assessed to ascertain the salient quality attributes on which restaurants are evaluated on the basic-level category level (cf. Parasuraman et al., 1988). The experience-based item scores were used to calculate the individual subordinate category expectations on these service-quality attributes. As they guarantee both better and faster assessments (Stone and Schkade, 1994), bipolar five-point "common context-relevant" rating scales were used to measure the item scores. The experience-based question and the disconfirmation question for the friendliness item, for example, were worded as, "The personnel in restaurants like this one are typically: (1) very unfriendly to (5) very friendly," and "During this particular encounter, the personnel were: (1) less friendly to (5) more friendly."

Analyses and Results

In order to verify our own category interpretation of the specific restaurants that we selected, respondents were asked to classify the restaurant visited according to the five restaurant categories. Of the 480 respondents, 86 percent classified the restaurant as we intended (78 percent in fast-food restaurants, 80 percent in lunchrooms, 78 percent in roadside restaurants, 94 percent in bistros, and 97 percent in atmosphere restaurants). As we wanted to base the analyses on the categorization perceptions of the respondents, 89 responses were from fast-food restaurants, 84 from lunchrooms, 66 from roadside restaurants, 124 from bistros, and 106 were from atmosphere restaurants.

Construct Validity and Reliability

Principal component analysis (PCA) was applied to examine the set of salient restaurant quality attributes. The factors were determined according to the eigenvalues greater than one procedure (cf. Parasuraman et al., 1988; Carman, 1990) and Varimax rotation.

Cronbach alphas were calculated to test the internal construct reliabilities.

It appears that, on the basic-level category level, consumers distinguish 7 service quality attributes when evaluating restaurants. These attributes are labeled as: empathy, ambiance, professionalism, reliability, service scapes, privacy, and access, showing eigenvalues of 2.98, 2.67, 2.64, 2.38, 1.86, 1.74, and 1.58 respectively.[3,4] The fit of the model and the reliabilities of the constructs are adequate, except for service scapes, whose reliability is below Nunnally's (1978) standard. By averaging the corresponding experience-based item scores for each subordinate restaurant category, the experience-based expectations are calculated for atmosphere, bistro, roadside, lunchroom, and fast-food restaurants.

EXPERIENCE-BASED EXPECTATIONS PER CATEGORY

One-way ANOVA shows that the experience-based expectations are significantly different across the subordinate categories (see Table 6.3). The Tukey HSD post-hoc statistics point out that these differences are widely spread, except for privacy. Apparently, privacy is selectively attended to when consumers want to distinguish atmosphere restaurants from nonatmosphere-restaurant (all other) categories. This finding supports the idea of local regions of attributes that has been suggested in the categorization literature (Goldstone, 1994). Most interesting is that whereas the experience-based expectations appear highly different between categories (high F-values), differences are low within categories (low standard deviations) on most of the service-quality attributes. In Figure 6.1, the average experience-based expectations on each of the seven salient quality attributes have been visualized for each of the five restaurant categories.

CONCLUSIONS AND MANAGERIAL IMPLICATIONS

Although the use of different types of consumer expectations has been demonstrated in the literature, experience-based expectations seem especially interesting in quality research. From a theoretical perspective, it appears that experience-based expectations match the conceptual characteristics of the quality construct better than, for ex-

TABLE 6.3. Experience-Based Category Expectations (ANOVA)

Source of Variation	F-value	Degrees of freedom	F-prob	Mean-scores (standard deviation)				
				Fast food	Lunchroom	Roadside	Bistro	Atmosphere
Quality attributes								
Empathy	43.01	4;458	.00	3.15_a (.54)	$3.45_a{}_c$ (.57)	$3.39^a{}_b$ (.50)	$3.62^{a,b}{}_d$ (.36)	$4.01^{a,b,c,d}$ (.43)
Ambiance	128.79	4;443	.00	2.77^a (.61)	$3.40^a{}_c$ (.51)	$3.32^a{}_b$ (.49)	$3.78^{a,b,c}{}_d$ (.41)	$4.29^{a,b,c,d}$ (.37)
Professionalism	51.09	4;417	.00	2.92_a (.58)	$3.24^a{}_c$ (.49)	$3.23^a{}_b$ (.50)	3.37_d (.41)	$3.89^{a,b,c,d}$ (.36)
Reliability	34.92	4;433	.00	3.61_c (.59)	3.57_b (.58)	3.52_a (.63)	$3.76^a{}_d$ (.45)	$4.33^{a,b,c,d}$ (.48)
Service scapes	21.46	4;457	.00	$3.64^a{}_b$ (.47)	$3.68^a{}_c$ (.46)	3.37^a (.50)	$3.74^a{}_d$ (.36)	$3.98^{a,b,c,d}$ (.40)
Privacy	84.92	4;447	.00	2.18_a (.68)	2.69_c (.58)	2.64_b (.68)	2.82_d (.60)	$3.74^{a,b,c,d}$ (.53)
Access	17.56	4;430	.00	$3.90^{a,b}$ (.58)	$3.77^{a,b}{}_c$ (.64)	$4.14^{a,b,c}$ (.73)	3.46_b (.60)	3.45^a (.64)

a,b,c,dTukey's HSD; superscript versus subscript indices indicate significant differences between category means at p = .05.

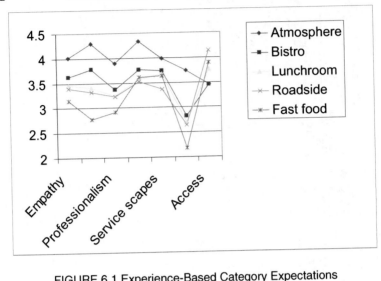

FIGURE 6.1 Experience-Based Category Expectations

ample, desired or adequate expectations do. From an empirical perspective, consumers can easily retrieve experience-based expectations from memory, and they appear equivalent among most consumers (objective) whereas the other types of expectations are usually very different from consumer to consumer (subjective).

Although adequate and desired expectations are widely used as the standards in service-quality research, reviewing the literature on the different types of consumer expectations and examining their true nature give reason to believe that they may not be the best choice. In earlier work, perceived service quality was distinguished from related constructs such as product value and customer satisfaction on six conceptual dimensions: time, basis, object, content, context, and aggregation, indicating that perceived service quality is a relativistic (not absolute), cognitive (not affective), product-related (not consumer-related), and postpurchase (not prepurchase) evaluation of "get" components (not sacrifices) (Roest and Pieters, 1997). Using this same conceptual framework to distinguish between different types of consumer expectations it is observed that whereas adequate and desired expectations (1) involve a trade-off between give and get components, (2) are highly affective, and as such (3) are affected by subjective and consumer differences, experience-based expectations seem to fit in perfectly with perceived service quality on all fundamental dimensions. Since product and service categories are based on differences in experiences, experience-based expectations may be regarded as category specific.

Focusing on experience-based expectations in this study we found that on the basic-category level, consumers evaluate restaurants on seven quality attributes: empathy, ambiance, professionalism, reliability, service scapes, privacy, and access. Checking whether these dimensions appeared in all distinct categories, it was concluded that this cognitive structure is robust, supporting the categorization premise of equivalence. Also in line with the categorization theory, the experience-based expectations on these attributes were found to be quite different between the five subordinate restaurant categories. Whereas large differences have been observed on the expectations held by consumers across the five restaurant categories, consumers have established more or less the same performance expectations within each category. These results indicate that consumers have a clear and shared picture of what exactly can be expected from each service category and which category may be expected to perform best on each of the service-quality attributes.

Because experience-based expectations are based on multiple encounters with different service providers within the same category, category expectations may be regarded as good benchmarks. In a competitive environment, customers will use these standards to determine the offer that is expected to fulfill their needs best, within the category. More insight into these benchmarks may help managers specify the brand performance levels that should to be achieved by the service and service organization in order to attract customers and prevent them from switching to competitors. Since experience-based expectations are to some extent interrelated within service categories, service brands have to be designed and communicated in a categorical manner. Restaurant managers, for example, have to decide whether their restaurant will focus on either quick lunch occasions (stress high performance on access) or on business dinner parties (high performance on ambiance), as these service propositions (and perhaps also their positioning) seem incompatible. Knowing that service categories are selected because they are expected to perform well on specific quality attributes, cue management should focus on prototypical cues too (i.e., cues that tell the consumer that the focal brand is a typical example of a certain category). This is an important issue, because consumers, when categorizing brands, convert the experience-based performance expectations of the category into the focal brand's will expectations. When consumers observe different cues that are typical for different categories, they may establish service-quality expectations that are too high or too low and which also are held with low confidence. In fact, the consumer may assess expectations the service manager is not able or willing to fulfill. Perhaps even the consumer may discard the brand when making a purchase decision as a result of perceived inconsistency and uncertainty of the focal service brand.

NOTES

1. One of the few studies is by Parasuraman and colleagues (1991), who conducted a number of focus-group interviews and found some evidence that emergency and service-failure situations tend to raise desired and adequate norms. They also claim that more experienced consumers generally have higher norms, arguing that experts have more to compare with.

2. The response was not equally distributed over specific restaurants and restaurant categories.

3. Repeating the same procedure for each of the five restaurant categories (cf. Parasuraman et al., 1988; Carman, 1990), it appeared that this dimensional structure is, to a large extent, consistent across these restaurant types. The results presented in Appendix A indicate that most items load on the same factors in the five replications and that the majority of the items expected to load together actually do so. Applying confirmatory factor analysis (Steenkamp and Van Trijp, 1991), reliabilities of the restaurant category factors averaged above .70 and appeared consistent with the reliabilities of the restaurant-class factors, except for "access" in lunchrooms and "privacy" in lunchrooms and roadside restaurants. These results should be treated as indicative as for the roadside restaurant analyses, for example, only 66 responses were available for 26 items.

4. We also verified whether differences in expertise have an impact on the cognitive dimensional structure. Using a median split, respondents were assigned to either the low-expert or the high-expert group. Although application of PCA with eigenvalues greater than 1 and Varimax rotation resulted in 6 and 7 quality dimensions respectively, differences are small. For example, 6 dimensions explain 59.2 percent and 59.0 percent of the variance respectively, and 20 of the 26 items load on corresponding factors in both groups (cf. Carman, 1990).

REFERENCES

Alba, J.W. and Hasher, L. (1983). Is memory schematic? *Psychological Bulletin,* March: 203-231.

Alba, J.W. and Hutchinson, J.W. (1987). Dimensions of consumer expertise. *Journal of Consumer Research, 13* (March): 411-454.

Barsalou, L. (1983). Ad hoc categories. *Memory and Cognition, 11*(3): 211-227.

Barsalou, L. (1985). Ideals, central tendency, and frequency of instantiation as determinants of graded structure in categories. *Journal of Experimental Psychology: Learning, Memory, and Cognition, 11*(4): 629-654.

Bettman, J.R. (1979). *An Informational Processing Theory of Consumer Choice.* Boston, MA: Addison-Wesley, Reading.

Bolton, R.N. and Drew, J.H. (1991). A multistage model of consumers' assessments of service quality and value. *Journal of Consumer Research, 17* (March): 375-384.

Boulding, W., Kalra, A., Staelin, R., and Zeithaml, V.A. (1993). A dynamic process model of service quality: From expectations to behavioral intentions,.*Journal of Marketing Research, 30:* 7-27.

Bridges, E. (1993). Service attributes: Expectations and judgments. *Psychology & Marketing,* 10 (May-June): 185-197.

Brown, S.W. and Swartz, T.A. (1989). A gap analysis of professional service quality. *Journal of Marketing, 53*(April): 92-98.

Burnkrant, R.E. (1978). Cue utilization in product perception. *Advances in Consumer Research, 5:* 724-729.

Cadotte, E.R., Woodruff, R.B., and Jenkins, R.L. (1987). Expectations and norms in models of consumer satisfaction. *Journal of Marketing Research, 14*(August): 304-314.

Carman, J.M. (1990). Consumer perceptions of service quality: An assessment of the SERVQUAL dimensions. *Journal of Retailing, 66* (Spring): 33-55.

Cohen, J.B. and Basu, K. (1987). Alternative models of categorization: Toward a contingent processing framework. *Journal of Consumer Research, 13*(March): 455-472.

Darby, M.R. and Karni, K. (1973). Free competition and optimal amount of fraud. *The Journal of Law and Economics, 16*(April): 67-88.

Deering, B.J. and Jacoby, J. (1972). Risk enhancement and risk reduction as strategies for handling perceived risk. In M. Venkatesan (ed.), *Proceedings of the 3rd Annual Conference of the Association for Consumer Research* (pp. 404-416). Duluth, MN: Association for Consumer Research.

Duncan, C.P. and Olshavsky, R.W. (1982). External search: The role of consumer beliefs. *Journal of Marketing Research, 19*(February): 32-43.

Einhorn, H.J. and Hogarth, R.M. (1985). Ambiguity and uncertainty in probabilistic inference. *Psychological Bulletin, 92:* 433-461.

Fishbein, M. and Ajzen, I. (1975). *Belief, Attitude, Intention and Behavior: An Introduction to Theory and Research.* Boston, MA: Addison-Wesley, Reading.

Fiske, S.T. (1982). Schema-triggered affect: Applications to social perception. In M.S. Clark and S.T. Fiske (eds.), *Affect and Cognition* (pp. 55-78). Hillsdale, NJ: Lawrence Erlbaum Associates.

Folkes, V. (1994). How consumers predict service quality: What do they expect? In R.T. Rust and R.L. Oliver (eds.), *Service Quality: New Directions in Theory and Practice* (pp. 108-122). Thousand Oaks, CA: Sage.

Furse, D.H., Punj, G.N., and Stewart, D.W. (1984). A typology of individual search strategies among purchases of new automobiles. *Journal of Consumer Research, 10:* 417-431.

Goering, P.A. (1985). Effects of product trial on consumer expectations, demand, and prices. *Journal of Consumer Research, 12*(June): 74-82.

Goldstone, R. (1994). Influences of categorization on perceptual discrimination. *Journal of Experimental Psychology: General, 123*(2): 178-200.

Grönroos, C. (1983). *Strategic Management and Marketing in the Service Sector.* Report No. 83-104. Cambridge, MA: Marketing Science Institute.

Helson, H. (1964). *Adaptation-Level Theory: An Experimental and Systematic Approach to Behavior.* New York: Harper and Row.

Hoffman, M.L. (1986). Affect, cognition, and motivation. In R.M. Sorrentino and E.T. Higgins (eds.), *Handbook of Motivation and Cognition: Foundations of Social Behavior* (pp. 244-280). New York: The Guilford Press.

Hunt, H.K. (1977). CS/D: Overview and future research directions. In H.K. Hunt (ed.), *Conceptualization and Measurement of Consumer Satisfaction and Dissatisfaction* (pp-455-488).Cambridge, MA: Marketing Science Institute.

Iacobucci, D., Ostrom, A.L., Braig, B.M., and Bezjian-Avery, A. (1996). A canonical model of consumer evaluations and theoretical basis of expectations. In T.E. Swartz, D.E. Bowen and S.W. Brown (eds.), *Advances in Services Marketing and Management: Research and Practice*, Volume 5 (pp. 1-44). Greenwich, CT: JAI Press.

Johnson, C. and Mathews, B.P. (1997). The influence of experience on service expectations. *International Journal of Service Industry Management, 8*(4): 290-305.

Jones, G.V. (1983). Identifying basic categories. *Psychological Bulletin, 94*(3): 423-428.

Jun, W.J. and Jolibert, A.J.P. (1983). Revealed versus hidden attribute's as determinants of perceived product quality. *Journal of Economic Psychology, 4:* 263-272.

Kahneman, D. (1992). Reference points, anchors, norms, and mixed feelings. *Organizational Behavior and Human Decision Processes, 51:* 296-312.

Kahneman, D. and Miller, D.T. (1986). Norm theory: Comparing realities to its alternatives. *Psychological Review, 93:* 136-153.

Kahneman, D. and Tversky, A. (1979). Prospect theory: An analysis of decision under risk. *Econometrica, 47:* 263-291.

Kahneman, D. and Tversky, A. (1982). The simulation heuristic. In D. Kahneman, P. Slovic and A. Tversky (eds.), *Judgment under Uncertainty: Heuristics and Biases* (pp. 201-208). New York: Cambridge University Press.

Lapierre, J., Filitrault, P., and Perrien, J. (1996). Research on service quality evaluation: Evolution and methodological issues. *Journal of Retailing and Consumer Services, 3*(2): 91-98.

Lee, D.H. and Olshavsky, R.W. (1994). Toward a predictive model of consumer inference process: The role of expertise. *Psychology and Marketing, 11* (March/April): 109-127.

Levitt, Th. (1980). Marketing success through differentiation—of anything. *Harvard Business Review,* January/February: 83-91.

Loken, B. and Ward, J. (1990). Alternative approaches to understanding the determinants of typicality. *Journal of Consumer Research, 17*(September): 111-126.

Meyer, R.J. (1981). A model of multi attribute judgments under attribute uncertainty and informational constraints. *Journal of Marketing Research, 18*(November): 428-441.

Miller, J.A. (1977). Studying satisfaction, modifying models, eliciting expectations, posing problems, and making meaningful measurement. In H.K. Hunt (ed.), *Conceptualization and Measurement of Consumer Satisfaction and Dissatisfaction* (pp.72-91). Cambridge, MA: Marketing Science Institute.

Miller, K.E. and Ginter, J.L. (1979). An investigation of situational variation in brand choice behavior and attitude. *Journal of Marketing Research, 16*(February): 111-123.

Miller, L.E. and Grush, J.E. (1988). Improving prediction's in expectancy theory research: effects of personality, expectancies, and norms. *Academy of Management Journal, 31:* 107-122.

Moorthy, K.S. (1991). *Measuring Overall Judgments and Attribute Evaluations: Overall First versus Attribute First.* Report No. 91-120. Cambridge, MA: Marketing Science Institute.

Murray, K.B. (1991). A test of services marketing theory: Consumer information acquisition activities. *Journal of Marketing, 55*(January): 10-25.

Nedungadi, P. and Hutchinson, J.W. (1985). The prototypicality of brands: Relationships with brand awareness, preference and usage. *Advances in Consumer Research, 12:* 498-503.

Nunnally, J.C. (1978). *Psychometric Theory.* New York: McGraw-Hill.

Oliver, R.L. (1977). A theoretical reinterpretation of expectation and disconfirmation effects on post exposure product evaluations: Experience in the Field. In R.L. Day (ed.), *Consumer Satisfaction, Dissatisfaction and Complaining Behavior* (pp. 2-9). Bloomington, IN: Indiana University Division of Business Research.

Oliver, R.L. (1981). Measurement and evaluation of satisfaction processes in retail settings. *Journal of Retailing, 57*(Fall): 25-48.

Oliver, R.L. (1993). A conceptual model of service quality and service satisfaction: Compatible goals, different concepts. In T.E. Swartz, D.E. Bowen and S.W. Brown (eds.), *Advances in Service Marketing and Management,* Volume 2 (pp. 65-85). Greenwich, CT: JAI Press.

Oliver, R.L. and Winer, R.S. (1987). A framework for the formation and structure of consumer expectations: Reviews and propositions. *Journal of Economic Psychology, 8:* 469-499.

Olson, J.C. and Dover, P.A. (1979). Disconfirmation of consumer expectations through product trial. *Journal of Applied Psychology, 64:* 179-189.

Olson, J.C. and Jacoby, J. (1972). Cue utilization in the quality perception process. In M. Venkatesan (ed.), *Proceedings of the 3rd Annual Conference of the Association for Consumer Research* (pp. 167-179). Duluth, MN: Association for Consumer Research

Olson, J.C. and Reynolds, T.J. (1983). Understanding consumers' cognitive structures: Implications for marketing strategy. In L. Percy and A. Woodside (eds.), *Advertising and Consumer Psychology* (pp. 77-90). Lanham, MD: Lexington Books.

Ozanne, J.L., Brucks M., and Grewal, D. (1992). A study of information search behavior during the categorization of new products. *Journal of Consumer Research, 18:* 452-463.

Ozga, S.A. (1965). *Expectations in Economic Theory*. London, UK: Weidenfeld and Nicolson.

Parasuraman, A., Berry, L.L., and Zeithaml, V.A. (1991a). Refinement and reassessment of the SERVQUAL scale. *Journal of Retailing, 67*(4): 420-450.

Parasuraman, A., Berry, L.L., and Zeithaml, V.A. (1991b). Understanding customer expectations of service. *Sloan Management Review, 32:* 39-48.

Parasuraman, A., Zeithaml, V.A., and Berry, L.L. (1985). A conceptual model of service quality and its implications for future research. *Journal of Marketing, 49*(Fall): 41-50.

Parasuraman, A., Zeithaml, V.A., and Berry, L.L. (1988). SERVQUAL: A multiple-item scale for measuring consumer perceptions of service quality. *Journal of Retailing, 64*(Spring): 12-40.

Pesaran, M.H. (1987). *The Limits to Rational Expectations*. Oxford, UK: Basil Blackwell.

Prakash, V. (1984). Personal values and product expectations. In R.E. Pitts and A.G. Woodside (eds.), *Personal Values and Consumer Psychology* (pp. 145-154). Lanham, MD: Lexington Books.

Ratneshwar, S. and Shocker, A.D. (1991). Substitution in use and the role of usage context in product category structures. *Journal of Marketing Research, 28*(August): 281-295.

Roest, H.C.A. (1998). *Service Quality Expectations: Assessment and Management.* Tillburg, the Netherlands: Tilburg University.

Roest, H.C.A. and Pieters, R.G.M. (1997). The nomological net of perceived service quality. *International Journal of Service Industry Management, 8*(4): 336-351.

Rosch, E. (1978). Principles of categorization. In E. Rosch and B.B. Lloyd (eds.), *Cognition and Categorization* (pp. 27-48). Hillsdale, NJ: Erlbaum.

Rosch, E., Mervis, C.B., Gray, W.D., Johnson, D.M., and Boyes-Braem, P. (1976). Basic objects in natural categories. *Cognitive Psychology, 8:* 382-439.

Steenkamp, J.B.E.M. (1989). *Product Quality.* Assen, the Netherlands: Van Gorcum.

Steenkamp, J.B.E.M. and Van Trijp, H.C.M. (1991). The use of LISREL in validating marketing constructs. *International Journal of Research in Marketing, 8:* 283-299.

Stone, D.N. and Schkade, D.A. (1994). Effects of attribute scales on process and performance in multiattribute choice. *Organizational Behavior and Human Decision Processes, 59:* 261-287.

Sujan, M. (1985). Consumer knowledge: Effects on evaluation strategies mediating consumer judgments. *Journal of Consumer Research, 12*(June): 31-46.

Sujan, M. and Bettman, J.R. (1989). The effects of brand positioning strategies on consumers' brand and category perceptions: Some insights from schema research. *Journal of Marketing Research, 26*(November): 454-467.

Surprenant, C.F. and Solomon, M.R. (1987). Predictability and personalization in the service encounter. *Journal of Marketing, 51*(April): 86-96.

Swan, J.E. and Trawick, I.F. (1981). Disconfirmation of expectations and satisfaction with a retail service. *Journal of Retailing, 57*(Fall): 49-67.

Teas, R.K. (1993). Expectations, performance evaluation, and consumers' perceptions of quality. *Journal of Marketing, 57*(October): 18-34.

Tolman, E.C. (1932). *Purposive Behavior in Animals and Men.* New York: Appleton Century Crofts.

Tse, D.K. and Wilton, P.C. (1988). Models of consumer satisfaction formation: An extension. *Journal of Marketing Research, 25*(May): 204-212.

Urban, G.L., Hulland, J.S., and Weinberg, B.D. (1993). Premarket forecasting for new consumer durable goods: modeling categorization, elimination, and consideration phenomena. *Journal of Marketing, 57*(April): 47-63.

Walker, B., Celsi, R., and Olson, J. (1987). Exploring the structural characteristics of consumers' knowledge. *Advances in Consumer Research, 14:* 17-21.

Ward, J.C., Bitner, M.J., and Barnes, J. (1992). Measuring the prototypicality and meaning of retail environments. *Journal of Retailing, 68* (Summer): 194-220.

Ward, J.C. and Loken, B. (1986). The quintessential snack food: Measurement of product prototypes. *Advances in Consumer Research, 13:* 126-131.

Ward, J.C. and Loken, B. (1988). The generality of typicality effects on preference and comparison: An exploratory test. *Advances in Consumer Research, 15:* 55-61.

Woodruff, R.B., Cadotte, E.R., and Jenkins, R.L. (1983). Modeling consumer satisfaction processes using experience-based norms. *Journal of Marketing Research, 20:* 296-304.

Zeithaml, V.A. (1988). Consumer perceptions of price, quality, and value: A means-end model and synthesis of evidence. *Journal of Marketing, 52*(July): 2-22.

Zeithaml, V.A., Berry, L.L., and Parasuraman, A. (1991). *The nature and determinants of customer expectations of service.* Report No. 91-113, Cambridge, MA: Marketing Science Institute.
Zeithaml V.A. and Bitner, M.J. (1996). *Services marketing: Integrating customer focus across the firm.* New York: McGraw-Hill.

Chapter 7

The Influence of Empowerment on Organizational Success: A Case Study on Flight Centre

Jiaolan Bowden
Andrew Martin

INTRODUCTION

Empowerment has been practiced as a tool for organizational effectiveness for decades. However, to many, the essence of empowerment is barely realized (Hales and Klidas, 1998; Lashley and McGoldrick, 1994; Pickard, 1993). Some believe that empowerment is no more than a buzzword of organizational control, or that it is only an illusion, not a reality, and that it does not necessarily lead to organizational success (Argyris, 1998; Claydon and Doyle, 1996; Cunningham and Hyman, 1999; Smith and Mouly, 1998).

The main aims of this chapter are to examine the meaning of empowerment, discuss related theories, evaluate the impact of empowerment practices on an organization, and reflect on their management implications. This is done with an examination of the empowerment practices in a case organization: Flight Centre Ltd. Flight Centre is an independent travel company that in two decades has grown from a single Australian travel shop to a multinational operation. The industrial context of this case organization is unique to empowerment study because the travel industry is characterized by a high intensity of competition, low barriers of entry, and low profit margins (Palmer and Dunford, 2002). Compared to many other industries, it is also burdened with a poor industrial image, a low level of professional-

Global Cases on Hospitality Industry
© 2008 by The Haworth Press, Taylor & Francis Group. All rights reserved.
doi:10.1300/5923_07

ization in terms of management styles, and acute employment problems (Baum, 1996; Choy, 1995).

Operating in such an industry, the success of Flight Centre can be largely attributed to an effective use of empowerment and associated management practices. The notion of empowerment is well understood by the management of this company, manifested by a people-centric organizational philosophy; empowerment is purposely induced through a gamut of management practices and ongoing activities. The successful use of empowerment by Flight Centre presents a promising benchmark for those operating in the travel and tourism industry.

The case study concludes that empowerment should not simply be viewed as a cognitive attitude or a management process of shifting organizational power from management to workers. These definitions confine the meaning of empowerment to a single management approach that has specific functions. Nor should empowerment be viewed as merely another humanistic management model, which, in general, still claims the ownership of the human resource of employees.

Empowerment should be viewed as a multidimensional concept that encompasses the integrated efforts of the employers and their endorsement of organizational power, the employees and their claims to power, and the setup of the social and structural antecedents to condition employee empowerment.

More important, empowerment should be lifted as a management philosophy that challenges the prerogative of management itself. The notion of power sharing in the concept of empowerment revolutionizes the interrelationship between management and workers. By sharing the central element of an organizational existence, empowerment enables these workers to ascertain their existence, that is, the employees' equal right to organizational control and the right to their own working life. According to the rules of empowerment, no boundary should exist between managers and employees. As they have the joint ownership of an organization, the differences between management and employee's should only be functional, not hierarchical.

THE CONCEPTUAL AND THEORETICAL FRAMEWORKS OF EMPOWERMENT

Empowerment Defined

At the onset of discussion, it is important to clarify the meaning of empowerment. According to the Oxford English Dictionary (2004b), the word *empower* has two basic meanings: (1) to invest legally or formally with power or authority; to authorize, license; and (2) to impart or bestow power to an end or for a purpose; to enable, permit. This simple definition gives a clue of the three central parts of *empowerment:* it is an act of shifting power between two parties, it is for the desired purpose of the one who initiated it, and it is also beneficial to those who are given power in the aspect that they are enabled with abilities to perform and act freely.

In the context of management study, various definitions of *empowerment* have been given by researchers. One common feature of these definitions, however, is that in essence they discuss the meaning, locus, extent, and impact of organizational power in the context of the interrelationship between employees, employers, and organizations. For example, Conger and Kanungo (1988) define empowerment as, "a process of enhancing feelings of self-efficacy among organizational members; it is a motivational process of employees" (p. 471). Relating to this notion, Thomas and Velthouse (1990) conceptualize empowerment as "changes in the cognitive variables of employees" (named "task assessments") (p. 667). Berry (1995) dismantles the cognition of employees into five states of mind: "feelings of control over job, awareness of the context of work, accountability of personal work output, shared responsibility for organizational or unit performance, and equality in the reward based on individual or collective performance" (p. 208).

An opposing view to this group of thoughts that puts employees' cognition as the focal point of employee empowerment proposes that empowerment is instead reflected in the function and impact on employees and management in the process of power reallocation. Lashley (1996) defines empowerment as an approach used to achieve greater employee commitment, to gain information from employees and improve the bottom line, and to increase the responsiveness to customers. In the same vein, Kanter (1977) defines empowerment as the process of giving power to people who are at a disadvantaged place in an organization.

Although these different schools of thought of empowerment have their own individual rationales, and contribute toward the understanding of empowerment, the diversity of these definitions reveals that the notion of empowerment is still fraught with ambiguities and disagreements (Claydon and Doyle, 1996; Eylon, 1998; Simon, 1990). Researchers have agreed that the concept of empowerment should not be viewed from a single perspective, but that it encompasses a multifaceted aspect (D'Annunzio-Green and Macandrew, 1999; Honold, 1997; Howard and Foster, 1999; Thomas and Velthouse, 1990; Wyer and Mason, 1999).

This chapter will attempt to explore the true meaning of empowerment from a multidimensional perspective; answer such questions as why empowerment is needed; and discuss the properties of power, how to achieve true empowerment, and what the contextual conditions and consequences of empowerment are.

The Hierarchy of Empowerment: An Employer's Perspective

As stated previously, one central part of empowerment is the investing of power in order to gain staff commitment. One primary question, therefore, is what the power is. According to Thomas and Velthouse (1990), power has several meanings. "Power can mean authority in a legal sense, capacity, and energy (p. 667)." It also can mean autonomy, control, and freedom of decision making (Appelbaum et al., 1999).

In the employment context, Howard and Foster (1999) refer to power as control, as influence and dominance over others. Empowerment, therefore, is about giving control (to employees) over decision making, work process, performance goals, and people (Fulford and Enz, 1995; Keller and Dansereau, 1995; Parker and Price, 1994; Pfeffer, 1994). However, empirical research has revealed that conceding control can lead to the various drawbacks of empowerment, such as management losing control and the abuse of power. One of the main causes is, as claimed, the incapacity of those who are given power. Factors such as lack of training and supportive organizational culture can contribute to this failure (Cunningham and Hyman, 1999; Roth and Potts, 2001).

Away from the basic idea of control, Burke (1986) views power as authority. "Empowerment, therefore, implies the delegation of authority" (p. 5). Likewise, Melhem (2004) brings in the idea of discretion in empowerment. He states that empowerment is mainly "concerned with giving employees more authority and discretion in task and context related issues" (p. 73). Compared with *control, authority* and *discretion* denote power and abilities that can be used to influence or persuade; they cannot be easily granted as can a commodity because they are derived from an individual's own knowledge and/or experiences. Therefore, the granting of authority and discretion is a level higher than simply the shifting of control, because the excising of power without matching abilities and knowledge is an abuse of power. Nurturing these abilities requires the efforts of both employers and employees.

A step further, the self-efficacy theory of employee empowerment proposed by Conger and Kanungo (1988) discloses a higher level of empowerment. *Efficacy* basically means "power or capacity to produce a desired effect and effectiveness" (Oxford English Dictionary, 2004a). It is also operationalized as knowledge and skills, information and communications (Spreitzer, 1995; Thomas and Velthouse, 1990), but it is more focused than authority and discretion in that it is a power carried out to achieve a desired purpose.

In review of these discussions, from an employer's perspective, the concept of empowerment can be seen as power bestowed by employers in exchange for employees' commitment. It also reveals that power has different properties. As a result, empowerment can be seen as having different levels (see Table 7.1). At the lowest level, empowerment is only a mechanical shift of the locus of control, and the granting of the power is at risk of management losing control to incapable employees. The second and the third levels of empowerment accommodate the idea of employees' abilities in undertaking control. These abilities are based on knowledge and experiences. Only the highest level of empowerment is what an organization should attempt to achieve—to enable the feeling of self-efficacy of employees. This implies that, in endorsing power, employers need to enable employees with the ability and capacity of taking power so that they can act effectively and responsibly to achieve the desired organizational goals.

TABLE 7.1. Extent of power and hierarchy of empowerment—an employer's perspective

Level of power	Hierarchy of empowerment
Control	Giving employees freedom to check and direct actions and exercise authoritative or dominating influence over others
Authority	Giving employees power to influence or persuade based on their own knowledge or experience
Discretion	Giving employees the quality to be discreet; ability to decide, discern, and judge what is right and wrong; and liberty or power of deciding to act on own judgment.
Self-efficacy	Giving employee power or capacity to produce a desired effect and effectiveness, to affect the object intended for the organization, and to take actions responsibly.

Source: Compiled from Burke (1986); Conger and Kanungo (1988); Howard and Foster (1999); Melhem (2004): Oxford English Dictionary (2004a,b,c) and Thomas and Velthouse (1990).

Cognitive Empowerment: An Employee's Perspective

The depiction of the hierarchy of empowerment also implies that it is far from a completed notion if empowerment is viewed only from an employer's perspective. This is because different levels of empowerment, particularly the empowerment of self-efficacy need the intervention of the "state of mind" (Berry, 1995; Bowen and Lawler, 1995; Melhem, 2004; Rafiq and Ahmed, 1998). It is also because the consideration of employees is indispensable as management science evolves from a one-dimensional paradigm, such as Taylorism (Taylor, 1911) and Fordism, to a multidimensional paradigm such as post-Fordism (Bowring, 2002; Gorz, 1982, 1985) and critical theory (Horkheimer and Adorno, 1947; Marcuse, 1964; Ogbor 2001). One-dimensional theories assert that "existing alternatives are those defined and presented by those who exercise control over instruments of social dominations," but multidimensional theories advocate that social discourse, such as corporate culture, should act as "a discursive practice" that legitimates the claim to power of the subordinate group (Ogbor, 2001: 590-591). As expressed by Alvesson and Deetz (1999) in their discussion of critical theory, the role of the multidimensional paradigm in management science should be to:

Create societies and workplaces which are free from domination, where all members have an equal opportunity to contribute to the production systems which need and lead to the progressive development of all. (p. 192)

Empowerment theorists have also pointed out that empowerment is not only structural, sociocultural, or technical, but also psychological (Howard and Foster, 1999; Spreitzer, 1995, 1996; Thomas and Velthouse, 1990). They agreed that the single-dimensional emphasis of employers' investing in power for employee commitment has the potential danger of overlooking the benefits and mind status of those who are given power, and creates the possible risk of "the exploitation of empowerment" (Appelbaum et al., 1999: 237). In this case, empowerment is simply "another manifestation of the manager acting as director and controller" (Randolph, 2000).

Looking at the self-efficacy theory of Conger and Kanungo (1988) from an employee's angle, empowerment is classified as having two levels. The first level of empowerment is relational, which is concerned with the delegation of power and related management styles. The second level is cognitive or motivational, which is defined in terms of employees' feeling self-efficacy. This conceptualization is closely related to the notion of "hierarchy of empowerment," despite that self-efficacy is viewed from an employees' perspective. It is basically concerned with an employee's judgment of or perception or confidence in his or her ability to perform well (Bandura, 1982; Melhem, 2004).

A more complex cognitive empowerment model was developed by Thomas and Velthouse (1990). They deconstructed the motivational empowerment proposed by Conger and Kanungo (1988) into four cognitive dimensions: personal meaning, a sense of self-determination, a sense of competence, and perceived impact. Personal meaning involves fitting the organizational goal into personal values and beliefs. Self-determination refers to a sense of freedom in making choices and decisions over the work process, and being accountable for personal work output. Competence is the belief of one's capacity to perform the work activities. Perceived impact refers to the value of an individual in the working environment achieved by adding value to and taking qualified responsibilities for their work (Berry, 1995). The four cognitions converge as motivational empowerment manifested as employees feeling of being empowered and their ability to accept the status and take the responsibility of empowerment.

The merger of power—the central part of an organizational existence and the emphasis of the cognitive construct of employees—gives the notion of empowerment a value beyond some of the humanistic concepts of management science, such as participation (Lawler, 1992), job enrichment (Hackman and Oldham, 1980), and quality management process (Flynn et al., 1996). The latter assume that employees are a special type of resources with knowledge and experiences that are under the domination of an organization system. A matching purpose of organizations with their motivation and job satisfaction can unleash these resources and benefit both parties.

Empowerment, on the other hand, challenges the convention of "management prerogative" (Ackers et al., 1992; Marchington et al., 1992) through obliterating the boundaries between the "management" and the "managed." It is fundamentally about the reclamation of freedom and emancipation of employees from managerial and administrative means (Ogbor, 2001). From the perspective of empowerment, employees and management are no longer opponents exchanging resources for vested interests, but are two idiosyncratic entities with an equal standing in and joint ownership of an organization; they make corresponding efforts to achieve a higher quality of worthiness for each other.

The Social Structural Antecedents of Empowerment

When accentuating the cognitive facet of empowerment, the influence of organizational context on empowerment should be looked at. This is because, as Thomas and Velthouse (1990) state, social and structural antecedents are constraints or conditions for subjective individual cognitions of empowerment. They argue that the "objective" external events and conditions are not independent of the employee empowerment, but are shaped by an individual's mental "interpretive process." This process has an addictive effect on the individual's task assessments, on the proximal cause of intrinsic working motivation and satisfaction, which are manifested by the four cognitive dimensions discussed in the previous section (meaning, self-determination, competence, and perceived impact), and, hence, on their empowerment (p. 668-669).

The basic promise of the concept of social and structural antecedents of empowerment is that organizational environment provides both constraints and opportunities for individuals' cognition and behavior. Therefore, better design of the antecedents can subdue constraints and increase the chances for individuals to develop cognitive empowerment (Blau, 1987; Lawler, 1992; Mowday and Sutton, 1993; Spreitzer, 1996; Walton, 1985). On the other hand, the relationship between employee cognition and social structural antecedents is not unidirectional. Over time, individuals' cognition will reshape and reinforce the environmental context through behavioral outcomes (Thomas and Velthouse, 1990).

Howard and Foster (1999) characterize the social structural antecedents of empowerment as

> open communications and opportunities to speak one's opinions without fear of reprisal, being integrally connected with a network of communications, and having access to influential people throughout the organization. It also means minimizing ambiguity in responsibilities and maximizing collaborative teamwork. (p. 9)

In empirical research, researchers such as Spreitzer (1996) have confirmed that the involvement of social structural environment, specifically, low role ambiguity, wide supervisory spans of control, sociopolitical support from top management, access to information, and a participative climate help to create opportunities for employee empowerment in the workplace. Chiles and Zorn's (1995) research bore that macrolevel culture is influential in shaping the sources of self-reported empowerment. This included generalizations about superiors, patterns of management, and communication of organization information and the like. Quinn and Spreitzer (1997) reported the importance of leadership as an empowerment antecedent. They state that although empowerment is a two-way process, the responsibility for creating an empowerment culture lies mainly with the top management who are the major forces in creating well-understood and accepted visions and culture for an organization. Employees' understanding of these vision and goals, and an emphasized openness and teamwork from top management will have a positive impact on employee empowerment.

In view of the previous, empowerment can be summarized as a multidimensional concept that addresses the interrelationships between organization and its employers and employees. It can be seen as the investment of power by employers to gain staff commitment, or as the attainment of self-efficacy by employees; power has various properties, and so does empowerment. Empowerment is also about setting the right conditions and using various management practices to facilitate the transfer of power and fostering the feeling of self-efficacy of employees. Figure 7.1 illustrates the conceptual framework of empowerment and related management practices.

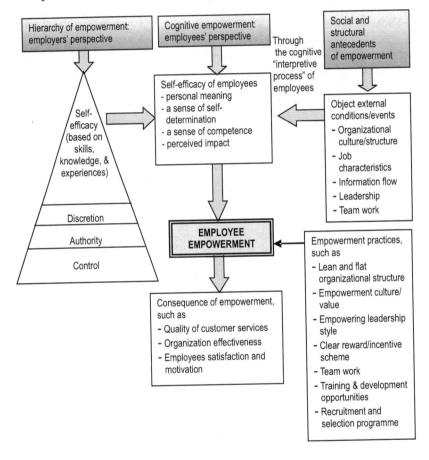

FIGURE 7.1. The conceptual framework of empowerment

However, empowerment is also beyond simple management strategies or practices, beyond the rationalization of the interrelationships between employees and employers in a workplace context, and even beyond the intention of mutual benefits or the respect of the human resources of employees. Empowerment should be viewed as an ideology that preaches equality and free will of employees, breaks the boundaries between employees and employers, and advocates a belief in the common goodness.

THE SERVICE AND TRAVEL INDUSTRY CONTEXT

The emphasis of the study context of empowerment is acknowledged by Lashley (1999), making the point that "despite the rhetoric of empowerment, service firms are in a different position in the relation with their customers and markets, and this impact how managers perceive and interpret empowerment" (p. 170).

The travel and tourism industry has a number of unique characteristics that make empowerment more important to organizational effectiveness. At the macrolevel, the travel and tourism industry is highly fragmented. It is easy for business entry, but it is intensively competitive. In addition, the recent decades' explosive development of e-tourism, through the extensive application of information and communication technology (ICT), has fundamentally changed the landscape of the tourism and travel industry. It is even harder for small brick-and-mortar travel agencies to compete as the tourism and travel industry is dis-intermediating due to the proliferation of direct contact between consumer and suppliers on the e-marketplace (Buhalis and Licata, 2002).

The tourism and travel industry also faces acute employment problems. Tourism jobs are dominated by manual and people-contact services—repetitive, experience-based, and relying on easily acquired skills. This leads to a high level of nonstandard jobs, high skill gaps and employee turnover rate, and low levels of pay and poor working conditions (Hjalager and Andersen, 2000; Jolliffe and Farnsworth, 2003; Weiss, 1997).

The tourism and travel industry is also typical of the service sector delivering intangible products. One difficulty of this is that it is hard to define a successful service encounter, hard to measure the quality, efficiency, and effectiveness of customer service (Lashley, 1999). However, the high level of employee-customer contact in the tourism and travel industry means that business success in this industry is defined by the effective performance of employees (Lashley and McGoldrick, 1994). High individual involvement in quality control, standard performance measurement, and a high degree of employee responsibility for customer-employer encounters is, therefore, particularly important. All these put momentous pressure on any business operating in this industry, especially those that require the effective services of frontline staff.

It follows that empowerment can play a unique role for the tourism and travel businesses because it encourages the maximum level of personal involvement to organizational goals and provides the necessary autonomy and discretion for them to maintain the high quality of customer service that is required (Lashley, 1995). Empowerment is also important because the tourism and travel industry is dominated by a large proportion of small- and medium-sized enterprises (SMEs), of which a high level of vagaries of the operating environment and a low level of professionalism in management styles make the adjustment of employee and employer relationship an urgency to this industry (Wyer and Mason, 1999).

However, though an increasing amount of attention has been given from academics and practioners in the service sectors (Ashness and Lashley, 1995; Bowen and Lawler, 1992; Holdsworth and Cartwright, 2003; Lashley, 1995, 1999; Melhem, 2004), the literature shows that empowerment studies in the travel and tourism sector is inadequate. It is expected that the following discussion of the active application of empowerment by Flight Centre, which has succeeded in a highly volatile and intensively competitive industry, can shed light on this literature gap. The information used in this case study was collected from various secondary publications, including published journal articles, newspaper articles, Flight Centre's Web site, published financial reports, and other related sources.

FLIGHT CENTRE: THE COMPANY BACKGROUND

Flight Centre Limited opened its first travel shop in Sydney, Australia, in 1981. It has since grown to become one of the world's largest independent travel retailers, with more than 1,200 stores, employing more than 5,500 people in Australia, New Zealand, the UK, South Africa, the United States, Canada, China, and Hong Kong. The company has made profits in every year of the first twenty-three years it has been in business ("Flight Centre Hails," 2003). In 2002, for the first time, the company was ranked the seventh largest travel company in the world (Tomlinson, 2002). Since floating in 1995, the company's share has risen sharply (see Figure 7.2). In 2004, the company achieved global revenue and pretax profit of $799 million ($A) (about £323.9 million; $656.6 million [U.S.]) and $117.8 million ($A) (about £47.74 million; 96.8 million [U.S.]), a growth of 27.6 percent and 21.9 percent respectively over the previous year (Flight Centre, 2004a).

Flight Centre used to sell cheap flights and holiday packages to cost-conscious travelers with low profit margins. It now owns twenty-one brands worldwide, offering hotel packages, coach and rail tours, cruises, car hire, and insurance for consumers from students to corporate travelers (see Table 7.2).

In 2002 and 2003, the company's UK Ltd. was voted, in two consecutive years, the third and fourth best company to work for and the highest new entrant on the *Sunday Times'* list of one hundred best em-

Share Price Performance

flight centre limited *company profile*

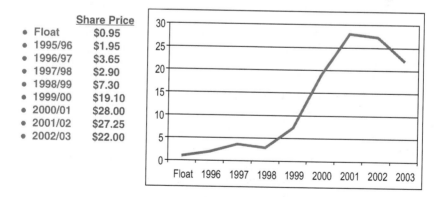

	Share Price
● Float	$0.95
● 1995/96	$1.95
● 1996/97	$3.65
● 1997/98	$2.90
● 1998/99	$7.30
● 1999/00	$19.10
● 2000/01	$28.00
● 2001/02	$27.25
● 2002/03	$22.00

FIGURE 7.2. Share Price Performance (1995-2003). *Source:* Flight Centre (2003a). Reprinted with permission from Flight Centre, Ltd.

TABLE 7.2. Flight Centre brands and Web sites

Category	Brand	Web site
Retail rands	Flight Centre	www.flightcentre.com
	Flight Centre Direct	An on-line and over-the-phone service
	Escape Travel	www.escapetravel.com
	Travel Associates	www.travel-associates.com.au
	Student Flights	www.studentflights.com
	Overseas Working Holiday	www.owh.com.au
	Cruiseabout	www.cruiseabout.com.au
	Fantastic Sport Tours	www.thefanatics.com
	Shopper Travel	www.shoppertravel.com.au
Corporate brands	FCm Travel Solutions	Encompasses the Corporate Traveler businesses throughout the world, incl. SBT (Aus), AIT (HK), Joint Venture (China), ITG and Britannic in Australasia and the UK.
	TQ^3 Travel Solution	www.tq3.com
	Britannic (UK)	www.britannic-travel.com/
	Kistend Travel	www.kistend.com.au
	Stage & Screen	www.stageandscreen.com.au
	Campus Travel	www.campustravel.com.au
	Ci Events	www.cievents.com.au
Wholesale brands	Infinity Holidays	
	Ticket Centre	
	VFR Flights	
Online brands	Travel there	www.travelthere.com
	Quick beds	www.quickbeds.com
Others	George Seymour College (NZ)	www.sirgeorge.co.nz/

Source: Flight Centre (2004). Reprinted with permission from Flight Centre, Ltd.

ployers in the UK ("100 Best Companies," 2003, 2004). It received similar awards in Australia, Canada, South Africa, and New Zealand (Flight Centre, 2003b). What makes these achievements valuable is that in comparison with other high profile winners such as Microsoft, Flight Centre has succeeded in a highly rivalrous environment that is troubled by a very poor industrial image and severe employment problems. An attempt to unveil its secret to success leads to an inevitable look at its distinct management practice.

EMPOWERMENT IN FLIGHT CENTRE

"Tribal" Organizational System

Flight Centre takes pride in its distinctive informal organizational structure. The management structure is established based on the anthropologist theories of family, village, and tribe. Staff in Flight Centre are divided into a maximum of four to five layers. The basic layer is the "families" (or teams), which are retail shops of between three to seven members. Above "families" are "villages," which are composed of five "families" overseen by an area manager. Above are "tribes" (or countries), which consist of a limit of three to ten "villages" bound in a geographical region. Above this are regional level leaders overseeing a limit of four to ten countries. Finally, the Global SWOT Board is the company's top management layer (Flight Centre, 2004a) (see Figure 7.3). The company's staff work on a "no privileges unless it is a must" basis; the company has no receptionists, no individual offices, no secretaries, and no cleaners, even at Flight Center's head office (Tomlinson, 2002).

The most obvious structural benefit of this system is that, first of all, the organization is lean and flat. It is particularly lean in the middle management level, which is crucial in delayering an organization and reducing the resistance to empowerment from middle-level management (Claydon and Doyle, 1996; Cluterbuck and Kernaghan, 1994; Cunningham et al., 1996). A lean organization is efficient in creating effective communication and easy information flows; these are essential antecedents of empowerment. These knowledgeable, informational, truthful, and up-to-date communications ensure that

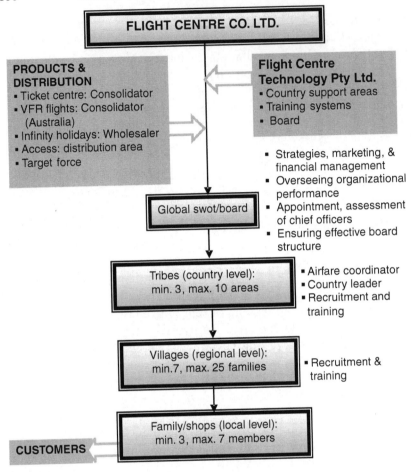

FIGURE 7.3. The Organizational Structure Chart of Flight Centre. *Source: Adapted from Dunford and Palmer (2002); Palmer and Dunford (2002; 1054); Flight Centre (2003a, 2004a,b).*

employees identify with the direction and values of an organization, and they lead to high employee involvement.

The second positive aspect of this system is its informality. The benefits of this informal system has been expressed by Gary Hogan, Managing Director of Flight Centre UK Ltd., who stated that this organizational structure has added efficiency to the organization as "staff feel involved rather than one small part of a homogenous mass"

("Inclusion of Staff," 2003). More metaphysically, it releases the power of the humanity imprisoned within the cage of organizational bureaucracy (Weber, 1947). Empirical research has proved that an informal organizational structure has made staff feel empowered to get on with their job and operate with a greater degree of individual autonomy than if they were in a more conventional, hierarchical organization (Palmer and Dunford, 2002: 1055). Smart et al. (2002) explained that an informal organization actively engages to overcome organizational boundaries and is organized based on self- managed, self-generated interrelationships, which forms the foundation of effective and efficient flows of information, experiences, knowledge, and ideas. It also builds trust between management and employees due to the increased openness, and it reduces barriers from bottom to top; therefore, the informality reinforces the cognitive empowerment of employees (Morton et al., 2004).

Perhaps the most intriguing contribution of this tribal system to empowerment should be the word *tribe* itself. Tribe originally means "a group of persons forming a community and claiming descent from a common ancestor" or a class of persons, a race of recognized ancestry, a family, etc. Tribalism means "loyalty to a particular tribe or group of which one is a member" (Oxford English Dictionary, 2004c).

These definitions provide a glimpse of the metaphorical functions of the tribal system of empowerment in Flight Centre. The most noticeable is the ability to convey a meaning of "group" or "family" solidarity. This capacity advocates staff loyalty. However, different from real tribalism in which loyalty is generated toward the tribe leaders, loyalty in Flight Centre is important in preaching a common belief and interest among staff, uniting their spirits toward a common goal and against the common enemies (i.e., the market rivals). This is particularly beneficial in curtailing one of the drawbacks of empowerment: internal competition, which can be detrimental to empowerment.

As discussed previously, the tribal system inoculates a sense of informality and therefore helps create an open organization with low levels of management hierarchy but high levels of staff egalitarianism, thus breaks down the psychological walls between management and workers. Finally, and most important, it helps generate a strong sense of culture. Researchers have confirmed that culture can act as an empowerment antecedent by managing "ambiguity and paradox" (Barnard, 1938; Peters and Waterman, 1982). The tribal system symbolizes the identity of Flight Centre by constructing a distinct organizational image. This strong and explicit group identity then acts as shaper and source of individuals' identity by drawing them together, insinuating their personal "meaning" and esteem, and ultimately informing and culturing their behavior.

Individual Autonomy versus Group Autonomy

A key feature of Flight Centre's management practice is its self-directed teamwork arrangement. The structure of the team (or a family) in Flight Centre is unique because of, as mentioned previously, its metaphorical "family" connotations. It has dual autonomy since the teams operate independently to achieve a team target with very little interference from the top. Within the teams, individual members maintain their own autonomy, but can reach one another and the team for support (Palmer and Dunford, 2002). Team members socialize with one another on a regular basis; occasionally, the teams from different regions get together ("Inclusion of Staff," 2003).

As one of the key antecedents of empowerment, the teams in Flight Centre empower employees through, first of all, acting as social units to bond individual members together. Members working in a team collaborate because they have to work together to achieve team targets; they are also interdependent on one another for support and advice, ranging from customer services and technical issues to new members' selection, performance evaluation, mentoring, and training. In this context, a team members' role evolves from a newcomer to someone gradually handling more of the groups' responsibilities as they integrate into the "family" and transform themselves from "being helped" to being "partners" or "family members." The teams in Flight Centre provide for a positive condition to reconcile the personal interests between team members.

The teams also create a vehicle for individuals to build up their equal membership and mutual trust, therefore breaking down the forces of management within an extended system (Walton, 1985). This is because this membership in support networks increases social exchange with one another, and this exchange enhances a sense of personal power that is manifested in enhanced feelings of "meaning" and "impact" of individuals. The interests of the individual are also best realized when people are working together. Effective support through coaching, reinforcing, and mentoring can also help build employee confidence and skills, which lead to another feeling of cognitive empowerment: "self-determination" (Crozier, 1964).

Besides these, the teams in Flight Centre are important in channeling individuals' and teams' autonomy along a common path. Power without a boundary can lead to power corruption. In this aspect, the self-directed teams in Flight Centre counterbalance this tendency effectively. The lowest layer in Flight Centre—the "families"—operate with a limit of three to eight people. This small number of team members ensures that members can reach one another for support quickly; they also are subject to the pressures of peer approval or disapproval within the autonomy of a given area or output so that they do not stray from achieving a collective goal of the whole team. The dual autonomy of individuals and a team guarantees that empowerment is achieved at both the frontline and the middle-management levels.

Empowering Leadership

Researchers have agreed that leaders have tremendous impact on the social structural antecedents and the degree of the cognitive empowerment of their employees. This is because empowerment reflects structural, cultural, and technical dynamics; therefore, a multidimensional perspective that is "perhaps only apparent at the highest levels of organization leadership" is needed (Howard and Foster, 1999, p. 17).

Leaders also push forward the empowerment process in a number of both explicit and implicit ways, such as a leader's personality and charisma, the establishment of organizational policies, the authority they delegate, the initiative they encourage, and the interaction they have with their staff. This is because, as researchers have found, the level of empowerment is dependent on the extent to which the culture and structure promotes and facilitates empowerment (such as Appelbaum et al., 1999; D'Annunzio-Green and Macandrew, 1999; Honold, 1997; Mallak and Kurstedt, 1996). Leaders can have a comprehensive and governing role in creating organizational cultures and values unique to their own styles and personalities. Leaders therefore leave their personal touches on every process, procedure, and communicating style of the operations of an organization. These clearly and repeatedly stated culture facets and values provide frameworks for people to refer to and that guide their action and their boundaries of responsibility, and provide a vision for future growth.

In Flight Centre, the clearly established organizational structure embodies Flight Centre's leadership style—open and informal. In 2003, Flight Centre (UK) Ltd. was in the third place on the list of the *Sunday Times'* best one hundred companies to work for in the UK ("100 Best Companies," 2003). Its managing director Gary Hogan was voted as the "best for leadership" across all the participants. However, to his employees, he was simply known by his nickname, "Boxer" (Boztas, 2003), which personifies the frank and open relationships between employees and employers. In the same competition, the criteria that ranked Flight Centre at the top of the best leadership list were "most appreciative managers," "most honest managers," "most inspirational managers," "most positive managers," etc. (see Table 7.3). These criteria symbolized the personalities of Flight Centre's leaders, but their real implication to employee empowerment is that the leaders' personalities are imprinted on the organization's "personality" and shape staff "individuality."

Despite the inspiring and culture-creating abilities of Flight Centre's leaders, the empowering leadership styles are also reflected in Flight Centre's approach of making leadership the vehicle to internalize staff and eliminate hierarchical boundaries. Under this approach, leadership in Flight Centre is seen as not only a person's prerogative or the characteristic of a leader, but as an organizational antecedent that contributes to the organizational effectiveness and is conditional to an employee's feeling of equality and autonomy. This is enhanced in the way that Flight Centre has a consistent record of promoting from within. The company has a leadership development program that provides an intensive set of training courses to nurture the future leaders of the company. Many key leaders in Flight Centre were grown in this manner. Currently, about 90 percent of their team leaders have come through the ranks in Flight Centre (Flight Centre, 2004b).

This principle coincides with the "process" theory proposed by Drath and Palus (1994) and Horner (1997). The theory stresses that leadership is a process in which everyone actively participates. The

TABLE 7.3. A summary of the empowerment practices in Flight Centre

Dimension of empowerment	Management practice	Content
Social structural antecedents	1. Tribal organizational structure	Lean and informal organization to reinforce open communication and reduce hierarchy
	2. Leadership Development programme	To train and nurture future Flight Centre leaders from within, and contribute to the organizational equality
	3. Self-directed team	Sociopolitical support to employees with dual autonomy
	• Buzz evening, conference, fun team, events	Regional or local events of socializing, meeting, etc.
Cognitive empowerment	4. Performance management	
	• Million dollar consultant award	A performance management scheme used to recognize the competitive performance of individuals relative to their peers
	• Global award event	An even to reward the winner across the global
	• Bronze awards	$80 per month per consultant if the profit per family is $500-$1,000
	• Diamond award	$220 per month per consultant if the profit per family is over $3,000
	• Hall of fame award	For high performers
	• In centos awards Scheme	Noncash bonus points that can be converted into travel or other Flight Centre products
	• Discounted travel and car	Incentive for high achievers
	5. Ownership and welfare scheme	
	• Employee option/share plan	Profit share schemes for company employees
	• Uncapped sales-driven commission	Sales commissions without ceiling
	• Money Wise	Free in-house financial advice service

TABLE 7.3 *(continued)*

Dimension of empowerment	Management practice	Content
	• MyCareer	Free in-house personal career development planning tool for staff
	• Employee assistance program	Free in-house employee help scheme
	• Health Wise	Free in-house personal fitness, health, and well-being advice
	6. Recruitment and Training: People Works	
	• Staff referral scheme	Members of staff recommend friends, family, or former colleagues for jobs with reward
	• In-house learning center	Provide free training to staff from the day one lasting throughout their career in the company
	• William James School of Business	Free in-house tertiary education program for staff toward bachelor's or master's degrees in management in an "on the job" environment
	• Centralized learning library	For staff development
	• The leadership center	Offer team leaders training courses
	• Conference	Team members attend minimum of 2; managers attend up to 7 conferences.

Source: Compiled from Flight Centre (2002; 2004a,b).

leadership principle practiced in Flight Centre puts forward the idea that an empowered organization gives everyone a vision of leadership legitimacy that they can be in control over their own task scope and are entitled to their own initiative and decision making. As an empowerment antecedent, empowering leadership sets to eliminate boundaries between leaders and subordinates and engages everyone as an active and organic part of an organization.

Clear Performance-Management Systems

In Flight Centre, incentive and reward schemes are generous and plenty. The salary package that Flight Centre offers to starters is above the industrial norm. New recruits can expect to earn at least £18,000 ($35,500 [U.S.]) in the UK (Flight Centre, 2004b). Individual performance awards include "Million Dollar Consultant Award" (Palmer and Dunford, 2002, p. 1036); Bronze and Diamond awards for high achievers and global reward events in different locations around the world. Individual achievements are also publicized in a comparative context with teams and peers. A team can be rewarded only if individual members fulfill their own targets. A range of other awards, including holiday, cash bonuses, cars, international travel awards, as well as financial planning and welfare services are available for all the staff (see Table 7.3).

The importance of a clear performance system is that it provides an explicit understanding of employees' responsibilities and methods for measuring their attainment in order to achieve their optimum productivity. Individuals need to know what their goals and performance expectations are, and they need to link these with overall objectives of the teams and the organization. They also need continuous feedback on how they are doing, suggestions for improvement, and coaching for success. Without these, individuals can lose their identity or suffer self-estrangement as they engage in corporate activities that are not intrinsically rewarding, and can even feel powerless as they have no control of their lives (Appelbaum and Honeggar, 1998; Seeman, 1975).

Clearly defined jobs and incentive schemes also delineate scopes of ownership and responsibilities and associate these with performance. People recognize their responsibilities as a meaningful process or output, and are, therefore, able to commit themselves with appropriate resources and have control over their own success.

What's more, tangible recognition and incentive programs enhance employees' feelings of self-esteem and pride. Through rewards, organizations express their encouragement of an organizational ideal, merge individual interests with the values and beliefs of an empowered organization, and acknowledge staff's meaning or worthiness and their impact on an organization. This enhances employees' identity and creates a psychological bond between the organizations and their employees.

Ownership Schemes

As was argued in the literature review, empowerment is fundamentally about the claiming of power by employees and their right to organizational ownership. Without recognizing this true meaning of empowerment, empowerment is merely rhetoric (Claydon and Doyle, 1996; Eylon, 1998; Hales and Klidas, 1998; Sewell and Wilkinson, 1992). For example Hales and Klidas (1998) in their empirical research of ten hotels in Amsterdam, the Netherlands, identified a wide gulf between rhetoric and the reality of empowerment. Empowerment was patronized in their vocabulary, official policy, and mission statements, but no transfer of real responsibilities and involvement in decision making occurred, which affected the organization as a whole. Employees were confined to participation in departmental meetings of varying frequency; their autonomy was only over technical choices about how to react to customers but they could not make proactive choices in raising the qualities of service. In essence, employees were still treated as a special type of asset that was to be utilized through motivational techniques, but were not allowed to share in the central parts of an organization. It is no wonder that empowerment in these organizations, in which employees and employers are ambivalent about its true meaning, is only another way in which management manipulates, influences, and controls their staff.

In contrast, the true meaning of empowerment and its essence of equality is well understood by Flight Centre. In their own words,

> We believe that every individual should have equal privileges. We will never have separate offices, receptionists or secretaries. Promotion from within will always be our fist choice. We believe that work should be challenging and fun for everyone. Within our company there is no "them and us." We are all going forward together. (Flight Centre, 2004a, p. 26)

Empowerment has become a reality through putting its people at the fore. Among the ten themes of Flight Centre's company philosophy, "people" (i.e., employees) are on the top of this list. More than half of the themes are about employees' benefits, from ownership, incentives, and structure, to egalitarianism and unity (see Figure 7.4).

Not only are "people" recognized at the top of the company's documents, Flight Centre practices all of the approaches necessary to eliminate the barriers between employees and management and involve employees as an organic part of the business. In addition to the practices used to build up the antecedents of empowerment, another defining feature of Flight Centre's empowerment practice is the financial ownership of the company achieved through the employee option plan, employee share plan, uncapped sales commission, and so on. These schemes are far ahead of many of its travel competitors. The first two schemes are profit-sharing practices to encourage staff to become shareholders. A full-time employee is eligible to participate in employee share plans whereby shares are issued at a 10 percent discount to the market price. About 65 percent of the employees own Flight Centre's shares (Flight Centre, 2004a).

Flight Centre also has an uncapped commission scheme based on profit increase and net income as well as turnover increase and staff

flight centre limited *company profile*

Our philosophies

1. **Our people**
2. **The customer is paramount**
3. **Profit**
4. **Ownership**
5. **Incentives**
6. **Brightness of future**
7. **Standard systems once best way**
8. **Our structure**
9. **Taking responsibility**
10. **Egalitarianism and unity in the workplace**

FIGURE 7.4. Flight Centre Philosophies *Source:* Flight Centre (2003a). Reprinted with permission from Flight Centre, Ltd.

retention (criteria for leaders) (Flight Centre, 2004a). As the name implies, sales commissions are given without a ceiling as long as consultants meet or exceed their "cost of seat," which is basically the average personal cost of running a shop. When consultants make a profit above the cost of the seats, they can earn 20 to 28 percent of this profit. The higher the profit, the higher the percentage. Employees' profit commissions can range from £500 ($986 [U.S.]) to £25,000 ($49,305 [U.S.]) per year. In 2004, at Flight Centre UK Ltd., 14 percent of its staff made an annual earning over £35,000 ($69,027 [U.S.]) (Best Companies, 2004). Team leaders can earn 10 percent of the profits and can buy 20 percent of their business if the whole team performs well (Flight Centre, 2004a; Palmer and Dunford, 2002). The performance of an individual consultant is also linked to the performance of the whole shop.

The importance of these ownership schemes is not only about the financial gains of individual employees, or about their effect on collaborative teamwork, but about their impacts on employee's cognitive empowerment. On Flight Centre's recruitment Web site, ownership of the company is one of the most prominent catchwords. "You will quickly find yourself effectively running your own business within a business" (Flight Centre 2004b). Under the uncapped commission scheme and through collaborative teamwork, staff are taught to run a small business within Flight Centre from day one. They bond with the organization because of the common interests and the responsibilities they share. Above all, the principle behind these practices is the belief that people "who work in it, own part of it" (Flight Centre, 2004a). Through these practices, the belief that employees are owners of their business but not "employees of anyone" (Flight Centre, 2004a) becomes a reality.

Recruiting and Selecting the Right Staff

The purpose of selection and promotion systems is to identify quality workers and leaders. But these procedures are particularly crucial to empowerment because, as researchers have pointed out, the "fear" that employees have of being empowered has been one of the biggest obstacles of empowerment (such as Cunningham et al., 1996; Cunningham and Hyman, 1999; Lowe, 1994). Not all people are equally interested in, or capable of, becoming empowered. Some can realize the benefits of empowerment faster and more cost-effectively than others can when they are equipped with appropriate skills and placed in an empowering environment. They also have to bear the responsibility to reinforce this process and carry on the organizational culture and values as well as realize their own self-actualization. Selection and recruitment are important initial steps in that they communicate organizational value and commitment to empowerment. Therefore, they must select people who are likely to take part in it, and who will align their personal beliefs and interests with those of the organization. It is also crucial that these selection and recruitment processes pick the right people from the beginning and guide them to the right position so that they can cope with the challenges of empowerment.

In Flight Centre, recruitment starts with an online application and a telephone interview. The next step is a computer assessment to find out about the working styles and characteristics of the candidates. The tests are emotional-quotient assessments and psychometric tests that are based on the scores of the company's best performers. If applicants pass they can have a panel interview with up to three or four other candidates. Success at this stage is dependent on behavioral and competency questions. Finally, they are asked to come to a storefront to meet their potential colleagues and team members to see if they could get along well with them (Flight Centre, 2004b; Vu, 2004). The aim of these steps is to guarantee that the people who are recruited have the appropriate attitude, are enthusiastic, and want to succeed and be celebrated for it. New employees undertake an extensive twelve-day induction program followed by a yearlong "progression" course. Team leaders and key organizational leaders have all progressed through the firm's leadership development program (Rodrigues, 2004).

At entry level, recruiters at Flight Centre do not want people with travel agency experiences as many of its rivals do. Nearly all new Flight Centre staff have no previous experiences in the travel industry. Instead, they look for people who have actually traveled and have been to at least two continents. In this situation, training to suit the company's culture, familiarization with technical procedures, systems, and product is essential (Flight Centre, 2004b). This process helps Flight Centre identify potential employees with the right psychological makeup. If they have had travel agency experiences somewhere else, they might be less likely to absorb Flight Centre's unique culture. They also insist on recruiting only university graduates as frontline travel consultants. In a travel industry in which the majority of agents and/or consultants have little or no degree level qualifications (Hospitality Training Foundation, 2003, p. 24), this practice is highly exceptional. Researchers have confirmed that "higher levels of education are critical for enhancing empowerment, particularly in terms of the providing skills and abilities that individuals need to feel competent" (Spreitzer, 1996, p. 498). Selection and recruitment is also crucial to Flight Centre in that it has only four to five layers; each recruit needs to be accountable and capable for business results, and be able to work with other members as a "family." They can take power, and, most important, develop and create power.

Since 2003, Flight Centre also started to use referral schemes to recruit staff. This means that members of staff can recommend their friends, family, or former colleagues for jobs. This has proven to be one of the most successful recruitment methods, second only to using consultancies. The company ensures that these referred people fit in with the company culture and reinforce the "tribal" spirit of the company. Referral schemes can also serve to improve staff morale, save money, and the procedure makes staff feel more personal, appreciated, and it is fun (Taylor, 2004).

Training and Staff Development

Flight Centre spends about £405,000 ($798,741 [U.S.]) a year on skills training and staff development (Rodrigues, 2004). The training starts as soon as staff join, and it lasts their entire career in Flight Centre. It is based partly at the office and partly in a learning center. For the first twelve months, staff have a regular program of training covering topics as diverse as advanced sales, goal setting, and time management, as well as airfares and packages. After that, staff can develop in any direction they choose by attending a range of courses and events in four key areas: sales and services, product and airfares, systems, and personal development. An in-house business school was established to assist staff's career development. In 2004, the company won the "Training and Development" award for excellence as voted by employees in the *Sunday Times'* 100 Best Companies to Work For competition (Flight Centre, 2004b; "100 Best Companies," 2004).

Training and development are empowering because people cannot be empowered unless they have got the ability and competence. Training prepares employees for these abilities. Also, as the travel industry provides intangible products and services, employees in Flight Centre tend to interact more often with co-workers, suppliers, and customers. Their abilities to independently identify problems and opportunities, take appropriate actions, control quality, and exceed customer satisfaction without appealing to higher authority are particularly indispensable in the service-sector provision of intangible products. Empirical research supports the theory that levels of education and training are positively linked to empowerment, particularly in terms of proving skills and abilities individuals need to feel competent (Appelbaum et al., 1999; Spreitzer, 1995, 1996). Ongoing training and management help employees assume their roles and responsibilities and enhance their feeling of self-determination and competence.

In summary, this section examines the unique management practices used in Flight Centre, evaluates their impacts on employee empowerment, and links back to the conceptual and theoretical frameworks discussed in previous sections. These practices range from creating a unique organizational culture to giving generous rewards to individual staff. Above all, work is designed to enhance the self-efficacy feeling of employees. Table 7.3 lists the unique practices used in Flight Centre and their implications to employee empowerment.

DISCUSSIONS AND CONCLUSIONS

This case study has reviewed the notion of empowerment and compiled a theoretical framework related to empowerment. The examination of the case organization, Flight Centre, not only provided a benchmark of empowerment for businesses operating in a similar industrial context, it illustrated some unique empowerment practices, and, most important, it also helped to answer some of the fundamental questions about empowerment.

Despite that empowerment does not have one universally accepted definition, the literature converges on a general recognition that empowerment is "in principle a good thing" and can "produce a win-win" situation (Lashley, 1999, p. 169). The rapid growth of Flight

Centre in a highly competitive industry, outperforming many of its rivals, testifies this point. It also demonstrates that putting people at the fore does not contradict business profitability. Employees and companies can gain outstanding benefits through empowerment. To employees, a decrease in job-related stress and an increase in job-related satisfaction are two explicit outcomes of empowerment (Holdsworth and Catwright, 2003). But fundamentally, empowerment changes the way employees interact with an organization, and it brings back their right to exhibit their individual identity in relation to others. A positive impact of Flight Centre's management practices on staff psychology can be seen from the key attitude measures of the employees from the survey of the *Sunday Times'* best one hundred employee competitions in the UK (see Table 7.4).

The success of Flight Centre also highlights the importance of correctly understanding the meaning of empowerment in its successful application. In Flight Centre, empowerment is not an illusion (Argyris, 1998), or a rhetoric (Claydon and Doyle, 1996; Hales and Klidas, 1998; Sewell and Wilkinson, 1992); nor is it simply a program to shift the locus of organizational control, or another management technique "cripples with innovation, motivation and drive" (Argyris, 1998). To Flight Centre, empowerment is a philosophy promoting the idea of egalitarianism in a workplace. The practices of empowerment helped to remove the barriers between management and employees, democratize organizational power, and enable employees with self-efficacy. These ultimately lead to the mutual worthiness of the organization and its people. The success of Flight Centre is, principally, a proclamation of the successful understanding of the essences of empowerment.

Empowerment is also multidimensional. It is a complex integration of the efforts of employees, employers, and a series of organizational antecedents. In Flight Centre, empowerment is practiced consciously, and is achieved through a combination of strategies such as the establishment of informal organizational culture, a lean and flat structure, self-directed teams, generous incentive schemes, genuine ownership schemes, and training and career development. From top to frontline, employees and employers in Flight Centre are cultured to embrace empowerment, mentally prepared for empowerment and supported with competence to share organizational power.

TABLE 7.4. The Performance of Flight Centre: A Summary of the Key Survey Results of "Sunday Times' 100 Best Companies to Work For" 2003-2004, UK

Attributes	Ranks*	%	Employee valuation**
2004			
Dream job	7	58.8	% positive score for having a dream job
Most appreciative managers	1	88.0	% whose manager praise a job well done
Most international leadership	4	81.9	% positive score for being inspired by the over-all boss
Most honest managers	2	87.6	% positive score for open and honest managers
Most inspirational leadership	4	81.9	% positive score for being inspired by the over-all boss
Best for fair pay	6	69.4	% positive score for fair pay compared to other companies
Most stimulating work	2	82.0	% positive score for work being stimulating
Most laughter	3	90.8	% positive score for laughing a lot with colleagues
Adding the most value	6	84.0	% positive score for contributing to firm's success
Wanting to quit	10	19.1	who would leave tomorrow if given another job
Best for training	2	83.8	% supported by managers when they want to learn new skills
2003			
Glad to be here	2	85.3	% who love working for their company
Best for treating customer well	9	90.0	% who say their company treats customers well
Don't feel taken advantage	8	65.8	% who don't fee taken advantage of
Most caring colleagues	1	90.4	% who say their colleagues care for each other
Most positive leadership	1	90.4	% who say the head of the company has positive energy
Best of job satisfaction	1	88.0	% who feel they contribute to company's success

Source: Compiled from "100 Best Companies to Work For" (2003) and (2004).

*Ranked among the 100 best company candidates involved in the survey;

**Performance attributes are evaluated by their own employees of the 100 organizations.

In conclusion, the case study maintains that although researchers have argued that the practices of empowerment are not universally applicable (such as Hughes, 2002; Lashley, 1996, 1997; Lashley and McGoldrick, 1994), the idea of empowerment exemplified by Flight Centre advocates a universal meaning of empowerment; that is, the reclaim of freedom by employees and their joint ownership of an organization with management. Flight Centre's effective use of empowerment practices suggests that it is only when all view one another equally within an organization that true empowerment can occur. Only under these circumstances can individuals draw on their full potential for the benefit of both the organization and themselves.

REFERENCES

Ackers, P., Marchington, M., Wilkinson, A., and Goodman, J. (1992). The use of cycles? Explaining employee involvement in the 1990s. *Industrial Relations Journal, 23*(4): 268-283.

Alvesson, M. and Deetz, S. (1999). Critical theory and postmodernism: Approaches to organizational studies. In S. Clegg and C. Hardy (eds.), *Studying Organizational: Theory and Method* (pp. 185-211). London, UK: Sage.

Appelbaum, S.H., Hébert, D., and Leroux, S. (1999). Empowerment: Power, culture and leadership—A strategy or fad for the millennium? *Journal of Workplace Learning: Employee Counseling Today, 11*(7): 23-254.

Appelbaum, S.H. and Honeggar, K. (1998). Empowerment: A contrasting overview of organizations in general and nursing in particular—An examination of organizational factors, managerial behaviors, job design, and structural power. *Empowerment in Organizations, 6*(2): 29-50.

Argyris, C. (1998). *Reasoning, Learning, and Action.*. San Francisco: Jossey-Bass.

Ashness, D. and Lashley, C. (1995). Empowering service worker's at harvester restaurants. *Personnel Review, 24*(8): 17.

Bandura, A. (1982). Self-efficacy mechanism in human agency. *American Psychologist, 37*(2): 122-147.

Barnard, C. I. (1938). *The Functions of the Executive.* Cambridge, MA: Harvard University Press.

Baum, T. (1996). Images of tourism past and present. *International Journal of Contemporary Hospitality Management, 8*(4): 25-30.

Berry, L.L. (1995). Relationship marketing of services growing interest: emerging perspectives. *Journal of the Academy of Marketing Science, 23*(4): 236-245.

Best Companies (2004). The workplace engagement specialists. Available at: http://www.bestcompanies.co.uk. Accessed September 22.

Blau, P. (1987). Contrasting theoretical perspectives. In J. Alexander, B. Giesen, R. Muench, and N. Smelser (eds.), *The Macro-Micro Link* (pp. 71-85). Berkeley, CA: University of California Press.

Bowen, D.E. and Lawler, E.E. (1992). The empowerment of service workers: What, why, how and when. *Slogan Management Review, 33*(3): 31-39.

Bowen, D.E. and Lawler, E.E. (1995). Empowering service employees. *Slogan Management Review, 36*(4): 73.

Bowring, F. (2002). Post-Fordism and the end of work. *Futures, 34*: 159-172.

Boztas, S. (2003). Britain's best employers are winning on all fronts. *Sunday Times,* March 9, p. 7.

Buhalis, D. and Licata, M.C. (2002). The future of e-tourism intermediaries. *Tourism Management, 23:* 207-220.

Burke, W. (1986). Leadership as empowering others. In S. Srivastva (ed.), *Executive Power* (pp. 51-77). San Francisco, CA: Jossey-Bass.

Chiles, A. M. and Zorn, T. E. (1995). Empowerment in organizations: Employees' perceptions of the influences on empowerment. *Journal of Applied Communication Research, 23*(1): 1-25.

Choy, D. J.L. (1995). The quality of tourism management. *Tourism Management, 16*(2): 129-137.

Claydon, T. and Doyle, M. (1996). Trusting me, trusting you? The ethics of employee empowerment. *Personnel Review, 25*(6): 13-25.

Cluterbuck, D. and Kernaghan, S. (1994). *The Power of Empowerment.* London, UK: Kogan Page.

Conger, J. A. and Kanungo, R. N. (1988). The empowerment process: Integrating theory and practice. *Academy of Management Review, 13*(3): 471-482.

Crozier, M. (1964). *The Bureaucratic Phenomenon.* Chicago, IL: University of Chicago Press.

Cunningham, I. and Hyman, J. (1999). The Poverty of empowerment? A critical case study. *Personnel Review, 28*(3): 192-207.

Cunningham, I., Hyman, J., and Baldry, C. (1996). Empowerment: The power to do what? *Industrial Relations Journal, 27*(2): 143-154.

D'Annunzio-Green, N. and Macandrew, J. (1999). Re-empowering the empowered: The ultimate challenge? *Personnel Review, 28*(3): 258-278.

Drath, W. H. and Palus, C. J. (1994). *Making Common Sense: Leadership As Meaning-Making in a Community of Practice.* Greensboro, NC: Center for Creative Leadership.

Dunford, R. and Palmer, I. (2002). Managing for high performance? People management practices in Flight Centre. *Journal of Industrial Relations, 44*(3): 376-396.

Eylon, D. (1998). Understanding empowerment and resolving its paradox: Lessons from Mary Parker Follett. *Journal of Management History, 4*(1): 16-28.

Flight Centre (2002). *Annual Report.* Brisbane, Australia: Flight Centre Ltd.

Flight Centre (2003a). Presentation to Queensland Institutional Roadshow. Flight September. Available at: http://www.flightcentre.co.uk/files/investors/2003/institutional-roadshow.ppt. Accessed November 2.

Flight Centre (2003b). Top-flight workplace, two years in a row. March 14. Available at: http://www.flightcentre.co.uk/aboutus/news/2003/2003-03-14. Accessed November 2.

Flight Centre (2004a). *Annual Report.* Brisbane, Australia: Flight Centre Ltd.

Flight Centre (2004b). Flight Centre Limited careers. Available at: http://careers.flightcentrelimited.co.uk/. Accessed November 3.

Flight Centre hails auspicious minds (2003). *News, Travel Trade Gazette,* 11 August, p. 32.

Flynn, B.B., Schroeder, R.G., and Sakakibara, S. (1996). The impact of quality management practices on performance and competitive advantage. *Quality Control and Applied Statistics, 41*(4): 407-408.

Fulford, M. D. and Enz, C. (1995). The impact of empowerment on service employee's. *A Journal of Managerial Issues, 7*(2): 161.

Gorz, A. (1982). *Farewell to the Working Class: An Essay on Post-Industrial Socialism.* London, UK: Pluto.

Gorz, A. (1985). *Paths to Paradise: On the Liberation from Work.* London, UK: Pluto.

Hackman, J.R. and Oldham, G.R. (1980). *Work Redesign.* Reading, MA: Addison-Wesley.

Hales, C. and Klidas, A. (1998). Empowerment in five-star hotels: Choice, voice or rhetoric? *International Journal of Contemporary Hospitality Management, 10* (3): 88-95.

Hjalager, A-M. and Andersen, S. (2000). Tourism employment: Contingent work or professional career? *Employee Relations, 23*(2): 115-129.

Holdsworth, L. and Cartwright, S. (2003). Empowerment, stress and satisfaction: An exploratory study of a call centre. *Leadership & Organization, 24*(3): 131-140.

Honold, L. (1997). A review of the literature on employee empowerment. *Empowerment in Organization, 5*(4): 202-212.

Horkheimer, M. and Adorno, T. (1947). *The Dialectics of Enlightenment.* London, UK: Verso.

Horner, M. (1997). Leadership theory: Past, present and future. *Team Performance Management, 3:* 4.

Hospitality Training Foundation (2003). *Labor Market Review 2003: For the Travel Service and Tourism Services and Event Industry.* London, UK: Hospitality Training Foundation.

Howard, L.W. and Foster, S.T. (1999). The influence of human resource practices on empowerment and employee perceptions of management commitment to quality. *Journal of Quality Management, 4*(1): 5-22.

Hughes, J.M.C. (2002). HRM and universalism: Is there one best way? *International Journal of Contemporary Hospitality Management, 14*(5): 221-228.

Inclusion of staff is key to success (2003). Special report. *Travel Trade Gazette,* June 23.

Jolliffe, L. and Farnsworth, R. (2003). Seasonality in tourism employment: Human resource challenge. *International Journal of Contemporary Hospitality Management, 15*(6): 312-316.

Kanter, R.M. (1977). *Men and Women of the Corporation.* New York: Basic Books.

Keller, T. and Dansereau, F. (1995). Leadership and empowerment: A social exchange perspective. *Human Relations, 48*(2): 127-145.

Lashley, C. (1995). Towards an understanding employee empowerment in hospitality services. *International Journal of Contemporary hospitality Management, 7*(1): 27-32.

Lashley, C. (1996). Research issues for employee empowerment in hospitality organizations. *International Journal of Hospitality Management, 15*(4): 333-346.

Lashley, C. (1997) *Empowering Service Excellence: Beyond the Quick Fix.* London, UK: Cassell.

Lashley, C. (1999). Employee empowerment in services: A framework for analysis. *Personnel Review, 28*(3): 169-191.

Lashley, C. and McGoldrick, J. (1994). The limits of empowerment: A critical assessment of human resource strategy for hospitality operations. *Empowerment in Organizations, 2*(3): 25-38.

Lawler, E.E. (1992). *The Ultimate Advantage: Creating the High Involvement Organization.* San Francisco, CA: Jossey-Bass.

Lowe, P. (1994). Empowerment: Management dilemma, leadership challenge. *Executive Development, 7*(6): 23-24.

Mallak, L.A. and Kurstedt, H.A., Jr., (1996). Understanding and using empowerment to change organizational culture. *Industrial Management, 38*(6): 8-10.

Marchington, M., Goodman, J., Wilkinson, A., and Ackers, P. (1992). *New Developments in Employee Involvement.* Employment Department Research Paper No. 2. London, UK: HMSO.

Marcuse, H. (1964). *One-Dimensional Man: Studies in the Ideology of Advanced Industrial Society.* New York, NY: Beacon Press.

Melhem, Y. (2004). The antecedents of customer-contact employees' empowerment. *Employee Relations, 26*(1): 72-93.

Morton, S.C., Smart, P.K., Brookes, N.J., Burns, N.D., and Backhouse, C.J. (2004). Managing the informal organization: Conceptual model. *International Journal of Productivity and Performance Management, 53*(3): 214-232.

Mowday, R.T. and Sutton, R.I. (1993). Organization behavior: Linking individuals and groups to organization context. In L. Porter and M. Rosensweig (eds.), *Annual Review of Psychology,* Volume 44 (pp. 195-229). Palo Alto, CA: Annual Reviews.

Ogbor, J.O. (2001). Critical theory and the hegemony of corporate culture. *Journal of Organizational Change, 14*(6): 590-608.

100 best companies to work for (2003). *Sunday Times,* March 3.

100 best companies to work for (2004). *Sunday Times,* March 7.

Oxford English Dictionary (2004a). s.v. "Efficacy." Available at: http://dictionary.oed.com/. Accessed November 7.

Oxford English Dictionary (2004b). s.v. "Empower." Available at: http://dictionary.oed.com/. Accessed November 7.

Oxford English Dictionary (2004c). s.v. "Tribalism." Available at: http://dictionary.oed.com/. Accessed November 7.

Palmer, I., and Dunford, R. (2002). Managing discursive tension: The co-existence of individualist and collaborative discourses in Flight Centre. *Journal of Management Studies, 39*(8): 1045-1070.

Parker, L.E. and Price, R.H. (1994). Empowered managers and empowered workers: The effects of managerial support and managerial perceived control on workers' sense of control over decision making. *Human Relations, 47*(8): 911.

Peters, T. J. and Waterman, R. H. (1982). *In Search of Excellence.* New York: Harper and Row.

Pfeffer, J. (1994). *Competitive Advantage through People.* Boston, MA: Harvard Business School Press.

Pickard, J. (1993). The real meaning of empowerment. *Personnel Management,* November: 28-33.

Quinn, R.E. and Spreitzer, G.M. (1997). The road to empowerment: Seven questions every leader should consider. *Organisational Dynamics, 26*(2): 37-49.

Rafiq, M. and Ahmed, P.K. (1998). Putting people first for organizational success. *The Academy of Management Executive, 13*(2): 37-48.

Randolph, W.A. (2000). Re-thinking empowerment: Why is it so hard to achieve? *Organizational Dynamic, 29*(November): 94-107.

Rodrigues, N. (2004). Top gun's right on target for a happy, harmonious workplace. *Sunday Times,* March 7.

Roth, W.F. and Potts, M. (2001). Doing it wrong: A case study. *Quality Progress, 34*(2): 63-66.

Seeman, M. (1975). Alienation studies. *Annual Review of Sociology, 1:* 91-123.

Sewell, G. and Wilkinson, B. (1992). Empowerment/exemplars of prevention: Toward a theory for community psychology. *American Journal of Community Psychology, 15:* 121-148.

Simon, B.L. (1990). Rethinking empowerment. *Journal of Progressive Human Services, 1*(1): 27-39.

Smart, P.K., Backhouse, C.J., and Brookes, N.J. (2002). Working the boundaries in the automotive industry. *Proceeding's of the Institution of Mechanical Engineers, Part B: Journal of Engineering Manufacture, 214*(10): 941-946.

Smith, A. and Mouly, V.S. (1998). Empowerment in New Zealand firms: Insights from two cases. *Empowerment in Organizations, 6*(3): 69-80.

Spreitzer, G.M. (1995). Psychological empowerment in the workplace: Dimensions, measurement, and validation. *Academy of Management Control, 38*(5): 1442-1465.

Spreitzer, G.M. (1996). Social structural characteristics of psychological empowerment. *Academy of Management Journal, 39*(2): 483-504.

Taylor, F.W. (1911). *The Principles of Scientific Management.* New York: Harper and Bros.

Taylor, K. (2004). Cutting Costs with a DIY Headhunter. *Mail on Sunday,* July 4.

Thomas, K.W. and Velthouse, B.A. (1990). Cognitive elements of empowerment: An interpretive model of intrinsic task motivation. *Academy of Management Review, 15*(4): 666-681.

Tomlinson, A. (2002). Top shops deliver more than flashy perks. *Canadian HR Reporter, 15*(2): 1-2.

Vu, U. (2004). Hire drills: A look at innovative recruiting policies. *Canadian HR Reporter, 17*(13): 11.

Walton, R. (1985). From control to commitment in the workplace. *Harvard Business Review, 63*(2): 77-84.

Weber, M. (1947). *The Theory of Social and Economic Change.* Glencoe, IL: Free Press.

Weiss, T. B. (1997). Show me more than the money (employee retention strategies). *HR Focus, 74*(11): 3-5.

Wyer, P. and Mason, J. (1999). Empowerment in small businesses. *Participation & Empowerment: An International Journal, 7*(7): 180-193.

Chapter 8

A Macroanalysis of Labor Productivity As a Value Driver in the Lodging Industry

Prakash K. Chathoth
Michael D. Olsen

INTRODUCTION

The success of firms depends on their ability to manage resources effectively (Olsen et al., 1998). Labor-intensive firms that form an integral part of the service industry are dependent on the productivity of their workforce to ensure overall firm productivity. Although labor productivity is a concern of service firms globally, the United States, whose economy for the most part is driven by service firms, has not improved service productivity over the past few decades. According to Sheehy and Schone (2003), "productivity gains are impressive in manufacturing—increasing at about four to five percent a year—but service sector productivity improvement is anemic" (p. 5). Although Bosworth and Triplett (2003) posit that the services sector productivity has grown faster than the manufacturing sector productivity during the post–1995 period, this chapter purports that the services sector productivity has not been impressive from a historical perspective. The impact of productivity is even more alarming since the service industry contributes approximately 75 to 80 percent of the overall U.S. gross domestic product.

The importance of labor productivity is felt as the lodging industry within the United States has faced the challenges of economic recession over the past years. This may be applicable to lodging firms that operate outside the United States. Lodging industry professionals understand that service productivity is an essential component of creat-

Global Cases on Hospitality Industry
© 2008 by The Haworth Press, Taylor & Francis Group. All rights reserved.
doi:10.1300/5923_08

ing and sustaining firm value, but does this generic understanding of the importance of productivity translate to effective strategies and tactics that reflect the firm's financial statements, which in turn impact the industry as a whole? We asked ourselves the same question: do managers really understand the importance of productivity?

In this study, our objective is to examine the productivity trend for lodging firms within the United States. We used a simple *ex post* approach to analyze productivity for the lodging industry. Defining and analyzing productivity from an industry perspective is the key, in that its definition as an outcome variable would have to be modified to include the causes and effects of productivity. Few analysts and industry professionals have used a sector-based approach to evaluate the reasons for decline in macroproductivity. To understand the service productivity of the hospitality industry, it is important that each sector (e.g., lodging sector, food service) within the hospitality domain be examined to see the overall growth/decline of productivity.

DEFINITION OF PRODUCTIVITY

Before we proceed any further, it is important to define productivity. Productivity is a ratio of output to input, and is measured by the ratio of output value to its related input value (Hodgkinson, 1999). When quantity is used as the surrogate for value, productivity is defined as quantity of output divided by the quantity of related input (Klassen et al., 1998). The quantity in the previous example could be units, hours, and measures that are quantifiable. Productivity is measured by comparing the amount of goods and services produced with the inputs that were used in production. According to (Vuorinen et al., 1998), "productivity has come to be interpreted as the ratio between output and input. In this way, productivity is conceptually defined as distinct from the value measurement of the monetary process" (p. 378). Drucker (1974) stated that a business may convert economic resources into something else either well or poorly. At this level, productivity is the balance between all production factors that will give the greatest return for the least effort (Drucker, 1974).

Labor productivity is the quantity of output per time spent or numbers employed.[1] From an efficiency perspective, Anthony (1965) points out that minimum consumption of inputs typically generate a given level of outputs. Or, contrarily, a given level of input generates the highest level of outputs. Furthermore, Vuorinen and colleagues (1998) describe efficiency in value terms: ". . . one tries to make compatible the effects of various input and output factors in the production process. This interpretation has led to formulations in which efficiency is seen as costs per product" (p. 378). We adopt this perspective while analyzing labor productivity for the lodging industry.

It should be noted that productivity can be defined from the customer's perspective also. Parasuraman (2002) defines productivity from the customer's perspective as the ratio of the service output experienced by a customer to the inputs provided by that customer as a participant in service production. Note that customers have influence on productivity from a service standpoint, as pointed out by several researchers (e.g., Lovelock and Young, 1979; Bateson, 1985; Ojasalo, 1999, 2003). In this study, we take labor productivity into consideration, and assume customer productivity to be a constant.[2]

LABOR PRODUCTIVITY AS A VALUE DRIVER

According to Ganchev (2000), the success of a hotel investment depends on value drivers, which include profit margin. "An investor who can make an improvement in any one or more of those drivers is able to create value and improve the return on the investment" (p. 78). Labor productivity is categorized as a value driver since it drives the revenue potential of a firm (Olsen et al., 1998). Moreover, a firm is able to manage costs through effective management of labor costs and labor productivity. For instance, a firm that is able to increase productivity of its labor force by being able to increase output at constant compensation rates per hour or at a compensation rate that increases but is lower than the rate at which productivity increases will have a lower unit cost of labor. This has an impact on the firm's cost of goods sold and on the gross margin that drives the firm's overall value.

Other ways of managing productivity to increase the overall value of the firm is for managers to be able to increase the level of output for a given number of employee hours worked. The firm's value will also increase even if the hours worked increases, but at a marginal rate as compared to the increase in output from period to period. Yet another way of measuring and using labor productivity to improve firm performance is to effectively manage employee contribution toward output. If the number of employees that produce a given level of output decreases, it is an indicator of increased productivity and hence increased value addition to the firm. In this study, we consider the productivity ratios mentioned previously to track the evolution of the lodging industry's labor productivity over the past four decades.

RESEARCH QUESTIONS

The research questions for the study include: (1) What has been the trend in labor productivity in the lodging industry over the past four decades? (2) What is the relationship between output and input factors within the context of labor productivity? (3) More specifically, how do these independent variables impact the output or dependent variables over the time period of this study? (4) Finally, how have the output variables varied over time for the years the data was collected?

The Sample and Unit of Analysis

We used a sample at the aggregate level of the lodging industry within the United States. In other words, the sample included firms from the U.S. lodging sector from whom the U.S. Bureau of Labor Statistics has collected relevant data. Therefore, the unit of analysis is the national economy level, using a given sector or industry as the sample; hence, productivity analysis in this case includes macroproductivity. Note that at the macrolevel or aggregate level, for instance, when the Bureau of Labor Statistics measures productivity, it is done so by using output value (in dollars) as the numerator, and input value, usually hours of labor, as the denominator.

Variables, Data, and Research Methodology

Variables included in this study were taken from the U.S. Bureau of Labor Statistics year by year data report on the lodging industry. The variables used in this study include: (1) output per hour, arrived at by taking firms output and dividing it by the total number of employee hours worked to produce that level of output; (2) output per employee; (3) output; (4) employee hours; (5) employees; (6) unit labor costs, calculated by dividing total labor compensation by real output, or, equivalently, it can be calculated by dividing hourly compensation by productivity [total labor compensation / hours] / [output / hours]; and (7) compensation per hour. Thus, increases in productivity lower unit labor costs whereas increases in hourly compensation raise them. If both series move equally, unit labor costs will be unchanged. Note that unit labor costs are a combination of internal as well as external value drivers.

The data was collected from secondary sources for the sample, which included firms within the lodging industry classified as "Hotel and Other Lodging Places" under the SIC code 701 reported by the U.S. Department of Labor. The department collects data and reports productivity measures including the variables used in the analysis period by period. They are reported in index format, the time line for which includes the years 1958 through 2000. The base year for the index is 1987, which equals 100.

DATA ANALYSIS AND RESULTS

Graphical Analysis of Data

Figure 8.1 provides a graphical analysis of all the variables used for the study. The data series for the indexes unit labor costs and compensation per hour are analyzed between the years 1987 through 1999. Note that output per hour and output per employee for the lodging industry increased steadily in the 1960s and the 1970s, reached a maximum point in 1979, and then began to decline. These labor productivity indexes in 1999 remained around the same level that was observed in the mid-1980s. However, in comparison to the late 1960s and the 1970s, labor productivity declined in the 1980s and the 1990s, although technology improved during the latter period. This is in contradiction to what is believed—that technology improves productivity. This must be researched in future studies in order to verify the impact of technology on productivity.

It should be pointed out that although highly correlated, output per hour was higher than output per employee in the 1960s and 1970s, which reversed in the 1980s and 1990s. This may indicate that the number of hours employees worked went up in the 1980s and 1990s

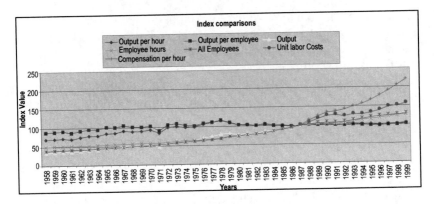

FIGURE 8.1. Productivity Ratio Comparisons

as compared to previous decades, or the number of employees decreased while the number of hours employees worked remained the same or increased.[3] According to Figure 8.1, employee hours were higher than the number of employees in the 1960s and the 1970s, and vice versa in the 1980s and the 1990s. This may explain why the output per employee was higher in the 1960s and 1970s and lower in the 1980s and 1990s, as compared to output per hour. Furthermore, this throws light on management issues in terms of the ways in which employees can maximize productivity at optimum levels of employees and the number of hours they work on a day-to-day basis to produce output.

On closer inspection of the graph, it becomes quite apparent that the growth rate for the sectoral labor-productivity-related variables, that is, output per employee and output per hour, decreased during periods of downturn (e.g. 1973, 1991). This indicates an emphasis on labor-productivity-related issues by management during times when the sectoral performance was affected by the external environment (e.g., economy). Variables such as employees, employee hours, and output also decreased in terms of growth rate during downturns. On the other hand, although the overall labor productivity vis-à-vis output per employee and output per hour showed an overall increasing trend, the rate of growth during periods of economic boom varied considerably. This raises the question: does management really con-

sider labor productivity as important when the external environment was favorable?

The unit labor costs increased during the time period 1987 through 1999 as employee compensation per hour was higher than the productivity ratios and was increasing at a higher rate than the latter. As seen in Figure 8.1, the unit labor costs increased during the period 1987 to 1999, the rate of increase was somewhat in correlation with compensation, while productivity was almost stagnant in comparison.

This has implications on the way the management defines its objectives and operates on a day-to-day basis. The compensation should be in tandem with productivity rates, although number of hours worked as well as number of employees will influence overall compensation. This raises the question of whether management paying for performance (related to productivity) would result in lower number of employee work hours while maintaining/increasing the level of output. To bring about superior performance, firms need to emphasize labor productivity and initiate this approach at the operational level.

Statistical Analysis of Lodging Industry Productivity

The statistical analysis of lodging industry productivity was conducted using time-series regression analysis. The analysis was done using two variables at a time, one being an input factor and the other an output factor. Therefore, the resulting regression line depicted the productivity for the time period. Regression analysis for the data was conducted using SPSS software. The curve that fitted the data as shown in Figure 8.2 is a logarithmic curve model represented by the equation $Y = b_0 + [b_1 * \ln(t)]$. The fit was indicated by r^2, which was 0.99, indicating an extremely good fit. The results indicate that the beta for the regression line output and employees as the variables was positive. A positive b_1 indicates that for the data set spanning the time period 1985 through 1999, productivity, i.e., output per employee hour, increased for the lodging sector. Similar curve estimation was done using output as the dependent variable and employee hours as the independent variable (see Figure 8.3). The curve fit was indicated by a high r^2 of 0.99, and the beta for the slope of the curve was positive. This further indicates that the output per employee was positive for the time period 1958 through 1999.

OUTPUT7

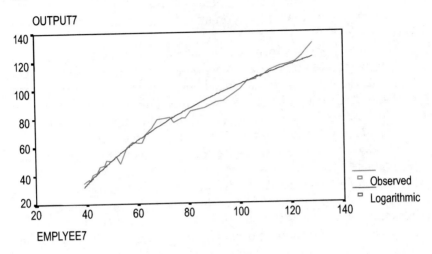

EMPLYEE7

FIGURE 8.2. Productivity: Output and Employee

OUTPUT7

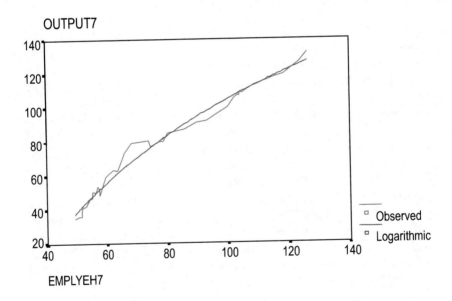

EMPLYEH7

FIGURE 8.3. Productivity: Output and Employee Hours

The second type of analysis conducted was the sequence analysis that was comprised of output per unit of input as the dependent variable and time as the independent variable. Results indicate that the cubic curve had the best fit in terms of fitting the observed data. The cubic function is defined by the model with the equation $Y = b_0 + (b_1 * t) + (b_2 * t^2) + (b_3 * t^3)$.

The r^2 for the curve was 0.99, which indicates an excellent fit. Results indicate that b_1 and b_3 were positive, whereas b_2 was negative. However, b_3 was not significant at the 0.05 level. Therefore, a quadratic function whose equation is $Y = b_0 + (b_1 * t) + (b_2 * t^2)$ was used to fit the curve on the observed data. Results indicate that the r^2 for the curve was 0.87, with positive and significant b_1 but negative and significant b_2. This further indicates that a curvilinear relationship existed between output per hour and time, and that output varied between the time period 1958 through 1999. It increased between 1958 and 1998 but went down between 1988 and 1998.

On the other hand, for the sequence analysis with output per employee as the dependent variable and years as the independent variable (see Figure 8.4), the curve that best fit the observed data was a cubic model whose equation is $Y = b_0 + (b_1 * t) + (b_2 * t^2) + (b_3 * t^3)$. Results indicate that b_0 was significant and positive, b_1 was significant but negative, and b_3 was significant but positive. The graph with the curve fit suggests that output per employee increased between 1958

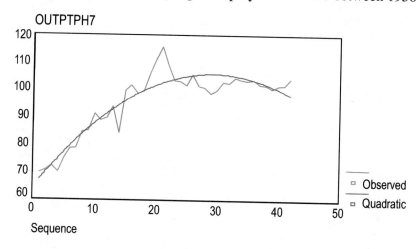

FIGURE 8.4. Sequence Analysis: Productivity and Time

and 1978, and then between 1978 and 1994 an overall decline in output per employee occurred, which flattened out and began to go up again in the mid to late nineties. When the ratio, output per unit of input (output/input), is the dependent variable and year is the independent variable, beta will be 0 if the output per unit of input over time does not change. Moreover, beta will be significantly different from 0 and positive if output increases and input remains the same or decreases, if output remains constant and input decreases, or if output decreases but input decreases at a faster rate over the time period analyzed. Furthermore, beta will be significantly different from 0 and negative if output decreases and input remains the same or increases, if output remains constant and input increases, or if output increases but input increases at a faster rate over the time period analyzed.

The present analysis reveals that in the case of output per employee hour, output increased with either constant or decreasing levels of input (employee hour) between 1958 and 1988. However, output either remained constant or decreased while input (employee hour) either decreased or remained constant, in that order. On further investigation of the graphical analysis, it can be stated that during the 1990s overall output increased but by a lower rate as compared to employee hour indexes, which increased at a higher rate.

On the other hand, in the case of output per employee (see Figure 8.5) the decline between 1978 and 1994 could be because output de-

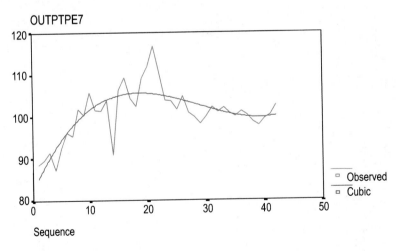

FIGURE 8.5. Sequence analysis: Output per Employee and Time

creased or remained constant while the number of employees either remained the same or increased, whereas the opposite was true for the preceding years 1958 through 1978. Further analysis of the graphical representation of the data reveals that output actually grew at a faster rate during the 1960s and the 1970s, and then declined in growth rate during the late 1970s to the early 1990s, which stabilized during the mid-1990s and began to grow toward the late 1990s as compared to the growth rate in the employee indexes. This explains the reason for the cubic curve fit.

DISCUSSION AND FUTURE RESEARCH

In this study, we used key variables to assess labor productivity and analyze them using graphical and regression analysis to report the direction of the relationship. It was found that the lodging industry in the past four decades has been able to improve productivity. However, the evolution of output per employee over the time period suggests that high volatility exists with respect to how much employees contribute to the production of given levels of output from year to year and from period to period. Although extraneous as well as within-firm factors exist that affect this productivity ratio, the variability of this factor over the time period is a function of the output and input factors (output levels and number of employees). As pointed out, this factor has a significant effect on firm value since it influences revenue levels and cost levels. However, on analyzing the variables that were used to calculate the ratio, it can be stated that the variation in levels of output and employees is a function of how the economic factors from the remote environment affect these variables individually.

We observed that as the economy went into a downturn, the number of employees within the sector went down. Furthermore, during periods of downturn, output per employee increased in the lodging industry. This may perhaps indicate that management's objectives during this period were to improve on productivity levels because of constraints on the firm. On the other hand, this was not the case during periods of economic boom, which further indicates that management of resources during boom and recession may be different as the focus shifts from efficient management of resources during recessions to focus on other factors that increase firm value during economic boom. This in itself is a deviation from the basic premise of the economic concept of the firm, which emphasizes maximum utility of resources at any given time. This argument is supported by the results obtained for "output per employee hour" showing similar patterns. It should be underscored that according to economic perspective on productivity, this may not be the case as noted by Becker (2003), "In the past, productivity almost always fell during recessions because both labor and capital were underutilized as output sagged or grew more slowly" (p. 29). The observation by Becker is in contrast to our findings for the lodging industry, which needs to be researched at the microlevel in more depth in future research efforts.

The changing objectives of the firm in terms of efficient management of resources during different periods could explain why overall sectoral productivity is on the decline. Since the United States has witnessed more periods of boom and moderate economic conditions over the past two to three decades, it could be argued that the overall decline is as a result of the external environmental conditions. Further analysis is required to be able to make firm conclusions on the cause-and-effect relationships.

The results also reveals that the relationship between output per employee and years was cubic, in that clear periods of crests and troughs existed over the past decade for this productivity ratio. Effective management of resources (employees) while at the same time managing output to maximize its value is the key to higher productivity levels. Management would have to pay more attention to how these variables vary with respect to one another. The same is true for the productivity ratio of output per employee hour. The curve that fit the data was a quadratic function, which indicates that periods of growth were followed by periods of decline. Again, management would have to lay more emphasis on the alignment between the firm and the environment in ensuring that this ratio is high in order to increase the levels of productivity. If number of hours that employees work is reduced during periods of downturn, management would need to ensure that output does not go below levels that result in decreased productivity. That the industry is not focusing on productivity-related measures of performance is evident in the varying levels of productivity from one time period to the other and from economic boom to recession.

It should be noted that as a result of varying levels of productivity during economic boom and recession, most industries have taken serious measures to adopt a "back to basics" approach to resource management, especially after the economic recession during the period 2000 to 2003. This approach is to maintain high levels of efficiency and productivity irrespective of the impact of the external economic environment on the firm. In other words, internal management of resources at the microlevel is key. To a large extent, firms have used technology as a permanent solution to ensure higher levels of productivity and efficiency. Note that this also translates to lower levels of rehiring of employees who were laid off during the recession.

This poses the question of what measures lodging industry managers have taken to address the variation in productivity reported in this chapter. Would technology at the operating level (e.g., check-in/check-out systems) be a solution? Some upscale lodging firms (e.g., Marriott, Hilton, and Starwood) have test marketed such technology in the past few months to see if it may be a good substitute for unreplaced employees. In the wake of recent technological developments that have helped hotels maintain the same level of service without compromising guest satisfaction, are as many employees needed to provide adequate services to customers in midpriced and upscale hotels? Note that this study reveals a downward trend in productivity during the 1980s and 1990s as compared to previous decades, although technological boom started in the mid-1980s. These are some of the questions that need to be answered by industry professionals as part of a micro approach to managing productivity at the firm level.

Lodging industries in developing economies could address the foregoing issue by incorporating state-of-the-art technology into the service production and delivery systems during the growth phase of the industry life cycle itself. It is imperative that labor-intensive lodging markets realize the importance of using technology to improve labor productivity in the wake of increasing international competition during the past decade, which has driven prices of lodging products and services down, especially in the upscale segment. Since the upscale hotel market has seen the highest growth in demand and supply in countries such as China and India, it should be underscored that labor productivity should be a priority in such markets in which labor costs are on the lower end of the spectrum. Even if hotel firms in developing markets could employ more employees per room as compared to developed markets, the productivity of these additional employees should be the basis of decision making, especially when new technology could be a very good substitute for human-resource-related functions in full-service firms. Since investments in technology are accompanied by increased productivity (Bosworth and Triplett, 2003) rather than incurring additional direct costs of labor to perform similar services at lower levels of productivity, such investments would enable firms to increase their gross profit margin. This is reflected in Bosworth and Triplett's (2003) statement that "IT investments now make a substantial contribution of labor productivity growth in services-producing industries" (p. 2), which might explain the increased growth of the services sector productivity levels in the United States during the post–1995 period in which technology-related investments was at the higher end of the spectrum as compared to previous periods.

Lodging firms in developing markets should realize that they could be more competitive in such markets if they implement state-of-the-art technology that enables increase in productivity levels. This calls for a shift in strategic thinking on the part of lodging firms' management in developing markets, which their counterparts in developed markets have gradually begun to realize. Such strategic thinking on part of management will help improve lodging firms' productivity globally.

LIMITATIONS AND CONCLUSIONS

This study has limitations. Since the data was collected from a secondary source, the sampling framework was not clear. Moreover, measurement errors that may have occurred during the data-collection process are also not apparent. This is echoed by Bosworth and Triplett (2003), who state that output measures used in national accounts for the hotel industry may not reflect productivity growth even though such a growth might have actually occurred but was not captured because of the way productivity was measured. Therefore, new measures of productivity may need to be used. Although this may be the case, it should be noted that the source, the Bureau of Labor Statistics, is reliable in collecting and processing data at the macroeconomic level.

Our findings clearly indicate significant increases and decreases in productivity levels within the lodging sector over the past four decades. These increases and decreases could be because of multiple factors; however, it is apt to pinpoint that an increase in productivity levels occurred during the periods of downturns over the previous year(s). What is even more interesting is that productivity levels of the lodging sector did not show improvement during economic boom, which was reflected in the variability in productivity levels reported for those years. Importance should be given to productivity as it was observed that factors such as "productivity per hour," which showed a significant increase during the 1960s and 1970s, declined during the 1980s and 1990s. This is true for productivity per employee also; however, the decline in productivity per employee has ceased, and this productivity ratio seems to be a gradually increasing.

Overall, as theory would suggest, the relationship between output and employee hours in terms of productivity for the data set was positive, which was observed for output and employees too. As pointed out in the previous section, contrary to economic perspective on productivity, the lodging industry showed increases in productivity during periods of recession and decreases in productivity during periods of economic boom. This needs to be investigated in future studies at the firm level. Also, further study needs to undertaken that focuses on the effects of the external economic environment on the sector's productivity level. The important step for industry professionals is to identify key measures that will improve industry productivity and sustain the value of the firms within the industry, which in turn will build industry value. Since productivity ratios declined during the 1980s and 1990s as compared to previous decades, even with the advent of superior technology, lodging firms should consider technological advances that could improve productivity at the operating level. Industry professionals would need to pay attention to productivity being the focus of management during economic boom as well as downturn.

NOTES

1. Definition extracted from http://economics.about.com/library/glossary/bldef-labor-productivity.htm.

2. Note that since this study is being pursued at the macrolevel of the lodging industry, which includes firms ranging from very less customer contact services to high customer contact services, customer productivity becomes difficult to capture. Moreover, from a secondary data standpoint, no macroeconomic databases exist that report this index for the lodging industry.

3. Note that the number of employees and employee hours would vary from period to period as a function of the number of lodging establishments included in the study. Since this is reported as an index, comparisons can be made between periods using the base year.

REFERENCES

Anthony, R. (1965). *Planning and Control Systems: A Framework for Analysis.* Boston, MA: Harvard Graduate School of Business Administration.

Bateson, J.E.G. (1985). Self service consumer: An exploratory study. *Journal of Retailing, 61*(3): 49-75.

Becker, G.S. (2003). The productivity boom is just warming up. *Business Week, 3854:* 29.

Bosworth, B.P. and Triplett, J.E. (2003). Service productivity in the United States: Griliches' service volume revisited. Presented at the CRIW Conference, September 19-20, Bethesda, MD. Washington DC: The Brookings Institution. Available at: https://www.nber.org/books/CRIW03-BH/bosworth-triplett3-24-05.pdf.

Drucker, P.F. (1974). *Management: Tasks-Responsibilities-Practices.* New York: Harper & Row.

Ganchev, O. (2000). Applying value drivers to hotel valuation. *Cornell Hotel and Restaurant Administration Quarterly, 41*(5): 78-89.

Hodgkinson, A. (1999). Productivity measurement and enterprise bargaining: The local government perspective. *The International Journal of Public Sector Management, 12*(6): 470 (obtained via ABI-Inform).

Klassen, K.J., Russell, R.M., and Chrisman, J.J. (1998). Efficiency and productivity measures for high contact services. *The Service Industries Journal, 18*(4): 1-18

Lovelock, C.H. and Young, R.F. (1979). Look to consumers to increase productivity. *Harvard Business Review, 53*(3): 168-178.

Ojasalo, K. (1999). *Conceptualizing Productivity in Services.* Helsinki, Sweden: Helsingfors, Svenska Handelshögskolan.

Ojasalo, K. (2003). Customer influence on service productivity. *S.A.M. Advanced Management Journal, 68*(3): 14.

Olsen, M.D., West, J.J., and Tse, E.C. (1998). *Strategic Management in the Hospitality Industry.* Boston, MA: Wiley.

Parasuraman, A. (2002). Service quality and productivity: A synergistic perspective. *Managing Service Quality, 12*(1): 6-9.

Sheehy, B. and Schone, B. (2003). Service productivity. *Executive Excellence, 20*(7): 5.

U.S. Department of Labor. Bureau of Labor Statistics, SIC code 701.

Vuorinen, I., Jarvinen, and R. Lehtinen, U. (1998). Content and measurement of productivity in the service sector: A conceptual analysis with an illustrative case from the insurance business. *International Journal of Service Industry Management, 9*(4): 377 (obtained via ABI Inform).

Chapter 9

Human Resources Initiatives in Designing and Developing Value-Delivery Systems in the Hospitality Industry

Shveta Singh
Vijayshri Tewari

INTRODUCTION

Over just a few years, the business environment facing hoteliers has changed radically. The new realities, if not permanent, are at least likely to persist for a while, and include the following:

- Consumer's value mind-set and sense of empowerment, contributing to real declines in average rates
- Potential of war and additional terrorist activity, coupled with general economic uncertainty and a shorter booking cycle in all segments, rendering forecasting more of a guessing game than at any other time in recent history
- Increased competition from nontraditional sources (cruise ships, corporate housing, time-share)
- Potential shift to new ways of conducting business

Companies that develop effective strategies for dealing with the impact of these issues, rather than hoping the issues will quickly fade away, will be the winners.

Global Cases on Hospitality Industry
© 2008 by The Haworth Press, Taylor & Francis Group. All rights reserved.
doi:10.1300/5923_09

WHY CONSIDER CUSTOMERS' PERSPECTIVES?

Some hotel managers may assume that improving a prevalent management practice ultimately contributes to customer value. In fact, managing customer value by "creating quality and service that customers can see" is now considered a critical component of companies' strategic marketing. Customer value, the experts assert, is what builds loyalty. It is, therefore, essential that managers can compare specific business practices in terms of their relative contributions to creating value and, ultimately, customer loyalty.

Focusing on Attributes that Are Visible to Customers

Analyzed was the customers' perception of attributes related to their favorite hotels in the areas of guest rooms (design and amenities), physical property (public spaces and exteriors), and overall atmosphere. For business travelers, the two most important sources of value were aesthetics and convenient location.

People and Process Management

It was found that although friendliness and attentiveness of personnel are valued across market segments, professionalism emerged as a particularly important quality for the two business segments—business travelers and conference attendees. Similarly, market segmentation exists in terms of guest room size, cleanliness, and prices. Cleanliness is a powerful source of customer value for leisure guests, whereas guest room size and comfort is most important for transient business guests. Conventions and meetings guests found the cost of goods and services as the most important factor.

Value for Money

Besides pricing and discounts, other value-added attributes mentioned included overall service quality, convenient location, uncommon services, and cleanliness. For leisure travelers, the importance of service quality was second only to cleanliness in establishing value for money, whereas business travelers identified a hotel's convenient location as being the second most important attribute after the hotel's various value-added services. Moreover, for business travelers, cleanliness trailed far behind when defining "value for money" (Burns, 1997).

THE NATURE OF WORK AND SKILLS IN HOSPITALITY

Hospitality work (and thus the skills that it demands) exhibits diversity in both horizontal and vertical terms. In a horizontal sense, it includes a very wide range of jobs, the extent depending on the definition of the sector that is employed. The traditional research focus on hospitality work concentrates on areas that provide, primarily, food and beverage and, to a lesser extent, accommodation. Research into wider areas of hospitality work, particularly those that have emerged with the expansion of services and functions in the area (front desk, leisure, entertainment, reservations call centers) is much more poorly served. The "newer" areas include functions and tasks that exhibit considerable crossover with work that falls out with normal definitions of hospitality in food and drink manufacture, office administration, IT systems management, and specialist areas of sports and leisure. Indeed, it is fair to say that although a long-standing debate exists as to whether the hospitality industry is "unique," little is unique about hospitality skills. Most of the skills that are employed within the sector also have relevance and application in other sectors of the economy. Those employed in areas in which a considerable skills overlap exists, such as the areas listed previously, may well see themselves in terms of their generic skills area rather than as part of the hospitality labor market. Some of these skills have been subject to separate assessment in a manner that has value and crossover implications for the hospitality sector.

The characteristics and the organization of the hospitality industry are subject to ongoing restructuring and evolutionary change. Major labor market and skills implications of such change become apparent as businesses reshape the range of services they offer or as they respond to fashion and trend imperatives in the consumer marketplace. A more traditional classification that ranges from unskilled to semiskilled and from skilled to supervisory and management represent vertical diversity in hospitality work. This "traditional" perspective of work and, therefore, skills in hospitality is partly described in terms that suggest that the proportionate breakdown of the workforce in hospitality is as follows (Brown et al., 2001):

1. Managerial: 6 percent
2. Supervisory: 8 percent
3. Craft (skilled): 22 percent
4. Operative (semiskilled and unskilled): 64 percent

This simplification masks major business organizational diversity in hospitality, reflecting the size, location, and ownership of hospitality businesses. The actual job and skills content of work in hospitality is predicated on these factors so that common job titles (e.g., restaurant manager) almost certainly mask a very different range of responsibilities, tasks, and skills within jobs in different establishments.

Peculiarities of the Hospitality Labor Market

The peculiarities of the hospitality market are the following: (Lashley and Morrison, 2000):

- Tendency to low wages, except where skills shortages act to counter this
- Prevalence of unsocial hours and family unfriendly shift patterns
- Rare incidence of equal opportunities policies and male domination of higher level, better paid work
- Poor or nonexistent career structures
- Informal recruitment practices
- Failure to adopt formalized "good practice" models of human resource management and development
- Lack of any significant trade union presence
- High levels of labor turnover
- Difficulties in recruitment and retention

However, we may question the basis for categorizing hospitality employment into "skilled" and "unskilled" categories, arguing the postmodernist case that this separation is something of a social construct. This construct is rooted in, first, labor-planning paradigms for the manufacturing sector, and, second, in the traditional power of trade unions to control entry into the workplace through lengthy apprenticeships. Skills within "organized" sectors, such as airlines and hotel companies with clearly defined staff relationship structures, such as Sheraton, are recognized and valued. Working in such an environment requires more than an ability to operate a cash register; emotional demands are made of employees to constantly be in a positive, joyful, and even playful mood. An ability to cope with such demands must be recognized as a "skill" par excellence. By contrast, catering and fast food operate within a business culture in which labor is seen in terms of costs that must be kept at the lowest possible level, and in which skills, therefore, are not valued or developed.

The new employees in hospitality must be trained to be loyal, flexible, tolerant, amiable, and responsible. At every successful tourism establishment it is the employees who stand out (technology cannot substitute for welcoming employees). Emphasis on "emotional demands" is an additional dimension of hospitality skills. Service employees are required to manage their emotions for the benefit of customers and are, in part, paid to do this.

The role of information technology in transforming work across a wide range of sectors in the economy does not really feature classification, and yet the impact of the information age can be seen as adding a new dimension to traditional or routine occupations. The new category of tourism work emerging as a result of the information revolution requires creative and information processing skills of an entirely different order to those traditionally associated with the sector. Assessment of the real impact of the information revolution on skills demands in hospitality work, therefore, must remain an issue for future consideration. The approach should be to consider skills in terms of personal attributes, job requirements, and the setting of work. This approach, with a focus on the context of work, both from an individual and organizational point of view, is much more sympathetic to the realities of diversity within hospitality work. This appears to accept that what is skilled work in one context may be less so in another, influenced by both the cultural context of the work and also by the availability and application of technology. It is argued, therefore, that a simple labeling of hospitality work as "unskilled" is both unhelpful and unjustifiable.

STRATEGIC ISSUES

Several strategic issues will serve to influence the nature of the relationship between the hospitality firm and those individuals it employs to meet the needs of the customer of tomorrow. In the case of organization and employee relations this will result in more complex interaction and individualized relationships throughout the workplace.

Workplace Concerns

Growing Expectations and Complexity in the Transaction between Guest Contact Employee and the Customer

This complexity is most challenging and will necessarily result in new demands for better leadership across all levels of responsibility within the organization. This will also be driven in correlation with another macroforce—the new worker (Seymour, 2000).

The New Worker

The workforce of tomorrow will reflect the broad-based changes occurring in education, which are taking place across the world. A shift from teacher-centered learning to student-centered learning is resulting in workforce entrants who are more independent in mind and spirit, who take responsibility for their own learning, and are plugged into a cyber-based knowledge work. They are less likely to emerge from this environment being interested in jobs that do not challenge their intellectual capacity. Leading this new workforce will require new approaches to understanding and developing leadership skills.

This new worker will participate in a continuing shift in cultural imperatives emerging from what is frequently being referred to as the *dot com* generation, a euphemism for those who are developing their views and values from the Internet. They will no doubt embrace such concepts as lifelong learning, greater matching of career and personal values, and the desire for personal development. Developing within this generation are growing expectations for equality for all races and genders, while at the same time the generation is witnessing the contradiction of a growing intolerance for these differences. This will no doubt create a more complex work environment for both leader and follower.

Growing Shortage of Qualified Labor

The issue affecting the management of human resources is meeting the increased complexity within all guest transactions. In the developed world, in the context of the current economic prosperity, unemployment is at its lowest in decades. With a growing demand for workers in the knowledge industry and the attractive working conditions it offers, few skilled workers are interested in working in basic service level occupations such as those available within the hospitality industry.

In addition, the demographics in the West are such that the size of the age group that has met many of the industry's labor force needs is shrinking compared to other groupings. In the developing world, the workforce is threatened due to the spread of disease, specifically those related to immunosuppressive disorders such as AIDS. In parts of southern Africa, it is not uncommon to lose as much as 10 percent of a firm's labor force as a result of this problem. These factors will no doubt compound the industry's existing struggles to obtain skilled employees.

In addition to the labor shortage resulting from a shrinking youthful labor supply, the growing number of the so-called "baby boomer" group who will be retiring in the near future also strains the industry. As older workers transition out of the labor force they will also have different job expectations that will change reward and compensation systems. Their work-related goals might often be as much social as economic. They also will seek work-scheduling alternatives toward a shorter, more flexible workweek.

Changing Workplace

This represents the issue affecting the human resource function. The workplace is changing as a result of influences from the previous forces. The major change here is the flattening of the organization structure as the individual who has transitioned from a learner-centered environment as a student now expects the workplace to resemble this more individualized setting. In this context, the organization must focus on setting standards and defining expected competencies. The old-fashioned notion of a hierarchical structure, often characterized by a "my way or the highway" leadership style, will evolve into a more shared, participatory approach to responsibility for organizational direction (Lashley and Morrison, 2000).

Global Capital Market System

The global market is imposing demands for greater focus on adding value throughout an organization. Simply put, managers are expected to direct their attention toward producing products and services that will help the firm go forward. The attention must be on industry-leading efforts to capture the customer of tomorrow and hold on to current ones. This does not means abandoning the romantic side of management, often interpreted as good food and service, the high touch element of the hospitality business; it simply means that the hospitality enterprises must be thought of as businesses that are required to perform in competitive markets and produce financial gains that reward investors with returns in excess of their opportunity costs. This is not an easy task in today's environment.

Technology

Technology will alter the landscape in many ways. In particular, the change in the way customers look at the price–value relationship will occur due to the increased transparency brought about by the Internet and electronic commerce. In particular, the growth of online auctions will force prices to remain highly competitive, almost to the point of commoditizing the industry. This then will focus the customers' attention on what products and services they really value and what they are willing to pay for them. This brings up the question of what will define the price–value relationship in the future? In addition to these demand-side issues, technology will change the internal management of human resources. From online sourcing of new employees to job change announcements within the firm, management information systems in support of the human resource function will change current practices.

These macroforces have resulted in many microforces that will create many challenges for human resource managers. The human resource as a function is changing in the current business environment (see Tables 9.1 and 9.2):

1. Creating a service culture
2. Building an empowered service-delivery system
3. Facilitating a "customer listening" orientation (Odgers and Baum, 2001)

Creating a Service Culture

"Seek opportunities to create memories" is the vision statement that guides the Boulders Resort, a luxury property located in Carefree, Arizona. Four Seasons and Regent Hotels maintain a high ratio

TABLE 9.1. Design of the Value Delivery System: The HR Perspective

Organizational Context	→	Market force and dynamics, business objectives/shareholder expectations, current business performance, change imperative.
Leading Change	→	How do we effectively implement our business strategy and build a positive and proactive approach to continuous change?
Leading Performance	→	How can we lead and develop our people in owning and growing their performance?
Leading Risk	→	How might we become more enterprising and creative without putting the business at risk?
Leading Communications	→	How should we communicate to ensure everyone is engaged in our brand and has real clarity of focus?

TABLE 9.2. Design of the Value Delivery System: HR Initiatives

Stage One	Stage Two	Stage Three	Ongoing
Explore key business issues	Deepen perspectives	Lead conversations	Become the change
Develop point of view and conviction	Develop ability to teach and role model	Facilitate others learning	Lead by example
Create actions	Learn to facilitate	Start to role model	Authentic behavior drives change in others
Engage in the Conversations	Own the conversations	Teach and role model new behaviors	Exemplify new attitudes and approaches

of employees to guests. New employees are given intensive orientation in the basics of the philosophy and culture of the hotel, which lasts over twelve weeks and culminates in an overnight stay in the hotel. The general manager of the Cincinnati Marriott Northeast implemented a twelve-point service program designed to encourage staff members to treat each guest as a family member who is on a visit to their homes. Employees carry pledge cards, and each daily meeting begins with a review of the importance of satisfying the guest. The credo of the Ritz-Carlton, "Ladies and Gentlemen Serving Ladies and Gentlemen," forms the basis for sophisticated methods of attaining high levels of guest service. The company hires only employees who share its values, as determined in a structured interview that is empirically scored. Interviewees also attend a series of receptions at which their conduct and personality are observed and judged (Ritz Carlton, 2007).

Developing Empowered Service Employees

Most of the champion companies rely on employees to deliver the enhanced guest services. For this they train and empower the employees to act on the spot to the best of their judgment, with the sole motto of satisfying the customer. Ritz Carlton Hotels empower all employees to spend up to $2,000 to solve a guest problem, if need be. The Inn at Essex has no detailed operational manuals; it has only a one-page policy statement, which includes guidelines such as "always find a way to say yes" and "when faced with a situation, if you make a decision for the benefit of the guest, 90% of the time you will be right, and management will back you 100% of the time"(Ritz Carlton, 2007).

Listening to Customers

All the best practice champions realize the importance of listening to their customers and seriously and promptly acting on the guest feedback. A coding system tracks the results of the quiz and indicates any actions needed to improve operations. Month-end summaries are provided to employees and departments and these are coded in red, yellow, and green colors. Green is "good"; yellow is "you are making progress, but there is still work to do here"; and red is "you are really below the expected performance." It is amazing to see the reaction when a particular team sees its performance in the red zone. The same information written on a plain piece of paper would not have the same impact as the red zone coding has, which hits the team like lightening. The Ritz-Carlton has extended the colored coding system in many other areas of communication as well (Keep and Mayhew, 1999).

DESKILLING WITHIN THE HOSPITALITY WORKPLACE

The deskilling is an inevitable consequence of growing standardization or routinization across the service sector. Evidence supports this process in hospitality and tourism in the form of a growing fast-food sector, within-budget accommodation, and through the growth of no-frills airlines. The growth of these sectors all point to a simplification of tasks in the workplace, aided in part by technology substitution, but also by changes in consumer demands and expectations. It is also arguable that these sectors have grown in response to new consumer demand as opposed to displacement of demand for traditional services. Therefore, although their growth may have had the global effect of "dumbing down" average skill levels in hospitality and tourism, it is difficult to argue that they have eliminated demand for higher-order skills within other sectors of the industry.

Analysis of research from the mid-1980s onward shows the following:

- Traditional skills and functional boundaries breaking down in many occupations, leading not to functional fragmentation, but to multiskilling in more integrated tasks
- The effect on skills not easily predicted, due to different management strategies on task reorganization
- Relatively little deskilling, disproportionately concentrated on lower skill and craft-level jobs for which barriers to cross-trade reskilling had reduced the potential for integration
- Much interoccupational hybridization of skills at all occupational levels and in manufacturing and service sectors, combined with both upskilling and deskilling
- Demand for higher-level occupations stimulated by the effect of structural trends and labor supply on employers' interpretation of skill needs

This analysis has relevance in the context of changing skills in hospitality. The argument that hospitality is moving toward increasingly multiskilled models of training and work has been aired since the early 1980s. The focus of this argument has been targeted toward meeting employer needs, particularly in smaller businesses in which the notion of flexible rotation between different hotel departments in a way to suit the demand cycle is presented as a logical business solution. In reality, such work represents multitasking because the level and nature of the work in question (food service, bar service, pottering, and housekeeping) offers little by way of enhancing the actual skills of employees other than extending the operational context within which they are exercised (Parsons and Marshall, 1995)

HUMAN RESOURCES INITIATIVES IN THE DESIGNING AND DEVELOPMENT OF VALUE-DELIVERY SYSTEMS IN THE HOSPITALITY INDUSTRY

Management Practices: The New Manager

The changes begin at the level of general management. The general manager must balance the traditional, internally focused view with one that incorporates an external, future-oriented view. Managers must be able to anticipate change, invest in products and services that are future oriented, and understand that these investments must produce returns in excess of the investor's cost of capital. The balance between craft and business skills has never been more important. This balance will set the stage for how the human resource function will be carried out. This ability to balance the art of hospitality with the demands for investment returns will alter the career paths of many in the industry today. The traditional route through the functional areas of hospitality enterprises will not ensure the top jobs. Expectations about career progress will have to shift from ensuring great service to ensuring great returns along with great service. The emphasis will be on owner relationships as well as on customer relationships. This will include a greater importance on managing the contract relationships with investors. Success will be based on competencies that will ensure performance in this area of owner–investor relations. Managing change and transmitting a value adding emphasis to all employees will become two of the most important of the competencies of tomorrow's manager. This will require greater creativity and vision on the part of managers with a focus on the future and the uncertainties presented by it. With the emphasis on adding value being driven by investors it is likely that pressure to restructure the organization and do away with many middle-level management positions will increase as responsibility is continually being pushed further down the organizational hierarchy. Those middle-management positions that remain will shift orientation from task management to knowledge management, as greater attention will be placed on the superior management of customer relationships and on enhancing products and services. Empowerment is being driven as much by this as it is by human resource professionals who advocate its use to improve leadership and motivation.

A shift will occur in the way management looks at the resource provided by employees. They will be considered as less of a cost and more of an asset. Management will have to invest in this asset as it does in all its fixed versions. This includes the idea of significant investment in the development of this asset without the long-held view that if this is done, the employee will leave and go someplace else and the investment will be used by the competition. This rather naive and incorrect view will be unacceptable to tomorrow's employee who will make an employment decision more often on what the firm can do for them, with their own development being probably the most important consideration. Performance evaluation and compensation systems will reflect the competency-based approach. Employees will expect to receive assistance in developing competencies, and once they are successful, they will expect to be paid for this accomplishment. In fact, they will expect compensation even if the organization is unable to put those competencies to work immediately. The point is that the employee of tomorrow will expect and seek development and personal growth opportunities and will not be willing to defer their rewards to some later time. Failure to manage this process successfully will result in difficulty retaining the new worker.

Leadership will change also. No more command control structures; participation will be essential. The manager of tomorrow will have to become a coach employing a learning organization model to solving the routine and exceptional problems of the business. With greater delegation of service delivery to the employee, they will grow more powerful in the formula of the business and will be expecting to be treated as partners, not task implementers in solving all types of problems. All this serves to make the entire human resource function more transparent. This will lead to many questions regarding what leadership styles and structures will work best in this new environment. What will leadership be and who will be responsible will also challenge the current thinking of today. The lines of authority and accountability will continue to blur.

Outsourcing will continue to develop across all functions of management. Entire departments such as housekeeping, accounting, front office, and food and beverage will be considered as possible candidates for outsourcing. Also, the entire labor pool in a hospitality enterprise is likely to be purchased from an outsourcing supplier. As this trend continues it will change the human resource management function and the responsibilities of both operations and staff management. In many cases the HR function will cease to exist as a function within the enterprise as the outsourcing firm will handle most of this activity. The responsibility left will be for leadership and motivation. Management will now have to concentrate on managing the outsourcing relationship. These evolving trends will impact how managers are trained and developed, and this will change the skill sets needed. This will force dramatic curricular changes in those institutions that focus on developing hospitality industry professionals. It will also change the role of the teacher. The current body of knowledge presently taught, and highly criticized by think-tank participants, will also have to change if these learning institutions are to succeed at developing tomorrow's new manager.

The New Worker

Individualism is a pattern of behavior on the increase, both from the customer and the employee. This can be expected to continue. This translates into a different set of conditions in the workplace environment. The idea that the workplace should be framed in an "obedience culture" is no longer acceptable. Power is now expected to be diffused throughout what was once referred to as the organization's hierarchy. This also suggests conditions that favor flexibility in everything from pay and work schedules to pension plans. Customization is no longer just the privilege of the customer. The new worker will expect greater self-development opportunities, desiring to improve and perfect their personal effectiveness. Not only will this allow them to improve their social skill set when interacting with customers, but it will also be of obvious benefit when seeking greater responsibility within the firm or when seeking other employment. This will become a very important benefit sought at all levels by all employees. In fact, the phrase often used by interviewers when considering a new hire—"what can you do for the firm"—will be replaced by the prospect asking, "What can the firm do for me"? In this case, especially in tight labor markets, the prospective employee is becoming more demanding and discriminating regarding their own development, and this can be expected to magnify as time goes by. The individuality translates into the concept of the "free agent," meaning that people will assess their personal skill and competency inventory and seek to market it to the firm that offers the best deal, including signing bonuses. This will be especially true for those workers who will possess special knowledge capabilities needed in this complex and changing world. They in turn will expect to bring their knowledge tools into a team-based environment, not one based on a command and control style of leadership.

The form of compensation and recognition expected will reflect both the individuality and team member effectiveness. Employees will be expecting to be compensated on their ability to translate the broad vision of the firm into everyday transactions. They anticipate being consulted in many areas and expect that their views will be honored. They will expect to be given all the tools necessary to accomplish their tasks and to be empowered to use them. They also expect to be trusted and viewed as a community of employees, helping the organization to achieve its goals.

Employees will no longer expect the firm to provide lifelong work. They however expect to develop themselves in order to maximize lifelong career capabilities. Thus, they will value lifelong learning and opportunities for career development. This will become increasingly difficult as firms downsize and eliminate middle management positions. Career development becomes more difficult in flattened organizations. Thus, they will seek to develop competencies that will allow lateral job change and interesting work. They will expect compensation for competencies developed. This set of expectations will require more coaching and personalized leadership skills by those in authority. The balance between work and private life will grow more important at all levels of the organization. For an industry that has betrayed this need for centuries, it raises perhaps the most significant challenge. In this context, participants in the think tanks have often come to the same conclusion, put simply as the industry provides poor working conditions, unpleasant jobs, often in unpleasant leadership settings, and poor compensation expecting them to give more to the firm than their families or private lives. Although many may argue with this assessment, the perpetually high turnover, labor shortage, and poor reputation of the industry seem to bear this out. Many changes will expected if this issue is to be resolved.

The new worker will expect a work environment that is safe and healthful. They can expect and will demand greater say in how this environment should be shaped, including the benefits associated with it. For example, they will expect health insurance coverage that is commensurate with the changes created by the work environment.

Ethics

Values and ethics become more important in the new work environment. Expectation is growing for a greater display of moral values and integrity, especially on the part of the employee with respect to management behavior. These issues will revolve around the employment, leadership, and social responsibilities of the firm. This includes compliance with laws and norms, including fairness. Employees would like to experience confidence in their leadership regarding this important new workplace expectation.

A growing spirituality exists throughout the workplace. This does not necessarily mean that people are becoming more religious; it implies only that everyone is expecting a higher moral ground, especially from leaders. Simply put, in a complex world in which many feel a great uneasiness with the uncertainty surrounding this complexity, many look for a moral compass to guide them. This need will change further the leadership styles expected in the near future. It will expand what leadership, broadening the expectations of today's hospitality manager, means.

Technology

Technology will continue to reshape the relationships between the employee and supervisor, and the employee and customer. First, management information systems will continue to enhance the human resource function and allow greater transparency between the employee and the firm. It will assist the employee in finding better work and self-development opportunities.

Managing information and data will become part of the job of every employee in increasing numbers. From data warehouses, to customized guest services information, the transaction between employee and customer is getting more sophisticated because of technology. This raises important questions about the jobs of tomorrow. Such questions as: what qualifications will be needed to meet technological changes in all jobs; how will this affect recruiting, compensation, and development; how will the balance between hi-tech and hi-touch be accomplished; what investments will be required; how will authority be diffused by technology; what competencies are required; how will retraining be handled for those who do not possess competencies; what new jobs will be created; and how will they affect the organization's structure? will continue to force new thinking about the relationships between employee, customer, and firm.

As the continuing challenge of finding qualified staff continues, it can be expected that looks toward technology will increase for assisting in alleviating this problem. This can be expected to evolve further in places where it is becoming increasingly difficult to obtain the necessary staff to meet heightened levels of service. What is left to be defined is what elements of the service delivery system will be enhanced or supplied completely by technology?

Communication will no doubt continue to be revolutionized by technology. This includes the exchanges in a business-to-business environment along with the customer-employee interaction. These exchanges will be more information rich, resulting in a growing set of expectations for quality, integrity, and responsiveness. It is probably in this realm that the impact of technology will be felt the greatest in the near future.

Education and Training

Changes will occur in the processes related to education and training as well as the content of what is communicated. Technology will influence how knowledge is shared, the timing of the sharing, and the location. As Web-based, cyber universities continue to expand their offerings, the learner will be able to enhance their skills anytime, anywhere, and at any pace. Education, similar to many other fields, will become more customized. The purchaser of this knowledge will become more discriminating. No longer will they accept marginal teachers, dated information, and stale learning opportunities. They will seek the best, both in terms of the teacher and of the delivery. In this new education marketplace, the merely passable teacher will not be eliminated, he or she will simply be relegated to the role of assisting the best by doing such tasks as grading, preparing materials, and managing the logistics of the learning experience. They will no longer be able to hold a center stage position.

Training programs, although always necessary for basic skill development, will also focus on developing personal effectiveness capability. As the new worker is required to do more and handle more complex settings, they will be expected to become more personally effective in managing customer transactions that will result in added value to both the firm and customer. They will also be expected to be more effective at handling relationships, which are growing more diverse between both customer and employee. Such skills as anticipation of customer and management needs, self-management, and personal responsibility for quality and economic value adding will be part of the training associated with the new worker and new manager. Along with this theme will be more efforts in multitasking and multiskill development, as jobs grow more complicated because the customer transaction grows more complex. Training will be necessary, on a continual basis, in technology, as this powerful element of business life becomes more of a competitive method. Such capabilities as managing information, the synthesis of ideas, and adapting and managing change are just a few of the areas in which training will be necessary. Technology will also influence how training will be done. Today, hospitality firms are developing personal coaches managed totally by multimedia components to guide the employee through everything from making pizza to serving as a help desk for night auditors. In many cases, these smart agent coaches are linked directly to the employee via microphones, earpieces, and digital cameras and are on demand. Today's youth will no doubt be more comfortable with this style of instruction as opposed to the stressed-out training manager or supervisor who often forgets basic behavioral skills when instructing employees on how to perform their jobs.

The entire education and training process will become more learner-centered. Everything from numeric to literacy skills will be capable of being learned in this new environment. New forms of certification and validation will emerge as cyber learning and customized development programs grow more important. If it will challenge the traditional benchmarks such as university degrees and trades recognition remains to be seen. However, many changes are occurring that will alter the landscape of all forms of training and education. The industry will face its most significant challenge in trying to bridge the gap between the contemporary employee and manager who was trained and/or educated in the old model and those who are experiencing the new learning environment. Not only has this environment changed, but so too has the body of knowledge. Thus, industry associations, consulting and training firms, schools and colleges, and corporate training programs will experience a powerful need to bring the body of knowledge, along with the current and collective intelligence of present-day management, into the new paradigm of management thinking.

THE LABOR ENVIRONMENT

Labor laws continue to mature within countries and across regions. In the international labor organization, a leader in improving the working conditions of all employees continues to be a driving force. Social conscience and awareness are bringing about greater focus on working conditions, especially in settings often characterized as "sweatshops." Child labor laws, moral issues such as prostitution, and exploitation of "have-nots" will help to shape a global standard for managing human resources. It can be expected that national governments will continue to feel the pressure to improve the working conditions for all people.

As diversity continues to impact the work environment, it can also be expected that governments and special interest groups will drive the cause for greater awareness, fairness, and tolerance. Training and education programs will grow in number as businesses try to grapple with this challenge. This will not be a simple task in the context of a growing level of nationalism and intolerance. Labor unions, although still influenced by regional and local environments, will find it necessary to adjust to the discipline that capital markets place on businesses. The rigidity of job descriptions, categories, and pay systems will have to change if businesses and countries try to compete in the global marketplace. Today, jobs are being transformed and transplanted as firms try to compete. Better partnerships will exist between management and labor.

Working conditions will in many ways be legislated if businesses do not provide for the safety and health of their employees. As people power grows, brought on by the rush of democracy and belief in the power of people to bring about change, it can be expected that businesses and entire industries will be asked, and in some cases required by law, to improve the entire work experience (Amoah and Baum, 1997).

CONCLUSION

The sector's long-standing skill problems are the consequence of wider factors that need to be addressed if significant and lasting improvements are demanded. Therefore, for the effective utilization of enhanced levels of skills among the broad mass of the workforce, would be development of better people management systems and practices and approaches to work organization that allowed for significant levels of job enrichment.

The skills debate in hospitality, therefore, questions the oversimplification of much of the wider discussion about skills within the wider service economy. It highlights problems of simplification in analysis, which uses the nature of technical work and associated skills as a starting point. Hospitality does not fit comfortably into any of the skills typologies outlined—rather it straddles several and moves between the categories in the shape of a "postmodern amoeba." Hospitality does more than question academic classification; it also raises questions relating to the globalization of labor mar-

kets and touches on policy concerns about sustained public investment in education and training. In conclusion, this chapter does not
find ready answers to the questions that are raised. Rather, it sign-
posts a rich agenda for skills researchers to pursue within the hospitality sector. The role of HR manager becomes even more challenging in streamlining the various employers and employees in the
development of a better environment to design an efficient and
effective value delivery-system for the hospitality sector.

REFERENCES

Amoah, V.A. and Baum, T. (1997). Tourism education: Policy versus practice. *In-
ternational Journal of Contemporary Hospitality Management, 9:* 5-12.
Brown, P., Green, A., and Lauder, H. (2001). *High Skills, Globalization Competi-
tiveness and Skill Formation.* Oxford, UK: Oxford University Press.
Burns, P.M. (1997). Hard-skills, soft-skills: Undervaluing hospitality's service with
a smile. *Progress in Tourism and Hospitality Research, 3:* 239-248.
Keep, E. and Mayhew, K. (1999). *The Leisure Sector.* Skills Task Force Research
Group, Paper 6. London, UK: Department for Education and Skills.
Lashley, C. and Morrison, A. (eds.) (2000). *In Search of Hospitality.* Oxford, UK:
Butterworth-Heinemann.
Odgers, P. and Baum, T. (2001). *Benchmarking of Best Practice in Hotel Front Of-
fice.* Dublin, Ireland: CERT.
Parsons, D. and Marshall, V. (1995). *Skills, Qualifications and Utilization: A Re-
search Review.* London, UK: Department for Education and Skills.
Ritz Carlton (2007). Working at the Ritz-Carlton. Available at: http://corporate
.ritzcarlton.com/en/Careers/WorkingAt.htm.
Seymour, D. (2000). Emotional labor: A comparison between fast food and traditional service work. *International Journal of Hospitality Management, 19:* 159-
171.

SUGGESTED READING

Andrew, R., Baum, T., and Morrison, A. (2001). The lifestyle economics of small
tourism businesses. *Journal of Travel and Tourism Research, 1:* 16-25.
Ashton, T. and Green, F (1996). *Education, Training and the Global Economy.*
Cheltenham, UK: Edward Elgar.
Bradley, H., Erickson, M., Stephenson, C., and Williams, S. (2000). *Myths at Work.*
Cambridge, UK: Polity Press.

Christou, E. (2000). Management competencies for graduate trainees of hospitality and tourism programs. *Annals of Tourism Research, 27*(4): 248-260.

Coombs, R. (1985). Automation, management strategies and the labor process. In D. Knights, H. Willmott, and D. Collinson (eds.), *Job Redesign: Critical Perspectives on the Labor Process*. Aldershot, UK: Gower.

Ecotec (2001). *Sector Skills Study: Food and Drink Manufacturing*. Final report to Wiltshire and Swindon Training and Enterprise Council, Birmingham, UK: Ecotec.

Foresight (2000). *The Learning Process in 2020 Task Force, Point and Click: Learners in the ICT Driving Seat*. London, UK: Foresight/ DTI.

Further Education Funding Council (1998). *Key Skills in Further Education*. Coventry, UK: FEFC.

Guerra, D. and Peroni, G. (1991). *Occupations within the Hotel Tourist Sector within the European Community*. Berlin, Germany: CEDEFOP.

Guerrier, Y. and Deery, M. (1998). Research in hospitality human resource management and organizational behavior. *International Journal of Hospitality Management, 17:* 145-160.

Hospitality Training Foundation (1998). *Skills Shortages', Labor Turnover and Recruitment in the Hospitality Industry: A Report to the National Skills Task Force*. London, UK: HtF.

International Labor Organization (1979). *Tasks to Jobs: Developing a Modular System of Training for Hotel Occupations*. Geneva, Switzerland: ILO.

Jenson, J. (1989). The talents of women, the skills of men: Flexible specialization and women. In S. Wood (ed.), *The Transformation of Work* (pp. 141-154). London, UK: Unwin Hyman.

Noon, M. and Blyton, P. (1995). *The Realities of Work*. Basingstoke, UK: Macmillan.

Pender, L. and Baum, T. (2000). Have the frills really left the airline industry? *International Journal of Tourism Research, 2*(6): 423-436.

Riley (1996). *Human Resource Management in the Hospitality and Tourism Industry,* 2nd edition, Oxford, UK: Butterworth-Heinemann.

Riley, M., Ladkin, A., and Szivas, E. (2002). *Tourism Employment: Analysis and Planning*. Clevedon, UK: Channel View Publications.

Ritzer, G. (1993). *The McDonaldization of Society*. Thousand Oaks, CA: Pine Forge Press.

Shaw, G. and Williams, A. (1994). *Critical Issues in Tourism: A Geographical Perspective*. Oxford, UK: Blackwell.

Sturdy, A. (1992). Clerical consent: Shifting work in the insurance office. In A. Sturdy, D. Knights, and H. Willmott (eds.), *Skill and Consent, Contemporary Studies in the Labor Process*. London, UK: Routledge.

Tas, R.E. (1988). Teaching future managers. *Cornell Hotel and Restaurant Administration Quarterly, 29*(2): 41-43.

Tesco (1999). *Critical Success Factors*. London, UK: Tesco plc.

Thomas, R. and Long, J. (2001). Tourism and economic regeneration: The role of skills development. *International Journal of Tourism Research, 3:* 229-240.

Warhurst, C., Nickson, D., Witz, A., and Cullen, A.M. (2000). Aesthetic labor in interactive service work: Some case study evidence from the new Glasgow. *Service Industries Journal, 20*(3): 1-18.

Wood, R.C. (1997). *Working in Hotels and Catering,* 2nd edition, London, UK: Routledge.

Chapter 10

Emotional Labor
Among the Frontline Employees
of the Hotel Industry in India

Sajith K. Augustine
Binoy Joseph

INTRODUCTION

"Now hiring smiling faces!"
"Friendly people wanted!"

These are typical "help wanted" ads that can be found everywhere in the hospitality industry. Whereas farms or factories are hiring "hands" or "heads," hospitality companies want to hire "people." The spirit of the hospitality industry is not only "getting a job done," but it also involves getting the job done with the right attitude, with the right degree of sincerity, and with the right amount of concern for the guests. Every company in the hospitality industry requires that employees, while interacting with customers, display certain types of emotions such as friendliness, cheerfulness, warmth, enthusiasm, or confidence.

Employers are very meticulous in selecting frontline employees in a hospitality industry because the interaction between the service provider and customer is the core of the service experiences that influence customers' perceptions of service quality. So it is necessary for managers or employers to regulate or manage employees' behavior or emotional expressions to ensure service quality. A common belief held by many employers is that a high correlation exists between em-

Global Cases on Hospitality Industry
© 2008 by The Haworth Press, Taylor & Francis Group. All rights reserved.
doi:10.1300/5923_10

ployees' smiling faces and increasing revenue (Ash, 1984; Rafaeli and Sutton, 1989). Displays of friendliness and enthusiasm, for example, are thought to increase customer satisfaction, improve sales immediately, and result in increased repeat business and financial success, ultimately (Hochschild, 1983; Rafaeli and Sutton, 1989). As a result, even when facing difficult customers, employees are still expected by the company to do what it takes to change the situation into a positive experience. Negative emotional displays are prohibited, and positive emotional displays are required. So it is necessary that the employees in the hospitality industry should be capable of displaying certain emotions and suppressing some other emotions.

Emotional labor is a crucial factor in the service industry, and in India, service industries, especially hospitality industry, has great significance to the economy. As the economy progresses, a higher percentage of the gross domestic product (GDP) comes from service sector, and it is true in the case of India too. In India, services sector accounts for 49 percent of the national product, and is growing by 7 percent annually. The hospitality industry in particular is experiencing a rapid growth rate, outperforming the GDP growth rate. Moreover, India earns a significant amount of money from tourism, and this facet of the hospitality industry is very crucial in earning substantial foreign earnings. The tourist inflows have risen by more than 26 percent (April to August 2004) and, more important, tourist spending is also higher. As a result, another record year for the tourist sector is expected. The cost of leadership and the service quality of the industry have much to do with this, and it gives India a competitive advantage over other nations. Emotional labor is one of the main factors that determines the perception of service quality, and, as mentioned earlier, the interaction between the service provider and customer is the core of service experiences that influences customers' perceptions of service quality.

After the literature review in the area of emotional labor it has been found that no previous studies have been done on emotional labor in the Indian context. This study's intent is to fill the lacunae in the emotional labor research in India. In this chapter the relationship between affectivity and emotional labor will be examined, as will the influence of emotional labor on job satisfaction and emotional exhaustion in the Indian context. The study has been done in Kochi, Kerala, a southern state in India.

THE SERVICE CONTEXT

According to the services management literature, the concept of emotional labor has particular relevance to service encounters for several reasons (Bowen and Schneider, 1988; Bowen et al., 1990, Brown et al., 1991). Frontline service personnel are situated at the organization-customer interface, and, thus, they represent the organization to customers. Service transactions often involve face-to-face interactions between service agents and customers. Given the uncertainty created by customer participation in the service encounter, such encounters often have a dynamic and emergent quality. The services rendered during an encounter are relatively intangible, thus making it difficult for customers to evaluate service quality. These four factors place a premium on the difficulty for customers to evaluate service quality. These four factors place a premium on the behavior of the service agent during the encounter, and this behavior often strongly affects customers' perceptions of product quality, both of goods and services (Bowen et al., 1989).

LITERATURE REVIEW

Emotional Labor

When the job roles require jobholders to display particular emotions and suppress others, jobholders do their own emotion management for a wage. Hochschild (1983) termed this regulation of one's emotions to comply with occupational or organizational norms as "emotional labor." She defined emotional labor as the management of feeling to manipulate ones physical expressions such as facial expressions and therefore emotional labor is sold for a wage. Therefore it has an exchange value (Hochschild, 1983).

Across a number of occupational roles, the act of expressing socially relevant emotions (Ashforth and Humphrey, 1993) during service transactions is the basis for emotional labor. Employees perform emotional labor when they regulate their emotional display in an attempt to meet organizationally based expectations specific to their roles. Such expectations determine not only the content and range of emotions to be displayed (Hochschild, 1983), but also the frequency, intensity, and the duration that such emotions should be exhibited (Morris and Feldman, 1996, 1997).

Emotional Labor Characteristics

According to Hochschild (1983), jobs involving emotional labor possess three characteristics: they require the workers to make facial or voice contact with the public, they require the worker to produce an emotional state in the client or customer, and they provide the employer with an opportunity to exert some control over the emotional activities of workers (Hochschild, 1983).

Hochschild (1983) argued that service providers and customers share a set of expectations about the nature of emotions that should be displayed during the service encounter. These expectations are a function of societal norms, occupational norms, and organizational norms. Rafaeli and Sutton (1989) and Ekman (1973) referred to such norms as display rules, which are shared expectations about which emotions ought to be expressed and which ought to be disguised (Ekman, 1973). Display rules are learned norms regarding when and how emotion should be expressed in public (Ekman, 1972).

The service industry in general, and the hospitality industry in particular, implement display rules to regulate employees' behavior. Based on these display rules, service providers are expected to act friendly and upbeat and to disguise anger and disgust, even toward annoying customers. Furthermore, employees must often relinquish part of their independence to the control of their company, including such compliances as wearing uniforms, and the regulation of their mannerisms, body language, and emotional expressions (Paules, 1991). The purpose is to ensure that employees will project the desired image of the company to the public, and that this image will elicit the desired response satisfaction and continued patronage from consumers.

SERVICE ACTING

Hochschild's (1983) emotional management perspective of emotional labor is based on the "acting" that service providers perform. Based on the dramaturgical perspective of social interactions, Hochschild theorized that service is a "show" in which the service

provider is an "actor," the customer is the "audience," and the work setting is the stage (Grandey, 1999). The workplace (restaurant) provides the setting and context that allows actors (waitstaff) to perform for audiences (diners). The interaction between actors and audiences is based on their mutual definition of the setting, which can be interpreted as occupational or organizational norms or display rules. In expressing the desired emotions, employees may experience emotional dissonance. This occurs when feelings differ from expressed emotions, owing to incompatibility between organizationally based expectations and actual feelings held by the workers (Morris and Feldman, 1996; Zerbe, 2000).

Acting Mechanisms

Researchers proposed that employees perform emotional labor through three types of acting mechanisms: surface acting, deep acting, and genuine acting (Hochschild, 1983; Ashforth and Humphrey, 1993). Hochschild's (1983) groundbreaking study found that workers dealt with this dissonance either by simply altering their displayed feelings (surface acting) or by "conjuring up" the appropriate feelings within themselves (deep acting). It should be noted that emotional labor does not always involve or lead to emotional dissonance (Zerbe, 2000). Indeed, both Ashforth and Humphrey (1993) and Morris and Feldman (1997) explicitly recognize that workers may genuinely feel the emotions displayed. In such cases, emotional labor has more to do with managing the appropriate emotions rather than faking (i.e., expressing unfelt emotions).

Surface Acting

Surface acting involves employees simulating emotions that are not actually felt, by changing their outward appearances (facial expression, gestures, or voice tone) when exhibiting required emotions. The use of surface acting does not mean that the agent experiences no emotion; it means that the displayed emotion differs from the felt emotion. Using the surface-acting technique, people alter the outward expression of emotion in the service of altering their inner feelings. Surface acting is the form of acting typically discussed as impression management.

Deep Acting

Another acting technique is deep acting. Deep acting occurs when employees' feelings do not fit the situation; they then use their training or past experience to work up appropriate emotions. In deep acting one attempts to actually experience or feel the emotions that one wishes to display. In deep acting, feelings are actively induced, suppressed, or shaped.

Unlike surface acting, deep acting involves changing inner feelings by altering something more than outward appearance. In surface acting, feelings are changed from the "outside in," whereas feelings are changed from the "inside out" in deep acting (Hochschild, 1983). Employees use their training or past experiences to help conjure up appropriate emotions or responses (empathy, cheerfulness) for a given scene (Kruml and Geddes, 2000). By practicing deep acting, emotions are actively induced, suppressed, or shaped.

Genuine Acting

As Hochschild's (1983) acting paradigm rests on the assumption that service providers are making efforts to actually feel the emotions they are displaying, many scholars claim that Hochschild ignores the instances whereby one spontaneously and genuinely experiences and expresses the expected emotion without exerting any effort (Ashforth and Humphrey, 1993). Therefore, genuine acting is used to imply the situation in which employees spontaneously experience and express the same emotions (Ashforth and Humphrey, 1993). Emotions are displayed with very little effortful prompting. However, Kruml and Geddes (2000) argued that these assertions about Hochschild's acting classification are incorrect because she described the genuinely expressed emotions of service employees as passive deep acting or genuine acting (Kruml and Geddes, 2000).

CONSEQUENCES OF EMOTIONAL LABOR

Ashforth and Humphrey (1993) described emotional labor as a double-edged sword. On the one hand, it can facilitate task performance by regulating interactions and precluding interpersonal problems. On the other hand, it can impair performance by priming expec-

tations of good service that cannot be met (Ashforth and Humphrey, 1993).

Negative Consequences

It has been proven that a clear correlation exists between one's emotional state and one's physical state. Laboratory research suggests that efforts to display positive emotions or suppress negative emotions often lead to patterns of physiological response that presage somatic illness (Schaubroeck and Jones, 2000).

In the emotional labor literature, substantial research in this field addresses unfavorable outcomes. The most often cited outcomes are burnout (Hochschild, 1983; Morris and Feldman, 1996) and job dissatisfaction (Morris and Feldman, 1996; Grandey, 1999; Wharton, 1993). Other impacts on the individual's psychological well-being are poor self-esteem, depression, cynicism, role alienation, and self-alienation (Ashforth and Humphrey, 1993; Wharton, 1993).

Hochschild (1983) theorized about the consequences of emotional labor based on service providers' capacity to strike a balance between the requirements of the self and the demands of the work role. Sustained performance of emotional labor may engender a fusion of self and work role, an estrangement between self and work role that comes at the expense of the self, or an estrangement between self and work role that comes at the expense of the work role (Hochschild, 1983).

The fusion of self and work role can be seen as the service providers' inability to depersonalize and detach themselves from the work roles. The estrangement between oneself and the work role is often presented in the forms of emotive dissonance or in authenticity, which can be seen as a result of surface acting.

Hochschild (1983) suggested that emotive dissonance is most harmful to employees' psychological well-being when it comes at the expense of the self, and is less harmful when it is at the expense of the work role. When emotive dissonance comes at the expense of the self, employees blame themselves for displaying feigned emotions and feelings of in authenticity. Thereafter, this estrangement of oneself leads to negative consequences such as depression (Ashforth and Humphrey, 1993), drug or alcohol abuse (Hochschild, 1983), and low self-efficacy (Seeman, 1991).

Antithetically, when emotive dissonance comes at the expense of the work role, employees attribute this false emotion or inauthentic expression to the demands of the job rather than to the desires of the self (Wharton, 1999), and thus it may be less harmful in terms of their psychological well-being.

Some of the negative consequences of emotional labor have received empirical support. Morris and Feldman (1997) found that greater emotive dissonance, which is a form of estrangement of self and work role, is significantly associated with increased emotional exhaustion and decreased job satisfaction. Similar relationships between emotive dissonance, job satisfaction, and emotional exhaustion are found in Abraham's (1998) research work.

Positive Consequences

Although substantial literature on emotional labor implies negative consequences, some researchers have suggested positive consequences for both organizations and individuals. For an organization, regulating employees' emotional display in a highly scripted manner can ensure task effectiveness and service quality (Ashforth and Humphrey, 1993), and increase sales and repeated business (Rafaeli and Sutton, 1987). For the individual, the positive aspects of emotional labor include financial rewards (e.g., tips or salaries) (Rafaeli and Sutton, 1987); increased satisfaction, security, and self-esteem (Wharton, 1993); increased self-efficacy and psychological well-being (Ashforth and Humphrey, 1993); and decreased stress (Conrad and Witte, 1994).

The reward or benefit aspect of performing emotional labor receives some empirical support. Wharton (1993) found that workers employed in jobs requiring substantial amounts of emotional labor experience higher job satisfaction and lower emotional exhaustion than other workers (Wharton, 1993). Adelman (1989) found a similar result for table servers. She concluded that, contrary to Hochschild's estrangement assumption, performing emotional labor does not adversely impact employees' psychological well-being, but enhances their job satisfaction (Adelman, 1989).

In a review of the negative and positive consequences, research in this area is still in its infancy. No universal conclusion exists about the consequences of emotional labor. Quantitative research has often found contradictory results—contradictory with one another or contradictory to predictions. A major reason for the confusion in results is a lack of clear definitions of what constitutes emotional labor. Without a clear definition of emotional labor, it is difficult to address its effects on service employees (Fisher and Ashkanasy, 2000).

Another reason for the contradictory conclusions about emotional labor's consequence is that researchers have failed to take into account the importance of individual factors. Researchers have posited that individual characteristics may play a primary role in explaining variation in the consequences (Rafaeli and Sutton, 1989). More and more researchers have recognized the importance of individual characteristics in determining the consequences of emotional labor (Refaeli and Sutton, 1989; Morris and Feldman, 1997; Jones, 1998; Wharton, 1999), and have acknowledged that the negative effects of emotional labor might be greater for some individuals than for others. As Pines (1982) noted, some service employees are unique in the way that they seem to enjoy working with people, helping meet their needs, and contribute in making the world a better place to live in.

EMOTIONAL LABOR FRAMEWORK

In earlier empirical studies, emotional labor has been conceptualized as a unidimensional construct solely concerned with the intensity and frequency of emotional displays. Researchers who employ this approach to emotional labor often separate samples into either an "emotional laborer" or a "nonemotional laborer" group. This classification creates problems since most jobs involve performing emotional labor to varying extend.

Wharton (1993) suggested that emotional labor should be treated as a multidimensional construct that delineates divergent consequences for different levels of emotional labor in different work settings. Understanding the dimensions of emotional labor would allow researchers to better differentiate emotional labor and examine its relationships with various individual and situational factors under different circumstances. The two major theoretical frameworks on the conceptualization of emotional labor are interactionist framework and dramaturgical framework.

Interactionist Framework

Morris and Feldman (1996, 1997) proposed a model of emotional labor based on the interactionist model of emotion, in which emotions are expressed and determined by the social environment. The interactionist view of emotion infers that emotion is partly socially constructed. Social factors determine the experience and expression of emotion during service transactions. Morris and Feldman (1996) conceptualized emotional labor based on the interactionist model, and defined emotional labor as the efforts in terms of planning and control needed to express organizationally relevant emotion during interpersonal transactions. Based on this definition, they proposed emotional labor as a four-dimension construct: frequency of emotional labor; attentiveness (intensity of emotions, duration of interaction); variety of emotions required; and emotive dissonance (the difference between felt emotions and expressed emotions).

Dramaturgical Framework

Recently, some researchers have constructed theories about emotional labor based on Hochschild's dramaturgical perspective of emotion management. The essence of this perspective rests on viewing customers as audiences, employees as actors, and the workplace as theaters. Therefore, by utilizing different acting techniques (surface acting, deep acting, or genuine acting), employees alter their outward appearances, behaviors, or inner emotional states to control emotional expression according to situational dictates or display rules.

Grandey (1999) asserted that theorizing emotional labor from a dramaturgical perspective can explain "how" emotion is managed (effort and control). Knowing the process and methods employees use to manage their emotions is most useful when researchers' purpose is to understand this mechanism and its relationships with other work outcomes (e.g., attitude, withdrawal behavior). Thus this dramaturgical perspective can gain utility for emotional labor theory development (Grandey, 1999).

EMOTIVE DISSONANCE AND EMOTIVE EFFORT

Kruml and Geddes (2000) identified two dimensions of emotional labor based on Hochschild's acting perspective. They developed an emotional labor scale based on three types of acting: surface acting, deep acting, and genuine acting. Factorial analysis resulted in two dimensions: emotive dissonance and emotive effort. According to Kruml and Geddes (2000), emotive dissonance represents the degree to which employees' expressed emotions align with their true feelings. Hochschild (1983) defined emotive dissonance as the difference between genuinely felt emotions and artificially feigned emotions. The dimension of emotive dissonance can capture surface and genuine deep acting as two opposite ends of a continuum (Kruml and Geddes, 2000). The more those employees adopt surface acting, the more emotive dissonance they experience. On the other hand, the more employees adopt genuine acting, the less emotive dissonance they experience.

Another dimension of emotional labor is emotive effort. Kruml and Geddes (2000) claimed that this dimension taps the domain of deep acting. Deep acting involves attempts to actually experience the emotions one is required to display.

Based on the dramaturgical perspective of emotional labor, and drawn from Grandey's (1999) and Kruml and Geddes's (2000) works, emotional labor is defined as the degree of manipulation of one's inner feelings or outward behavior to display the appropriate emotion in response to display rules or occupational norms. This working definition emphasizes the different degrees of effort employees exert to manipulate or change their emotional state and behavior (see Figure 10.1).

In the center of this theoretical model lies the construct of emotional labor. The two dimensions of emotional labor are emotive dissonance and emotive effort. In the theoretical model, the individual characteristic affectivity is treated as the antecedent of emotional labor. Affectivity represents a general tendency of an individual to experience a particular mood or to react to occurrences in a particular way or with certain emotions (Lazarus, 1993). Researchers have identified two types of affectivity: positive affectivity (PA) and negative affectivity (NA). High PA individuals experience more positive emotions, such as cheerfulness or enthusiasm. High NA individuals experience more negative emotions, such as irritation or nervousness.

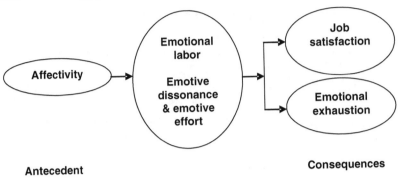

FIGURE 10.1. Theoretical Frame Work of the Study. *Source:* Modified from Chu (2002).

Researchers have suggested that affectivity is the precursor of whether a person will engage in emotional labor, or whether that labor will have a detrimental outcome (Rafaeli and Sutton, 1989; Grandey, 1999).

Concerning emotional labor and its consequences, this model gives both positive (low emotional exhaustion and high job satisfaction) and negative (high emotional exhaustion and low job satisfaction) consequences. Emotional exhaustion refers to feelings of being emotionally overextended and worn out by one's work (Maslach, 1982). Job satisfaction is defined as a pleasurable feeling that results from the perception that ones job fulfills or allows for the fulfillment of important job values. It refers to the attitude and feelings people have about their work. Positive and favorable attitudes toward the job indicate job satisfaction and negative and unfavorable attitude toward the job indicate job dissatisfaction.

RESEARCH METHODS

The relationship being examined in this study is among affectivity, emotional labor, job satisfaction, and emotional exhaustion. The hypotheses of this study based on literature review are the following: (1) employees with high positive affectivity may experience less emotive dissonance than employees with low positive affectivity, (2) employees with high negative affectivity may experience more emotive dissonance than employees with low negative affectivity, (3) employees with high positive affectivity may exert less emotive effort than employees with low positive affectivity, (4) employees with high negative affectivity may exert more emotive effort than employees with low negative affectivity, (5) employees with high emotive dissonance may experience less job satisfaction than employees with low emotive dissonance, (6) employees exerting high emotive effort may experience more job satisfaction than employees exerting low emotive effort, (7) employees with high emotive dissonance may experience more emotional exhaustion than employees with low emotive dissonance, and (8) employees exerting high emotive effort may experience less emotional exhaustion than employees exerting low emotive effort.

A sample survey was designed to test the hypotheses on the relationship among affectivity, emotional labor, job satisfaction, and emotional exhaustion. Using stratified random sampling, a study was conducted among one hundred employees, both male and female, with at least six months work experience in the food and beverages service department or front office department of four-star and five-star hotels in Kochi, Kerala. The term *employee* refers to any person working in these departments, having designations such as manager, executive, captain, steward, waiter, or assistant. Data was collected from six hotels, which belong to the four- and five-star category in Kochi. The hotels were also selected randomly. Data collection took around three to four weeks to complete. The human resources (HR) department was first approached to get permission for data collection. The questionnaires were handed over to the respondents randomly through the HR department in most of the cases, and in some cases to the front office and/or the food and beverages department. The filled questionnaires were collected from the particular department. The response rate was very high, as the researchers administered the questionnaires personally to the respondents.

MEASURES

Emotional Labor

Emotive dissonance and emotive effort, which are the two forms of emotional labor, were measured on a nineteen-item hospitality emotional labor scale by Lin Chu (2002). Emotional labor was measured on a seven-point Likert scale ranging from (1) rarely to (7) always, with no verbal labels for scale points 2 through 6.

Affectivity

Positive affectivity negative affectivity scale [PANAS] questionnaire by Watson and colleagues (1988) was used to measure the individual characteristics of positive affectivity and negative affectivity. The questionnaire had twenty items, and the affectivity was measured on a seven-point Likert scale ranging from (1) rarely to (7) always, with no verbal labels for scale points 2 through 6.

Emotional Exhaustion

Emotional exhaustion subscale of the twenty-two-item Maslach burnout inventory by Maslach and Jackson (1981), which had seven items, was used to measure emotional exhaustion. Emotional exhaustion was measured on a seven-point Likert scale ranging from (1) strongly disagree to (7) strongly agree, with no verbal labels for scale points 2 through 6 in the study.

Job Satisfaction

In the study, job satisfaction was measured using the job satisfaction scale derived from job diagnostic survey (JDS) of Hackman and Oldham (1975). It had five items, and was measured on a seven-point Likert scale ranging from (1) strongly disagree to (7) strongly agree, with no verbal labels for scale points 2 through 6.

RESULTS

The sample consisted of one hundred frontline employees, both male and female, with at least six months experience working in the food and beverages service department or in the front office of four-star and five-star hotels in Kochi, Kerala, India. After collection of research data, an analysis of the data and interpretation of the results were made (see Table 10.1).

TABLE 10.1. Descriptive Statistics of the Sample for Positive and Negative Affectivity, Emotive Dissonance and Emotive Effort, Job Satisfaction, and Emotional Exhaustion.

	Mean	Standard Deviation	Skew	Kurtosis
Positive affectivity	49.83	13.6	−.596	−.583
Negative affectivity	31.2	7.7	−.454	0.25
Emotive dissonance	39.48	9.6	0.35	−.84
Emotive effort	33.6	9.3	0.37	−.75
Job satisfaction	23.48	6.53	0.9	−.14
Emotional exhaustion	19.4	7.9	0.68	−.21

Hypotheses Testing

The tabulated data has been subjected to statistical tests such as regression analysis. A summary of the regression analysis is given in Table 10.2.

Based on Table 10.2, the relationship between positive affectivity and emotive dissonance was found to be negative. Hence hypothesis (1) employees with high positive affectivity may experience less emotive dissonance than employees with low positive affectivity was accepted ($R = 0.628$, $R^2 = 0.39$, $b = -0.462$, and beta $= -0.628$). It was also found that the gender difference is not significant in the relationship between positive affectivity and emotive dissonance.

The data from the Table 10.2 depicts the relationship between negative affectivity and emotive dissonance to be positive ($R = 0.404$, $R^2 = 0.163$, $b = 0.504$, and beta $= -0. 0.404$). Therefore, hypothesis (2) employees with high negative affectivity may experience more emotive dissonance than employees with low negative affectivity was accepted. High negative affectivity employees have more negative emotions and will experience more emotive dissonance when they have been asked to display positive emotion. It was also found that being female has an advantage in the relationship between negative affectivity and emotive dissonance. Females experience less emotive dissonance when compared to males.

TABLE 10.2. Regression Analysis

Independent variable(s)	Dependent variable	R	R²	B Value	Beta value
Positive affectivity	Emotive dissonance	0.628	0.39	−0.462	−0.628
Negative affectivity	Emotive dissonance	0.404	0.163	0.504	0.404
Positive affectivity	Emotive effort	0.571	0.326	−0.406	−0.571
Negative affectivity	Emotive effort	0.475	0.226	0.572	0.475
Emotive dissonance	Job satisfaction	0.421	0.177	−0.296	−0.421
Emotive effort	Job satisfaction	0.237	0.056	−0.173	−0.237
Emotive dissonance	Emotional exhaustion	0.362	0.131	.309	0.362

Hypothesis (3) employees with high positive affectivity may exert less emotive effort than employees with low positive affectivity was accepted, as the relationship between positive affectivity and emotive effort was found to be negative from the above data with ($R = 0.571$, $R^2 = 0.326$, $b = -0.406$, and beta $= -0.571$). It was also found out that the gender difference is not significant in the relationship between positive affectivity and emotive effort.

Hypothesis (4) employees with high negative affectivity may exert more emotive effort than employees with low negative affectivity hypothesis was accepted, as the Table 10.2 shows the relationship between negative affectivity and emotive effort to be positive with ($R = 0.475$, $R^2 = 0.226$, $b = 0.572$, and beta $= 0.475$). It was also found that the gender differences did not have any significance in the relationship between negative affectivity and emotive effort.

As per the data from Table 10.2, the relationship between emotive dissonance and job satisfaction was found to be negative ($R = 0.421$, $R^2 = 0.177$, $b = -0.296$, and beta $= -0.421$), thus hypothesis (5) employees with high emotive dissonance may experience less job satisfaction than employees with low emotive dissonance was accepted. It was also found that the gender difference had significance in the relationship between emotive dissonance and job satisfaction: being female has got an advantage in the relationship between emotive dissonance and job satisfaction. Females experience more job satisfaction when compared to males.

Hypothesis (6) employees exerting high emotive effort may experience more job satisfaction than employees exerting low emotive effort was rejected, as the relationship between emotive effort and job satisfaction was found to be negative with ($R = 0.237$, $R^2 = 0.056$, $b = -0.173$, and beta = -0.237). It was also found that the difference in gender is not significant in the relationship between emotive effort and job satisfaction.

The relationship between emotive dissonance and emotional exhaustion was found to be positive in Table with ($R = 0.362$, $R^2 = 0.131$, $b = .309$, and beta = $.362$). Hypothesis (7) employees with high emotive dissonance may experience more emotional exhaustion than employees with low emotive dissonance was accepted. It was also found that the difference in gender is significant in the relationship between emotive dissonance and emotional exhaustion: being female has an advantage in the relationship between emotive dissonance and emotional exhaustion. Females experience less emotional exhaustion when compared to males.

Hypothesis (8) employees exerting high emotive effort may experience less emotional exhaustion than employees exerting low emotive effort hypothesis was rejected, as the data from Table 10.2 shows that the relationship between emotive effort and emotional exhaustion is not found significant with ($R = 0.362$, $R^2 = 0.131$, $b = 0.309$, and beta = 0.362).

DISCUSSION

The study was aimed at providing a better understanding of the relationship among affectivity, emotional labor, job satisfaction, and emotional exhaustion. Research studies have highlighted the importance of affectivity as a major contributing factor of emotive effort and emotive dissonance, which are the two forms of emotional labor in individuals. The relationship between positive affectivity and emotive dissonance was found to be negative, and it was also found that the relationship between negative affectivity and emotive dissonance was found to be positive. The relationship between positive affectivity and emotive effort was found to be negative, and negative affectivity was positively related with emotive effort. The relationship obtained between affectivity and emotional labor in this study substantiates earlier studies by Lin Chu (2002) and Morris and Fieldman (1996).

The more positive affectivity employees have the less emotive dissonance they will experience when the job requires employees to display positive emotions. They can express it very naturally. High positive affectivity employees experience less emotive dissonance because their personalities and job characteristics fit together well. This low emotive dissonance is an outcome of a good fit. This result corresponds to what Rafaeli and Sutton (1987) suggested, that if a good fit exists between individual characteristics and job characteristics, employees experience more emotional harmony than emotional dissonance. Individuals may be better suited for their position when expected emotional behavior on their jobs and their own predisposition to experience the same type of emotions converge. High positive affectivity employees can display more genuine positive emotions with less effort than can low positive affectivity employees. In other words, high positive affectivity employees do not need to use "deep acting" to have a positive emotional expression; they can enact genuine hospitality naturally and easily. As a result, they are very popular in the hospitality industry. High negative affectivity employees tend to use deep acting to call up desired positive emotions.

This study provides a better understanding of how employees perform emotional labor, and how this labor affects employees' work outcomes. Results of this study reveal that the consequences of emotional labor can be either positive or negative, depending on how it is performed. The relationship between emotive dissonance and job satisfaction was found to be negative, and the relationship between emotive effort and job satisfaction was also negative. Employees who experience emotive dissonance are not expressing genuine emotions. They are faking the emotions, and this continued faking will lead to job dissatisfaction. Rutter and Fielding (1988) found that the perceived need to suppress the genuinely felt emotions in the workplace is negatively associated with job satisfaction. Employees display positive emotions by putting in more effort. This will make them feel that they are putting in more effort and hence will lead to job dissatisfaction. The previous studies conducted by Rutter and Fielding (1988) and Morris and Fieldman (1996) also showed a significant negative relationship between emotive effort and job satisfaction. In performing emotive effort, workers must expend energy to display the required emotions, and this reduces job satisfaction.

The relationship between emotive dissonance and emotional exhaustion was found to be positive, and it corroborates the findings of the earlier studies by Brotheridge and Grandey (2002), Brotheridge and Lee (2003), Glomb and Tews (2004), Kruml and Geddes (2000), Gross and Levenson (1997), and Pennebaker and Beall (1986). The reason for emotional exhaustion is the conflict between the predisposition of the individual and the demands of the job. Emotive dissonance is a conflict between the felt emotions and the expressed emotions, and hence it will lead to emotional exhaustion. Emotional exhaustion stems largely from the effort required to hide one's true feelings or to pretend to feel those that were expressed (Brotheridge and Lee, 2003).

The relationship between emotive effort and emotional exhaustion was not found significant. Only the previous study by Brotheridge and Grandey (2002) had a similar result. Hochschild (1983) argued that doing "emotion work" was a way of decreasing a state of emotional dissonance and may also result in a feeling of accomplishment if the performance is effective. Thus, deep acting (emotive effort) might not relate to emotional exhaustion because it minimizes the tension of dissonance.

Employees in the hospitality industry are paid to be nice. The ability to be consistently nice to strangers requires incredible effort. When such effort succeeds, it is a remarkable accomplishment. Emotional labor should be taken seriously, since it affects customer satisfaction, customer loyalty, and, eventually, organizational financial performance. Emotional labor deserves hospitality researchers' attention. People performing emotional labor deserve the public's respect. Beyond this, the study could make the hotel industry aware of their employees' emotional contribution to the organization's performance.

Implications of the Study

This study found that emotional labor is significantly related to affectivity, which is a personal factor. From a practical perspective, at the organizational level, this impacts the selection of employees in hospitality industry. This study found that high positive affectivity employees could perform emotional labor in a genuine and natural way. For jobs that require high levels of emotional labor, training also plays an important role. Providing training programs to develop necessary skills to perform emotional labor may require more concerted efforts by organizations than reliance on selection. If companies could provide appropriate training that would help employees learn to deep act emotional labor, employees could learn how to provide sincere hospitality. They would also gain a sense of satisfaction from their ability to act out emotional labor. As more and more workers of all kinds find themselves with few opportunities other than service employment, organizations should shift their attention to create the conditions for satisfying work.

Limitations of the Study

One limitation of the study is, while concentrating on the dynamics of personal characteristics, emotional labor, and its outcomes, the influence of situational factors such as training, frequency of customer interactions, variety of emotional displays, and duration of the interactions between the employees and customers in the way employees perform emotional labor was not accounted for. These factors also influence emotional exhaustion that is experienced by employees, and it was not considered in this study. Here no effort was done to find a fit between the personal characteristics and the consequences of emotional labor and the influence of personal characteristics on emotional exhaustion.

RECOMMENDATIONS FOR FURTHER RESEARCH

The present study opens the doors for a wider and deeper study of the relationship among personal characteristics, emotional labor, and work outcomes of employees in a hospitality industry by accounting for the various personal characteristics and work outcomes and the situational factors of the units of study. It would be interesting to study how the situational factors—that is, the variety of emotional displays, and the presence of organizational display rules—influence the previously discussed relationships. Future studies can be done on the influence of frequency, intensity, and duration of emotional displays on emotional labor in the Indian context. The moderating effect of job autonomy, social support, self-identity, etc. in the relationship between emotional labor and work outcomes need to be studied in India. This study failed to find out the relationship between emotive effort and emotional exhaustion. Future studies should concentrate on this area, to explore the relationship. The impact of individual factors such as empathy on emotional labor also needs to be studied in the Indian context. This study is done in four- and five-star hotels, which is a part of hospitality industry. Further research on emotional labor can be done in other categories of hotels and other industries in the service sector in India. A layered understanding and investigation of the concepts under study will enable a more comprehensive analysis of the relations among them.

REFERENCES

Abraham, R. (1998). Emotional dissonance in organizations: Antecedents, consequences, and moderators. *Genetic, Social, and General Psychology Monographs, 124:* 229-246.

Adelman, P.K. (1989). *Emotional Labor and Employee Well-Being.* Unpublished Doctoral Dissertation, University of Michigan, Ann Arbor, Michigan.

Ash, M.K. (1984). *Mary Kay on People Management.* New York: Warner Books.

Ashforth, B.E. and Humphery, R.H. (1993). Emotional labor in service roles: The influence of identity. *The Academy of Management Review, 18:* 188-115.

Bowen, D.E., Chase, R.B., Cummings, T.G., et al. (1990). *Service Management Effectiveness: Balancing Strategy, Organization and Human Resources, Operations and Marketing.* San Francisco: Jossey- Bass.

Bowen, D.E. and Schneider, B. (1988). Service and marketing management: Implications for organizational behavior. In B.M. Staw and L.L. Cummings (eds.), *Research in Organizational Behavior* (pp. 1-42). Greenwich, CT: JAI Press.

Bowen, D.E., Siehl, C., and Schneider, B. (1989). A framework for analyzing customer service orientations in manufacturing. *Academy of Management Review, 14:* 75-95.

Brotheridge, C.M. and Grandey, A. (2002). Emotional labor and burnout: Comparing two perspectives of people work. *Journal of Vocational Behavior, 60:* 17-39.

Brotheridge, C.M. and Lee, R.T (2003). Development and validation of emotional; labor scale. *Journal of Occupational and Organizational Psychology, 76:* 365-379.

Brown, S.W., Gummesson, E., Edvardsson, B., and Gustavsson, B (1991). *Service Quality: Multidisciplinary and Multinational Perspectives.* Lanham, MD: Lexington Books.

Chu, L. (2002); The effects of emotional labor on employee work outcomes. Unpublished doctoral dissertation, College of Human Resource Education, Virginia Tech, Blacksburg, Virginia

Conrad, C. and Witte, K. (1994). Is emotional expression repression oppression? Myths of organizational affective regulation. In S. Deetz (ed.), *Communication Yearbook,* Volume 17 (pp. 417-428). Thousand Oaks, CA: Sage Publications.

Ekman, P. (1972). Universals and cultural differences in facial expressions of emotion. In J. Cole (ed.), *Nebraska Symposium on Motivation 1971,* Volume 19 (pp. 207-283). Lincoln, NE: University of Nebraska Press.

Ekman, P. (1973). Cross culture studies of facial expression. In. P. Ekman (ed.), *Darwin and Facial Expression: A Century of Research in Review* (pp. 169-222). New York: Academic Press.

Fisher, C. D. and Ashkanasy, N. M. (2000). The emerging role of emotions in work life: An introduction. *Journal of Organizational Behavior, 21:* 123-129.

Glomb, T.M. and Tews, M.J. (2004). Emotional labor: A conceptualization and scale development. *Journal of Vocational Behavior, 64:* 1-23.

Grandey, A. (1999). *The Effects of Emotional Labor: Employee Attitudes, Stress and Performance.* Unpublished Doctoral Dissertation, Colorado State University, Fort Collins, Colorado.

Gross, J. and Levenson, R. (1997). Hiding feelings: The acute effects of inhibiting negative and positive emotions. *Journal of Abnormal Psychology, 106*(1): 95-103.

Hackman, J.R. and Oldham, G.R. (1975). Development of the job diagnostic survey. *Journal of Applied Psychology, 60:* 574-580.

Hochschild, A. (1983). *The Managed Heart: Commercialization of Human Feeling.* Berkeley, CA: University of California Press.

Jones, J. R. (1998). *An Examination of the Emotional Labor Construct and its Effects on Employee Outcomes.* Unpublished Doctoral Dissertation, University of Nebraska, Lincoln, Nebraska.

Kruml, S.M. and Geddes, D. (2000). Exploring the dimensions of emotional labor: The heart of Hochschild's work. *Management Communication Quarterly, 14:* 8-49.

Lazarus, R.S. (1993). From psychological stress to the emotions: A history of changing outlooks. In L.W. Porter and M. Rosenzweig (eds.), *Annual Review of Psychology,* Volume 44 (pp. 1-2). Palo Alto, CA: Annual Reviews.

Lin Chu, K.H. (2002). *The Effects of Emotional Labor on Employee Work Outcomes.* Unpublished Doctoral Dissertation, College of Human Resource Education, Virginia Tech, Blacksburg, Virginia.

Maslach, C. (1982). *Burnout: The Cost of Caring.* Englewood Cliffs, NJ: Prentice-Hall.

Maslach, C. and Jackson, S.E. (1981). The measurement of experienced burnout. *Journal of Occupational Behavior, 2:* 99-113.

Morris, J. and Feldman, D. (1996). The dimensions, antecedents and consequences of emotional labor. *The Academy of Management Review, 21*(4): 986-1010.

Morris, J. and Feldman, D. (1997). Managing emotion's in the workplace. *Journal of Managerial Issues, 9:* 257-274.

Paules, G.F. (1991). *Dishing it Out: Power and Resistance among Waitresses in a New Jersey Restaurant.* Philadelphia, PA: Temple University Press.

Pennebaker, J. W. and Beall, S (1986). Confronting a traumatic event: Toward an understanding of inhibition and disease. *Journal of Abnormal Psychology, 58:* 528-537.

Pines, A. (1982). Helpers' motivation and the burnout syndrome. In T.A. Wills (ed.), *Basic Processes in Helping Relationships* (pp. 453-475). San Diego, CA: Academic Press.

Rafaeli, A. and Sutton, R. (1987). Expression of emotion as part of the work role. *Academy of Management Review, 12:* 23-37.

Rafaeli, A. and Sutton, R. (1989). The expression of emotion in organizational life. In B.M. Staw and L.L. Cummings (eds.), *Research in Organizational Behavior* (pp. 1-42). Greenwich, CT: JAI Press.

Rutter, D.R. and Fielding, P.J. (1988). Sources of occupational stress: An examination of British prison officers. *Work and Stress, 2:* 292-299.

Schaubroeck, J. and Jones, J. R. (2000). Antecedents of work place emotional labor dimensions and moderators of their effects on physical symptoms. *Journal of Organizational Behavior, 21:* 163-183.

Seeman, M. (1991). Alienation and Anomie. In J. Robison, P. Shaver, and L. Wrightsman (eds.), *Measures of Personality and Social Psychological Attitudes* (pp. 291-295). San Diego, CA: Academic Press.

Watson, D., Clark, L.A., and Tellegen, A. (1988). Development and validation of brief measures of positive and negative affect: The PANAS scales. *Journal of Personality and Social Psychology, 54:* 1063-1070.

Wharton, A. (1993). The affective consequences of service work. *Work and Occupations, 20:* 205-232.

Wharton, A. (1999). The psychosocial consequences of emotional labor. *The Annals of the American Academy of Political and Social Science, 561*(1): 158-176.

Zerbe, W.J. (2000). Emotional dissonance and employee well-being. In N.M. Ashkanasy, C.E.J. Hartel, and W. J. Zerbe (eds.), *Emotions in the Workplace: Research, Theory, and Practice* (pp. 189-214). Westport, CT: Quorum/Greenwood.

Chapter 11

Understanding the Impact of Situational Components in Hospitality Retailing: The Case of Irish Theme Pubs

Barry O'Mahony
John Hall
Wayne Binney

INTRODUCTION AND RESEARCH TRADITION

The impact of situational components on consumer choice has long been recognized as an important aspect of retail marketing. The theoretical foundation of situational influences dates back to Lewin's field theory (Lewin 1935, 1936, 1938, 1951), which concluded that human motivations, intentions, and behavior are a function of the interaction between consumers and situations. In Lewin's view, situation was a dual construct comprised of the "objective" world outside of the individual, which could be described in terms of physical and social variables, and the "subjective" world or psychological environment, which referred to the individual's perception and constructions of the physical environment described in terms of psychological variables.

Frederiksen (1972) argues, however, that since not all aspects of a situation affect behavior, it is pertinent to focus only on those aspects of the situation that do influence behavior. Consequently, he defined consumption situations as social surroundings, physical surroundings, and task definition.

Belk (1974) refined situation to include a temporal dimension defining situation as a discrete time and place occupied by one or more

Global Cases on Hospitality Industry
© 2008 by The Haworth Press, Taylor & Francis Group. All rights reserved.
doi:10.1300/5923_11

persons. More recent studies also give credence to time, proposing that situation entails all of those factors particular to a time and place of observation that have a demonstrable and systematic effect on current behavior (Lai 1991; Quester and Smart 1998).

The research reported by Foxall (1983, 1990, 1996, 1997a,b), Foxall and Greenley (1998, 1999), and Leek and colleagues (2000) extends our understanding of situation, concluding that situational influences on consumer behavior can be comprehended in terms of the consumer behavior setting, consumption history, utilitarian reinforcement, informational reinforcement, and aversive consequences. Indeed, Leek and colleagues (2000) include all of these dimensions in their summary of situation, indicating that the consumer situation is the point in time and space at which a particular consumption history and a specific consumer setting intersect, providing opportunities for the individual to gain from purchasing, consuming, or avoiding either or both of these actions and their consequences. In their discussion, the consumer's consumption history refers to previous buying behavior for the product concerned and its positive (rewarding or reinforcing) and negative (punishing or costly) outcomes. Thus the consumer behavior setting, experience, and its consequences, transform the social and physical stimuli that comprise the setting into environmental cues.

Three types of situations are relevant to marketing strategy: the communication situation, the purchase situation, and the consumption situation (Hansen 1972; Belk 1979; Lai 1991). A review of literature has found that an extensive body of research utilizes these variables to evaluate consumers' attitudes toward products. These include investigations of the effects of situational variation on consumer purchase intentions (Richins and Bloch 1986) and brand choice (Chow et al. 1990) as well as the promotion and consumption of alcoholic and nonalcoholic beverages (Sandell 1968; Belk 1974; Bearden and Woodside 1977; Woodside et al. 1977; Lai 1991; Quester and Smart 1998; Hall and Lockshin 2000; Olsen and Thach 2001; Hall et al. 2002).

The review found, however, that although some studies have been conducted into the effects of situational components within the service sector, the majority of these studies focus on physical issues, such as the design of shopping precincts and store layout (Donovan and Rossiter 1982; McGoldrick and Pieros 1998; Turley and Millman

2000; Turley and Furgate 1992), or on financial services (Srivastava 1980; Zeithaml et al. 1990). As a result, a research gap exists in that the influence of situation on consumption within a pub setting has not been adequately investigated.

Over the past decade, Irish-theme pubs have been exceedingly popular and profitable entities within the leisure and hospitality sector, both at national and international levels (Goldsmith 1996; Walk-up 1997; Brown and Patterson 2000; West 2001). Moreover, a recent UK–based study proposes that the phenomenal success of Irish-theme pubs can be attributed to the added value experience that is provided by the environment in which the product is sold (Knowles and Howley 2000).

Having discussed the research tradition, this paper will provide a brief background to the conceptual frameworks of situational research. The aims and research questions are then presented and the research methodology is described. The results are presented and discussed, and the implications of the research for marketing practitioners and for further research are highlighted.

RESEARCH ORIENTATION

As noted in the introduction, no previous studies have been conducted into the influence of situation within Irish-theme pubs. Consequently, a research framework that could incorporate both physical and social aspects as well as consumer perceptions of the theme pub environment was sought. Bitner's "servicescape" model was one possible approach (Bitner 1990). In Bitner's evaluation of service encounters (1992, p. 58) she coined the term "servicescape" to describe the "... built environment (i.e. the manmade, physical surroundings as opposed to the natural or social environment)."

However, research by Brown and Patterson (2000, p. 658) concludes that theme pubs are all about "capturing the essence of the represented phenomenon" in both a physical and sociocultural sense. Their study highlights the strong social dimension of theme pubs, a feature that is commensurate with the nature of leisure services in general. A major feature of this social dimension is the interaction between various entities, including employees and customers as well as customers with other customers (O'Mahony 2002). This type of consumer interaction is accounted for in the servuction model, a services marketing framework that is comprised of two principal components: the invisible aspects of service that occur backstage and the visible or front-stage dimensions (Langeard et al. 1981).

In 1995, Berman and Evans (1995) incorporated the dimensions of servicescape and servuction in a model developed to investigate service-based retail encounters. Hoffman and Turley (2002) subsequently modified this framework to incorporate a number of theoretical aspects of situation that can influence the consumer experience. The model, which Hoffman and Turley titled the *atmospherics* model, was deemed appropriate to guide this study because many of the dimensions incorporated in the model have a significant influence on attracting, serving, and satisfying the needs of on-premises consumers (Hoffman and Turley 2002), which is an important aspect of hospitality retailing.

COMPONENTS OF THE HOFFMAN
AND TURLEY MODEL

The principal components of the Hoffman and Turley (2002) model are the visible and invisible situational components also referred to as atmospherics. An outline of these dimensions is provided in the following sections.

Invisible Atmospherics

In the Hoffman and Turley model, the term "invisible atmospherics" incorporates two elements. First is the invisible organization and systems, which involves managing the environment, the provision of goods and services, and the selection, training, and management of personnel. This encompasses various management styles as well as the often extensive documented management procedures that form part of the system of management. These procedures can vary greatly between different entities within the hospitality retail sector, especially in the provision of food and alcoholic beverages. At McDonald's restaurants, for example, the major management focus is on implementing a rigid set of management principles, recipes, and guidelines in order to ensure that both the product and service are uniform and consistent. It is important to note, however, that consumers are often not aware of this controlling influence.

The second element of the invisible environment includes intangible situational influences, such as perceptions of service quality, friendliness of staff, and general atmosphere. These dimensions have also been found to be influential in the service-quality literature in which they are associated with the willingness of staff to respond to customer's needs, as well as product knowledge and competency (Zeithaml et al. 1990).

Visible Atmospherics

Visible atmospherics include the inanimate environment as well as contact personnel. In themed environments this can include colors such as known national colors (e.g., the green, white, and orange associated with Ireland), posters, artifacts, and other theme-related decorations. The pint-sized glasses used for beer in pubs in Ireland for example are currently used to reinforce the theme in Irish-theme pubs in Melbourne, a practice that does not normally occur in pubs in Australia.

Inanimate Environment

The inanimate environment includes both the exterior and the interior of the sales environment. The exterior environment in the atmospherics model operates on two levels: The first of these relates to the location of the outlet, the provision of parking, windows, colors, and signage. The second is concerned with the macroenvironment of the venue, including issues such as whether the sales environment is located within a shopping center and what kind of other businesses are in the vicinity.

The interior environment includes the overall interior environment as a whole (image), music and sounds, ambient colors, lighting, design and layout, product displays, internal signage, decorative style, and provision for patron comfort. Within Irish-theme pubs each of these components is strongly connected to the notion of authenticity (O'Mahony 2002).

Contact Personnel

The term *contact personnel* includes the number of service providers, their appearance, and skill level or ability to perform the retail task. Recognized links exist between this dimension of the atmospherics model and the "tangible" dimension of service quality outlined by Zeithaml and colleagues (1990). In the hospitality industry, in general, tangible aspects of the environment can include uniform and personal grooming with a strong emphasis on those aspects of employee presentation that relate to hygiene such as hair, makeup, and the amount of jewelry worn by contact personnel.

Customer

A central part of the model is customers and their interaction with other components of the model, including the environment and the nature and level of interaction with other customers.

Other Customers

The manner in which customers' interact as well as issues such as crowding or the lack of customer numbers is a key aspect of the hospitality retail experience.

Aims of the Study

The aim of the study was to identify and evaluate the situational components that influence consumers within Irish-theme pubs in Melbourne and to gauge the influence of each of the dimensions of the Hoffman and Turley model on customer behavior among gender and age cohorts.

METHODOLOGY

Since little research has been conducted within Irish-theme pubs, a "sequential mixed method design" approach was employed (Tashakkori and Teddlie, 1989). When using "sequential mixed method designs, the researcher conducts a qualitative phase of a study and then a separate quantitative phase, or vice versa" (Tashakkori and Teddlie,

1989, p. 46). This study began with a quantitative survey of Irish-theme-pub customers, which was designed to identify the physical and social atmospheric variables that might have an impact on attracting customers to Irish-theme pubs. Using a convenience sampling method, a quantitative questionnaire was distributed to customers in six Irish-theme pubs in Melbourne. The main focus of the investigation was the relatively new Irish-theme pubs, because these pubs were perceived to have set a particular trend in terms of situational influences. Five of these pubs were selected for the study; however, for the purpose of comparison, one of the older, established Irish pubs was also included. An important aspect of the collection of data was that customers had to be there during their leisure time. Consequently, the surveys were conducted at specific times on Friday and Saturday nights.

A further sampling consideration was that some Irish-theme pubs are located in the city of Melbourne, while others are in the suburbs. In this study three pubs were chosen from within the city of Melbourne and the other three were suburban. A nonprobability quota sample of 320 respondents was obtained from the six Irish-theme pubs. The quantitative data was used to build a profile of Irish-theme pub customers and to solicit information about the reasons why those respondents were attracted to Irish-theme pubs. It was further used to gain a demographic profile of Irish-theme pub customers; to collect data on age, gender, average spending, and frequency of visitation; and to select a broad-based, inclusive sample of respondents for a more in depth, qualitative study.

The inclusion of qualitative methods was important because few studies have been conducted into Irish-theme pubs, and according to Strauss and Corbin (1990), "qualitative methods can be used to uncover and understand what lies behind any phenomenon about which little yet is known" (p. 19). Following the analysis of the questionnaire data, four respondents from each pub were selected to take part in an in-depth interview. The sample comprised a range of age groups and occupational types and was gender balanced.

At interview the variables of the atmospheric construct were further explored and elaborated on, and a culturally aligned code name was given to each respondent. This meant that if a respondent's name was Michael Murphy, an obvious Irish name, a similarly Irish name was given as the code name, for example, Patrick O'Brien.

This allowed for some tracking to occur during the analysis so that those of Irish heritage could be grouped if necessary. Although the sample was a purposeful, nonprobability quota sample, Table 11.1 shows some of the characteristics of respondents highlighting the gender balance, range of age groups, and occupational status.

Finally, in order to corroborate the findings of the customer-oriented research, interviews were also conducted with the owners or

TABLE 11.1. List of Respondents, Including Their Culturally Aligned Code Names

Code Name	Gender	Age	Occupation
Anne Brennan	Female	34	Entertainer
Chris Brennan	Male	36	Entertainer
Katrina Womax	Female	20	Secretary
Daniella Rhodes	Female	19	Student
Jane Williams	Female	19	Students
Jonathon Harvey	Male	20	Barman
Trevor Edwards	Male	20	Service station attendant
Anthea Stuart	Female	26	Employment consultant
Robert Hill	Male	20	Bar manager
David Phillips	Male	39	Business consultant.
Kevin Richards	Male	37	Tour operator
Lawrence Hopkins	Male	34	Economist
Liz Steiner	Female	41	Office administrator
Stephanie McEvoy	Female	34	Social worker
Lauren Davison	Female	33	Public servant
Jack Parker	Male	55	Lecturer
Paul Murphy	Male	23	Retail manager
Rosemary Martens	Female	47	Teacher
Ben Davison		30	Plumber
Ron McIntosh	Male	41	Business Manager
Deirdre O'Sullivan	Female	36	Home Duties
Vincent Flood	Male	19	Student
Richard Ellis	Male	28	Manager
Patricia Jones	Female	24	Student

managers of the six theme pubs. Using a semistructured interview format, this involved presenting the various themes identified as important by customers and soliciting the owners' views on the importance of these issues to the theme-pub product.

ANALYSIS AND RESULTS

From the quantitative study, a sample of 320 respondents were surveyed, of which 298 usable questionnaires were obtained. This comprised of 44.3 percent male and 55.7 percent females, of which 87 percent visit a "pub" at least once a month, with 75 percent visiting an "Irish pub" at least once per month. Approximately 77 percent of respondents raised atmospherics or situational components as an important characteristic in relation to their choice to visit an Irish pub. The major emphasis was on social aspects, for example, friendliness (21 percent), people (21 percent), fun (9 percent), culture (7 percent), staff (6 percent), welcome (4 percent), and accents (4 percent). The average amount spent per visit for respondents was $44.00, with 70 percent of respondents spending at least $25.00 per visit.

Atmosphere and Gender

Although atmosphere is important for both genders, it was found to be far more important for females, as 85.0 percent of females believed atmosphere to be important, compared with 70.1 percent of males ($p = 0.05$).

Age and Atmosphere

Atmosphere is important for all age groups with a somewhat decreasing trend with age (see Table 11.2).

TABLE 11.2. Importance of Atmosphere to Age Cohorts

Age range (years)	18-20	21-25	26-30	31-40	41+
Percentage	82.4	81.8	80.8	71.8	69.4

Influence of Atmosphere Across Age and Gender Cohorts

Atmosphere is very important for females of all age groups; it is significantly less for males, with a somewhat decreasing emphasis with older age groups, but nevertheless, still an important consideration for males also (Table 11.3).

Having demonstrated the importance of atmospherics from a quantitative perspective, further insights are provided using the qualitative data. The interviews were transcribed, coded, and analyzed, and a summary is presented under the individual constructs proposed in the Hoffman and Turley model. Selected quotations from respondents are included using the code names presented earlier in Table 11.1. Qualitative quotes from the owners or managers of the Irish-theme pubs are also presented in this format.

INVISIBLE ORGANIZATION AND SYSTEMS

The invisible organization and systems includes the way the environment is managed. Although all of the respondents were positive about the Irish-theme pub environment, authenticity was raised as an important theme in this study and also permeated a number of other themes. One respondent, code named Ron, offered a view on Slim Finnigans's, a large Irish-theme pub in Melbourne that is licensed to cater to up to 700 customers. Ron observed that it was bright and clean but not new looking, which he believed was a deliberate attempt to make it look old. "It's like an artifice of what these pubs are expected to be but at the same time appealing to people's sensibilities," he asserted. Ron was one of a number of respondents who compared

TABLE 11.3. Importance of Atmosphere to Gender and Age Cohorts

Age range (years)	18-20		21-25		26-30		31-40		41+	
Gender	M	F	M	F	M	F	M	F	M	F
Percentage	75.0	88.9	74.2	88.6	77.1	86.7	66.7	80.8	57.6	82.8

Chi-square sig. diff. = 0.05

Slim Finnigan's to McDonald's, asserting that it was contrived as a marketing exercise rather than an effort to share Irish culture. Several other respondents also felt that Slim Finnigan's was overdone, leading them to conclude that it is not authentically Irish. It was curious that the majority of these respondents had never been to Ireland and so they were expressing their perceptions of what an authentic Irish pub might be like. Similar to Ron, however, they believed that Irish-theme pubs should be vectors for the sharing of Irish culture.

Nevertheless, all of the respondents expressed the view that Irish-theme pub owners have created a point of difference from other pubs that is recognizable to customers. Indeed, Jack reported that a number of visible distinguishing features about these pubs identify them as distinctly Irish. He went on to say:

> I think if I were blindfolded and taken into a pub and it's revealed to me I could tell immediately that it is an Irish pub. So in saying that I think that, yes, I think that they have tapped into something that's recognizable. Whether it is fair dinkum Irish or not is a bit hard to say.

Invisible

The invisible environment is different from the invisible organizations and systems in that it includes intangible situational components such as friendliness. When questioned about the reasons for the popularity of Irish-theme pubs all of the respondents stated that a major attraction was the atmosphere. This invisible aspect was perceived to be positive and was summarized by Robert who reported that "there was no trouble [which he believes was] probably because of the atmosphere that was generated. It's happy, there's no negativity in there whatsoever." Liz concurred stating, "I have never been in a situation in an Irish pub where I felt uncomfortable or have seen any problems. I'm sure that they have their problems, but it's never been obvious to me." Rosemary agreed, but also noted a cultural element, advising that going to an Irish pub from outside the culture is a different kind of experience than going to a pub within your own culture.

Robert also believes that the positive atmosphere in Irish-theme pubs is created and enhanced by the interaction between customers and the bar staff. "If they [the staff] see someone sitting there they'll go up and they'll most likely talk to them, they'll chat to them," he reported, asserting that something is unique or special about the way Irish people interact with others. Jack was also impressed with the interaction he had with a non-Irish staff member when he visited an Irish-theme pub. When he asked what the word *shîbîn*, written on the waitress's apron, meant, she replied, "It's an illegal drinking house; if you hear the police coming run out this door." He had enjoyed the joke and remarked how this kind of humor adds to the Irish atmosphere.

Inanimate Environment

In this study, the external environment was not rated as important by respondents, however, they placed a great deal of emphasis on the interior décor, especially the fabrics, tones and materials used, the design and positioning of the seating, and the artifacts and memorabilia that are incorporated. When asked about décor Anne advised, "each pub that I have seen, so far, has been quite unique, to a degree." Despite her Irish background, she was impressed by the decor in a number of city and suburban Irish-theme pubs, noting that one had a printing press and all sorts of books while another seemed to concentrate on agricultural implements. The major similarity between them, she felt, was the antiquity of the items that were on display. She firmly believes that this is a sharing of Irish culture. She also felt that the open display of Irish culture in the form of historical artifacts provides an insight into Irish history.

Lauren also reported that the Irish-theme pubs that she has visited "have all been quite different." The major attraction, in terms of design, for Trevor was the booths or nooks, as he referred to them, which he liked because they "offer . . . a little privacy for your own conversations and a sense that 'this is my area' and you can invite people into that little area."

Another aspect was the music, and the majority of respondents expressed the view that the music that they wanted to hear in Irish-theme pubs is authentic Irish music. They specifically noted, however, that they did not want token Irish jigs and reels, insisting that they wanted to hear both traditional and contemporary Irish music, especially that which is currently available in Ireland. This would seem to suggest that, at least with respect to music, respondents are

seeking authenticity rather than some romantic notion of Irishness contrived purely for their benefit.

Contact Personnel

As previously noted, contact personnel includes the number of service providers, their appearance, and their ability to perform the retail task. In this study, all of the respondents reported that the service personnel were an important aspect of the Irish-theme pub, especially in terms of the creation of a positive, friendly atmosphere. This was seen as different to other entertainment venues. As Jonathan noted, "It's different—you can chat to the security guys at the door and they're friendly—not like at the clubs." Robert also advised that the atmosphere is "mainly due to the staff. The staff there they're always friendly, always bubbly, always wanting to have a joke, and that's just part of the service that I'd go back for. . . ."

Jack was adamant that "in an Irish pub you have to have Irish staff or you lose everything you've tried to set up." Several other respondents shared this view and identified Irish accents as an attractive component of Irish-theme pubs. This was linked to the issue of authenticity and led to the question of whether the staff in Irish-theme pubs should be Irish. According to the Irish Pub Company (2000, p. 1) "friendly, efficient, Irish bar staff" are among the success factors in the creation of an authentic Irish-theme pub. This was confirmed in this study. Indeed, many respondents expressed the view that at least some Irish staff ought to be present to complement the theme. For example, Liz reflected, "I think Slim Finnigan's must have some policy where they only appoint people with an Irish accent and that certainly adds to the atmosphere." Rosemary supported this view asserting that the Irish accent "is a very highly valued attraction." Siobhan, who is Irish, was more direct, advising that it is vital to have Irish bar staff. She explained that:

> very often it's the bar staff who set the tone of the pub itself, be they male or female. You know, the welcome that you get from them is crucial, and I think that the Irish have a very particular way of welcoming, particularly strangers. They seem to know how much to give and how much to reserve so there's a welcoming, but they're not totally "in your face." There's an invitation to friendliness but it's not overpowering.

Customer

In this study, the behavior and disposition of customers was also linked to a notion of Irishness. Lauren believes, for example, that part of the attraction of Irish-theme pubs is the Irish attitude to life. When asked what she perceived this to be she stated that "it is a 'such is life' attitude, 'I'm here to have a good time: if I have one beer, I have one beer; if I end up under the table, well, that's life.'" Most respondents felt that Irish people know how to have fun, and those respondents who had either been to Ireland or had some experience of Irish culture used the Gaelic term *craic* when describing their reasons for going to, or their experiences at, Irish-theme pubs. Siobhan believes that people have fun at Irish-theme pubs because:

> there is an unwritten code amongst Irish people that when you are in the pub you're there to have a good time . . . when you go into a pub . . . you take everything in with you, you know, you take your problems and everything, but there's a certain kind of expectation that you'll have a relaxed sort of jovial time.

One thing that can quickly transform a fun atmosphere, however, is drunkenness. One of the most significant themes that emerged during the interviews was a perceived lack of drunkenness in Irish-theme pubs. Katrina attempted to articulate this, stating "that there wasn't any drunk, I mean they were drunk but they weren't like, do you know what I mean?" This statement seems contradictory, however, Katrina explained that Irish-theme pubs didn't seem to have customers who were drunk or sleazy or drowning their sorrows in a drunken depression. "People were there to have a good time. I don't like pubs, the whole pub atmosphere does nothing for me, but this is not your typical average corner pub." Daniella agreed, and suggested that security is unnecessary at Irish-theme pubs because "you just never really see anybody getting feisty about anything, everybody's pretty happy-go-lucky." Similar to Katrina, she felt that people didn't go there to get drunk.

Other Customers

Several respondents identified other customers as important, especially in the creation of atmosphere. Andrew noted, for example, that "everybody's up and moving and talking and laughing out loud, so it's got that pub atmosphere where you know people are more likely to mix and move through the room." Lauren also believes that "it's the attraction of the clientele—it's drawing a crowd that actually just want to go and have a conversation and a drink."

This begins with the welcome, which respondents opined creates an atmosphere in which one can relax and have fun. Jonathan explained that a level of inclusiveness exists in the atmosphere of Irish-theme pubs. He reported that the atmosphere at the Maude Gonne "is just unreal. Its not like your classy pub crowd where it's 'who are you.' It's sort of 'hey come on,' it doesn't matter who you are, if you're sixty or eighteen." Inclusiveness was important to Liz as well. She advised, for example, that "you don't have to feel like you're a member of a club or that you come from a particular country to feel comfortable there." In contrast, she felt that some other pubs and clubs in Melbourne were a bit more exclusive, and she feels that this openness and inclusiveness was one of the most attractive aspects of Irish-theme pubs.

Pub Owners' Views

Most pub owners were aware that customer's and, more important, the kinds of customer that frequent Irish-theme pubs are in fact an essential ingredient in these pubs. They also recognized the value of Irish accents in enhancing the authenticity of the venue. When asked if it is important to customers to be served by Irish bar staff, for example, one publican stated that "in a perfect world we'd have all Irish staff, but unfortunately it's not a perfect world." By this he meant that the current equal opportunities legislation was restrictive because "you need to get the staff that relate to the country that its from [the theme pub]." He asserted that "if you can't get them it looks a bit silly. If you have ninety-nine percent Australians in an Irish bar, it might as well be just another bar." One pub manager reported that he was currently employing 80 percent Australian bar staff because he was not allowed to advertise for Irish-born staff.

As noted earlier, an important aspect of Irish-theme pubs is the manner in which they are designed. The manager of one of the larger Irish pubs asserted that creating an authentic, recognizable environment was vital "so that when they [the customers] come in, it is recognized as an Irish pub." Authenticity in the design of the pub was also seen as an important feature. At one of the suburban, Irish-theme pubs, for example, the bar manager, explained that:

> it's just the way they're done, and the owner of this place has done a really good job, I think, in the way that he's actually set it out. Ninety percent of the Irish pubs that are in Melbourne have got that old feeling, I mean all the old bric-a-brac and stuff; I mean it's got to be put in the right way to have effect, and it does.

He went on to caution that "you can't just open an Irish pub and put stickers up and flags up and think you've got an Irish pub."

This issue was also explored with the owner an established Irish pub. He stated that he doesn't need to rely on artifacts because the long and rich history of the establishment resonates within it, creating a vibe that is almost tangible. He reported that he has seen some of the toughest of men who are known in the local community for their violent tendencies become calm and respectful because the atmosphere in the pub is pervasive. He went on to say that each night is targeted toward a community of people in the city that is diverse in age range and professions: "In here the 'wharfie' rubs hands with the laborer, the doctor, and the lawyer." Finally, the owner was asked why the atmosphere in that pub was so spellbinding. Revealing a spiritual dimension, he answered, "I just believe that there's been a lot of souls in this place that have been very well respected and very well judged by their creator."

IMPLICATIONS

Three-quarters of those surveyed identified the atmosphere of the retail setting as influential in their decision to visit an Irish pub. The survey also indicated that all age groups and both genders shared this attitude, although females tended to place more importance on the physical setting. In addition, the level of inclusiveness and the manner in which customers interact with one another was found to be an extremely important factor and is an aspect that has tended to be overlooked in consumer behavior, especially in terms of age and gender.

The rapport between customers and employees was also extremely important, as was the overall décor and ambience. This suggests that

the disposition of staff and indeed landlords, as well as the creation of a comfortable leisure environment, is highly valued by pub patrons. In this study, the behavior of customers was also linked to a perception of Irishness, to which customers felt that they ought to conform. To these respondents, Irishness represented a happy-go-lucky attitude to life, which they believe is reflected in the atmosphere created within Irish-theme pubs. This intangible dimension was most obvious in the established Irish pub where the owner asserted that the establishment resonates with a pervasive calming atmosphere.

One unexpected finding of the research was that Irish-theme pub operators were perceived to be custodians of Irish culture. There was also a dominant view that Irish-theme pubs needed to conform to a perceived level of authenticity, a feature that several respondents associated with pub size as well as other physical situational components.

The results and implications of this study should be of interest to both marketing theorists and practitioners. First, Lewin's theory, which identified the "subjective" world or psychological environment, is still valid, albeit in a revised form. Evidence also suggests that the Hoffman and Turley framework is a useful tool to predict, identify, and evaluate the situational influences that are important to customers of Irish-theme pubs. Further research is required, however, in order to enhance the literature and to provide opportune strategic advice to those who are considering investing in theme-related venues. Moreover, the limited local focus of this study, coupled with the sampling criteria and sample size indicates that ongoing research should be undertaken particularly in relation to age and gender. An opportunity exists, for example, to look at issues of security and gender within the Irish-theme pub environment and compare the findings with similar research in non-Irish pubs. The issue of authenticity of themed hospitality venues is also worthy of further, in-depth study.

REFERENCES

Bearden, W.O. and Woodside, A.G. (1976). Interaction of consumption situations and brand attitudes. *Journal of Applied Psychology, 61*(December): 764-769.

Belk, R.W. (1974). An exploratory assessment of situational effects in buyer behavior. *Journal of Marketing Research, 11:* 156-163.

Belk, R.W. (1979). A free response approach to developing product-specific consumption situation taxonomies. In A.D. Shocker (ed.), *Analytic Approaches to Product and Market Planning* (pp. 77-196). Cambridge, MA: Marketing Science Institute.

Berman, B. and Evans, J. (1995). *Retail Management: A Strategic Approach*, 6th Edition. Englewood Cliffs, NJ: Prentice-Hall.

Bitner, M. (1990). Evaluating service encounters: The effects of physical surroundings and employee responses. *The Journal of Marketing, 54:* 69-82.

Bitner, M. (1992). The impact of physical surroundings on customers and employees. *Journal of Marketing, 56*(2): 57-71.

Brown, S. and Patterson, A. (2000). Knick-knack paddy-whack, give pub a theme. *Journal of Marketing Management, 16*(6): 647-662.

Chow, S., Celsi, R., and Abel, R. (1990). The effects of situational and intrinsic sources of personal relevance on brand choice decisions. *Advances in Consumer Research, 17:* 755-759.

Donovan, R.J. and Rossiter, J.R. (1982). Store atmosphere: An environmental psychology approach. *Journal of Retailing, 58*(1): 34-57.

Foxall, G. (1983). *Consumer Choice.* London, UK: MacMillan.

Foxall, G. (1990). *Consumer Psychology in Behavioral Perspective.* New York: Routledge.

Foxall, G. (1996). *Consumers in Context: The BPM Research Program.* New York: Routledge/ITBP.

Foxall, G.R. (1997a). Affective responses to consumer situations. *International Review of Retail, Distribution, and Consumer Research, 7:* 191-225.

Foxall, G.R. (1997b). The emotional texture of consumer environments: A systematic approach to atmospherics. *Journal of Economic Psychology, 18:* 505-523.

Foxall, G.R. and Greenley, G.E. (1998). The affective structure of consumer situations. *Environment and Behavior, 30:* 781-798.

Foxall, G.R. and Greenley, G.E. (1999). Consumers' emotional response to service environments. *Journal of Business Research, 30:* 781-798.

Fredericksen, N. (1972). Toward a taxonomy of situations. *American Psychologist 27:* 114-123.

Goldsmith, C. (1996). Prefab Irish pubs sell pints worldwide. *Wall Street Journal,* October 25, pp. B1, B8.

Hall, J. and Lockshin, L. (2000). Using means end chains for analyzing occasions: Not buyers. *Australasian Marketing Journal, 8*(1): 45-54.

Hall, J., O'Mahony, G.B., and Lockshin, L. (2002). A comparative evaluation of wine attributes and consumption occasions and consumer perceptions. In *Proceedings of the Council for Australian University Tourism and Hospitality Education,* February 6-9, Fremantle, Western Australia. Queensland, Australia: CAUTHE.

Hansen, F. (1972). *Consumer Choice Behavior.* New York: The Free Press.

Hoffman, K. and Turley, L. (2002). Atmospherics, service encounters, and consumer decision making: An integrative perspective. *Journal of Marketing Theory and Practice, 10*(3): 33-46.

Irish Pub Concept (2001). Pub galleries. Available at: www.irishpubconcept.com/galleries/. Accessed May 24.

Knowles, T. and Howley, M.J. (2000). Branding in the UK public house sector: Recent developments. *International Journal of Contemporary Hospitality Management, 12:* 366-370.

Lai, A.W. (1991). Consumption situation and product knowledge in the adoption of a new product. *European Journal of Marketing, 25*(1): 55-67.

Langeard, E., Bateson, J., Lovelock, C., and Eigler, P. (1981). *Marketing of services: New insights from consumers and managers.* Report No. 81-104. Cambridge, MA: Marketing Science Institute.

Leek, S., Maddock, S., and Foxhall, G. (2000). Situational determinants of fish consumption. *British Food Journal, 102*(1): 18-39.

Lewin, K. (1935). *A Dynamic Theory of Personality Selected Papers.* New York: McGraw-Hill: 11-70.

Lewin, K. (1936). *Principles of Topological Psychology.* New York: McGraw-Hill.

Lewin, K. (1938). The conceptual representation and the measurement of psychological forces. In D.K. Adams and H. Lundholm (eds.), *Contributions to Psychological Theory,* Volume 1 (pp.). Durham, NC: Duke University Press.

Lewin, K. (1951). *Field Theory in Social Science Selected Theoretical Papers.* New York: Harper.

McGoldrick, P.J. and Pieros, C.P. (1998). Atmospheres, pleasures and arousal: The influence of response moderators. *Journal of Marketing Management, 14*(1): 173-185.

Olsen, J. and Thach, L. (2001). Consumer behavior and wine consumption: A conceptual framework. *The Australian and New Zealand Wine Industry Journal, 16*(6): 123-129.

O'Mahony (2002). *Food and Beverages in Australia: An Irish Perspective.* Unpublished Doctoral Dissertation, The University of Melbourne, Melbourne, Australia.

Quester, P. and Smart, J.G. (1998). The influence of consumption situation and product involvement over consumers' use of product attributes. *Journal of Consumer Marketing, 15*(3): 220-238.

Richins, M. and Bloch, P. (1986). After the new wears off: The temporal context of product involvement. *Journal of Consumer Research, 13*(2): 280-285.

Sandell, R.G. (1968). The effects of attitudinal and situational factors on reported choice behavior. *Journal of Marketing Research, 4:* 405-408.

Srivastava, R.K. (1980). Usage-situational influences on the perceptions of product markets response homogeneity end: Its implications for consumer research. In J.C. Olson (ed.), *Advances in Consumer Research* (pp. 644-649). Ann Arbor, MI: Association for Consumer Research.

Strauss, A. and Corbin, J. (1990). *Basics of Qualitative Research: Grounded Theory Procedures and Techniques*. Newbury Park, CA: Sage.

Tashakkori, A. and Teddlie, C. (1989). *Mixed Methodology: Combining Qualitative and Quantitative Approaches*. Thousand Oaks, CA: Sage.

Turley, L.W. and Furgate (1992). The multidimensional nature of service facilities: Viewpoints and recommendations. *The Journal of Services Marketing, 6*(3): 37-45.

Turley, L.W. and Millman, R.E. (2000). Atmospheric effects on shopping behavior: A review of the experimental evidence. *Journal of Business Research, 49:* 193-211.

Walkup, A. (1997). Irish pubs pour pints of Guinness, store up golden guineas. *Tampa Tribune, 31*(11): 60-61.

West, P. (2001). Last order's down at McFoney's. *New Statesman, 130:* 14.

Woodside, A.B., William, O., and Clokey, J.D. (1977). Effects of consumption situations and multibrand attitudes on consumer brand choice, moving ahead with attitude research. In Y. Wind and M. Greenberg (eds.), *Moving Ahead with Attitude Research* (pp. 58-65). Chicago, IL: American Marketing Association.

Zeithaml, V.A., Parasuraman, A., and Berry L.L. (1990). *Delivering Quality Service: Balancing Customer Perceptions and Expectations*. London, UK: Collier Macmillan.

Chapter 12

Internationalization of Services: The Global Impact of U.S. Franchise Restaurants

Mahmood A. Khan

INTRODUCTION

Franchising has become the dominant force in the distribution of goods and services in the United States and many parts of the world. It is predicted that it will become the primary method of doing business and expansion worldwide. In order to understand the global impact of franchising, it is essential to fully understand its definition and the way it works. According to a report by the Committee on Small Business (1990), U.S. House of Representatives, "franchising is essentially a contractual method for marketing and distributing goods and services of a company (franchisor) through a dedicated or restricted network of distributors (franchisees)." The International Franchise Association defines franchising as a "continuous relationship in which the franchisor provides a licensed privilege to do business, plus assistance in organizing, training, merchandising, and management in return for a consideration from the franchisee" (International Franchise Association). In short, franchising is designed to provide a symbiotic and mutually beneficial relationship between the franchisor and franchisees. The same guidelines work whether the business is run locally, regionally, or internationally. A distinct differentiation exists between franchising and other business methods. Multiunit operations and groups of restaurants owned by an individual or corporation that have the same trademark may not be franchises. What constitutes a franchise is the legal agreement and bond-

Global Cases on Hospitality Industry
© 2008 by The Haworth Press, Taylor & Francis Group. All rights reserved.
doi:10.1300/5923_12

ing between a franchisor and a franchisee for the conduct of specific business, after meeting prearranged sets of legal requirements. A franchise-granting corporation may itself be a wholly owned subsidiary of another corporation. A good example is Pizza Hut, a subsidiary of Yum! Brands, Inc., which also owns Taco Bell, KFC, A&W, and Long John Silver's corporations. Components of conglomerates are not considered franchises, although some of them may individually be franchise-granting corporations. In summary, under the terms of the franchise contract, a franchisor grants the right and license to franchisees to market a product or service, or both, using the trademark and/or the business system developed by the franchisor. The entire process of franchising starts with a concept, which may be based on an idea, innovation, process, product, service format, or a combination of all these. The franchisor grants a license to another party to use this concept. Due to the legal agreement, room for flexibility is strictly limited, which leaves a distinct impact wherever this concept is carried. Hence this concept in its totality has to survive within the cultural, social, economical, and political environments. In other words, a fairly rigid concept has to flourish in variable environments based on the country in which it is transposed. This results in a sort of give and take, causing positive and negative impacts, which are discussed in this chapter.

Franchising in the international market is expanding rapidly; in particular, restaurant franchises have a seen a tremendous increase in recent years. Despite temporary setbacks during the global downturn after the turn of the millennium, franchising is still expected to be the fastest-growing market-entry strategy (Ziedman, 2003). American restaurant franchises are now prevalent in every corner of the world. The United States, pioneer in the field of franchising, continues to be the worldwide leader in restaurant franchising. The quick-service segment of the restaurant industry is the fastest-growing segment in foreign markets. Restaurant franchises were often among the first types of American businesses to open in the emerging market economies of the former republics of Russia, Eastern Europe, China, and many of the Southeast Asian countries. Some of the most successful business stories came from McDonald's in Moscow (700 seat restaurant with 27 cash registers and long waiting lines) and KFC in China, with the Beijing store having the highest sales volume among all restaurants worldwide. Most notable trends that favor the increase in international franchising include (1) increased educational status of the local population; (2) technological advancement facilitating travel, intercultural cooperation, and instant dissemination of information; (3) exposure to different foods, the willingness of younger generations to try new products and unconventional types of foods; (4) rapid development of rural areas, construction of highways, improved transportation methods, and overall industrial development; (5) improved economies and increased disposable family income; (6) the increased numbers of women in the workforce and of two-income families; (7) the increased significance of convenience as a result of one or more factors mentioned previously; and (8) the popularity of take-out or home-delivered meals (Khan, 1999). International fast-food chains came to Hong Kong with core products: hamburger, chicken, or pizza. Since their products are limited, their strategies are focused on image building through aggressive marketing. To attract consumers, they try to establish a clear and unique image of their brand. For instance, KFC is the expert in American-style chicken, and McDonald's serves the American hamburger (Lan and Khan, 1995).

In the fight to gain extra share of stomach in a $440 billion U.S. food-service market in 2004, according to the National Restaurant Association (2004), strategy is obviously a huge determinant of success. The most intriguing strategic response to the marketplace comes from Louisville, Kentucky–based Yum! and its efforts to develop multibrand units across the globe. Yum! includes multiunit concepts featuring KFC and Long John Silver's or Taco Bell and A&W and a number of other combinations (Cunneen, 2004).

METHODOLOGY

This chapter is based on case studies and a qualitative assessment approach, drawing assumptions from limited published studies on the subject. Several models were examined both for presumptive as well as comparative purposes. The primary intent of this chapter is to outline the major impact of restaurant franchises, which may be positive or negative. It is expected that from this exploratory study further issues will be delineated for future empirical studies. Also, McDonald's Corporation is used primarily for case study examples since it has the largest number of franchise units worldwide and has very distinct impact on aspects discussed in this chapter. McDonald's has more than 30,000 restaurants in 119 countries, serving 47 million customers per day. The ten largest markets in McDonald's system are in Australia, Brazil, Canada, China, France, Germany, Japan, Spain, the United Kingdom, and of course the United States. These markets represent approximately 24,000 McDonald's restaurants and account for approximately 72 percent of their business. McDonald's is used as an example since its restaurants are widely present internationally; however, the aspects discussed apply in general to all American franchise restaurants.

BASIC CONCEPTS

The basic core of franchising is based on a symbiotic relationship between franchisor and franchisees, which is supposed to result in a mutually beneficial relationship. Legally in the United States, franchises must meet three criteria to be classified as a franchise: (1) the franchisee distributes products or services associated with the franchisor's trademark or identifying symbol, (2) the franchisor provides significant assistance and/or exercises significant control over the franchisee's method of operation, and (3) the franchisee is required to pay at least $500 to the franchisor during the first six months of operation of the franchise. If properly executed, franchising is a win-win-win situation for franchisor, franchisees, and consumers. Above all, franchising provides a cost-effective and systematic strategy for marketing and rapid expansion with a minimum of direct involvement and financial investment. In order to implement it in practice, the basic requirement is that the franchise concept be simple and one that can be replicated easily. It is this attribute of franchising, which is analogous to "breeding rabbits," that makes franchises, particularly the business-format franchises, follow a rigid pattern of standardization. It is this rigidity that causes impacts wherever the franchises are expanded and transformed.

BASIC FRANCHISOR SERVICES
AND THEIR GLOBAL IMPACT

Typical services provided by franchisors and their impact is listed in Table 12.1. These services pertain to site selection, building and architecture, equipment and facilities, training, marketing, communications, territorial expansion, purchasing, operations, management,

TABLE 12.1. Global Impact of the Basic Franchor's Services to Franchisees

Typical services provided by franchisors	Global multi-dimensional impacts
Site selection	Prominent sites and real estate selected in commercial areas such as malls and shopping centers, providing visibility and frequent exposure
Building and architecture	Building design, logo, colors, and overall appearance are representative and symbolic
Equipment and facilities	Custom-made standardized equipment imposes process changes and leads to technology transfer
Training	Educational, language, and cultural impacts leading to development of special skills
Marketing	Global advertisement and promotional methods
Communication link	Use of informational technology for global secure communication with franchisees
Territorial expansion	Provides for regional growth and expansion
Purchasing	Development of highly sophisticated and customized specifications for products and services to be obtained locally or from abroad
Operations	Special operational parameters for products and services, which are uniquely aligned with the franchise concept
Management	Tools for comparative assessment on regional and global basis; reports; financial assistance; and other management assistance
Legal Aspects	Different franchising laws aligning with local laws, rules and regulations
Research and development	Related to all aspects including customization of products and services in line with the primary franchise concept
Community development	Community development activities to help as well as gain acceptance
Financial	Financial aspects including transactions; monetary help; book-keeping; cash registers; etc.

legal aspects, research and development, community development, and financing. Since these services are provided by the franchisors, a sort of standardization emerges wherever that particular franchise goes. It is this standardization that has an impact, which may be useful or adverse based on the circumstances. These impacts are briefly described here as well as in Table 12.1.

The site selected for a first-time restaurant franchisor is a location at a prime shopping area in order to provide visibility and frequent exposure. Based on the building and architectural design of the concept it has its own impact. Colors used become source of brand recognition as well as the basics of franchise concept, which cannot be altered significantly by any franchisee. For example, McDonald's restaurants are prominently located at choice locations, and with golden color and arches, establish its presence in the midst of the existing shopping area. This may or may not blend with the cultural environment and atmosphere of the locale, as seen in Paris, where the building of a restaurant in a historical district was met with much resistance. Also, fast turnovers in many franchise restaurants require bright light, warm colors, less comfortable seating, and drive-throughs. This again creates an ambiance and environment that may either not blend well or conflict with the existing atmosphere. If it blends well, it becomes a positive impact. When competitors try to compete with such businesses they develop a similar atmosphere, thus multiplying the effects of the impact.

In order to provide similar products and services, franchisees are bound to use specialized equipment and facilities. For example, Burger King uses a flame-broiling method, which may not be the traditional method in a country. In many countries, pizza, tacos, french fries, pepperoni, squids, etc. are very unfamiliar items. Thus methods and materials used may have an impact on the ingredients, procedures, and equipments used. Also, restaurant franchising is based on quantity preparation in a short period of time, using simple menus that are not complex and can be duplicated easily. Custom-made standardized equipment imposes process changes and leads to technology transfer.

One of the most important services provided by the franchisor is training, which provides a thorough understanding of the operational aspect of a franchise concept. This training requires specific media, mode, and exercises to develop required skills. Language and educational background are needed in order to accomplish goals of training. Similar requirements pertain to the communications, which are essential between franchisees and franchisors.

Franchises are also very well known for their advanced marketing methods, particularly when it comes to advertising and promotion. Due to the collective assessment of advertising fees from all franchisees, it becomes economically feasible to advertise nationally or internationally. This may shadow promotions by smaller, nonfranchised businesses and put them at a disadvantage.

Since franchising exists because of the property of territorial expansion, the number of franchises multiply in a region, and all impacts discussed are not confined to an area but will gradually expand, thereby bringing adverse or beneficial results.

For standardization, uniformity, and operational purposes of restaurant franchises, products and services that meet rigid specifications are extremely important. This requires the availability of products and services locally. McDonald's in China and Russia had difficulty getting the exact variety of vegetable products to a point that they had to grow their own or import from other regions. Unfamiliarity or unavailability of items such as pepperoni and certain cheese and meat products requires importation from sometimes far distances. If not, it leads to the cultivation, development, or manufacture of specialized products or ingredients locally. Also, large-quantity preparation requires large-quantity purchasing, which may have a distinct impact on the price structure and stabilization. The balance of supply and demand also gets altered.

Each franchise has their own style and management techniques, which are passed on to the franchisees. This provides tools for managing efficiently that particular type of restaurant operation. Reports, financial controls, reporting, tools for comparative assessment, and other management assistance can also have an impact on the existing systems. Also data comparing units within an area are provided, which is very helpful in running a successful restaurant franchise. In addition, laws and legal requirements vary from country to country. As franchising is a legal agreement, it has to be aligned to the prevalent laws and regulations. Many countries had to amend, add, or introduce new laws in order to bring franchises within their boundaries.

Research and development are continuous aspects of franchisors in order to keep their concepts in line with the demands. This research can involve consumer surveys, consumer preferences, competition analysis, and new product development. Newer techniques for these assessments are introduced. Also, community development activities provide another source for introducing newer ways of helping the community, such as by social activities and having specialized events.

FRANCHISING AND MARKETING MIX

Franchising and its relation with different aspects of the expanded marketing mix are shown in Table 12.2. Although marketing mix is applicable to all types of businesses, the intent of this comparison is to show the rigidity and standardization that takes place in franchising. Every aspect becomes a part of the concept, and thus it is carried wherever the franchise goes with its impact on those aspects. Manuals that are provided by the franchisor to franchisees outline specifics of operations and management. These specifics are legally binding on franchisees and are used for auditing purposes.

TABLE 12.2. Expanded Marketing Mix for Services Provided through Restaurant Franchises

Expanded marketing mix	Primary franchise components
Product	Menu items, standard quality, packaging with branding, menu combinations, concept theme
Place	Franchise outlets, location, channel management, building and facilities, site development, drive-throughs, and parking
Promotion	Promotion blend, sales/counter persons;,incentives, advertising, sales promotion, publicity, and public relation
Price	Price level, value pricing, discounts, price bundling, discounts, and allowances
People	Employee recruitment, training, compensation, and work ethics; and customer information/education
Physical evidence	Signage, facility design, equipment, employee uniform, supplies, color combination, business stationary, reports, menu board, and other tangibles
Process	Standardized and customized process flow, operational guidelines, entire business procedures, turnkey operation, and customer service processes.

Using the example of McDonald's, the relationship between franchising and marketing mix is shown and discussed in the following sections.

Product

For any franchise restaurant, foods become the major component of the concept. Menu becomes the core around which the entire concept is developed. According to McDonald's 2002 Annual Report (McDonald's Corporation, 2002), their plan is to serve food and beverages people prefer to enjoy regularly. As with any franchise, McDonald's tries to standardize major items that taste similar, whether they are purchased in Australia, Africa, Asia, or anywhere else. This standardization itself has an impact on the lifestyle, eating habit, food preferences, and food habits. In one of their statements, McDonald's sums up by saying, "We will make McDonald's the Brand people grow up with . . . and never outgrow; we intend to remain constantly relevant in a constantly changing world" (McDonald's Corporation, 2002). Although the core products remain similar everywhere, adaptations are made based on consumer tastes, preferences, laws, customs, and religious requirements. Even with these changes, the overall character is maintained by offering the main menu items. For example, in China, in addition to serving the traditional favorites such as Big Mac and McChicken sandwiches, McDonald's offers a Spicy Chicken Filet Burger and Spicy McWings to provide items that appeal to local tastes. Similarly, in India they offer vegetable McNuggets and Maharaja Mac, another form of Big Mac made with mutton rather than beef, to meet the religious requirements. In Malaysia and the Middle East they offer their favorite items, but the meat used is slaughtered according to Islamic requirements, with complete exclusion of items containing pork or pork products. In tropical countries, sugarcane juice or guava juice is offered and in Germany beer is served. Other special items include chilled yogurt drinks in Turkey, espresso and cold pasta in Italy, teriyaki burgers in Japan, grilled salmon sandwich in Philippines, Samurai Pork Burger in Thailand, and Croque McDo ham and cheese and Le 280 beef sandwich in France. Almost every other franchise restaurant is also making such adaptations to meet the demands of the local population.

In addition to the standardized products and ingredients, quality assurance is an important aspect of franchising. The continuous monitoring, inspections, and audits of all restaurants, production facilities, distribution centers, indirect suppliers, and farms create a series of quality consciousness and upkeep. This not only affects the local affiliated businesses but also competitors, who have to meet the quality standards.

The impact of products provided by franchise restaurants on health safety and well-being of the population cannot be ignored. The growth of fast-food restaurants worldwide has had a large impact. This impact needs to be monitored very closely so that any adverse consequences can be checked. McDonald's as well as other franchise restaurants are putting much emphasis on menu choices and physical activity by introducing different menu items and consumer information programs. Product variety and portion sizes are taken into consideration while adding menu choices. Programs promoting physical activities are being introduced. For example, in Brazil, McDonald's menu now include two meal-size salads—a mixed greens salad and a mixed greens salad topped with chicken. In addition, McFruit juice's is offered with 70 percent juice-based drinks in orange, grape, and passion fruit flavor. McDonald's China added several choices to their Happy Meal offerings, including two new options, a cheese and egg sandwich on a steamed bun, potato and chicken Dino McNuggets, and a new drink option: milk.

People

Each franchise restaurant has their own training programs, which helps in developing knowledge, skills, and attitudes. McDonald's itself can be credited with providing lifetime skills, work ethics, and attitudinal changes, particularly among younger generation, that will last for a lifetime. Currently, the number of employees of McDonald's exceeds 1.6 million people worldwide. Employees range from different professions such as construction workers, agricultural workers, engineers, interior designers, architects, etc. With franchise restaurants opening every hour worldwide, this has a major impact on building individual's basic skills, which will lead to gaining experience for future leadership and management opportunities. Training is one of the essential services provided by franchisors, and such programs are well structured and designed for employees ranging from crewmembers through executive officers. In addition to men worldwide, women and minorities also get an opportunity to work either full or part time after completing ongoing or hands-on training. Well-established training centers are built in major business centers, which also cater to local population by providing continuing education. The training focus covers all business aspects from food preparation to customer service to management. The diversity of laws and customs has an impact on selection of appropriate employees for various jobs. Thus labor laws have to be modified, changed, or established in order to meet those criteria in different countries.

Place

The criteria used to select franchise restaurants are very sophisticated, which takes into account various aspects of demographics and future area development. For example, with 30,000 restaurants in 119 countries, the economic impact of each restaurant can be enormous. It involves the investment of money in the community as a taxpayer, employer, and purchaser of goods and services, and the consequent multiplier effect in the region. Site selection is one of the primary aspects of McDonald's restaurants. Based on the country, the site selected varies. For example, Switzerland was the first place that McDonald's ever offered food on a train. They expanded their services to include boats, and they opened on the ferry that crosses the Baltic Sea between Sweden and Finland.

Process

Franchise restaurant concepts are based on a systematic process, which varies from operation to operation. This process is strictly controlled by the franchisor and is included in the services provided to the franchisees. An elaborate "operations manual" is provided, which details every little step of the operation. This is key to the success of a franchise system. For example, McDonald's also have their own process, which helps in standardization and quality control. This system is transferred from restaurant to restaurant and thus facilitates the understanding of the systems approach. In order to meet this systemization, suppliers have to meet very strict guidelines, and other aspects back-of-the-house and front-of-the-house have to work in complete sequence. Facilities layout and design have to be carefully planned in order to facilitate the food flow and align with the franchise concept. It is noteworthy that in fast-food restaurants speed is of paramount importance, and this type of facilities and processes helps in serving food in a record time period. This layout and design may prove to be very different than what is followed traditionally. Since language and understanding may be different in other countries, visual signs and pictographs are used to facilitate understanding.

Price

Prices are based on a number of factors, including demand and supply. With large quantity food production and sales, franchise restaurants are bound to have an impact on prices worldwide. Also, the concept of franchising is based on territorial expansion. This in turn results in a cycle of more sales, more use of resources, and more overall purchasing. Also, prices have to be reasonable and well within the reach of an average person worldwide. Because of the standardization and ease of comparability, Big Mac indexes were developed that provided an indication of the purchasing power of the country or region. McDonald's states that they have a responsibility to maintain their values and high standards as they provide food that is affordable to a wide range of customers. Prices are based on the cost of resources needed, affordability by customers, competitor's prices, and value provided. The size of the population segments willing to pay offered prices is also an important consideration. A balance between quality and value is essential for survival. Competition with other local restaurants is the main basis of judgment since consumers will be comparing the value received from one restaurant to another. Thus, in order to make it more affordable, the major impact of franchising is seen in the introduction of a keen competition in the local restaurant business. Sometimes the competition can be between different menu items, for example, burger items competing with noodles in Hong Kong and Thailand. Depending on the country, the strategic decision is based on whether market penetration/share or competitive edge is desired. The PLC, or the product life cycle, also becomes important in making decisions about the prices and how to compete with different products in the existing market. For some local businesses it may become very hard to compete since franchising has the collective power and can sustain losses when necessary. As evident, many of the sandwich bakeries in UK, soup and noodles shop in Thailand, and street vendors in most of the Asian countries were affected by the rise of franchise restaurants, where readily available hot food is sold at an affordable price in a relatively inviting ambiance.

Promotion

Marketing and promotion are other important services provided by franchisors for which a set percentage of fees are charged to respective franchisees. It is this collective marketing done on national or regional basis that becomes difficult to match by local businesses. The frequent exposure on all advertising media by franchise restaurants may overshadow whatever limited marketing is done by local restaurants. McDonald's states that they have a responsibility to maintain and build trust with all their stakeholders by ensuring that their marketing and communications efforts are truthful and appropriate. This power of advertising, promotion, and public relation cannot be underestimated. Children particularly are attracted to different ways by which marketing is done by fast-food restaurants. Also a feeling of belonging is created by frequent exposure to these ads, thereby indirectly promoting brand loyalty. This is successfully done by utilizing the local celebrities, events, familiar faces, locale, etc. In order to appeal to the local populations, special features such as showing restaurants as environmental friendly, as being sports fans, as representing families, as animal friendly, and/or as a community component are used in marketing.

Physical Evidence

One of the basic features of franchising is the physical evidence, which comprises of number of different aspects such as logo, trademark, colors used, ambience, cleanliness, appearance, uniform, seating, menu boards, napkins, etc. The consistent appearance of these physical attributes identifies the brand and is a requirement for any franchise unit. McDonald's is very easily recognized worldwide by the golden arches, logo, colors of the uniform, and the ambiance of the restaurant. Even where adaptations have been made to meet the local environment, it is evident that the restaurant is McDonald's. The same is true for other restaurant franchises. Physical evidence has an impact on the local environment, which may lead to either enrichment of the place or in some cases objections by the local population. For example, people do not prefer to disturb the historical or aesthetic environment by having something that is or symbolic of modernization or outside interference.

Newer services or items introduced may also have an impact, for example, play facilities or computers in a restaurant may add to the near environment as well as influence other competitors to add such facilities. Parking and drive-throughs also impact the traffic pattern of a shopping center or other business areas. Interior decorations and equipment may be new to the country, and the utilities used may have an impact on their consumption pattern in the area. The service area, personnel uniform, and style of services all represent a particular franchise and may affect the local patterns. For example, it is not very common in many countries to provide service with a smile, or have counters with cash registers.

QUALITY DIMENSIONS FOR SERVICES PROVIDED BY RESTAURANT FRANCHISES

It has been proven by empirical research that customers do not perceive quality in a unidimensional way, but rather judge quality based on multiple factors relevant to the context (Zeithaml and Bitner, 2003). Five specific dimensions of service quality that apply across a variety of service contexts were identified (Parsuraman et al., 1988). These five dimensions are described here and shown in Table 12.3. These dimensions align very closely with basic aspects of franchising, and moreover by the requirements of conduct by the franchisor and franchisees.

Reliability: Delivering on Promises

Reliability is the ability to perform the promised service dependably and accurately. This is considered as the most important determinant of service perception, and the success of restaurant franchising is very much based on this dimension. Due to the quality requirement and standardization, franchises perform dependably and

TABLE 12.3. Quality Dimensions for Services Provided through Restaurant Franchises

Service quality dimension	Primary franchise focus
Reliability	Standardized service provided dependably and accurately. Maintaining quality standards. Information provided through operations manuals.
Responsiveness	Service attributes defined and importance on prompt service. Emphasis on mandatory training and use of training manuals.
Assurance	Employee knowledge, courtesy, and ability enhanced through training at different levels.
Empathy	Individualized customer attention focused through training. Treating franchisees as customers.
Tangibles	Signage, facility design, equipment, appearance and employee uniform, supplies, color combination, business stationary, reports, menu board, and other tangibles.

accurately. A consumer going to McDonald's in Malaysia expects the same quality of service as in the United States although the environment is different. Reliability means that the company delivers on its promises—promises about delivery, service provision, problem resolution, and pricing (Zeithaml and Bitner, 2003). Franchises have reliability as one of the cornerstone of their services.

Responsiveness: Being Willing to Help

Responsiveness is the willingness to help customers and to provide prompt service. Responsiveness is communicated to customers by the length of time they have to wait for assistance, answers to questions, or attention to problems (Zeithaml and Bitner, 2003). Frontline workers and staff are mostly responsible for responsiveness. Clear definition of service attributes and importance of prompt service are integral part of operations of franchise restaurants, particularly fast-food restaurants.

Assurance: Inspiring Trust and Confidence

Assurance is defined as employees' knowledge and courtesy and the ability of the firm and its employees to inspire trust and confidence (Zeithaml and Bitner, 2003). Mandatory training programs provided by franchisors instill assurance in services. The ongoing training required by employees from crew workers to executives results in building customer trust and confidence. Long-standing reputation and existence also results in building assurance.

Empathy: Treating Customers As Individuals

Empathy is defined as the caring, individualized attention the firm provides its customers (Zeithaml and Bitner, 2003). Training programs offered by the franchisors emphasizes individualized customer attention. Detailed explanation of services such as smile while you serve, how to greet customers, developing customer relations, etc. are all included in the lessons provided through training manuals, which also come a service provided by the franchisor. Frequent audits and inspections ensure that these attributes are followed.

Tangibles: Representing the Service Physically

Tangibles are defined as the appearance of physical facilities, equipment, personnel, and communication materials. All these provide physical representations or images of the service that customers will use to evaluate quality (Zeithaml and Bitner, 2003). Franchises are well known for providing tangibles, which become their brand identity. Logos, colors, uniforms, lighting, seating, equipment, menu boards, pamphlets, tray liners, and ambience are well planned to match with the concept of any franchise restaurants.

As evident from the aforementioned quality dimensions for services, franchise restaurants come very close to adhering to all service dimensions. The degree to which it is followed may vary from one franchise to another; however, these dimensions are built into their franchise concept. By agreeing to franchise, these dimensions are transposed and become legally binding wherever the franchise goes.

GLOBAL IMPACTS OF FRANCHISING

The global impacts of franchising can be visualized by examining them from different angles. McDonald's is used as an example under each category for the reasons mentioned previously. Figure 12.1 il-

a went to Japan in 1985, the company discovered that
d for pepperoni. Domino's imported pepperoni until
were trained to make this product. After more than ten
oni pizza is the number-one-selling pie in Japanese
ot only a new product was introduced but also its prefer-
nportation of certain products that are already available
y is restricted in some countries. In South Korea, pepper-
t be imported because of the restriction on importation of
cts. This led to establishing some methods of production
cial slaughtering restrictions, such as halal foods in Ma-
Middle-Eastern countries, led to the development of prod-
meet those requirements. Thus, franchising is not only
dating local food preferences but also developing new food

imings and eating patterns are also affected by introduction
ood restaurants. The popularity of breakfast meals in the
States does not get translated very easily in many countries,
in Middle East, where eating breakfast away from home is not
mmon. With the introduction of breakfast menu items and
eating patterns are changing, if not getting homogenized all
he world. Eating styles and mannerism have also been im-
d. A vast number of people in many countries do not like the
of eating away at a food stand or eating while standing. More-
holding sandwiches in hand, and not using knife, fork, or chop-
s to eat, is considered out of etiquette. Slowly this pattern is get-
impacted in many parts of the world. Another major aspect
acted is the family ritual of eating together at home. Some cul-
es are very particular about family members getting together to eat
one time. Eating away from home or the habit of grazing has se-
rely dented this opportunity of getting together and interacting with
e another. The idea and design of a food court with common seat-
g area is now being accepted in many European countries. Previ-
usly consumers ate at home or frequented restaurants serving china,
cloth napkins, and silverware. Reusable items and eating while standing or driving were not considered civilized.

Though indirectly, McDonald's has introduced certain words and
phrases in local languages, such as the addition of Mac or Macados,
"super size it," "I'm loving it," "You deserve a break today," etc. To
many the golden arches represent more than fast foods to mean

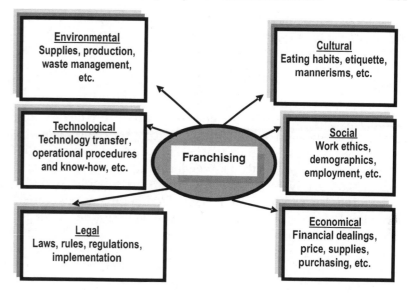

FIGURE 12.1. Global Impacts of Franchising

lustrates the major aspects of the global impact of franchising. The
experiences learned by U.S. franchisors in Asia bear testimony to the
importance of understanding foreign cultures' ways of doing business (Chan and Justis 1990). For U.S. franchisors seeking to expand
globally, these include greater cultural universalism, a younger population willing to try new products, more women working, and, thus, a
higher percentage of two-income families with more disposable income (Justis and Judd, 1989). Franchisors must consider a number of
strategic factors in making the decision to expand their franchising
system globally, namely: (1) economic factors, (2) political/legal factors, (3) sociocultural factors, and (4) infrastructure. For example,
U.S. firms intending to franchise in Europe must be prepared to cater
to local tastes rather than to a "pan-European" ideal. With the elimination of geographic and other barriers, European consumers will
have access to an increased variety of new products, many of which
will be produced by new entrants. It is likely that many of these new
entrants will be smaller businesses that do not have the resources required for research and development, sophisticated marketing, or
quality control. The franchising concept, with its emphasis on trade-

name/product recognition, quality control, and cooperative advertising, seems well suited to succeed in this type of environment (Chan and Justis, 1990).

Cultural

According to Gilbert and colleagues (2004), in today's ever-increasing globalization of services and brands, service-oriented businesses need to attend to the satisfaction of their customers both domestically and abroad while transcending unique cultural differences from country to country. Their study reveals two empirically derived, cross-cultural, fast-food customer satisfaction dimensions: satisfaction with the personal service and satisfaction with the service setting. Services involve people-to-people contact, and thus culture plays a much bigger role in services than in merchandise trade. McDonald's requires Polish employees to smile whenever they interact with customers, and such a requirement is considered by many employees as artificial and insincere. (Cateora and Graham, 2005). This is also noticed in many countries where smiling at customers is not customary and is considered hypocritical. However, the ways to serve, greet customers, and other aspects are all being standardized and are integral part of the services provided by the franchisors.

It is very difficult, if not impossible, to distinguish the intricacies involved in any culture. One of the ways of examining some of the major dimensions of culture has involved a comparison of behavioral aspects. The most often used cultural dimensions are by Hofstede (1980), which primarily focus on power distance, uncertainty avoidance, individualism/collectivism, and masculinity/femininity. Other cultural analysis by Trompenaars and Hampden-Turner (1998) is more recent and looks from a broader angle. The impact of franchise restaurants on these dimensions needs to be studied empirically.

Manners and customs represent a culture's views of appropriate ways of behaving. It is important to monitor differences in manners and customs since they can have a direct effect on the service encounter (Ziethaml and Bitner, 2003). The most prominent impact on culture due to franchise restaurants is on food habits, etiquettes, and mannerisms. Sandwiches, such as burgers, are new to many cultures and do not resemble the staple foods and menus that have been followed traditionally for a number of years. It is the method of prepara-

tion and ingredients used
to region. Now with franc
very significant differences
arches have become a symbo
American style. As seen in Cl
iar American setting was the m
English in smaller print). Peop
Cokes. It was, deja vu all over
(Watson, 2000). In many countrie
by vendors and mom-and-pop re
studied U.S. and Korean fast-food c
tations and perceptions of McDonal
results indicate that significant diffe
and South Korean patrons in terms of
tions of fast-food restaurant services, o
U.S. consumers, low food prices are of p
evaluations of fast-food establishments.
significantly important to Americans. Or
customers, service dimensions other than l
ity and empathy, increase in relative impo
pected to be just that: fast in selection as w
less time is spent the expectation of the pric
that food will be of consistent quality and serv
ans and other Asian cultures, service speed an
be important, but do not dominate their percep
features. McDonald's is considered in many co
dining restaurant symbolizing U.S. culture and no
food restaurant with less expensive menu items. Fe
conditioning, ambience, visual appeal, and conveni
portant in many cultures where U.S. fast foods are p
many countries food is relatively expensive at U.S. f
rants. For Koreans the expectations are higher, and the
cheap and is imbued with the cultural messages of the r
on earth. As a result, Lee and Ulgado (1997) find Korea
likely disappointed by McDonald's. They look for a mo
experience, which includes the food, the speed of servi
association with American culture.

Products that are acceptable and extremely popular in th
States may not be acceptable and familiar in many countrie

Domino's Pizz
no word existe
the Japanese
years, pepper
units. Thus, n
ence. Also, i
in the countr
oni could no
pork produ
locally. Sp
laysia and
ucts that
accommo
choices.
Meal
of fast-f
United
such as
very c
coffee
over
pacte
idea
over
stick
ting
im
tur
at
v
o
i

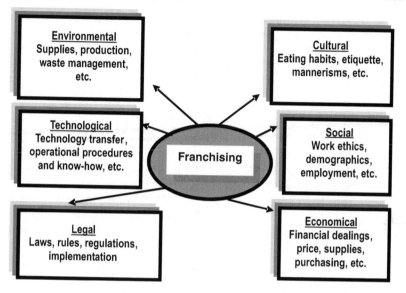

FIGURE 12.1. Global Impacts of Franchising

lustrates the major aspects of the global impact of franchising. The experiences learned by U.S. franchisors in Asia bear testimony to the importance of understanding foreign cultures' ways of doing business (Chan and Justis 1990). For U.S. franchisors seeking to expand globally, these include greater cultural universalism, a younger population willing to try new products, more women working, and, thus, a higher percentage of two-income families with more disposable income (Justis and Judd, 1989). Franchisors must consider a number of strategic factors in making the decision to expand their franchising system globally, namely: (1) economic factors, (2) political/legal factors, (3) sociocultural factors, and (4) infrastructure. For example, U.S. firms intending to franchise in Europe must be prepared to cater to local tastes rather than to a "pan-European" ideal. With the elimination of geographic and other barriers, European consumers will have access to an increased variety of new products, many of which will be produced by new entrants. It is likely that many of these new entrants will be smaller businesses that do not have the resources required for research and development, sophisticated marketing, or quality control. The franchising concept, with its emphasis on trade-name/product recognition, quality control, and cooperative advertising, seems well suited to succeed in this type of environment (Chan and Justis, 1990).

Cultural

According to Gilbert and colleagues (2004), in today's ever-increasing globalization of services and brands, service-oriented businesses need to attend to the satisfaction of their customers both domestically and abroad while transcending unique cultural differences from country to country. Their study reveals two empirically derived, cross-cultural, fast-food customer satisfaction dimensions: satisfaction with the personal service and satisfaction with the service setting. Services involve people-to-people contact, and thus culture plays a much bigger role in services than in merchandise trade. McDonald's requires Polish employees to smile whenever they interact with customers, and such a requirement is considered by many employees as artificial and insincere. (Cateora and Graham, 2005). This is also noticed in many countries where smiling at customers is not customary and is considered hypocritical. However, the ways to serve, greet customers, and other aspects are all being standardized and are integral part of the services provided by the franchisors.

It is very difficult, if not impossible, to distinguish the intricacies involved in any culture. One of the ways of examining some of the major dimensions of culture has involved a comparison of behavioral aspects. The most often used cultural dimensions are by Hofstede (1980), which primarily focus on power distance, uncertainty avoidance, individualism/collectivism, and masculinity/femininity. Other cultural analysis by Trompenaars and Hampden-Turner (1998) is more recent and looks from a broader angle. The impact of franchise restaurants on these dimensions needs to be studied empirically.

Manners and customs represent a culture's views of appropriate ways of behaving. It is important to monitor differences in manners and customs since they can have a direct effect on the service encounter (Ziethaml and Bitner, 2003). The most prominent impact on culture due to franchise restaurants is on food habits, etiquettes, and mannerisms. Sandwiches, such as burgers, are new to many cultures and do not resemble the staple foods and menus that have been followed traditionally for a number of years. It is the method of preparation and ingredients used that have differentiated foods from region to region. Now with franchising, standardizations take place with very significant differences in the products and services. Golden arches have become a symbol of consistent product and services with American style. As seen in China, the only departure from the familiar American setting was the menu board (which was in Chinese, with English in smaller print). People were downing burgers, fries, and Cokes. It was, deja vu all over again in dozens of other countries (Watson, 2000). In many countries fast foods are traditionally served by vendors and mom-and-pop restaurants. Lee and Ulgado (1997) studied U.S. and Korean fast-food customers, comparing their expectations and perceptions of McDonald's restaurants. In general, study results indicate that significant differences may exist between U.S. and South Korean patrons in terms of their expectations and perceptions of fast-food restaurant services, of McDonald's in particular. To U.S. consumers, low food prices are of paramount importance in their evaluations of fast-food establishments. In addition, assurance is also significantly important to Americans. On the other hand, to Korean customers, service dimensions other than low prices, such as reliability and empathy, increase in relative importance. Fast foods are expected to be just that: fast in selection as well as service, and when less time is spent the expectation of the price is low, with assurance that food will be of consistent quality and service. However, for Koreans and other Asian cultures, service speed and low food prices may be important, but do not dominate their perceptions as other service features. McDonald's is considered in many countries a prestigious dining restaurant symbolizing U.S. culture and not necessarily a fast-food restaurant with less expensive menu items. Features such as air-conditioning, ambience, visual appeal, and convenience are more important in many cultures where U.S. fast foods are popular. In fact, in many countries food is relatively expensive at U.S. fast-food restaurants. For Koreans the expectations are higher, and the product is not cheap and is imbued with the cultural messages of the richest country on earth. As a result, Lee and Ulgado (1997) find Koreans to be more likely disappointed by McDonald's. They look for a more complete experience, which includes the food, the speed of service, and the association with American culture.

Products that are acceptable and extremely popular in the United States may not be acceptable and familiar in many countries. When

Domino's Pizza went to Japan in 1985, the company discovered that no word existed for pepperoni. Domino's imported pepperoni until the Japanese were trained to make this product. After more than ten years, pepperoni pizza is the number-one-selling pie in Japanese units. Thus, not only a new product was introduced but also its preference. Also, importation of certain products that are already available in the country is restricted in some countries. In South Korea, pepperoni could not be imported because of the restriction on importation of pork products. This led to establishing some methods of production locally. Special slaughtering restrictions, such as halal foods in Malaysia and Middle-Eastern countries, led to the development of products that meet those requirements. Thus, franchising is not only accommodating local food preferences but also developing new food choices.

Meal timings and eating patterns are also affected by introduction of fast-food restaurants. The popularity of breakfast meals in the United States does not get translated very easily in many countries, such as in Middle East, where eating breakfast away from home is not very common. With the introduction of breakfast menu items and coffee, eating patterns are changing, if not getting homogenized all over the world. Eating styles and mannerism have also been impacted. A vast number of people in many countries do not like the idea of eating away at a food stand or eating while standing. Moreover, holding sandwiches in hand, and not using knife, fork, or chopsticks to eat, is considered out of etiquette. Slowly this pattern is getting impacted in many parts of the world. Another major aspect impacted is the family ritual of eating together at home. Some cultures are very particular about family members getting together to eat at one time. Eating away from home or the habit of grazing has severely dented this opportunity of getting together and interacting with one another. The idea and design of a food court with common seating area is now being accepted in many European countries. Previously consumers ate at home or frequented restaurants serving china, cloth napkins, and silverware. Reusable items and eating while standing or driving were not considered civilized.

Though indirectly, McDonald's has introduced certain words and phrases in local languages, such as the addition of Mac or Macados, "super size it," "I'm loving it," "You deserve a break today," etc. To many the golden arches represent more than fast foods to mean

American, the Western culture, capitalism, and a foreign competitor. Also, it is the homogenization of tastes and elimination or reduction of local cuisines that will have a slow but long-term impact.

Although effort is made to include and localize menu items, such as adding more spices in South America or Malaysia, the main items must have the identity of the franchise. Some of the prominent examples of menu changes made by McDonald's restaurants worldwide include frankfurters, beer, and a cold four-course meal in Germany; McLaks, a grilled salmon sandwich with dill sauce, and McSpaghetti, pasta in a sauce with frankfurter bits in the Philippines; Chicken tatsuta, a fried chicken sandwich spiced with soy sauce and ginger in Japan; Kiwi burger, a hamburger with a fried egg and a slice of beet in New Zealand; Samurai Pork burger, a sandwich marinated with teriyaki sauce in Thailand; and McHuevo, a hamburger with a poached egg on top in Uruguay. McDonald's makes heroic efforts to ensure that its food looks, feels, and tastes the same everywhere. A Big Mac in Beijing tastes virtually identical to a Big Mac in Boston. Menus vary only when the local market is deemed mature enough to expand beyond burgers and fries. Consumers can enjoy Spicy Wings (red-pepper-laced chicken) in Beijing, kosher Big Macs (minus the cheese) in Jerusalem, vegetable McNuggets in New Delhi, or a McHuevo in Montevideo. Nonetheless, wherever McDonald's takes root, the core product, at least during the initial phase of operation, is not really the food but the experience of eating in a cheerful, air-conditioned, child-friendly restaurant that offers the revolutionary innovation of clean toilets (Watson, 2000). It is also argued that it is other conveniences provided by fast food that establishes their permanence. Also, one of the major impacts of franchising is developing food habits in children, which will be hard to change for generations. Even with all the adaptations that McDonald's does to suit local tastes, the local culture seems to be changing due to its presence and business strength.

Social

According to McDonald's (McDonald's Corporation, 2002) plan, they pride themselves in having well-trained employees who will proudly provide fast, friendly, and accurate service with a smile, in a way that delights their customers. They have a responsibility to maintain a work environment in which everyone feels valued and accepted for personal and professional growth, and to promote job satisfaction. This plan and responsibility have the positive impact of developing "work ethics," which is inculcated particularly in younger generation. Also, the concept of part-time work for students, elderly, and home-makers was also introduced in many countries. In the United States, McDonald's has taught work ethics to millions of college students who are starting their professional career or who would like to support part or whole of their educational expenses. In a study done by Royle (1995) McDonald's workers in UK and Germany were found to be fundamentally similar: largely deskilled, owing to high levels of automation, and were part-time and shift workers. Usually only management had full-time contracts. Broad similarities were evident in the makeup of the workforce in both countries, which can be put into two categories: First, those who have difficulty finding work due to lack of education or they do not speak the language fluently or because they are economic migrants. The second group perceive themselves as having a limited stake or interest in the company, either because they are not financially dependent on the work or because they are transitory, as in the case of students. Most notable differences were seen in the numbers of youth workers, especially those under 18. In the UK approximately 64 percent of the workforce was under 20, whereas in Germany this figure was nearer to 24 percent.

In many countries, working for McDonald's is considered as a highly preferred job. They receive many applications from well-educated candidates. This is also true for other franchise businesses. The initial and ongoing training, which is a part of franchising, has a distinct impact on the work habits of people worldwide. It teaches teamwork, coordination, planning, synchronization, and execution in a timely fashion. In addition to excellent training opportunities, stepwise promotion from line workers to managers were unheard of in many countries where only seniors based on age alone were given priority. The age-old requirement in some countries to work only for one corporation during a lifetime has changed partly due to the influx and availability of jobs provided by franchising.

According to Watson (2000),

McDonald's opened in Beijing in 1992, a time when changes in family values were matched by a sustained economic boom. The startup date also coincided with a public "fever" for all things American—sports, clothing, films, food, and so on. American-style birthday parties became key to the McDonald's expansion strategy. Prior to the arrival of McDonald's, festivities marking youngsters' specific birth dates were unknown in most of East Asia. . . . Until the late 1970s and early 1980s, most people paid little attention to their calendar birth date if they remembered it at all.

Arranging birthday parties have become a very popular activity for most of the franchise restaurants, particularly in countries where celebrating birthdays were not known. According to Watson (2000),

For the first time in Chinese history, children matter not simply as future providers but as full-scale consumers who command respect in today's economy. . . . In effect, the fast-food industry helped start a consumer revolution by encouraging children as young as three or four to march up to the counter, slap down their money, and choose their own food.

Children are major target consumers and driving force most of the fast-food restaurants worldwide. It is more than food that has made American restaurant franchises popular in other countries. It is a unique combination of cleanliness of restaurant, toilet facilities, quick service, value meals, air-conditioned atmosphere, different ambience, and the association of a super power. School and college kids go to fast-food operations to socialize, enjoy the lighted atmosphere, and spend hours after school in those places. Elderly use it to get out of crowded living quarters, enjoy the openness, and read newspapers provided by these restaurants. Thus it is a place of socialization in many countries as opposed to being a fast turnover place in the United States. The changing demographics in many countries, with large proportions of teenagers have also increased the development of franchise restaurants worldwide. Sometimes social and religious dilemmas pop up due to certain restrictions imposed by franchisors. For example the short-sleeve shirts worn by many in fast food restaurants is frowned upon by people in countries such as Malaysia and Middle East, where women normally follow a strict dress code.

Most companies build their human resources (HR) programs by adapting to specific cultural differences in each Asian country. But McDonald's takes a different approach by looking at how the cultures are the same. As part of recruitment process, McDonald's looks for people who are seeking advancement, such as training, and think they will be rewarded for hard work ("McDonald's Focuses," 1997).

Another indirect or direct impact of fast foods is the creation of public civility, which was ignored in many countries. Crowded counters, customer rage, noisy atmosphere, breaking lines, discriminatory customers, and impatience were witnessed in many restaurants. However, with standard procedures and providing an attendant as well as with peer customer pressure, lines are well organized, discipline is noted in little actions such as picking up and disposing trash. This is a very gradual and subtle change that is becoming evident, although its full credit may not be imparted to franchising.

One of the most severe criticisms of fast foods is related to the health consequences of fast-food consumption on a long-term basis. Numerous studies have or are focused on health consequences of most food items served by fast-food restaurants. Although the exact impact can be judged only after carefully planned longitudinal studies, it is widely presumed and shown that one of the causes in recent dietary changes is resulting in obesity. Such a study (Lowell, 2004) considered various possible causes of worldwide obesity, such as genetics, modern lifestyles, and particularly food. The author points a finger at the food industry, and particularly the fast-food industry, which, over the past few decades, has perfected various marketing techniques designed to make people eat more food ("super sizing"), more often. The leaders of this industry are also accused of putting its balance sheet before the health and welfare of young people by targeting children and schools. It can be safely presumed that fast-food consumption has some impact that may be overtly negative or sometimes positive.

McDonald's places much emphasis on employee training to attain a standard level of service, regardless of the restaurant or the country they are in. This training program is very carefully designed and covers all aspects of the service from meeting and greeting, to food preparation, to cleaning the restrooms. McDonald's has traced a number of other benefits to ongoing training, particularly in terms of improved morale and productivity. This training program is an integral and mandatory part of franchising agreement. Training leads to personal development and creates a sense of achievement and belonging, which is highly valued in many countries.

Historically, many family-owned restaurants in Europe were closed on certain days of the week, on holidays, and for about two weeks during the late summer for family vacation. Most of the franchise restaurants including McDonald's are open on more days and hours than local businesses. This has imposed on the local restaurant practices as well as for employees who would like to avail of the former break periods.

Economical

Great interest is shown in franchising because of the recent and projected impact of franchising on the U.S. economy and global markets in the next decade. Franchising is one means of providing capital, needed services, and management training to businesses in communities that are experiencing rapid and discontinuous change in their economy. The enthusiasm for global expansion in franchising is fueled by many of the same factors that drove the growth of franchising in the United States. Purchasing food in large quantities itself has helped local growers and purveyors. Out of necessity and demand, many restaurants have must on growing their own products, thereby employing a local workforce. For instance, the demand for french fries in China and Russia encouraged local suppliers to provide potatoes with specific requirements and variety.

Referring to the example of McDonald's "Plan to Win Vision" (McDonalds, 2006), they will be the most efficient provider so that they can be the best value to the most people. They have a responsibility to maintain their values and high standards as they provide food that is affordable to a wide range of customers. This affordability has been the hallmark of franchising, since the survival of franchising is based on their growth. Prices set by McDonald's restaurants worldwide is used as a barometer to measure the purchasing power of a country. The Big Mac Index has become a comparative tool to assess certain financial parameters. The index is also an indicator of the pricing flexibility and differentiations that McDonald's allows for its products as well as an indication of local economy and purchasing power. Table 12.4 shows the differences among Big Mac prices served in selected countries. The *Economist*'s Big Mac index is based on the theory of purchasing-power parity (PPP), based on the notion that exchange rates should move to equalize the prices of a basket of

TABLE 12.4. Big Mac Prices in Selected Countries

Country	Big Mac Price $*	Country	Big Mac Price $*
Switzerland	5.46	South Africa	2.44
Denmark	4.97	South Korea	2.36
Sweden	4.46	Taiwan	2.32
Euro area	3.75 **	Singapore	2.19
ntblBritain	3.61	Mexico	2.12
New Zealand	3.16	Poland	2.06
United States	3.00 ***	Brazil	1.99
Hungary	2.85	Egypt	1.67
Turkey	2.80	Argentina	1.60
Peru	2.74	Indonesia	1.57
Canada	2.60	Hong Kong	1.54
Chile	2.56	Thailand	1.52
Japan	2.50	Russia	1.49
Australia	2.46	Philippines	1.42
Czech Republic	2.45	Malaysia	1.33
		China	1.26

*At market exchange rate (December 13, 2004)

**Weighted average of member countries

***Average of four cities

Source: Adapted from *The Economist* using McDonald's price data

goods and service across different countries ("The Big Mac Index," 2004). As seen in the table, the cheapest Big Mac is in China compared to the United States. This differential is used for the comparative valuation of currency in respective countries.

Political/Legal

Fast food can even trump hard politics. After NATO accidentally bombed the Chinese embassy in Belgrade during the war in Kosovo, Beijing students tried to organize a boycott of American companies in protest. Coca-Cola and McDonald's were at the top of their hit list, but the message seemed not to have reached Beijing's busy consumers: McDonald's were packed with Chinese tourists, local yuppies, and grandparents treating their "little emperors and empresses" to Happy Meals (Watson, 2000).

For different political motives, McDonald's restaurants have been the targets of protests, sometimes violent, worldwide such as seen in California, Mexico City, Taiwan, Beirut, France, etc. McDonald's is often the preferred site for anti-American demonstrations, even in places where the local embassies are easy to get at. McDonald's is more than a purveyor of food; it is a saturated symbol for everything that environmentalists, protectionists, and anticapitalist activists find objectionable about American culture. McDonald's even stands out in the physical landscape, marked by its distinctive double-arched logo and characteristic design (Watson, 2000). Through successful global marketing of the McDonald's franchise, the "golden arches" have come to symbolize American fast food and its related services such as convenience, quality, value, and cleanliness. In Europe, anger behind the protests stems from a set of interrelated issues: escalating trade tensions and the importation of hormone-treated beef, dispute over the openness of the Europe Union markets to U.S. goods, and French fears of the decay of their national culture as the U.S. burrows deeper into French society (Kramer, 2000).

An area of great concern to franchising relates to laws governing the franchisor-franchisee relationship. Laws, rules, and regulations vary from country to country. The very success of franchising is based on sound laws, which can be defended when necessary. In some countries either such laws are nonexistent or problems with their implementation exist. Even major differences exist between the U.S. and the EC systems. Whereas the United States has detailed state and federal laws regulating the franchisor-franchisee relationship, the EC has regulated it only through the general antitrust provisions in the Treaty of Rome and the competition law of each member state. The antitrust provisions of the treaty prohibit anything that tends to prevent or restrict competition between member states, which in franchising terms means exclusive territories and price controls. To facilitate the growth of franchising, the EC Commission passed the new Franchising Block Exemption in November 1988 to enable franchisors to gain exemption from the treaty provisions.

Compliance with the provisions of the block exemption will mean that the franchisor is now able to grant exclusive territories, among other things. Problems in many countries also relate to the copyright and patent laws. Franchising concepts are closely guarded by franchisors, and any infringement leads to unfair competition. Thus the impact of franchising has been on either development of franchising laws or modifications in existing laws.

Technological

Every franchise restaurant concept is based on specific operational and management criteria, which include technology in one form or other. The use of equipment, special control devices, temperature regulators, point-of-sales systems, inventory upkeep, financial information, and communications are all linked to different technologies. Thus major technology transfer takes place when one franchise concept moves into another country. Both tangible and nontangible technological aspects are transferred, which are necessary to provide standard quality of products and services. Constant communication links between the franchisor and franchisees are essential for keeping healthy relationships. Technology is used for this communication, which may range from day-to-day operation to occasional problem solving. Many of the equipment used in franchise restaurants are custom made and therefore have to be imported. This not only brings in new innovative technology, but also needs provisions for parts, accessories and services.

Biotechnology is also a major factor, which is becoming one of the major issues confronting franchise restaurants. In order to meet demands of the growth of restaurants and for quality reasons biotechnology is being used increasingly. Concern related to the genetically altered products is evident in several countries. It is predictable that product and nutrient quality of crops raised using biotechnology will become a debatable issue in many parts of the world.

Environmental

Rapid development of restaurant franchises worldwide will also have an impact on external and near environments. The continuous and enormous use of natural resources can disturb the balance in the ecosystem. McDonald's has a rain forest policy that declares its commitment to beef purchasing practices that do not contribute to tropical deforestatation. Natural habitat can be disturbed by extensive deforestation and overcultivation. Soil erosion and fertility can also be affected if appropriate measures are not taken. Other environmental concerns include water-use efficiency, water being a very scarce and valuable resource in many countries. Harmful by-products may be released into air, which may be due to the functioning within the restaurant or due to the harvest and transportation of needed supplies. Fertilizers and pesticides used for raising corps for animal feeds also add to the environmental concerns. In addition, energy use and sources used for energy also becomes a very major impacting factor in many countries.

Another major impact is related to the amount of waste produced from preproduction practices, leftover items, detergents and cleaning agents, garbage and trash, and packaging materials. Millions of tons of plastic and paper packaging are used per year, which in turn uses chemicals and forest products. McDonald's alone is the largest consumer of beef products in many countries, and some of the cattle were raised on the former rain forest land. Deforestation not only removes vegetation, but also adds to the moving of communities into the cleared areas thereby multiplying the impact. Cleaning compounds, insecticides, antibiotics, and pesticides can have an impact on human, animal, and environmental health, which requires effective management. This is not confined only to the restaurant facility since some of this waste originates when consumers carry food to different places. The use of foam materials or materials that do not disintegrate easily has also become a major concern. Thus recycling becomes extremely important to minimize the impact of waste produced on environment. McDonald's has developed social, environmental, and animal welfare actions in order to address most of the aforementioned concerns.

CONCLUSION

A brief and disjointed effort has been made in this chapter to highlight the major impact of rapidly growing franchise restaurant services globally. Further empirical studies are imperative to explore each impact individually, particularly those related to services management.

REFERENCES

The Big Mac index (2004). *The Economist,* December 16. Available at: http://www.economist.com/markets/indicators/displaystory.cfm?story_id=E1_PVDPGQT.

Cateora, C. and Graham, J.L. (2005). *International Marketing,* 12th edition. Boston, MA: McGraw-Hill Irwin.

Chan, P.S. and Justis, R.T. (1990). Franchising in the EC: 1992 and beyond. *Journal of Small Business Management, 30*(1): 83-89.

Committee on Small Business (1990). Special Report. Washington, DC: U.S. House of Representatives. Available at: http://sbc.senate.gov/republican/HTML/news/SnoweUrgesOMBNomineePortman.html.

Cunneen, C. (2004). Recipe for success: Fast-food bigwigs vary strategies, menus to make it in 2004 market. *Nation's Restaurant News, 38*(2): 30.

Gilbert, R.G., Veloutsou, C., Goode, M.M.H., and Moutinho, L. (2004). Measuring customer satisfaction in the fast food industry: A cross-national approach. *The Journal of Services Marketing, 18*(4/5): 371.

Hofstede, G. (1980). *Culture's Consequences: International Differences in Work Related Values.* Beverly Hills, CA: Sage.

International Franchise Association (2007). Available at: http://www.franchise.org.

Justis, R.T. and Judd, R.J. (1989). *Franchising.* Cincinnati, OH: South-Western Publishing.

Khan, M. A. (1999). *Restaurant Franchising,* 2nd edition. New York: John Wiley & Sons, Inc.

Kramer, G. (2000). McDomination. *Harvard International Review, 22*(2): 12-14.

Lan, L. and Khan, M.A. (1995). Hong Kong's fast-food industry: An overview. *Cornell Hotel & Restaurant Quarterly, 36*(3): 34-42.

Lee, M. and Ulgado, F.M. (1997). Consumer evaluations of fast-food services: A cross-national comparison. *The Journal of Services Marketing, 11*(1): 39-52.

Lowell, J. (2004). The food industry and its impact upon increasing global obesity: A case study. *British Food Journal, 106*(3): 238-248.

McDonalds (2006). Available at: http://www.McDonalds.com.

McDonald's Corporation (2002). 2002 annual report. Available at: http://www.mcdonalds.com/corp/invest/pub/annual_rpt_archives/2002_annual.html.

McDonald's focuses on similarities (1997). *HR Magazine, 42*(7): 107.

National Restaurant Association (2004). Available at: http://www.restaurant.org.

Parasuraman, A., Zeithaml, V.Z., and Berry, L.L. (1988). SERVQUAL: A multiple-item scale for measuring consumer perception of service quality. *Journal of Retailing, 64:* 12-40.

Royle, T. (1995). Corporate versus societal culture: A comparative study of McDonald's. *International Journal of Contemporary Hospitality Management, 7*(2/3): 52-57.

Trompenaars, F. and Hampden-Turner, C. (1998) *Riding The Waves Of Culture.* London, UK: Nicholas Brearley.

Watson, J. L. (2000). China's Big Mac attack. *Foreign Affairs, 79*(3): 120-135.

Zeidman, P.F. (2003). The global brand: Asset or liability? *Franchising World,* (May/June): 4.

Zeithaml, V.A. and Bitner, M.J. (2003). *Service's Marketing,* 3rd edition. Boston, MA: McGraw-Hill Irwin Publishing.

Chapter 13

The Strategic Behavior of German Tour Operators in Croatia

Nadine Sulkowski
Angela Roper

INTRODUCTION

Previous research into the international holiday industry (Dale, 2000; Evans and Stabler, 1995) and contemporary industry reports (Deloitte, 2004) reflect that the typical mass-market strategy of conventional tour operators is being challenged by a growing trend toward individualized holidays. For tourism firms operating in today's dynamic environment, strategic management becomes a balancing act between offering personalized service and generating sales volume as well as developing packages that are economically viable for today's travelers while meeting their rising quality expectations. For those tourism firms operating globally, this task is challenged further by host country conditions that often differ considerably and thus threaten international product consistency and standardization.

German tourism firms are increasingly investing into building or upgrading capacity in the growing holiday destination of Croatia ("South-East Europe Invests," 2002; Birnmeyer, 2003; Münster, 2002). Croatia is a small destination with a market share of 4.5 percent within the Mediterranean region (Deutsche Entwicklungsgesellschaft, 2001). See Figure 13.1.

Accounting for 14 percent, tourism is one of the main contributors to the country's GDP (Central and Eastern European Business Information Centre, 2002). After a shortfall during the Yugoslavian war, Croatia recorded about 6.9 million visitors in 2002 and was thus close

Global Cases on Hospitality Industry
© 2008 by The Haworth Press, Taylor & Francis Group. All rights reserved.
doi:10.1300/5923_13

FIGURE 13.1. *Source:* Adapted from University of Texas (2004). Perry-Castañeda library map collection. Available at: http://www.lib.utexas.edu/maps/cia04/croatia_sm04.gif.

to reaching prewar levels (Croatia National Tourist Board [CNTB], 2003b). Although unaffected by the current international crisis, Croatia's image is still affected by Yugoslavia's previous mass-market strategy and by an outdated tourism infrastructure (Deutsche Entwicklungsgesellschaft, 2001). However, a gradual development of strategic tourism planning aiming to enhance Croatia's competitiveness is occurring (Cizmar, 1996; Pirjevac, 1997; Dragicevic et al., 1998).

Three global tourism firms, TUI, Thomas Cook, and LTU Touristik (REWE), account for 60 percent of all package tours to Croatia sold in Germany (CNTB, 2003a), which equals the proportion of the total number of package tours sold by the integrated conglomerates on the German market (Cavlek, 1994). The remaining tours are sold by Croatia specialists (CNTB, 2003a), which are almost exclusively targeting Germany and are typically integrated to a minor extent compared to the large firms. The German market for Croatia holidays is thus oligopolistic, with the three conglomerates and the specialist I.D. Riva (2003a,b,c) as the main players. All operators have diversified their Croatia portfolio and now offer a range of holidays targeted at the volume, exclusive, and specialist segments.

RATIONALE AND OBJECTIVES

The recent trends toward more individualized holidays and enhanced quality standards as well as integration and diverse host country conditions suggest that the attention of the academic arena is required to conceptualize the strategic behavior of firms in tour operating. Until now, only a few academics have researched this subject.

Gauf and Hughes' (1998) case study of TUI's diversification into coach tourism provided valuable empirical insights into the strategic behavior of integrated tourism firms and concluded that the suitability of different strategies depended on organizational size and the structure. Meanwhile, Roper and colleagues (2003) conducted a comprehensive empirical study of the strategic approaches taken by a sample of multinational tour operators managing the source market of Norway. Their study focused on how the sample firms organized different activities in the package tour value chain, including the design, preproduction activities, marketing and distribution, production and consumption, as well as postpurchase activities. Their study also highlighted that the structure of tour operating firms must be considered when attempting to conceptualize their strategic behavior. Moreover, the effect of the services offered by different agents in the supply chain on overall tourist satisfaction and the need to respond to industry dynamics were identified as key factors impacting the strategies pursued by firms. Further qualitative research in this field (Curtin and Busby, 1999; Klemm and Parkinson, 2001; Medina-Munoz et al., 2003) has focused on analyzing the relationship between tour operators and local suppliers in destinations. Although these contributions did not aim to take a holistic approach to analyzing the management of value chain activities, they were, however, useful in identifying the key issues in analyzing the strategic behavior of tour operating firms.

Overall, the findings from previous research suggest that external dynamics, company internal factors, and the relationship to agents in the tourism supply chain must be addressed when attempting to conceptualize the strategic behavior of tourism firms. However, a need still exists for more comprehensive empirical studies of the approaches taken by tourism firms in managing package tours. Davies and Downward (2001b) in particular pointed to the need for more qualitative and case-specific investigations in collaboration with practitioners to enable a more specific assessment of the dynamics featuring the industry and the internal environment of tourism firms.

The rationale for conducting a comparative analysis of how different tour operators manage inclusive tours to a particular holiday destination thus emerges from a lack of empirical research into the strategic behavior of tourism firms. Whereas conventional theory on industry economics holds that strategic success is mainly determined by favorable market conditions, it is increasingly argued that a firm's ability to operate efficiently and effectively under various external conditions is positively correlated to its success (D'Aveni, 1995; Davies and Downward, 2001b). Given the lack of case-specific studies in this field and the recent debate about the significance of internal factors in contributing to strategic success, this chapter aims to provide empirical insights into the determinants of the strategies pursued by German tourism firms in operating package tours. The objectives of the chapter are the following:

- To review previous research into the package tour industry with focus on the European short-haul market
- To explore the approaches taken by four German firms in operating package tours to Croatia
- To analyze the emerging key issues that influence the strategies pursued by tourism firms and to identify the determinants that must be taken into consideration when attempting to conceptualize their strategic behavior
- To make recommendations and suggest areas for further research

The exploration of the strategic approaches taken by tourism firms in managing inclusive holidays is based on a comparative study of four German tourism firms in operating package tours to Croatia. Since TUI, Thomas Cook, and LTU Touristik are among the five main players on the European holiday market (Kuoni, 2001), an empirical exploration of their approaches toward managing activities in the package tour value chain seems to offer potentially valuable insights into the factors influencing the strategic behavior of tourism firms. Moreover, it was considered that the approaches taken by integrated firms and specialists vary significantly. To gain empirical insights into this phenomenon, the strategies pursued by both types of firms were explored.

Since Croatia is in the process of postcommunism transition after the Yugoslavian war in the early 1990s, the challenging business environment facing incoming tour operators was regarded as an ideal setting for this study. Similar to D'Aveni (1995) and Davies and Downward (2001b), this study challenges the traditional assumption that strategic success is mainly determined by favorable market conditions. Moreover, it can be observed that the strategic approaches taken by the four firms in Croatia vary in terms of geographical focus, product portfolio, and arrangement of different inclusive tour elements.

This chapter first assesses the potential of Croatia as a destination for package tours sold in Germany. Second, the main findings from previous research in the strategic behavior of tourism firms are reviewed. The methodology employed is then outlined and primary research findings from a comparative case study into the strategic approaches taken by four German tourism firms are analyzed. Triangulating the findings from the comparative case study with the findings from previous research, the chapter finally attempts to conceptualize the determinants of strategic behavior in tour operating and suggests areas for further research.

ISSUES IN MANAGING GERMAN PACKAGE TOURS TO CROATIA

The following assessment of demand-and-supply issues in operating inclusive tours to Croatia is based on information derived from secondary research. The following seven key themes emerged:

1. The buying power and travel behavior of German tourists
2. Croatia's image as a holiday destination
3. The length of the holiday season

4. The state of the accommodation sector
5. Management expertise and availability of financial resources
6. The state of the transportation infrastructure and ground services
7. Sustainability

These themes will be briefly discussed.

Germany is Croatia's most important source market, with the uniqueness of Croatia's coast and its diverse opportunities for water sports being the key selling points (CNTB, 2002, 2003c). The proportion of German inclusive tourists is 34 percent (approximately 419,000 holidays sold), compared to 66 percent traveling individually (Deutsche Entwicklungsgesellschaft, 2001). Despite the adverse effect of the German recession, Croatia and Bulgaria were the only countries recording increasing visitor numbers in 2002 (Köster-Hetzendorf, 2002). Following the aftermath of the Yugoslavian war, Croatia experienced a prior image as being a destination for cheap mass-market holidays. However, the now higher costs of living have affected Croatia's attractiveness in both the volume and the up-market segments (Deutsche Entwicklungsgesellschaft, 2001).

Secondary research findings illustrated that Croatia's accommodation sector required substantial upgrading, whereby particularly the four-star plus sector was seen as underdeveloped (Bunja, 2003; Deutsche Entwicklungsgesellschaft, 2001; Pirjevac, 1993; Köster-Hetzendorf, 2002). Since Croatia lacks sufficient resources and management expertise, the Croatian government has tried to attract foreign investors knowledgeable in hotel and tourism management through privatizing state-owned properties (Cizmar, 1995; Dulcic, 2000; Fox, 2000; Horvat-Jokic, 1997; Jordan, 2000; Kunst, 1998). Particularly in areas dominated by monopolistic competition, for example, in Mid Dalmatia, local hoteliers often depend on support from foreign investors (Kunst, 1998). However, privatization is proceeding slowly and corruption and cronyism are threatening foreign investors who cannot build on the expertise of a local partner ("South-East Europe Invests," 2002).

The most problematic aspect of Croatia's transportation infrastructure is its underdeveloped road system and lack of parking facilities in important destinations (CNTB, 2003b,c; Deutsche Entwicklungsgesellschaft, 2001). Contrarily, the two oligopolists for air charters between Germany and Croatia were rated as excellent in terms of service and punctuality and were identified as an important source contributing to overall guest satisfaction (Deutsche Entwicklungsgesellschaft, 2001). The same applies to the services provided by Croatia's various ground handling agents during airport transfers and excursions, whereby foreign tour operators are legally obliged to organize ground services in conjunction with local agents (Udruga Hrvatskih Putnickih Agencija , 2001).

The academic literature on Croatia's tourism industry (see Cizmar, 1996; Pirjevac, 1997; Dragicevic et al., 1998) widely recognizes the need for sustainable tourism development. Moreover, governmental policies restricting the building of new capacity to prevent environmentally and culturally adverse effects have been implemented (Deutsche Entwicklungsgesellschaft, 2001).

PREVIOUS RESEARCH INTO THE EUROPEAN TOUR OPERATING INDUSTRY

Appendix 13.A evaluates previous research into the package tour industry, and the main issues identified from this review are discussed.

Although the process of integration has led to contestable market conditions within the British inclusive tour industry, featuring fierce price wars, the German market is characterized as a stable oligopoly dominated by TUI, Thomas Cook, and LTU/REWE (Evans and Stabler, 1995; Gratton and Richards, 1997). All firms operate their own charter airlines, tour operators, travel agencies, hotel chains, and other related subsidiaries. Whereas TUI and Thomas Cook serve various European and several overseas markets, LTU specifically targets Germany and Austria. Due to exclusive arrangements binding travel agents to one operator, German tourism firms have been able to protect market share, turnover, and profitability more effectively than UK operators. It follows that German operators are challenged in increasing their share on the home market and thus tend to grow by internationalizing their business, particularly through exploring other European source markets (Gratton and Richards, 1997) and by the integration of upstream activities (Cavlek, 1994). Contrarily, British operators have focused mainly on the integration of downstream activities through the acquisition of distribution channels to protect their share (Gratton and Richards, 1997; Klemm and Parkinson, 2001). However, it is increasingly argued that in times of uncertain market conditions more focus should be placed on profitability by keeping capacity tight (Davies and Downward, 2001a; Roper et al., 2003). Despite the differences, a gradual convergence of the German and the UK market is occurring (Gratton and Richards, 1997), which was demonstrated by the acquisition of the British operators Thomson and Thomas Cook by TUI and C&N Touristik and the transformation of the latter into one conglomerate under the name Thomas Cook.

Large operators are currently challenged by the maturity of the mass-market tour product and the trend toward increasingly differentiated markets and individualized holidays (Curtin and Busby, 1999; Evans and Stabler, 1995). Middleton (2003) however acknowledged that since many tourism destinations were characterized by decades of mass tourism, the process of transformation into destinations offering individualized quality products might occur slowly, which implies that mass, customized, and personalized products exist in parallel, and that operators hence tend toward portfolio diversification. Although being powerful in producing economies of scale, integrated firms operating in the specialist segment are facing serious competition from small- and medium-sized operators that are more agile and thus more flexible in adapting their products to changing traveler demands (Dale, 2000; Evans and Stabler, 1995; Gauf and Hughes, 1998; Laws, 1997; Middleton, 1991). Large operators typically tend to control more value chain activities through up- and downstream integration, which enables them to control the design of physical products and service standards (Cavlek, 1994; Gauf and Hughes, 1998; Tribe, 1997; Pender, 2001). Contrarily, specialists are characterized by informal and flat hierarchies and by their flexible approach to developing products and procuring tourism services, which enables them to deliver personalized holiday packages (Laws, 1997; Gauf and Hughes, 1998). Consequently, Gauf and Hughes (1998) concluded that concentration and specialization were the most viable strategies for large firms, whereas Dale (2000) suggested that large firms could increase their responsiveness to changing consumer demands by the continued acquisition of niche operators. He also emphasized that tight linkages with agents in the supply chain were crucial to consistently satisfying consumer demands.

Following their research into the competitive strategies of British tour operators and their impact on the image of particular destinations, Klemm and Parkinson (2001) argued that sustainable tourism development was threatened by the domination of distribution channels by large operators, their continued aggressive price competition, and tour operating branding policies. However, according to the business attitudes toward sustainable tourism development expressed by a sample of British tour operators, Curtin and Busby (1999) concluded that a sustainable tourism product was also desired by incoming tour operators since it enhanced the quality of the overall product and contributed to higher profit margins. Whereas Klemm and Parkinson (2001) emphasized that a sustainable tourism product depended on equal relationships between incoming operators and local suppliers, Middleton (2003) assigned particular importance in this process to small- and medium-sized firms on both the demand and supply side. His main arguments were that due to their typical collaboration with multiple local suppliers, smaller operators were supporting local entrepreneurs, and that small suppliers owned by locals enabled a more authentic image projection than large and standardized suppliers.

In summary, in terms of the strategic behavior of tour operating firms it can be observed that they are very much in the process of integration and concentration as well as of developing internationally. Operationally, a growing tendency is toward keeping capacity "tight." In terms of the market for package tours, an increasing trend is toward differentiated products and more individualized holiday packages. A mounting need exists for incoming tourism firms to contribute to sustainable tourism development at the destination in order to gain financial and promotional benefits.

METHODOLOGY

The findings presented in this chapter originate from a larger study (Sulkowski, 2003). Due to a lack of previous data, an inductive approach was taken. Previous research into the European holiday industry, academic literature on industry organization, and the tourism value chain as well as the consulting report provided by the EU Commission on the Airtours/First Choice merger procedure (European Commission, 1999) were reviewed to identify the main dynamics of the industry and to provide a broad conceptualization of how tourism firms operated strategically.

To enable the evaluation of Croatia's current and future potential as a destination for package tours sold in Germany and to identify the main players dominating this market, a case study research strategy was employed. The applied sampling technique was purposive, whereby two homogeneous subgroups, large integrated tourism firms and two specialists were selected. Although a purposive sample is seldom representative (Saunders et al., 2000), the approaches taken by two of the three largest players in the German market were investigated. However, the sample of German specialist operators was not regarded as representative since specialists are numerous and differ considerably in terms of size and target markets. Since a case study involves multiple data-collection techniques (Jankowicz, 1995), primary and secondary data on each firm was collected. Primary data was obtained through semistructured interviews with one key informant from each German sample firm:

R1: Chief contract manager from the second largest tour operating firm (ITF1)

R2: Director, product department South Eastern Europe, from the third largest tour operating firm (ITF2)

R3: Director from the largest Croatia specialist in the German market (S1)

R4: Manager from a small, highly individualized specialist in the market for Croatia holidays (S2)

The interview questions focused on discussing the firm's perception of the external conditions it faced when operating package tours to Croatia and on the firm's approach toward managing different value chain activities. Since the process of data collection took place just before the start of the summer holiday season, unfortunately not more than one interview could be arranged as the firms were restricted by the high level of internal activity. In the case of both specialists, the interviews were frequently disrupted by incoming phone calls; therefore the data was a little less detailed than that gathered from the interviews with respondents from the large operators. However, the interviewer was given the unexpected opportunity to observe the day-to-day procedures of the two specialist operators and thus gained insights into organizational structures and dynamics characterizing these two companies.

Interviews were also carried out with three experts in the Croatian tourism industry. These included a director from the Croatia National Tourist Board in Frankfurt (R5), an investment manager at a German investment and development institution (R6), and a visiting academic and director of one of the top hotels in Zagreb (R7). These expert informants provided important data about the demand and supply features of the German market for package tours to Croatia; in addition, they provided an external view of the strategic behaviors of sample tour operators. Moreover, secondary data was gathered by studying the brochures and Web sites of the firms. In addition, articles published in one of Germany's largest tourism journals, the touristic master plan for Croatia, Croatia country reports, and previous research into the Croatian holiday industry were reviewed to obtain secondary data on demand-and-supply characteristics. Statistical evidence on incoming travelers and tour operators was obtained from the Croatia National Tourist Board.

The findings from secondary data were used to establish a set of key issues (K1-Kn, see Figure 13.2), which were considered relevant to the exploration and evaluation of the approaches taken by the four sample firms in operating package tours to Croatia.

This included an assessment of the current dynamics featuring the European holiday industry, demand-and-supply issues impacting the operation of tours to Croatia, and typical approaches of integrated tourism firms and specialists in managing different value chain activities. In terms of the latter, the package tour value chain devised by Roper and colleagues (2003) was utilized as a framework for analysis of the findings in this study (Figure 13.3). The themes subsequently identified were used to categories the data obtained from primary research and to enter units of data (U1-Un) into data sheets (see Appendixes 13.B and 13.C), which allowed the views of the respondents and secondary research findings on the identified key themes to be juxtaposed systematically. This process also enabled a triangulation of secondary and primary research findings. The analysis of different data units enabled the identification of emerging key themes that

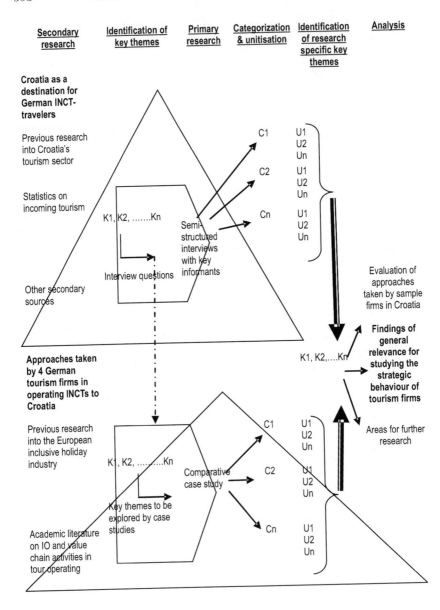

FIGURE 13.2. The Process of Data Analysis. *Source:* Adapted from Saunders et al. (2002).

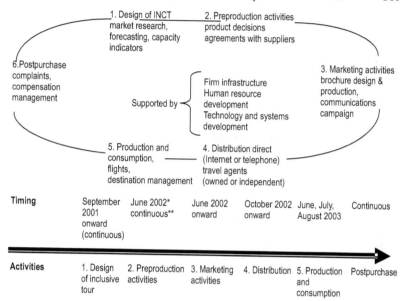

1. Design of INCT
market research,
forecasting, capacity
indicators

2. Preproduction activities
product decisions
agreements with suppliers

6.Postpurchase
complaints,
compensation
management

3. Marketing activities
brochure design &
production,
communications
campaign

Supported by — Firm infrastructure
Human resource
development
Technology and systems
development

5. Production and
consumption,
flights,
destination management

4. Distribution direct
(Internet or telephone)
travel agents
(owned or independent)

Timing	September 2001 onward (continuous)	June 2002* continuous**	June 2002 onward	October 2002 onward	June, July, August 2003	Continuous

Activities	1. Design of inclusive tour	2. Preproduction activities	3. Marketing activities	4. Distribution	5. Production and consumption	Postpurchase

*Final decisions of product components
**Agreements with local suppliers

FIGURE 13.3. The Package Tour Value Chain and the Typical Time Frame of Holiday Packaging. *Source:* Adapted from Roper et al. (2003).

seemed relevant in developing a deeper understanding of the strategic behavior pursued by tourism firms. Moreover, areas for further research were identified.

FINDINGS

All sample firms illustrated a certain level of integration. On an international basis, both large firms operated their own charter airlines, hotel chains, tour operators, and travel agency chains. However, in managing tours to Croatia, only some upstream activities were integrated. For example, ITF1, which is currently developing its redesigned international up market product, owns and operates seven key properties near Croatia's five-star destination Dubrovnik. Offering a more diversified Croatia portfolio than ITF2, R1 also mentioned a planned joint venture with one of Croatia's largest ground handling agents. The third largest player, S1, owns four ground handling agencies in Istria, where most of the operator's highly diversified business is concentrated. The family-owned operator S2 displayed a comparatively high level of integration. Apart from one travel agency that simultaneously functioned as the head office, S2 owned three hotels in Mid Dalmatia, where most of the operator's activity was taking place and a fleet of five coaches.

In terms of value chain activities, all operators started the design of package tours for summer 2004 around eighteen months in advance, whereby trends observed during previous seasons served as indicators for customer demand. ITF1 additionally used external marketing reports and competitor information, whereas the most diversified operators S1 extensively researched the activities by tourists at the destination. S2 obtained most information from loyal customers. Both large operators concentrated on a few key segments, whereby ITF1 pursued a volume and up-market strategy and ITF2 focused on the volume segment and the all-inclusive market. S1 based its product design largely on the variety of niche markets available in Istria and, apart from their own ground service agencies there, collaborated with a multiplicity of small local suppliers to design the Croatia experience as authentic as possible (R3, 2003). Contrarily, S2 focused on individualized service. The predesigned product range concentrated largely on the volume segment, but due to S2's flexible approach to supplying different package tour elements, personalized packages were available on request. According to R4 (2003), its intention was not to grow but to maintain a loyal customer base. To maintain these linkages, S2 offered additional services such as flight-only arrangement at more competitive rates than the usual scheduled service. Whereas the marketing department of ITF1 carried out the design of tours, ITF2 had a product department for air-inclusive tours and arrivals by car. Being characterized by very flat hierarchies, both specialists said that the director, managers, and assistant managers were directly involved in the design process.

All operators started their preproduction activities for the season 2004 in May 2003, whereby previous buying behavior was used as an indicator for the capacities required in different locations. Whereas in the case of ITF2, one product department carried out most value chain activities, the marketing activities and contractual agreements of ITF1 were arranged in different departments. In the case of the two specialists, again directors, managers, and assistant managers were directly involved in the purchase of capacity and services. Due to currently exceeding demand, good personal relationships with local suppliers were seen as imperative in negotiating favorable deals (R4, 2003). Although all operators apart from ITF2 controlled some upstream activities through integration, most of them were managed through contractual agreements. Typically starting with the arrangement of accommodation, both large operators and S1 mostly agreed guaranteed capacities. ITF1 and ITF2 tended toward guaranteeing key properties through three- to five-year contracts, whereby ITF1 also owned and operated seven key properties in South Dalmatia. Both operators were investing in upgrading properties that were guaranteed through long-term commitments, for example, through financing a swimming pool. The financially restricted specialists refrained from such investments. The smallest operator, S2, made additional use of allocations and ad hoc agreements to maintain a certain level of flexibility and to minimize the risk of financial losses. After starting the distribution of packages, operators still had the opportunity to increase the agreed capacity, whereby ITF1 also kept some flexibility in reducing capacity by offering any excess to smaller players. All firms offered charter flights from the major airports in Germany on fixed travel days. Flights were arranged on the basis of contracted accommodation. The estimation of required charters seemed easier for the large operators who, unlike the two specialists, were able to specify the proportions of air-inclusive tours sold in different Croatian regions. Again, both large operators and S1 used almost exclusively guaranteed part-charters on Croatia Airlines and AeroLloyd. Due to comparatively low levels of volume, both large operators stated that flights operated with their own aircraft would be unprofitable. S2 made additional use of allocations and ad hoc agreements and collaborated in the exclusive segment with scheduled carriers. For both specialists, transport by coach was another crucial element of tour design. Both large operators collaborated with one large national agent that operated ground services (transfers, excursions, and sportive activities) in all coastal regions. To maintain their flexibility in holiday packaging, the specialists typically collaborated with multiple local agents.

In terms of marketing and distribution, both ITFs mainly sold their products through their integrated or allied travel agency chains, whereas the specialists sold most holidays directly. Both ITFs were promoting Croatia through two mass-market brochures, one designed for air-inclusive and one for arrival by car. The properties promoted by the latter were generally concentrated in the north of Croatia and included a large number of apartments, and the air-inclusive brochures promoted destinations in the south and properties slightly higher in category. Croatia was promoted in the same brochures among other Mediterranean, Southeast, and North African holiday destinations, where the design of the brochures was largely standardized without differentiating Croatia from other destinations. Both operators included their specialist products, particularly cruises, on no more than two pages in the brochures. ITF1 also included a small number of southern destinations in its brochure for up market holidays. This brochure was divided into four different themes, which were active holidays, cultural trips, exclusive tours, and relaxation. Croatia, renowned for being a destination offering diverse opportunities for sports and culture, was interestingly promoted these opportunities under the theme "relaxation." Significant for ITF1 was that the properties that were owned or management contracted were particularly highlighted in the brochures. Moreover, the mass-market brochures offered a huge range for families, pointed out through specific icons next to the picture of the property indicating that children were welcome and thus directing the purchasing decision of families toward these properties. ITF2 particularly focused on promoting all-inclusive clubs, which was demonstrated by the relative higher proportion of all-inclusive clubs included in their brochure. This observation is in line with the firm's strategic intent to expand the family all-inclusive business, a segment that R2 (2003) stated was seen as having the highest potential in this destination.

Both specialists were promoting their products through one brochure covering both their mass-market and specialist products, whereby S1 dedicated about a third of its brochure to niche products and used extra supplements for cruises and biking. S2 promoted just a limited range of specialist products through its brochure, which corresponded with their flexible and personalized approach to holiday packaging. According to R4 (2003), a number of collaborative partners at the destination could be contacted on an ad hoc basis to personalize products either for individual travelers or for groups. This implies that for S2, tight linkages with customers were imperative to keep them informed about the opportunities the operator was offering. Despite the specialist orientation of the two firms, the brochures promoted largely properties in the three-star range, which for both reflected a considerable reliance on the volume market. Although only a few all-inclusive clubs were offered and no specific indication was given about the suitability of different properties for particular segments, the hotels owned by S2 were highlighted to catch the customers' attention.

In all four cases, ground services, such as sporting activities or excursions, were either sold through the brochure or directly by ground handling agents at the destination, whereby obviously the number of destination-based activities sold in advance was greater for S1 than for the other operators.

During the production and consumption phase, direct control over the quality of products and services was executed by ITF1 over key properties in the up-market destination South Dalmatia, by S1 over most ground services in Croatia, and by S2 over key properties in Mid Dalmatia and the transport by coach. ITF1 admitted that in all properties that were operated by the firm, changes to the workforce had to be made to enable the delivery of a satisfactory service quality. Moreover, a planned joint venture between ITF1 and one of Croatia's largest ground handling agents will allow the German conglomerate to execute more control over the activities taking place at the destination. All operators, apart from ITF2, thus controlled the core activities of their differentiation strategy. Nearly all leisure activities at the destination were designed, sold, and operated by local agencies, which highlighted the important role of ground handling agents in contributing to the overall holiday experience. Correspondingly, the respondents mentioned that the range and quality of ground services delivered by particularly smaller agents depended on good relationships between the operator and suppliers. The same applied to the supply of accommodation, for which, in critical situations, such as an overbooked resort, personal relationships with local hoteliers proved to be of advantage in obtaining the best possible service for the operator's travelers (R4, 2003).

Only ITF2 and S2 provided some information about their post-purchase activities. ITF2 mentioned that sources of common guest complaints were traced and unsatisfactory performance was discussed with the supplier. However, R2 lamented that many discussions with local suppliers about product and service deficiencies, most commonly inadequate food and beverage (F&B) products, were fruitless, and that in some cases the only option was to impose financial claims for the losses incurred by compensation payments or to choose a different supplier. S2 obtained most customer feedback directly from frequent customers, which again highlighted their strong focus on building a loyal customer base. For S2, strong linkages with loyal customers also proved beneficial in the operator's attempt to improve its product and services on a continuous basis.

DISCUSSION

The current trend toward increasingly differentiated segments and individualized holiday packages implies that operators will have to diversify their portfolios. However, previous research into the European holiday industry has led to the conclusion that the structure of large operators is not suited to highly individualized products. Thus, it was suggested that the most viable strategy for large operators was concentration, whereas small- and medium-sized should compete through their agility and their ability to respond quickly to changing consumer demands (Dale, 2000; Evans and Stabler, 1995; Laws, 1997; Middleton, 1991). In this study, in a similar way, a positive correlation between the size of the firm and the level of standardization or personalization was observed. Both integrated operators concentrated on a few segments, whereby the products fitted into the regional strategies pursued in each segment and displayed only little adaptation to Croatia through a selection of typical niche products. In the case of ITF2, one product department carried out most value chain activities, whereas the marketing activities and contractual agreements of ITF1 were arranged in different departments. Correspondingly, R1 noted that this split in organizational responsibilities was not ideal since those directly involved in negotiating the contracts with suppliers were usually more informed about the features of individual properties or locations at the destination. That individual value chain activities were carried out by different departments or subsidiaries of the large operators also implied that those involved in selling holiday packages to the end consumer probably lacked sufficient knowledge about the supplier structures at the destination to personalize holiday packages on request. The largest Croatia specialist offered mainly customized holidays through a highly differentiated portfolio. Segmentation thus occurred on a psychocentric basis according to the preference for certain activities (e.g., biking, hiking, or cruising) or destination experiences, such as ecotourism. However, according to R3 (2003), the operator's largest business was in the volume segment. The smallest operator, which kept the approach to holiday packaging flexible through the use of allocations and ad hoc agreements, offered the most personalized packages, which was crucial in maintaining a loyal customer base. Due to the flat hierarchy, the directors, managers, and assistant managers of S2 were directly involved in contracting as well as sales activities and could thus establish close relationships with customers as well as suppliers, which proved to be highly beneficial in individualizing holiday packages on an ad hoc basis.

Traditionally, the strategic aim of players within the inclusive holiday industry was to increase their market share, however, previous empirical investigations (Curtin and Busby, 1999; Davies and Downward, 2001a; European Commission, 1999; Roper et al., 2003) demonstrated that in times of uncertain market conditions, more importance was assigned to maximizing profitability by keeping capacity tight. Primary research findings showed that the sample firms tended to keep initial capacity tight but at the same time flexible through agreements allowing them to extend their capacity up to a certain date in early spring. Typical to large operators, ITF1 also maintained some flexibility in decreasing capacity by offering excess seats or beds to smaller operators to avoid financial losses incurred by overcapacity. At the same time, it could be observed that the operators strategically fixed a part, or, in the case of S1, all of their capacity to secure market share within the segments and the regions they were mainly targeting. As R2 (2003) mentioned, the market leader and ITF1 had negotiated five-year contracts with various properties in the region they were strategically targeting (see Appendix 13.C) and thus secured their market share, which forced other operators to focus on alternative destinations (R2, 2003). A significant correlation also existed between the regions in which ITF1 and S2 had fixed their capacity through ownership and the locations in which the strategically most important activities pursued by the operators were taking place. For instance, ITF1, which is currently developing its redesigned international up-market product, owns and operates seven key properties near Croatia's five-star destination Dubrovnik. S2, which is focusing on Mid Dalmatia, owned three properties in this region. In the case of the specialist S1, the atypical approach to arrange exclusively guaranteed capacity displayed the operator's attempt to extend its overall market share (R3, 2003). Here, a significant focus on the northern region of Istria, which is offering the most diverse range of destination activities, was observed, which correlated to the operator's customized portfolio. Moreover, S1 agreed one-year contracts with the owners of sixty eco-farmhouses and twenty-nine motor sailing ships, and thus secured capacity in two of its key niches. The strategic behavior of S1 suggests that organizational type and structure are not the only internal determinants of the approaches taken toward managing different activities in holiday packaging. It seems that, in addition, the strategic goals as well as differentiation strategies must by considered when attempting to conceptualize the strategic behavior of tourism firms. Another factor that requires consideration is the correlation between strategy and financial risk taking. ITF2, which did not reveal any particular plans to change its current strategy, pursued a low risk strategy by keeping capacity tight and limited financial investments to the upgrading of key properties, whereas the other three operators took higher risks either through the ownership of properties in key location (ITF1, S2) or through an atypically high number of commitments (S1). Due to S1's heavy reliance on their only source market of Germany, which is currently in recession, and the operator's relatively low brand awareness in the volume segment, such inflexibility in decreasing capacity, appeared particularly risky, but matched the firm's aggressive growth strategy. In the case of ITF2, the willingness to take financial risks through the acquisition of key properties in the up-market destination Croatia was correlated to the firm's attempt to expand its international up-market product.

It was argued by authors such as Dale (2000) and Klemm and Parkinson (2001) that tight linkages with individual agents in the supply chain were crucial in meeting customer expectations and delivering package tours of high quality. As this comparative study demonstrated, three of the sample firms had invested in the integration of upstream agents involved in the operation of Croatia holidays. In the case of ITF1, the acquisition of key properties in Croatia's up-market destination South Dalmatia was in line with the firm's strategic intent to develop its global up-market product, whereby R1 also argued that Croatia could not be treated as a typical family destination because the stony beaches were not suitable for small children. Correspondingly, a significant observation was that ITF1 sold its up-market product under the umbrella brand that was created following ITF1's acquisition of a British operator of the same name. Also the firm's charter airline, which previously carried a different name, was rebranded and named after the umbrella brand, which probably relates to a strategic intent to achieve more global visibility and to project a more consistent image of the parent company. Contrarily, the volume products for Croatia were sold under one of the conglomerates subbrands carrying the historical name of the firm. According to R1, the original brand from which the conglomerate evolved over the past decades still has a higher market acceptance in Germany's volume segment. Contrarily, ITF2 sold its volume product under the name of the umbrella brand and included a number of destinations in Mid and South Dalmatia under the name of a subbrand targeting mainly singles and couples in the midmarket segment. As the parent brand is generally concentrating on the volume and the family segment, the firm's intent to extend its all-inclusive offer for families in Croatia conformed to the overall strategy, whereby investments into the upgrading of key properties were aimed at making the properties more suitable for this market segment. The key niche S1 focused on was biking holidays. As many travelers wished to carry their own bicycles to the destination the operator collaborated with five bus companies connecting all German regions. Some especially designed coaches carried the operator's logo, reflecting its intention to increase brand awareness. In the case of S2, the operation of a small bus fleet was a crucial strategic predisposition to personalizing group tours. The planned joint venture between ITF1 and one of Croatia's largest ground handling agents will enable the firm to exercise greater control over products and services and will lead to a more diversified portfolio in the Croatia business. This strategic move appears to be an attempt to defend ITF1's market share against the growing competition from S1, which is enjoying competitive advantage in Istria through its ownership of strong ground handling agents.

Academic literature on tour operating (Laws, 1997) highlighted that large operators were usually maintaining tight linkages with downstream agents through the integration of distribution channels, whereas due to their personalized approach in holiday packaging, the more viable option for specialists was to sell directly. This implies that customer closeness and the ability to sell directly is of paramount importance for small operators. The findings generated by the comparative case study complied with the previous assumption. Whereas the integrated conglomerates sold the majority of their largely standardized holiday packages through subsidiaries or allied travel agents, the specialists sold most tours directly. As observed during the interviews, both specialists operated the direct selling function at their head office under the direct supervision and involvement of their directors and managers who were at the same time directly engaged in the contracting activities. This flat structure logically enabled a quick response to individual customer requests and thus facilitated the establishment of a loyal customer base, which for S2 was crucial in maintaining their market share, whereby added-value offers such as S2's flight-only arrangement proved advantageous. Maintaining tight linkages with customers seems also important in preventing the effects of disintermediation. As discussed by Kunst (1998), principals should aim to establish close relationships with incoming tourists to encourage direct bookings, which would reduce the bargaining power of incoming operators, particularly in destinations that were easily accessible.

Moreover, the findings of the study suggest that tight linkages with customers are also of paramount importance in monitoring and controlling the performance of suppliers. As R2 (2003) explained, ITF2 traced the sources of guest complaints, often through comment cards, and approached the underperforming supplier either on a consultative basis or, in drastic cases, imposed financial grievances by deducting any compensation payments from the invoice of the respective supplier, whereby the effect of these actions on future service levels varied. S2 confirmed a similar approach, whereby customer feedback was mainly obtained during conversations with loyal customers.

Some academics (for example, Curtin and Busby, 1999; Middleton, 1991) have argued that the contribution to sustainable tourism development is of particular concern to incoming tour operators who could benefit from higher profits and higher levels of stability in destinations characterized by high quality levels. Moreover, Middleton (1991) argued that sustainable tourism development, through the implementation of environmental policies or the commitment to the preservation of local heritage, is increasingly demanded by consumers, which implies that the contribution to this process could be used as a marketing tool. Unfortunately, no evidence proving a formal commitment of the firms to sustainable tourism development was produced, whereby both specialists saw their contribution to Croatia's economic development in their collaboration with many small suppliers and their attempt to exploit the destination's numerous niches. However, it should be considered that some specialist holidays bringing tourists into direct contact with local inhabitants bear the danger of incurring a gradual acculturation and might thus be more destructive than volume strategies accumulating incoming tourists in restricted tourist spots (Klemm and Parkinson, 2001). This begs the question as to what extent S1's strategy to sell "authentic Croatia" to a large customer base will be viable in the long term?

Unlike the financially less advantaged specialists, both large operators made key investments into properties that were guaranteed through three- to five-year contracts, whereby the main motivation was to adjust the physical standard of the properties to the demands of the operator's guests. R2 (2003) perceived the collaboration between local hoteliers and ITF2 as effective and saw some improvements in overall quality levels, whereby ITF1's tight control over key properties in the up-market destination Dubrovnik could be expected to have a similar positive effect and might be used as a benchmark for quality standards in competing hotels. This observation shows that the branding policies of incoming tour operators can positively influence tourism development at the destination and thereby challenges Klemm and Parkinson's (2001) argument that the branding policies of tour operators often have an adverse effect on sustainable tourism development. However, since the level of control exercised by incoming tour operators over local suppliers varied, their contribution toward increased levels of quality and profit margins remains subject to further research, which conforms to the conclusions drawn from previous studies (Medina-Munoz et al., 2003).

As stated in the rationale of this study, conventional theory on industry economics is based on the assumption that strategic success is mainly determined by favorable market conditions. However, recent insights into this subject have concluded that a firm's ability to operate efficiently and effectively under various external conditions is positively correlated to its success (D'Aveni, 1995; Davies and Downward, 2001b). Previous research also led to the conclusion that large operators were currently challenged by the maturity of the mass-market tour product and the trend toward increasingly differentiated markets and individualized holidays. Thus, they were facing serious competition from small- and medium-sized operators that were more agile and thus more flexible in adapting their products to changing traveler demands (Dale, 2000; Evans and Stabler, 1995; Gauf and Hughes, 1998; Laws, 1997; Middleton, 1991). The last assumption could be partly triangulated with primary research findings that showed that the smallest of the four investigated operators proved to be the most flexible in personalizing holiday packages. However, it could be observed that ITF1 and S1, which were among the three largest operators for Croatia holidays, focused mainly on the volume segment, took strategic action by operating their own ground handling agents (or in the case of ITF1, planning a joint venture with an existing agent), which allowed them to customize holidays at the destination. Moreover, the study into the strategic behavior pursued by the sample firms demonstrated that the evaluation of the external conditions in Croatia depended on their pursued strategies. ITF1, which is currently developing its up-market product particularly bemoaned the lack of adequate four-star accommodation and took strategic action by acquiring key properties or agreeing management contracts and thus executed tight control over the product delivery in this segment. Contrarily, ITF2 particularly lamented the poor quality of F&B products that obviously had a detrimental effect on the overall quality of the family all-inclusive product the operator aimed to extend in Croatia. Moreover, the operator rated the leisure facilities of many hotels as inadequate for families and took action by investing in the upgrading of those. The two specialists that sold a large amount of coach tours obviously lamented the poor quality of roads toward southern destinations, whereas the representative of ITF2 stated that the company was benefiting from the underdeveloped road system in Mid and South Dalmatia since 90 percent of all travelers to Dalmatia were thus choosing more profitable air-inclusive packages.

　　Overall, the comparative case study highlighted that all operators focused on slightly different segments and concentrated their business in different regions along Croatia's coast, whereby the characteristics of the respective region matched the strategies pursued by the firms. This phenomenon was underlined by R2, who saw all-inclusive clubs as the most promising future product and stated that the operator was already successfully expanding this business in Croatia. He however stressed that other firms were likely to see a greater potential in other products, which, as he explained, is the condition for long-term competitiveness of the strategies pursued by different tour operators in one destination.

Generally, the findings of the study suggest the validity of D'Aveni's (1995) and Davies and Downward's (2001b) argument that a firm's ability to operate efficiently and effectively under various external conditions is positively correlated to its success.

CONCLUSIONS AND FURTHER RESEARCH

The themes that emerged from the above research were the following:

- The impact of business strategy on the relative importance of external conditions
- The link between organizational size and structure and the focus on concentration or individualization
- The tendency to keep capacity tight to maximize profits and strategically fixed to secure market share
- The link between differentiation and branding strategies and the management of tourism value chain activities
- The importance of maintaining tight linkages with customers to secure market share and monitor supplier performance
- The role of incoming tour operators in contributing to sustainable tourism development and thus in elevating quality levels as well as profit margins

This research suggests that in an attempt to conceptualize the strategic behavior of tourism firms in operating inclusive tours to a short-haul destination, both internal as well as external factors must be considered. Figure 13.4 illustrates those factors that were found to determine the value chain activities of tour operators in holiday packaging.

From an external perspective, the structure and dynamics of the inclusive holiday industry, the demand characteristics of the source

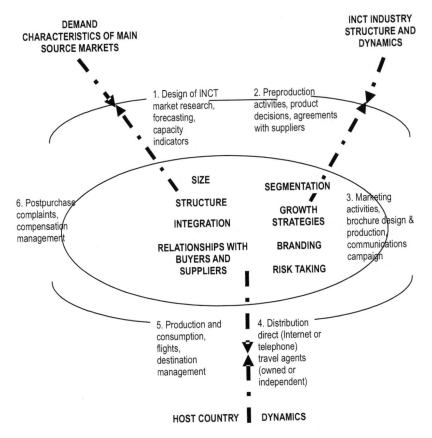

FIGURE 13.4. The Determinants of Strategic Behavior in Operating Package Tours

market and host country dynamics were found to be important determinants. From a company internal perspective, size and structure of the firm, the level of integration, segmentation, growth, and branding strategies, relationships with buyers and suppliers and the preparedness to take financial risks were identified as determinants with a significant impact on a firm's strategic behavior in holiday packaging.

Overall, it was observed that the extent to which external conditions were regarded as problematic depended on how much they were affecting the success of the strategy pursued by different operators, whereby the financially strong players took strategic action by investing into facilities that were critical to the success of their international strategies. The financially less advantaged operators targeted segments that could be satisfied with existing tourism facilities and affordable company assets.

This research has shown that due to their flat structure and flexible approach to holiday packaging, specialist operators enjoy competitive advantage through their responsiveness to the growing demand for individualized holidays. However, financially strong large players can compete in the specialist segment through the acquisition of specialist operators or ground handling agents that enable a customization of holiday packages at the destination, whereby a seamless collaboration between the product design department, contractors, and distributors is imperative to gain knowledge of customer demands and exploit tourism facilities at the destination effectively.

The most important segment for all operators remains to be the volume segment, whereby specialists with lower brand awareness aiming to compete with integrated conglomerates in terms of sales volume may adopt aggressive and financially risky strategies and secure their market share through high proportions of guaranteed capacity. However, large integrated players enjoy competitive advantage in the volume segment through scale economies.

It was observed that all operators, apart from the expanding specialist S1, tended to keep capacity tight to minimize the risk of financial losses. However, a positive correlation existed between the regions in which different operators had fixed their capacity through ownership or long-term contracts and the regions in which most activities of the respective operators took place. In each case, the features of the region matched the differentiation strategy pursued by the operator, which implies that a targeted arrangement of fixed capacity can act as a source of competitive advantage.

Another source of competitive advantage that emerged from this research is the integration of tourism value chain activities that are critical to the differentiation or branding strategy of the operator, whereby this phenomenon of tight control is equally valid for integrated operators and the financially less advantaged specialists.

Customer closeness proved to be of paramount importance in monitoring supplier performance, whereby integrated operators have developed formal customer feedback systems and small players tended to obtain feedback informally from their small but loyal customer base.

Although this study has provided some empirical insights into the determinants of the strategic behavior pursued by four sample operators, the demand for more case specific research into this subject matter remains to gain a deeper understanding of how internal factors enable a firm to cope successfully with external dynamics. One aspect explored by this research that should be addressed further is how volume operators react to the trend toward increasingly differentiated markets and the increasing demand for individualized holiday packages. Moreover, further research into the branding strategies pursued by integrated tourism firms and their subsidiaries in marketing inclusive tours to different destinations is required. Another aspect that should be addressed is the effect of tour operator branding policies on sustainable tourism development, whereby it seems equally important to investigate in how far a potential contribution of incoming tour operators to sustainable tourism development is hindered by the unwillingness of suppliers to cooperate.

Comparing the increase in incoming visitors from different source markets recorded by the Croatia National Tourist Board in 2003, a significant growth between 2001 and 2002 was in the number of tourists from countries where the travel markets have been shaped by the merger and acquisition activities pursued by TUI and Thomas Cook (Hartung, 2002; Lindner, 2003). This seems to indicate that the two firms are increasingly attracting travelers from alternative source markets to Croatia. Thus another area for future research could be in how far the flexibility of globally operating tourism firms in shifting capacity between different source markets affects their strategies pursued in these markets, and in how far the numbers of incoming tourists are shaped by the expansion strategies of integrated tourism firms.

APPENDIX 13.A. PREVIOUS RESEARCH INTO THE PACKAGE HOLIDAY INDUSTRY

Authors	Subject	Methodology	Conclusions
Medina-Munoz et al. (2003)	Empirical study of the control exercised by tour operators over accommodation companies	Review of previous research and secondary data sources; survey of British and German tour operators	The level of control exercised by different tour operators varies, whereby it is generally neither considerably significant nor nonexistent. The aspects most controlled are those referred to in contractual agreements, i.e., (in descending order of importance), the financial side, the characteristics of the accommodation facilities, internal operation and condition of the accommodation company, marketing and sales activities, the characteristics of other tour operators having agreements with the accommodation company, and investment and growth activities.
Roper et al. (2003)	Assesses the dynamics of the Norwegian package tour industry and evaluates how multinational package tour firms strategically manage the source market Norway	Review of previous research and secondary data sources; comparative case study using secondary data sources, semi-structured interviews and document analysis	Package tour brands will be pressurized towards enhancing their profitability rather than just extending their market share. Tourism research appears to be underrepresented and demands for more specific attention.
Davies and Downward (2002a)	Investigates the nature of competition shaping the UK tour operator	Review of secondary data sources Quantitative empirical data generated for the purpose of econometric analysis and causality tests	More qualitative research is needed to investigate the dynamics of profitability and market share further. The industry organization approach is useful in investigating the tourism industry and the UK tour operator and travel agent industry, but to allow a more specific analysis firms must be segmented according to similar size and interest.
Davies and Downward (2001b)	Assesses the applicability of the industry organization model to the UK package-tour industry and its implications for research	Review of previous research	More qualitative and case-specific analysis is needed to give a broader perspective than provided by the industry organization model, which demands a new agenda of tourism research.

325

Authors	Subject	Methodology	Conclusions
Klemm and Parkinson (2001)	Investigates the competitive strategies of British tour operators and their impact on the image and quality of tourist destinations	Review of previous research and secondary data sources; empirical data obtained from discussion with key informants inside the firms and at the destination	The domination of distribution channels by tour operators, continued aggressive price competition, and tour operating branding policies are a threat to the sustainable tourism development at many destinations, whereby the short-term economic pressure driving international tour companies is the major determining factor. More equal partnerships between tour operators and local suppliers are required. More research into the relationship between tour operators and local suppliers is needed.
Cavlek (2000)	Investigates the process of horizontal and vertical integration on the European travel market and the multinationalization and globalization of this business	Review of secondary data sources	The competition between and integration of European tour operators is expected to intensify. In terms of integration, major targets of large operators will be small and medium-sized operators and specialists. Increasing individualization will force tour operators into greater portfolio diversification. The fact remains that it is impossible for one tourism firm to satisfy the demands of *all* possible global target markets.
Dale (2000)	Examines the growth and structure of the UK tour-operating industry using the competitive analysis model developed by Porter and Thurlby	Review of previous research	"Organizations are now focusing on change, determining their optimum response and then reinventing themselves to exploit the opportunity" (p. 365). For enhancing the service delivery of the holiday product and to satisfy consumer demands on a sustainable basis, tight linkage's with individual agents in the supply chain are the key to success. Flexibility and responsiveness to changing consumer demands can be achieved through the continued acquisition of niche operators, the development of high value niche products, and through virtual integration/collaboration.

Authors	Subject	Methodology	Conclusions
Curtin and Busby (1999)	Investigates the business attitudes toward sustainable tourism development expressed by some members of the British Federation of Tour Operators and the Association of Independent Tour Operators	Review of previous research and secondary sources; survey of six British tour operators by conducting in-depth interviews	Due to changing demand structures, a need exists for more clearly defined markets rather than just mass and specialist. Sustainable tourism development is also desired by tour operators to enhance quality and thus to increase profit margins and stability. Due to unlimited growth opportunities, large tour operators are unable to regulate themselves. It remains unclear whether the responsibility for environmental problems lies with tour operators or destinations.
Davies and Downward (1998)	Explores competition and contestability in the UK package tour industry using econometric analysis • Compares with Evans and Stabler (1995) • Contrasts with Gratton and Richards (1997)	Review of previous research and secondary data sources; quantitative empirical data generated for econometric analysis	The industry is segmented according to the size of the firm; therefore, more research offering less generalized conclusions about the industry as a whole is needed, whereby the liaison with practitioners is imperative. Relationships between large firms require further investigation and conceptualization.
Gauf and Hughes (1998)	Examines the attempt of TUI to diversify into coach tourism	Review of previous research and secondary data; case study using observation, semistructured interviews, and unpublished data sources	Large firms are suited to mass standardized products, such as air inclusive tours, rather than to the highly individualized coach tourism markets. Despite their assumed ability to exploit economies of scope, large operators were unable to challenge smaller players in the coach tour business. Specialization and concentration are thus considered to be more promising strategies for large firms than diversification.
Gratton and Richards (1997)	Analyzes the development of the European package tour market by comparing the UK and the German market	Review of previous research and secondary data sources	Due to contestable market conditions, the UK market is featured by a fierce price competition and a focus on the home market to protect market share. A stable oligopoly in Germany has resulted in the inability of tour operators to grow on the home market, which has led to their expansion into other European markets. A gradual convergence of the UK and German market could be observed over the past decade.

327

APPENDIX 13.A (continued)

Authors	Subject	Methodology	Conclusions
Evans and Stabler (1995)	Examines and explains the structure and history of the UK packaged holiday market and assesses its future development	Review of previous research	Portrays a gloomy future of the UK inclusive holiday industry, which is likely to be shaped by recurrent price wars. Due to changing consumer demands toward more individualized, innovative, and flexible holiday packaging, mass-market strategies are no longer viable, whereby small to medium-sized operators are more effective in delivering individualized packages. The strategic choice of operators will be to standardize or to specialize. Large operators will have to diversify, possibly in a different sector.
Cavlek (1993)	Assesses the future of the European packaged holiday market	Review of previous research and secondary data sources; possible use of empirical data (no clear methodology provided)	The competition between tourism firms and between different destinations (also between short- and long-distance destinations) will become stronger. The mass-market has reached the state of saturation, which demands that tour operators to become more flexible in responding to changing consumer demands. Small and agile tour operators are quicker and more flexible in adjusting to changing demands, but will not be able to compete with large integrated operators in terms of economies of scale. Sustainable tourism development will become more important on both the demand and supply side.
Middleton (1991)	Assesses the future of the UK market for outbound air-inclusive tours	Review of previous research and secondary data sources	The UK air-inclusive market has reached the stage of maturity. Tour operators will have to become more creative in producing and presenting competitive packages tailored to meet the identified demands of segmented markets. The contribution to sustainable tourism development at the destination by tour operators is beneficial for marketing. The advantages of air-inclusive tours are unassailable.

APPENDIX 13.B. PRIMARY RESEARCH FINDINGS
ON THE DEMAND-AND-SUPPLY ISSUES
OF MANAGING PACKAGE TOURS TO CROATIA

Key themes	Secondary research	R1 Purchasing director ITF1	R2 Director product development SE Europe ITF2	R3 Director S1	R4 Assistant junior manager S2	R5 Director CNTB Frankfurt	R6 Investment manager	R7 Representative of Croatia's academic field
Buying power and travel behavior of German tourists	Germany is the most important source market	Germany is the most important source market	Germany is the most important source market	Germany is the most important source market	Germany is the most important source market	Germany is the most important source market	Germany is the most important source market	Germany is the most important source market
		Three-star volume market is the most important segment	Three-star volume market is the most important segment	Three-star volume market is the most important segment	Three-star volume market is the most important segment			
		Decline in inclusive tours sold in Germany	Decline in inclusive tours sold in Germany				Decline in inclusive tours sold in Germany	
		In 2002 Croatia and Bulgaria were the only countries to experience tourism growth	In 2002 Croatia and Bulgaria were the only countries to experience tourism growth			In 2002 Croatia and Bulgaria were the only countries to experience growth	In 2002 Croatia and Bulgaria were the only countries to experience growth	
	Tendency toward more individualized holidays	Trend toward shorter holidays		Tendency toward more individualized holidays			Increasing trend toward shorter and individualized holidays	

Key themes	Secondary research	R1 Purchasing director ITF1	R2 Director product development SE Europe ITF2	R3 Director S1	R4 Assistant junior manager S2	R5 Director CNTB Frankfurt	R6 Investment manager	R7 Representative of Croatia's academic field
	Recession in Germany led to a decline in package tours sold			Biking is the most important sportive holiday activity	Compared to the entire German market, S2's key market has less spending power, therefore there is less demand for up market products Due to size of operator, the buying power of its loyal customers dictates a highly individualized product			
Croatia's image as a holiday destination	Renowned for its preserved environment Affected by aftermath of Yugoslavian war and still regarded as mass destination Comparatively high costs of living	Renowned for its preserved environment Comparatively high costs of living	Renowned for its preserved environment Affected by aftermath of Yugoslavian war and still regarded as a mass destination Comparatively high costs of living	Renowned for its preserved environment Comparatively high costs of living	Renowned for its preserved environment Aftermath of Yugoslavian war and previous low quality image not regarded as problematic anymore Comparatively high costs of living	Renowned for its preserved environment Comparatively high costs of living	Renowned for its preserved environment Affected by aftermath of war and still regarded as mass destination Comparatively high costs of living	Renowned for its preserved environment Comparatively high costs of living

Potential for the development of a multiplicity of niches	Potential for spa holidays and for active holidays and cruising, stony beaches unsuitable for children	Potential for all inclusive clubs	Potential for ecotourism and further development of cruising, biking and water sports	Potential for cultural tourism and coach tours for seniors	Potential for spa and golf holidays and for cultural tourism	Potential for cultural holidays and ecotourism
	Image of a low quality destination affects Croatia's competitiveness in the up market segment	N/A		Cruising and sailing are the most important niches	Sailing and cruising are currently most important niches	
Holiday seasons	Short (May until October)	Short, should be extended by developing Dubrovnik as a winter destination, but airlines unwilling to cooperate	N/A	Short, but should be extended by developing Dubrovnik as a winter destination	Short, should be extended by developing Dubrovnik as a winter destination	Short, should be extended by developing Dubrovnik as a winter destination
State of the accommodation sector	Underdeveloped due to slow privatization hindered by bureaucratization, corruption and cronyism	Privatization of the accommodation sector is hindered by bureaucratic system	Privatization of accommodation sector is hindered by bureaucratic system	Particularly Dubrovnik is dominated by the investment activities of ITF1	Underdeveloped due to slow privatization, particularly the three and four-star sector require extension and upgrading	Underdeveloped due to slow privatization, particularly the three and four-star sector require extension and upgrading

APPENDIX 13.B. (continued)

Key themes	Secondary research	R1 Purchasing director ITF1	R2 Director product development SE Europe ITF2	R3 Director S1	R4 Assistant junior manager S2	R5 Director CNTB Frankfurt	R6 Investment manager	R7 Representative of Croatia's academic field
State of the accommodation sector	Particularly four-star sector requires extension and upgrading	Requires upgrading, particularly in four-star range, many hotels lack standard facilities such as swimming pools / Quality of three-star accommodation is satisfactory	Requires some upgrading, particularly in the up market segment		Requires some upgrading, but accommodation in general satisfactory			
			Mid-market accommodation is in general satisfactory	Generally satisfactory, but requires some upgrading in the up market segment		Generally satisfactory, but requires some upgrading in the up market segment		
			The range and quality of F&B offers is the main subject of guest complaints		The range of F&B offers is the main subject of guest complaints			
Management expertise and availability of financial resources	Severe lack of management expertise and financial resources demands for the attraction of foreign investors	Severe lack of management expertise and financial resources demands for the attraction of foreign investors	Lack of management expertise in terms of quality, but the friendliness of staff is generally perceived as satisfactory	Lack of management expertise in terms of quality, but the friendliness of staff is generally perceived as satisfactory	Lack of management expertise in terms of quality, but the friendliness of staff is generally perceived as highly satisfactory	Sufficient management expertise, but lack of financial resources to bring tourism product up to international standards	Severe lack of management expertise and financial resources demands for the attraction of foreign investors	Lack of management expertise and financial resources demands for the attraction of foreign investors, particularly hoteliers

	State of tourism infrastructure	Sustainability
	Airports satisfactory. Routes to resort centers and local transport services are underdeveloped	Focus should lie on up-market holidays to maximize profits. Demand for sustainable tourism development to preserve country's natural uniqueness. So far ineffective tourism strategy
	Performance of local ground handling agents is very satisfactory. Airports satisfactory. Routes toward resort centers must be overhauled	Focus should lie on up-market holidays to maximize profits
	Performance of local ground handling agents is very satisfactory. Airports satisfactory. Routes to particularly Southern resort centers require substantial overhaul and more parking spaces are require	Focus should lie on up-market holidays to maximize profits. The attitude of locals towards incoming tourism is problematic
	Performance of local ground handling agents is very satisfactory. Airports satisfactory. Routes to resort centers are underdevelopedd	The range of tourist activities on has improved. Focus should lie on up-market holidays to maximize profits
	Performance of local ground handling agents is very satisfactory. Airports satisfactory. Routes to resort centers are underdeveloped	The range of tourist activities on offer has improved. Focus should lie on up-market holidays to maximize profits
	Airports satisfactory. Routes to coast are underdeveloped, but corrective action is being taken	The range of tourist activities on has improved. Focus should lie on up-market holidays to maximize profits
	Airports satisfactory. Routes to resort centers are underdeveloped	Lack of tourist activities on offer. Focus should lie on up-market holidays to maximize profits
	Routes to resort centers are underdeveloped, but corrective action is being taken. Airports satisfactory	The range of tourist activities on has improved. Focus should lie on up-market holidays to maximize profits. Foreign investors should take more responsibility in educating local staff

APPENDIX 13.C. VALUE CHAIN ACTIVITIES OF THE FOUR SAMPLE FIRMS

Value chain activities	ITF1	ITF2	S1	S2
Information provided by	R1: Chief contract manager of accommodation	R2: Director product department south-eastern Europe air inclusive tours	R3: Director	R4: Assistant junior manager
Design of inclusive tours	Product design based on trends observed during previous season, market research reports developed by external institutions and activities of competitors	Product design based on trends observed during previous season. Possibly use of other indicators (n/a)	Product design based on trends observed during the previous season and extensive marketing research into the activities pursued by tourists at the destination	Product design based on trends observed during the previous season
	Carried out by marketing department	Carried out by product department	Directors and managers directly involved in the design of packages	Directors and managers directly involved in the design of packages
	Packages adjusted to fit into different product ranges offered by the firm, whereby each product range covers one particular region and concentrates on a main segment	Packages adjusted to fit into different product ranges offered by the firm, whereby each product range covers one particular region and concentrates on a main segment	Packages adjusted to niche products typical to Croatia (cruising, yachting, biking, trekking, water sports). Some packages adapted to current lifestyle products (ecotourism)	Pre-designed packages mainly concentrate on the volume segment. Some packages adapted to niche products typical to Croatia (yachting and cruising)
	Southeastern Europe Air inclusive tours: volume tending towards up market. Europe, Arrival by car: volume tending towards low cost and self-catering	Southeastern and North Africa Air inclusive tours: volume tending towards up market. Southeastern Europe, arrival by car: volume tending towards low cost and self-catering		

Mediterranean, Black Sea and North Africa: up market	Southeastern Europe and North Africa: midmarket, singles and couples		
Some adaptation to Croatia in the volume segment through offering niche products typical to Croatia (particularly cruising)	Some adaptation to Croatia through offering niche products typical to Croatia (particularly cruising)	High level of localization through collaboration with a multiplicity of small local suppliers to maximize the experience of "authentic Croatia"	On request high level of individualization, mainly due to a loyal customer base and considerable activity in the business of group tours (i.e. sports clubs, seniors etc.) enabled through the collaboration with a multiplicity of suppliers
Notable standardization of products in the up market segment through offering niche products adapted to the overall product range			Offers also flight-only arrangements
Currently focus on developing Dubrovnik as up market destination		Focus on Istria	Focus on Mid-Dalmatia
Preproduction activities			
Contracts with suppliers were made in May and June of the ongoing year (2003) for the following season (2004)	Contracts with suppliers were made in May and June of the ongoing year (2003) for the following season (2004)	Contracts with suppliers were made in May and June of the ongoing year (2003) for the following season (2004)	Contracts with suppliers were made in May and June of the ongoing year (2003) for the following season (2004)
Carried out by the Chief Contract Manager	Carried out separately for Air inclusive tours and holiday packages involving arrival by car	Carried out by directors and managers	Carried out by director, junior managers and assistant junior manager
Findings from market research are used to estimate required capacity	Findings from market research are used to estimate required capacity	Findings from market research are used to estimate required capacity	indings from market research are used to estimate required capacity

Value chain activities	ITF1	ITF2	S1	S2
Accommodation	First, agreements with hoteliers are made and based on guaranteed number of bed nights, flights and ground services are arranged	First, agreements with hoteliers are made and based on guaranteed number of bed nights, flights and ground services are arranged		
	Some integration in South Dalmatia through ownership of three hotels (expansion of subsidiary hotel chain)	60 eco-farmhouses and 29 motor sailing ships hired from private investors		Some integration through ownership of three properties
	Three- to five- year contracts, whereby investments tend to be made in key properties guaranteed through five-year contracts	One and five-year contracts, whereby investments tend to be made in key properties guaranteed through five-year contracts		
	Agreements through commitment	Arrangements made through commitment	Arrangements made through commitment	Arrangements made through commitment
	Mainly agreements with three-star properties, but the current emphasis is on developing the up market segment	Mainly agreements with three-star properties, current emphasis lies on developing all inclusive offers for families	Mainly agreements with three-star properties	Mainly agreements with three-star properties
Transport	Air travel through guaranteed seats with Croatia airlines and Aerolloyd	Air travel through guaranteed seats with Croatia airlines and Aerolloyd	Air travel through guaranteed seats with Croatia airlines and Aerolloyd	Air travel through guaranteed seats or ad hoc agreements with Croatia Airlines and Aerolloyd or in individual cases with Lufthansa or Austrian Airlines
	Flights from all major German airports and on typical travel days	Flights from all major German airports and on typical travel days	Flights from all major German airports and on typical travel days	
	90% arrival by car in Istria	90% arrival by car in Istria		

	90% arrival by air in Dalmatia	90% arrival by air in Dalmatia	Collaboration with five coach companies to establish a network serving all parts of Germany Travel by coach particularly used by travelers taking their own bike	Part of coach business integrated through fleet of five coaches, which are mainly used for tours that have been designed on initial request by a group of travelers (i.e. clubs, seniors) Rest of coach business is arranged through contractual agreements with German and Croatian coach companies
Ground services	Intended integration through joint venture with one Croatian ground handling agent Collaboration with one ground handling agent which organizes transfers, excursion and other activities in all destination, but employs own destination managers	Collaboration with two Croatian ground handling agents which organizes transfers, excursions and other activities in all destinations, but employs own destination managers	Partly integrated through a ground handling agency comprising four offices in Istria Depending on location, there is a collaboration with various smaller players handling transfers, excursions and other activities	Collaboration with multiple local partners to enable flexible and individualized packaging
	Excursions and activities are sold in advance through a brochure or arranged at the destination	Excursions and activities are sold in advance through a brochure or arranged at the destination	Excursions and activities are sold in advance through a brochure or arranged at the destination	Excursions and activities are sold in advance through a brochure or arranged at the destination
Marketing and distribution	Largely integrated	Largely integrated	No own travel agencies	One own travel agency
	Probably similar as ITF2	Approximately 90% of all inclusive tours sold through travel agents	Probably largest proportion of inclusive tours sold direct	60 to 70 percent of all holidays sold directly
	Uses three main brochures: volume Air inclusive tours, volume car and up market	Uses three main brochures: volume Air inclusive tours, volume car and up market	Uses one main brochure and one supplement for cruises	Uses only one brochure

APPENDIX 13.C. *(continued)*

Value chain activities	ITF1	ITF2	S1	S2
Production and consumption	Quality control in up-market segment and key properties through ownership and management contracts			Product and quality control largely based on personal relationships with suppliers, so trust in their performance is of paramount importance
	Quality control through investment into the upgrading of key properties	Quality control through investment into the upgrading of key properties	Product control of ground services and thus key part of this operator's packages through integration of ground handling agents	
	Product control in terms of ground services through close collaboration with one ground handling agent			
	Own destination managers (resort representatives)	Own destination managers (resort representatives)	Own destination managers (resort representatives)	Own destination managers (resort representatives)
				In critical situations, i.e. an overbooked hotel, personal relationships with hoteliers are helpful
Postpurchase	N/A	Quality control through customer feedback and discussing negative performance with suppliers	N/A	Quality control from feedback obtained from loyal customers
		If ITF2 has to refund guests as the result of a complaint, the balance is deducted from the hotelier's bill		

REFERENCES

Birnmeyer, S. (2003). RIU hotels erhöhen Investitionen auf 300 mill, Euro—Zum 50, Firmenjubiläum zwölf neue Hotels. *FVW International, 2*(January): 52.

Bunja, D. (2003). Modernizing the Croatian tourism industry. *International Journal of Contemporary Hospitality Management, 15*(2): 126-128.

Cavlek, N. (1993). The outlook of the European tourist package holiday market. *Acta Turistica, 5*(2): 2-39.

Cavlek, N. (1994). Processes of horizontal and vertical concentration within the European travel market. *Acta Turistica, 6*(1): 3-39.

Cavlek, N. (2000). The global development trends of European tour operators. *Acta Turistica, 48*(2): 119-124.

CEEBICnet – Central and Eastern European Business Information Centre (2002). Investment climate. Available at: http://www.mac.doc.gov/EEBIC/COUNTRYR/Croatia/ccg2002/investmentclimate/htm. Retrieved March 24, 2003.

Cizmar, S. (1995). Mogucnostu uvodenja fransizinga u turisticko-ugostiteljsko gospodarstvo Hrvastke. [Possibilities for the introduction of franchising within the Croatian tourism and hospitality industry]. *Turizam, 5*(6): 102-108.

Cizmar, S. (1996). Strategic management in the hospitality industry in Croatia. *Turizam, 46*(5-6): 109-125.

Croatia National Tourist Board (2002). *Hrvatski turizam u brojkama 2001.* Zagreb, Croatia: Republika Hrvatska, Ministarstvo Turizma.

Croatia National Tourist Board (2003a). *Hrvatska ponuda na Europskom turistickom trzistu 2003, godine.* Zagreb, Croatia: Croatia National Tourist Board.

Croatia National Tourist Board (2003b). *Press Information.* Frankfurt, Germany: Croatia National Tourist Board.

Croatia National Tourist Board (2003c). *Tourist Information Brochure.* Frankfurt, Germany: Croatia National Tourist Board.

Curtin, S. and Busby. G. (1999). Sustainable destination development: The tour operator perspective. *International Journal of Tourism Research, 1:* 135-147.

Dale, C. (2000). The UK tour operating industry: A competitive analysis. *Journal of Vacation Marketing, 6*(4): 357-367.

D'Aveni, R. (1995). Coping with hyper competition: Utilizing the new 7S's framework. *Academy of Management Executive, 9*(3): 45-57.

Davies, B. and Downward, P. (1998). Competition and contestability in the UK package tour industry: Some econometric observations, *Tourism Economics, 4*(3): 241-251.

Davies, B. and Downward, P. (2001a). Industrial organization of the package tour industry: Implications for research, *Tourism Economics, 7*(2): 149-161.

Davies, B. and Downward, P. (2001a). Industrial organization and competition in the UK tour operator/travel agency business, 1989-1993: An econometric investigation. *Journal of Travel Research, 39*(May): 411-425.

Davies, B. and Downward, P. (2001b). Industrial organization of the package tour industry: Implications for research. *Tourism Economics, 7*(2): 149-161.

Deloitte (2004). *Executive Report,* Issue 4, July. Available at: http://www.deloitte .com/dtt/cda/doc/content/UK_THL_ExecReport_July04.pdf.

Deutsche Entwicklungsgesellschaft (2001). Touristic master plan for Croatia . CD-ROM. Cologne, Germany: DEG.

Dragicevic, M., Cizmar, S., and Paljanec-Boric, S. (1998). Contribution to the development of Croatian tourism. *Turizam, 46*(5-6): 243-253.

Dulcic, A. (2000). Croatian tourism, transition and global development processes. *Tourism, 48*(2): 175-187.

European Commission (1999). *Case No IV/M.1524—Airtours/First Choice.* Regulation EEC No. 4064/89 Merger Procedure, Article 8(3): Incompatibility. September 22. Available at: http://www.cerna.ensmp.fr/Enseignement/CoursEU CompetionLaw/11-AirtoursFirstChoice.pdf.

Evans, N.G. and Stabler, M.J. (1995). A future for the package tour operator in the 21st century. *Tourism Economics, 4*(3): 245-263.

Fox, J. (2000). Approaching managerial ethical standard's in Croatia's hotel industry. *International Journal of Contemporary Hospitality Management, 13* (1): 43-46.

Gauf, D. and Hughes, H. (1998). Diversification and German tour operators: The case of TUI and coach tourism. *Tourism Economics, 4*(4): 325-337.

Gratton, C. and Richards, G. (1997). Structural change in the European package tour industry: UK–German comparisons. *Tourism Economics, 3*(3): 213-226.

Hartung, T. (2002). Thomas cook schwebt über allen wolken. *FVW International, 13*(May).

Horvat-Jokic, B. (1997). Croatian tourism in a socio-cultural perspective. *Acta Turista, 9:* 58-69.

I.D. Riva (2003a). Kreuzfahrten auf klassischen Motorseglern zwischen tausend Inseln. *I.D. Riva Summer Brochure,* Munich: I.D. Riva.

I.D. Riva (2003b). Kroatien. 2. Auflage. *I.D. Riva Summer Brochure,* Munich: I.D. Riva.

I.D. Riva (2003c). Radreisen in Kroatien. *I.D. Riva Summer Brochure,* Munich: I.D. Riva.

Jankowicz, A.D. (1995). *Business Research Projects,* 2nd edition, London, UK: International Thompson Business Press.

Jordan, P. (2000). Croatian tourism and the challenges of globalization. *Tourism, 48*(2): 167-174.

Klemm, M. and Parkinson, L. (2001). UK tour operator strategies: Causes and consequences. *International Journal of Tourism Research, 3:* 367-375.

Köster-Hetzendorf, M. (2002). Die Adria hat die Deutschen wieder: Finanzspritze für kroatische hotels. *FVW International, 7*(March): 56.

Kunst, I. (1998). Market structure of the Croatian tourism sector. *Turizam, 46*(3): 123-129.

Kuoni (2001). The European travel market: Nearly no change in Europe's top ten. *Annual Report,* Zurich: Kuoni.

Laws, E. (1997). *Managing Packaged Tourism.* Boston, MA: International Thompson Business Press.

Lindner, K. (2003). Neckermann will's wieder möglich machen. *FVW International, 5*(February). .

Medina-Munoz, R.D., Medina-Munoz, D.R., and Garcia-Falcón, J.M. (2003). Understanding European tour operators' control on accommodation companies: An empirical evidence. *Tourism Management, 24:* 135-147.

Middleton, V.I.T (1991). Whither the package tour? *Tourism Management,* September: 185-192.

Middleton, V.I.T. (2003). Guest lecture. Department of Hospitality, Leisure and Tourism Management, Oxford Brookes University, Oxford, UK. July.

Münster, M. (2002). Iberostar eröffnet Hotels und steigert Umsatz, *FVW International,* No. 13, May 5th. p. 68.

Pender, L. (2001). *Travel, Trade and Transport: An Introduction.* London, UK: Continuum.

Pirjevac, B. (1993). Should the structure of accommodation facilities in the republic of Croatia be changed? *Acta Turistica, 5:* 71-85.

Pirjevac, B. (1997). Survey and assessment of the real potentials for the development of the Croatian tourism. *Acta Turistica, 9:* 5-45.

Roper, A., Jegervatn, R-H, and Jensen, O. (2003). Internationalization of inclusive tour firms: A case study of Norwegian subsidiaries. *11th Nordic Symposium in Tourism and Hospitality Research,* Goteborg University, School of Economics and Commercial Law, Goteborg, Sweden, November 14-17.

Saunders, M.., Lewis, P., and Thornhill, A. (2000). *Research Method's for Business Students,* 2nd Edition. Upper Saddle River, NJ: Prentice Hall.

South-East Europe invests in tourism as demand grows (2002). *FVW International,* August 1. Available at: http://www.fvw.com/index.cfm?ID=602. Retrieved April 9, 2003.

Sulkowski, N. (2003). A comparative analysis of how German tourism firms are operating inclusive tours to Croatia. Unpublished master's thesis in international hotel and tourism management, Oxford Brookes University, Department of Hospitality, Leisure and Tourism Management, Oxford, UK.

Tribe, J. (1997). *Corporate Strategy for Tourism,* London: Thompson Business Press.

Udruga Hrvatskih Putnickih Agencija (Association of Croatian Travel Agencies) (2001). *Legal Framework.* Zagreb, Croatia: UHPA.

WEB RESOURCES

I.D. Riva Tours
http://www.idriva.de

Map of Croatia
http://www.lib.utexas.edu/maps/cia04/croatia_sm04.gif

Misir
http://www.misir.de

Thomas Cook
http://www.thomascookag.de

PERSONAL COMMUNICATIONS

Dezeljin, Z. (2003). Personal communication, May 12. Frankfurt, Germany: Croatia National Tourist Board.

Lukinowic, Z. (2003). Personal communication, May 12. Oberursel, Germany: Thomas Cook AG.

Misir, R. (2003). Personal communication, May 20. Essen, Germany: Misir Sonnenlandreisen.

Ognjenovic, S. (2003). Personal communication, May 21. Munich, Germany: I.D. Riva.

Thimme, P.M. (2003). Personal communication, May 19. Cologne, Germany: Deutsche Investitions-und Entwicklungsgesellschaft.

Tomasevic, A. (2003). Personal communication, May 29. Zagreb, Croatia: Hotel Esplanade.

Urbschat, J. (2003). Personal communication, May 13. Cologne, Germany: LTU Touristik (REWE).

FURTHER READING

Cavlek, N. (1993). The outlook of the European tourist package holiday market. *Acta Turistica, 5*(2): 2-39.

ITS (2003a). Autoreisen Sommer: Italien, Slowenien, Kroatien, Ungarn, Tschechien, Slowakei. *ITS Summer Brochure,* Cologne: REWE.

ITS (2003b). Flugreisen Sommer: Tunesien, Marokko, Ägypten, Vereinigte Arabische Emirate, Türkei, Malta, Italien, Rumänien, Bulgarien, Montenegro, Kroatien. *ITS Summer Brochure,* Cologne: REWE.

Misir, S. (2003). Kroatien: Ein kleines Land für den grossen Urlaub. *Misir Summer Brochure.* Essen: Misir Sonnenlandeisen.

Neckermann (2003a). Europa. *Neckermann Summer Brochure.* Oberursel: Thomas Cook AG.

Neckermann (2003b). Flugreisen Bulgarien und Rumänien, Türkei und Ägypten, Tunesien und Marokko, Montenegro, Kroatien, Zypern, Malta. *Neckermann Summer Brochure.* Oberursel: Thomas Cook AG.

Tjäreborg (2003). Viel Urlaub für wenig Geld: Mittelmeer/Nordafrika. *Tjäreborg Summer Brochure.,* Cologne: REWE.

Chapter 14

Working Capital in Hospitality Sector: A Case of Maruti Hotels

Vinayshil Gautam

This case study is about a heritage property that is entering into a professional partnership with a well known branded hotel. Traditional heritage properties in India have been targets of bigger firms for either a takeover or a management agreement to run them as professionally managed hotels. The case study gives an insight into the financial condition of a hotel property entering into a relationship with a larger brand. The challenge is to either survive and sustain one's existence a stand-alone unit, or become a part of another brand and enhance longevity. The names of the hotels used have been disguised to ensure confidentiality. The case study demonstrates and encourages the risk from a perspective of business, financial, and ownership in the long run.

Maruti Hotels Private Limited (MHPL) was incorporated on March 12, 1992, in Suratgarh. The company was promoted by a local celebrity, hereafter called the Raja, who gave a substantial part of his ancestral home (a princely *haveli,* a heritage building) for this purpose. Apart from this heritage property, MHPL also operates other heritage resort/hotels at different locations in the Bilaspur region of the state. These properties are owned by the Raja's family members individually or through other corporate entities, and MHPL operates these properties under an operating fee structure.

MHPL is a closely held company. As against the authorized share capital of Rs 10 crores (approximately 247,218.79 USD, 1 USD = 40.4500 INR), the issued and paid-up capital as on March 31, 2004, stood at 50,000,000 (Rs) ($\approx$$1,236,093.94), which was represented

Global Cases on Hospitality Industry
© 2008 by The Haworth Press, Taylor & Francis Group. All rights reserved.
doi:10.1300/5923_14

by 500,000 shares of Rs at 100 Rs (≈$2.47) each. The entire paid-up equity share capital is held by the promoters, namely Raja and his family. MHPL is managed by a board comprised of eleven directors headed by the chairman Raja. An average of two-thirds of MHPL's customers are foreign nationals. The foreign tourists served by MHPL are mainly from Germany, United States, France, Britain, Italy, and Spain, among other countries.

Tour operators and travel agents both domestic as well as foreign are the originating points for MHPL's customers. Tour operators and agents together bring about 70 percent of the total customers of MHPL, while 20 percent are through Internet or referrals. MHPL approached a financial institution for sanction of a term loan of Rs 50 crores (≈ $12,360,939) as a corporate loan toward general corporate purposes including replacement of existing debt. A snapshot of MHPL's revenues and PAT for the past ten years as given in Table 14.1. MHPL has consistently been recording profits until FY 2000-2001, thereafter the company slipped into loss due to market conditions.

In the past, the company had consistently been performing reasonably well in terms of revenue and profitability. However, consequent to events such as the Kargil War between India and Pakistan in 1999-2000, the 9/11 terrorist attack in the United States in 2001, the outbreak of SARS (severe acute respiratory syndrome) in Southeast Asia in 2002, and the subsequent Gujarat communal riots, the tourist inflow into India was adversely affected, which impacted the perfor-

TABLE 14.1. A snapshot of MHPL's revenues and PAT'

For the year ended	3/31/ 95	3/31/ 96	3/31/ 97	3/31/ 98	3/31/ 99	3/31/ 00	3/31/ 01	3/31/ 02	3/31/ 03	3/31/ 04
Total revenue	32	37	38	39	40	38	38	35	38	39
Operating expenses	29	31	32	33	33	33	34	36	36	34
EBIDTA	3	6	6	6	7	5	4	–1	2	5
Depreciation	0.75	0.75	1.00	1.75	1.75	1.25	1.25	1.75	1.75	2.50
Interest	0.67	2.28	2.81	2.47	3.39	3.07	3.30	2.58	4.51	5.11
Profit/(loss) after tax	1.4	2.75	2.5	1.65	2	0.4	(0.75)	(4.95)	(4.15)	(3.02)

Note: Currency in Rs. crores

mance of MHPL. The domestic tourist inflows too were affected by the Gujarat riots since the affluent section of Gujarat accounted for a significant part of domestic tourist traffic. The fiscal year (FY) 2001-2002 was the worst year for the company, with net revenues falling to a low of Rs 35 crores (≈ $8,652,657), and as a result the company suffered a gross loss with a negative EBIDTA (earnings before interest, depreciation, taxes, and amortization) of Rs 1 crore (≈ $247,218). However, in FYs 2002-2003 and 2003-2004, driven by higher foreign currency earnings as a result of increasing inflow of foreign tourists and a modest growth in RevPar (revenue per available room), the company's net revenues increased to Rs 38 crores (≈ $9,394,313) and Rs 39 crores (≈ $9641,632) respectively, which helped the company post positive EBIDTA of Rs 2 crores (≈ $494,437) in FY 2002-2003 and Rs 3 crores (≈ $741,656) in FY 2003-2004. MHPL's current gross margins of Rs 12 percent compares well with that of the industry. However, on account of high interest costs, the company posted net losses of Rs 4.15 crores (≈ $1,025,197) (interest of Rs 4.51 crores [≈ $1,114,130]) in FY 2000-2003 and Rs 3.02 crores (≈ $746,047) (interest of Rs 5.11 crores [≈ $1,262,351]) in FY 2003-2004. Foreign currency earnings increased from Rs 22.99 crores (≈ $5,679,347) in FY 2001-2002 to Rs 29 crores (≈ $7,164,031) in FY 2003-2004.

The ratio on March 31, 2004, was 1.11, as opposed to 1.35 as on March 31, 2003. The drop in the most recent ratio was mainly on account of the increase debt due to creditors from Rs 16 crores (≈ $3,952,569) for the year ended March 31, 2003, to Rs 21 crores (≈ $5,187,747) for the year ended March 31, 2004. This increase was a result of the liquidity crunch that company was facing on account of the continuous losses the company was suffering. MHPL's debtors in turn saw an increase of around 22 percent on March 31, 2004, from 15 percent as on March 31, 2003. The increase in amount owed by debtors is an aberration to the past debtor position. In 2003-2004 debtors jumped to almost 81 days, mainly because of bunching of last quarter sales and also some delay in transmission of funds by the company's foreign travel agents. However, all the realizations are reportedly up to date and the company is back to normal, with and average holding of 45 to 50 days.

The total capital employed by MHPL on March 31, 2004, was Rs 80 crores (≈ $19,762,845), comprising of Rs 55 crores (≈ $13,586,956) of net worth and Rs 25 crores (≈ $6,175,889) of debt funds. In FY 2002-2003, the promoters brought in Rs 5 crores (≈ $1,235,177) toward application money for equity share capital, which was subsequently issued in FY 2003-2004. In FY 2002-2003, the company also contracted an agreement with a leading Mumbai-based real estate developer for developing a high end, premium residential complex on 125 acres of land owned by the company. As per the agreement, the company sold 100 acres of land (out of the company-owned 300 acres) to limit the incidence of long-term capital gains. MHPL's debt comprises Rs 20 crores (≈ $4,940,711) of long-term debt and working capital bank borrowings of Rs 5 crores (≈ $1,235,177). The term debt lenders were all leading financial institutions, commercial banks, etc. On March 31, 2004, the debt to equity ratio of the company was 0.4:1.

As on March 31, 2004, the company had investments of Rs 4 crores (≈ $988,142) in private companies controlled by the promoters of the company. Out of Rs 4 crores (≈ $988,142), an amount of Rs 1 crore (≈ $247,035) was by way of share application money. MHPL's unaudited operational results for FY 2004 for the period ending December 31, 2004 is given in Table 14.2.

During the current year, driven by increase in inflow of foreign tourists, MHPL has shown an improved performance in terms of occupancy and average room revenue (ARR). With thirty of forty rooms undergoing renovation (being undertaken under the ECL's management) the occupancy rate of the available forty rooms is close to 95 percent and the ARR is around Rs 8,900 (≈ $219.86). The company's EBIDTA is around 43 percent of net revenues, and although the company has had a loss of 50 lakhs (≈ $123,517), it has earned cash profit

TABLE 14.2. Profit and Loss Account

Profit and Loss Account	12/31/2004
Net revenue	38
EBIDTA	6
Depreciation	2.5
Interest and finance charges	4
Profit/(loss) before tax	(.50)

Note: Currency in Rs crores

of Rs 200 lakhs (2 crores; ≈ $494,071). As is evident from the previous interim results, the company's operating performance was seeing an upturn, and with ECL having took over the reins of the management of the hotel and with three months of peak season for hotel remaining, it was estimated that the company would close the FY 2004-2005 with a profit at the net level. The revenues for FY 2004-2005 was estimated to be in the region of Rs 42 crores (≈ $10,375,494), profit before tax of Rs 1.27 crores (≈ $313,735), and cash profit of Rs 3 crores (≈ $741,106).

In November 2004, MHPL entered into a hotel operations and management (O & M) agreement with a leading hotel chain, hereafter called ECL, for managing and operating the *haveli* in conformity with standards comparable to first class international hotels. The agreement with ECL was for a period of thirty years, and is renewable mutually for a further period of ten years. Under the agreement, MHPL agreed to renovate, refurbish, and upgrade the existing structures and its related facilities and amenities to standards comparable to the first class luxury palace hotels at a cost not exceeding 30 crores (≈ $7,411,067), which will be raised by MHPL by way of debt and would be guaranteed by ECL. The project management task of the upgrade of the hotel will be undertaken by ECL, and ECL would be completing the same by September 30, 2006, with partial opening of the upgraded portion of the hotel by September 30, 2005. ECL would ensure that the upgrade project does not suffer any time, and that ECL would get approval from MHPL for necessary operating expenses, which would cover the following:

1. Payroll expenses
2. Marketing expenses
3. Opening stock of food and beverage
4. Operating equipment and furniture, fixtures, and equipment
5. Software costs

The agreement provided that ECL will render certain technical services to MHPL for the upgrade of the hotel, which included the following:

- Facilities allocation
- Guest room configuration recommendations

- Interior design/decoration and furniture, fittings, and equipment recommendations
- Mechanical and electrical engineering design recommendations
- Operating equipment recommendations
- Property management information system recommendation
- Training of staff
- Commissioning and handover

ECL would have the full operating control and discretion in all matters pertaining to operation of the hotel. ECL would render consultancy and advisory services (CAS) to MHPL during the agreement period for smooth functioning of the hotel as a luxury palace hotel. MHPL will have the advantage of using the services of ECL's global sales and reservation offices. The prorated costs of such facilities and services shall be charged to the operating expenses of the hotel.

As per the O&M agreement with ECL, the management fees will be earned by ECL for rendering its services in operating the *haveli* as a hotel. Although ECL will be paid a one-time flat technical service fee of Rs 35 lakhs (≈ $86,462.40) for rendering the technical services, ECL will be entitled to a basic management fee at the rate of 2.5 percent of the gross income of the hotel plus service tax. In addition to the basic management fee, ECL also would be entitled to an incentive fee equivalent to 12.5 percent of the gross operating profit of the hotel plus service tax. Thus, the fee structure is designed to make ECL gear itself to drive both revenue growth as well as higher profitability. The payment of basic management fee and incentive fee shall be subordinated to the periodic servicing of the proposed debt from a financial institution.

MHPL approached the financial institution, as mentioned previously, for a corporate loan of Rs 50 crores (≈ $12,351,778). The proceeds of the loan would be utilized toward replacement of existing debt of around Rs 25 crores (≈ $6,175,889) and to upgrade the *haveli* to standards comparable to first class international hotels at a total cost not exceeding Rs 25 crores (≈ $6,175,889). The present 125 rooms in the *haveli* would be converted into 90 rooms with varying sizes. As part of the O & M contract MHPL has with ECL, ECL will guarantee part of the proposed loan, not exceeding Rs 25 crores (≈ $6,175,889), being raised by MHPL for upgrading the hotel. Hence, the proposed loan of Rs 50 crores (≈ $12,351,778) would be broken into two components, as given in Table 14.3.

The proposed loan would be secured first by way of mortgage of the *haveli* and hypothecation of all the moveable fixed assets therein. In addition, ECL would be provided a corporate guarantee for term loan component A (Rs 25 crores [≈ $6,175,889]) and cash support to the extent of Rs 12.50 crores (≈ $3,087,944) to service debt relating to term loan component B (Rs 25 crores; ≈ $6,175,889) should a shortfall in the cash flows of MHPL occur. All the credit card receivables, which account for more 50 percent of the total cash flows of the company, would also be securitized. In addition, the Raja would provide his personal guarantee to guarantee term loan component B of the proposed loan. Both loans would be for a period of ten years, with term loan component A being repaid in sixteen quarterly installments commencing in year seven and term loan component B being paid in a ballooning amortizing repayment commencing from the fourth year from the date of disbursement. The interest rates will be reset at the end of three to five years from the date of disbursement.

Financial projections have been drawn based on certain assumptions. The summarized projected profitability of MHPL is given in Table 14.4. ECL would use its brand name for the upgraded hotel, and MHPL would also benefit from the global agent and marketing network of ECL, which would put it on the marketing forefront among

TABLE 14.3. Term Loan Components A and B

Term Loan Component A Rs 25.00 crores	Term Loan Component B Rs 25.00 crores
Loan to be utilized for the upgrade of the hotel	Loan to be utilized for replacement of existing debt
The loan is guaranteed by ECL	Cash flow support from ECL to the extent of Rs 12.50 crores for debt servicing on a revolving basis
Second priority for debt servicing out of cash flow from operations/escrow of credit card receivables	First priority for debt servicing out of cash flow from operations/escrow of credit card receivables

Fees/ compensation to ECL under the management contract with MHPL will have a lower priority than the debt servicing of both of the loans, Component A and B

TABLE 14.4. Financial Projections

	2005	2006	2007	2008	2009	2010	2011	2012	2013	2014	2015
Total revenue	42	44	45	45	47	47	48	48	50	50	50
Total expenses	22.18	29.55	26.02	26.06	26.71	26.23	27.05	26.09	27.63	27.92	28.47
	52.82	67.16	57.83	57.92	56.85	55.81	56.37	54.37	55.26	55.85	56.94
Operating profit	19.81	14.48	18.95	18.91	20.28	20.76	20.92	21.90	22.35	22.06	21.53
	47.18	32.91	42.13	42.04	43.15	44.19	43.60	45.63	44.71	44.12	43.06
Depreciation	11.84	4.90	5.59	5.43	5.35	4.90	4.93	4.58	4.69	4.62	0.44
	28.20	11.14	2.43	12.08	11.39	10.44	10.28	9.56	9.39	9.24	0.88
Finance expenses	6.86	6.79	7.78	7.38	6.93	5.96	5.53	4.71	4.28	3.58	1.59
	16.35	15.45	17.31	16.41	14.75	12.70	11.54	9.83	8.56	7.16	3.18
Income tax	0	0	1.98	2.19	2.88	3.55	3.73	4.50	9.80	4.96	5.51
	0	0.00	4.42	4.87	6.13	7.57	7.78	9.39	19.61	9.92	11.03
PAT	1.18	2.78	3.56	3.92	5.13	6.34	6.70	8.05	8.57	8.88	9.87
	2.82	6.32	7.92	8.72	10.92	13.50	13.96	16.79	17.14	17.76	19.74
Gross cash accruals	13.02	7.68	9.15	9.36	10.48	11.25	11.63	12.64	13.26	13.50	10.31
	31.02	17.46	20.35	20.80	22.31	23.95	24.24	26.34	26.53	27.00	20.62
Debt repayment	163	208	421	546	548	581	560	580	677	660	2475
DSCR	1.78	2.55	2.41	2.07	2.19	2.25	2.35	2.47	2.14	2.2	0.58
Average DSCR						1.88					

Note: Currency in Rs crores

other hotels in the state. Major strengths of the proposal are the following:

1. MHPL operates one of its "Heritage Havelis" in India, located in the state, which is a popular destination among tourists.
2. MHPL has signed a long-term agreement of thirty years with ECL and would benefit from ECL's expertise in operating the hotel. ECL would be guaranteeing the loan to the tune of Rs 25 crores (≈ $6,175,889), with cash support to meet further possible shortfalls of Rs 12.50 crores (≈ $3,087,944).
3. The hotel will be positioned at the top end of the ECL portfolio (in the luxury palace category) and leverage its ECL brand name.

4. MHPL would gain from the global arrangements with travel agents that ECL has in place and would thus put itself on the global marketing front.
5. The present proposal enables MHPL to replace high-cost debt bearing an average interest rate of Rs 14 percent with a lower interest bearing debt, which is expected to improve its financial position.
6. The global tourism industry is presently doing very well, and the Indian government is also promoting India as a favorite tourist destination, which augurs well for MHPL.

The risks associated with the proposal may be said to be in terms of promoter risk, financial risk, and industry risk.

BIBLIOGRAPHY

Agrawal, N. K. (1983). *Management of Working Capital.* Sterling, MI: University of Michigan.

Block, S.B. and Hirt, G.A. (1997). *Foundations of Financial Management.* New York: McGraw-Hill.

Brigham, E.F. (2003). *Fundamentals of Financial Management.* Belmont, CA: Thomson South-Western.

Brigham, E.F. and Ehrhardt, M.C. (2005). *Financial Management: Theory and Practice.* Belmont, CA: Thomson South-Western.

Hrishikes, B. (2004). *Working Capital Management: Strategies and Techniques.* New Delhi, India: Prentice-Hall of India.

MacMenamin, J. (1999). *Financial Management: An Introduction.* London, UK: Routledge.

Madura, J. (2006). *International Financial Management.* Belmont, CA: Thomson South-Western.

Marsh, W.H. (1989). *Case Problems in Financial Management.* Upper Saddle River, NJ: Prentice Hall.

Mathur, S.B. (2004). *Working Capital Management and Control: Principles and Practice.* New Delhi, India: New Age International.

Peterson, P.P. and Fabozzi, F.J. (2003). *Financial Management and Analysis.* Hoboken, NJ: John Wiley and Sons.

Powell, G.E. (2005). *Understanding Financial Management: A Practical Guide.* Boston, MA: Blackwell Publishing.

Sametz, A.W. (1963). *Financial Management: An Analytical Approach.* Homewood, IL: R.D. Irwin.

Shim, J.K. and Siegel, J.G. (2000). *Financial Management.* Hauppauge, NY: Barron's Educational Series.

Chapter 15

Entrepreneurship in Indian Hotel Industry: Financial and Strategic Perspective

Vinnie Jauhari

INTRODUCTION

Hotels are tourism's major component. They account for half the tourism earnings, of more than Rs 12,000 crores (approximately $2,964,426,877 [U.S.]) in the foreign exchange market, and ninety percent of investments (The Hindu, 1998). The tourism sector in India has the potential of creating employment opportunities for 3,845,000 jobs between 2004-2013 (WTTC, 2007). Tourism is one of the biggest employment-generating industries in India, with a capacity to absorb an additional investment to the tune of $10 billion (U.S.). As stated in the Preface, according to the World Travel and Tourism Council (WTTC), tourism accounted for 10.6 percent of global gross domestic product, 12.0 percent of the total world exports, and 8.3 percent of global employment in the year 2005 (Ministry of Finance, 2007).

Entrepreneurship in hotel industry has an immense significance. Between the years 1991 and 2006 almost Rs 227,431.7 million were earned as foreign exchange earnings from Tourism (Hindua Indiastat, 2007). This study looks at the entrepreneurship experience in the Indian hotel industry. The study is conducted on ninety-nine listed hotels for which financial data is available in the Centre for Monitoring Indian Economy (CMIE) database "Prowess." The chapter traces the evolution of the hotel industry with an insight into the emergence of national chains. It brings in a competitive analysis for market leaders such as Indian Hotels, EIH, ITC, and ITDC hotels. Select financial

Global Cases on Hospitality Industry
© 2008 by The Haworth Press, Taylor & Francis Group. All rights reserved.
doi:10.1300/5923_15

ratios have been discussed for evaluating the liquidity, risk-taking capability, and profitability of selected hotels in India. The chapter also delineates the strategic possibilities for growth and suggests the potential for growth in the budget segment in hotels.

HOTEL INDUSTRY IN INDIA

Kamra and colleagues (2000) traces the growth of modern hotel industry in India. The concept of a modern hotel was initiated way back in 1840 when the first Western style hotel was set up in Mumbai. This was followed by Auckland Hotel in Calcutta in 1843, and subsequently the Great Eastern Hotel in 1858. In 1871, John Watson opened Esplanade Mansion with 130 rooms and qualified man power. In India, many large chains of hotels emerged such as Indian Hotels, EIH, ITC, ITDC, Asian Hotels, and Jaypee Hotels. India itself has a strong tradition of hospitality. Most of the properties that were set up were sprawling properties and magnificent in their appearance. All were the outcome of Indian entrepreneurs, and were set at a grand scale. Along with these big properties, the smaller properties such as guesthouses, *sarais,* lodges, and *dharamshalas* coexisted.

On one hand, sophistication and standardized operations existed, and on the other hand, entrepreneurial initiative of thousands of entrepreneurs was manifested as small properties. These were characterized by low levels of competence, scant training, and meager compensation. On the supply side of labor, almost all educational institutions were set up under the aegis of Ministry of Human Resource Development, and were focused on operational skills for the hospitality industry. The hospitality sector education was skewed toward operations. Very little by way of management education went into the education curriculum.

In India, hotels are classified per the following nomenclature: five star deluxe, five star, four star, three star, two star, others, resort, and heritage properties. The budget hotels could be in all categories other than five star and four star category. In terms of product offering, a huge vacuum exists in terms of value for money and quality of services in categories other than the five star category of hotels. Appendix 15.A contains the top ninety hotels listed in terms of sales turnover in March 2003.

THE MODERN INDIAN HOTEL INDUSTRY

The entrepreneurial growth pattern in about ninety-eight listed hotels featured in Prowess is indicated in Table 15.1. The analysis of Table 15.1 reveals that most growth took place in the large hotels in the 1980s. This was the time when the seeds of liberalization were being sown in India. Big hotel groups were expanding and had service standards in place. The key top-of-the-line hotel brands that have existed in India are Taj Hotels, Resorts, and Palaces; Oberoi Hotels and Resorts; and ITC Limited. In fact, the luxury hotels in India earned a formidable reputation for themselves in terms of product offering, nature of infrastructure, and training of staff.

The market leaders also invested in educational institutions that could train employees to deliver per the required service levels. The market leaders either initiated their own training and education setups or supported some hotel management institutions. The Manipal Institute of Technology, The Institute of Hotel Management at Aurangabad (in collaboration with Taj Hotels and Resort Palace) are illustrations of the this trend. All of these institutions had curriculum focused on operations in hotels.

Ownership Pattern

The ninety-nine listed hotels are categorized on the basis of ownership as indicated in Table 15.2. A fair balance exists between the growth of chain and independent properties. Hotel brands such as Taj, Oberoi, Ashok, and ITC-Welcomegroup were characterized by standardized service standards. These were systems-oriented groups. In-

TABLE 15.1. Growth of Hotels Industry by Year of Incorporation

Year	No. of hotels set up	Expressed as %
1902-1979	29	30
1980-1989	37	38
1990-2001	32	32
Total	98	100

Source: Adapted from CMIE database "Prowess" August 2004.

TABLE 15.2. Classification of Hotels on the Basis of Ownership

Ownership type	No. of Hotels
Government	3
Private Indian	51
Group hotels	42

Source: Adapted from CMIE database "Prowess" August 2004.

ternational collaborations for some of these groups brought in the required service standards. Investments were made and the chains became national brands. Some of them also looked at international expansion. Brands such as Taj and Oberoi also ventured in some other Asian countries as well. The globalized brands still did not emerge.

Geographical Location

Table 15.3 indicates that western India has the highest number of properties. This is on account of Mumbai being a commercial port city, with other cities such as Pune and Goa in the vicinity. It is also a business hub. The state of Maharastra attracts a great amount of tourism in western India. It is the policy of the state government to provide infrastructural support. The state government of Maharshtra has taken several steps to promote state tourism. It extends over the Sahyadri Mountains (or Western Ghats), a vast stretch of 720 kilometers of Arabian Sea coast and provide a beautiful backdrop. It is estimated that nearly 40 percent of the tourists who visit India come to Mumbai. Maharashtra also has rich historical and cultural heritage and a strong political base. Nearly 80 percent of the cave temples in India are located in Maharashtra. North and South India almost have a similar number of properties. Expansion in eastern India was limited on account of limited industrialization in this part.

MARKET LEADERS IN INDIAN HOTEL INDUSTRY

Appendix 15.A details the largest hotels in terms of sales turnover in March 2003. The Indian Hotels Company is the market leader. It

TABLE 15.3. Geographical Spread of Hotels

Location	No. of Hotels
North	24
South	23
East	8
West	35

Source: Adapted from CMIE database "Prowess" August 2004.

owns the luxury brand Taj. The other hotels at the top are EIH, which owns the Oberoi brand, and the ITC-Welcomegroup chain with their very famous luxury property, Maurya Sheraton at Delhi.

The Indian Hotels Company

The Indian Hotels Company caters to a wide cross section of travelers with its luxury, business, and budget hotels. It has beach, resort, garden, and palace hotels. This company was incorporated on April 1, 1902, by Jamsetji Nusserwanji Tata, the founder of the Tata Group for the ownership and operation of Taj Mahal Hotel in Mumbai. It targets its products across the entire gamut, with a product offering targeted at luxury and business hotels. It has expanded its product offering through fourteen subsidiary companies. It was awarded the "best hotel group in India" honor in 2002 Selling Long Haul Travel Awards and was voted the best local hotel chain in 2002 by TTG Asia. The Taj Group has fifty-three hotels in India, and has twelve properties at various international destinations such as Sri Lanka, Dubai, Oman, Nepal, the UK, and Maldives. The group sees much opportunity in cities such as London, New York, Shanghai, and Beijing. The Australasian and Gulf markets are also opportunity regions. The aspirational brands for Indian Hotels are Four Seasons and Ritz-Carlton. For a distinct brand to emerge, the core competence needs to be well defined. It's important to focus on few key areas such as unique competencies, people, and a distinct offering.

The luxury hotels contribute to more than 70 percent of the company's profits, and they attract international guests. They have a presence in diverse areas such as business, leisure, and heritage properties. Though the brand connotes hospitality and warmth, a clear connotation still does not seem to emerge.

The analysis of the market leader in the hotel industry on select variables in India with respect to the other ninety-eight listed hotels is indicated in Table 15.4. The market leader contributes to 25 percent of the sales of the listed hotels. The advertising expenses incurred by the market leader are 52.4 percent. The market leader spends 4.4 percent of the sales on advertising, while as the rest of the industry spends 2.2 percent of its sales on advertising. It employs 22 percent of the capital employed. It is responsible for 20 percent of the profits of the organized sector. It contributes 27.3 percent of the export earning, and 25.5 percent of the wages paid by the organized sector.

EIH Ltd.

The East India Hotels Calcutta was set up in 1949. The EIH Ltd. owns the Oberoi as a brand. The Oberoi Hotel Pvt. Ltd. was established with a capital of Rs 5 lakh ($\approx$ \$12,351.70) in 1946. The hotel went in for collaboration with InterContinental Hotels group, New York, for its hotel in New Delhi. For the Mumbai property Oberoi went in for collaboration with Sheraton Hotel International, Boston.

Table 15.5 indicates that EIH Ltd. contributes 13.6 percent of sales to total hotel sales (out of ninety-eight hotels). It incurs 15.7 percent of the total advertising expenses for ninety-eight hotels. It also con-

TABLE 15.4. Comparison of Indian Hotels with the Other 98 Listed As of March 2003

Variable	Indian hotels Rs (crores)*	Other 98 hotels Rs (crores)
Sales	590.19	2337.94
Advertisement	25.97	49.48
Capital employed	1516.39	6636.14
Total export	248.91	911.12
Land and built	304.36	3866.05
PAT	40.48	200.66
Wages	145.56	569.04

*1 Crore = 10^9

Source: Derived from CMIE database, "Prowess" August 2004.

TABLE 15.5. Comparison of EIH Hotels with Other 98 Hotels in India As of March 2003

Variables	EIH (Cr.)	Other 98 hotels
Sales	384.09	2544.04
Advertising	10.25	65.02
Marketing	7.12	45.17
PAT	15.11	226.03
Capital employed	1205.12	6947.41
Total export	918.43	3251.98
Net Worth	116.64	597.96
Land and building	918.43	3251.98
Wages	116.64	597.96

Source: Derived from CMIE database "Prowess" August 2004.

tributes 6.68 percent of PAT (profit after tax). It employs 17.3 percent of the total capital employed. In terms of land and buildings, its share is about 28 percent. This means that the growth strategy is linked with making its own investments in land and buildings. This is a resource-intensive means of growing. EIH also owns the Trident brand, which has been conceived to target the growing market in the budget sector.

India Tourism Development Corporation

The ITDC (India Tourism Development Corporation) is responsible for the construction and management of hotels in the public sector. The ITDC's Ashok group has thirty-five hotels segmented into three categories: Elite, Ashok Classic, and Ashok Comfort. The Elite brand is the five star deluxe category. The Classic group comprises sixteen units and is targeted at the business traveler and midmarket guests. The Comfort category is available at eleven destinations in the country. Table 15.6 indicates the findings.

ITC

The ITC group is a diversified group with a presence in a range of different business areas. ITC is owns the brand Welcomegroup.

TABLE 15.6. Comparison of ITDC with Other 98 Listed Hotels

	ITDC	Other 98 hotels
Sales	227.83	2700.3
Advertising	1.73	73.72
PAT	6.7	247.84
Capital employed	101.34	8051.19
Net Worth	98.41	4108.8
Exports	100.77	1059.26
Land and building	33.14	4137.27
Wages	66.37	4137.23

Source: Derived from CMIE database "Prowess," August 2004

Welcomegroup is targeted at the luxury segment. It also has the Fortune brand, which is targeted at the budget sector, as well as WelcomeHeritage.

STRATEGIC PERSPECTIVE

In India, most of the profitable hotel brands are clustered in the luxury segment with brands such as Oberois, Taj, ITC, and other multinational brands such as Hyatt and Marriott. These brands are luxury brands. The product offering is outstanding, and they have international presence as well. However, some of the leading Indian brands until few years back did not have a well defined international strategy. A vacuum seems to exist in the budget/economy segment. Though thousands of properties are established in the mass market, very few are national brands. The market leaders have forayed into this segment by developing new brands for this sector. Multinational brands such as Choice Hotels, Country Inns and Suites, Best Western, and Comfort Inns have made an entry. Some of the hotel properties have been indicated in Figure 15.1, characterizing the various brands on price and quality of services.

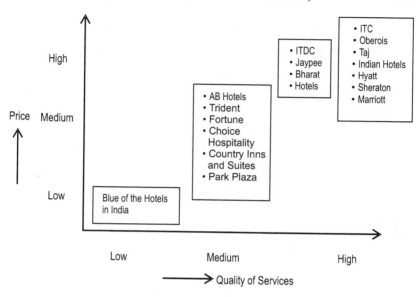

FIGURE 15.1. Hotel Properties Various Brands on Price and Quality

CHALLENGES FOR BECOMING NATIONAL/ INTERNATIONAL BRANDS

The challenges for the market leaders in each segment whether luxury or business traveler are the following:

- Ability to become an international brand
- Have a sustainable presence in India (100 cities)
- Have a unique product for each segment
- Range of products to diffuse the risk

For a growth strategy to emerge, it is essential that the brand achieves the following:

- Standardization
- USP (unique selling point)
- Ease of replication
- Good brand reputation

Brand Insight

Most of the brands in India have been growing by acquiring the properties. The expenditures incurred by some of the market leaders as indicated in Tables 15.2, 15.3, and 15.4 are evidence. This is a capital-intensive method of expansion and requires immense coordination to set up various offices and recruit and manage employees. It is also a slower process that requires a time lag before profits start coming in. The financial data indicates that funds are limited. This means that the other options such as joint ventures, management contract, franchising, and strategic alliance would have to be explored.

Emerging Budget Segment

An immense amount of potential exists in the budget segment. The budget segment has the potential to generate higher profits through huge volumes. The Indian consumer is discerning and would like to have value for money. The majority of the Indian market in the hotel industry comes in from domestic business travelers. So brands that offer value for money are those that will survive. Brands have to be functional and chic.

Financial Management in Indian Hotels

Financial health will ensure longevity. The traditional hotels have had a resource-intensive strategy for growth. This reflects in their expenditure on assets in the form of land and buildings. Second, these investments have been in metropolitan areas where the competition is intense.

LIQUIDITY ANALYSIS

Current Ratio

Table 15.7 indicates the current ratio and the quick ratio for 67 Indian hotels. The rule of the thumb for current ratio is 2 to 1. The higher the current ratio, the greater the margin for safety. Table 15.7 indicates that out of the 67 listed properties whose data is available, 12 properties have a higher current ratio. The range varies for 9.56 to

TABLE 15.7. Current ratio for select Indian hotels (March 2003)

Company Name	March 2003 Current Ratio
Northern India Hotels Ltd.	9.56
Gujarat Hotels Ltd.	7.47
Sterling Enterprises Ltd.	3.62
Benares Hotels Ltd.	3.09
Mahindra Holidays & Resorts India Ltd.	2.91
Indus Hotel Corpn. Ltd.	2.74
Fortune Park Hotels Ltd.	2.67
Viceroy Hotels Ltd.	2.62
Country Club (India) Ltd.	2.58
CHL Ltd.	2.56
Cindrella Hotels Ltd.	2.53
ITC Hotels Ltd.	2.5
Hotel Rugby Ltd.	2.15
Sinclairs Hotels & Transportation Ltd.	1.77
Jindal Hotels Ltd.	1.77
Khyati Multimedia Entertainment Ltd.	1.69
Kamat Hotels (India) Ltd.	1.66
Srinivasa Resorts Ltd.	1.61
Indian Resort Hotels Ltd.	1.6
Bihar Hotels Ltd.	1.45
AB Hotels Ltd.	1.4
Nehru Place Hotels Ltd.	1.38
India Tourism Devp. Corpn. Ltd.	1.33
Hotel Leelaventure Ltd.	1.33
Oriental Hotels Ltd.	1.29
Golkonda Hospitality Services & Resorts Ltd.	1.26
Fomento Resorts & Hotels Ltd.	1.21
Kedia Infotech Ltd.	1.2
Royale Manor Hotels & Inds. Ltd.	1.18
Indian Hotels Co. Ltd.	1.18

TABLE 15.7 *(continued)*

Company Name	March 2003 Current Ratio
Sayaji Hotels Ltd.	1.12
EIH Associated Hotels Ltd.	1.1
Venkataramana Hotels Ltd.	1
UP Hotels Ltd.	1
Peerless Hotels Ltd.	0.99
Associated Hotels Ltd.	0.95
Savera Hotels Ltd.	0.91
Spencer International Hotels Ltd.	0.9
Taj GVK Hotels & Resorts Ltd.	0.89
Jaypee Hotels Ltd.	0.89
Sagar Tourist Resorts Ltd.	0.86
EIH Ltd.	0.84
Adayar Gate Hotel Ltd.	0.82
GL Hotels Ltd.	0.78
Ras Resorts & Apart Hotels Ltd.	0.75
Howard Hotels Ltd.	0.74
Gujarat JHM Hotels Ltd.	0.71
Mac Charles (India) Ltd.	0.68
Hotel Corpn. Of India Ltd.	0.66
Asian Hotels Ltd.	0.56
Best Eastern Hotels Ltd.	0.48
Advani Hotels & Resorts (India) Ltd.	0.44
Piem Hotels Ltd.	0.42
Sterling Holiday Resorts (India) Ltd.	0.32
Ishwar Bhuvan Hotels Ltd.	0.29
Velan Hotels Ltd.	0.26
HS India Ltd.	0.24
UG Hotels & Resorts Ltd.	0.23
Vedant Hotels Ltd.	0.18
Island Hotel Maharaj Ltd.	0.17

Company Name	March 2003 Current Ratio
Noorjahan Hotels Ltd.	0.17
Polo Hotels Ltd.	0.12
Marwar Hotels Ltd.	0.09
Dolphin Hotels Ltd.	0.08
Cross Country Hotels Ltd.	0.07
Bharat Hotels Ltd.	0.04
James Hotels Ltd.	0.02

Source: Derived from CMIE database "Prowess," August 2004.

0.02. In terms of sales, the market leader is behind the smaller unknown hotels in terms of liquidity. This means that it needs to manage its liquid assets better for a better availability of working capital. Higher sales do not necessarily lead to a better working capital management practices, which could be a high risk situation for the firms. ITC however has more cash available to meet its current liabilities as compared to the firms at the top of the table.

Quick Ratio

An analysis of Table 15.8 reveals that, as against a standard benchmark of 1 to 1, most properties have a lower quick ratio. This indicates that the firm is operating in thin margins in terms of meeting its current liabilities. The market leaders such as ITC hotels has a quick ratio of 0.44, ITDC has 0.37, EIH is at 0.34, and Indian Hotels is at 0.2. This reveals that the ability of large hotels to take large debts and expansion through its own investments may be a difficult proposition. Another very interesting trend that is seen here is that budget hotels such as Fortune Park Hotels, CHL, Indus Hotel Corporation, Indian Resort, and AB Hotels have better liquidity as compared to the market leaders.

Leverage Ratios

The bankers and suppliers of raw material are more concerned with a firm's current debt-paying ability. On the other hand, long-

TABLE 15.8. Quick Ratio for select Indian Hotels for the year 2002-03

Company Name	March 2003 Quick Ratio
Northern India Hotels Ltd.	7.94
Gujarat Hotels Ltd.	6.2
Benares Hotels Ltd.	2.24
Mahindra Holidays & Resorts India Ltd.	2.11
Cindrella Hotels Ltd.	1.66
Fortune Park Hotels Ltd.	1.51
CHL Ltd.	1.27
Indus Hotel Corpn. Ltd.	0.89
Srinivasa Resorts Ltd.	0.89
Sinclairs Hotels & Transportation Ltd.	0.85
Bihar Hotels Ltd.	0.77
Indian Resort Hotels Ltd.	0.74
Jindal Hotels Ltd.	0.74
AB Hotels Ltd.	0.63
Venkataramana Hotels Ltd.	0.59
Golkonda Hospitality Services & Resorts Ltd.	0.58
Kamat Hotels (India) Ltd.	0.57
Country Club (India) Ltd.	0.48
Royale Manor Hotels & Inds. Ltd.	0.48
EIH Associated Hotels Ltd.	0.47
Gujarat JHM Hotels Ltd.	0.45
Fomento Resorts & Hotels Ltd.	0.44
ITC Hotels Ltd.	0.44
Howard Hotels Ltd.	0.43
UP Hotels Ltd.	0.4
GL Hotels Ltd.	0.39
Taj GVK Hotels & Resorts Ltd.	0.39
India Tourism Devp. Corpn. Ltd.	0.37
Kedia Infotech Ltd.	0.37
Sagar Tourist Resorts Ltd.	0.36
EIH Ltd.	0.34

Company Name	March 2003 Quick Ratio
Viceroy Hotels Ltd.	0.29
Best Eastern Hotels Ltd.	0.28
Peerless Hotels Ltd.	0.28
Savera Hotels Ltd.	0.28
Sayaji Hotels Ltd.	0.25
Sterling Enterprises Ltd.	0.25
Hotel Rugby Ltd.	0.24
Jaypee Hotels Ltd.	0.23
Nehru Place Hotels Ltd.	0.23
Adayar Gate Hotel Ltd.	0.2
Associated Hotels Ltd.	0.2
Indian Hotels Co. Ltd.	0.2
Advani Hotels & Resorts (India) Ltd.	0.18
Oriental Hotels Ltd.	0.18
Ras Resorts & Apart Hotels Ltd.	0.18
Asian Hotels Ltd.	0.16
Hotel Corpn. Of India Ltd.	0.16
Spencer International Hotels Ltd.	0.16
UG Hotels & Resorts Ltd.	0.16
Mac Charles (India) Ltd.	0.14
Hotel Leelaventure Ltd.	0.13
HS India Ltd.	0.12
Piem Hotels Ltd.	0.1
Velan Hotels Ltd.	0.07
Ishwar Bhuvan Hotels Ltd.	0.04
Island Hotel Maharaj Ltd.	0.03
Sterling Holiday Resorts (India) Ltd.	0.03
Marwar Hotels Ltd.	0.02
Polo Hotels Ltd.	0.02
Khyati Multimedia Entertainment Ltd.	0.01

Source: Derived from CMIE database "Prowess," August 2004.

term creditors lending to institutions are concerned with a firm's long-term financial strength (Pandey, 2001). Higher use of debt is a more risky proposition from a firm's point of view. However, if the firm earns a rate of return on capital employed higher than the interest rate in the borrowed funds, the earning would be magnified.

Table 15.9 indicates that entrepreneurship financed by the debt is almost equal to self-financial ventures in the Indian hotel industry. Most of the upcoming or smaller properties have a higher degree of reliance on the debt. Firm's such as Mahindra Holidays and Resorts, Vedant Hotels, Spencer International, Sagar Tourist Resorts, Sayaji Hotel, and Royal Manor have extremely high levels of debt as compared to owners' contributions. In such properties, the professional management becomes a necessity as any deviation from the desired standards could result in a working capital crisis.

The market leaders such as Indian Hotels, EIH, and ITC have a conservative approach, and owner funds have been the main source of expansion for such firms.

INTEREST COVERAGE CAPACITY OF INDIAN HOTELS

The interest coverage ratio or the times interest earned is used to test the firm's debt servicing capacity. The interest coverage ratio is computed by dividing earnings before interest and taxes by interest charges. This ratio shows the number of times the interest charges are covered by funds that are ordinarily available for their payment. A high ratio is desirable, but too high a ratio indicates that the firm is very conservative in using debt and that it is not using credit to the best advantage of shareholder. A lower ratio indicates excessive use of debt or inefficient operations. Table 15.10 indicates select ratios for ability to cover interest for the market leaders.

Table 15.10 indicates that the interest coverage ratio is declining for all the hotels other than Oriental hotels and Jaypee Hotels. This signifies the use of higher debt and a growing interest rate. Table 15.10 indicated the use of lesser debt by the market leaders. This points at the use of short-term debt to maintain the liquidity of the hotels at a higher rate of interest.

The cash profits/interest ratio is also declining steeply. The steepest fall is in the case of ITDC, the public sector firm that has also been

TABLE 15.9. Debt Equity Ratio for the Hotels in India in March 2003

	March 1999 Debt equity ratio	March 2000 Debt equity ratio	March 2001 Debt equity ratio	March 2002 Debt equity ratio	March 2003 Debt equity ratio
Mahindra Holidays & Resorts India Ltd.		−616.93	53.65	−328.17	34.09
Vedant Hotels Ltd.	2.21	3.11	5.09	11.08	28.66
Spencer International Hotels Ltd.		19.48	15.83	15.47	13.77
Sagar Tourist Resorts Ltd.	3.33	4.56	5.01	7.63	12.36
Sayaji Hotels Ltd.		4.11	4439	−8.25	11.25
Royale Manor Hotels & Inds. Ltd.	1.82	1.96	2.76	4.84	8.82
EIH Associated Hotels Ltd.	1.77	2.56	3.01	3.64	4.27
Advani Hotels & Resorts (India) Ltd.	1.29	1.35	1.52	3.01	3.68
UG Hotels & Resorts Ltd.	4.26	11.38	0.58	−6.44	3.04
GL Hotels Ltd.	1.48		2.17	0.8	2.92
Nehru Place Hotels Ltd.	0.64	0.38	0.71	0.67	2.46
Cross Country Hotels Ltd.	1.33	1.48		1.93	2.15
HS India Ltd.	1.75	1.98	2.16	2.27	2.1
Hotel Leelaventure Ltd.	2.36	2.42	2.15	2.26	1.98
Gujarat J H M Hotels Ltd.	2.59	4.77		6.35	1.87
Velan Hotels Ltd.	6.76	11.13	2.16	1.86	1.83
Viceroy Hotels Ltd.	2.09	1.78	1.38	1.68	1.81
Fomento Resorts & Hotels Ltd.	1.8	1.74	1.11	1.68	1.55
Kamat Hotels (India) Ltd.	1.25	1.38	1.26	1.33	1.37
Sterling Enterprises Ltd.			1.53	1.38	1.25
Asian Hotels Ltd.	0	0.01	0.39	0.88	1.14
Howard Hotels Ltd.	1.4	2.07	1.41	1.36	1.13
Indus Hotel Corpn. Ltd.		1.17	2.28	1.08	1.12
Adayar Gate Hotel Ltd.	0.92	1.01	0.93	0.99	1.1
Marwar Hotels Ltd.					1.06
Savera Hotels Ltd.	0.56	0.43	0.55	0.82	1.05
Piem Hotels Ltd.	0.54	0.15	0.17	0.11	1
Polo Hotels Ltd.	0.56	0.95	0.96	0.84	0.98
Indian Hotels Co. Ltd.	0.16	0.42	0.57	0.91	0.85
Best Eastern Hotels Ltd.	6.85	1.7	1.25	1.1	0.84
Associated Hotels Ltd.	0.41	0.5	0.61	0.72	0.8
Country Club (India) Ltd.	2.49	1.34	1.29	0.8	0.8

TABLE 15.9 *(continued)*

	March 1999 Debt equity ratio	March 2000 Debt equity ratio	March 2001 Debt equity ratio	March 2002 Debt equity ratio	March 2003 Debt equity ratio
EIH Ltd.	0.39	0.38	0.39	0.6	0.8
Sinclairs Hotels & Transportation Ltd.	0.85	1.07	0.99	0.83	0.71
U P Hotels Ltd.	0.23	0.23	0.33	0.5	0.69
James Hotels Ltd.	0.61			0.67	0.68
Jindal Hotels Ltd.	0.1	0.1	0.34	0.64	0.67
Jaypee Hotels Ltd.	0.92	1.19	0.77	0.81	0.62
Khyati Multimedia Entertainment Ltd.	0.75	0.84		0.74	0.6
CHL Ltd.	0.06	0.11	0.46	0.62	0.59
AB Hotels Ltd.	1.68	1.09	0.95	0.63	0.54
Peerless Hotels Ltd.	0.36	0	0.08	0.16	0.53
Bharat Hotels Ltd.	0.26	0.29	0.37	0.82	0.5
Hotel Rugby Ltd.	0.16	0.25	0.34	0.39	0.49
Srinivasa Resorts Ltd.	0.86	0.99	0.74	0.6	0.44
Bihar Hotels Ltd.	0.65	0.77	0.75	0.42	0.36
Noorjahan Hotels Ltd.	1.06	0.82	0.3	0.28	0.31
Taj GVK Hotels & Resorts Ltd.		0.24	0	0.01	0.16
ITC Hotels Ltd.	0.12	0.08	0.1	0.13	0.11
Ras Resorts & Apart Hotels Ltd.	0.46	0.54	0.58	0.13	0.1
Indian Resort Hotels Ltd.	0.41	0.28	0.1	0.08	0.08
Golkonda Hospitality Services & Resorts Ltd.		−1.86	−4.45	0.17	0.04
Oriental Hotels Ltd.	0.09	0.08	0.13	0.04	0.04
India Tourism Devp. Corpn. Ltd.	0	0	0.01	0.06	0.03
Cindrella Hotels Ltd.	0.01	0.01	0.01	0.04	0.02
Benares Hotels Ltd.	0	0	0	0.01	0.01
Fortune Park Hotels Ltd.	0	0	0.19	0.2	0.01
Mac Charles (India) Ltd.	0.07	0.17	0.16	0.04	0.01
Aramusk Infrastructure Investments Ltd.				0	0
Bay Islands Hotels Ltd.	0	0	0	0	0
Gujarat Hotels Ltd.	0	0	0	0	0
Hotel Corpn. Of India Ltd.	0.18	0.11	0.69	−5.75	0

	March 1999 Debt equity ratio	March 2000 Debt equity ratio	March 2001 Debt equity ratio	March 2002 Debt equity ratio	March 2003 Debt equity ratio
Kedia Infotech Ltd.	0	0	0	0	0
Northern India Hotels Ltd.	0	0	0	0	0
Venkataramana Hotels Ltd.	−1.23	−1.23	−1.3	−2.16	−2.01
Ishwar Bhuvan Hotels Ltd.	1.08	1.55	2.77	10.84	−5.28
Sterling Holiday Resorts (India) Ltd.	2.61	1.79	−53.64		−7.16
Dolphin Hotels Ltd.	−26.85	−13.42	−4.33	−16.47	−17.28
Island Hotel Maharaj Ltd.				−6.15	−29.55
Abhinav Homes & Resorts Ltd.	0.07	0	0	0	
Aruna Hotels Ltd.	0.13	0.04	0.06		
Asia Pacific Hotels Ltd.	7.2	20.78	2.09	2.64	
Benchmark Homes & Resorts Ltd. [Merged]					
Blue Coast Hotels & Resorts Ltd.	1.19	1.37	0.25	0.97	
Budget Hotels Ltd.	0.76	0.56	5.01	−55.21	
Coromandel Hotels Ltd. [Merged]	0.75	0.48	0.31		
Covelong Beach Hotel (India) Ltd. [Merged]	0.2	0.14	0.1		
East West Hotels Ltd.	0.19		0	0	
Empire Hotels & Resorts Ltd.					
Gandhinagar Hotels Ltd.	0.23	0.2	0.28	0.26	
Hazoor Media & Power Ltd.			0	0	
Hotel Sree Krishna Ltd.	0.54				
Ideal Hotels & Inds. Ltd.	0.98				
Indo Hokke Hotels Ltd.	0	0	0	0	
Joymat Hotel Resorts Ltd.	0.2	0.21			
KTC Hotels Ltd.	4.79	3.98	3.24	3.5	
Lakeland Hotels Ltd.					
Mahindra Hotels & Resorts Ltd.	−1.42	−1.42	−1.39		
Nalanda Hotels & Properties Ltd.		0			
Neelkanth Motels & Hotels Ltd.	0.07	0.07	0.05	0.05	
Pan India Resort & Land Devp. Ltd.					
Poona Industrial Hotel Ltd.	0.33	0.02	0.01	0	
Rajgarh Palace Hotel & Resorts Ltd.	0	0	0	0	
Royal Resorts & Hotels Ltd.					
Shivgarh Resorts Ltd.					
Suman Motels Ltd.	2.42	2.7	5.5		

TABLE 15.9 *(continued)*

	March 1999 Debt equity ratio	March 2000 Debt equity ratio	March 2001 Debt equity ratio	March 2002 Debt equity ratio	March 2003 Debt equity ratio
Trade Wings Hotels Ltd.	−6.72	−3.56	−2.25		
Woodside Parks Ltd.	11.25		−1.3	−1.28	

Source: Derived from CMIE database "Prowess," August 2004.

TABLE 15.10. Interest Coverage Ratio for select Indian Hotels

Interest Cover						
Hotel	1999	2000	2001	2002	2003	2004
Indian Hotel						
PBIT/interest	6.38	4.63	3.37	2.63	2.01	2.83
Cash profits/interest	5.71	4.2	2.86	2.02	1.41	2.5
Operating cash flow/interest	4.78	3.9	2.24	1.45	1.64	2.37
EIH Hotels						
PBIT/interest	15.74	1.31	0.21	0.81	0.56	0.38
Cash profits/interest	16.87	1.1	−0.2	0.36	0.12	0.07
Operating cash flow/interest	18.76	1.9	0.68	1.45	0.63	1.19
ITDC						
PBIT/interest	784.14	1116		−10.36	−153.57	−25.8
Cash profits/interest	744.57	1984		−6.66	−139.52	7.96
Operating Cash flow/interest	438.71	3829		−0.7	−16.29	21.12
Jaypee Hotels						
Interest cover						
PBIT/ interest	1.72	2.31	1.12	1.22	1.04	1.1
PBIT (NNRT)/interest	2.11	2.36	1.16	1.24	1.05	1.07
PBDIT (NNRT)/interest	2.43	3.01	1.44	1.54	1.25	1.31
Cash profits/interest	0.97	1.9	0.4	0.51	0.28	0.33
Operating cash flow/interest	1.97	4.63	0.92	0.5	0.79	0.95
Oriental Hotels						
Interest cover						
PBIT/ interest	11.64	7.16	3.94	6.3	7.18	13.92
PBIT (NNRT)/interest	11.62	7.41	4.95	5.19	8.06	15.15
PBDIT (NNRT)/interest	13.47	9.33	6.7	9.59	17.21	26.25
Cash profits/interest	10.89	6.88	4.14	7.68	13.28	19.51
Operating cash flow/interest	6.45	12.22	4.75	6.06	15.76	25.26

Source: Derived from CMIE database "Prowess," August 2004.

selling off its properties. The EIH hotels also indicate a declining cash/interest ratio along with Indian Hotels and others, except for Oriental Hotels, whose situation is strengthening.

Appendix 15.B indicates the cross-sectional view for interest coverage for ninety-eight hotels listed in CMIE database (Prowess). The smaller hotels, such as Mac Charles, Spencer, and Fortune Park Hotels, indicate that have a high capacity to raise debt and need to utilize funds for expansion strategy.

About eight to ten hotels have a reasonable interest coverage ratio. A substantially large number of properties have expansion plans that will be difficult to fund on account of inability to service the debt. This has grim pointers toward the extent of entrepreneurship existing in the hotel industry. This also has an implication for the existing inefficiencies in large number of Indian properties. About 50 percent of the properties out of sixty-three indicated in Appendix 15.B would have problems in raising funds for growth.

Any branding-related activity is resource extensive. Brand building requires investments in understanding customer needs and in product development matching with changing environmental context. The perception of quality is impossible without qualified and trained staff. It is therefore pertinent that the hotels invest in such areas so as to raise their cash flow.

PROFITABILITY

Return on equity indicates how well the firm has used the resources of owners. This ratio is one of the most important relationships in financial analysis. It is calculated as a ratio of PAT and net worth. It indicates that smaller hotels have a high return on equity. Table 15.11 indicates that the smaller hotels have a higher return on equity as compared to the larger hotels such as EIH, ITC, Indian Hotels, and ITDC. Hotels such as AB Hotel, Sayaji, Mahindra, Furtune, and Taj GVK, can utilize the return to fund their expansion plans.

Table 15.12 indicates the net profit margin for select hotels. Only about one-third of the ninety-nine properties have a positive net profit margin. The smaller properties have a higher net profit margin as compared to the market leaders. A small hotel such as Bay Island has a higher margin as compared to hotels such as Indian Hotels, EIH,

TABLE 15.11. Return on Equity for select Hotels in India

Company Name	March 2003 (100*pat_nnrt/ avg_net_worth)
Ishwar Bhuvan Hotels Ltd.	545.76
Sayaji Hotels Ltd.	255.41
Mahindra Holidays & Resorts India Ltd.	198.98
Island Hotel Maharaj Ltd.	113.73
Sterling Holiday Resorts (India) Ltd.	97.62
Gujarat J H M Hotels Ltd.	83.87
Kedia Infotech Ltd.	32.29
Mac Charles (India) Ltd.	26.27
AB Hotels Ltd.	19.77
Fortune Park Hotels Ltd.	18.54
Bihar Hotels Ltd.	15.99
Golkonda Hospitality Services & Resorts Ltd.	15.71
Spencer International Hotels Ltd.	14.88
Srinivasa Resorts Ltd.	14.70
Nehru Place Hotels Ltd.	10.59
Taj GVK Hotels & Resorts Ltd.	10.42
Jindal Hotels Ltd.	9.78
Best Eastern Hotels Ltd.	7.87
Fomento Resorts & Hotels Ltd.	7.61
Sterling Enterprises Ltd.	7.51
Piem Hotels Ltd.	6.48
Velan Hotels Ltd.	6.43
Venkataramana Hotels Ltd.	6.22
Dolphin Hotels Ltd.	5.63
Indian Resort Hotels Ltd.	3.62
Asian Hotels Ltd.	3.39
Oriental Hotels Ltd.	3.21
Viceroy Hotels Ltd.	2.92
CHL Ltd.	2.72
Indian Hotels Co. Ltd.	2.56

Company Name	March 2003 (100*pat_nnrt/ avg_net_worth)
HS India Ltd.	2.55
EIH Ltd.	1.45
Cindrella Hotels Ltd.	1.11
Jaypee Hotels Ltd.	0.63
Polo Hotels Ltd.	0.57
ITC Hotels Ltd.	0.44
Bharat Hotels Ltd.	0.02
Aramusk Infrastructure Investments Ltd.	−0.18
Howard Hotels Ltd.	−0.22
Kamat Hotels (India) Ltd.	−0.41
Hotel Rugby Ltd.	−1.25
Hotel Leelaventure Ltd.	−1.71
Adayar Gate Hotel Ltd.	−1.97
GL Hotels Ltd.	−2.12
Ras Resorts & Apart Hotels Ltd.	−2.77
Khyati Multimedia Entertainment Ltd.	−2.94
Country Club (India) Ltd.	−3.06
India Tourism Devp. Corpn. Ltd.	−6.53
Associated Hotels Ltd.	−6.69
James Hotels Ltd.	−6.8
Indus Hotel Corpn. Ltd.	−8.03
Savera Hotels Ltd.	−8.78
Cross Country Hotels Ltd.	−10.75
UP Hotels Ltd.	−17.78
Peerless Hotels Ltd.	−26.6
Royale Manor Hotels & Inds. Ltd.	−40.06
Hotel Corpn. Of India Ltd.	−41.62
Advani Hotels & Resorts (India) Ltd.	−43.61
E I H Associated Hotels Ltd.	−54.73
Sagar Tourist Resorts Ltd.	−56.36
G Hotels & Resorts Ltd.	−92.20

Source: Derived from CMIE database "Prowess," 2004.

TABLE 15.12. Net Profit Margin for the Select Hotels in India

Company Name	March 2003 Net profit after taxes/sales
Bay Islands Hotels Ltd.	51.35
Noorjahan Hotels Ltd.	46.00
Gujarat Hotels Ltd.	31.56
Mac Charles (India) Ltd.	31.38
Northern India Hotels Ltd.	19.48
Gujarat J H M Hotels Ltd.	14.86
A B Hotels Ltd.	14.62
Sterling Enterprises Ltd.	14.19
Golkonda Hospitality Services & Resorts Ltd.	14.04
Taj G V K Hotels & Resorts Ltd.	13.15
Spencer International Hotels Ltd.	12.32
Benares Hotels Ltd.	11.96
Nehru Place Hotels Ltd.	11.06
Srinivasa Resorts Ltd.	11.00
Fortune Park Hotels Ltd.	10.05
Best Eastern Hotels Ltd.	8.99
Jindal Hotels Ltd.	8.39
Asian Hotels Ltd.	8.38
Bihar Hotels Ltd.	7.96
Piem Hotels Ltd.	7.49
Indian Resort Hotels Ltd.	7.04
Oriental Hotels Ltd.	6.7
Mahindra Holidays & Resorts India Ltd.	6.55
Kedia Infotech Ltd.	5.61
Fomento Resorts & Hotels Ltd.	4.79
Viceroy Hotels Ltd.	4.67
Cindrella Hotels Ltd.	4.5
Indian Hotels Co. Ltd.	3.85
Velan Hotels Ltd.	3.61
EIH Ltd.	2.89
CHL Ltd.	2.64
HS India Ltd.	2.39
Polo Hotels Ltd.	1.85
Sinclairs Hotels & Transportation Ltd.	0.98

Company Name	March 2003 Net profit after taxes/sales
ITC Hotels Ltd.	0.52
Jaypee Hotels Ltd.	0.52
Bharat Hotels Ltd.	0.07
Howard Hotels Ltd.	−0.36
Dolphin Hotels Ltd.	−0.62
Kamat Hotels (India) Ltd.	−0.67
Adayar Gate Hotel Ltd.	−2.25
India Tourism Devp. Corpn. Ltd.	−2.86
Hotel Leelaventure Ltd.	−4.26
utoRas Resorts & Apart Hotels Ltd.	−5.06
Country Club (India) Ltd.	−5.83
Savera Hotels Ltd.	−6.08
Peerless Hotels Ltd.	−9.94
Hotel Rugby Ltd.	−10.18
Sayaji Hotels Ltd.	−10.21
Associated Hotels Ltd.	−11.89
Royale Manor Hotels & Inds. Ltd.	−13.74
UP Hotels Ltd.	−15.64
Advani Hotels & Resorts (India) Ltd.	−15.88
UG Hotels & Resorts Ltd.	−25.00
Sagar Tourist Resorts Ltd.	−27.19
Indus Hotel Corpn. Ltd.	−34.15
Khyati Multimedia Entertainment Ltd.	−35.63
EIH Associated Hotels Ltd.	−48.16
Ishwar Bhuvan Hotels Ltd.	−54.21
Sterling Holiday Resorts (India) Ltd.	−59.77
Hotel Corpn. Of India Ltd.	−68.14
Island Hotel Maharaj Ltd.	−94.37
Aramusk Infrastructure Investments Ltd.	−200.00
Venkataramana Hotels Ltd.	−225.00
Marwar Hotels Ltd.	−472.88
Cross Country Hotels Ltd.	−650.00
James Hotels Ltd.	−1,500.00
Vedant Hotels Ltd.	−3,800.00

Source: Derived from CMIE database "Prowess," 2004.

and ITC, which have the net profit margins as 3.85, 2.89, and 0.52 respectively. Hotels such as Sterling and EIH, which indicated a good interest coverage ratio, have negative ratios here.

MARKETING ORIENTATION OF FIRMS IN THE HOTEL INDUSTRY IN INDIA

Marketing is an essential ingredient for creating brand awareness and consumer acceptance. Table 15.13 indicates the marketing and advertising expenses of select hotels in India. It can be seen that in terms of advertising expenses, Indian Hotels leads with Rs 25.97 crores (≈ $6,380,835), and EIH follows it. The other hotels' expenditures on advertising is minimal, and is almost negligible. The extent of expenditure clearly indicates that with such a budget, targeting national media on a regular basis is impossible. So most of the reliance is on the local media. Hence this is also a constraint for smaller firms. The expenses on marketing are also minimal. In fact, the smaller firms have higher expenditure on marketing efforts than bigger firms. The smaller firms invest on sales promotion, public relations, and other related activities.

CONCLUSIONS AND RECOMMENDATIONS

The emergence of national brands and international presence requires a planned strategy. A selective analysis of listed hotels in India reveals that entrepreneurship in this industry is still at a nascent stage. The stage is dominated by few major Indian firms. In this particular set of firms, the top four firms contribute to 50 percent of the market share. The other 50 percent of the share is split between ninety-five firms.

The reliance on self-efforts and expansion through investments of owner funds have been the major route for initiation of entrepreneurship in this segment. A need exists for exploring other possibilities, such as expansion through management contracts, joint ventures, franchising, or strategic alliances. These options are less resource extensive. They elicit a stronger commitment from the other party as individual entrepreneurs are more committed to producing higher returns on their investments.

TABLE 15.13. Advertising and Marketing Expenditures of Select Indian Hotels

Company name	March 2003 Advertising expenses Rs. (cr.)	March 2003 Marketing expenses Rs. (cr.)
Mahindra Holidays & Resorts India Ltd.	4.18	13.37
Oriental Hotels Ltd.	0	7.75
EIH Ltd.	10.25	7.12
Asian Hotels Ltd.	2.77	3.38
Nehru Place Hotels Ltd.	0.62	2.54
Adayar Gate Hotel Ltd.	1.39	2.16
Sterling Holiday Resorts (India) Ltd.	0.06	2.15
A B Hotels Ltd.	1.39	1.75
Bharat Hotels Ltd.	0.71	1.08
Advani Hotels & Resorts (India) Ltd.	0.71	1.05
Taj G V K Hotels & Resorts Ltd.	1.47	0.97
rsid16729343 Kamat Hotels (India) Ltd.	2.37	0.93
Fomento Resorts & Hotels Ltd.	1.40	0.91
Kedia Infotech Ltd.	0.52	0.89
Savera Hotels Ltd.	0	0.76
Mac Charles (India) Ltd.	0	0.70
EIH Associated Hotels Ltd.	1.59	0.60
Jaypee Hotels Ltd.	0.84	0.53
Indian Resort Hotels Ltd.	1.46	0.49
CHL Ltd.	0.07	0.37
Peerless Hotels Ltd.	0.16	0.33
Sagar Tourist Resorts Ltd.	0.03	0.28
Indus Hotel Corpn. Ltd.	0.78	0.26
ITC Hotels Ltd.	4.22	0.22
Sayaji Hotels Ltd.	0.28	0.22
Viceroy Hotels Ltd.	0	0.21
Benares Hotels Ltd.	0.49	0.16
Royale Manor Hotels & Inds. Ltd.	0.23	0.15
Jindal Hotels Ltd.	0.06	0.14
UG Hotels & Resorts Ltd.	0.06	0.11
Hotel Corpn. Of India Ltd.	0.09	0.09
Dolphin Hotels Ltd.	0.03	0.08
Golkonda Hospitality Services & Resorts Ltd.	0.09	0.08
Bihar Hotels Ltd.	0.07	0.06

TABLE 15.13 *(continued)*

Company name	March 2003 Advertising expenses Rs. (cr.)	March 2003 Marketing expenses Rs. (cr.)
HS India Ltd.	0.02	0.06
UP Hotels Ltd.	0.28	0.05
Velan Hotels Ltd.	0.01	0.05
Cindrella Hotels Ltd.	0.01	0.04
Island Hotel Maharaj Ltd.	0.19	0.04
Hotel Rugby Ltd.	0.04	0.03
Marwar Hotels Ltd.	0.07	0.03
Ras Resorts & Apart Hotels Ltd.	0.04	0.03
Howard Hotels Ltd.	0.02	0.02
Ishwar Bhuvan Hotels Ltd.	0.05	0.02
Sterling Enterprises Ltd.	0.12	0.02
Associated Hotels Ltd.	0.16	0.01
Aramusk Infrastructure Investments Ltd.	0	0
Bay Islands Hotels Ltd.	0	0
Best Eastern Hotels Ltd.	0	0
Country Club (India) Ltd.	0	0
Cross Country Hotels Ltd.	0	0
Fortune Park Hotels Ltd.	0.05	0
GL Hotels Ltd.	0.01	0
Gujarat Hotels Ltd.	0	0
Gujarat JHM Hotels Ltd.	0.28	0
Hotel Leelaventure Ltd.	2.58	0
India Tourism Devp. Corpn. Ltd.	1.73	0
Indian Hotels Co. Ltd.	25.97	0
James Hotels Ltd.	0	0
Khyati Multimedia Entertainment Ltd.	0	0
Noorjahan Hotels Ltd.	0	0
Northern India Hotels Ltd.	0.01	0
Piem Hotels Ltd.	4.44	0
Polo Hotels Ltd.	0	0
Sinclairs Hotels & Transportation Ltd.	0.12	0
Spencer International Hotels Ltd.	0	0
Srinivasa Resorts Ltd.	0.86	0

Source: Derived from CMIE database "Prowess," 2004.

Franchising as a strategy would again mean that the product and delivery methods would need to be standardized. The systems orientation needs to be strong along with the a good brand equity at a local level. The profitability also needs to be high to attract potential entrepreneurs. However, in India, as the analysis indicates, the market leaders have a diffused strategy with their product primarily directed at the luxury market. They all have come out with the brands specifically targeted at the budget segment. Indian Hotels with Indi One (now renamed as Ginger Hotels), Oberoi with Trident, ITC with Fortune, Carlson Hospitality with Park Plazas, are all examples of such a strategy. The entry of multinational businesses in such areas further points out at the potential for growth in this market. Brands such as Choice Hotels, Best Western, Courtyard, and Country Inns and Suites are all brands that have aggressive action plan for Indian market.

The need is to standardize products and ensure delivery standards. The key to success in employees. The Indian hotel industry would benefit immensely by having human resources managers drawn from the manufacturing sector or people who have professional MBA degrees. A huge vacuum exists in management orientation in hospitality education in India. An entrepreneurial venture requires the nurturance from a visionary leader. The hospitality industry is replete with examples of success on account of visionary leadership. The managers who create and build these brands will benefit immensely from exposure to general management functions. The skew toward operational training in 98 percent of hospitality management institutes produces employees with a specific focus. On the other hand, job training does not bring in the required development of an appropriate knowledge level. This enlarges the learning curve and hence the organization cannot benefit from the enhanced capability of the individual employees. So education inputs could have an impact on the quality of entrepreneurship in this sector.

The large base of assets lying with small entrepreneurs or ITDC could be turned around by either tying with a national or international brand through management contract or a strategic alliance. The issue that could constrain this is the huge management fees and share in profit, which most international firms demand. However, if it ensures success in the long run, it may be a worthwhile investment. Some outstanding initiatives are being taken by some entrepreneurs that are creating products that are more contemporary. Initiatives such as

Lemon Tree are an innovation in India. Lean hotels, multiskilled workforce, energy-saving devices, clear market and product strategy, and a grand vision to think at the global scale will lead to successful entrepreneurship in the hotel industry in India.

APPENDIX 15.A. SALES OF SELECT INDIAN HOTELS FOR THE YEAR 2002-2003

Company name	Sales (Rs crore) March 2003
Indian Hotels Co. Ltd.	590.19
EIH Ltd.	384.09
India Tourism Devp. Corpn. Ltd.	227.83
ITC Hotels Ltd.	177.49
Hotel Leelaventure Ltd.	134.42
Asian Hotels Ltd.	106.66
Piem Hotels Ltd.	99.2
Oriental Hotels Ltd.	97.28
Jaypee Hotels Ltd.	96.58
Bharat Hotels Ltd.	74.59
Taj GVK Hotels & Resorts Ltd.	70.04
Nehru Place Hotels Ltd.	60.41
Mahindra Holidays & Resorts India Ltd.	59.58
Adayar Gate Hotel Ltd.	56.43
AB Hotels Ltd.	55.83
Kamat Hotels (India) Ltd.	44.84
Sterling Holiday Resorts (India) Ltd.	44
Hotel Corpn. Of India Ltd.	39.39
Srinivasa Resorts Ltd.	38.82
Kedia Infotech Ltd.	32.97
Mac Charles (India) Ltd.	27.44
EIH Associated Hotels Ltd.	26.95
CHL Ltd.	26.47
Dolphin Hotels Ltd.	25.89
Country Club (India) Ltd.	25.56

Company name	Sales (Rs crore) March 2003
Viceroy Hotels Ltd.	23.76
UP Hotels Ltd.	22.25
Fomento Resorts & Hotels Ltd.	20.45
Advani Hotels & Resorts (India) Ltd.	20.22
Indian Resort Hotels Ltd.	19.45
Savera Hotels Ltd.	19.07
Sayaji Hotels Ltd.	18.52
Indus Hotel Corpn. Ltd.	18.33
Gujarat J H M Hotels Ltd.	15.75
Peerless Hotels Ltd.	10.86
Benares Hotels Ltd.	10.79
Spencer International Hotels Ltd.	10.39
Sinclairs Hotels & Transportation Ltd.	10.17
Royale Manor Hotels & Inds. Ltd.	9.24
Bihar Hotels Ltd.	8.92
Golkonda Hospitality Services & Resorts Ltd.	7.69
Velan Hotels Ltd.	6.38
Jindal Hotels Ltd.	6.32
Hotel Rugby Ltd.	5.01
HS India Ltd.	4.61
Associated Hotels Ltd.	4.54
Island Hotel Maharaj Ltd.	3.73
Sterling Enterprises Ltd.	3.1
Ishwar Bhuvan Hotels Ltd.	2.97
Howard Hotels Ltd.	2.77
Best Eastern Hotels Ltd.	2.67
Gujarat Hotels Ltd.	2.63
UG Hotels & Resorts Ltd.	2.6
Ras Resorts & Apart Hotels Ltd.	2.37
Fortune Park Hotels Ltd.	1.89
Northern India Hotels Ltd.	1.54
Marwar Hotels Ltd.	1.18

Company name	Sales (Rs crore) March 2003
Sagar Tourist Resorts Ltd.	1.14
Cindrella Hotels Ltd.	1.11
Khyati Multimedia Entertainment Ltd.	0.87
Polo Hotels Ltd.	0.54
Noorjahan Hotels Ltd.	0.5
Bay Islands Hotels Ltd.	0.37
Venkataramana Hotels Ltd.	0.32
Cross Country Hotels Ltd.	0.1
James Hotels Ltd.	0.03
Vedant Hotels Ltd.	0.02
Aramusk Infrastructure Investments Ltd.	0.01

Source: Derived from CMIE database "Prowess," 2004.

APPENDIX 15.B. INTEREST COVERAGE FOR SELECT INDIAN HOTELS FOR THE YEAR 2002-2003

Company Name	March 2003 Interest Coverage
Mac Charles (India) Ltd.	157.13
Spencer International Hotels Ltd.	49.75
Fortune Park Hotels Ltd.	30
Kedia Infotech Ltd.	15.6
Taj GVK Hotels & Resorts Ltd.	15.52
Golkonda Hospitality Services & Resorts Ltd.	11.83
Oriental Hotels Ltd.	8.06
Piem Hotels Ltd.	7.24
Bihar Hotels Ltd.	5.41
Srinivasa Resorts Ltd.	4.94
AB Hotels Ltd.	4.84
HS India Ltd.	4.67
Asian Hotels Ltd.	4.28

Company Name	March 2003 Interest Coverage
Indian Resort Hotels Ltd.	4.13
Gujarat J H M Hotels Ltd.	3.36
Best Eastern Hotels Ltd.	3.29
Cindrella Hotels Ltd.	3.25
EIH Ltd.	2.3
Jindal Hotels Ltd.	2.1
Sterling Enterprises Ltd.	2.1
Fomento Resorts & Hotels Ltd.	1.83
Indian Hotels Co. Ltd.	1.69
ITC Hotels Ltd.	1.68
Nehru Place Hotels Ltd.	1.6
Velan Hotels Ltd.	1.57
Mahindra Holidays & Resorts India Ltd.	1.54
CHL Ltd.	1.51
Viceroy Hotels Ltd.	1.38
Howard Hotels Ltd.	1.18
Polo Hotels Ltd.	1.08
Jaypee Hotels Ltd.	1.07
Bharat Hotels Ltd.	1.03
Kamat Hotels (India) Ltd.	1
Dolphin Hotels Ltd.	0.95
Hotel Leelaventure Ltd.	0.91
Adayar Gate Hotel Ltd.	0.84
Country Club (India) Ltd.	0.77
Royale Manor Hotels & Inds. Ltd.	0.61
Sayaji Hotels Ltd.	0.61
Savera Hotels Ltd.	0.56
Hotel Rugby Ltd.	0.42
Associated Hotels Ltd.	0.41
UG Hotels & Resorts Ltd.	0.39
Advani Hotels & Resorts (India) Ltd.	0.2

Company Name	March 2003 Interest Coverage
Khyati Multimedia Entertainment Ltd.	0.11
Sterling Holiday Resorts (India) Ltd.	0.05
James Hotels Ltd.	-0.13
Ishwar Bhuvan Hotels Ltd.	-0.25
Indus Hotel Corpn. Ltd.	-0.38
UP Hotels Ltd.	-0.44
Marwar Hotels Ltd.	-0.65
Ras Resorts & Apart Hotels Ltd.	-0.71
Island Hotel Maharaj Ltd.	-0.9
Aramusk Infrastructure Investments Ltd.	-1
EIH Associated Hotels Ltd.	-1.04
Cross Country Hotels Ltd.	-1.1
Peerless Hotels Ltd.	-5.35
GL Hotels Ltd.	-5.4
Sagar Tourist Resorts Ltd.	-9.33
Hotel Corpn. Of India Ltd.	-16.12
India Tourism Devp. Corpn. Ltd.	-25.04
Venkataramana Hotels Ltd.	-35

Source: Derived from CMIE database "Prowess," 2004.

REFERENCES

The Hindu (1998). *Survey of Indian Industry.* Tamil Nadu, India: The Hindu.
Hindu Indiastat (2007) Tourism receipts. Available at: http://www.indiastat.com/india.
Kamra, K.K., Mill, R.C., and Kaushil, S. (2000). *Hospitality Operations and Management.* New Delhi, India: Wheeler.
Ministry of Finance (2007). Union budget and economic survey: Economic survey 2006-2007. Government of India. Available at: http://indiabudget.nic.in/es2006-07/esmain.htm.
Pandey, I.M. (2001). *Financial Management.* New Delhi, India: Vikas.
WTTC (2007) Blueprint for new tourism 2003. Available at http://www.wttc.travel/bin/pdf.

FURTHER READING

Geller, L. (2001). The demands of globalization on the lodging industry. Presentation at Credit Lyonnaise Lodging Conference, March 1998, Paris, France. Available at: http://www.fiu.edu/~review/deman-sp98.htm. Retrieved July 19.

Hisrich, R.D. and Peters, M.P. (2000). *Entrepreneurship*. New Delhi, India: Tata McGraw Hill.

Jones, P. (2002). *Introduction to Hospitality Operations*. London, UK: Continuum.

Kondaiah, C. (2002). *Entrepreneurship in the New Millennium*. New Delhi, India: Tata McGraw Hill.

Morrison, A. Rimmington, M., and Williams, C. (1999). *Entrepreneurship in the Hospitality Tourism and Leisure Industries*. Oxford, UK: Butterworth Heinemann.

Chapter 16

Hospitality and Tourism:
International Industries Experiencing
Common Problems

Hadyn Ingram

INTRODUCTION

This chapter covers some select entries from the *International Journal of Hospitality Management (IJHM)* since 1989. Seven themes are identified in the chapter, which are categorized as issues relating to international locations and generic issues. The themes are presented in table form, listing the authors, the theme, and the focus of the research (see Appendixes 16.A and 16.B). These themes are international tourism planning, the development and operation of hotels, Europe and the single market, planning issues and techniques, service improvement, finance and performance, and the psychology of management.

INTERNATIONAL TOURISM PLANNING

Tourism is an important international industry, generating welcome additional income for smaller countries, but needing to be care-

This chapter was originally published in Ingram, H. (1995). Hospitality and tourism: International industries experiencing common problems. *International Journal of Contemporary Hospitality Management,* 7(7): 44-54. Adapted with permission by Emerald Group Publishing Limited.

fully managed in an increasingly sophisticated market. The articles selected show the positive relationship between effective planning and successful national tourism, even for established tourism destinations. Countries new to tourism, however, need to consider the primary needs of discerning foreign visitors whose standards of living may differ from their own. In a study by Olokesusi (1990) in Abeokuta in Nigeria, for example, tourists are encouraged to visit the densely populated town that is suffering from noise pollution, lack of telephones, and unreliable water and electricity supplies. The recommendation is that physical infrastructure, facilities, and security be a prerequisite for attracting foreign visitors to the area. Once established, tourism continues to present national government and hospitality operators with dilemmas that are difficult to reconcile. Such a dilemma is shown in Gibbons and Fish's (1999) analysis of international tourism in Indonesia, where the small and densely populated island of Bali has become the primary tourist attraction. The pattern of growth in tourism is characterized by greater representation by lower spending market segments whose average length of stay is only four days. The dilemma for Bali is to how to direct its marketing policy so as to meet its objectives, and to match hotel and recreation facilities to serve the market segment. Mexico is another country with a developed tourism industry that has planned effectively to maintain the comparative market attractiveness of its tourism. Faced with recent poor economic growth, political controversy, and dire international debt, Mexico's international tourism plays an increasingly important part in contributing toward the country's gross national product. Fish and Gibbons (1993) report the beneficial effects of periodic peso devaluation in Mexico in offsetting internal inflation and increasing tourism receipts. This strategy of manipulating currency devaluation has been successful in maintaining high levels of tourism volume that support the national economy (see Table 16.1).

The message suggested by these articles is that tourism is an attractive and important industry for many small countries throughout the world. Continued success, however, depends on careful marketing planning in order to offer the international tourist benefits and facilities that compare favorably with competing tourism destinations.

TABLE 16.1. International Tourism Planning

Authors	Focus	Subtheme
Gibbons and Fish (1989)	Growth in Bali's international tourism and its effects on attracting both lower and higher spending tourists. Future policy in relation to the socioeconomic objectives of the island	Tourism customer segmentation
Olokesusi (1990)	An assessment of hotels in beokuta, Nigeria and its implications for tourists	Shortcomings of Nigerian infrastructure
Fish and Gibbons (1991)	Assessment of the importance of tourism to Mexico in view of its falling market share, particularly since monetary devaluation	Tourism as a means of settling foreign debt
Slater and Cheung (1991)	Assessment of residents' attitudes towards tourism in Hong Kong in the light of its position as a major tourist destination	Effects of high volume tourism
Bauer et al. (1993)	The changing demand for hotel facilities in the Asia Pacific region	Comparative rating of hotel and service attributes

THE DEVELOPMENT AND OPERATION OF HOTELS

Many of the articles published in the *IJHM* originate from a variety of locations throughout the world, reinforcing the view that hospitality and tourism organizations are becoming truly international, and the issues they face equally universal. The articles featured in this section reflect some of those problems, ranging from preopening development to key operational issues such as marketing and safety. Kim and Olsen (1993) emphasize the importance of external environment. They investigated the economic, sociocultural, political, technological, and ecological factors that multinational hospitality chains should consider when contemplating expansion in newly industrialized countries in Asia. Scanning of the political domain is found to be particularly important, as it is often the most volatile element in these areas (see Table 16.2).

Political upheavals have also affected the emerging development of hospitality in China, and Yu's (1992) article records the losses in international tourism as a result of political turbulence in 1989. International tourist arrivals decreased by almost one quarter while hotel beds continued to increase, resulting in a dramatic fall in hotel occupancy rates, especially in the major towns. Yu (1992) suggests that coordinated planning is essential to the future success of China's hospitality industry with, for example, a central reservation system and systematic training programs. Established hotels must also relate to their immediate environment by taking adequate precautions against fire, especially if they are situated in densely populated urban areas. A study by Chow and Kot (1992) of hotel fires in Hong Kong high-

TABLE 16.2. The Development and Operation of Hotels

Authors	Focus	Subtheme
Chow and Kot (1992)	A study of the fire risk of hotels in Hong Kong by carrying out a survey on the fire load, local design considerations and past records	Adequacy of safety and accident control
Falk and Pizam (1992)	The significance of the US meetings market, projected growth in terms of revenue, occurrence and attendance	Variables which assist in obtaining meetings business
Yu (1992)	Development of hotel structures in China	Need to systemize tourism in China
Chan (1993)	Managerial roles of hotel pre-opening teams in developing countries such as China	Differences in Chinese work culture
Kim and Olsen (1993)	A framework for the identification of political environmental issues faced by multinational hotel chains in newly industrialized countries in Asia	Importance of monitoring the political environment
Simons (1992)	Resolving disputes in management contracts in Australia	Mediation as an alternative to litigation

lights estimated reports that up to 8,000 hotel fires worldwide may claim 10,000 lives annually. The authors were at pains to point out that the level of reported fires in Hong Kong hotels at the time of writing was small, but that the lessons of tragic past cases should influence future fire strategy. In particular, due emphasis should be placed on adequate fire awareness training for hotel managers and staff as well as the proper maintenance of fire protection systems.

The articles reviewed emphasize the need for hospitality firms, no matter where they are located, to be constantly aware of factors in the external domain that can have a profound effect on levels of business and unit operations.

EUROPE AND THE SINGLE MARKET

The first issue of *International Journal of Hospitality Management* of 1993 (volume 12, issue 1) concentrates on the potential effects on hospitality and tourism sectors of the enactment of the single European market. At that time, many were excited at the new opportunities afforded by the lowering of European barriers (Table 16.3), but Robinson and Mogendorff (1993) argue that some countries have not realized the decline of revenues from declining tourism receipts. They suggest that this lack of urgency should be replaced by a response from the sectors in terms of strategy, internal organization, and quality improvements if the traditional tourism market in Europe is to be successfully defended. Baum (1993) points out that the sectors' human resources have an important part to play in this market defense. He suggests that increased tourism flows would be matched by greater labor mobility within the European Community resulting from enhanced education and training opportunities. Although central funding would concentrate on investment in peripheral regions of the community, labor mobility would flow in the reverse direction, from peripheral to core regions. The effects of this scenario would be local labor shortages in those poorer peripheral areas, which would also need to invest heavily in training to improve skill levels in line with those in other member states. Baum (1993) argues for a strategic response to these important human resources issues.

A coordinated and strategic response is also advocated by Akehurst et al. (1993) in a study that evaluates tourism policy in the

TABLE 16.3. Europe and the Single Market

Authors	Focus	Subtheme
Hoffman and Schniederjans (1990)	An international strategic management/goal programming model for structuring global expansion decisions in the hospitality industry of Eastern Europe	Use of technology to aid site location decisions
Smith (1991)	Investigation of the specialized professional organizations in the European meetings industry	Increasing sophistication and competitive nature of this industry
Robinson (1993)	Tourism and tourism policy in the European Community: an overview of the challenges it faces for the future	Problems such as mass tourism and the loss of global market share
Robinson and Mogendorff (1993)	Assessment of the European tourism industry and its readiness for the Single Market in the light of Europe's declining share of global tourism receipts	Effects of cross-border mobility
Akehurst et al. (1993)	Tourism policies in the European Community states and the link between clear central government strategy and tourism success	Trends towards self-financing tourism projects
Wanhill (1989, 1993)	European regional development funds for the hospitality and tourism industries and the methodology of appraising projects for submission	The economies of this form of grand-in-aid
Baum (1993)	Human resource concerns in European tourism which are important in retaining market share	Labor mobility in the single market
Lucas (1993)	The Social Charter as an opportunity or threat to employment practice in the UK hospitality industry	Efficient employment of people in hospitality

European Community member states. The survey results show a clear link between coherent central government strategy through national tourist organizations (NTOs) in member states and success in attracting higher-spending international tourists. Although a heavy dependence on central government financing currently exists, the 1990s saw NTOs become self-financing. The authors suggest that the European Commission should coordinate the efforts of tourism in member states so as to develop national policies that clearly identify relevant problems and produce effective strategies to address them. This theme suggests that Europe should not be complacent about traditional tourism markets and that, although central planning bodies might provide coordinated support, member states should develop their own strategies to maximize tourism in their own countries. Fellow members are also in competition with each other for tourism revenue.

PLANNING ISSUES AND TECHNIQUES

The period since 1989 has been characterized by more difficult trading conditions in both hospitality and tourism sectors (Table 16.4). In 1989, the U.S. restaurant sector in the United States experienced overcapacity and poor growth that particularly affected the performance of smaller operations. West and Olsen's (1989) article of that year predicts greater difficulty in the operating environment of this sector and espouses systematic environmental scanning in order to monitor, and respond to, environmental changes. West and Olsen (1989) note that the level of environmental scanning in the industry is unsophisticated, and this is later supported by Gilbert and Kapur's (1990) research into strategic marketing planning in the U.S. hospitality industry. Their study shows that the four hospitality groups investigated follow very different planning processes in their attempts to gain inroads into the same market. Interestingly, one group took a systematic and integrated approach to planning over the long term of ten years, while another group had no mechanism in place for long-term planning. The authors comment on the polarity of approaches and suggest that further research is needed to link the success rates of each of these diverse approaches to business planning.

TABLE 16.4. Planning Issues and Techniques

Authors	Focus	Subtheme
West and Olsen (1989)	Environmental scanning, industry structure and strategy making: concepts and research in the hospitality industry	Planning in the restaurant industry
Gilbert and Kapur (1990)	A study of contemporary strategic marketing planning and the hospitality industry through a comparison of strategic theory with practice from international hotel groups	Differences in hotels' strategic orientations
Jones (1990)	The role of innovation in systems design to provide strategic competitive advantage for organizations. The need to understand and operate these systems efficiently over the long term	Improving productivity and efficiency
Dev and Brown (1990)	Research investigating how the co alignment of an organization's task environment, business strategy and structure affects its performance	The relationship between environmental uncertainty and planning in the hotel sector
Quain et al. (1990, 1991)	Using decision theory for strategic decision making in the convention industry	Techniques for attracting larger Conventions
Tse (1991)	An empirical analysis of the links between organizational structure and financial performance in the restaurant sector	Little "hard" research evidence in this area
Quain et al. (1990, 1991)	Marketing decision making in the convention sector to determine the most important type of advertising medium used by the travelers in selecting a hotel	Using advertising for hotel selection between market segments
Gartrell (1991)	Strategic partnerships for convention planning: the role of convention and visitor bureaux in convention management	Making convention events productive

Authors	Focus	Subtheme
Lucas and Jeffries (1991)	The "demographic time bomb" and how some hospitality employers are responding to the potential challenge	The special problems which face the hospitality industry
Brotherton and Mooney (1992)	Maximization of sales and profits using the technique of yield management in the profit-market configuration	Accommodation planning and budgeting
Reich (1989)	Application of related economic theories to the emerging field of hospitality management	Optimal decision making for cost reduction

Hospitality planners were also concerned about the effects on marketing and employment of structural changes in the population of working age. The implication of this "demographic time bomb" for hospitality employers is studied by Lucas and Jeffries (1991), who suggest that changes in labor force can be turned into opportunities. In order to plan for this eventuality, the industry should develop a more systematic approach to labor planning that is more anticipatory than reactive. The authors reject the view that the hospitality industry is lagging behind others in its planning, but they recognize that it faces special problems. The articles reviewed suggest that systematic scanning of the environment by hospitality operators and diversity of approaches is lacking. It would appear that more collaborative research is needed in this field to suggest ways in which hospitality firms might further systemize their planning methods while enhancing the creativity of their people.

SERVICE IMPROVEMENT

Service improvement is a major concern for managers in the restaurant sector, and it is linked with quality and customer satisfaction (Table 16.5). This section features a cross-section of some of the articles that address the systems or the people involved in the provision of service delivery. McCleary and Vosburgh (1990) suggest that interpersonal understanding and communication are at the heart of ser-

TABLE 16.5. Service Improvement

Authors	Focus	Subtheme
Pavesic (1989)	Quantitative and qualitative criteria in menu pricing and the role of psychological aspects of choice	The nature of the customer purchase decision
McCleary and Vosburgh (1990)	An analysis of the value systems of food service managers and hospitality students, in order to improve communications and motivation	Differences in personal values in the fast-food industry
Brownell (1990, 1993)	The role of effective communications strategies in managing the change process in services	Importance of listening skills by managers
Hsu et al. (1991)	Restaurant managers' learning styles and their implications using the Kolb Inventory. The implications of convergent styles in management	Differences between unit and district-level managers
Gardner and Wood (1991)	The role of theatricality in food service work in the expanding market niche of themed restaurants	Skills of service staff
Thomas and Thomas (1992)	State regulation of the hospitality industry and the way in which units might influence local planning process	Hot food takeaways
Sparks and Callan (1992)	Using the communication accommodation theory to investigate improving interpersonal communication in service encounters	Training of service staff
George and Tan (1993)	A comparison of the importance of selected service-related factors as perceived by restaurant employees and managers	Service delivery quality and interpersonal relationships
Lennon and Mercer (1994)	Service quality in practice: customer service in Scotland's tourist information centers	Service training and assessment

vice improvement in the hospitality industry and that "understanding builds bridges." Their comparative study of the value systems of fast-food service managers and hospitality students suggests differences in personal values, which inhibits effective communication. They conclude that improved understanding of the way employees' values change over time would be of assistance in addressing the enormous problems of recruitment and retention that face hospitality firms.

Understanding is linked with learning, and Hsu et al. (1991) contend that each person learns differently and displays a preferred learning method. They conducted a study of the learning styles of unit and district level managers using Kolb's Learning Style Inventory, which identifies four categories of learning styles: assimilators, divergers, accommodators, and convergers. Both sets of managers exhibited a predominantly convergent style of learning; that is, they learn best through "hands on" experiences. The study hypothesizes that an awareness of the learning styles of managers could assist in developing appropriate management development programs. Managers with each type of learning style would benefit from instructional methods such as lecture, group discussion, and self-instruction. The article by Gardner and Wood (1991) emphasizes the centrality of the server in the food service process and explores the role of theatricality in enhancing the meal experience. It is suggested that theatrical food styles in themed restaurants are becoming a growing market niche that relies on creating a physical atmosphere that is supported by often costumed staff service "performance." Effective meal "staging" can create enjoyment for both staff and customers. It depends on three factors: the relationship between diner and server, use of social and technical skills, and rituals and the environment of the operation. These articles suggest that people involved in the provision of food need to be open to new and innovative ideas to improve service delivery. This implies that managers should seek to create an organizational "atmosphere" that both supports product quality and enhances communication with employees and customers.

FINANCE AND PERFORMANCE

The principles of judicious planning apply equally to business finance, and the articles in this section show some techniques and skills that may be of interest to managers in the hospitality industry (see Table 16.6). Harris's (1991) article offers an example of the expanding role of technology in supporting the finance function. He proposes an approach to financial planning using computer spreadsheets and suggests that these spreadsheet models need not be large or complex, yet can provide a powerful aid to management decision making. Spreadsheet design principles may be applied to financial planning and control situations such as cost-volume profit analysis, food and beverage

TABLE 16.6. Finance and Performance

Authors	Focus	Subtheme
Wanhill (1989, 1993)	Matching pricing strategies and company objectives to arrive at an optimal solution for pricing in event catering	Catering contracting
Spengler and Uysal (1989)	Considerations in the hotel taxation process	Effects of elastic and inelastic demand
Harris (1991)	An approach to financial planning using computer spreadsheets	Profit planning
Nichols (1991)	Sound financial management for successful meetings	Standardization of financial techniques
Damitio and Schmidgall (1991)	A comparison of hospitality executives', educators' and students' views on the importance of accounting skills	Accounting training in hospitality education
Cranage and Andrew (1992)	A comparison of time series and econometric models for forecasting restaurant sales	Benefits of systematic approaches over judgment
Fields and Kwansa (1993)	Assessment of a technique called "pure-play" to calculate the cost of equity capital in the divisions of multi-divisional firms in the restaurant industry	Financial frameworks for multi-divisional firms
Jeffrey and Hubbard (1989)	A model of hotel occupancy performance for monitoring and marketing in the hotel industry	Local and national factors affecting performance

budgeting, flexible budgetary control, comparative analysis, stock control, credit management, cash forecasting, menu engineering, profit sensitivity analysis, pricing decisions, and so on.

Jeffrey and Hubbard (1989) explore the use of hotel occupancy as a primary indicator of performance and an aid to marketing planning. They contend that occupancy data can be exploited for more rigor. It is suggested that a more rigorous approach to occupancy analysis is a useful tool in achieving high occupancy rates. The model assists in the identification of the strengths and weaknesses of the hotel's performance in relation to similar units, and it narrows the search for solutions to marketing and investment decisions. The inference from this article is that more systematic analysis of important generators of income, such as accommodation, may lead to greater overall performance in hospitality organizations.

Damitio and Schmidgall's (1991) survey of executives, educators, and students in the hospitality field sought to measure the extent of agreement of the importance of accounting skills. Respondents were asked to rate the importance of thirty-one accounting skills using a Likert scale both at the beginning of employment and after three years in the industry. The research shows that all three groups considered accounting skills important, and should be a part of the skill hospitality programs. The articles selected demonstrate the need for systematic financial analysis and suggest a positive relationship between analytical rigor and organizational performance. Financial analysis and decision making can be improved by the use of computer technology, but a consensus exists between the hospitality industry and its education providers of the importance of accounting skills to its managers.

THE PSYCHOLOGY OF MANAGEMENT

The practice of management is constantly developing, altering the nature of the demands placed on managers and skills that may be needed by them (see Table 16.7). This section considers some articles that address psychological trends, particularly the mental qualities and behavior of managers in the hospitality industry. In 1989, Worsfold (1989a,b) investigated the personality profile of the hospitality manager with a view to developing selection techniques that could effectively predict management performance. His study sug-

TABLE 16.7. The psychology of Management

Authors	Focus	Subtheme
Worsfold (1989a,b)	A personality profile of the hospitality manager	Management selection techniques
Shortt (1989)	Application of Mint berg's managerial roles to work activities of hospitality managers in Northern Ireland	Role of hospitality managers and their work
Whitney (1990)	Ethics in the hospitality industry; with a focus on hospitality managers	Stress caused by the conflict between ethics and business realities
Worsfold (1989a,b)	Leadership and managerial effectiveness in the hospitality industry	Leadership requirements in hospitality
Chitiris (1990)	A study of the relationship between demographic differences and work motivation of managers in the hospitality industry	Hospitality managements and culture in Greece
Brymer et al. (1991)	Managerial job stress in the hospitality industry	Stress prevention
Brownell (1990, 1993)	Hospitality managers' communication practices	Differences in perception
Yamaguchi and Garey (1993)	The relationship between central life interest of restaurant managers and their level of job satisfaction	Motivation and ambition of managers
Ghei and Nebel (1994)	The successful manager and psychological androgyny: a conceptual and empirical investigation of hospitality executives	Ideal management behaviors and success

gests that personality is considered less important than other necessary attributes such as assertiveness, independence, mental stamina and manageable levels of anxiety. In addition, he found that hotel managers were more venturesome, uninhibited, and imaginative than managers in other industries. Interestingly, he found that female managers had higher scores for independence and tough poise than their male counterparts.

Goal-oriented management behavior is also studied by Whitney (1990), who considers the conflicts caused by the business realities of the 1990s. He identifies "ethical dissonance," the mental discord in managers that arises from conflict in "what they believe" and "what they practice," as a source of stress. Managers particularly at risk from "ethical burnout" are those with strong traditional orientation and relatively weaker career orientation. Whitney (1990) suggests that excellent managers are marked by the maturity to "hold high ethical ground under fire," as they have the internal qualities to deal with confusing external phenomena. Solutions to this increasingly common and complex problem require holistic and long-term responses and are philosophical as well as operational in nature. Managerial job stress was also studied by Brymer and colleagues (1993), who attempt to link the relationships between perceived job stressors and experienced strain. Some suggestions were made for strain reduction based mostly on greater employee control over their work. These articles infer that, although managers in the hospitality industry may possess positive psychological attributes, they perceive that their jobs are becoming more stressful. This increased stress may be caused by mental conflicts between perceptions and reality, all of which reinforce the view that the practice of management became more difficult in the 1990s.

SUMMARY

This review has identified seven themes that exemplify some emerging issues of importance to the hospitality and tourism industries in recent years. The first three themes address issues facing organizations and governments in international locations. They show the wealth of new opportunities that exist for the tertiary sector in many parts of the world, but emphasize that these opportunities need to be carefully managed if they are to be sustained over the long term.

The final four themes addressed generic issues concerning planning, service, finance, and management. A common message is that organizations should adopt a more planned and professional approach to managing operations if they are to achieve and maintain long-term success.

APPENDIX 16.A. EDITOR'S SUMMARY TABLE AND THEMATIC RELATIONSHIP DIAGRAM

Hospitality and tourism: International industries experiencing common problems—themes, subthemes, and observations based on a review of 118 entries (1989-1994) in the *International Journal of Hospitality Management*

Theme	Subtheme	Observations
Theme 1: *International tourist planning*	Tourism customer segmentation; the infrastructure for tourism; tourism as a means of settling foreign debt; the impacts of high volume tourism; the demand for hotel facilities and the comparative rating of hotel service attributes	Tourism is an attractive and important industry for many small and developing nations. Commercial success depends on careful marketing planning so as to offer the international tourist an array of benefits and facilities which compare favorably with competing tourism destinations
Theme 2: *The development and operation of hotels*	The adequacy of accident and safety controls; market segments and the importance of the meetings segment; the role of hotels in tourism development; culture and the working environment; monitoring the hotel operating environment; hotels and management contracting	Stresses the impact of internal systems and procedures and the need to monitor continually events occurring in the external domain and assess the potential impact on business and unit level operation
Theme 3: *Europe and the single market*	The application of technology to assist with selecting sites for European expansion; the nature of competition in Europe; European tourism policy and the impact of mass tourism; the effects of cross-border mobility; self-financing tourism projects in Europe; (European regional development funding; labor mobility in the Single Market; the European Social Charter and employment issues	Europe cannot afford to be complacent about traditional tourism markets. Although European tourism policies provide co-ordination and support on planning and other matters, member states need to develop their own strategies too if they with to maximize incoming tourism. This is partly because fellow EU members compete with one another for tourism revenue
Theme 4: *Planning issues and techniques*	Planning in the US restaurant sector; strategic marketing planning; improving productivity and efficiency by innovations in systems design; strategy, structure and the hotel business, environment; decision theory and its application to strategic decision making; organizational structure and financial performance in the US restaurant sector; the role of advertising in marketing decisions; strategic partnerships for convention planning;	The broad-ranging nature of the material reviewed in this theme area points to a lack of systematic planning, especially in relation to external analysis and the application of decision-making models and techniques to planning tasks and activities. Evidence suggests that more collaborative research is needed in these areas with the objective of enabling hospitality firms to systemize their planning effort and

Theme	Subtheme	Observations
	demographics and human resource planning; the application of yield management to accommodation planning and budgeting; economic modeling and decision making	release more time for creative thinking and innovation
Theme 5: Service improvement	Criteria for menu pricing and the role of psychological aspects of choice; the relative value systems of food service managers and students in the US fast-food sector; the role of the effective communication strategies in managing the change process; differences between the learning styles of restaurant managers; interpersonal skills and food service staff; interpersonal communication and the service encounter; quality, service delivery and interpersonal relationships; service training and assessment	If service standards are to improve, food service personnel need to be open to new and innovative ways of improving service delivery. The key implication of this is that managers should seek to create an organizational atmosphere which supports efforts to improve quality and enhances the nature of communications between employees and customers
Theme 6: Finance and performance	Matching pricing strategies and company objectives in contract catering; hotels and the factors affecting demand; profit planning; the application of financial techniques; the importance of accounting skills and its relevance to hospitality education; methods for forecasting restaurant sales; assessing the cost of equity capital; modeling hotel occupancy performance	Evidence shows that systematic financial analysis produces a number of positive outcomes, especially in terms of organizational performance. While computer technology can assist financial analysis and decision making, a consensus of opinion exists both in industry and education that hospitality managers need to be able to interpret financial data in order to derive benefits from investing in financial information systems
Theme 7: The psychology of management	Management selection techniques; the managerial roles and work activities of hospitality managers; business ethics; leadership and managerial effectiveness; motivational factors; stress prevention; managerial communications; the motives and ambitions of hospitality managers; managerial behavior, success and effectiveness	While many experienced hospitality managers have enjoyed successful careers and seem well suited to the nature of the work involved, it is generally felt that managerial roles are becoming more stressful. Further collaborative research is needed to identify the reasons for this more precisely and to assess the implications for management education and development

APPENDIX 16.B. SERVICE PERFORMANCE
AND COMPETITIVENESS

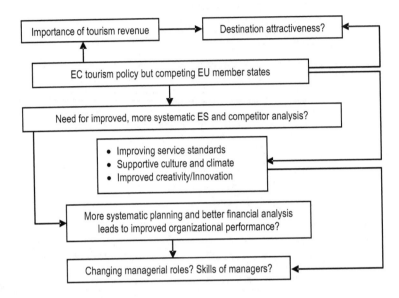

REFERENCES

Akehurst, G., Bland, N., and Nervin, M. (1993). Tourism policies in the European community member states. *International Journal of Hospitality Management, 12*(1): 33-66.

Bauer, T., Jago, L., and Wise, B. (1993). The changing demand for hotel facilities in the Asia pacific region. *International Journal of Hospitality Management, 12*(2): 313-322.

Baum, T. (1993). Human resource concerns in European tourism: Strategic response and the EC. *International Journal of Hospitality Management, 12*(1): 77-88.

Brotherton, B. and Mooney, S. (1992). Yield management – Progress and prospects, *International Journal of Hospitality Management, 11*(1): 23-32.

Brownell, J. (1990). Hospitality managers' communication practices. *International Journal of Hospitality Management, 9*(3): 191-205.

Brownell, J. (1993). The symbolic/culture approach: Managing transition in the service industry. *International Journal of Hospitality Management, 11*(2): 111-128.

Brymer, R.A., Perrewe, P., and Johns, T.R. (1991). Managerial job stress in the hotel industry. *International Journal of Hospitality Management, 10*(1): 47-58.

Chan, W.-H.W. (1993). Managerial roles of hotel pre-opening teams in developing countries such as China. *International Journal of Hospitality Management,* 12(2): 156-161.

Chitiris, L., (1990). Who are the work-motivated managers in the hotel industry? An exploratory study. *International Journal of Hospitality Management,* 9(4): 293-304.

Chow, W.K. and Kot, H.T. (1992). Hotel fires in Hong Kong. *International Journal of Hospitality Management,* 8(4): 271-281.

Cranage, D.A. and Andrew, W.P. (1992). A comparison of time series and econometric models for forecasting restaurant sales. *International Journal of Hospitality Management,* 11(3): 129-142.

Damitio, J.W. and Schmidgall, R.S. (1991). A comparison of hospitality executives', educators' and students' views on the importance of accounting skills. *International Journal of Hospitality Management,* 10(3): 219-228.

Dev, C.S. and Brown, J.R. (1990). Marketing strategy, a vertical structure, and performance in the lodging industry: A contingency approach. *International Journal of Hospitality Management,* 9(3): 269-282.

Falk, T.E. and Pizam, A. (1992). The United States meetings market. *International Journal of Hospitality Management,* 10(2): 111-118.

Fields, B.J. and Kwansa, F.A. (1993). Analysis of the pure-play technique in the hospitality industry. *International Journal of Hospitality Management,* 12(3): 271-287.

Fish, M. and Gibbons, J.D. (1991). Mexico's devaluation's and changes in net foreign exchange receipts from tourism. *International Journal of Hospitality Management,* 10 (1): 73-80.

Gardner, K. and Wood, R.C. (1991). Theatricality in food service work, *International Journal of Hospitality Management,* 10(3): 267-278.

Gartrell, R.B. (1991). Strategic partnerships for convention planning: The role of convention and visitor bureaux in convention management. *International Journal of Hospitality Management,* 10(2): 157-165.

George, R.T. and Tan, Y.F. (1993). A comparison of the importance of selected service-related factors as perceived by restaurant employees and managers. *International Journal of Hospitality Management,* 12(3): 289-298.

Ghei, A. and Nebel, E.C. (1994). The successful manager and psychological androgyny: A conceptual and empirical investigation of hotel executives. *International Journal of Hospitality Management,* 13(3): 247-264.

Gibbons, J.D. and Fish, M. (1989). Indonesia's international tourism: A shifting industry in Bali. *International Journal of Hospitality Management,* 8(1): 63-70.

Gilbert, D.D. and Kapur, R. (1990). Strategic marketing planning and the hotel industry. *International Journal of Hospitality Management,* 9(1): 27-43.

Harris, P.J. (1991). An approach to financial planning using computer spreadsheets. *International Journal of Hospitality Management,* 10(1): 95-106.

Hoffman, J.J. and Schniederjans, M.J. (1990). An international strategic management/goal-programming model for structuring global expansion decisions in the hospitality industry: The case of Eastern Europe. *International Journal of Hospitality Management, 9*(3): 175-190.

Hsu, C., Smith, F.M., and Finley, R.A.H. (1991). Restaurant managers' learning styles and their implications. *International Journal of Hospitality Management, 10*(1): 81-93.

Jeffrey, D. and Hubbard, N.J. (1989). A model of hotel occupancy performance for monitoring and marketing in the hotel industry. *International Journal of Hospitality Management, 13*(1): 57-71.

Jones, P. (1990). Managing food service productivity in the long term: Strategy, structure and performance. *International Journal of Hospitality Management, 9*(2): 143-154.

Kim, C.Y. and Olsen, M.D. (1993). A framework for the identification of political environmental issues faced by multinational hospitality chains in newly industrialized countries in Asia. *International Journal of Hospitality Management, 12*(2): 163-174.

Lennon, J.J. and Mercer, A.T. (1994). Service quality in practice: Customer service in Scotland's tourist information centres. *International Journal of Hospitality Management, 13*(2): 129-141.

Lucas, R. (1993). The social charter: Opportunity or threat to employment practice in the UK hospitality industry? *International Journal of Hospitality Management, 12*(1): 89-100.

Lucas, R. and Jeffries, L. (1991): The demographic time bomb and how some hospitality employers are responding to the challenge. *International Journal of Hospitality Management, 10*(4): 323-337.

McCleary, K.W. and Vosburgh, R.M. (1990). Towards a better understanding of the value systems of food service managers and hospitality students,.*International Journal of Hospitality Management, 9*(2): 111-123.

Nichols, B.C. (1991). Sound financial management for successful meetings. *International Journal of Hospitality Management, 10*(2): 127-136.

Olokesusi, F. (1990). An assessment of hotels' in Abeokuta, Nigeria and its implications' for Tourists. *International Journal of Hospitality Management, 9*(2): 25-34.

Pavesic, D.V. (1989). Psychological aspects of menu pricing. *International Journal of Hospitality Management, 8*(1): 43-49.

Quain, W.J., Render, B., and Herman, P.W. (1991). A multivariate approach towards marketing decisions in the convention segment. *International Journal of Hospitality Management, 10*(2): 147-155.

Quain, W.J., Render, B., Higgins, J.M., and James, H. (1990). Using decision theory for strategic decision making in the convention industry. *International Journal of Hospitality Management, 9*(3): 237-246.

Reich, A.Z. (1989). Applied economics of hospitality production: Reducing costs and improving the quality of decisions through economic analysis. *International Journal of Hospitality Management, 12*(2): 337-352.

Robinson, G. (1993). Tourism and tourism policy in the European community: An overview. *International Journal of Hospitality Management, 12*(1): 12-20.

Robinson, G. and Mogendorff, D. (1993). The European tourism industry: Ready for the single market? *International Journal of Hospitality Management, 12*(1): 21-31.

Shortt, G. (1989). Work activities of hotel managers in Northern Ireland: A mintzbergian analysis. *International Journal of Hospitality Management, 8*(2): 121-130.

Simons, H.S. (1992). Hotel management contracts, some recent trends in relation to dispute resolution in Australia. *International Journal of Hospitality Management, 13*(2): 143-153.

Slater, B. and Cheung, V. (1991). Residents' attitudes towards' tourism in Hong Kong. *International Journal of Hospitality Management, 10*(3): 289-293.

Smith, G. (1991). Professional organizations in the European meetings industry, *International Journal of Hospitality Management, 9*(2): 119-126.

Sparks, B. and Callan, V.J. (1992). Communication and the service encounter: The value of convergence. *International Journal of Hospitality Management, 11*(3): 213-224.

Spengler, J.O. and Uysal, M. (1989). Considerations in the hotel taxation process. *International Journal of Hospitality Management, 8*(4): 309-316.

Thomas, R. and Thomas, H. (1992). State regulation of the hospitality industry: The case of hot food take-aways. *International Journal of Hospitality Management, 11*(3): 197-211.

Tse, E. (1991). An empirical analysis of organizational structure and financial performance in the restaurant industry. *International Journal of Hospitality Management, 10*(1): 59-71.

Wanhill, S.R.C. (1989). Pricing for event catering. *International Journal of Hospitality Management, 8*(4): 299-308.

Wanhill, S.R.C. (1993). European regional development funds for the hospitality and tourism industries. *International Journal of Hospitality Management, 12*(1): 67-76.

West, J.J. and Olsen, M.D. (1989). Environmental scanning, industry structure and strategy making: concepts and research in the hospitality industry. *International Journal of Hospitality Management, 8*(4): 283-298.

Whitney, D.L. (1990). Ethics in the hospitality industry: With a focus on hotel managers. *International Journal of Hospitality Management, 9*(1): 59-68.

Worsfold, P. (1989a). Leadership and managerial effectiveness in the hospitality industry. *International Journal of Hospitality Management, 8*(2): 145-155.

Worsfold, P. (1989b). A personality profile of the hotel manager. *International Journal of Hospitality Management, 8*(1): 51-62.

Yamaguchi, Y. and Garey, J.G. (1993). The relationship between central life interest of restaurant managers and their level of job satisfaction. *International Journal of Hospitality Management, 12*(4): 385-393.

Yu, L. (1992). Hotel development and structures in China. *International Journal of Hospitality Management, 11*(2): 99-110.

FURTHER READING

Ross, G.F. (1992). Tourism and hospitality industry job-attainment beliefs and work values among Australian school leavers. *International Journal of Hospitality Management, 11*(4): 319-330.

Schmidgall, R.S. (1991). A comparison of hospitality executives', educators' and students' views on the importance of accounting skills. *International Journal of Hospitality Management, 10*(3): 219-228.

Vosburgh, R.M. (1990). Towards a better understanding of the value systems of food service managers and hospitality students. *International Journal of Hospitality Management, 9*(2): 111-123.

Chapter 17

The Heritage Tourism of George Town, Penang: Setting the Right Tourism Culture

Azizi Bahauddin
Aldrin Abdullah
Badaruddin Mohamed

INTRODUCTION

This chapter examines the impact of British colonialism on the heritage tourism development of George Town, Penang, in the Malaysian northern region. Malaysia is situated geographically in the heart of Southeast Asia and is made up of eleven states in the Malay Peninsula and another two states in the northern part of Borneo Island. Malaysia (formerly known as Malaya) gained her independence from England in 1957. In 1963 the Federation of Malaysia was formed, consisting of the thirteen states and Singapore. However, due to political circumstances, Singapore became an independent nation in 1965. Malaysia now has a population of 23 million people, comprised of: Malays, 51 percent, Chinese, 35 percent, Indians, 10 percent, and other ethnic groups, 4 percent. The system of government in Malaysia is a constitutional democracy with a prime minister as the head of government and an elected *Yang di-Pertuan Agong* (king) as the supreme head of state.

HISTORY OF MALAYSIA AND THE WESTERN POWERS

Historically, Malaysia was built on the legacy of the Malay Sultanate of Malacca. It came to an abrupt end when the Portuguese con-

Global Cases on Hospitality Industry
© 2008 by The Haworth Press, Taylor & Francis Group. All rights reserved.
doi:10.1300/5923_17

quered Malacca in 1511. Successions of colonial powers then took possession of the Malay Peninsula: the Portuguese (1511-1641), Dutch (1641-1795), and British (1795-1957). Today the remains of their colonial architecture can still be found in most major cities including Malacca, George Town, Kuala Lumpur, Johor Bahru, Ipoh, Taiping, Kuching, and Kota Kinabalu. The Portuguese and Dutch architecture is primarily found in Malacca. Examples of Portuguese architecture include the Porta de Santiago gate (1511) and St. Paul's Church (1590). Dutch architecture includes the Stadhuys (1641-1660) and the Christ Church (1753). All these buildings remain intact and are well maintained to the present date. The 160 years of British occupation in Malaysia has brought about major changes in the local architectural scenes through the erection of mainly institutional buildings. These buildings portray distinct design features that are similar to that of their contemporaries in England (Ahmad, 1997). The reigning of Portuguese, Dutch, and British colonial powers for more than three hundred years has bared its mark significantly on the country's town planning, commerce, and administrative patterns. The unique colonial architectural styles of these buildings have played a major role in the creation of heritage cities throughout Malaysia, such as the cities of George Town, Ipoh, Malacca, Taiping, Kuala Lumpur, and Kuching. Historic buildings usually provide significant physical characteristics to a city. They build a lucid image and distinct identity of a heritage city that differentiates it from other regular cities elsewhere. Urban conservation is a practice of urban planning and development whereby significant historical, architectural, and cultural values in the urban areas are highlighted and accentuated as far as heritage tourism is concerned. It is fast gaining momentum in Malaysia, particularly in cities with outstanding historical, architectural, and cultural heritage.

OBJECTIVES

Malaysia's historic cities generally portray unique local cultures, exciting historical sites, and outstanding heritage buildings that arguably should be maintained for national pride and be cherished for posterity. The growing tourism industry has highlighted the important roles of the heritage cities, namely George Town, as distinguished tourist destinations in Malaysia. Paralleled with the rising interest in heritage tourism and the global influx of the alternatives tourists, the number of tourist arrivals in George Town has increased steadily over the past decade. Accordingly, George Town has diversified the tourism products and cultural activities in order to attract more foreign and local visitors. Thus, the objectives of this chapter are the following:

- To highlight role of George Town as a heritage city in a heritage tourism context
- To examine the steps taken in setting the right tourism culture in George Town
- To suggest and recommend methods for making tourism successful for George Town

METHODOLOGY

This chapter discusses several issues and challenges that confront George Town as the focus of the research. It is justified particularly in the light of rapid growth of new townships, depopulation of historic inner-city areas, intensive development pressures, as well as changing lifestyles and consumption patterns among city inhabitants and tourists. All of these challenges are likely to pose a significant impact on the sustainability of George Town. The management of visitors and the involvement of the local community in heritage cities are also discussed in this chapter. The methodology applied for this research includes literature review, visual data collection, and interviews and surveys with the various local authorities, tourists, and tourist-related industries.

PENANG

Penang is comprised of Penang Island (Pulau Pinang) and Province Wellesley (Seberang Perai) on the mainland of Peninsula Malaysia. The Island of Penang is connected to the mainland by a 13.5 kilometer bridge, the longest bridge in Asia. The city of George Town (the second biggest city in Malaysia) is located on the northeastern cape of the island. The local Malays simply refer the city as "Tanjung." The history of Penang goes back to the year 1786, when Captain Francis Light established the first British trading post on the island for trade between India, China, and the archipelago. In 1832, along with Malacca and Singapore, Penang became part of the British Straits Settlements. Since Penang Island is situated on the trading route of Straits Malacca, during the sixteenth and seventeenth century, Europeans, including the Dutch and British, were competing to open up the East Indian trading routes. The settlement quickly lured people of all descents.[1] Chinese and Indians were drawn to the Straits settlement during the second half of the nineteenth century by the booming tin and rubber industries.

Over the years, a consolidation of these cultural influences has brought about the manifestations of British colonial architecture on the island. With the independence of Malaysia (or Malaya) on August 31, 1957, Penang became a state, governed by an appointed head of state and administered by an elected chief minister. George Town has become the capital city of Penang, and today the different ethnic groups of the inner city still exist and can be traced from their heritage buildings and diverse cultures and languages. Initially, Penang was ruled by the Sultan of Kedah and was populated by the Malays. After Penang became the British trade cenetr, traders from various regions gathered and settled down in the island. Among them were two prominent groups—the Indian Muslims and Chinese, who took Malay wives and became a part of the earliest permanent settled community. These two groups were urban elites and cultural hybrids, and were more receptive to European influence than other contemporary groups. The two communities were the Jawi Peranakan (Indian Muslim) and Cina Peranakan, locally known as the Baba Nyonya (Straits Chinese). Besides these prominent groups, Penang had also attracted various other peoples,[2] making Penang Island a unique place. As observed by Tjoa-Bonatz (2000), the migration of various people from all over Asia has constituted a society of multiethnic sojourners, and although this cultural pluralism was often highlighted, the degree of cultural assimilation has varied over time, and ethnicity has become the main criterion for cultural stratification.

HERITAGE TOURISM IN PENANG

Heritage tourism is a growing segment of the tourism marketplace. Clearly, heritage tourism crosses many lines and may more appropriately be seen as a target market within a destination. Heritage tourists appear to be motivated for different reasons than traditional tourists. Some tourism destinations see heritage tourism as a promotion for tourism products, and this has been lamented.

Millar (1989) and others (Hardy, 1988; Tighe, 1986) suggest that heritage tourism gives importance to cultural traditions, places, and values that people and groups across geographies are happy to conserve. Cultural traditions such as family patterns, religious practices, folklore traditions, and social customs attract individuals interested in heritage (Collins, 1983; Weiler and Hall, 1992), as do monuments, museums, battlefields, historic structures, and landmarks (Konrad, 1982; McNulty, 1991). According to Tassell and Tassell (1990), heritage tourism also includes natural heritage sites—gardens, wilderness areas of scenic beauty, and valued cultural landscapes. Regardless of the heritage attraction, Prentice (1993) argue that heritage tourism is about searching for something that links the past and the present. It is integrally tied to nostalgia.

Heritage tourism can be classified as a subclass of cultural tourism, defined by the World Tourism Organization (1985) as the movements of persons for essentially cultural motivations such as study tours, performing arts, and cultural tours, and travel to festivals and other related events. Essentially, in tourism, the term *heritage* has come to mean landscapes, natural history, buildings, artifacts, and cultural traditions that are "either literally or metaphorically passed on from one generation to the other, but those among these things which can be portrayed for promotion as tourism products" (Prentice, 1993). Heritage culture and buildings in George Town have become among the most valued assets in Malaysia, consisting of a jumble of old temples, churches and mosques, white stucco colonial mansions, rows of tiled Chinese and Muslim Indian shop houses, and ornate clan houses guarded by stone dragons. The streets of George Town keep thousands of untold stories of human interaction with humankind, with the built environment and with God.

The architecture of George Town is seen as an eclectic mixture of the European classical style, mainly British, with Islamic, Malay, Indian, Chinese, and later art deco motifs. Interestingly, the different religions, cultures, and architecture portrayed by the groups coexist in harmony. As a result, it is a common scene to see mosques, churches, and Buddhist and Hindu temples standing side by side on the same street in George Town.

The Penang Municipal Council has taken a bold step in adopting planning and conservation guidelines to control the development of inner-city areas. The city of George Town has currently identified and designated several conservation areas, each with its distinctive flavors, building characteristics, social fabric, and cultural ambience. The council has made provisions for historic buildings[3] of categories I and II to be restored and adapted into new uses without destroying the original building structure and materials. This practice is essential to maintain such buildings in their authentic characters for tourist appreciation.

Heritage in essence refers to the remains of history. Some have argued favorably for the conservation of heritage for national pride, a jewel to be treasured and cherished for successive generations. Oth-

PHOTO 17.1. Acheen Street Mosque

PHOTO 17.2. Restoring the Acheen Street Mosque

ers for some reason have refused to recognize the values of heritage. Urban conservation refers specifically to the protection and preservation of elements of urban heritage from being destroyed forever or from being restored without proper guidance, planning, control, and management. The major elements of urban heritage include buildings of significant architectural values, historical sites, and unique local cultures that can be classified into three of the following general categories:

- *Building conservation:* Refers to the practice of keeping intact all buildings bearing significant historical and architectural values implemented through various stages, including listing and grading of historic buildings, evaluating buildings to be reported under the law, preparing proposals for building conservation, and implementing conservation projects under expert supervision.
- *Area conservation:* Refers to the preservation of specific sites having elements, buildings, and monuments of significant historical and architectural values. Area conservation includes the adoption of building control measures, façade treatments, building height, design control, and landscaping.

- *Cultural conservation:* Refers to the preservation and maintenance of the vigor and authentic character of the daily routines
and cultural heritage of the local communities including cultural
items, mannerisms, and expressions.

According to Collins (1983), heritage is about cultural traditions,
places, and values that people proudly preserve. It is about the present
generation continuing to cherish and learn about the vibrant and glorious history, culture, and past civilization. Walking through George
Town's narrow old streets within the inner city transports one through
the relics of time. The much intact buildings have been hosts and eye-
witnesses to some very important development of Penang's history.
Although George Town has been included in the United Nations list
of the world's one hundred most endangered sites, the town has taken
measures to apply to United Nations Educational, Scientific, and Cultural Organization (UNESCO) to be a World Heritage site, together
with Malacca, another strait settlement. Strict controls have been enforced on any renovation to these buildings. Guidelines have been introduced on the color, facade, motifs, height, and various architectural aspects of any work to be carried out on these buildings. George
Town has more than 12,000 old buildings, comprised of shop and ter-
race houses, churches, mosques, bungalows, villas, government offices, and monuments. In 1996, the Penang State Conservation Committee consisting of government agencies, local authorities, and
private sectors was formed to monitor and control any development
in the conservation areas. Many heritage buildings in George Town
have been protected under a Rent Control Act, introduced in 1948
(Tjoa-Bonatz, 2000)[4] as well as the Antiquities Act of 1976. In a further effort to conserve the historic buildings of George Town, the state
government and local authorities have designated several conservation areas in the inner city, and these zones have been forwarded to
the UNESCO to be nominated as World Heritage sites. The zones are
the following:

- Seven Street precinct
- Cultural precinct: Chulia-Love-Muntri Street
- Historic commercial center: Little India and traditional business
communities

- Waterfront business-financial district: Banking, shipping, and corporate business
- Mosque and clan house enclave: Religious buildings, clan houses, and small businesses
- Market and shopping precinct: Traditional retail and neighboring markets

A 1994 census showed that the state had 12,453 rent control premises, with 8,259 located in the inner city of George Town. With the repeal of the Rent Control Act on December 31, 1999, many tenants who had been living in the city for the past fifty years had to be relocated. This has led to an exodus of town dwellers of ethnic communities and raised the fear that heritage cultures will eventually disappear.

The historic buildings in George Town, some aged more than two hundred years, were once regarded as "outdated." Not until recently have these buildings been revisited, appreciated, and revitalized. Conservation and tourism activities have given these "old" buildings a new life. Examples of the "recycling" of buildings are the Eastern & Oriental Hotel (Photo 17.3) and the Hotel 1926, which stand among

PHOTO 17.3. The E & O Hotel, Popular Hotel in George Town

the most popular hotels in George Town. A more recent case is the privatized project by the state government on the five state bungalows on Penang Hill that will be refurbished, restored to their original British architecture, and eventually turned into boutique hotels ("Penang Hill Boutique Hotels," 2002). Some measures have already been taken by the state government and nongovernmental organizations to encourage the emerging heritage tourism industry. Among the measures are (1) creating heritage trail maps, (2) erecting signboards with information on respective heritage buildings, and (3) organizing walking (by the Penang Heritage Trust, a nongovernmental organization).

HERITAGE ROUTES IN GEORGE TOWN

George Town, where most of Penang's architectural treasures are located, can be divided and drawn into several zones, along various ethnic lines. Its culture has been molded by the successions of civilizations that arrived and shaped its urban growth. A closer look at these zones and the locations of some heritage buildings that dot the inner city exposes a strong sense of compromise between the pioneers, earlier settlers, and later immigrants. The street names give some indications of the history and the significance of an area. Bishop Street, Church Street, and Buckingham Street indicate the influence of Christianity on that part of the city, proved by the existence of several churches along the streets.

Acheen Street and Farquhar Street mark the arrival of Muslim Acheenese and Arabs in the early days of Penang. China Street, as the name clearly states, denotes the congregation of the early Chinese community in Penang. At Little India, a line of shops owned by Indian shopkeepers originating from South India selling necessities, for example, fabrics such as sari, accessories, statues, and music instruments. The dates on the building walls denote the succession of settlers that fought their way to this "Pearl of the Orient." The Kapitan Keling mosque (Photo 17.4), the oldest in the island, was built by the East India Company at the end of eighteenth century, marking the growing number of Indian Muslims in Penang. Their leader, Cauder Mohhidden who was popularly known as the "Kapitan Keling," developed the land. The mosque has been the focus of both social and economic activities, which can still be seen around the mosque. This

PHOTO 17.4. Kapitan Keling Mosque

area was a service center for those going to perform hajj in Mecca via sea route when Penang was one of the departing points. Eventually this became less popular due to the development of modern aircraft.

The evidence of Chinese civilization can be traced to some of most beautiful religious structures in the island—the Kong San Tong Khoo, best known as the Khoo Kongsi (or clan association), the Cheah Kongsi, and Yap Kongsi.

Khoo Kongsi (Photo 17.5) is located at Cannon Square. The clan members who later built a great temple in 1901 formally established the Kongsi in 1884. The temple, however, was burned down soon afterward. Today, it becomes one of the most visited sites in George Town, receiving some eight hundred visitors a day all year round. For Hindus, the Sri Maha Mariamman temple, located at Queen Street, is a showcase of temple architecture of East India. Built in 1883, it is the oldest temple in Penang, and is currently the host of various religious celebrations and ceremonies related to Hinduism.

George Town can be explored either on foot or by trishaw. Presently, two heritage trails are set up by the American Express Company for the inner city. However, what these trails do is merely con-

PHOTO 17.5. Khoo Kongsi

nect places of interests found within the walking zones. Thus, a different approach is suggested here in which the heritage sites of George Town can be divided into three overlapping zones, separated by their respective ethnic characters: Indian, Indo-Malay-Arab, and Chinese. This ethnic divide is both historical as well as physical, and their dynamic coexistence and intermingling is the strongest selling point of the heritage communities. Over centuries, through constant interaction, intermarriages, and a shared history and purpose, each culture has absorbed and adopted the accruements and traditions of its neighbors. Although still recognizable Indo-Malay-Arabian, Chinese, or Indian as individuals, most heritage zone natives would be more at home with each other than they would be back in their respective countries. The purpose of separating these cultures, which have existed side by side for so long, is to be inclusive, rather than divisive.

The Indo-Malay-Arab Zone

This community covers the areas of Acheen Street, part of Armenian Street and Kapitan Keling Road, up to the Kapitan Keling Mosque, behind which is a sizeable area of *waqf* land. The starting point for this zone is the Kapitan Keling Mosque, which is highly visible from the main road.

The Chinese Zone

The Chinese community covers the largest area on the site, and contains living communities (such as the Khoo Kongsi), religious facilities, business premises, craftsmen guilds, and individual homes. The starting point for this zone is the Khoo Kongsi, and it covers other kongsis such as Cheah Kongsi, Tan Kongsi, Lim Kongsi, Yap Kongsi, and Yeoh Kongsi and their extensive trust properties.

The Indian Zone

The Indian community in the heritage site covers the area between Queen Street, Market Street, and Penang Street (Photo 17.6). Bustling spots with hawkers offer traditional Indian fare and titbits, and colorful sari shops and traditional Indian moneychangers and barbers dot the entire route. The area is a contrasting mixture of vernacular shop houses, ornate European style buildings, and modern office blocks.

PHOTO 17.6. Busy Morning at the Little India

ISSUES

The inscription of Penang into a UNESCO World Heritage list will mark a new era in the sense that it will now become a world heritage product. The inscription will locate Penang among the top priority destinations for the mass travelers and specifically "heritage tourists." The expected growth of heritage tourism will bring both positive and negative changes to the social and economic environment of Penang.

The Arrival of Tourists and the Demands of New Tourists

The listing is expected to benefit Malaysia in general, in terms of promoting the good image of the country, and will increase tourist revenues from taxes and foreign exchange. Growth in heritage tourism spurs infrastructure development, promotes heritage conservation, and builds up a modern cultural identity. It encourages nations to open up to international contacts and exchanges in order to build up a productive economy that may benefit many (Sereyvuth, 2000). Studies show that once a site is listed as a World Heritage site, the number of tourists will increase. Examples include Angkor Wat, Cambodia (Richardson, 2000), and Luang Prabang, Laos, the capital of an ancient kingdom that was covered by the present day Laos for more than six hundred years (Cam Ly, 2003). Increased numbers of tourists are encouraged, especially by the tourism-related businesses such as the accommodation and transportation sectors, travel and ticketing agencies, street vendors, etc. Popularized by an increasing number of what is known as the "new tourists" worldwide, visitations to places with historical significance quickly gain popularity. Buildings with a historical background attract these tourists. This new trend boosts the value of old buildings, pressing the local authority to take proper measures to ensure the authenticity of these assets remains intact. As mentioned by Boniface and Fowler (1993), colonizers have now become tourists to the land from which they or their ancestors once conquered. They no longer visit a place only for the sake of visiting, but they demand much more. They not only desire to observe the culture in the galleries, but also to experience it. Conserving authenticity—as demanded by these tourists—can be rather costly and challenging.

Overconcentration

Heritage sites around Penang attract the curiosity of both allocentric and psychocentric tourists (Plog, 1991). They are mostly Westerners, allocentric, and travel in a small group. Many stay at low-budget hotels, which are found in abundance along Chulia Street, an important tourist district. They travel on shoestring budgets and can be found wandering through every little corner of the streets. Psychocentric tourists, on the other hand, usually come from Europe, the Arab world, China, and Japan. They prefer to travel in groups and stay at classy hotels found at Ferringhi Beach. Continuous promotion and marketing, without proper route planning, will result in tourists concentrating around heritage attractions and around areas known as "tourist enclaves."

Increased numbers of tourists means increased tourist activities, especially in tourist enclaves and in inner-city areas. Without proper tourists management, more tourists may mean that more people will end up concentrating on specific areas, which can result in social, economic, and environmental stress on the place and its communities. Tourists walking on monuments and gathering in enclosed areas to look for features in monuments can cause extensive wear and deterioration through time. The quantum effects of thousands of people walking on monuments wear them down (Sereyvuth, 2000). A study on local population in Oxford, England, revealed that tourism is perceived to bring congestion, overcrowding, and longer queues (Glasson, 1994). In the inner city, parking spaces are harder to find and are more expensive today compared to years past. The concentration of tourists affects the carrying capacity of the city's infrastructure. As Penang opens itself to greater number of global tourists, it must also be ready to contend with possible conflicts that may occur between tourists and locals competing for the same facilities. This conflict, if not addressed, can cause resentment among the locals, and can create uneasiness among the visitors and subsequently reduce their joy of visitations.

Paranoia of Tourism and Overdependency

Local authorities, believing that tourism, in any form, is the panacea of economic ills, quickly jump onto the bandwagon and blatantly offer resources they deem potential to attract tourists. The notion is "the more the merrier." The higher the number of visitors that a place receives means greater economic income as well as negative impacts. Tourism growth changes the social structures of a community. Tourism opens areas for more tourists, and brings businesses and job offers. Tourism, in any form, is a fragile and sensitive sector in nature that is comprised of a chain of industries that rely and affect one another. Problems occurring in a link of the chain can cause the whole chain to collapse in this enjoyment experience.

The Commodification of Heritage

Tourism may act as the catalyst for culture preservation and product development. One may argue that tourism is the by-product of conservation, but tourism can form the basis of cultural or heritage revitalization. Demands from tourists on local handicrafts have enlivened villagers to produce arts and crafts for tourist consumption. This, however, has also led to the commodification and commercialization of heritage and culture. Cam Ly (2003) reported that although heritage scenes surround Angkor Wat seem perfect, local girls have started offering for sale to tourists glutinous rice wrapped in a banana leaves that had been up to now offered to monks. Robinson (1999) wrote that the very presence of tourists can chip away local culture and can reinvent it to fit the demand of tourism the industry in a staged authenticity.

The Diminishing Culture

The growth of tourism, whether it is new tourism or mass tourism, affects local communities. In addition, the repeal of the Rent Control Act in George Town creates an atmospheric change when many people who live their lives in the old shop houses have to move out due to higher rental charges, according the market value, endangering traditional trades and businesses. According to Robinson (1999), one of the immediate impacts is that the host communities find their culture and traditions under threat from the purchasing power of the usually more affluent tourists. The worst scenario is when tourist businesses are preferred rather than traditional homes, turning many once culturally vibrant homes into places of different character. However, calls and efforts have been made for a more affordable alternative housing for the poor to induce urban dwellers, but it is difficult to stop the exodus of especially the younger generation to the suburbs, preferring modern, detached houses and condominiums than the perceived dirty and congested dwellings (Thieme et al., 1999). Perhaps tourism can also be blamed for the rampant destruction of authentic heritage buildings. As noted by Cohen (1978), face lifting, refurbishing, and restoration of towns and neighborhoods that have become tourist attractions are a general phenomenon. George Town can be much admired, but recent observation sees an increasing trend of overmodifications that somehow result in the original buildings not only losing their original uses, but also their original facades and thus their charm.

Design of New Township Development

Heritage cities in the developing nations including Malaysia currently face intensified urban problems as a result of rapid population growth, economic development, and urbanization. More than half of the Malaysian population in 2001 resided in urban areas. The government perceives the development of new townships as a necessary measure to disperse population pressures from central cities and to cater for the ever-growing population. Nonetheless, the establishment of new townships at the edge of the heritage cities has exposed the cities to severe pressures of commercialization, poor design, and cultural uniformity that fade away individuality and identity. Modern buildings should be regarded as potential additions to the urban heritage and they should create harmony with the prevalent urban design vision, thus enriching the aesthetic quality of the urban environment. Unfortunately, the new townships around George Town are visually sterile and reflect poorly on the urban design guidelines adopted (Majlis Perbandaran Pulau Pinang, 1987).

Depopulation of Inner City

Cultural heritage is widely considered an economic asset that could attract investments and mass tourism. Nonetheless, technological advancements in transportation and telecommunications have decentralized many urban functions to the city limits and beyond, and have encouraged urban sprawl. George Town has been losing its population especially among the younger age group due to poor housing, lack of employment opportunities, congestion, etc. (Masters Planning Studio, 1999). Although the repeal of the Rent Control Act in Penang and other heritage cities is expected to refresh urban revitalization efforts within the cities, it is feared that such a move would drive away more businesses and city dwellers from the city as they could no longer afford the higher market rates, thus creating the "dead town" syndrome.

Intensive and Uncontrolled Development Pressures

In city growth dynamic, an attractive city blessed with remarkable historical heritage may entice inward migration of new residents and visitors as well as new businesses and investments (Kotler et al., 1993). However, such an inflow of people and capital should be moderated and gauged. The designation of the conservation zones within George Town has indeed provided a breathing space to heritage conservation. However, other areas within the city should also qualify for protection. They are subject to real estate speculations and potential encroachments. According to Kamarul Baharin Buyong (2002), the director general of the Department of Museum and Antiquities, the idea of conservation and preservation of heritage is still new in Malaysia, and the ideas have to be promoted to the owners of buildings so that they can see the economic advantages of two-story shop houses over fifty-story buildings (Holland, 2001). Urban conservation approaches including adaptive reuse, restoration, and urban infill should be encouraged to maintain the original structure and fabric of the heritage buildings and sites.

Insufficient Legislation and Enforcement

Currently, six acts and enactments related to urban conservation in Malaysia are in place. In retrospect, these acts and enactments have been rather insufficient in addressing the various aspects of urban conservation in Malaysia in an integrated manner.

Changing Lifestyles and Consumption Patterns of City Dwellers

Heritage cities represent a unique place of intense social life and cultural events. The lifestyles of the city as a whole should be considered as part of the cultural heritage that needs to be conserved for the future generations. George Town is blessed with various religious ceremonies and multicultural festivals. However, factors of demographic changes, overconsumerism, and changing lifestyles and consumption patterns among the city dwellers have imposed a major turnabout in the way of life in this city. Many young urban professionals admit that living in a heritage inner city is boring. Traditional lifestyles are changing, and these changes toward modern society have affected the rhythm and pulse of George Town.

Expectations of the New Tourists

As mentioned by Boniface and Fowler (1993), across the globe, colonizers have become the tourists to the land from which they or their ancestors originated. Their expectations may be both different and greater than those of traveling companions who are solely on holiday. Today's new tourists have a different approach in their traveling behavior. Traveling has evolved, and centers around enrichment of knowledge. The profile of these new tourists is rather different than their normal counterparts. When compared to travelers overall, individuals who travel to heritage and cultural sites (heritage tourists) are better educated and have a higher average annual income (Travel Industry Association, 1997). They more often travel in couples or large groups and are twice as likely to take group tours. On average, heritage tourists spend significantly more than general travelers (Travel Industry Association, 1999). Fun, according to Hawley (1990), is secondary to learning for heritage tourists because they travel to increase their knowledge of people, places, and things, to experience a sense of nostalgia for the past. Prentice and Prentice (1989) and Thomas (1989) have suggested that heritage tourists have increased interest in knowing more about the places over the past twenty years (Photo 17.7). George Town, however, faces the risks of damage to its tourist appeal from the success of the tourist industry itself, as it brings increasing number of visitors. It is a well-known fact that tourists often come and destroy the very thing they come to visit. Among potential impacts are the following:

- Any significant arrivals of tourist and their concentration at certain zones will bring changes to the local population.

- Threats to the present heritage products such as the Khoo Kongsi, Masjid Melayu, etc. bring various social and cultural changes.

One important tourism product policy is the setting of priorities in the planning and development of new tourist products where sociocultural and heritage based resources, encompassing the past and present lifestyles of the people of Malaysia, have been identified (Ministry of Tourism Malaysia, 1990). Tourism products constitute anything that supports and enhances the traveling experience of a traveler. It can be generally divided into two categories: tourist attractions and tourist supporting facilities. From the destination point of view, important tourism elements are: transportation (which relates to image and accessibility), accommodation, attractions, and services (which includes all kinds of infrastructure for both locals and tourists) and information (and promotion).

Public Awareness

Most of the buildings in heritage zones in George Town belong to the colonial occupation period. Some quarters of society argue the

PHOTO 17.7. A Row of Old Shop Houses, Now a Famous Heritage Hotel

significance of these buildings as some of them reflect a darker period in Malaysian history. Some claim glorifying the buildings is a new colonialism, causing them to stay away from becoming a part of the conservation effort. Simultaneously, drive from the government to educate the public on the value of these buildings has been lacking. George Town, by virtue of its glorious past life, possesses historical, cultural, and political assets, which could support and survive a shift in leadership and vision but fails due to poor public participation and varying levels of heritage awareness.

Environmental Degradation

Heritage cities throughout the world are not only the center of long civilization, but often become main tourist destinations. The three top destinations in Malaysia for instance, are major heritage cities—namely Kuala Lumpur, Penang, and Malacca. The transformation in the types of city dwellers and users in the heritage centers can create environmental problems. Human-induced factors have resulted in such environmental degradations as deforestation, soil erosion, land reclamation, traffic congestion, and water and airborne chemical pollutants from automobile and factory emissions. Heritage sites such as Fort Cornwallis in George Town have been cautioned against the risks of heavy traffic vibrations.

INITIATIVES AND MEASURES

The respective local authorities of Penang have undertaken various initiatives and measures in dealing with the challenges of heritage conservation and tourism. Some of the initiatives involve are discussed in the following sections.

Zoning of Conservation, Buffer Zones, and Pedestrianization

George Town has taken deliberate and conscious effort to designate its respective conservation zones. This step is basic and essential to protect the image and the identity of a heritage city among other areas of social and cultural activities that should also be labeled as conservation zones. A pedestrianized area is a good urban design element, which facilitates heritage trails and walkabouts for tourists to allow appreciation of heritage products. The semi-pedestrianization of the heritage area protects the historic structures from the damaging effects of air pollution and constant vibrations caused by heavy traffic.

Diversification of Tourism Products and Heritage and Tourism Management

The entire heritage has an array of exciting tourism products, ranging from historic buildings and monuments to traditional activities and handicrafts. Several historic buildings have been converted into museums, shops, and other centers for the tourist. Local cultures and cottage industries should be promoted further to enhance the tourist experience. Elements associated with the eras of colonialism, the influx of migrants of various origins, and the culmination of cultures are useful information to present to tourists. Tourists are able to experience the history of these cities through exhibits and displays of heritage products, including historic buildings, sites, and local cultures. All heritage and tourism activities should be managed effectively to enhance the development of the heritage cities. Important aspects of tourism management include authentic product development and presentation, information dissemination, provision of facilities for tourists and local use, financial management, and heritage marketing strategies. Updates of heritage and tourism products, together with important guidelines at the sites, should be provided effectively through various channels such as Web sites, mass media, and advertisement boards. Management of heritage also includes improving the quality of the tourist experience at a site. In its effort to reduce traffic congestion, which resulted from a tourist influx into George Town, the local government had redesigned some of the routes from two-way to one-way traffic.

Local Involvement in Heritage Conservation

Heritage sites consist of not only physical structure, but also the living communities. Thus, to keep the city vibrant, the Penang state government has taken measures to ensure the city populace also values this heritage (see Photo 17.8). Various NGOs have been set up to encourage active participation from the public. A good example is the

PHOTO 17.8. Cheong Fatt Tze Mansion

awareness program conducted by Penang Heritage Trust (PHT) at schools in Penang. The Malaysian government on the other hand has started to acknowledge the importance of youth tourism as well as heritage as an educational tool.

LESSONS LEARNED

The previous discussion has shown that all is not well in the heritage cities in Malaysia. More concerted efforts are needed to navigate the problems experienced in the heritage cities into this new millennium. Efforts should be geared at various levels, qand should address the measures discussed in the following sections.

More Transparent Local Initiatives

In a networked global economy driven by rapid and free flow of information, ideas, cultural values, capital, goods and services, and people, it is important to emphasize the need for local action, local decision-making power, and accountability in urban development issues. It is necessary to link and coordinate more effectively the various bodies and agencies that carry out important work for urban heritage and heritage tourism.

Provision of Grants and Technical Advice

Provision of grants, incentives, and support to building owners are still lacking in Malaysia. Without the necessary grants, private building owners are more inclined to resort to total demolition of old buildings to make ways for cheaper and new ones. In George Town, strict controls and the abolishment of the Rent Control Act without acceptable financial incentives have left many building owners without choices but to deliberately tear down their buildings.

Sufficient Laws and Enforcement

Introducing sufficient and effective laws and design guidelines regarding heritage and urban conservation are vital for heritage survival. Those involved in the development of the heritage cities including policymakers, town planners, urban designers, and architects need to have a greater understanding of heritage and urban tourism. While introducing various laws and legislation is important, it is much more crucial that they are enforced effectively. Despite the existence of various laws, heritage buildings in Malaysia are constantly threatened by demolition and incompatible extensions reflecting the lack of serious enforcement of the law by the authority.

Introducing Sustainable Measures and Planning

The issue of massive population increase could be dealt with by a review of the production and consumption of resources of the urban masses. As more people rely on the city's services and infrastructure, governments, planners, and the society have not managed to keep pace with the demands and the pressures. Programs of sustainable resources should be launched to reduce waste, recycling, more efficient use of energy, use of mass public transport, etc. This requires better planning, development, and action plans for the conservation areas and cultural zones with stronger political will and a more balanced distribution of resources. The conservation[5] of heritage cities should be a continuous and dynamic process involving comprehensive planning and development of the townscape, architecture, historical sites, local cultures, and the community livelihood (Majlis Perbandaran Pulau Pinang, 1987).

Heritage Partnership

It would be a great symbol of global urban solidarity if more cities were to form partnerships with one another for the transfer of know-how, technology, and the exchange of experience. George Town needs the power of this vision, and the imagination and the talent of related people. Generating more public awareness on the importance of heritage and urban conservation for tourism becomes the utmost vital move. This could be channeled through exhibitions, seminars, and hands-on workshops.

MANAGING TOURISM IN GEORGE TOWN

We often tend to implement all sorts of strategies and programs to attract tourists without even considering the ability of the destination to absorb tourism. The heavy promotional strategies managed to generate demand for tourism, but the space for tourism is shrinking. George Town is one of the examples of destination that has gone beyond its capacity for accommodating tourists. Thus, George Town has to consider issues relating to number of tourist arrivals in planning for the future development of its tourism. The island recorded an arrival of more than three million visitors every year. Capacity has also been associated with a realization that destination areas and resorts display cycles of popularity and decline.

As expressed by Butler (1980), it is contended that the number of visitors to a destination will decline as certain capacities are exceeded or as overcommercialization occurs. Consequently, Butler stressed that developments should be kept within predetermined capacity limits. Crowding is often seen to be a major influence on visitor satisfaction. Dissatisfaction of visitors and negative experiences can act to restrict the growth of tourism or to cause a decline in popularity of a destination. It is the role of planners to forecast and project the capacity of tourist infrastructure to be used by the tourists. One of the biggest challenges faced by a planner is to make sure that the infrastructure supplied is not only sufficient for the use of tourists, but also for the local populations. Often, use of infrastructure by the tourists and the locals overlaps. Between the shared infrastructure or facilities of the locals and the tourists are road networks, urban parks, public transportation, and restaurants (see Figure 17.1).

The tourism industry is a key economic sector for Penang, contributing significantly to income and job generation. The Penang Development Corporation (PDC) is the agency responsible for the promotion and development of tourism in Penang. In carrying out its role, PDC works in close liaison with the Ministry of Culture, Arts, and Tourism; the Malaysia Tourism Promotion Board; and various trade organizations such as the following:

- Penang Tourism Centre
- Penang International Hotel Association
- Penang Tourist Guides Association
- Malaysian Association of Tour and Travel Agents, Penang chapter
- Malaysian Food and Beverage Executives Association, Penang chapter
- Chefs Association of Malaysia, Penang chapter

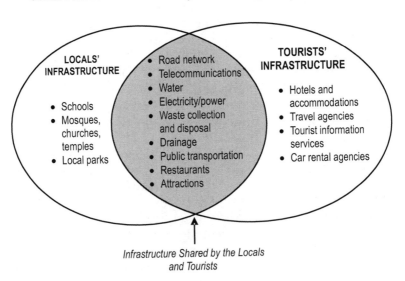

Infrastructure Shared by the Locals and Tourists

FIGURE 17.1. Facilities and Infrastructure Shared By Both Tourists and Local Population

CONCLUSION

The move to nominate George Town as UNESCO World Heritage site should be supported by all parties involved. The listing bid by the state government of Penang faces various levels of challenges from many parties. Whereas nominating a site is already a great experiment, maintaining the status as a World Heritage site is an even greater challenge. Maintaining cultural authenticity in the wake of a constant threat of globalization is not going to be an easy task. Robinson (1999) noted that little thought is given to tourism being a globalizing influence that can initiate dramatic and irreversible changes within the cultures of host communities. Perhaps the obvious conflict is between tourist and host. This is in part engendered by the fundamental difference in goals; while the tourist is engaged in leisure, the host is engaged in work.

This chapter illustrates in brief that many crucial issues need attention in anticipating more tourist activities that are expected to bundle with the world listing. As Prideaux and Kininmont (1999) conclude, the demands of the tourism industry may create the potential for conflicting aspirations between the desire to conserve and the need to develop exhibits that are of interest to tourists. However, good heritage management that focuses on heritage interpretation and presentation should be able to do both. The future and the growth of heritage tourism in George Town not only depends on the conservation efforts to preserve the historic buildings in the inner city but also requires strong involvement of the local people who make up the bulk of "living" and "moving" culture of George Town. It also depends on continued support from the tourists who should not only be exposed to the classic beauty of the buildings, but also should be exposed to the reality of the life of the people. In other words, heritage tourism should have an educational role.

Having a list of laws and enactments is applauded, but Malaysia has learned that it takes strong government commitment and leadership to push forward effective legislation that would protect this heritage from continuous threats of rapid industrialization and modernization. Although various measures have been employed to protect the buildings, efforts to maintain the city populace and its integrity remain to be seen. As being exemplified by the case of George Town, the vibrancy of a heritage site is only significant when its original community remains. Thus, George Town learns that a heritage city can carry a soul only when its population understands, wants, and participates in the conservation efforts. Conservation in the name of heritage tourism is not only about the past, it is also about the future.

NOTES

1. Europeans, Chinese, Indians, Bugis, Arabs, Armenians, Persians, Siamese, Burmese, and Sumatrans.

2. Europeans, Arabs, Armenians, Jews, Burmese, Thais, Achenese and other Malay groups, Tamils, Gujeratis, Sikhs of India, Hokkien and other southern Chinese groups, and later the Japanese and the Filipinos.

3. Historical attractions in the city of George Town today include the Kapitan Keling Mosque (1801), Fort Cornwallis (1808), Acheen Street Mosque (1808), (see Photos 17.1 and 17.2), St. George's Church (1817), Penang Museum and Art Gallery (1821), St. Xavier's Institutions (1852), Old Town Hall-the Esplanade (1900), Khoo Kongsi, Chong Fatt Tze Mansion, and Syed Al-Attas Mansion.

4. The Rent Control Act (RCA) was enacted to address the issue of social inequity of half a century ago. By controlling the rent of certain properties and protecting the tenants from easy evictions, RCA easily housed poorer citizens and redistributed wealth. An overwhelming 12,609 premises were under the act. "Repeal of Rent Control Act," 2000).

5. This should not only involve building preservation and renovation of facade treatments, building materials, height, functions, maintenance, and interior renovation, but also city beautification strategies and the provision of community facilities as an important part of the heritage and urban tourism development.

REFERENCES

Ahmad, A.G. (1997). *British Colonial Architecture in Malaysia 1800-1930.* Kuala Lumpur: Museums Association of Malaysia.

Boniface, P. and Fowler, P.J. (1993). *Heritage and Tourism in the Global Village.* London, UK: Routledge.

Butler, R.W. (1980). The concept of a tourism area cycle of evolution: Implications for managers of resources. *Canadian Geographer, 24*: 5-12.

Buyong, K.B. (2002). Personal communication. Department of Museum and Antiquities, National Museum of Malaysia.

Cam Ly, N.B. (2003). Tourists threaten fragility of ancient sites. *Inter Press Service,* April 7.

Cohen, E. (1978). The impact of tourism on the physical environment. *Annals of Tourism Research, 5*(2): 215-237.

Collins, R. (1983). Tourism and heritage conservation: The pacific experience. *Heritage Australia, 2*(2): 58-59.

Glasson, J. (1994). Oxford: A heritage city under pressure—visitors, impacts and management response. *Tourism Management, 15*(2): 137-144.

Hardy, D. (1988). Historical geography and heritage studies. *Area, 20:* 333-338.

Hawley, P. (1990). Historic preservation and tourism., In J. Ziegler (ed.), *Enhancing Rural Economies through Amenity Resources: A National Policy Symposium*. University Park, PA: The Pennsylvania State University.

Holland, L. (2001). Malaysia: Whose heritage? *Far Eastern Economic Review,* May 3.

Hoon, Y.S. (1996). Malaysia: Penang Pangs. *Travel Asia,* May.

Konrad, V. (1982). Historical artifacts as recreational resources. In G. Wall and J. Marsh (eds.), *Recreational Land Use: Perspective on its Evolution in Canada* (pp. 392-416). Ottawa, Canada: Carleton University Press.

Kotler, P. et al. (1993). *Marketing Places Attracting Investment, Industry and Tourism to Cities, State's and Nations*. New York: The Free Press.

Light, D. and Prentice, R. (1994). Who consumes the heritage product? In G. Ashworth and P. Larkham (eds.), *Building a New Heritage* (pp. 90-116). London, UK: Routledge.

Majlis Perbandaran Pulau Pinang. (1987). *Design Guidelines for Conservation Areas in the Inner-city Area of George Town, Penang*. Pulau Pinang, Malaysia: MPPP.

Master's Planning Studio (1999). *Kajian Tren Pembangunan Sektor Perniagaan Runcit di Pulau Pinang: Pusat Bandaraya George Town*. Technical Report, Pulau Pinang, Malaysia: Universiti Sains Malaysia.

McNulty, R. (1991). Cultural tourism: New opportunities for wedding conservation to economic development. In *Conservation and Tourism: Second International Congress on Architectural Conservation and Town Planning* (pp. 34-41), London, UK: Heritage Trust.

Millar, S. (1989). Heritage management for heritage tourism. *Tourism Management, 10*(3): 9-14.

Ministry of Tourism Malaysia (1990). Brief profile. Available at: http://www.motour.gov.my/laman_web/index.php?page=profile.

Penang Hill boutique hotels to be new attraction (2002). *The Star,* October 11, p. 25.

Plog, S. (1991). *Leisure Travel: Making it a Growth Market Again*. New York: Wiley.

Prentice, M. (1993). *Tourism and Heritage Attractions*. London, UK: Routledge.

Prentice, M. and Prentice, R. (1989). The heritage market of historic sites such as education resources. In D. Herbert, R. Prentice, and C. Thomas (eds.), *Heritage Sites: Strategies for Marketing and Development*. Hants, UK: Avebury.

Prideaux, B.R and Kinimont, L-J. (1999). Tourism and heritage are not strangers: A study of opportunities for rural heritage museums to maximize tourism visitation. *Journal of Travel Research, 37*(3): 299-303.

Repeal of Rent Control Act (2000). *Utusan Konsumer,* February, p. 10.

Richardson, M. (2000). Angkor Wat: After the war, here come the tourists. *International Herald Tribune,* August 25. Available at: http://www.iht.com/articles/2000/08/25/phnom.2.t.php.

Robinson, M. (1999). Is cultural tourism on the right track? *Unesco Courier, 52*(7): 22-23. Available at: http://www.unesco.org/courier/1999_08/uk/dossier/txt11.htm.

Sereyvuth, V. (2000). Angkor Wat: The pillar of the Cambodia tourism industry. Presentation at the International Conference on Cultural Tourism, December 11-13, Siem Reap, Cambodia.

Sudarskis, M. (2000). Competitive trends in the wake of internationalization and globalization of mediterranean cities. Available at http://www.comen.org/principale_inglese_2000.html.

Tassell, C. and Tassell, M. (1990). The Tasmanian rural landscape. *Heritage Australia, 9*(4): 12-15.

Thieme, S., Knigge, M., and Schenke, D. (1999). *Survey on the Perception of the Historic Centre of in Young People's Minds.* Penang, Malaysia: ASA Project.

Thomas, C. (1989). The roles of historic site's and reasons for visiting. In D. Herbert, R. Prentice, and C. Thomas (eds.), *Heritage Sites: Strategies for Marketing and Development* (pp.)Hants, UK: Avebury.

Tighe, A. (1986). The arts/tourism partnership. *Journal of Travel Research, 24:* 2-5.

Tjoa-Bonatz, M.L. (2000). Penang's historic city centre before the repeal of the rent control act. *Journal of the Malaysian Branch of the Royal Asiatic Society, LXXlll*(2): 53-69.

Travel Industry Association (1997). *1997 Outlook for Travel and Tourism.* Washington, DC: Travel Industry Association.

Travel Industry Association (1999). Fast facts. Available at: www.tia.org/press/fastfacts8.stm.

Weiler, B. and Hall, C. (1992). *Special Interest Tourism.* London, UK: Belhaven Press.

World Tourism Organization. (1985). *The State's Role in Protecting and Promoting Culture as a Factor of Tourism Development and the Proper Use and Exploitation of the National Cultural Heritage of Sites and Monuments for Tourists.* Madrid, Spain: World Tourism Organization.

FURTHER READING

Mohamed, B. (2000). Heritage tourism in Penang. Paper presented at Workshop on the Listing of Tentative Heritage Sites of Melaka and Penang, September 28-29, Melaka, Malaysia.

Mohamed, B. and Nordin, N.A. (2001). Future trends and scenarios in tourism: A case study on the capacity of tourist infrastructure in Malaysia. Paper presented at the First Hospitality and Tourism Educators National Conference, June 14-15, Kuala Lumpur, Malaysia.

United Nations Development Programme. (1997). International Survey of Mayors: Urban Problems Remain Similar Worldwide. Presentation at the International Colloquium of Mayors, International Conference on Governance for Sustainable Growth and Equity, July 28-31, New York, NY. Available at: http://mirror .undp.org/magnet/Docs/urban/Maysur.htm.

Chapter 18

Effects of Tourism Development on the Local Poor People: A Case Study in Taibai Region China

B. Zeng
R. W. Carter
T. De Lacy
Johannes Bauer

INTRODUCTION

Tourism has grown rapidly to become an activity of worldwide importance. Economic effects of tourism on a nation or specific region are highly significant. These effects include the positives of increased foreign currency earning and government revenues, increased employment and skills of local community members, and regional development. Tourism also can bring inflation, market dependency, financial leakage, and imbalances in the distribution of tourist spending, which can lead to host-community dissatisfaction (see Oppermann and Chon 1997).

Most economic studies focus on the magnitude of benefits and the multiplier effects of tourism at national or regional levels. Few, however, consider cash flows through the different components of the tourism system and ultimately to local households. Understanding the flow is important for developing strategies for equitable distribution of tourism benefits and poverty alleviation.

Tourist expenditure is ultimately the source of cash that directly influences flows within local tourism systems. Goodwin (2000) identified four different types of local cash income generated from tourism:

Global Cases on Hospitality Industry
© 2008 by The Haworth Press, Taylor & Francis Group. All rights reserved.
doi:10.1300/5923_18

- Wages from formal employment
- Earnings from selling goods, services, or casual labor (e.g., food, crafts, building materials, guide services)
- Profits arising from locally owned enterprises
- Profit from a community-run enterprise, dividends from a private sector partnership, and land rental paid by an investor

Because different categories of local people are involved in tourism activities, cash can flow to local people through all four means. However, the magnitude of each flow depends on local institutional arrangements, local participation in tourism, and community or people's capacity to respond to opportunities. This chapter reports the results of a study that mapped cash flow to determine the benefits of tourism to local households. Special attention is given to the poor in the interest of clarifying strategies for effective poverty alleviation. Communities living adjacent to a series of protected areas in China were the focus of the study.

CASE STUDY AREA

Protected areas are one of the most important attractions for tourism. Progressively, protected areas in China, including forest parks, scenic sites, and nature reserves, are being opened to tourism. About 82 percent of nature reserves have developed tourism since the early 1990s, and of these, 15.9 percent have achieved more than 100,000 annual visits (China Man and the Biosphere Programme 2000). It is also seen by all levels of government as a means of spreading wealth and a means of bringing economic development to isolated areas and improving the well-being of the rural poor.

The study was conducted in a group of protected areas in the Taibai Mountain region in Shaanxi, a western province of China. The field survey sites included Taibai Mountain Nature Reserve, Taibai Mountain National Forest Park, Heihe Forest Park, Laoxiancheng Nature Reserve, and Changqing National Nature Reserve, along with their adjacent communities.

Shaanxi is one of the less developed provinces in China. The annual net income per rural resident in Shaanxi Province was a mere $192.88 (U.S.), that is, $0.53 per day. This is much lower than the average national level of $299.22. It means that people here are living in poverty according to the international poverty indicator, which sets the poverty level at under $1 (U.S.) per day (World Bank 2001). The case study area has an even lower economic development level than the province. Meixian County, where Taibai Mountain Nature Reserve and National Forest Park are located, has a lower per capita net income for rural residents and per capita gross domestic product (GDP).

Since the 1990s, tourism development in China has increased sharply. In 1978, annual international visitor arrivals were 1.8 million (China National Tourism Administration 2003a). In the same period, international tourism receipts increased from $2.63 billion (U.S.) to $20.39 billion (China National Tourism Administration 2003b). Tourism development stimulates national economic growth. In western China, where it is relatively less developed, tourism development is considered important for accelerating economic development.

Shaanxi is an important tourist destination in China. In 2002, international visitors numbered 0.85 million, 12.0 percent up on 2001. The annual receipts from international tourism was $351.0 million, a 14.0 percent increase on 2001. In addition, domestic tourism continues to increase. The annual arrival of domestic tourists was 37.3 million, an 11.0 percent increase on 2001. Annual receipts from domestic tourism was $1,909.4 million, an 11.3 percent annual growth (see Figure 18.1).

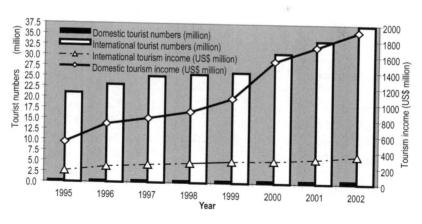

FIGURE 18.1. Tourism Growth in Shaanxi Province, China. *Source:* Compiled from National Bureau of Statistics of China, *China Statistical Yearbooks*, 1996-2003.

The Taibai Mountain Region is one of the most important habitats for giant pandas, golden monkeys, and golden takin, three endangered species listed on the IUCN Red Book (International Union for Conservation of Nature and Natural Resources 2004). The Taibai Mountain region is presently undergoing rapid development to cater to an increasing number of tourists. Although it is of international interest, because of international recognition of giant panda, international tourist arrivals are low, and the rapidly growing local market is largely based on outdoor recreation and scenery rather than on wildlife tourism.

SURVEY METHODS

To understand tourist spending patterns, tourists (n = 271) were surveyed at different regional locations. Local households (n = 108) and employees (n = 54) of tourism businesses or park/reserve authorities were also interviewed to obtain details of their income and spending structures. In addition, local tourism businesses (n = 20) were surveyed to trace cash flows. The resultant combination of receipt and expenditure data permits tracing of cash flow, verified by tracing expenditure and receipts separately for each interview group. This permits triangulation of results.

RESULTS

Who Is Really Poor?

Referring to the category system of rural resident net income adopted by the Shaanxi Provincial Bureau of Statistics (SPBS 2003), local households can be categorized into six groups by per capita annual net income:

1. Absolute poor: ≤ CN ¥627 ($75.78 [U.S.])
2. Relative poor: CN ¥627- ¥869 ($75.78-$105.02)
3. Low income: CN ¥869- ¥1,500 ($105.02-$181.28)
4. Middle income: CN ¥1,500- ¥2,142 ($181.28-$258.86)
5. Upper middle income: CN ¥2,142- ¥5,000 ($258.86-$604.25)
6. High income: > CN ¥5,000 ($604.25)

This criteria system applies in the case study. The households with per capita annual net income lower than $105.02 (U.S.) are poor in the local area.

Poor's Economic Benefit from Tourism

A significant positive correlation exists between per capita income and tourism income proportion (n = 108, p = 0.245, sig. = 0.010 [< 0.05]). It means that the proportion of household income from tourism increases with the increase in per capita net income. It suggests that tourism is a very important income source for local households.

By quantitative analysis, it is found (see Figure 18.2) that in poor household groups (including absolute and relative poor), average tourism income values were $14.60, much lower than the whole region average ($189.2), as well as lower than other groups. The proportions of tourism income were 6.5 percent, also much lower than the whole region average (20.1 percent) and other groups. The results suggest that local poor people get much less benefit from tourism than other household groups.

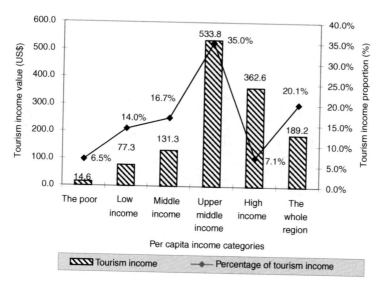

FIGURE 18.2. Differences in Contribution of Tourism Income to Total Cash Income in Different Household Groups

Equality and Security for the Poor

Equality Issues in Households Benefiting from Tourism

When especially considering "local poor people," 82.4 percent of stakeholders in the region believed "local poor people" got some financial benefit, but 17.6 percent considered they received no benefit. All related agency employees still insisted poor people received benefit, although 81.3 percent considered the benefit to be "low" or "too low" (see Figure 18.3). In comparison, most local households (55.2 percent) in tourism development areas reckoned "local poor people" got no benefit at all, while those households living in areas without tourism had a more optimistic expectation about poor benefit (only 13.1 percent answered no).

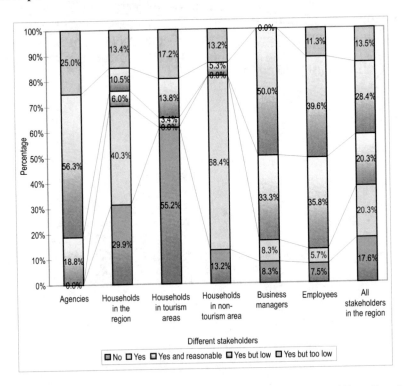

FIGURE 18.3. Different Perspectives on Financial Benefit to Local Poor People from Tourism

The results suggest that local people do gain some economic benefit from tourism, but that it is low. Local poor people gain even less. Local households with close linkage to tourism development are not as optimistic about these benefits as other stakeholders and households expecting tourism development in their areas. It appears that agency employees, business managers, and tourism employees overestimate the economic benefit of tourism to local people, including the poor. Meanwhile, households in areas without existing tourism have high expectations that tourism development would greatly benefit them. Although overestimation and overexpectation may be traits of tourism, these false perceptions by people of influence may have significant consequences for public policy and the tourism development agenda, and may even extend beyond national investment in tourism to include well-meaning international aid programs expected to assist the poor.

Considering different household groups (see Figure 18.4), 38.9 percent of poor households admitted they received no income, 11.1

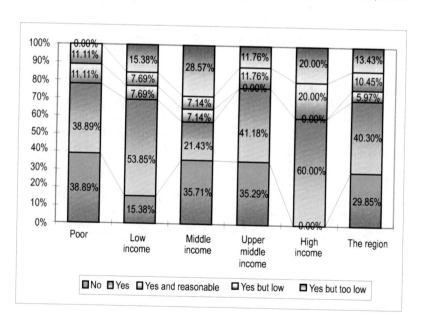

FIGURE 18.4. Households' Perspectives on Tourism Benefit to Local Poor People

percent admitted they received some but low. Meanwhile, more than 35 percent middle and upper middle income households believed no benefit went to local poor people, and 23.6 percent to 35.7 percent of them considered some benefit, but that is was "low" or "too low." All high-income households believed local poor people received benefit, although 40 percent admitted it was "low" or "too low." It is interesting that most low-income households (94.6 percent) believed poor people received benefit. The results suggest that poor people realized their disadvantage in getting benefits from tourism, as did middle and upper middle income households.

Based on a seven-point scale (−3 to +3), local households were scored on tourism effect on local households (see Table 18.1). Poor people gave the lowest average score (0.95) to economic effect, much lower than the region average (1.41). High-income households scored a highest point (2.00), followed by low-income (1.76), upper-income (1.60), and middle-income households (1.23). The results suggest that although all households believed generally tourism development had a positive effect on economic development, poor people were not as optimistic as others.

The results suggest that although all households admitted generally tourism development had positive effects on local households, many of them believed no benefit or low and too low benefit to local poor people. Local poor households realized their disadvantage and were not as optimistic as other households. High-income groups believed tourism had a very strong positive effect on local households, including the poor, because they are one of the major beneficiaries in tourism development. It is interesting that low-income groups also

TABLE 18.1. Household Scoring Tourism Effects on Local Households

	Economic effect	Cultural effect
Poor	0.95	1.05
Low income	1.76	1.18
Middle income	1.23	1.31
Upper middle income	1.60	1.42
High income	2.00	0.80
The region	1.41	1.20

claimed a very strong positive tourism effect on household economic situation, and they had a relatively optimistic judgment about the tourism effect on local poor people. It can be explained by that the low-income group had a low expectancy on their living standards, so they were quite content with even a small benefit from tourism. The lack of desire from low-income groups to improve their life is actually an obstacle and dilemma for tourism development targeting poverty elimination.

Employment Opportunity

The primary employment opportunities through tourism appear to be in jobs such as hospitality servicing, craft making, shop ownership, tour operation, government agency staff, and park rangers (Wearing 2001). It must be noted that currently a general lack of host community skills and resources has meant that many tourism ventures are often owned and operated by expatriates, and the employment opportunities for local communities are not as many as expected (Weiler and Hall 1992).

Estimated by local governments, around 7,000 people were employed in tourism-related businesses in Meixian County in 2002. Meanwhile in Tangyukou Town, around 1,500 people were serving for tourism development in such services as hotel, food, and guide. A survey in local tourism hotels shows that each hotel averagely creates 37.3 employees, 77.6 percent being taken by employees from the local county, including the local town, with the rest being from other counties in Shaanxi Province, and without employees from other provinces. Especially considering local poor people, it is found that half of them (50.0 percent) believed that tourism had a positive effect on employment, but another half (50.0 percent) considered neutral or negative impact (see Table 18.2). Checking the employment in tourism businesses, it is found that very few employees were from poor households. Obviously, hotels provide local households with a good employment opportunity, however, very few local poor people can be employed in the tourism businesses, and they generally had a neutral judgment about tourism's effect on employment opportunity, which is a more conservative judgment than other households in the region.

TABLE 18.2. Poor's Perspective on Employment Affected by Tourism Development

	Negative	Neutral	Positive
Poor	9.1%	40.9%	50.0%
Low income	0.0%	0.0%	100.0%
Middle income	0.0%	33.3%	66.7%
Upper middle income	9.1%	0.0%	90.9%
High income	0.0%	0.0%	100.0%
The region	6.1%	22.4%	71.4%

Education Opportunity

Of total spending, education is the biggest expenditure for households, accounting for about 18.4 percent of total expending (see Figure 18.5). Food consumption, production materials, and health care follow respectively as 8.8 percent, 7.4 percent, and 5.4 percent.

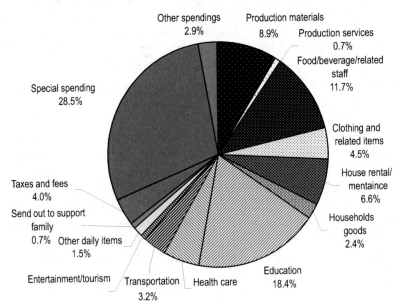

FIGURE 18.5. Household Spending Structure

The total annual cash income was much lower than the total annual spending for poor households; the gap between income and spending is much higher than other households (see Figure 18.6). It means they have to rely on loans or previous savings to sustain their education investment. Therefore, for local poor people it was very hard to support their children's schooling, although they were still doing so. It must be noted that although the cost of education is so high, almost every household sent their children to school, even if via loan. This shows an opportunity to get higher human resource quality in the future. It is important for local sustainable development.

Livelihood Security

Food supply is selected to indicate household livelihood. It is found that no significant difference existed in food supply amount among different income groups. However, especially considering "food diversity," 54.1 percent of poor households believed they had not much higher than the region average (44.4 percent), as well as much higher than other households (see Figure 18.7). This suggests that although generally local households can get enough food for their basic livelihood, higher-income households could buy much

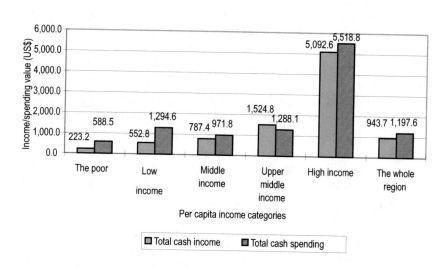

FIGURE 18.6. Balance Between Cash Income and Spending

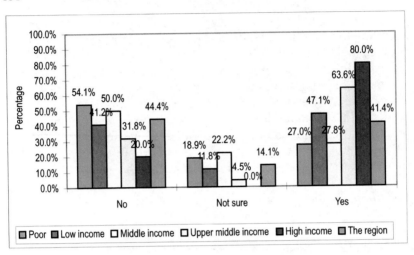

FIGURE 18.7. Household Perspective on Their Food Diversity

more variety of food rather than just grains and vegetables, and may arrange their meals ample and alternative, while local poor people could just meet their preliminary food demands.

Considering household living standard improvements, taking ten years before (year 1993) as a benchmark, the poor people and low-income households generally believed that although standards improved they improved much slower (point = 15.2) than the region average (point = 17.7), as well as much slower than relatively wealthy households (point = 20.1 to 23.4) (see Figure 18.8). Since tourism development started in the early 1990s, the contribution of tourism to regional economic growth and household living standard improvement is obvious.

Considering contentment with life, most households (64.6 percent) were content with their lives (see Figure 18.9). A relatively high proportion of poor (64.7 percent) and low-income households (74.7 percent) expressed their contentment, much higher than middle (55.6 percent) and upper middle income households (60.0 percent).

Combining these two groups of results, it is found that although local poor and low-income households believed they had a slower improvement in their living standards, they were quite content with their

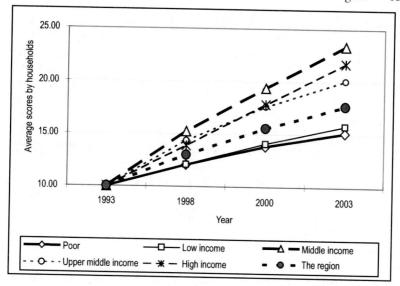

FIGURE 18.8. Households' Perspective on Their Living Standard Improvement

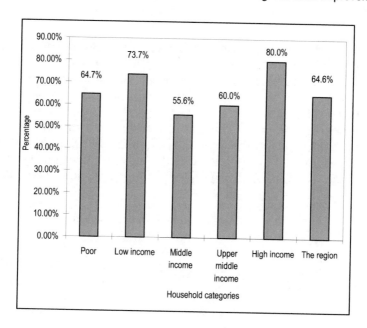

FIGURE 18.9. Percentage of Households Content with Their Lives

current lives. It suggests that they generally had a lower expectation of life quality than did other groups. It can also reversely explain why fewer proportions of middle and upper middle income households were content with their life even though they admitted their living standards had much improvemed compared to other households in the region. The low life quality expectation embodied in poor and low-income households is a dilemma in tourism development targeting poverty elimination in the region.

Considering tourism's effect on livelihood security, although most households (77.6 percent) believed that it reduced the numbers of poor people in the region, many households (36.7 percent) reckoned the gap between poor and wealthy has enlarged (Table 18.3). The poor people and low-income households agree that this enlargement has occurred.

The results suggest that poor people and low-income households were in a dilemma. On one hand, they were quite happy their life improved with tourism development; on the other hand, they worried about the gap between poor and wealthy being enlarged.

Social Security

Quantitative analysis based on a seven-point scale (-3 to $+3$) indicates that local households trended to consider a strong ($1.0 <$ score $= 1.2 < 2.0$) tourism effect on cultural aspect of households (see Table 18.1). Although different household groups had different scores, no significant difference was found.

Considering the social changes caused by tourism development, most of households in the region (57.1 percent to 58.3 percent) believed that tourism development had a positive effect on social aspects such as criminal cases, traditional customs, and local culture

TABLE 18.3. Percentage of household perspective on tourism effect on poverty issues

	Reducing in number of poor people	Change of gap between poor and wealthy
Negative	6.1%	36.7%
Neutral	16.3%	22.4%
Positive	77.6%	40.8%

(see Table 18.4). In terms of different household groups, it is found that more local poor people, low-income, and middle-income households believed a positive effect from tourism was had on social aspects than the region average, while relative wealthy households, including upper middle and high income households, believed few positive effects occurred, and instead reported tourism having a neutral or even negative effect. This suggests that tourism development strengthened the poor's perspective on social security, but wealthy people did not accepted this judgment.

It may be explained by that poor people and relatively low income households were more tolerant of tourism's negative effects on social aspects, as they were expecting to get more economic benefit from it. Reversely, wealthy households were more sensitive to the negative effects from tourism on their vested interests since they had a low dependency on income from tourism development.

DISCUSSION

Since in China many tourism destinations are located in underdeveloped areas, local residents, including local poor people, are willing to participate in development activities for benefits. However, the local households in particular with poor people could not effectively participate in tourism activities, and thus got few benefits. Difficul-

TABLE 18.4. Percentage of Household's Perspective on Social Security

		The poor	Low income	Middle income	Upper middle income	High income	The region
Criminal cases	Negative	0.0%	0.0%	0.0%	27.3%	0.0%	6.3%
	Neutral	38.1%	33.3%	16.7%	36.4%	100.0%	35.4%
	Positive	61.9%	66.7%	83.3%	36.4%	0.0%	58.3%
Traditional customs	Negative	0.0%	0.0%	16.7%	18.2%	0.0%	6.3%
	Neutral	19.0%	33.3%	50.0%	54.5%	100.0%	35.4%
	Positive	81.0%	66.7%	33.3%	27.3%	0.0%	58.3%
Local culture	Negative	0.0%	0.0%	0.0%	9.1%	0.0%	2.0%
	Neutral	22.7%	44.4%	33.3%	72.7%	100.0%	40.8%
	Positive	77.3%	55.6%	66.7%	18.2%	0.0%	57.1%

ties and barriers exist for local households to be fully involved in tourism development.

Lack of Personal Capacity

Low education, lack of funding, and shortage of effective government intervention are major factors causing local poor a lack of personal capacity to be involved in tourism development. Since few people are educated, their ability to access job opportunities, especially those requiring knowledge and skill, is low. Lacking of funding, it is possible to set up some self-employing business to access tourism benefit. Moreover, financial aid from governments or NGOs are more available for relatively wealthy households than by the poor, just because these aids tend to match some existing small fund to initiate some projects or programs.

Disadvantage in Competition

Households serve in the tourism system as basic supporters or supplementary labor sources, not as one of the most important roles in the system. Since generally overestimated by other stakeholders, involvement of local people, especially local poor people, in tourism has actually been neglected in tourism development.

Laws and regulations state many obligations, but few rights for local people. Normally authorities take themselves as law executers, not as partners of the local community. In this situation, it is very difficult for local people to participate in tourism. When problems occur in competition, local residents are usually in an unfavorable position. In general, it is impossible for them to be on equal footing with the authorities because the latter represent "the national interests" and the former represent "the interests of only a few people."

Government's Crucial Role in Overcoming Barriers

By government intervention, to force cash to flow to the poor by special policies such as encouraging *nong jia le,* which is a tourism form based on farmhouse and local traditional food; raising special funding from tourism to support poor involvement; leading government anti-poverty funding to support poor involvement; and advocating local tourism services and businesses to purchase local products is important.

Sustainable Tourism–Eliminate Poverty (ST–EP) model

Sustainable tourism–eliminate poverty (ST–EP), which is being explored in developing countries, may be a suitable model for nature-based tourism in rural areas. Since many natural tourism destinations are located in underdeveloped areas, the local residents are willing to participate in development activities for benefits, but they have low ability to be involved. Therefore, to stimulate poor and low-income households' desire to improve their life, encourage their belief, and do some necessary training are crucial to their role in ST–EP as a key partner.

Developing tourism activities suitable to local people's involvement is key in ST–EP. Households participate in not just garbage collecting and labor but also in such direct services such as guide, farm-house hotel, restaurant, community lifestyle, and traditional handcraft courses (such as paper, traditional food cooking, and knitting).

In Taibai Region, in comparison with employees from outside the local area, locals are employed at lower pay rates and are involved in unskilled jobs such as house cleaning, luggage handling, and street sales of produce and food. The barrier appears to be related to the hand-to-mouth existence of the poor and the consequent inability to invest in a tourism future through business development or the upgrading of skills. The balance of income versus subsistence expenditure for the poor is such that the relatively rich will get richer and the poor poorer. Such a situation is far from the ideals of sustainable tourism, but it is the reality being faced by the Taibai poor.

Improving the skill level of local households to serve existing tourists is part of the solution. Developing skills to create new tourism products is another. However, the largest gains are likely to occur if the local community is ready to meet the demands of more wealthy nationals and the inevitable international tourist traffic attracted to the wildlife and scenic values of the region. Maximizing the economic benefits will not just require skill upgrading for providing tourist products and services, but skills to serve the whole of the tourism system, so that people are ready to fill the commercial and general work void created when others move their income source directly to tourism. The strategy for reducing poverty is possibly not to train the poor to take on tourism-related income generation activity but to take on activity that serves the system. These are activities that the poor currently undertake, largely within an economically stagnant society, despite rapid economic growth elsewhere in the province. Without this general upgrading of skills for the poor, the danger is that they will become slaves to the tourist entrepreneur who will probably emerge from the middle and upper middle income brackets who have excess financial capital to invest.

REFERENCES

China Man and the Biosphere Programme (2000). *Study on Sustainable Management Policy for China's Nature Reserves.* Beijing, China: Scientific Literature Press.

China National Tourism Administration (2003a). Annual visitor arrivals 1978-2000. Available at: http://old.cnta.gov.cn/lyen/2fact/annual.htm.

China National Tourism Administration (2003b). International tourism receipts 1978-2000. Available at: http://old.cnta.gov.cn/lyen/2fact/international-3.htm.

Goodwin, H. (2000). Pro-poor tourism: Opportunities for sustainable local development. *D+C Development and Cooperation,* 5(September/October): 12-14.

International Union for Conservation of Nature and Natural Resources (2004). 2004 IUCN red list of threatened species. Available at: http://www.iucnredlist.org.

McIntosh, R.W., Goeldner, C.R., et al. (1995). *Tourism: Principles, Practices, Philosophies.* New York: John Wiley & Sons.

National Bureau of Statistics of China (2003). *China Statistical Yearbook.* Beijing: China Statistical Press.

Oppermann, M. and Chon, K.S. (1997). *Tourism in Developing Countries.* London, UK: International Thomson Business Press.

Shaanxi Provincial Bureau of Statistics (SPBS) (2003). *Shaanxi Statistic Yearbook 2003.* Beijing, China: Chinese Statistics Press.

Wearing S. L. (2001). Exploring socio-cultural impact's on local communities. In Weaver, D.B. (ed.), *The Encyclopaedia of Ecotourism* (pp. 385-410). Wallingford, UK: CABI Publishing.

Weiler, B. and Hall, C. (eds.) (1992). *Special Interest Tourism.* London, UK: Belhave Press.

World Bank (2001). *World Development Report 2000/2001: Attacking Poverty.* New York: Oxford University Press.

Chapter 19

Barriers to Hotel Chain Development in China

Ray Pine
Pingshu Qi

INTRODUCTION

By the year 2020 China will become the world's number one tourist destination, with annual arrivals of 130 million (WTO, 1999). This is quite an incredible statistic when one remembers that China's international tourism industry started only in 1979 as a result of the Open Door Policy.

In 2001 China had 33 million tourist arrivals, spending $17.8 billion (U.S.) (CNTA, 2002). The stock of hotels in 2000 stood at 10,481, with a total of 948,185 rooms (CNTA, 2001). China's stock of hotels will need to expand and upgrade very significantly to serve its potentially massive market in line with the expected growth of international arrivals, in addition to increasing domestic tourist demand (Pine, 2002a,b).

China's own increasingly affluent population is also traveling more and more within the country, adding to the need for additional hotels. Affluence has resulted from continual average annual economic growth in China of 9.8 percent between 1979 and 1997 (State

This chapter was originally published in Pine, R., and Pingshu, Q. (2004). Barriers to hotel chain development in China. *International Journal of Contemporary Hospitality Management,* 16(1): 37-44. Adapted with permission by Emerald Group Publishing Limited. The work described in this paper was substantially supported by funding from the Hong Kong Polytechnic University (Project Account No. V808).

Statistics Bureau, 1998). The dynamic economy stimulates more business travelers. Changes in government policies have also loosened travel restrictions and introduced a strict five-day working week and three weeks of annual holidays, swelling the already massive leisure tourism movements. This resulted in a total of 784 million domestic travelers in 2001 with revenues of around $40 million (U.S.) (CNTA, 2002).

Firms have a variety of inducements to expand, but also external and internal difficulties to overcome in expansion. Such difficulties create conditions enhancing or restricting the profitability or practicability of expansion. Limitations might include managerial ability, product or factor markets, and uncertainty and risk (Penrose, 1995). In addition to these general factors, the barriers to hotel chain growth in China have some particular aspects, which influence not only the development of indigenous hotel companies, but also expansion by multinational hotel corporations.

The global hotel industry is dominated by hotel chains. In 1998 a total of 15.4 million rooms were available in hotels and similar establishments throughout the world (WTO, 2000a,b). Given this situation, it is not unreasonable to speculate that a significant part of China's future hotel industry will be in the form of hotel chains.

This chapter will look at barriers to such development within the following four main areas:

1. Economic and political systems
2. Hotel ownership
3. Management capability and resources
4. Competition between local and foreign chains

METHODOLOGY

The research was undertaken in three stages. First, a comprehensive literature review was undertaken to understand the concepts of hotel chains, then secondary data were collected and analyzed to describe hotel chain development in China. Finally, primary data were collected to further explore chain formation.

For primary data the case study approach was employed to examine several hotel chains and independent hotels in three of China's gateway cities. Qualitative methodology was deemed more appropriate, as it emphasizes processes and meanings that cannot be rigorously examined or measured in terms of quantity, amount, intensity, or frequency, and it seeks to answer questions that focus on how social experience is created and given (Denzin and Lincoln, 1994).

After an extensive literature review and examination of secondary data, a research instrument for use in in-depth interviews was developed. Both closed- and open-ended questions relating to hotel chains and independent hotels were used during interviews to obtain extensive insights into hotel chain formation and expansion in China. Of all the qualitative methods, the in-depth interview may be argued as being the most powerful tool to gain insights into the socially constructed realities of individuals (Kvale, 1983; McCracken, 1988). By using the in-depth interview, the interviewees are introduced to the topic through general questions. Then through probing and prompting of interviewees for deeper descriptions (Howe, 1985) the interviewer could understand replies from their respondents' perspectives and then interpret them for contextualization. In April 1999, pilot testing of the interview questions was conducted in Beijing with three local and two international groups along with the Department of Industry Management of the China National Tourism Administration. Subsequently, two final instruments were developed, one for chain hotels and one for independent properties. (The complete question lists are reproduced in the Appendix 19.A.)

Hotel Management Companies Survey

Of the thirty-nine hotel management companies in China at the time of the research, ten companies in the gateway cities of Beijing, Shanghai, and Guangzhou were selected for interview. These three cities were the earliest to start the modern hotel industry in China and have a relatively higher standard of development. More important, most hotel chains are headquartered in these three cities, using them as a base for expansion. The criteria of selection of companies were their size, portfolio, location of hotels, management style, and ownership to try and ensure that all possible types of hotel management companies were included. The Guangdong Provincial Tourism Administration was also interviewed.

Independent Hotels Survey

Each of the three target cities has more than one hundred hotels, most being independently operated. Several hotels in each city were selected for an in-depth interview to explore the major factors and problems of independent hotels joining hotel chains. The major considerations in selecting hotels were their star level, ownership, location, business type, history, and the need to cover all types of hotels.

FINDINGS

The combination of literature review, secondary data, and interview findings indicated four main categories of barriers to chain development, namely economic and political systems, hotel ownership, hotel management capability and resources, and competition between local and foreign firms. These four areas will be discussed in the following sections.

Economic and Political Systems

Paradox of a Transitional Economy

Since 1978 China has adopted an opening and reforming policy to gradually transform toward a market-oriented economy. This kind of reform created a better business environment for hotel development; even the investment in and management of hotels was a reflection of this reform. However, China has not yet finished its economic transition and remains a mixed economy system in which market principles and the central planning system interact and conflict. Although China is in a period of transition from planned to market economy, state-owned hotels are still obedient to the traditional administrative system. State hotels, which account for the great majority of hotel rooms, belong to different government bodies and administrative departments, and their ownership is very complicated. They are not actual firms and cannot act as a commercial business. Even though the government has conglomerated some hotels, they still cannot break the barriers of ownership and protectionism to generate market competitiveness.

Until recently, overseas involvement in China's hotel business, although encouraged and supported by the state politically and financially, was still under government control. However, China's entry to the World Trade Organization has effectively removed such controls and exposed the local industry to extensive penetration by and competition from foreign companies. China will lose the ability to control the activities of overseas companies within its own borders.

Government Intervention

Government officials heavily influence the hotel industry, and they may interfere with actual hotel management and operation (Tisdell and Wen, 1991). Too much bureaucratic control over hotels may cause a waste of resources, low efficiency, and a lack of innovative entrepreneurs (Yu, 1999), while preventing the growth of hotels and hotel companies. For example, a typical phenomenon in China is local protectionism, when the government of one region bars investment and commodities from other regions into its territory. These policies greatly affect an indigenous hotel company; it is easier for foreign companies to establish a nationwide presence.

Policy Restriction and Interest Groups

Policy restrictions and interest groups influence hotel chain formation. The current regulations limit the free flow of state-owned assets in the market. As state-owned hotels are invested by different government agencies with various interests, most hotels are difficult to incorporate into chains. It is also difficult for existing chains to handle these hotels. For example, the *China Post* and Telecom Tourism Group is a holding company created by the Ministry of Information Industry (MII) to manage all MII hotels. However, most of these MII hotels are owned in the name of local bureau, and, during the course of reorganization, constant conflicts shift these assets to the holding company. Different government bodies control hotel assets, and they are seldom willing to give up the right of control that brings them benefits, even though some hotels are losing money. Reform of some basic disciplines of regulations is still needed to create a better business climate for hotel chain development in China.

Lack of Motivation and Drive

Traditional firms are conservative in ideology and new ideas, and lack vitality and sensitivity to changes in the environment and market. They are still backward in internal management and decision-making mechanism. Hotels belonging to government departments rely heavily on the political administrative system to form chains rather than the market mechanism. This mechanism is distorted in China in this transition period. Some firms cannot compete freely in a normal business environment, because government "owners" interfere from a nonbusiness perspective (e.g., they influence recruitment, choice of suppliers, etc.).

Market economy approaches have been tolerated for only a few years in China, and have only recently been encouraged. Hence appreciation and actual utilization of market economy mechanisms are far from mature. The administrative system of the planned economy is being dismantled step by step, while the market mechanism is not yet fully established. Some "firms" cannot be considered as a firm and cannot act as if a firm in the existing nonmarket environment. In addition, existing obstacles raise their transaction costs, for example, local protectionism and monopoly by some industries.

Hotel Ownership

Complexity and Diversity of Hotel Ownership Types

The issue of ownership and control over assets and operations is one of the central problems in the negotiation and subsequent use of hotel-management or partnership agreements (Saunders and Renaghan, 1992), especially in China, where hotel ownership is quite complex. In the "seventh five-year plan" (State Planning Commission, 1986-1990), a policy called "bringing into play the five sectors" was implemented to attract more capital, which meant that state, departments, collectives, and private capital owners were all encouraged to invest in the hotel and travel industry (He, 1992). This resulted in the intended acceleration of hotel development (Liu and Liu, 1993), but the complicated ownership resulting from decentralization led to a severe lack of coordination in decision making in hotel construction (Tisdell and Wen, 1991).

Dominance of the State-Owned Hotels

Decentralization resulted in a variety of different types of hotel ownership (Tisdell and Wen, 1991), now totaling nine different categories: state-owned, collective, private, alliance, shareholding cooperative, limited liability, limited liability shares, foreign-invested, and Hong Kong-, Macau-, and Taiwan-invested (CNTA, 2000, p. 92).

However, state ownership is still the dominant mode, accounting for 64 percent of total hotels and 61 percent of total rooms (CNTA, 2000). State ownership can cause many problems for chain affiliation, with the leading problems being failure to separate hotel management and ownership (Tisdell, 1990) and lack of effective monitoring of state assets.

Du and Dai (1998) analyzed the behavior of the state-owned hotels that restrict chain operation and found the following:

- The noncommercial objectives of the state-owned hotels restrict their renovation; the owner or its representative worries about losing benefits during the course of chain operation.
- The pressure of the vested interest group, including employees, retired employees, etc. affect operations.
- Ineffective monitoring of hotel management companies after contracting hotels to the management party is restrictive to growth.

It seems that hotel chain formation in China should start from the change of the ownership system. Wang (1998) suggested that an ownership trading market should be established, leading to restructuring of the assets of Chinese hotels (Xu, 1998; Wan and Hu, 1998).

Comparison between Different Ownership Types

Overseas-invested hotels have better performance than other hotels, as reflected in higher occupancy rates and higher annual average revenue per room of foreign-invested and Hong Kong/Macau/Taiwan-invested properties (Pine, 2002b). This is generally because overseas-invested hotels are usually operated by multinational hotel corporations according to the rules of market economy and international business practices.

Most state-owned hotels lack strategy in management; they pay more attention to the daily operation and management procedures, but neglect branding, corporate culture and innovation and, most important, the effective use of capital in the market.

Hotel Management Capability and Resources

Managerial Capacity

Since the hotel industry in China is a comparatively fledgling one, most local hotel chains are new players in the market and are still weak in providing satisfactory service to their client hotels. Many standard international business practices are unknown or unfamiliar within China (EIU, 1989). For example, strategies and expertise, such as standardization, branding, ecology programs, frequent guest programs, and strategic alliances are still new concepts. Information technology is another weak point, with only one indigenous chain having an online, real-time reservation system. Zou (1998) specified four severe problems of Chinese hotel chains: lack of marketing network and reservation system, lack of hotel managerial expertise, problems of the capital market and loans, and protectionism of local authorities.

The weakness of the environment for the Chinese hotel chain development made it difficult to get contracts from individual hotels and to expand. Most Chinese hotel owners would prefer self-management rather than contracting hotel management to an incapable party.

Resources for Chinese Hotel Companies

Improvement of management skills and the service provided by hotel management companies are key factors for chain growth and expansion. Further market segmentation and establishment of a central reservation system are major concerns of China's lodging industry (Yu, 1992). According to Horsburgh (1991), a hotel company should use its resources to develop its assets, core competence, knowledge, and the ability to learn to create and sustain a critical competitive advantage for hotel development, such as superior knowledge of brand management, real estate development, operation of management contracts, and franchising. The lack of necessary resources (e.g., human resources, capital, management expertise) makes it difficult for Chinese hotel chains to create their organizational capability.

Competition between Foreign and Local Hotel Chains

Presence of Foreign Hotel Companies

As globalization is an obvious trend, most giant hotel chains have expanded to China, attracted by its rapid economic growth and tourism development potential (Wise, 1993). Among the world's top 300 corporate chains ranked by *Hotels* magazine (Dela Cruz and Wolchuk,1999), about 10 percent have entered China, for example, Hilton, Hyatt, InterContinental Hotels, Shangri-La, Marriott, Accor, Club Med, Days Inn, and some megachains such as Starwood and Wyndham Worldwide.

The brands that already have a presence in China are in the higher category of hotels, mainly four and five star. Many of the brands held by these companies have not yet entered China, but they represent the diversity of operations and different market level experience of these companies. This is especially important in the budget market, two-star and below hotels, which will prove to be the biggest sector of China's hotel industry and for which a latent demand already exists from increasingly affluent and mobile domestic tourists: 784 million domestic travelers in 2001 with revenues of around $40 million (U.S.) (CNTA, 2002). Many hotel chains have set China as a strategic target for their future growth and have increased their stocks in this market.

Joint venture hotels account for only 10.22 percent of the hotels and 15.75 percent of hotel rooms, but generate 31.78 percent of the total hotel revenue in China (CNTA, 2000). Most of the joint venture hotels are managed by multinationals, whereas state-owned hotels have a worse performance in terms of room occupancy and average room revenues, as discussed previously.

Advantages for Foreign Companies

In China, the advantages of chain operation by international hotel management companies are significant. Once a hotel stops its contract with the chain, business is affected greatly. For example,

Starwood's distribution channel generates 60 percent of its hotels' revenues (Wang, 1998). China's hotel management companies are small in scale and unable to fulfill the potential advantages of chain operation. Most of the four- or five-star hotels are operated by international hotel chains, whereas local chains mostly operate three-star and below hotels (Shi, 1997). The most competitive advantages of multinational hotel corporations over local chains are economies of scale, management expertise, and technology, especially networking by their distribution channels and centralized reservation systems, which can directly lead the overseas tourists to chain hotels. In addition, foreign hotel chains entered the Chinese market earlier and dominated the market, enjoying favorable policies set by the Chinese government (EIU, 1989).

Competition between multinational hotel corporations and indigenous hotels is not fair, as foreign-invested hotels enjoy more preferential policies and treatment than indigenous hotels regarding taxation, tariff, foreign exchange, pricing, human resources policies, etc. This is an important reason why many investors seek foreign partners for joint venture and hire a foreign hotel management company.

CONCLUSIONS AND RECOMMENDATIONS

The hotel industry in China will need to grow, and grow significantly. China's entry into the World Trade Organization should open the door fully to foreign hotel companies, and these hotel companies are looking to the very significant growth potential in China. As most of these companies, especially the giant ones, involve the business formats of management contracting, franchising, or consortia, they need to continue growing to provide a meaningful increase in company revenues. China is a very obvious target for their necessary expansion.

At the same time, hoteliers within China are making great progress in adapting overseas hotel-operating and business concepts, and in initiating their own ideas. Local companies have learned a great deal by studying how foreign companies work within China. This process of technology transfer (Pine, 1992) started with attention to the physical facilities and service standards needed to match international hotel offerings. Attention was then given to the different management and business techniques used by foreign companies. Finally, local companies are now adapting hotel facilities and business formats to the particular needs and advantages of the Chinese environment. In addition to being able to match foreign companies in these three areas, local companies benefit from having excellent knowledge of the internal workings of the Chinese political, regulatory, financial, and social systems.

With China's increasingly important role as a major destination for international travelers and with its own internal growth in domestic travelers, vast expansion will be needed in hotel provision throughout the country. Much of that expansion will be achieved by the growth of existing local and international hotel chain companies as well as the creation of new ones, but an awareness and appreciation of the potential barriers to such expansion are crucial for the success of both local and foreign hotel companies.

In principle, the formation of hotel chains appears to be a logical way to develop and advance China's hotel industry, but care must be taken to fully understand and appreciate the full range of consequences and possibilities before fully committing to that direction. The following considerations are recommended:

- Ensure that any policy for chain development creates the most appropriate formats within the peculiar China context.
- Be fully aware of the intensely competitive business environment that exists, which is dominated globally by giant hotel companies.
- Appreciate the national and organizational differences in culture that determine differences in behavior and expectations of domestic travelers, hotel staff, and, especially, the large variety of types of owners.
- Understanding and appreciation of such differences are crucial for any foreign company considering entering the China domain.

APPENDIX 19.A. INTERVIEW QUESTIONS

Questions for Hotel Management Companies

1. Can you briefly describe the origins and historical development of your company?

2. What is the current situation of your hotel management company in terms of (a) size, (b) speed of expansion, and (c) performance?
3. What drives your company to expand and grow—internal and external factors?
4. Environment issues:
   - Do you scan the business environment when expanding? If you do, what factors influence the growth and expansion of your hotel management company?
   - How do government policies and regulations influence hotel chain development?
   - What could be improved in the environment for hotel chain development?
   - How do you evaluate the competition between hotel management companies?
   - How do you evaluate the competitiveness of Chinese hotel management companies versus foreign hotel management companies?
   - What do you think about the impact of China's WTO entry on hotel chains?
5. Ownership and mechanism:
   - What is the ownership type of your company?
   - How is the decision made for such an ownership system?
   - How does the ownership type affect the growth and expansion of your chain?
   - Are management rights separated from the ownership? Why or why not?
   - Which type of hotel would you like to manage? Why?
6. Formation issues:
   - How do you expand? For example, by direct investment, merger/acquisition, management contract, franchising, consortia, referral system, or any other?
   - Why do you use that form of expansion?
7. Management and operation issues:
   - Do you have a management model or management style in your company? If yes, can you describe it?
   - How do you view branding for hotel chains? Do you have a branding strategy? If yes, what is your branding strategy?
   - How do you finance chain development?
   - How do you operate and manage your hotel management company?
   - How about the application of technologies in your hotel chain?
   - How do you manage the individual hotels in the chain?
   - What are the factors influencing independent hotels joining your chain?
   - How is the effectiveness of your management in those hotels? What are the major achievements and barriers?

- What are the advantages and disadvantages of your company?
8. Strategy issues:
   - What factors influence the future expansion and growth of your company?
   - What are the future development plans and strategies of your company?

Questions for Independent Hotels

1. Briefly describe your hotel: its history, investment, facilities, and performance?
2. Are you willing to join a hotel chain? Why or why not?
3. How is the business environment of your hotel—internal and external?
4. How do you compare the differences between chain-operated hotels and independent hotels?
5. What are the major considerations in joining chain operation?
6. If joining a hotel chain, what considerations are used to choose a hotel management company?
7. Which way would you choose to join a chain? For example, by direct investment, merger/acquisition, management, franchise, consortia, referral system? Why?
8. What are the emerging issues in the operation and management of a hotel after joining a chain? Why is that important to your business?
9. How will you deal with the relationship with the hotel management company after they take on management of your hotel?
10. What would be the main influence on your hotel to join a chain?
11. What are the major difficulties or problems for your hotel business?
12. What is the plan or strategy for your hotel's future development?

REFERENCES

China National Tourism Association (CNTA) (2000). *The Yearbook of China Tourism Statistics*. Beijing, China: China Travel and Tourism Press.

China National Tourism Association (CNTA) (2001). *The Yearbook of China Tourism Statistics*. Beijing, China: China Travel and Tourism Press.

China National Tourism Association (CNTA) (2002). *The Yearbook of China Tourism Statistics*. Beijing, China: China Travel and Tourism Press.

Dela Cruz, T. and Wolchuk, S. (eds.) (1999). Hotels' 325: Mergers and acquisitions, albeit of smaller magnitude, still define the global lodging industry *Hotels, 33* (7). Available at: http://www.hotelsmag.com/archives/1999/07/hotel-giants-consortia-325.asp

Denzin, N.K. and Lincoln Y.S. (eds.) (1994). *Handbook of Qualitative Research.* Thousand Oaks, CA: Sage.

Du, J. and Dai, B. (1998). Market base and development strategies of the national hotel groups. Paper presented at the Seminar on Theories and Practices of Conglomerates in Chinese Hotels, November 20-22, Beijing, China.

Economic Intelligence Unit (EIU) (1989). Foreign investment in China's hotel sector. *Travel & Tourism Analyst, 3:* 17-32.

He, G.W. (ed.) (1992). *China Reform Series: Reform of Tourism Mechanism.* Dalian, China: Dalian Publishing House.

Horsburgh, S. (1991). Resources in the international hotel industry: A framework for analysis. *International Journal of Contemporary Hospitality Management, 3*(4): 30-36.

Howe, C. (1985). Possibilities for using a qualitative research approach in the sociological study of leisure. *Journal of Leisure Research, 17:* 212-224.

Kvale, S. (1983). The qualitative research interview: A phenomenological and hermeneutical understanding, *Journal of Phenomenological Psychology, 14:* 171-196.

Liu, Z.Q. and Liu, J.C. (1993). Assessment of the hotel rating system in China. *Tourism Management,* December: 440-452.

McCracken, G. (1988). *The Long Interview.* Newbury Park, CA: Sage.

Penrose, E. (1995). *The Theory of the Growth of the Firm,* 3rd edition, New York: Oxford University Press.

Pine, R. (1992). Technology transfer in the hotel industry. *International Journal of Hospitality Management, 11*(1): 3-22.

Pine, R. (2002a). China's hotel industry: Serving a massive market. *Cornell Hotel and Restaurant Administration Quarterly, 43*(3): 61-70.

Pine, R. (2002b). Performance comparisons of hotels in China. In Chon, K. and Zhang Qiu, H. (eds.), *Conference Proceedings: The 8th APTA Annual Conference* (pp. 603-609) July 10-13,Dalian, China.

Saunders, H.A. and Renaghan, L.M. (1992). Southeast Asia: A new model for hotel development. *The Cornell Hotel and Restaurant Administration Quarterly,* October: 16-23.

Shi, X. (1997). Perspectives of hotel management market. *Hotels China and Overseas, 4:* 5-6.

State Planning Commission (1986-1990). *Seventh Five-Year Plan of National Economy and Society Development.* Beijing, China: State Planning Commission.

State Statistics Bureau (1998). A comparison of economy increase rate between China and other countries and regions in the world. *People's Daily,* September 25, p. 1.

Tisdell, C. (1990). Separation of ownership and management, markets, their failure and efficiency: Possible implications for China's economic reforms. *Asian Economies,* June: 41-55.

Tisdell, C. and Wen, J. (1991). Foreign tourism as an element in PR China's economic development strategy. *Tourism Management,* March: 55-67.

Wan, D.M. and Hu, J.W. (1998). The development of Chinese national hotel groups and market competition. Paper presented at the Seminar on Theories and Practices of Conglomerates in Chinese Hotels, November 20-22, Beijing, China.

Wang, Y.Z. (1998). Study on the trading system of property rights for Chinese hotel conglomeration. Paper presented at the Seminar on Theories and Practices of Conglomerates in Chinese Hotels, November 20-22, Beijing, China.

Wise, B. (1993). Hotel chains in the Asia-Pacific region. *Travel & Tourism Analyst,* 4: 57-73.

World Tourism Organization (WTO) (1999). *Tourism 2020 Vision: Intraregional and Long-Haul Flows,* Volume 3: East Asia/Pacific. Madrid, Spain: World Tourism Organization.

World Tourism Organization (WTO) (2000a). *Tourism Highlights 2000.* Madrid, Spain: World Tourism Organization.

World Tourism Organization (WTO) (2000b). *Tourism Market Trends: Europe 2000.* Madrid, Spain: World Tourism Organization.

Xu, D.K. (1998). Restructuring assets and management: Views on national hotel conglomeration. Paper presented at the Seminar on Theories and Practices of Conglomerates in Chinese Hotels, November 20-22, Beijing, China.

Yu, L. (1992). Hotel development and structures in China. *International Journal of Hospitality Management, 11*(2): 99-110.

Yu, L. (1999). *The International Hospitality Business: Management and Operations.* Englewood Cliffs, NJ: Prentice-Hall.

Zou, T.Q. (1998). Strategies of Chinese hotel groups: Development model and policy guidance. Paper presented at the Seminar on Theories and Practices of Conglomerates in Chinese Hotels, November 20-22, Beijing, China.

Chapter 20

Employee Behavioral Intentions Toward Adoption of Information and Communication Technology

Terry Lam
Vincent Cho
Tom Baum

INTRODUCTION

Information and communication technology (ICT) has profound impacts on hotels, as a large amount of information must be processed and communicated among internal and external customers. The hotel industry extensively relies on information and communication technology to improve employees' productivity and efficiency, and accordingly to improve customer satisfaction.

Previous studies have shown that information and communication technology plays an important role in improving the effectiveness of the business operations and in enhancing customer satisfaction (e.g., Zahra and Covin, 1993; Hoof et al., 1995; Powell and Dent-Micallef, 1997; Byrd and Turner, 2001). However, previous studies found that new information and communication technology would not be fully accepted if employee factors are overlooked (e.g., Ross et al., 1996; Lee and Miller, 1999; Roepke et al., 2000). Such barriers of the human factors hindering successful implementation of information and communication technology in an organization includes employees' willingness and ability and managers' support. Thompson and Richardson (1996) also lamented that technologies are designed, developed, and implemented with little or no attention to the needs of em-

Global Cases on Hospitality Industry
© 2008 by The Haworth Press, Taylor & Francis Group. All rights reserved.
doi:10.1300/5923_20

ployees or to the impact that the technologies might have on the workforce. It appears that the impact of technological change on human behavior has not been extensively studied, and has not received sufficient attention in academic literature (Baker and Riley, 1994). Although the hotel industry is a labor-intensive sector, hotel managers are willing to increase technology investment to enhance their business thrust on employee productivity. Yet, disregarding human aspects will affect effective use of information technology (Hoof et al., 1995). Therefore, this study filled the gap by investigating employee factors based on the theory of planned behavior developed by Fishbein and Ajzen (1975) toward adoption of information technology in hotels. The objectives of this study were the following:

1. To identify the importance of attitudinal attributes affecting ICT adoption
2. To assess the relationship between attitude and ICT adoption
3. To assess the relationship between subjective norm and ICT adoption
4. To examine the impacts of attitude and subjective norm on behavioral intention of ICT adoption

LITERATURE REVIEW

Theory of Reasoned Action

Previous studies have used behavioral intention models or behavioral decision theories to explain usage of information systems (e.g., Davis, 1989; Liao and Landry, 2000), and results further show that behavioral intentions are significantly and positively correlated with actual behavior. The findings imply that an effective use of information technology relies on positive intention toward adoption of ICT. In the context of social science study, Fishbein and Ajzen's (1975) developed and refined the theory of reasoned action (TRA) over time (Ajzen and Fishbein, 1980; Fishbein and Ajzen, 1975). This theory has been utilized by researchers to investigate human behavior in the disciplines of social psychology (Conner et al., 2001; Buttle and Bok, 1996), and was found in the literature to support in the prediction of various social behaviors.

According to Fishbein and Ajzen (1975), an individual's intention to perform a specific act, or a behavioral intention with respect to a given stimulus object, in a given situation is a function of the individual's attitude toward the behavior and his or her subjective norm. Subjective norm (SN), as another determinant of attitude, is a perception of general social pressures to perform or not to perform a particular act. Therefore, individuals are more likely to perform an act if they perceive the existence of greater social pressure from salient referents to perform that act.

Attitude

TRA postulates a set of relations among attitude, subjective norm, and behavioral intention. Attitude is an individual's feeling of the favorableness or unfavorableness of his or her performance of the behavior. According to Fishbein and Ajzen (1975), an attitude is the function of behavioral beliefs and evaluation of outcomes. Behavioral belief is one's belief in performing a specific behavior that will lead to a specific consequence, and evaluation of outcome is one's assessment of that specific consequence. An attitude is, "an individual's disposition to respond favorably or unfavorably to an object, person, institution, or event" (Ajzen, 1989, p. 241). A hierarchical model, which includes cognition (beliefs), affect (feelings), and conation (intentions) as first-order factors and attitude as a single second-order factor has served as a starting point for many attitude-behavior theories.

Attitudes toward information systems have been extensively studied in the past. For instance, Liao and Landry (2000) argued that employee's attitude toward the acceptance of ICT would affect the intention of ICT adoption. Thus, a hypothesis (H1) was suggested that attitudes are related to the intentions of adopting ICT (H1).

Subjective Norms

Subjective norms are important in an organizational setting (Taylor and Todd, 1995). According to Fishbein and Ajzen (1975), subjective norms refer to perceived pressures on a person to perform a given behavior and the person's motivation to comply with those pressures, and a person's behavioral intentions were found to be correlated with subjective norms. A number of studies have supported such correlation in the context of social psychology (e.g. Conner et al., 2001; Buttle and Bok, 1996). Fishbein and Ajzen (1975) further state that subjective norm is related to the normative beliefs that a person comply with expectations from other people, such as a person's family or friends, supervisor, or society at large. Social norms represent perceived external pressures to use (or not to use) the system. Individuals who perceive that others expect that they should use the system will have high score on intentions to use the system, even when they may personally not feel positive about the system. Thus, the social normative component captures the collective effect of these influences on behavioral intention. Lucas and Spitler (1999) and Venkatesh and Davis (2000) reported that organizational variables such as social norms are more important than users' perceptions of the information technology in predicting system usage and acceptance. A hypothesis (H2) was suggested in this case that subjective norms toward ICT directly affect intentions to use ICT. The model in Figure 20.1 presents the hypothesized interrelationships among the variables described previously.

METHODOLOGY

The population of the study consisted of employees of international hotels in Hangzhou of China and Hong Kong. A self-adminis-

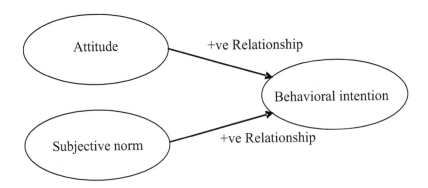

FIGURE 20.1. Model of Interrelationships among Attitude, Subjective Norm, and Behavioral Intention of ICT Adoption

tered questionnaire was used to collect data. The questionnaires were distributed to respondents via their human resources managers. Respondents were asked to complete the questionnaire upon receipt at the time in the human resources office. The questionnaire was developed based on a comprehensive literature review. Based on Ajzen and Fishbein (1980), attitude was measured by five statements using a five-point semantic differential scale. Four statements were used to evaluate subjective norm, ranging from strongly agree (5) and strongly disagree (1). Behavioral intention was measured by three items with a five-point Likert scale, again ranging from strongly agree (5) to strongly disagree (1). A pilot test was conducted to test the validity and reliability of the questionnaire with thirty-three hotel employees randomly selected from the hotels in Hong Kong. In the pilot test, the reliability coefficients (Cronbach's alpha) for the questionnaire constructs ranged from .83 to .95, which exceeded the recommended satisfactory level of .70 (Nunnally and Bernstein, 1994).

Scale reliability analysis was used to measure the internal consistency. Descriptive statistics were used to measure the degree of attitude toward ICT adoption. Correlations were used to measure the relationship between respective attitude and subjective norm and behavioral intention of ICT adoption. Linear multiple regression was used to assess relative importance of the attitude and subjective norm in predicting behavioral intention of ICT adoption. The relative importance of the dimensions was based on their beta weights.

FINDINGS AND DISCUSSION

Of the 788 questionnaires distributed, 678 were received. Among 678 completed questionnaires, 458 were usable. About one-third of respondents were from of the front office (30.4 percent), followed by sales and marketing (24.5 percent), human resources (14.7 percent), and finance (14.4 percent). A few of respondents were from housekeeping (7.5 percent), food and beverage (3.5 percent), and others (4.2 percent). Females dominated the sample (66.9 percent). The majority of respondents were operational employees (58.3 percent), followed by supervisors (36.1 percent), and assistant managers or above (4.6 percent).

As shown in Table 20.1, the reliability coefficients (Cronbach's alpha) of the constructs ranged from .813 to .910, which exceeded the recommended acceptable level of .70 (Nunnally and Bernstein, 1994). This indicates that the measuring instrument was reliable.

Table 20.2 shows that hotel employees will tend to adopt ICT if they perceive that the technology is relevant, significant, and important to their job performance. Relatively, whether ICT is attractive or interesting was not that essential factors leading to a high intention of ICT adoption.

TABLE 20.1. Reliability analysis of observed variables

	Mean	Standard deviation	Cronbach's alpha
Attitude			0.876
• IT is important to my job,	4.10	0.92	
• IT is relevant to my job	4.12	0.89	
• IT is trifle	4.12	0.97	
• IT is interesting	3.83	0.93	
• IT is attractive	3.91	0.96	
Subjective Norm			0.813
• My supervisor always encourages me to use information systems	3.89	0.70	
• My colleagues think that I should use information systems	3.79	0.61	
• My guests perceive using information systems to be useful in a hotel	3.76	0.71	
• My hotel manager believes that there are advantages of using information systems	3.90	0.79	
Behavioral Intention			0.910
• I intend to work with IT more increasingly in the future	3.61	0.74	
• I want to use IT for my work	3.54	0.77	
• It is likely that I will use IT for my future work	3.92	0.69	

TABLE 20.2. Means of attitudinal attributes

	Attitudinal Attributes	Mean	SD
1.	Relevant to my job performance	4.12	.89
2.	Significant to my job	4.12	.97
3.	Importance to me in the workplace	4.10	.92
4.	Attractive ICT	3.91	.96
5.	Interesting ICT	3.83	.93

Note: SD = standard deviation.

Means, standard deviations, and correlations among the three measuring scales are shown in Table 20.3. Significant correlations (at $p <$ .01) existed between behavioral intention of ICT adoption and respective attitude (a = .39) and subjective norm (a = .27). Thus, the more positive the attitude and the higher degree the subjective norm, the higher the intention of ICT adoption will be. Furthermore, social pressure from the referent group to the employees did have an influence on their behavioral intention. This referent group might include immediate supervisors, team members, colleagues, and family members. It can be concluded that both the hypotheses (H1 and H2) received support in this study.

Table 20.4 depicts the results of stepwise regression with the nonsignificant variables. The coefficient of determination R^2 is significant at .01 (F = 58.55, df = 2,443, p < .01). The result shows that 20.9 percent of the variance in the behavioral intention of ICT adoption is explained by the two independent variables of attitude and of subjective norm. The low percentage shows that some other unknown factors may be influencing the behavioral intention in the model. Based on the beta values, the conclusion can be drawn that the impact of attitude is slightly greater than that of subjective norm in predicting behavioral intention, and the two variables are positively related to the intention. The results may provide an indication for hotel managers that those "most important persons" to employees can play an important role in influencing the latter on their intention to adopt ICT. This may suggest that managers should ensure that those important persons provide positive influence on the employees. The influence may be obtained through encouragement and counseling.

TABLE 20.3. Mean, Standard Deviations, and Correlation Matrix (N = 458)

Variables	Mean	SD	1	2	3
1. Attitude	4.03	.75	—		
2. Subjective norm	3.83	.51	.08	—	
3. Behavioral intention of ICT adoption	3.69	.57	.39*	.27*	—

*p < .01.

TABLE 20.4. Stepwise Regression of Behavioral Intention with Independent Variables

R	R Square	Adjusted R Square	Standard error	F(58.55)	p-value
0.457	0.209	0.205	0.508	58.55	0.000*
	Unstandard-ized coeffi-cient B	Standard error	Standardized coefficient. beta	T	p-value
(Constant)	1.522	0.217	—	7.018	0.000*
Attitude	0.278	0.032	0.367	8.655	0.000*
Subjective norm	0.275	0.048	0.243	5.723	0.000*

*the significant level (α) < .01

CONCLUSION AND IMPLICATIONS

The hypothesized research model explained behavioral intention of adopting ICT by hotel employees in China moderately well. Both attitude and subjective norm were related to behavioral intention of adopting ICT. The study has provided some preliminary evidence concerning employees' psychological factors to ICT adoption. Based on these findings, a number of salient implications were suggested for hotel managers to consider. First, relevant training should be provided for employees to improve their competency in using ICT, especially during the early stage of implementation of new ICT in hotels. Hotels should work closely with trainers of ICT suppliers to provide on-the-job and off-the-job training. Second, those persons who are considered by the employees as most important should be encouraged to provide support and motivation during the early stage of ICT implementation. Hotel managers are likely those important persons. Thus hotel managers should counsel their employees as soon as they have problems with ICT adoption. They should also provide continuous feedback, support, and encouragement for employees so that they can master the technological skills within a short period of time.

Limitations of the study included the limited sampling frame. Data were collected only in Hangzhou, China, and results might not be representative of the general hotel employees in China. Another limitation includes the convenience sampling method used to select subjects, so the results may not be generalizable to other samples in China.

REFERENCES

Ajzen, I. (1989). Attitude structure and behavior. In A. Pratkanis, S. Breckler, and A. Greenwald (eds.), *Attitude Structure and Function* (pp. 241-274). Hillsdale, NJ: Laurence Erlbaum Associates.

Ajzen, I. and Fishbein, M. (1980). *Understanding Attitudes and Predicting Social Behavior.* Englewood Cliffs, NJ: Prentice-Hall.

Baker, M. and Riley, M. (1994). New perspectives on productivity in hotels: Some advances and new direction. *International Journal of Hospitality Management, 13*(4): 297-311.

Buttle, F. and Bok, B. (1996). Hotel marketing strategy and the theory of reasoned action. *International Journal of Contemporary Hospitality Management, 8*(3): 5-10.

Byrd, T.A. and Turner, E.T. (2001). An exploratory examination of the relationship between flexible IT infrastructure and competitive advantage. *Information and Management, 39:* 41-52.

Conner, M., Kirk, S.F.L., Cade, J.E., and Barrett, J.H. (2001). Why do women use dietary supplements? The use of the theory of planned behavior to explore beliefs about their use. *Social Science and Medicine, 52:* 621-633.

Davis, F.D. (1989). Perceived usefulness, perceived ease of use, and user acceptance of information technology. *MIS Quarterly, 13:* 319-340.

Fishbein, M. and Ajzen, I. (1975). *Belief, Attitude, Intention, and Behavior: An Introduction to Theory and Research.* Boston, MA: Addison-Wesley Pub. Co.

Hoof, H.B.V., Collins, G.R., Combrink, T.E., and Verbeeten, M. J. (1995). Technology needs and perceptions. *Cornell Hotel and Restaurant Administration Quarterly,* October: 64-69.

Lee, J. and Miller, D. (1999). People matter: Commitment to employees, strategy and performance in Korean firms. *Strategic Management Journal, 20:* 579-593.

Liao, Z. and Landry Jr., R. (2000). An empirical study on organizational acceptance of new information system's in a commercial back environment. *Proceedings of the 33rd Hawaii International Conference on System Sciences,* January 4-7. Los Alamitos, CA: Computer Society Press. Available at: http://csdl2.computer.org/comp/proceedings/hicss/2000/0493/02/04932015.pdf.

Lucas, H.C. and Spitler, V.K. (1999). Technology use and performance: A field study of broker workstations. *Decisions Sciences, 30*(2): 291-311.

Nunnally, J.C. and Bernstein, I.H. (1994). *Psychometric theory,* 3rd Edition. New York: McGraw-Hill.

Powell, T.C. and Dent-Micallef, A. (1997). Information technology as competitive advantage: The role of human, business and technology resources. *Strategic Management Journal, 18*(5): 375-405.

Roepke, R., Agarwal, R., and Ferratt, T. W. (2000). Aligning the IT human resource with business vision: The leadership initiative at 3m. *MIS Quarterly, 24*(2): 327-353.

Ross, J.W., Beath, C.M., and Goodhue, D.L. (1996). Develop long-term competitiveness through IT assets. *MIT Sloan Management Review, 38*(1)*:* 31-42.

Taylor, S. and Todd, P.A. (1995). Understanding information technology usage: A test of competing models. *Information Systems Research, 6*(2): 144-176.

Thompson, J. and Richardson, B. (1996). Strategic and competitive success: Towards a model of the comprehensively competent organization. *Management Decision, 34*(2): 5-14.

Venkatesh, V. and Davis, F.D. (2000). A theoretical extension of the technology acceptance model: Four longitudinal field studies. *Management Science, 46*(2): 186-204.

Zahra, S. and Covin, J. (1993). Business strategy, technology policy, and firm performance. *Strategic Management Journal, 14*(6): 451-478.

Chapter 21

Improving the Effectiveness of Hotel Loyalty Programs through Data Mining

Vishnuprasad Nagadevara

INTRODUCTION

The hospitality product is essentially a service experienced by the customer. The industry creates expectations, and these expectations are further influenced by prior experience and opinions of friends and associates. The intangible product of service is reinforced by the tangibles such as food, physical comforts, space, etc. Traditionally, the emphasis in the industry had been on acquiring new customers. Of late a strong attempt to retain customers has been made and a realization has occurred that the lifetime value of the customer is more important in improving profits (Mukhopadhyay, 2001). It is not enough to retain the customers; they need to be drawn into the hotel repeatedly. To achieve this end, various hotels started loyalty programs patterned on the lines of "frequent flier" programs of the airlines.

It is known that frequent visitors account for only 11 percent of all hotel guests, but they contribute to about 44 percent of the revenue. According to a survey conducted by Paul Brown of McKinsey & Company (now president of Expedia North America), the frequent travel segment represents $40 to $50 billion (U.S.) in revenues each year (Brown, 2004). These guests spend only part of that money in their preferred hotel chains, but a considerable percentage (estimated to be about 40 percent) is spent in other hotels. Many of these customers are known to be members of more than one loyalty program. Persuading such customers to return to one or two favorite chains can add considerable increases to revenues. To achieve this objective, the

Global Cases on Hospitality Industry
© 2008 by The Haworth Press, Taylor & Francis Group. All rights reserved.
doi:10.1300/5923_21

hotel chains should make their loyalty programs more focused and make them more attractive to members. This requires appropriate classification of the members (proper segmentation) as well as understanding of the customers in each of these segments.

Many types of loyalty programs are offered by different hotel chains. For example, Hilton Hotels has a loyalty program called "Hilton HHonors." The members are offered a dedicated reservation service with a special number. The members get special attention, especially during peak periods. Since the details of the members are already available (collected at the time of enrolment), the check-in process is expedited and members are checked in quickly when they arrive at the hotel. Similarly, the members can avail express checkout. It is also possible for the members to avail late checkout (beyond the normal checkout time), within reasonable limits. Other facilities include eFolio (hotel bill organization online), free stay for the spouse on every qualifying HHonors stay, and online communications with respect to the reward points.

The HHonors program is linked with airline miles so that the members can earn both hotel reward points as well as airline miles. The program offers a certain amount of flexibility by combining the reward points with air miles. The reward points can be earned with the following options:

1. *HHonors points and variable miles:* Earn at the rate of 10 HHonors points + 1 airline mile per eligible U.S. dollar spent.
2. *HHonors points and fixed miles:* Earn 10 HHonors points per eligible U.S. dollar spent + 500 miles per stay.
3. *HHonors points and HHonors points:* Earn 10 HHonors points + 5 bonus points per eligible U.S. dollar spent.

Members can avail any of the previous options and change the preferences any time without any restrictions.

The HHonors program offers four different levels of membership. The more frequent the stay at Hilton hotels, the more generous the HHonors benefits become, including HHonors point bonuses, complimentary room upgrades, and health club privileges. These levels are Blue, Silver VIP, Gold VIP, and Diamond VIP (Hilton HHonors, 2007).

Another type of loyalty program is offered by Taj Hotels, Resorts, and Palaces. The program, called Taj InnerCircle, has three membership levels namely Blue, Silver, and Gold. All members begin with Blue membership. As the members earn more points, they move up from Blue through Silver to Gold. The level of service benefits increases with each membership level.

As a Silver Member of the InnerCircle, members enjoy the following benefits when they check in at a participating Taj hotel:

- They are greeted with flowers and fruit in their rooms.
- Check-in and departure formalities are easier and faster.
- Members receive a 10 percent discount on room rates at leisure hotels.
- Members receive a 10 percent discount on telephone and fax usage.
- Members receive a 15 percent discount on laundry services.
- Members receive a 20 percent discount on business center services.
- Members can receive double occupancy benefits at no extra cost.
- Members are entitled to a priority waiting list.
- Members enjoy free use of the health club and can take a complimentary steam bath or sauna.

Gold members enjoy the following additional benefits:

- Points are accrued at 1 point for every Rs. 80 (approximately $1.98 [U.S.]) spent (net of taxes).
- A nonalcoholic welcome drink is provided.
- Preferred daily newspapers are given at metro hotels.

The InnerCircle program offers a special experience to the members along with the other benefits in terms of discounts and free room nights (Hilton HHonors, 2007).

Although these programs differ in the approach, they aim to increase their share of customer spending, and to do so it is important to identify the high spenders. The hotel should be in a position to classify, a priori, members into different categories and predict their potential spending. Once such predictive models are generated, the characteristics that differentiate each of the categories need to be identified so that a clear understanding of each of these categories or segments exists. The classification of the members into different categories is done in this chaper, using artificial neural networks.

ARTIFICIAL NEURAL NETWORKS

Artificial neural networks (ANNs) are generally based on the concepts of the human (or biological) neural network consisting of neurons, which are interconnected by the processing elements. ANNs are composed of two main structures, namely the nodes and the links. The nodes correspond to the neurons and the links correspond to the links between neurons. An ANN accepts the values of inputs into what are called input nodes. This set of nodes is also referred to as the input layer, as shown in Figure 21.1. These input values are then multiplied by a set of numbers (also called as weights) that are stored in the links. These values, after multiplication, are added together to be-

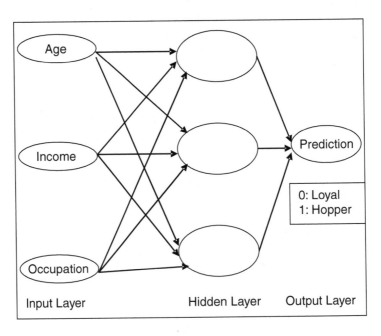

FIGURE 21.1. Artificial Neural Network

come inputs to the set of nodes that are to the right of the input nodes. This layer of nodes is usually referred to as the hidden layer. Many ANNs contain multiple hidden layers, each feeding into the next layer. Finally, the values from last hidden layer are fed into an output node, where a special mapping or threshold function is applied and the resulting number is mapped to the prediction.

The ANN is created by presenting the network with inputs from many records whose outcomes are already known. For example, the data on age, income, and occupation of the first customer (first record) are inputted into the input layer. These values are fed into the hidden layer, and after processing (by combining these values using appropriate weights), the prediction is made at the output layer. If the prediction made by the ANN matches with the actual known status of the customer (either loyal or hopper), then the prediction is good and the ANN proceeds to the next record. If the prediction is wrong, then the extent of error (expressed in numerical values) is apportioned back into the links and the hidden nodes. In other words, the values of the weights at each link are modified based on the extent of error in prediction. This process is referred to as backward propagation.

The artificial neural networks are found to be effective in detecting unknown relationships. ANNs have been applied in many service industries, such as health (to identify the length of stay and hospital expenses) (Nagadevara, 2004) and airlines (Chatfield, 1998), and ANNs are used in this chapter for predicting the categories of the members of the loyalty program.

DATA

The data was obtained from a major hotel chain in India that has a loyalty program. The database contained information on 752 members. Data with respect to many demographic characteristics such as gender, age, marital status, nationality, and employment status (called VIP code depending on whether the member belonged to senior or junior management) was collected from each member at the time of enrollment into the loyalty program. In addition, the preferences, if any, of the members with respect to the type of newspapers, type of room, type of bed, smoking or nonsmoking, were also identified. Data on revenue generated from each member on various services in the hotel was also obtained. The various services involved in generating the revenue are food and beverages (outdoor, chambers, coffee shop, bar, pastry and cake shop, lounge, nightclub, restaurants), fax and business center, domestic as well as international long distance telephone, beauty salon and health club, and, finally, room nights. The room nights are also classified based on the room type, such as budget rooms, economy rooms, executive rooms, villas, etc. The information on the length of stay as well as the number of visits was also available. The number of complaints received under different categories was also recorded.

PROFILE OF THE MEMBERS

The members were predominantly male, with female members accounting for only 7 percent. About one-third of the members were married, as shown in Table 21.1. The majority of the members were middle aged, belonging to the age group between 40 years and 60 years. Marital status appears to be influenced by the age group, as reflected by a high value of chi-square ($c^2 = 14.99$ with 4 degrees of freedom). As expected, the proportion of married members increased with age group. At the same time it may be noted that the marital status was well below the national average for these age groups. About 50 percent of the members are of Indian nationality, whereas another 30 percent are from the UK and the rest of Europe. The members from United States and Canada accounted for only 11 percent. Very few of the members belonged to other nationalities. More than 60 percent of the members belonged to the senior management cadre.

RESULTS

The database had information on the revenues collected from different services, such as food and beverages, laundry, room nights, fax, and other facilities. The total revenue from all of the sources is clubbed together for each member. The members are classified into three categories: high, medium, and low spenders, depending on the total revenue contributed. The categories are created using equidepth binning. The objective of the binning is to achieve equal number in each category, but because of ties at the point of categorization, the

TABLE 21.1. Distribution of the Members Based on Marital Status and Age Group

Age Group		Marital Status		
		Single	Married	Total
Less than 30	Number	50	9	59
	Percentage	84.75	15.25	100.00
30 to 40	Number	81	23	104
	Percentage	77.88	22.12	100.00
40 to 50	Number	129	67	196
	Percentage	65.82	34.18	100.00
50 to 60	Number	110	75	185
	Percentage	59.46	40.54	100.00
More than 60	Number	76	49	125
	Percentage	60.80	39.20	100.00
Total	Number	446	223	669
	Percentage	66.67	33.33	100.00

number of members in each category are slightly different. The low spender category has 259 members, the medium spender category has 276 members, and the high spender category has 217 members, as shown in Table 21.2.

These categories or classes of members are used as the prediction variable for the artificial neural network. The variables used for prediction are classified into five groups: room related, member segment, demographic characteristics, member preferences, and nature of complaints. The room-related variables consisted of budget nights, club nights, executive nights, and health club. The member segment variables are corporate, conference, compliment, group, leisure, event, and long-stay segments. The demographic characteristics included age, gender, marital status, nationality, and VIP code. The member preferences consisted of newspaper preference (Indian, foreign, or financial newspaper), bed preference, special interests, room preference, smoking preference, and view preference. The nature of complaints are classified into those relating to front office, housekeeping, food and beverage, and maintenance.

The artificial neural network was generated using the previous variables. The network was generated using IBM's data mining software Intelligent Miner. The predictive accuracy of the model is presented in Table 21.3.

The ANN was able to predict the categories with an overall accuracy level of 85.64 percent. It misclassified 12.43 percent and unable to identify the categories for only about 1.73 percent of the cases.

Most often the mathematical relationships developed by the ANNs are complex and not available to the user. As a result these are treated as black boxes, to be used only to obtain the prediction results. Nevertheless, it is important to know the relative importance of each of the variables in predicting the categories. The software used provides the sensitivity of the prediction with respect to each of the variables, and this can be viewed as an indicator of the relative importance of the variables in question. Table 21.4 summarizes this information, with variables grouped under each of the five groups mentioned earlier and the corresponding sensitivity.

Among the room-related variables, the club nights and executive nights appear to be most important. Similarly, among the member

TABLE 21.2. Details of Different Categories of Members

Sl No	Category	Revenue range	Number
1	Low spender	Less than Rs. 7,00,000	259
2	Medium spender	Rs. 7,00,000 to Rs. 10,00,000	276
3	High spender	More than Rs. 10,00,000	217

TABLE 21.3. Prediction Accuracy of the Artificial Neural Network

			Prediction				
	Category	Item	Low	Medium	High	Unknown	Total
	Low	Number	239	15	4	1	259
		Percentage	92.20	5.70	1.50	0.30	100
Actual	Medium	Number	31	228	12	5	276
		Percentage	11.20	82.60	4.30	1.80	100
	High	Number	8	14	188	7	217
		Percentage	3.60	6.40	86.60	3.20	100

TABLE 21.4. Sensitivity of Prediction with Respect to Different Variables

Room related		Member segment		Demographic characteristics		Member preferences		Nature of complaints	
Budget nights	3.5	Corporate	10.2	Age	5.1	Indian newspaper	0.8	Front office	3.0
Club nights	7.6	Conference	3.4	Gender	1.6	Foreign newspaper	0.6	Housekeeping	0.6
Executive nights	4.5	Compliment	5.2	Marital status	0.9	Financial newspaper	0.8	Food and beverage	2.2
Health club	3.1	Group	0.6	Nationality	5.4	Type of bed	0.7	Maintenance	2.9
		Leisure	7.5	VIP code	1.1	Type of room	1.4		
		Event	4.7			Special interest	0.6		
		Long Stay	15.7			Smoking	1.8		
						Nonsmoking	1.0		
						View	0.8		

segment, long-stay and corporate segments are most important. Age and nationality are most important among the demographic characteristics. The variables with respect to member preferences do not seem to be having a large impact on the categorization. On the other hand, complaints related to the front office and maintenance are most important.

The previous analysis helps the hotel chain in classifying each member into one of the three categories, that is, high, medium, or low spenders. It should be kept in mind that this classification is not a one-time exercise, and the classification needs to be reviewed regularly as new data become available. For example, each stay with the hotel, type of room for the current stay, and each new complaint is additional data, and the classification needs to be revised based on the new information, accordingly. The objective is obviously to move the members up the value pyramid. In other words, the strategy of the hotel chain is to move the low spenders into the medium-spender category and the medium spenders into high-spender category. In order to achieve this, the hotel chain needs to understand the members in each category. Some of the distinguishing features of the three categories are discussed.

The members from UK and Europe have the highest percentage in the high-spender category, while the members from India have the highest percentage in the low-spender category, as shown in Table 21.5. A large percentage of the members from the United States, Canada, and other countries are concentrated in the medium-spender category. In other words, more concentration needs to be placed on the Indian members to move them up to high-spender category. Little more than 25 percent of the members who are single are in the high-spender category. At the same time, about 35 percent of the members who are married are in the high-spender category. One of the benefits of the loyalty program is free stay for the spouse during the qualifying stay of the member. This facility is likely giving dividends by pushing more married members toward the high-spender category. Obviously the loyalty program needs to create strategies aimed at the members who are single in order to push them up to high-spender category. Similarly, the loyalty program needs to concentrate on members belonging to junior management.

The spending pattern of each of the categories of members can be analyzed to identify appropriate strategies for encouraging members to move into the high-spender category. The data with respect to reve-

TABLE 21.5. Distribution of Members Based on Demographic Characteristics

	Member Category			
	Low	Medium	High	Total
Nationality				
Indian	36.89%	37.16%	25.96%	100.00%
US & Canada	34.15%	37.80%	28.05%	100.00%
UK & Europe	31.96%	33.33%	34.70%	100.00%
Others	30.59%	42.35%	27.06%	100.00%
Marital status				
Single	36.15%	37.50%	26.35%	100.00%
Married	30.60%	34.91%	34.48%	100.00%
VIP code				
Senior management	33.62%	35.55%	30.84%	100.00%
Junior management	36.10%	37.91%	25.99%	100.00%

nue earned from different services such as laundry, food and beverages, fax and business center, etc. are available. A simple analysis of the revenue from laundry and continental restaurant is carried out. Table 21.6 presents the data on the revenue earned from the members in these two services. It can be seen from the table that 53 percent of the high spenders contributed to more than Rs. 30,000 ($\approx$ $740.74) per member with respect to laundry services, whereas the corresponding percentage for the low spenders is only 8.11 percent. Similarly, more than 33 percent of the high spenders contribute to more than Rs. 10,000 ($\approx$ $246.91) per member with respect to continental restaurant. The corresponding percentages for the low spenders and medium spenders are 14 percent and 21 percent respectively. In addition, room service is as significantly different between the member categories. If this information is to be strategized, the policy is to attract low-spender category members more toward the continental restaurants and offer enough incentives for them to use more laundry services. At the same time, strategizing on the food and beverages from room service unless a differentiating strategy could be created to increase the revenue from room service as a whole.

TABLE 21.6. Revenue Earned from Laundry and Continental Restaurant

Range (Rs.)	Low	Medium	High	All
		Laundry		
Nil	11.20%	6.88%	2.30%	7.05%
Up to 10,000	45.17%	30.43%	17.05%	31.65%
10,000-30,000	35.52%	43.48%	27.19%	36.04%
> 30,000	8.11%	19.20%	53.46%	25.27%
		F & B: Continental restaurant		
Nil	55.21%	53.62%	37.33%	49.47%
Up to 10,000	30.12%	25.00%	29.49%	28.06%
> 10,000	14.67%	21.38%	33.18%	22.47%
		F & B: room service		
Nil	82.63%	73.19%	70.05%	75.53%
Up to 10,000	14.29%	21.38%	19.35%	18.35%
> 10,000	3.09%	5.43%	10.60%	6.12%
Total	**100.00%**	**100.00%**	**100.00%**	**100.00%**

Similar analysis could be done with respect to the various services contributing to revenue and the three categories of members, combined with other variables or factors that are used for classifying the categories through the ANNs. Such an analysis could provide information for focusing the strategies toward a particular group of members so as to move them up the value pyramid. It could also identify the appropriate demographic characteristics for better targeting of the incentives.

CONCLUSION

Many hotel chains offer loyalty programs with special rewards for members. These rewards or incentives are expected to draw them more toward the hotel chain and improve revenues. It is important to focus these programs and target them toward appropriate group of customers to achieve the objective of increasing the share of customer spending. A classification technique called artificial neural network was used to first classify the members into different categories and identify the variables that influence the classification. The members were classified into three categories: high, medium, and low spenders in this particular case. Once the members were categorized and the influencing variables identified, it was possible to analyze the data further to generate appropriate strategies and target them toward the appropriate segment. The database contained information on 752 members only. Three-fourths of the data is used for training the ANN and the remaining one-fourth is used for calculating the prediction accuracy and model improvement. Once the model was finalized, the prediction was carried out for the entire set of data. This was resorted to because of the small number of observations. Also, the revenue figures in the database refer to the revenue contribution of the members since enrolment. Annual breakup of the data could have provided better insight into the profile of the members.

REFERENCES

Brown, P. (2004). Better rewards for hotel loyalty. *McKinsey Quarterly,* September 28. Web exclusive. Available at: http://www.mckinseyquarterly.com/article_abstract_visitor.aspx?ar=1490.

Chatfield, C. (1998). Time series forecasting with neural networks: A comparative study using eh airlines data. *Applied Statistics, 47*(2): 231-250.

Hilton HHonors (2007). About Hilton HHonors. Available at: http://hhonors1 .hilton.com/en_US/hh/about/index.do?it=Hnav,About

Mukhopadhyay, S. (2001). Relationship management practices in hospitality industry: A case study of hotels and restaurants in Calcutta. In Sheth, J.N., Parvatiyar, A., and Shainesh, G. (eds.), *Customer Relationship Management Emerging Concepts, Tools and Applications* (pp. 388-398). New Delhi, India: Tata McGraw Hill.

Nagadevara, V. (2004). Application of neural prediction models in healthcare. *Proceedings of the 2nd International Conference on e-Governance* (pp. 139-148), November 29-December 1 , Colombo, Sri Lanka.

Chapter 22

Performance Evaluation of Worldwide Hotel Industry Using the Data Envelopment Analysis

João C. Neves
Sofia Lourenço

INTRODUCTION

Performance determines a company's survival in the long term (Anderson et al., 2000). Consequently, performance measurement is crucial for management. Among the techniques of performance evaluation, ratio analysis is probably the most used in practice with ratios such as EBITDA (earnings before interest, taxes, depreciation, and amortization) margin, operating margin, assets turnover, return on assets, return on capital employed, return on investment, return on sales, and return on equity. More recently, economic value added (Stewart, 1991) emerged as a measure related to the management goal of creating shareholder value, and the balanced scorecard (Kaplan and Norton, 1992) has been established as a requirement for linking multidimensional managerial decisions to the implementation of the strategy of the firm. Many authors emphasize a firm's need to reflect a multidimensional nature of management in performance evaluation (Anthony and Govindarajan, 2003; Kaplan and Norton, 1993; Zhu, 2000; Reynolds, 2003; Phillips, 1999a,b; Avkiran, 2002). However, the weighting of multifactor models to generate a single indicator of performance is a problem derived by its subjectivism, which is a constraint for its utilization in practice.

Global Cases on Hospitality Industry
© 2008 by The Haworth Press, Taylor & Francis Group. All rights reserved.
doi:10.1300/5923_22

Data envelopment analysis (DEA) overcomes some of the previous criticisms and emerges as an alternative methodology that has been used to evaluate the performance of decision-making units (DMUs) such as companies, divisions, nonprofit organizations, public departments, persons, etc. The most efficient DMUs are used for generating the efficient frontier that is used to compute a score that measures the level of efficiency of each DMU. Thus, DEA is not only a methodology to evaluate performance but also a benchmarking technique for learning about gaps of performances and the management of resources supporting the management decisions for improvement.

DEA was initially used by Charnes and colleagues (1978) for evaluating an educational program in the public sector, but it spread quickly to other organizations and economic activities (Seiford, 1996) because of its features (Zhu, 2004).

In this chapter, DEA is used for evaluating the performance of hotels and corporations around the world. Wober and colleagues (2003) emphasize the increasing importance of tourism as a source of employment, revenue, international awareness, and opportunity for growth. The remainder of the chapter presents briefly the basics of DEA and a literature review on the performance evaluation of the hospitality sector, the methodology used in the research, an analyses of the results obtained in the empirical study, and a comparison of the DEA results with the typical ratio analysis. The final section discusses the conclusions.

LITERATURE REVIEW

Data envelopment analysis is a linear, nonparametric, and multifactor methodology used by Charnes and colleagues (1978) to evaluate DMUs, in an educational program in the United States. The efficiency index created by these authors (CCR, named after its authors) used constant returns to scale (CRS), that is, all DMUs had the same possibility to obtain a constant transformation ratio from inputs to outputs. An increase in the inputs should be followed by the same proportion increase in the outputs. This assumption ignored a firm's scale or size. This CCR index is known as technical efficiency (TE). Subsequently, Banker and colleagues (1984) presented a new version of the model with variable returns to scale (VRS), thus the efficiency is evaluated attending to a different firm's scale. The BCC score (again named after its authors) is known as the pure technical efficiency (PTE). With such assumption, the efficiency index is exclusively related to the transformation process from inputs into outputs, ignoring eventual inefficiencies of scale. The DMUs could operate in a CRS region, in an increasing returns to scale (IRS) region, or in a decreasing returns to scale (DRS) region. The IRS means that if the DMU increases its inputs, the outputs will be increased in a more than proportionate way. The DRS is the inverse situation: an increase in the inputs will have a less than proportionate impact in the outputs.

Notice that the difference between the two indexes (CCR and BCC) is the type of returns to scale. The ratio between the CCR index and the BCC index is the scale efficiency (SE). If the two indexes are equal, the SE is one, meaning that the DMU operates under constant return to scale (CRS) and is scale efficient. As a result, with CRS, the average productivity is maximized and the marginal productivity equals the average productivity (Banker, 1984; Banker and Thrall, 1992).

This chapter uses the Zhu (2004) formulation of the envelopment model. This model was mentioned not only for its capacity to evaluate the efficiency of each unit (technical, pure technical, and scale efficiency), but also for finding targets and slacks, evaluating returns to scale, and finding the efficient peers that are used to benchmark its performance for each inefficient DMU.

Where:

- θ is efficiency index (input-oriented)
- ϕ is efficiency index (output-oriented)
- y is outputs
- x is inputs
- s is number of outputs
- m is number of inputs
- n is number of DMUs
- y_{rj} is output r from DMU *j*
- x_{ij} is input *i* from DMU *j*
- λ is model variables to compute the DMU efficiency
- s_i^- is input *i* slack variable
- s_r^+ is output *r* slack variable
- ε is non-Archimedean infinitesimal

Notice that s_i^- and s_r^+ are the slacks for the input i and output r of the DMU being analyzed. The DMU will be efficient if and only if θ^* = 1 or ϕ^* = 1and if s_i^- = s_r^+ = 0. The DMU reference set or benchmarking units are identified by the non-zero . The coefficients also allow the DMU projection in the efficient frontier, showing the possible inputs reduction or outputs increase, according to the model: input-oriented or output-oriented.

Since the efficiency index is always between 0 and 1, DEA is a simple and fast technique to rank the units by their performance. DEA allows multiple inputs, outputs, and different units of measurement. A DMU is efficient if its index is equal to one and inefficient if less than one. For each inefficient DMU, the model identifies its efficient DMU of reference benchmark by the smaller distance of the mix of inputs and outputs.

The set of efficient DMUs constitutes the efficient frontier. This frontier represents the lowest level of inputs for a given level of outputs (input-oriented model) or the maximum level of outputs for a given level of inputs (output-oriented model). Inefficient DMUs use a higher level of input for the same level of output or produce lower a level of output for the same level of input.

To our knowledge, this is the first study that analyzes the hotel industry performance with the DEA in a worldwide basis sample. Most of the previous studies in the hotel industry used traditional ratio analysis or subjective performance indexes (Anderson et al., 2000). More recently, Enz and colleagues (2001) use the average daily rate (ADR), revenue per available room (RevPAR), and occupancy in hotels in the United States between 1988 and 2000, concluding, however, that these are inappropriate measures of performance because of the higher daily rates per room of luxury hotels and their lower occupancy rates. Thus, the typical hotel has lower than average ADR and RevPAR but higher occupancy.

Other studies in the hotel industry assess performance through lodging index sales (Wassenaar and Stafford, 1991) and growth rates in several regions (Van Doren and Gustke, 1982). The lodging index is a ratio against the average revenue per room in a given period. These measures of performance are criticized because of their partial focus. Brown and McDonnell (1995) suggest the use of the balanced scorecard (BSC) to overcome this problem and Huckestein and Duboff (1999) applied it to the Hilton Hotels.

Morey and Ditman (1995) use the DEA to analyze the efficiency of fifty-four units of a hotel chain, which were geographically disperse. The variables in the study are exogenous inputs (number of rooms, average market occupancy, market ADR, and unionized employees), controllable inputs (room expenditures, food and beverage expenditures, etc.), and outputs (room revenue, average guest satisfaction related with the physical facilities, and average guest satisfaction related with the service provided). The study concludes that the average efficiency is 89 percent, that is, the inputs can be reduced 11 percent and the lowest efficiency score was 64 percent.

Anderson and colleagues (2000) use the DEA to evaluate the efficiency of forty-eight North American hotels. They considered the following variables as outputs: room revenue, gaming revenue, food and beverage revenue, and other revenues; and as inputs: full time equivalent employees, the number of rooms, total gaming related expenses, total food and beverage expenses, and other expenses. The findings indicate an average total efficiency of 42 percent, which is lower than the previously mentioned study. Anderson and colleagues (2000) consider that this low efficiency is due to the broad selection of variables in the study. The origin of such inefficiency is mainly allocative (average allocative efficiency is 51 percent) and not technical inefficiency (average of 81 percent), with a scale efficiency of 90 percent and pure technical efficiency of 87 percent. This conclusion is important, as it directs the management attention to the resources allocation.

Avkiran (2002) uses the DEA to study the productivity of twenty-three Queensland, Australia's hotels. The variables use the number of full-time employees, number of part-time employees, number of beds as inputs, and total revenues and room rate as output. The findings show average pure technical efficiency of 87.6 percent, scale efficiency of 92.9 percent, and technical efficiency of 81.4 percent. Avkiran (2002) concludes that potential exists for a reduction in the number of beds and part-time staff and simultaneously a revenue increase.

Chiang and colleagues (2004) use the DEA to evaluate the performance of three types of hotel operations: franchised licensed, those managed by international hotel operators, and independently owned and operated hotels. The variables used are number of rooms, food and beverage capacity measured by area, number of employees, and total costs of the hotel as inputs; and yielding index (which evaluates hotel room performance since it is the ratio between hotel RevPAR and market RevPAR), food and beverage revenues, and other revenues as outputs. With a sample of twenty-five hotels of four and five stars in Taipei, the study concludes that the efficiency is not statistically different for the three type of operations analyzed.

METHODOLOGY AND RESEARCH DESIGN

This study uses the DEA to assess the hotel corporation's performance in a worldwide basis for the period 2000-2002. The sample is composed of all hotels found in the Corporate Focus In Financials database (Corporate Focus, 2003) using the search by sector: FT 464—restaurants and hotels, and SIC 70—hotels; and by subject: hotels and hospitality. The main activity of each company was checked through the business summary provided by Corporate Focus, the firms' Web sites, and business Web sites such as http://www.business.com, http://www.crmz.com, and http://www.shibuimarkets.com. Firms with activities other than hospitality were also accepted, if hotel management was the main activity. The diversification of activities found in the sample includes restaurants, casinos, real estate, and other tourism activities.

The duplicated data were deleted, resulting in total 284 hotels. However, because of incomplete or incompatible data with the DEA envelopment model, data greater than zero are required, thus the number of hotels in the sample was reduce to 145 in 2000, 146 in 2001, and 103 in 2002.

Given the number of companies with incomplete data, the study uses all the companies for the period 2000-2002, and subsequently it tested the 83 companies that were in the sample for every year of the study. Because the results are very similar, this study presents the results of the sample with a constant number of companies per year. The sample used is shown in Table 22.1. The geographical origin of the companies is shown in Table 22.2.

The selection of variables of inputs and outputs is a fundamental task in the DEA methodology. The outputs should reflect the business goals and the inputs the required resources for achieving the goals. The availability of data is a serious constraint for the empirical study since the only data available in the Corporate Focus database are fi-

TABLE 22.1. Business Segmentation of the Companies in the Sample

DMUs	2000-2002		2000		2001		2002	
	N.	%	N.	%	N.	%	N.	%
Hotels	51	61%	98	68%	94	64%	59	57%
Hotels: holding	20	24%	24	17%	26	18%	22	21%
Hotels: casinos	2	2%	6	4%	5	3%	4	4%
Hotels: real estate	1	1%	2	1%	4	3%	3	3%
Hotels: restaurants	4	5%	8	6%	8	5%	8	8%
Hotels: others	5	6%	7	5%	9	6%	7	7%
Total	83	100%	145	100%	146	100%	103	100%

TABLE 22.2. Geographical home-based of the companies in the sample

DMUs	2000-2002		2000		2001		2002	
	N.	%	N.	%	N.	%	N.	%
Europe	26	31%	40	28%	38	26%	27	26%
Asia	36	43%	69	48%	71	49%	46	45%
Africa	1	1%	1	1%	1	1%	1	1%
North America	4	5%	14	10%	9	6%	8	8%
Central and South America	9	11%	13	9%	14	10%	9	9%
Oceania	7	8%	8	6%	13	9%	12	12%
Total	83	100%	145	100%	146	100%	103	100%

nancial data from financial statements. It would be of interest, for example, to know the number of rooms, occupancy rates, and number of employees. Considering the mentioned constraints, the variable selection was based on the purpose of evaluating a firms' capacity to generate revenues and its transformation in earnings (outputs), and the resources used as inputs in this process are assets (fixed and current), capital (the total shareholders' equity and liabilities), and the cost of goods and services. The final set of variables was chosen from the results obtained from the three sets shown in Table 22.3 for the sample in 2000.

TABLE 22.3. Inputs and Outputs Selection

Variables selection		5 inputs/ 2 outputs	4 inputs/ 2 outputs	3 inputs/ 2 outputs
Inputs	Total net fixed assets	X	X	
	Total current assets	X	X	
	Total assets			X
	Total shareholders equity	X	X	X
	Total liabilities and debt	X		
	Cost of goods and services	X	X	X
Outputs	Total revenues	X	X	X
	EBITDA: Earnings before interests, taxes, depreciation and amortization	X	X	X
Variables number		7	6	5
Number of DMUs		145	145	145
Heuristic rule 1—[m * s]		10	8	6
Heuristic rule 2—[3 * (m + s)]		21	18	15
CRS efficient units %		27%	18%	6%
VRS efficient units %		37%	28%	16%

The number of units in the sample satisfies the minimum required by the heuristic rules described by Cooper and colleagues (2001): , with n as the number of DMUs, m the number of inputs, and s the number of outputs.

The set with seven variables generates a large number of efficient units, and the set with five variables generates a few numbers of efficient units and excludes the structure of assets (i.e., asset management). The set with six variables is apparently more balanced than the other two sets. Nevertheless, it is important to check the correlations between the different variables as suggested by Thanassoulis (2001) and Avkiran (2002), for which inputs and outputs should exhibit strong correlation to ensure the cause-effect relationship, and the correlation between the inputs (and between the outputs) should be weak to avoid redundancy (see Table 22.4).

The correlations between the inputs and outputs are strong as required, but the correlations between the inputs (and between the two

TABLE 22.4. Bivariate Correlations (Year 2000)

Correlations	Current assets	Net fixed assets	Total assets	Liabilities	Shareholders equity	Cost of goods & services	Total revenues	EBITDA
Current assets	1.00	0.69	0.84	0.84	0.71	0.77	**0.81**	**0.84**
Net fixed assets	0.69	1.00	0.94	0.87	0.92	0.61	**0.70**	**0.87**
Total assets	0.84	0.94	1.00	0.97	0.91	0.76	**0.83**	**0.96**
Liabilities	0.84	0.87	0.97	1.00	0.77	0.76	**0.84**	**0.99**
Shareholders equity	0.71	0.92	0.91	0.77	1.00	0.64	**0.70**	**0.78**
COG and services	0.77	0.61	0.76	0.76	0.64	1.00	**0.99**	**0.80**
Total revenues	**0.81**	**0.70**	**0.83**	**0.84**	**0.70**	**0.99**	1.00	0.88
EBITDA	**0.84**	**0.87**	**0.96**	**0.99**	**0.78**	**0.80**	0.88	1.00

Note: Correlations between inputs and outputs are in bold

outputs) are also strong, denoting some overlapping between inputs (and outputs). Excluding total assets and total liabilities, the set chosen include the following variables: total current assets, total net fixed assets, total shareholders equity and cost of goods and services as inputs, and total revenues and EBITDA as outputs.

The diversity of DMUs is apparent not only in terms of segmentation of businesses and geographical origin, as previously observed, but also in size, financing strategies, and asset structure (see Table 22.5).

The reported results were obtained using the input-oriented DEA envelopment model. The differences with the output-oriented model for the year 2000 were not significant. Consequently, the study uses the input-oriented model exclusively, and the DEAFrontier software, developed by Joe Zhu.

Before the presentation of results in the next section, it is worth mentioning the following limitations of the study. First, the use of a worldwide sample narrowed the choice of variables. It was not possible to get some relevant inputs and outputs of hotel management such as the number of beds available, employees' education levels, occupancy rates, guest satisfaction, or even the number of employees. Consequently, the study uses exclusively financial variables, which does not benefit from the DEA advantages of blending different type of variables in the performance measurement. Second, the financial statements are subject to different accounting standards and currencies, in spite of the use of revenue and EBITDA as outputs allowing for the minimization of the effect of accounting policy on amortization, depreciation, and provisions. Finally, DEA is a nonstochastic method that is unable to measure eventual effects of data errors and the reliability of the results.

RESULTS FROM THE EMPIRICAL STUDY

The efficiency derived from the DEA input-oriented model can be found in Table 22.6. Table 22.6 exhibits that the scale efficiency is higher than the pure technical efficiency for every year (average and median), which is similar to Anderson and colleagues (2000) and Avkiran (2002) findings. Because technical efficiency is the product

TABLE 22.5. Variables: Year 2000 (Millions of USD)

Variables	Current assets	Net fixed assets	Total assets	Liabilities	Share-holders equity	Cost of goods & services	Total revenues	EBITDA
Average	89.5	344.7	585.1	321.4	263.7	191.0	272.2	57.8
Standard deviation	342.4	794.0	1,556.4	1,022.2	628.3	879.8	1,043.4	171.1
Maximum	3,692.6	4,423.6	11,260.7	7,640.6	3,620.1	8,900.0	10,017.0	1,223.7
Minimum	0.2	0.1	0.7	0.0	0.2	0.0	0.3	0.0
Median	16.1	53.5	114.5	43.9	56.0	17.7	33.0	9.5
Coef.of variation	3.8	2.3	2.7	3.2	2.4	4.6	3.8	3.0

TABLE 22.6. DEA Envelopment Input-Oriented Results: Variable Firms' Sets

	2000			2001			2002		
Efficiency	Technical efficiency	Pure technical efficiency	Scale efficiency	Technical efficiency	Pure Technical efficiency	Scale efficiency	Technical efficiency	Pure technical efficiency	Scale efficiency
Average	72.46%	80.67%	89.62%	64.39%	75.46%	84.66%	64.26%	74.53%	84.87%
Standard deviation	21.83%	20.61%	11.15%	25.00%	24.15%	13.73%	24.42%	22.89%	12.15%
Minimum	29.45%	29.61%	54.02%	21.46%	22.74%	37.49%	24.53%	31.80%	50.70%
Median	72.79%	86.01%	94.02%	67.01%	80.36%	86.90%	65.74%	75.96%	87.09%

of pure technical efficiency and scale efficiency, the management of those companies should ask themselves what is the best way to increase technical efficiency. Based on the results of the empirical study, apparently the best way is through pure technical efficiency, as it has higher percentage of potential to increase. Consequently, the strategy should give priority to the efficiency of operations in transforming inputs into outputs, while the firm's size or scale should be a secondary goal.

Table 22.6 also evidences a significant decrease of efficiency in the year 2001 (average, median, and minimum) and a small increase in year 2002. The t-test shows it is apparent that the efficiency in 2000 is significantly different from 2001, and the efficiency in 2002 is not statistically different from 2001. Consequently, the decline of performance observed in 2001 was not completely reverted in 2002 (see Table 22.7).

One possible explanation for the performance decline is the observed contraction in the tourism. According to the World Tourism Organization, worldwide tourism revenue dropped from $473.4 billion (U.S.) in 2000 to $459.5 billion in 2001; however, it reverted to $474.2 billion in 2002. The number of tourists, measured by the number of arrivals, has also declined from 687.3 million in 2000 to 684.1 million in 2001. However, in 2002 the number of tourists increased by 2.7 percent to 702.6 million (World Tourism Organization, 2004).

Appendix 22.A presents the efficient DMUs identified by the DEA envelopment model for the 83 DMUs, with available data for every year of the study and detailed information about these efficient units, such as the type of efficiency, the year of the efficiency, and the number of times the DMU was considered an efficient peer or a reference or benchmark.

TABLE 22.7. T-Test

	T-Test	T	p value
	2000-2001	4.900	0.000*
TE	2000-2002	1.273	0.207
	2001-2002	-1.704	0.092

*Rejection of the null hypothesis with a significance level of 1%

As previously mentioned, efficient units are the reference of themselves, but the inefficient units may have one or more references. The diversity of efficient DMUs can be observed in Appendix 22.A:

- Efficient DMUs that are not used as benchmarks for themselves, such as Accor and Club Med
- DMUs that are rarely classified as efficient peers, such as City Lodge and Grand Hotel Group
- DMUs with important number of references, but for only one year or two, as is the case of Rajadamri Hotel PLC
- DMUs that are important references for several years, but only with pure technical efficiency, such as Central Plaza Hotel
- Finally, some DMUs are efficient peers for several years and with both types of efficiency, which is the case of Blue Tree, CHE Group, Club Crocodile, Hilton Hotels, and Kingsgate International

Table 22.8 shows that companies following strategies concentrated in the hotel business tend to have higher efficiency than those with diversified strategies. It is also apparent, from Table 22.9, that North American home-based corporations exhibit higher efficiency because of the number of DMUs in the efficient frontier.

Another interesting output from the DEA envelopment models is the type of returns to scale that each DMU is operating. Table 22.10 shows that the majority of DMUs operate in decreasing returns to

TABLE 22.8. DMUs' Activities: Total Sample and Efficient Units

DMUs	Total sample No. of units	%	Efficient units No. of units	%
Hotels	51	61%	30	71%
Hotels: holding	20	24%	9	21%
Hotels: casinos	2	2%	1	2%
Hotels: real estate	1	1%	0	0%
Hotels: restaurants	4	5%	1	2%
Hotels: others	5	6%	1	2%
Total	83	100%	42	100%

TABLE 22.9. DMUs' Origin Country: Total Sample and Efficient Units

DMUs	Total sample		Efficient units	
	No. of units	%	No. of units	%
Europe	26	31%	12	29%
Asia	36	43%	15	36%
Africa	1	1%	1	2%
North America	4	5%	4	10%
Central and South America	9	11%	4	10%
Oceania	7	8%	6	14%
Total	83	100%	42	100%

TABLE 22.10. Types of Returns to Scale: Three Year Period Study

Returns to Scale	2000		2001		2002	
	No.	%	No.	%	No.	%
CRS	18	22%	13	16%	11	13%
DRS	47	57%	57	69%	56	67%
IRS	18	22%	13	16%	16	19%

scale, meaning that a decrease in their size would allow an increase in technical efficiency. The study suggests the resources are in excess for the level of output, which has a negative influence in the efficiency scores. This analysis should be made jointly with the findings from the technical efficiency—scale efficiency was higher than the pure technical efficiency, which suggests that management should focus more on operation procedures and less in the increase of operation's scale. The decreasing returns to scale mode is also coherent with some industry studies and common knowledge of underused capacity and low occupancy rates (Enz et al., 2001). The decline of efficiency in 2001 caused an increase of firms operating in decreasing returns to scale.

The stability of the returns to scale was analyzed for the three-year period of the study in which 71 percent of the 83 firms in the sample operate under the same type of returns to scale for every year of the study. This is indicative that the excess of scale is not a problem of a specific year, but is a structural problem of the industry.

COMPARISON BETWEEN DEA AND RATIO ANALYSIS

In this section, the DEA results are compared with the return on assets and the return on equity calculated respectively as the quotient of EBIT (earnings before interests and taxes) to the year average total assets and the quotient of net profit to the year average total shareholders equity.

The ROA (return on assets) and ROE (return on equity) indicate a clear decline in the performance for the year 2001, which is similar to the DEA analysis, but by 2002 the level of performance was higher than 2000, which contrasts with the DEA (see Table 22.11).

After the evidence from the Kolmogorov-Smirnov test that ROA and ROE ratios do not follow a normal distribution, the statistical significance of differences between the years was performed by the Wilcoxon test, concluding that the difference between 2000 and 2001 is statistically significant, which is similar to the DEA conclusion, and that 2002 is not statistically different from 2001 (see Table 22.12). Consequently, the year 2000 is distinct from 2001 and 2002, structural decline of performance between the two periods.

TABLE 22.11. ROA and ROE: Three Year Period Study

Three year period study	ROA			ROE		
	2000	2001	2002	2000	2001	2002
Average	6.50%	5.46%	6.64%	5.50%	4.18%	5.70%
Standard deviation	5.35%	5.90%	6.98%	9.88%	9.03%	9.26%
Maximum	35.31%	26.25%	33.61%	23.89%	32.84%	39.11%
Minimum	−2.30%	−9.40%	−1.71%	−50.86%	−25.74%	−14.21%
Median	5.81%	4.37%	4.81%	6.39%	3.87%	3.25%
Number of DMUs	67	83	83	67	83	83

Note: In the year 2000, sixteen DMUs were excluded because it was not possible to compute the average of assets and the average of equity.

TABLE 22.12. Wilcoxon Test for the ROA and ROE

Wilcoxon Test		z	p value
ROA	2000-2001	−4.689	0.000*
	2000-2002	−2.265	0.024**
	2001-2002	−1.658	0.097
ROE	2000-2001	−4.002	0.000*
	2000-2002	−2.683	0.007*
	2001-2002	−0.855	0.393

*Rejection of the null hypothesis with a significance level of 1%

**Rejection of the null hypothesis with a significance level of 5%

A linear regression was used to analyze the relationship between the performance measure by the DEA and the traditional ratios of ROA and ROE:

$$Y_i = \alpha + \beta x_i + \varepsilon$$

The efficiency index (TE or PTE) is the independent variable (x); the returns (ROA or ROE) the dependent variable (y). Both are measures of performance and consequently one expects to find a positive and strong relationship between the independent variable (efficiency) and the dependent variable (return) (see Table 22.13).

It is apparent the existence of positive relationships of both technical efficiency and pure technical efficiency with the ROA, as the null hypothesis of $\beta = 0$ is rejected for every single year with at least 5 percent significance level. However, the coefficient of determination evidences that only a small portion of the total variation of the dependent variable (return) is explained by the efficiency obtained through the DEA model.

For the ROE, the coefficient β is always positive, but the null hypothesis is accepted in three situations at 5 percent significance, and the coefficient determination is lower than before. A possible explanation for this weaker relationship is that the output variables are exclusively related to operations, whereas ROE includes performance factors such as financial leverage, financial expenses, extraordinary items, and taxation.

TABLE 22.13. Linear Regression: Three Year Period Study

Linear regression		ROA				ROE				n
		t	p value	R^2	β	t	p value	R^2	β	
TE return	2000	2.201	0.031**	0.069	0.263	0.130	0.897	0.000	0.016	67
	2001	4.300	0.000*	0.186	0.431	2.798	0.006*	0.088	0.297	83
	2002	2.877	0.005*	0.093	0.304	2.906	0.005*	0.094	0.307	83
PTE return	2000	2.373	0.021**	0.080	0.282	0.579	0.565	0.005	0.072	67
	2001	3.573	0.001*	0.136	0.369	2.561	0.120	0.075	0.274	83
	2002	2.340	0.022**	0.063	0.252	2.514	0.014**	0.072	0.269	83

* Rejection of the null hypothesis with a significance level of 1%

** Rejection of the null hypothesis with a significance level of 5%

Finally, the average difference of return (ROA and ROE) of the efficient and inefficient units of the DEA classification was compared. Although the average of the efficient firms was higher than the inefficient, the differences were not statistically significant at 5 percent level by the Mann-Whitney test for two independent samples. In spite of the use of financial inputs and outputs in the DEA, these results indicate that DEA measures performance more broadly than the financial measures of performance such as ROA and ROE.

CONCLUSIONS

This research used the DEA to analyze the worldwide performance of the hotel industry. Very few studies have used this methodology in this industry, but the most distinct features of the research is the use of worldwide hotel companies data, the size of the sample being larger than previous studies, and the period analyzed being a single year analysis.

In terms of efficiency, the study shows a possible improvement with a 30 to 40 percent reduction in the inputs without decreasing the outputs. From a strategic point of view, companies that concentrate on their core businesses evidence better performance than those who are diversified. The efficient frontier was also composed of a higher proportion of companies originated from North America or Oceania than the sample structure, which signals the better performance of the companies originated from these two geographical areas.

The majority of the DMUs operate under decreasing returns to scale, and consequently a decrease in size would benefit the efficiency. Moreover, the primary origin of the technical inefficiency comes from the pure technical efficiency and not from the scale efficiency. This also suggests that managers should give priority to the improvement of the process of transforming inputs into outputs (productivity), and searching for economies of scale should be secondary goal.

The longitudinal study exhibits a statistically significant decline of performance in 2001 (average and median), which may result from the decline of worldwide tourism demand as reported by the World Tourism Organization (2004). The regression analysis also indicates a positive relationship between the computed DEA efficiency and the ROA. The cause-effect relationship between efficiency and ROE was not so evident, probably, because the output variables used in the DEA model are of operational in nature.

The study presents several limitations, however. One of most relevant is related to the database and the exclusive use of financial data, which is affected by the accounting standards practices in each country and the evolution of foreign-exchange rates. The DEA has also its own limitations as (1) the performance index is relative to the sample used and not an absolute measure, (2) the results depend on the selected variables for inputs and outputs, and, finally, (3) the method used was deterministic, which does not allow a confidence level or an error estimation in the results obtained.

Future research could relate DEA efficiency index with economic development of the countries or regions where the DMUs are located, extend the performance analysis of the DMUs to the capital market performance, and relate the measures of the balance scorecard with the DEA measures.

APPENDIX 22.A.
EFFICIENT PEERS IN THE THREE-YEAR PERIOD STUDY

Efficiency/Year	TE				PTE				
DMUs	2000	2001	2002	Total	2000	2001	2002	Total	Total
Accor					1	1	1	3	3
Blue Tree Hotels & Resorts	8	25	18	51	6	3	7	16	67
CH e group	16	2	11	29	22	30	32	84	113
Central Plaza Hotel						11	10	21	21
Choice Hotels Scandinavia	19	8	11	38	12	22	17	51	89
City Lodge Hotels	8			8	6			6	14
Club Crocodile	5	67	70	142	3	31	40	74	216
Club Med						1	1	2	2
Dalian Yicheng Group					3		1	4	4
Extended Stay America	1	4	11	16	16	10	5	31	47
Four Seasons Hotels Inc	13	20	9	42	10	19	8	37	79
Grand Central Enterprises Berhad							2	2	2
Grand Hotel Group			14	14			3	3	17
Grand Plaza Hotel			14	14	1	5	4	10	24
Grupo Posadas						13		13	13
Hamilton Island	13			13	4			4	17
Hanover International						3		3	3
Hilton Hotels Corp	7		33	40	21	13	43	77	117
Hong Kong & Shanghai Hotels	8			8	14	13	15	42	50
Hotels c Deauville					2			2	2
Hotel Grand Central Ltd							11	11	11
Hotel Holiday Garden	7			7	3			3	10
Hotel Negara Ltd							3	3	3
Hunan Ginde Development					5			5	5

| Efficiency/Year | TE | | | | PTE | | | | Total |
DMUs	2000	2001	2002	Total	2000	2001	2002	Total	Total
Jarvis Hotels					2	4		6	6
Jolly Hotels		1		1		2		2	3
Kingsgate International	43	56	42	141	26	46	26	98	239
Marriott International	2			2	16	3	2	21	23
Millennium and Copthorne						1		1	1
Newhaven Park Stud					5			5	5
Oriental Hotel Thailand	7	25		32	2	10		12	44
Peel Hotels		10		10	4	5	8	17	27
Pierre & Vacances		2		2	4	3	2	9	11
Rajadamri Hotel Plc	54			54	32			32	86
Real Turismo					5			5	5
Royal Garden Resort					8			8	8
Shanghai New asia Group					2		13	15	15
shangri La Asia Ltd					2	1		3	3
shangri La Hotels Malaysia	1			1	4			4	5
Shenzhen Century Plaza Hotel	22			22	6			6	28
Sundowner Group	6	7	2	15	5	7	2	14	29
Thistle Hotels		2		2	3	4		7	9
Efficient peers' references	240	229	235	704	255	261	256	772	1476
Number of efficient peers	18	13	11	24	32	25	23	42	42
Average number of efficient peers by DMU	2.89	2.76	2.83	2.83	3.07	3.14	3.08	3.10	2.96
Average number of efficient peers by inefficient DMU	3.42	3.09	3.11	3.20	4.37	4.07	3.88	4.09	3.60
Efficient DMUs %	22%	16%	13%	29%	39%	30%	28%	51%	51%
Inefficient DMUs %	78%	84%	87%	71%	61%	70%	72%	49%	49%
DMUs' total number				83					

REFERENCES

Anderson, R.I., Fok, R., and Scott, J. (2000). Hotel industry efficiency: An advanced linear programming examination, *American Business Review, 18*(1): 40-48.

Anthony, R. and Govindarajan, V. (2003). *Management Control Systems,* 11th edition. New York: McGraw-Hill.

Avkiran, N.K. (2002). Monitoring hotel performance. *Journal of Asia-Pacific Business, 4*(1): 51-66.

Banker, R.D. (1984). Estimating most productive scale size using data envelopment analysis. *European Journal of Operational Research, 17*(1): 35-44.

Banker, R.D., Charnes, A., and Cooper, W.W. (1984). Some models for estimating technical and scale efficiencies in data envelopment analysis. *Management Science, 30:* 1078-1092.

Banker, R.D. and Thrall, R.M. (1992). Estimation of return's to scale using data envelopment analysis. *European Journal of Operational Research, 62:* 74-84.

Brown, J. Brander and McDonnell, B. (1995). The balanced score-card; short-term guest or long-term resident?, *International Journal of Contemporary Hospitality Management, 7*(2): 7-11.

Charnes, A., Cooper, W.W., and Rhodes, E. (1978). Measuring the efficiency of decision making units. *European Journal of Operational Research, 2*(6): 429.

Chiang, W.E., Tsai, M.H., and Wang, L.S.M. (2004). A DEA evaluation of Taipei hotels. *Annals of Tourism Research, 31*(3): 712-715.

Cooper, W. W., Li, S., Seiford, L. M., Tone, K., Thrall, R. M. and Zhu, J. (2001). Sensitivity and stability analysis in DEA: Some recent developments. *Journal of Productivity Analysis, 15*(3): 217-246.

Corporate Focus (2003). In financials. Available at: http://www.infinancials.com/Eurofin/page.jsp?nav=1_1.

Enz, C.A., Canina, L., and Walsh, K. (2001). Hotel-industry averages: An inaccurate tool for measuring performance. *Cornell Hotel and Restaurant Administration Quarterly, 42:* 22-32.

Huckestein, D. and Duboff, R. (1999). Hilton hotels: A comprehensive approach to delivering value for all stakeholders. *Cornell Hotel and Restaurant Administration Quarterly, 40*(4): 28-38.

Kaplan, R. and Norton, D.P. (1992). The balanced scorecard: Measures that drives performance. *Harvard Business Review,* (January-February): 71-79.

Kaplan, R.S. and Norton, D.P. (1993). Putting the balanced scorecard to work. *Harvard Business Review,* September-October: 134-143.

Morey, R.C. and Dittman, D.A. (1995). Evaluating a hotel GM's performance: A case study in benchmarking. *Cornell Hotel and Restaurant Administration Quarterly, 36*(5): 30-35.

Phillips, P.A. (1999a). Hotel performance and competitive advantage: A contingency approach. *International Journal of Contemporary Hospitality Management, 11*(7): 359-366.

Phillips, P.A. (1999b). Performance measurement systems and hotels: A new conceptual framework. *International Journal of Hospitality Management, 18*(2): 171-182.

Reynolds, D. (2003). Hospitality-productivity assessment using data envelopment analysis. *Cornell Hotel and Restaurant Administration Quarterly, 44*(2): 130-137.

Seiford, L.M. (1996). Data envelopment analysis: The evolution of the state of the art (1978-1995). *Journal of Productivity Analysis, 7:* 99-137.

Stewart, G., III (1991). *The Quest for Value,* New York: Harper Business.

Thanassoulis, E. (2001). *Introduction to the Theory and Application of Data Envelopment Analysis.* Norwell, MA: Kluwer Academic Publishers.

Van Doren, C.S. and Gustke, L.D. (1982). Spatial analysis of the U.S. lodging industry. *Annals of Tourism Research, 9*(4): 543-563.

Wassenaar, K. and Stafford, E. R. (1991). The lodging index: An economic indicator for the hotel/motel industry. *Journal of Travel Research, 30*(1): 18-21.

Wober, K.W., Hwang, Y.H., and Fesenmaier, D.R. (2003). Services and functions provided by European city tourist offices: A longitudinal study. *International Journal of Tourism Research, 5*(1): 13-27.

World Tourism Organization (2004). Facts and figures. Available at: http://www.world-tourism.org/facts/wtb.html.

Zhu, J. (2000). Multi-factor performance measure model with an application to fortune 500 companies. *European Journal of Operational Research, 123:* 105-124.

Zhu, J. (2004). *Quantitative Models for Performance Evaluation and Benchmarking,* 2nd edition. Norwell, MA: Kluwer Academic Publishers.r

Chapter 23

Ethics in the Hospitality Industry: An Applied Model

Randall S. Upchurch

INTRODUCTION

According to Longenecker (1985), management affects an organization's ethical performance by the establishment of priorities that direct the ethical conduct of the organization. He also asserts that the "management process," and particularly the setting of organizational priorities, affects the attainment of ethical performance by identifying those values that seem important to management. Longenecker's points are very critical to organizational vitality given that management is often empowered to maintain the following:

- The highest level of services as possible
- The highest guest satisfaction ratings
- An optimal degree of financial return on investment to the organization as a whole

In order to satisfy these duties, lodging management must deliver services that meet the needs and wants of its guests. However, during the provision of daily services, management is often confronted with a variety of ethical situations that can leave a lasting either positive or

This chapter was originally published in Upchurch, R.S. (1998). Ethics in the hospitality industry: An applied model. *International Journal of Contemporary Hospitality Management,* 10(6): 227-233. Adapted with permission by Emerald Group Publishing Limited.

negative impression with the guest, staff, and other members of management. Undoubtedly the image that these constituent bodies collectively hold is directly related to organizational success as directed by management.

The belief that an organization's ethical climate is strongly influenced by management's ethical conduct has generated a body of academic research that has focused on determining the type and nature of ethical issues that are present in lodging organizations. In general, hospitality researchers have determined that management is confronted with ethical issues surrounding guests rights, empowerment, sexual harassment, equal opportunity, departmental relations, vendor relationships, yield management, community and public relations, and the balance of personal and organizational values (Enghagen and Hott, 1992; Hall, 1993; Hall and Enghagen, 1991; Kwansa and Farrar, 1991; O'Halloran, 1991). Overall, these studies have reflected on profiling ethical situations and on understanding management's role in resolving particular ethical situations within a service based setting.

NEED FOR THE STUDY

The current hospitality and tourism research has generally not tested nor profiled the theoretical principles that are at management's disposal to cope with the ethical issues as previously listed. The exception to this view is research conducted by Upchurch and Ruhland (1996). These authors sought to determine ethical principles and referent sources that are at management's disposal in hotel and motel lodging organizations. They concluded that management based their ethical decisions on the following:

- The three main ethical precepts of egoism (e.g., self-interest), benevolence (e.g., care and concern for others), and principle (e.g., adhering to internalized or external rules and regulations)
- The three referent sources of individual values (e.g., individual), values emanating from the immediate work setting (e.g., local), and from values exerted from society at large (e.g., cosmopolitan)

However, more important, management operated from a predominant ethical precept, and this ethical precept was strongly influenced by a particular referent source. That is to say, hotel and motel managers relied heavily on benevolence precepts emanating from the immediate work setting. Still, a problem exists in that ethical decision making in the bed-and-breakfast industry has not been subject to empirical research.

PURPOSE OF STUDY

The purpose of the current study was to profile the ethical decision-making foundations and referents that influenced ethical decision making for bed and breakfast and country inns operators in the United States. In particular, this study reviewed the following:

- The primary normative ethical precepts of egoism, benevolence, and principle used as a criterion in ethical decision making
- The predominant referent sources of individual, local, and cosmopolitan used in applying ethical precepts to ethical decisions for bed-and-breakfast and country inn operations located in the United States

QUESTIONNAIRE ADMINISTRATION

The sample consisted of 1,500 bed-and-breakfast and country inn operations randomly selected from nine geographical regions as reported by the consulting firm of Coopers & Lybrand (1996). For the purposes of this study, the researcher classified bed-and-breakfast and country inn operations as a lodging facility with 1 to 30 rooms. The first phase represented a mailing to 1,500 bed-and-breakfast and country inn properties. In two weeks, a follow-up letter was sent reminding the nonrespondents to complete and return the survey. This sampling process resulted in 607 usable surveys, for a return rate of 40 percent.

The respondents completed a questionnaire packet consisting of the ethical climate questionnaire (ECQ) and a section containing demographic variables of gender, years of experience, education attainment level, property classification, and position classification. The ECQ questionnaire as developed by Victor and Cullen (1988) consists of a six-point Likert-type scale. The scale ranged from 0 to 5 with completely false = 0, mostly false = 1, somewhat false = 2, somewhat true = 3, mostly true = 4, and completely true = 5. The midpoint of this scale was 2.5. The means of the ethical work climate type represented the respondents' rating of the ethical work climate type that existed in their lodging operation. The ECQ contained twenty-six questions designed to measure the three ethical foundations of egoism, benevolence, and principle. In addition, the ECQ measured the referent from which the ethical decision originated (i.e., individual, local, and cosmopolitan referent sources). According to Victor and Cullen (1998) the ethical precepts interact with the referent sources by influencing the individual's ethical decision process. Therefore, the combination of the ethical foundation and referent source interacts to produce a unique ethical response set by the individual. The following is a brief description of the model as developed and tested by Victor and Cullen (1988).

CLIMATE FOUNDATION AND REFERENT DESCRIPTION

Egoism Climate Type

The criterion used in ethical reasoning for an egoism climate is maximizing self-interest at the personal, company, or the societal level. Ethical decisions based at the individual level represent an individual's internalized values and beliefs. Decisions at the local level satisfy the organization's best interest, whereas ethical decisions at the cosmopolitan level of analysis symbolize societal or economic interests.

Benevolence Climate Type

The basic criteria used in ethical reasoning for the benevolence ethical climate is on maximizing the best interest of organizational members within prescribed boundaries. Individuals using the benevolence criteria and an individual locus develop friendships without regard to belonging to the organization. Local referents exert a collective influence that exists within the immediate work setting (e.g., work teams). An individual operating from the cosmopolitan perspective makes ethical decisions based on external factors that guide socially responsible behavior.

Principle Climate Type

When an individual utilizes principle precepts he or she makes decisions based on the equitable application of ethical rules and principles. Although, if the person operates from the individual perspective, he or she uses internalized rules and principles. When the individual operates from the local perspective he or she makes ethical decisions in alignment with company rules. Often these rules exist in a code of ethics that originate outside of the organization.

RESEARCH QUESTIONS AND HYPOTHESES

The research questions for this study were:

> *R1:* Is a predominant ethical foundation utilized for ethical decisions for a bed-and-breakfast or country inn organization as practiced by the owner/partner?
> *R2:* Is a predominant referent source utilized by bed-and-breakfast and country inn organizations as practiced by the owner/partner?

RESEARCH FINDINGS: DEMOGRAPHIC FINDINGS

The descriptive findings of this study indicated that bed-and-breakfast and country inn operators were the following:

- A seasoned group of individuals in terms of length of industry experience
- Formally educated past the high school level
- Relatively balanced in the numbers of males and females responding to the questionnaire

- Almost equally balanced as classified as a bed-and-breakfast or a country inn
- Approximately equally represented throughout the nine geographical regions of the United States (see Table 23.1)

Research Question 1 Summary

It is noteworthy that Victor and Cullen (1988) found that differences existed between manufacturing and service industries in the type of ethical foundations (e.g., otherwise known as ethical precepts in this chapter) utilized when making ethical decisions. The primary ethical foundation used by the bed-and-breakfast or country inn operator was determined to be egoism followed by principle and the benevolence dimensions (see Table 23.2). This multiple dimension profile is indicative of the service sector in that many constituencies and ethical situations arise.

In contrast, Upchurch and Ruhland (1996) found that managers of limited and full-service lodging operations based their ethical decisions primarily from the benevolence perspective. However, by design, a bed-and-breakfast or country inn operation is a single unit managed by the owner or owners. This fact enhances the personal ownership and self-interest in operating the property. Hence, the finding in the bed-and-breakfast study indicated that managers/owners operated from an egoism perspective. This finding makes conceptual sense given the relatively flat structure that incorporates the owner/manager as the sole advocate and supporter of operational outcomes. In other words, the owner/partner maximized their self-interest and investment in the operation by retaining control over the entire operation.

Still, the bed-and-breakfast lodging provider did not rely entirely on one primary ethical precept. Table 23.1 indicates that decision making in this setting relied on all three ethical precepts, and these precepts were influenced by the referent sources.

Research Question 2 Summary

The research conducted by Victor and Cullen (1988) and Upchurch and Ruhland (1996) found differences within management ranks in the referent source used when making ethical decisions. For instance, middle management within manufacturing companies re-

TABLE 23.1. Sample respondent profile

	Frequency	Percent
Respondent experience in the industry		
2 years	19	3.1
3 years	34	5.6
4 years	37	6.1
5+ years	517	85.2
Educational level		
High school	166	27.3
2 year college	124	20.4
4 year college	240	39.5
Master's degree	38	6.3
Doctoral degree	36	5.9
Certificate	3	0.5
Gender		
Male	363	59.8
Female	244	40.2
Property classification		
Bed and Breakfast	335	55.2
Country inn	272	44.8
Respondent position		
Owner	409	67.4
Partner	198	32.6
Geographic region		
New England	72	11.9
Middle Atlantic	30	4.9
South Atlantic	69	11.4
East North Central	27	4.4
East South Central	66	10.9
West North Central	124	20.4
West South Central	54	8.9
Mountain	84	13.8
Pacific	81	13.3

lied more heavily on immediate workplace norms and values, whereas lodging businesses were driven by social obligations and civic beliefs (cosmopolitan perspective) external to the organization.

Here, again, differences occurred between the limited and full-service lodging sector versus the bed-and-breakfast and country inns sector in that the latter operated primarily from an individual referent (see Table 23.3). This is logical given the limited management structure of the bed-and-breakfast and country inn operation. In general, the limited and full-service operation has layers of management on site, whereas the management structure of the bed-and-breakfast and country inn is often limited to a single owner or a partnership structure. This means that ethical decisions based at the individual level of analysis represents an individual's internalized values and beliefs. However, ethical decisions at the property (local referent) also had to satisfy the customer's best interest that comprised the cosmopolitan referent. Again, this profile indicates the difficulty in isolating a single determinant factor influencing ethical decision making within an organization.

In summary, the outcomes of this research support Victor and Cullen's (1998) contentions that individuals utilize multiple ethical precepts when resolving an ethical dilemma. Second, this study indicates that bed-and-breakfast and country inn owners/partners relied on egoism as the predominant ethical precept from a local referent

TABLE 23.2. Ethical Percept Profile

Predominate ethical dimension	Mean	SD
Egoism	2.33	0.77
Principal	2.19	0.96
Benevolence	2.10	0.82

TABLE 23.3. Ethical Referent Source

Predominate ethical dimension source	Mean	SD
Individual	2.35	0.75
Cosmopolitan	1.97	0.74
Local	1.91	0.69

source, with benevolence being equally influenced from the individual and cosmopolitan perspectives, and principle being largely influenced from an individual referent source. In all, these findings indicate that management is challenged to produce an ethical decision in a highly complex decision-making environment (see Table 23.4).

APPLICATION OF ETHICS RESEARCH OUTCOMES: A PROPOSED MODEL

The ultimate outcome of ethical decision-making research should be on the value that it provides the practitioner. This is especially true regarding the study of ethics due to the linkage of management's ethical conduct and practices on organizational performance and image. Hence, the utility of the findings reported in this chapter are threefold. First, the practitioner needs to conceptually understand the theoretical ethical precepts and referent sources that have been proven to influence ethical decision making in a variety of service based organizations (Upchurch and Ruhland, 1996; Victor and Cullen, 1988). Second, management should be aware of the range of ethical situations that will confront them during daily operation of a service-based business. Last, a structured approach must be taken that actively challenges the "learner" to solve a given ethical dilemma by properly applying ethical precepts from the various referent sources.

Developing the Process

The following model is based on the practices used by Strike and Soltis (1985) in their text titled *The Ethics of Teaching*. These authors developed realistic case studies centered around ethical issues and

TABLE 23.4. Ethical Decision-Making Style Matrix

	Individual		Local		Cosmopolitan	
	Mean	SD	Mean	SD	Mean	SD
Egoism	2.26	0.71	2.50	0.78	2.21	0.83
Benevolence	2.11	0.69	1.85	0.80	2.08	1.0
Principal	2.41	0.78	1.90	0.75	2.24	0.80

way of ethical decision making for instructors and administrators in educational institutions.

First, Strike and Soltis (1985) evaluated two major types of ethical theories: consequentialism and nonconsequentialism. The former theoretical perspective is based on whether the consequences of the decision maker's actions were moral or immoral. In short, a consequentialist asserts that the morality or immorality of an action is determined by the consequences of the ethical decision. The nonconsequentialist believes morality or the immorality of an action is determined by sense of duty, obligation, and universal and impartial adherence to principles. However, the current model expands on Strike and Soltis's model by incorporation of ethical theories of egoism, benevolence, and principle into the context of consequentialism and nonconsequentialism. For the purpose of this proposed model, egoism aligns with consequentialism and benevolence and principle align with nonconsequentialism.

Second, vignettes must be developed based on current and pressing ethical dilemmas as extracted from the organizational setting. This phase allows the learner an opportunity to absorb and identify with the issue as applied to the learner's operational setting. However, it would be a good practice to utilize focus groups to validate a vignette's content prior to incorporating the issue into a vignette. The purpose of the focus group is to ensure that the issue has relevance to the setting and to management.

Third, the "learner" is challenged to read and review the key points of the vignette. Basically, the learner is challenged to reflect on on "what" (i.e., the issue) is going on in the vignette. Here the learner enters the situation with their own "experiential baggage." Furthermore, it is the presence of preexisting internalized values and beliefs (e.g., baggage) that strongly impact the learner's reliance on a preferred ethical precept.

Fourth, the learner is challenged to analyze the issue from each theoretical perspective. This process is intended to raise the learner's level of understanding of the unique differences between the theoretical approaches. This, of course, requires an extreme amount of facilitation by the trainer/instructor because it challenges the learner to adopt an ethical stance that varies from his or her own personal value system. This stage is also quite complex because it not only analyzes the theoretical perspective, but includes an analysis of how the referent sources (i.e., personal values, immediate work setting, and societal values) interact to influence an individual's ethical decision.

The last step in the proposed model is to compare and contrast the theoretical approaches available to the learner. This process provides an overview and synthesis of the key concepts germane to each theoretical perspective. It is the latter stage of the model that is expected to offer the learner a deeper appreciation of how his or her ethical conduct is directly linked to organizational effectiveness. Hence, the learning process utilized by Strike and Soltis (1985) provides an overview of introducing the learner to an ethical dilemma, the awareness of the issue by conceptualizing through a chosen ethical precept in combination with the immediate influencing referent source, a consideration of the consequences (e.g., trial), application of the ethical decision, and then an evaluation of the consequences. Also, this model indicates that a feedback loop is part of the process. This feedback loop allows the decision maker the opportunity to make the necessary adjustments in "how" they might resolve a similar situation if the occasion arises again. Still, a caveat to this proposed process of ethical training is that the proper application of ethical theory must be reviewed by a content expert in ethical theory. More specifically, this "expert" can assist in the development and validation of ethical responses based on the ethical derivatives of consequentialism and nonconsequentialism.

In actual practice, ethical decision making proceeds through the typical decision-making steps of awareness, information search, alternative evaluation, application, and evaluation (see Figure 23.1). In the first step of the model the individual becomes aware that a problem exists. Next, information is sought that aids the individual in conceptualizing and in coping with the problem. In this stage of decision making the individual considers various resolution strategies. Third, the individual adopts one strategy in an attempt to resolve the ethical dilemma. Fourth, the individual applies the selected ethical strategy to the ethical dilemma. The last step of the ethical decision-making model involves the individual (ethical decision maker) in a monitoring process. Here the decision maker weighs the positive and negative outcomes of the imposed strategy in an effort to adjust the principles to match the situation better. Of course, the type of adjustment taken is contingent on whether a consequentialist or a nonconsequentialist approach is taken.

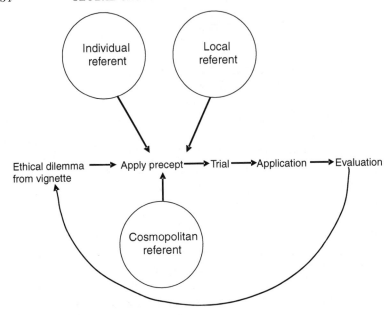

FIGURE 23.1. Ethical Decision-Making Process

CONCLUSION

In conclusion, it is the knowledge gained from understanding the underlying ethical precepts and referent sources that will shed light on how effectively an individual reacts to an ethical situation. Hence, a comprehensive understanding of these ethical precepts and referents can prove quite beneficial to the resolution of an ethical situation. In agreement with Sheldon (1989), the outcome of a structured approach to ethical awareness training raises the level of professionalism by the following:

- Focusing on training individuals in these ethical principles
- Providing information on ethical principles and sources of influence
- Establishing a body of knowledge concerning how an individual approaches ethics in the workplace
- Demonstrating competence in coping with ethical situations

REFERENCES

Coopers and Lybrand (1996). *Hospitality Directions: Forecasts and Analyses for the Hospitality Industry.* New York: Coopers and Lybrand.

Enghagen, L. and Hott, D. (1992). Students' perceptions of ethical issues in the hospitality and tourism industry. *Hospitality Research Journal, 15*(2): 41-50.

Hall, S. (1993). *Ethics in Hospitality Management.* East Lansing, MA: Educational Institute of the American Hotel and Motel Association.

Hall, S. and Enghagen, L. (1991). Ethics in hospitality: Two tested, full credit models for teaching [Abstract]. *Annual CHRIE Conference Proceedings,* pp. 252-253. Richmond, VA: International Council on Hotel, Restaurant and Institutional Education.

Kwansa, F. and Farrar, A. (1991). A conceptual framework for developing a hospitality educators' code of ethics [Abstract]. *Annual CHRIE Proceedings,* pp. 49-50. Richmond, VA: International Council on Hotel, Restaurant and Institutional Education.

Longenecker, J. (1985). Management priorities and management ethics. *Journal of Business Ethics, 4:* 65-70.

O'Halloran, R. (1991). Ethics in business curricula: A Denver University model [Abstract]. *Annual CHRIE Conference Proceedings,* pp. 180-190. Richmond, VA: International Council on Hotel, Restaurant and Institutional Education.

Sheldon, P. (1989). Professionalism in tourism and hospitality. *Annals of Tourism Research, 16*(4): 492-503.

Strike, K. and Soltis, J. (1985). *The Ethics of Teaching.* New York: Teachers College Press.

Upchurch, R. and Ruhland, K. (1996). The organizational bases of ethical work climates in lodging operations as perceived by general managers. *Journal of Business Ethics, 9:* 1083-1093.

Victor, B. and Cullen, J. (1988). The organizational bases of ethical work climates. *Administrative Science Quarterly, 33:* 101-125.

FURTHER READING

Whitney, D. (1990). Ethics in the hospitality industry. *International Journal of Hospitality Management, 9*(1): 187-192.r

Chapter 24

The Ethical Challenges of Managing Pilgrimages to the Holy Land

Stephen R. Sizer

INTRODUCTION

Israel and the occupied territories comprise a unique location, born out of the ravages of war and the Holocaust, its 20,000 square miles of territory claimed by two peoples, the Jews and Palestinians, its holy sites shared uneasily by three religions, Judaism, Islam, and Christianity, often in close proximity, as at the Temple Mount in Jerusalem or the Tomb of the Patriarchs at Hebron. According to Tuchman (1957), "more blood has been shed for Palestine than for any other spot on earth" (p. viii). To Protestant England it was, as Lord Curzon eulogized, "the holiest space of ground on the face of the globe," not only the land of the Scriptures and of the Crusades, but also the land "to which all our faces are turned when we are finally laid in our graves in the churchyard" (Tuchman, 1957, p. viii). It is the geographical junction between East and West, the bridgehead between three continents, and, throughout history, the focal point in the military strategies of succeeding empires. Few countries attract so much media coverage, or arouse such intense religious feeling and political controversy.

This chapter was originally published in Sizer, S. (1999). The ethical challenges of managing pilgrimages to the Holy Land. *International Journal of Contemporary Hospitality Management* 11(2/3): 85-90. Adapted with permission by Emerald Group Publishing Limited.

The pilgrimage and tourist industry, which brings just under two million people from around the world to the Holy Land every year, is both a microcosm and perpetuator of these tensions and divisions. In 1994 300,800 people visited from the UK, of whom approximately 20 percent were pilgrims. In the period January to June 1996 109,638 people visited from the UK (Israeli Government Tourist Office, 1996). Sadly, the indigenous Church is largely ignored by the many thousands of Christian pilgrimage groups whose itineraries involve visiting a predictable succession of archaeological sites and Christian shrines, which vary only according to the denomination of the group and number of days present in the land. That so many Western Christians visit the Holy Land and yet have little or no contact with the indigenous Christian community is a serious ethical issue with important theological implications, not only for the unity and vitality of the Church but also for its very survival in Israel and the occupied territories.

THE DETRIMENTAL IMPACT OF RELIGIOUS TOURISM TO ISRAEL AND THE OCCUPIED TERRITORIES

Many Western pilgrims appear not only ignorant of recent Middle East history but surprised to find an Arab Christian presence at all. Even where Christian visitors are aware of this fact, their behavior obliterates it. Worshipping with their own priest or minister in a closed chapel, shrine, or even hotel, their pilgrimage would be no different if the oldest Christian communities in the world had been obliterated long ago (Macpherson, 1993).

"The ethical issues involved in promoting pilgrimages to the Holy Land and their impact on the Palestinian Christian community are therefore considerable" (Council of Churches for Britain and Ireland [CCBI], 1992, pp. 2-3). "Typical Western perceptions of orientals still appear to be based on nineteenth century colonial stereotypes, formed at a time when Europe controlled 85 percent of the world" (Eber, 1993, pp. 2-3). "These are further reinforced and exploited by Zionist propaganda" (Said, 1978, p. 166). The Palestinians, whether Muslim or Christian, are often branded as terrorists because of their support for violent as well as nonviolent opposition to continued Israeli settlement of the occupied territories.

Western Christians have, for a variety of reasons, tended to show greater sympathy for the state of Israel than for the condition of the Palestinian people. At the same time, during the Cold War and subsequently, U.S. and UK foreign policies have consistently viewed Israel as an important ally in the Middle East. With the demise of Soviet communism, the new enemy, for both right-wing religious fundamentalists and politicians alike, is militant Islam.

These perceptions inevitably exacerbate the vulnerability of Palestinian Christians since they are a minority among Muslim Arabs as well as among Jews within a Zionist state. For Muslim fundamentalists who equate "Arabism" with Islam, Palestinian Christians are an anomaly, guilty by association with European imperialism dating back to the Crusades (Armstrong, 1988).

Contemporary pilgrimage research reveals that "in this century there has been a gradual decline in the level of contact between pilgrim parties and Palestinian Christians" (Ekin, 1990, p. 25). This has, in part, been due to tighter control of the pilgrimage industry by the Israeli Ministry of Tourism, especially since 1967, when the main sites of biblical significance were appropriated by Israel from Jordan, along with the registration of Palestinian guides, hotels, and travel agencies (Bowman, 1992).

This problem is compounded by semantics and propaganda. Is the "Holy Land" Palestine or Israel, and if Israel, which Israel? Neutrality is a rare luxury, and difficult to sustain, linguistically or ethically, given the Palestinians' demand for justice and Israel's need for security, more so since language is both a subtle indicator of presuppositions and a powerful tool of propaganda.

TYPES OF PROTESTANT PILGRIMAGES

Within the very broad diversity of Christian tradition, three particular types of protestant pilgrimage may be discerned: evangelicals, fundamentalists, and living stones (see Table 24.1).

Evangelicals go essentially to visit the sites of biblical significance on what are primarily educational tours. These in themselves will only perpetuate and reinforce a pietistic faith rooted in the first century, without addressing either the present Middle East conflict or necessarily engaging in theological praxis. The presence of an an-

TABLE 24.1. Types of Protestant Christian pilgrimage to the Holy Land

Type of pilgrimage	Emphasis of the tour	Effect on indigenous church
Evangelical	Biblical sites	Indifference and ignorance
Fundamentalist	Eschatological signs of the future	Antipathy and antagonism
Living stones	Human significance in the present	Empathy and solidarity

cient Christianity is either ignored, misunderstood, or even criticized for desecrating the archaeological sites with what are often regarded as pagan shrines.

Fundamentalist pilgrims visit the Holy Land for similar reasons, but with the added eschatological dimension, believing themselves to be witnessing and indeed participating in the purposes of God, at work within Israel in these "Last days." They believe they have a divine mandate to support the state of Israel.

The third, most recent, and smallest category of pilgrimage to emerge is associated with the term "living stones." These pilgrimages in contradistinction seek to counter the ignorance of many evangelicals and the harm caused by fundamentalists by engaging in acts of solidarity with the Palestinian church. These pilgrimages include opportunities to meet, worship with, listen to, and learn from the spirituality and experience of the indigenous Christians.

CATEGORIES OF HOLY LAND TOUR OPERATORS

Four categories of pilgrimage tour operator emerge: First, a small number of secular companies offer what are really religious tourist package holidays. Second, the majority of companies offer biblical-educational tours. Third, a small but influential group of Zionist- or Israeli-owned companies concentrate on the Jewish dimension to the Christian faith. And fourth, only a handful of operators actively encourage contact with the Palestinian church. In terms of comparative influence, if the first group is benign, and the second blind, the third appears bigoted, and only the fourth offers any genuine dialogue or intercourse between pilgrims and Palestinian Christians (see Table 24.2). Based on a series of interviews, the majority of operators ap-

TABLE 24.2. Categories of Holy Land tour operators

Type of tour operator	Nature of tour offered	Effect on indigenous Christians
Secular	Specialist package	Irrelevant
Christian	Biblical archaeology and sites	Ignored
Israeli or Zionist	Bible from Jewish dimension	Antagonistic
Living stones	Encountering the people	Encouragement

pear ignorant of the ethical issues implicit in their business, fail to recognize how they are manipulated by the Israeli authorities, or see how detrimental their trade is to the indigenous Christian community. Based on this evidence it is not surprising that so few pilgrimage groups ever meet with Palestinians.

CONSEQUENCES FOR THE INDIGENOUS PALESTINIANS

The consequences of the ignorance or indifference of UK Christians and tour operators results in significant detrimental effects felt by Palestinians living in the Holy Land, especially by the Christian minority (see Exhibit 24.1). These cumulative consequences have led to a seriously diminished Christian presence that now threatens their very survival in the Holy Land.

DEFICIENCIES INHERENT IN MOST PROTESTANT PILGRIMAGES

The deficiencies inherent in the majority of protestant pilgrimages undertaken to the Holy Land appear essentially threefold (see Exhibit 24.2). For pilgrimage groups and organizers to continue to ignore the presence of a local Christian community is a perversion of what pilgrimage could and should be about. The lack of contact between Christians perpetuates ignorance and complacency for pilgrims and injustice and despair for Palestinians. It is ultimately to treat the Holy Land as nothing more than an entertaining religious theme park, and

EXHIBIT 24.1. Deleterious Consequences of Traditional Pilgrimages Experienced by Palestinians

Consequence

- Dispossession of their land by quasi-judicial confiscation
- Pervasive racial discrimination inherent in an apartheid system denying basic human rights
- Invisibility, hidden from the touristic gaze of Western pilgrims
- Persistent misrepresentation through the Israeli exploitation of the media and propaganda
- Emigration and depletion of the Palestine Christian community in Israel and the West Bank

EXHIBIT 24.2 Three Essential Deficiencies Inherent in the Majority of Protestant Pilgrimages

Deficiency

- A preoccupation with a pietistic religious experience based on visits to locations of Biblical significance which perpetuates the separation of Christian faith from practice
- The absence of any contact with the indigenous Christian church reinforces the ignorance of, and stereotyping by, each community of the other
- The failure of pilgrims to question or challenge the causes of the deep suffering and injustice - Palestinians continue to face in the very land where Jesus Christ came, contradicting his work of bringing peace and reconciliation to the world

will only hasten the day when Palestinian Christians become extinct in the Holy Land, their heritage forgotten and their churches turned into museums.

The litmus test for distinguishing between different kinds of pilgrimages and religious tourism is, it is suggested, the attitude of the organizers and participants toward the presence of an indigenous Christian church. Is the Church visible or invisible? Respected or repudiated? Visited or ignored?

Local Christians are caught in a degree of museumization. They are aware of tourists who come in great volume from the West to savor holy places but who are, for the most part, blithely disinterested in the people who indwell them. The pain of the indifference is not eased insofar as the same tourism is subtly manipulated to make the case for the entire legitimacy of the statehood that regulates it. (Cragg, 1992, p. 28)

Probably as many as 95 percent of Christian pilgrimage groups visiting the Holy Land have a detrimental effect on the indigenous Christian community (see Figure 24.1).

THE ETHICAL ISSUES ENCOUNTERED IN PROMOTING RESPONSIBLE TOURISM TO THE HOLY LAND

The ethical issues and decisions encountered in promoting responsible tourism to the Holy Land are considerable and complex. They may, however, be broken down into two categories: those issues over which tour operators and pilgrimage group leaders have little or no

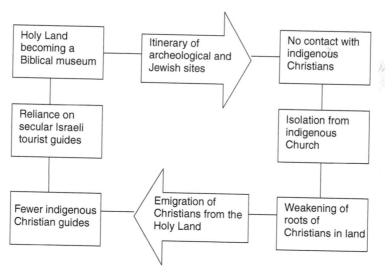

FIGURE 24.1. The Cumulative Effect of Traditional Pilgrimages on the Indigenous Church in the Holy Land.

control, owing to the policies of the Israeli government (see Exhibit 24.3); and those decisions over which they have some influence (see Exhibit 24.4).

To a large degree, acceptance of these restrictions and the orchestrated Israeli agenda for Holy Land pilgrimages is difficult to resist

---

EXHIBIT 24.3. Ethical Issues Encountered on Pilgrimages Determined by the Israeli Government Policy

Ethical issue

- Intensive questioning at British and Israeli airports by Israeli security personnel often occurs well beyond that required for flight security. Questions asked relating to travel plans and contact with Palestinians are probably designed to intimidate and gather intelligence. How far should tour groups comply or refuse to answer questions beyond those that relate to baggage, flight and airport security?
- Restricted access by pilgrims to locations in the Occupied Territories, on the spurious grounds of security measures, e.g. travel to places like Bethlehem, Hebron, Jericho, Nablus and Gaza may be curtailed under locally imposed "closed military orders". Should tour groups protest at these restrictions or seek to evade them by choosing alternative routes?
- Tourist hotel and restaurant facilities on Kibbutzim such as at Ein Gev in Galilee, Banias in the Golan and Engeddi on the Dead Sea are built on confiscated land within the Occupied Territories of former Jordan and Syria. Should pilgrimage groups make use of these facilities and become complicit by association?
- Access to Christian guides is severely restricted. Only a handful of Palestinian guides have been trained and licensed since 1967 by the state of Israel. This means that invariably Christian pilgrimage groups will be led by an Israeli guide. Should pilgrimage groups employ non-licensed Palestinian guides?
- Restrictions imposed on the renovation or extension of Palestinian hotels in locations such as East Jerusalem means that the number of beds within the Arab sector has remained static since 1967 while Israeli West Jerusalem has benefited from Government subsidies and massive expansion. Should tour operators continue to use poorer quality Palestinian hotels or the better Israeli ones?
- Guide books, maps and promotional literature provided by the Israeli Government Ministry of Tourism renders invisible the presence of an indigenous Christian community. Should tour operators use this free literature?

EXHIBIT 24.4. Summary of Ethical Decisions Faced by Holy Land Tour Operators and Group Leaders

Ethical decision

- Choice of airline carrier between BA and El Al, the State controlled and funded Israeli airline on grounds of commercial interest or on principle
- Wording of own promotional literature and maps. To include reference to Israel and the Occupied Territories or use the euphemism "Holy Lands"
- To provide maps that distinguish or hide the Green Line.
- Whether or not to accept Israeli Government Ministry of Tourism subsidies and promotional literature in advertising tours to Israel; e.g. State-sponsored free glossy brochures which operators may overprint with their own details come stamped with the controversial "Jerusalem 3000" logo
- Choice of Israeli tour agents, guides, coach company and hotels. To choose Jewish or Palestinian services on grounds of commercial interest or on principle
- Content of itineraries promoted. To offer what is popular and avoids controversy or encourage tour group leaders to address the contemporary issues on their pilgrimages
- To encourage contact with the indigenous Christian communities or to leave it to individual tour group leaders to decide
- Level of payment made for local services and recommended amount for baksheesh. On the basis of market forces or what is fair. NB Palestinians tend to be paid much less than Israelis fulfilling the same role

without causing inconvenience or anxiety to tour participants; endangering the future licensing and livelihood of Palestinian agents, guides, or coach drivers; or decreasing the profitability of tour operators. For example, following the shooting, allegedly by an Arab, of two UK tourists near Eilat in southern Israel in August 1997, in what the UK Foreign Office described as "a straightforward criminal act," the Israeli Embassy in London exploited the tension by claiming in advice to foreign tourists: "Entry to the West Bank and the Gaza Strip is being very tightly controlled, and visitors are very strongly discouraged from trying to go there. Elsewhere normal rules apply" (Owen, 1997, p. 2).

Subsequently it transpired that the attack was the work of an Israeli who had been a member of an undercover military team involved in the assassination of Palestinian political activists in Gaza.

However, some ethical choices and decisions exist that tour operators and individual tour group leaders have considerable freedom to make, whether intentionally or by default (see Exhibit 24.4).

RESPONSIBLE PILGRIMAGES: SOME PROPOSALS

In addressing these complex and controversial ethical issues associated with managing and promoting pilgrimages and religious tourism to Israel and the occupied territories, what constitutes responsible tourism? In the light of this research, nine distinctive characteristics are offered as a basis for further discussion and investigation (see Exhibit 24.5).

EXHIBIT 24.5. Summary of the Distinctive Characteristics of Responsible Pilgrimages to the Holy Land

Ethical issue

- Preparation before visit with reading material on the historical and political background to the Arab-Israeli conflict, preferably including texts by indigenous Christian leaders
- Meetings with indigenous Christians and representatives during pilgrimage
- Visits to Christian projects within itinerary such as schools, hospitals and other agencies
- Worship on Sundays with local Christians avoiding travel where possible
- Employment of indigenous Christian guides and Palestinian services whenever available
- Stay at Christian hospices and hostels or Palestinian hotels
- Meet with Jewish and Moslem representatives working for peace through justice and reconciliation
- Seek to develop long-term partnership relationships with indigenous Christian communities and serving mission agencies
- Become advocates for the indigenous Palestinian Church on return from pilgrimage

---

The essential task for those who aspire to promote responsible tourism and religious pilgrimages to Israel and the occupied territories is to face the twofold challenge of discovering and then implementing the ways and means by which the tourism industry can bring benefit to the Palestinian economy and Christian communities. The Palestinians need contact and work while tourists need local guides, hotels, and transport services. If the creation of a Christian Disney World managed by expatriates but devoid of indigenous Christians is to be avoided, it is imperative that these communities be given the opportunity to become self-sustaining, ensuring not merely their survival into the next millennium but also their growth and prosperity. Solidarity and partnership through responsible tourism is one answer.

KEY QUESTIONS FOR DISCUSSION

1. What parallels, if any, cab be drawn with ethical issues encountered in tourism to other countries experiencing political tension?
2. How can the cause of responsible tourism to the Holy Land be enhanced from the experience of those engaged in tourism to other countries?
3. What practical steps should be taken to enhance the Palestinian tourist economy?

REFERENCES

Armstrong, K. (1988). *Holy War, The Crusades and Their Impact on Today's World.* London, UK: Macmillan.

Bowman, G. (1992). The politics of tour guiding, Israeli and Palestinian guides in Israel and the occupied territories. In Harrison, D. (ed.), *Tourism and the Less Developed Countries* (pp. 121-134). London, UK: Belhaven.

Council of Churches for Britain and Ireland (CCBI) (1992). *Holy Land Pilgrimage: A Guide for Visitors.* London, UK: CCBI.

Cragg, K. (1992). *The Arab Christian, A History in the Middle East.* London, UK: Mowbray.

Eber, S. (1993). Reflections on images, tourism in focus. *Tourism Concern,* 6(Winter): 2-3.

Ekin, L. (1990). From pilgrimage to packaged tours: Jerusalem and tourism. *Perspectives,* 8 (July): 25-28.

Israeli Government Tourist Office (1996). *Survey of British Tourists Departing from All Borders and Eilat/Ovda, March 1995-February 1996.* London, UK: IGTO.

Macpherson, D. (1993). A living stones pilgrimage. *Living Stones,* December 9, pp. 12-3.

Owen, G. (1997). Tourists warned to avoid flashpoints. *The Times,* August 14, p. 2.

Said, E.W. (1978). *Orientalism.* New York: Vintage.

Tuchman, B.W. (1957). *Bible and Sword, How the British Came to Palestine.* London, UK: Macmillan.

FURTHER READING

Assal, R.A.E. (1992). The identity of the Palestinian Christian in Israel. In Ateek, N.S., Ellis, M.H., and Ruether, R.R. (eds.), *Faith and The Intifada, Palestinian Christian Voices* (pp. 77-84). New York: Orbis Books.

Ateek, N.S. (1990). *Justice and Only Justice, a Palestinian Theology of Liberation.* Maryknoll, NY: Orbis Books.

Bowman, G. (1991). Christian ideology and the image of the holy land, the place of Jerusalem pilgrimage in the various Christianities. In Eade, J. and Sallnow, M.J. (eds.), *Contesting the Sacred, The Anthropology of Christian Pilgrimage* (pp. 98-121). London, UK: Routledge.

Bowman, G. (1992). Pilgrim narratives of Jerusalem and the holy land, a study in ideological distortion. In Morinis, A. (ed.), *Sacred Journeys, The Anthropology of Pilgrimage* (pp. 149-168). Westport, CT: Greenwood Press.

Bowman, G. (1993). Christian pilgrimage, structures of devotion/structures of obedience. *The Month,* December, pp. 491-498.

Eber, S. (1991). Getting stoned on holiday, tourism on the front line, in focus. *Tourism Concern,* 2(Autumn): 4-5.

Eber, S. and O'Sullivan, K. (1989). *Israel and the Occupied Territories, The Rough Guide.* London, UK: Harrap & Columbus.

Prior, M. (1994). Pilgrimage to the holy land, yesterday and today. In Prior, M. and Taylor, W. (eds), *Christians in the Holy Land* (pp. 169-199). London, UK: World of Islam Festival Trust.

Sizer, S.R. (1994). Visiting the living stones, pilgrimages to the Un-Holy Land: An investigation of the perceptions of British and Palestinian Christians on the subject of pilgrimages to the Holy Land, with particular reference to their impact on the indigenous Anglican Church in Israel and the occupied territories. Unpublished master's thesis in applied theology, University of Oxford, Oxford, UK.

Sizer, S.R. (1994). A word after a word after a word is power: With semantics and scripture, Zionists have crafted a peculiar and powerful labyrinth of belief. *Living Stones,* 11(Autumn): 5-6.

Sizer, S.R. (1996). Where to find Christ in the promised land. *Evangelicals Now,* October, p. 16.

Sizer, S.R. (1997). The hidden face of holy land pilgrimage tourism. *International Journal of Contemporary Hospitality Management, 9*(1): 34-35.

Sizer, S.R. (1997). The mountain of the wall: The battle for Jerusalem. *Evangelicals Now,* May, p. 9.

Sizer, S.R. (1997). Pilgrimages to the holy land. Presentation at the International Living Stones Conference, Christian Continuity and the Quest for Peace in the Holy Land, June 21, St. James the Less–Pimlico, London, UK.

Sizer, S.R. (1997). Pilgrimages and politics: A survey of British holy land tour operators. *Living Stones, 14*(Spring): 14-17.

Sizer, S.R. (1998). Render to Caesar: The politics of pilgrimage tourism to the holy land. *International Journal of Contemporary Hospitality Management, 10*(1). Available at: http://www.cc-vw.org/articles/pilgrimage.html.

Turner, V. and Turner, E. (1978). *Image and Pilgrimage in Christian Culture: Anthropological Perspectives*. Oxford, UK: Blackwell.

Wagner, D.E. (1995). *Anxious for Armageddon*. Scottdale, PA: Herald Press.

Chapter 25

State of Practice of Ethics in the Hotel Industry in India: Some Conclusions

Umashankar Venkatesh

INTRODUCTION

The origins of hospitality, as a paid form of service, dates back to the ancient times when grateful travelers would leave a gratuity for their previously unknown hosts more as a mark of their gratitude to the hosts rather than recompense. In India too it has been no different with travel related to trade and commerce, religious motivations, and social commitments being evident since time immemorial. Hospitality as a social manifestation integrated into the personal and group values and behavioral norms of the average Indian is best represented by the adage *Atithi devo bhavah* (Guests are manifestations of god). The scenario in the contemporary context has however changed to organized hospitality, with large corporations having multiple properties all over the country along with small, independent properties usually catering to the budget or economy segments.

What one therefore gets in the Indian context is a range of hospitality businesses from the small, owner-managed, stand-alone properties to large (both Indian and multinational), professionally managed chain hotels.

THE INDIAN HOTEL SECTOR

Indian hotels are categorized into approved and unapproved category hotels. India's Ministry of Tourism grants approval to the hotels

Global Cases on Hospitality Industry
© 2008 by The Haworth Press, Taylor & Francis Group. All rights reserved.
doi:10.1300/5923_25

during the project stage and then the hotels are classified into one of the star categories. This whole process of approval is contingent on the hotel company seeking an approval, but only approved hotels can avail various incentives the government declares for the hospitality sector, namely income tax exemptions, import licenses (especially important for importing equipment as well as certain consumables such as wines, cheeses, etc.), and other approvals. Currently hotels are categorized into seven classes: five star deluxe, five star, four star, three star, two star, one star, and heritage hotels.

Average occupancy in India across all hotel categories in 2003-2004 was 59.7 percent, and the average room rate improved by 34.2 percent in 2003-2004. As far as the tourism sector is concerned, inbound tourists to India in 2004 was 3.37 million, amounting to a 23.8 percent increase over 2003, whereas the 2005 estimate is 4.25 million (HVS International, 2005). The foreign exchange earning from inbound tourism in 2004 is estimated to be $4.8 billion (U.S.), a 36.1 percent increase over 2003. Domestic tourism has also grown by 19 percent from 2003 to 2004, and amounts to 367.6 million tourists. The year 2004 surpassed all previous years for inbound travel. This impressive performance in tourist arrivals is attributable to a strong sense of business and investment confidence in India. The offshoring boom in support services and the information technology sector has caused overseas business travel to take off, and it has increased the inbound business travelers. As per estimates of the World Travel and Tourism Council (2006), Indian tourism demand will grow by 8 percent per annum between 2007 and 2016, which would place India as the second most rapidly growing tourism market in the world after Montenegro and before China. India's travel and tourism industry is expected to contribute 2.1 percent to the gross domestic product (GDP) in 2006, contributing 5.4 percent to the total Indian employment.

The future outlook as reported by HVS International (2005) is pretty good for the Indian hotel sector. Before the slump in the period immediately after 1999, when India tested an atomic device, the industry was at its peak. This was followed by the Kargil conflict with Pakistan. The World Trade Center incident followed by the SARS (severe acute respiratory syndrome) outbreak and then the Iraq invasion kept a leash on the sector till about 2002. But strong demand from the domestic leisure travel and continued travel within India, especially business travel, enabled hotel demand to grow. In 2003-2004, most hotel markets had recovered, across all star categories, and were recording impressive growth in terms of occupancy. During the period of 2003 to 2007, hotel operators have been able to optimize demand and implement proactive rate management strategies. The average rate performance in the majority of markets clearly reflects this. With projections of strong demand growth and limited addition to supply expected, most cities are likely to maintain high occupancies and witness average rate growth in the range of 25 to 30 percent annually for the next three years.

HOW MANAGEMENT STYLE AND OPERATIONAL NATURE CONTRIBUTES TO UNETHICAL PRACTICES

The traditional hotelier in India has been one who has usually come into the business because of ownership of landed properties and buildings that could then be put to some economic use. In earlier times, taking care of needs of travelers was considered a part of community service by local communities or patrons who would build wayside serais (inns) where travelers could stay without any payment and who would usually leave a small gratuity for the caretaker. This was followed by dak bungalows made in the British period mainly meant for government officials on tour but also open to general travelers on payment basis. Hotels for leisure tourists really took off with development in the numerous hill stations of India.

For a long time the management of operations as well as the overall management of hotels in India has vested with the owners and their family members, and frequently with those with no real qualification to do so. Managing hotels was not considered to be a profession and was more seen as a "trade" that required very few skills and little expertise. A telling statistics is that on an average about 65 percent of managers in Indian hotels were found in a survey result published by Federation of Hotel and Restaurant Association of India (2001) not to possess any formal training or qualification in this hotel/hospitality management. Even today it is not rare to overhear senior executives (including human resources executives) in Indian hotels emoting that hotel management is not "rocket science," indicating the poor esteem in which the industry is held and as a consequence the neglected and decrepit status of the employees. For very a long time (and the trend continues even today to an extent), hospitality and hotels have not been the first career choice for most people, and even for those who have joined the industry it is not out of choice. Those who do so do it either for the glamour associated with the hotel industry or for other reasons.

Second, the shop-floor or factory routine and environment dominate the organizational culture and ethos, and organizational structures are prevalently hierarchical and multitiered. Command and control is the religiously followed managerial style, and rank and file is expected to blindly adhere to these norms. Federation of Hotel and Restaurant Associations of India (2001) reports that five star deluxe hotels in India have on an average four levels in managers, two levels in supervisors, and two to four levels in staff positions. However, in best practice hotels these went down to 3, 2, and 2 for managers, supervisors, and staff respectively. The same survey also crucially reveals that the ratio of managers/supervisors to staff ranges from 1:3 to 1:4 for the five star deluxe hotels in India, to 1:10 for the three star categories. This confirms the intense command and control environment in the hotel organizations.

Overstaffing at the lower levels, especially as easy availability of entry-level people drives down wages to very low levels, is a common phenomena. In the survey of general managers' opinions on overstaffing in Indian hotels (Federation of Hotel and Restaurant Associations of India, 2004), on an average across all hotel categories the view was equally divided on the reasons for overstaffing. The most important determinant of overstaffing was reported as lack of trained staff, low wages, concern for quality service, and union pressure. Absenteeism and lack of automation and interest on the part of the owners were also cited as factors leading to overstaffing, but not by all categories. Crucially, lack of trained staff seemingly is the major factor causing overstaffing.

The conclusion therefore is that the operating environment within Indian hotels is conducive for practices that lead to exploitation of rank and file, poor work conditions, a high degree of control and supervision, lack of empowerment, poor wages, and high staff turnover. On the other hand, the degree of autocratic power coupled with a relatively demotivating organizational climate implies toward a compromised state of ethical practices within the Indian hotel sector.

THE GROWTH IMPERATIVES
FOR THE INDIAN HOTEL SECTOR

Externally, the hotel sector must look for opportunities in a structured manner to disseminate the advantages among a wider cast of recipients, including benefits for local communities and economies to ecological conservation. This could be achieved by including and integrating the local populace and their skills in the business model and delivery, and with training and developing new skills and knowledge among the local people. Hotels must also look at developing the local businesses by developing and expanding suppliers/channel partners from among the local community as far as possible. The overarching concern should be one of conservation, balance, and equity in all facets of the business they pursue. Enhancing the sector's commitment to local people and their communities and environments can harness this power. This would not only benefit those who work in the sector, or use its services, or spend the tax revenues it generates, but also these benefits can flow through to people at the receiving end of tourism, namely local citizens in destinations, and entire populations for whom tourism can radically improve prospects of growth and prosperity.

Regarding organization design and strategy, Indian hotel organizations need to align and adjust their business objectives, planning, product, and quality of their service delivery through adopting policies that respect the interests of the people for and with whom it works.

In the new millennium, with India slated to become a global economic and knowledge hub, along with its cultural heritage, the Indian hotel companies need to strengthen their operations with a longer-term focus and a shift from quarter-to-quarter financial growth objectives to building shareholder value and ensuring long-term sustainability and security by respecting the communities in which they operate. The business logic of such an approach is proven, but obviously not in the short run. Integration and respect of local identities and cultures in one's business model and planning is an imperative that can be ignored only at the cost of lost franchise both among customers (internal as well as external) and local communities.

The World Travel and Tourism Council (2003) has delineated the following touchstones that the private sector tourism companies must meet in order to balance economics with environment, people, and cultures, which could be easily adopted by the Indian hotel sector:

1. Expanding markets while promoting and protecting natural resources and local heritage and lifestyles
2. Developing careers, education, and employee relations; promoting smaller firms; raising environmental awareness; and helping in its own way to narrow the gap between the "haves" and "have-nots"
3. Sensitive provision of traditional tourism products and imaginative product diversification that reduces seasonality and increase yields
4. Improving the quality of tourism products and services, and adding value for money while increasing consumer choice
5. Agreeing and implementing quality standards at all levels and in all areas, including staff training
6. Transfer of industry skills and best practice that spreads the benefits widely and efficiently
7. Increasingly sophisticated and more precise measurement of the sector's own activity, to feed into strategic business decisions
8. Communicating more effectively with the world in which it operates, including energetic input from travel and tourism umbrella organizations to government, at strategic and local levels

If we try and analyze the previous eight tenets almost all of them have direct and immediate connotations for ethical business practices and leadership. For instance, item 3 looks innocuously to be a marketing/business decision, but the qualification that provision should be "sensitive" reveals the ethical underpinning. The previous list could therefore very well form the business philosophy of Indian hotels and shape their market orientations.

THE STAKEHOLDERS

The stakeholders as far as the hotel sector is concerned could include the following:

- The board of directors
- Employees
- Franchisees (if it is a franchising company)
- Hotel owners (if it is a management company)
- Shareholders (if it is a listed company)
- Vendors/suppliers of products and services
- Channel partners and associates
- Customers (internal and external)
- Local communities
- Public at large

AREAS IN WHICH UNETHICAL PRACTICES ARE MORE EVIDENT

In the context of employees and customers only, the following areas are important in the Indian context as far as studying ethical practices:

1. Food safety and sanitation
2. Adherence to company policy
3. Theft, pilferage
4. Misrepresentation of facts or prevarication (e.g., excuses for failure to deliver to internal/external customers)
5. Human and customer relation
6. Managerial systems and responses to employee complaints and problems

Josephson (1992, cited in Vallen et al., 2000) provides a set of principles that can form the basis for ethical decision making and for establishing standards or rules of behavior within which a future hospitality manager must function. These are discussed in the following sections.

Accountability

This principle holds that people are morally accountable for their actions and treatment of others, particularly in relation to their specific professional position and role in the workplace. Morally responsible hospitality managers should be accountable for the welfare of the employees they supervise given that, in most cases, the workers' livelihood depends on them.

In the Indian context some evidence to the contrary exists in the context of hotel employees. The traditional organizational structure of the Indian hotel is highly hierarchical and regimented, with flat or team structures being very rare to find. This coupled with the feudal mindset and paternal styles of management results in hierarchies that are seen as power/authority differentiators rather than work expeditors. Venkatesh and Kulkarni (2002) indicate that it is quite possible that the entire industry (Indian hotel sector) has been traditionally based on feudalism rather than on modern hospitality (managerial) tenets, and that today's industrial culture is a mix between understanding hospitality as a concept and this embedded philosophy of feudalism. This deep-rooted feudalism has led to a great deal of belief in hierarchies and their ability to deliver results. Venkatesh and Kulkarni (2002) conclude that these hierarchical structures deliver results that tend to satisfy only a few. Migration to other industry sectors and high employee turnover in the Indian hotel sector could be one of the manifestations also stemming from this.

Commitment to Excellence

Commitment to excellence determines the necessity to deliver the best service possible for the price obtained. Hospitality managers who deviate from this principle would cheat their guests of their right to have their money's worth for services received.

It is not at all uncommon for customers to frequently feel that they have been "ripped-off" as far as the service experience in the Indian hotel sector is concerned, compared to the prices they may have paid. Lack of professionalism resulting in variable levels of commitment to excellence across the industry is quite evident. This obviously has connotations to employee training as well as managerial systems and practices. It could be said that larger chain hotels with a corporate management structure do look at training and development investment for employees favorably, but with stand-alone hotels this is hard to envisage. This is corroborated by the findings that for hotels with up to 50 rooms, only 20.3 percent were found to have a training department, whereas it was 29.1 percent for hotels with 50 to 150 rooms, and 56.8 percent for hotels having more than 150 rooms. Another telling statistic is that among all chain-affiliated hotels, this figure was found to be 50.4 percent, whereas for independent hotels it was a lowly 17.2 percent (Federation of Hotel and Restaurant Associations of India, 2004). This is indicative of the wide variance in standards and practices within the industry and in the management outlook toward training as a function and its relative importance. It is obvious that training is most probably looked at by hotel owners in India as a preserve of the large (corporate/chain) brands, and is considered at best a deferrable expense.

Second, the basis of managerial decision making—until the time it has economic justification, at least—could be termed as professional, beyond which it may breach the limits of ethical practices. As an example of this, the current dilemma of the Indian hotel sector, which is coping with unprecedented boom in demand, is aptly described by Mansukhani (2005) through the dilemma faced by hospitality marketers:

> extended periods of buoyancy are not that much of a party either when there is not enough to sell and suddenly, they (hotel sales people) find themselves victims of guest angst over either inflated tariffs or simply no availability at any tariff. If they are a tad accommodative of their loyal niche, then the ownership or management strains its eyebrows at their ignorance of a revenue management mechanism that works on a more straightforward logic. All this raises a nightmarish specter of a tight ropewalk and erring on either side is virtually inevitable.

Another fact in point is that the difference between the "rack rates" published by the hotels vary from the actual tariff charged by a variable margin of up to an astounding 70 to 75 percent (on the lesser side obviously). Keeping this in view, the government of India has promulgated a policy to tax room earnings of hotels on the basis of the published rack rates and not on the actual tariff charged to the customer. As a result of this the customer ends up paying an amount (to cover for the extra tax amount) that he or she should not have to pay.

What this indicates is a contingency approach that does not really augur well as far as consumer welfare is concerned. On the flip side, the adverse impact that this may be having on employees should also not be ignored.

Concern for Others

At the minimum, the golden rule, "do unto others as you would have them do to you," applies in having a human concern for the needs of others. This principle is hard to observe from the lofty position of managers looking down on contracted/temporary workers performing menial jobs.

In Indian hotels this is especially visible during banquets and outdoor catering for which as a rule contracted (read: usually poorly trained and paid) workers are taken on for menial and operative jobs for the event. Another generic and chronic issue is long work hours that usually extend beyond the scheduled eight-hour shift. It is not exceptional to find operative as well as junior management staff regularly working extra hours almost as a norm. Scheduling for paid overtime is rare, and department heads and managers expect staff to routinely work extra hours. In the context of student interns, as discussed before, this problem of extra work is more acute, as these interns are not even paid the minimum daily wage defined by the government. This is a practice that is common across small, independent hotel companies as well as large chains.

Another aspect is one of whether the management system provides for employee welfare and whether a formal grievance handling mechanism exists. Although the government of India has enunciated guidelines for companies to prepare a manual that delineates the rights and procedures thereof for employees, very few hotels have this in place.

This concern for others needs to be extended to include the interests of the local communities and society at large. This could be manifested variously, through a concern for environment, a spirit of conservation, limiting profligate behavior and approach sustainability, using local skills and labor in the business model, etc.

Fairness

A basic policy is to deal with people evenhandedly for equal performance. In violation of this principle, hotel managers tend to deal discriminatingly between permanent/confirmed employees and contracted/temporary workers. Also, stories of ill treatment of the multitude of hotel management student (interns) who work in Indian hotels for various periods of time as part of their course requirements are legion. Student interns are not paid the minimum daily wage and are routinely paid Rs. 250 to Rs. 450 ($6.16 to $11.09 [U.S.] approximately) per month during their period of internship.

Contract employees are routinely hired in various departments such as security, maintenance, transport, etc. In many such occasions outsourcing firms are usually contracted with this work, but usually they only supply people who are then supposed to work as per the instructions of the managers of the hotel. The negotiation of fee to be paid to these firms is usually ruthless and in turn leads to very poor compensation being paid to the actual worker by the outsourcing firm.

Another aspect of fairness could be paying of wages/compensation commensurate with other industries. Starting salaries for trainees in Indian hotels have traditionally been very low, most probably a function of their relative inexperience and lack of skills, but the situation is improving, albeit very gradually. This aspect is emphasized by the employee turnover figures of Indian hotels as reported by the Federation of Hotel and Restaurant Associations of India (2001), which indicates that in case of five star deluxe hotels the highest turnover of staff, including managers/supervisors, was in the area of food and beverage service at 16.2 percent, followed closely by food and beverage production, front office, and then housekeeping. The turnover in departments such as sales and marketing, maintenance, human resources, and finance were relatively low. This pattern was reported in similar percentage levels in five star, four star, and three star hotels. However, the annual turnover of staff in two and one star was as high as 27.9 percent in the food and beverage service area. Obviously, operations-related departments experience a higher degree of employee churn. This could be attributed partially to a sense of being poorly compensated on part of the operating staff as compared to staff from marketing/sales and other staff function areas.

Honesty

Being able and willing to state the truth (no matter how painful) is ethically essential. This is true not only because deceiving or misleading others often results in costly lawsuits, and in some cases jail sentences. In the context of Indian hotels a basic level of transparency between management and staff needs to be established and enhanced over time. Moving to a less hierarchical and more team-based structure may be also helpful.

Integrity

Although soundness of moral principle and character may be qualities of an individual's moral code, managers and employees may feel conflicting pulls of moral conscience and self-interest. The hospitality industry offers many examples of situations that can damage individual integrity and responsibility. One instance would be a manager's willingness to continue daily operations even as the property is polluting the local environment, overcharging clients (all in the name of yield/revenue management practices), mistreating employees (for example, by not paying for overtime), not investing in training and staff development, delayed payment to vendors, etc. This may be addressed, at least to an extent, by investing in systems that take away some of the ambiguities in decision-making processes. These could take the form of written manuals and codes of conduct for each level of staff and management. Standard operating procedures need to be created, communicated, and adhered to. For instance, it will be rare in Indian hotels to find a manual explaining the employee grievance handling procedure that an employee can look to for succor in case of any such event.

Law Abiding

An action's legality does not guarantee that the action is morally right. While laws codify customs and mores, they can reflect political compromise and, thus, are not sufficient to establish the moral standards that should guide individuals or professions. As a result, hospitality managers can follow the letter of the law while still acting against their values. An example might be taking advantage of lax pollution/environmental laws and exploit groundwater in a profligate and irresponsible manner. (This applies especially in water-deficient areas, namely the state of Rajasthan in India where inbound tourism is one of the mainstays of the state economy. The historic city of Udaipur suffered because of depletion of water from all of the lakes that supply water to the entire city, part of the blame being attributed to the large number of luxury and other category hotels catering to inbound and domestic tourists.)

Leadership

To restore trust in business, ethical leadership is more necessary than ever before. Ethical leadership not only in the context of setting a good example but also in stimulating ethical conduct of employees, having a sound understanding of the ethical quality and ethical progress of the organization, and taking appropriate measures on the basis of this knowledge (Trevino et al., 2000; Kaptein, 2003).

Another aspect of ethical leadership is to enhance the management's awareness of the irregularities in the organization as well as their sensitivity regarding the extent to which the organizational structure and culture stimulates unethical conduct. It is crucial therefore for the leadership to help create an organizational culture of openness and transparency in which unethical conduct will become visible and in which employees and managers can assess one another as accountable individually as well as departmentally (Kaptein and Avelino, 2005).

An example of ethical leadership in the hospitality industry would be to refuse to employ student interns at below minimum wage rates even when competitors are doing so.

Loyalty

Faithfulness to engagements and obligations toward laws, companies, guests, and employees should be part of the moral behavior of all professionals. This faithful adherence may be difficult if one's own benefit or social comfort is at stake. A hospitality manager might, for instance, find it difficult to abide by legal or company principles if his or her quarterly bonus for improving the bottom line is in jeopardy. Again, this could be implemented by setting up stringent and transparent systems and standard operating procedures, with strict and universal adherence to the same.

Promise Keeping

Some time ago, a business deal made orally with another person carried all the necessary assurance that the expectations would be fulfilled. Today, most deals must be closed in the presence of attorneys lest one of the parties involved breaks the original promise. Hospitality managers intending to make use of another person as a means to an end would be acting untrustworthily. A common and rampant practice is to delay payments to be made to vendors, suppliers, and third party service providers, even when this is against the agreed-upon terms and conditions. This becomes possible as most vendors/suppliers exist in a highly competitive supply market and they value the existing relationship to the extent of letting themselves be exploited. In another context, it is almost impossible to see an Indian hotel company manifesting a policy of "satisfaction guaranteed" and communicating the same to all concerned. Internally, a system of ombudsman who can look into such complaints along with adherence to SOPs (standard operating procedures) may help.

Reputation

The community's and guests' estimation of a company is important for conducting business. Attempts by hotel managers to resist employees' organizing could cast an unfavorable shadow on the company's ethical values. Brand building through enhancing reputation is still nascent in its inception as far as the Indian hotel sector is concerned, and is also largely limited to the chain hotel companies.

Corporate social responsibility (CSR) is gradually forming an integral part of a hotel's nonoperational activity, at least for chain hotels in India. The thrust of corporate social responsibility of most hotels is to build livelihoods with a clear focus on women, craftspeople and artisans, and education of children. For instance, the Tata ethos places a special emphasis on community and environmental and ecological issues; this emphasis also percolates to its hotel division. The greater portion of what the group does in this sphere is by choice and conviction. The central tenet of this philosophy is people and communities, often in rural regions and frequently facing inequitable struggles to secure livelihoods. Taj Group's community development program in Chennai found a different sort of supplier for its seafood requirements: women's self-help groups (SHG). The success of this venture encouraged the Taj to look for more SHGs who could supply other requirements. It soon tied up with the Ullasa Paravaigal Women's SHG to supply vegetables. Here, too, the women were trained by Taj personnel in hygiene and taught to clean vegetables with chlorine solution in pure water ("The Good Samaritan," 2005). Another example is the Orchid Hotel (Ecotel) in Mumbai that has enhanced its reputation through its conduct based on ecologically friendly business practices and hotel design.

One area needing action by Indian hotels is the provision of customer guarantees in cases of service failure. This is rare in existence as well as rarely dispersed or advertised by Indian hotel companies.

Respect for Others

One of Kant's principles states that everyone should be treated as an end, not merely as means to an end. Every human being deserves to be treated with respect, as an independent moral agent. The previous example of "hiring" student trainees at low wages (conveniently named as a stipend) also violates this principle of respecting other human beings.

The previous discussion leads to an overall picture of ethical practices in the Indian hotel sector that is not really very encouraging. Instances and statistics that have been mentioned tend to indicate clearly toward the broad-based malaise ailing the industry. Professionalism and investing in rigorous systems of governance and management is the logical way out, with attendant structural rationalization.

REFERENCES

Federation of Hotel and Restaurant Associations of India (2001). *HR Practices in the Indian Hospitality Industry.* New Delhi, India: FHRAI

Federation of Hotel and Restaurant Associations of India (2004). *Staffing Patterns in Indian Hotels: Improvement in Productivity through Multiskilling, Outsourcing, and Other Means.* New Delhi, India: FHRAI.

Federation of Hotel and Restaurant Associations of India (2004). *Indian Hotel Industry Survey: 2003-2004.* New Delhi, India: FHRAI.

The Good Samaritan (2005). *Express Hospitality,* December 15. Available at: http://www.expresshospitality.com/20051215/management01.shtml.

HVS International (2005). *Hotels in India: Trends and Opportunities.* New Delhi, India: HVS International.

Kaptein, M. (2003). The diamond of managerial integrity. *European Management Journal, 21*(1): 99-108.

Kaptein, M. and Avelino, S. (2005). Measuring corporate integrity: A survey based approach. *Corporate Governance, 5*(1): 45-54.

Mansukhani, B. (2005). Selling during good times. *Express Hospitality,* December 31. Available at: http://www.expresshospitality.com/20051231/management01 .shtml.

Trevino, L.K., Hartman, L.P., and Brown, M. (2000). Moral person and moral manager: How executives develop a reputation for ethical leadership. *California Management Review, 42*(4): 128-142.

Vallen, G. and Casado, M. (2000). Ethical principles for the hospitality curriculum. *Cornell Hotel and Restaurant Administration Quarterly, 41*(2): 44-51.

Venkatesh, U. and Kulkarni, A. (2002). Employee motivation and empowerment in hospitality, rhetoric or reality: Some observations from India. *Journal of Services Research, 2*(1): 31-53.

World Travel and Tourism Council (2003). *Blueprint for New Tourism.* London, UK: WTTC.

World Travel and Tourism Council (2006). *India Travel and Tourism Climbing to New Heights.* London, UK: WTTC.

FURTHER READING

World Travel and Tourism Council (2004). *India: Travel and Tourism Forging Ahead.* London, UK: WTTC.

Chapter 26

Work Values of Chinese Food-Service Managers

Chak-Keung Simon Wong
Kam-Ho Manson Chung

INTRODUCTION

Globalization, with its vast influence on the global economy, society, and culture, has brought significant impacts in its wake. Likewise, the global diffusion of Chinese food culture has occurred during the past two hundred years, under the impact of Western capitalism and colonialism (Li, 2001).

Nowadays, Chinese food has become one of the three major popular cuisines in the United States and the UK ("Chinese Food Wins," 2001; "International Foods," 2001). Chinese flavors and cooking techniques have become commonplace on many menus, and Chinese-concept restaurants sport truly mainstream images. In all likelihood, Chinese cuisine seems to be making more headway on the international palate (George, 2001).

Chinese food-service operation is a Chinese-dominated profession. In the same vein, Collins and Williams (2000) concluded from their interviews that at many Chinese, Japanese, Italian, and other ethnic restaurants, for instance, owners said that they needed to hire employees sharing their own backgrounds. They said that customers

This chapter was originally published in Wong, C-K. S. and Chung, K-H. M. (2003). Work values of Chinese food service. *International Journal of Contemporary Hospitality Management,* 15(2): 66-75, Adapted with permission by Emerald Group Publishing Limited.

demanded the authenticity implied by the presence of ethnic waiters in ethnic restaurants. However, on many occasions, it is inevitable that the Chinese restaurants are managed by non-Chinese managers. Especially in the context of multinational hotel companies, managers employed to be in charge of the food and beverage department of a hotel are usually expatriates. Modern expatriates are often younger, better qualified, more likely to be female, and come from many different countries across the globe (Gliatis and Guerrier, 1993). A study by Yu and Pine (1994) reported that the Hong Kong hotel industry employed quite a high proportion of expatriate managers, particularly in luxury hotels. Although only 16.8 percent of hotel managers in Hong Kong were expatriates, they tended to dominate the top management positions.

Expatriates often face problems when entering a foreign work culture. The differences in managerial values and practices among countries often confuse and frustrate expatriate managers, and cause the ineffectiveness or even failure of the overseas assignment. Estimates show an average failure rate of approximately 30 percent across all locations for U.S. expatriates, and this is significantly higher for expatriate appointments in developing countries (Dowling et al., 1994). It is also recognized by some theorists that an expatriate's ability to understand culture and manage in a cross-cultural fashion has an important part to play in their management capabilities (Go and Pine, 1995; Hoecklin, 1995; Littlejohn, 1997; Overstall, 1997). One of the three most common reasons for expatriate failure was that the manager was unable to understand the values of the home culture and the host culture and was lacking the ability to differentiate between the two on various dimensions (Powers, 1992). A person's attitudes and values are all, to a large extent, shaped by culture. What is valued by the people of one country may not be valued by the people of another country (Hofstede, 1980a; Dillon, 1999). Managers tend to behave in ways that reflect what is valued in their own particular country, especially when making difficult or complex decisions (Lai and Lam, 1986). In international business relations, managers frequently face highly uncertain situations and fall back on their value systems to make decisions (Tung and Miller, 1990). Likewise, some food-service managers used information from studies of personnel behavior in other industries, even though such studies may not be relevant, because data are not available from the food-service industry (Morgan, 1971).

Results of an experimental study indicated that culturally homogeneous groups of workers had higher performance than did culturally heterogeneous groups of workers on five group tasks (Thomas, 1999). Other researchers supported workers being more satisfied and committed when their values were congruent with the values of their supervisors (Spinale, 1980; Mullins, 1985; Meglino et al., 1989). Thus, awareness of similarities and differences should help managers better understand and appreciate their international counterparts and, ideally, should lead to improved cross-national working relationships (Ralston et al., 1992). The results of various surveys demonstrated that the workers were more satisfied and committed when their values were congruent with the values of their supervisors (Spinale, 1980; Mullins, 1985; Meglino et al., 1989).

Moreover, China's accession to the World Trade Organization (WTO) is expected to attract more multinational hotel and catering companies to China, and opportunities for expatriates to work in China are fast increasing. Yet, as Shay and Tracey (1997) alluded, most studies on expatriate manager performance have been conducted across a variety of industries and fail to consider the specific requirements of hospitality management. Even less studies address the specific work-related values of the Chinese food-service personnel in both China and Hong Kong. Because of the lack of research focusing specifically on the Chinese food service industry, the goal of this study is to identify the work values of the hotel Chinese restaurant managers by targeting Hong Kong as a case study. Tanner and Tucker (1996) concluded that the Chinese food in Hong Kong was of consistently high caliber, and that the best food in Hong Kong was to be found in hotels. Thus, hotel Chinese restaurant managers were chosen as the targeted sample of this study.

Therefore, the scope of this study focuses on understanding the work values of Hong Kong Chinese managers so that it can provide solid knowledge and inspiration for any hotel chain entering into Hong Kong. Nevertheless, this research does not attempt to conduct comparative surveys between different independent Chinese restaurants or Chinese restaurants in different countries.

OBJECTIVES

Three major objectives are established for this research, which are the following:

1. To find out the underlying dimensions of work values of the hotels' Chinese restaurant managers in Hong Kong
2. To investigate any significant differences among Chinese restaurant managers' demographic variables and industrial experience variables, including age, gender, number of years in attaining education, length of service in present hotel, length of service in Chinese restaurant industry, level of work and type of hotel (the null hypothesis will be that no significant difference exists between different demographic variables over the underlying dimensions)
3. To recommend possible strategies for foreign hotel companies when they want to enter the Chinese food service industry or operate Chinese restaurants

CONCEPTS OF WORK VALUES

Numerous studies have examined work values, rewards, and their relationships with other work-related organizational behaviors, such as work commitment and job satisfaction (Kalleberg, 1977; Walker et al., 1982; Pinfield, 1984; Mottaz, 1986, 1988; Loscocco, 1989; Kanchier and Wally, 1989; Wood et al., 2000). Before proceeding to review the concept of work values, it is necessary to give some initial attention to the meaning of values.

One of the most prominent and influential writers on values and value systems is Rokeach (1973), who defines a value as "an enduring belief." Central to these definitions is that values and value systems are thought of in relative terms: values in terms of preferences for behaviors or end-states relative to their converses, and value systems in terms of the relative importance of any given value relative to others in the system.

Hofstede (1980a), in a massive cross-cultural study of employees working internationally for IBM, found significant national differences in work-related values. Hofstede (1980a) defined the following four dimensions of culture that differ across countries:

1. Power distance
2. Uncertainty avoidance
3. Individualism versus collectivism
4. Masculinity versus femininity

Hofstede's cultural dimensions are richly suggestive of psychological process. However, his work was based solely on evaluative instruments developed in the West, leading to the question: Can the Eastern value system be captured with instruments based on Western ideology? (Hofstede and Bond, 1984). In response to this concern, the Chinese Culture Connection, an international network of colleagues, orchestrated by Bond (1987), developed an instrument called the Chinese Value Survey (CVS). The CVS, which was developed to identify values indigenous to the Chinese culture, focuses on the fundamental values held by Chinese people. In their study of twenty-two countries, they identified four dimensions within the CVS instrument. These dimensions are the following:

1. Confucian work dynamism
2. Human heartedness
3. Integration
4. Moral discipline

Although the CVS was developed solely as a measure of the basic values held by Chinese people, it has proved to be valuable in identifying significant differences in values among managers in the United States, People's Republic of China (PRC), and Hong Kong (Ralston et al., 1992, 1999).

On the other hand, researchers have been able to compare the CVS dimensions to Western developed measures. For example, when compared with Hofstede's (1980b) IBM research, three of the four CVS dimensions aligned closely with three of the four Hofstede dimensions (Hofstede and Bond, 1988). The nonmatching CVS dimension was Confucian dynamism. Moreover, Hofstede's dimensions and the Rokeach Value Survey dimensions align closely (Hofstede and Bond, 1988). Thus, the CVS, which focuses on Eastern value, is comparable to Western instruments while adding an element missing from the Western developed measures.

Values of Chinese Workers

The Chinese people have shared a common culture, which developed through a 5,000-year evolution. Researchers in the study of Chinese cultural values may find it amazing that Chinese values have formed a clear and consistent system for generations (Kindle, 1982; Hsu, 1970). The Chinese cultural values are largely formed and created from interpersonal relationships and social orientations. This is shown in the work of Confucius, whose doctrine is still a basic pillar of Chinese life today. Confucian philosophy, preaching the values of filial piety, loyalty, righteousness, friendship, and the importance of education, took root in China, strongly influencing the moral code of Chinese society.

The fundamental Confucian assumption is that humans exist in relationship to others (Bond and Hwang, 1986). Bond and Hwang (1986) stated that the Western starting point of the anemic individual is alien to Chinese consideration of humans' social behavior, which sees humans as relational beings, socially situated and defined within an interactive context. Confucius' teachings are lessons in practical ethics without any religious content.

The prevalent type of bureaucracy in Hong Kong is the personal bureaucracy, which resembles an Asian family (Hofstede, 1980a). Hong Kong was included in Hofstede's survey sample in 1980. Along with several other Asian countries, Hong Kong was classified as high power distance, medium to low uncertainty avoidance, low individualism, and medium masculinity. Work values have subtle but powerful influence on work life (Hofstede and Bond, 1984).

A recent study on the job factors that may motivate Hong Kong's hotel employees divulged that the top three factors for Hong Kong hotel employees were, in order:

1. Opportunities for advancement and development;
2. Loyalty to employers
3. Good wages

The top three factors for food and beverage (F&B) employees were the following:

1. Opportunities for development
2. Job security
3. Good wages (Siu et al., 1997)

In another study (Redding, 1984), Hong Kong culture appeared to stress formality, power distance, and acceptance of authority. It also scored high on centralization, autocracy, paternalism, and collectivism. Lai and Lam (1986) compared the work values of managers from Hong Kong to those from the People's Republic of China. They reported that the Hong Kong sample ranked challenge, desirable living area, good working relationship with superior, recognition, freedom to adopt own approach, opportunity for advancement, and sufficient time for personal and family life as being more important than the samples from Beijing and Wuhan. Chau (1977) compared Hong Kong workers' work values with those of other countries. The main finding from her study was that overwhelming concern for monetary reward and self-interest seemed to characterize the Hong Kong workers. Mok and Finley (1986) surveyed 373 Hong Kong food-service workers and reported that more than 53 percent of their respondents ranked pay as the most important aspect of their job followed by opportunity for promotion.

Very little has been reported in the literature on work values of Chinese food-service workers, particularly in the Asia-Pacific region. Pizam (1993) lamented that more research is needed in this important area to provide information that will be industry specific and relevant to various national and ethnic cultures. Even in the same culture, different people behave and react differently. Hong Kong Chinese behave differently from Taiwanese and, of course, mainland Chinese. This research attempts to focus the scope of study in the Hong Kong Chinese hotel managers.

METHODOLOGY

Population Frame and Targeted Sample

In accordance with Hong Kong Tourists Association's (1999) (reconstituted as the Hong Kong Tourism Board in 2001) hotel supply situation report, issued in May 1999, there were altogether seventy-six hotels in Hong Kong by the end of March 1999; therefore, these seventy-six hotels were adopted as the population frame for this study.

Since the purpose of this study is an attempt to determine the work values of Chinese restaurant managers in Hong Kong hotels, only those employees belonging to the managerial ranking were selected for this study. Moreover, managers who match the following sampling specifications are the subjects of this study:

- Chinese ethnic origin
- Educated locally to primary or above levels
- Employed as a full-time employee in a Chinese restaurant managed by a hotel

Questionnaire

The questionnaire for this research is composed of the 1980 version of Hofstede's VSM (value survey module) and demographic questions. The original survey is a score of thirty-three items tapping perceptions, personal behavior, and beliefs.

This research does not attempt to test the generalizability of Hofstede's VSM model. In fact, it aims to study only the work values of the Chinese restaurant managers in Hong Kong. In this connection, the first eighteen work value research questions were adopted from the VSM model. Five additional questions, which have relation with work values, were adopted from the CVS. As a result, section one of the questionnaire for this research was composed of twenty-three questions altogether.

Section two of the questionnaire was comprised of demographic items, such as gender, age, and length of service in the Chinese restaurant industry, etc. The questionnaire was translated and back-translated from English to Chinese.

RESULTS AND DISCUSSION

Profile of Respondents

By the end of August 1999, a total of 152 valid questionnaires were collected from 58 hotels by mail, with an overall response rate of 67 percent. Table 26.1 reveals the demographic profile of the sample. Over 87 percent of the respondents were male. The majority of the respondents fell within the age range of 30 to 49 years, and around 80

TABLE 26.1. Profile of Respondents

Demographic items (N = 152)	Valid percentage
Gender	
Male	87.5
Female	12.5
Age group	
Under 35	38.8
35-39	27.0
39 or above	34.2
Number of years in attaining education	
10 years or less	27.0
11-12 years	42.7
13 years or above	30.3
Length of service in present hotel	
Less than 3 years	26.3
3-5 years	32.9
Over 5 years	40.8
Length of service in Chinese restaurant industry	
Less than 6 years	35.5
6-10 years	28.9
Over 10 years	35.5
Kind of work	
Manager	69.1
Manager of other managers	30.9
Race	
Chinese	100.0
Type of hotel	
High tariff A	42.8
High tariff B	38.2
Medium tariff	19.1

percent of them had an education level of 13 years or below. The average lengths of service in the present hotel and the Chinese restaurant industry were 3 to 5 years and 6 to 10 years, respectively. All the respondents were Chinese with almost 70 percent of them being frontline managers. The number of respondents from both high tariff A and high tariff B hotels were quite similar to each other at about 40 percent, while the rest, 20 percent, were from medium tariff hotels.

Factor Analysis

The overall mean value of all 23 statements was 3.64, with 0.38 standard deviation. This implies that most respondents perceived these 23 statements as being of moderate importance in general. The perceived importance of the 23 statements was factor-analyzed, using principle component analysis with orthogonal Varimax rotation to determine the underlying dimensions (see Table 26.2). Prior to factor analysis, the Kaiser-Meyer-Oklin (KMO) measure of sampling adequacy and the Bartlett test of sphericity were pursued to test the fitness of the data. The KMO was 0.776, which was greater than 0.5. The Bartlett test of sphericity was found to be 945.834, with significance lower than 0.000. Both statistical data supported the use of factor analysis for these items. "Latent root/eigenvalue" and scree plot were applied as the criteria for selecting the right number of factors (Kim and Mueller, 1994; Hair et al., 1995; Norusis, 1994).

This research does not intend to test the fitness of Hofstede's VSM model, instead it concentrates on the discovery of underlying dimensions of work values only. Pursuant to the results of the factor analysis, this study successfully identified the underlying dimensions of hotel Chinese restaurant managers' work values. The following five factors were derived:

- *Factor 1:* "Congenial job context" (eigenvalue = 5.64, alpha reliability = 0.71).
- *Factor 2:* "Desirable job content" (eigenvalue = 1.67, alpha reliability = 0.69).
- *Factor 3:* "Job status and prospect" (eigenvalue = 1.55, alpha reliability = 0.59).
- *Factor 4:* "Self-fulfillment and accountability" (eigenvalue = 1.47, alpha reliability = 0.59).

- *Factor 5:* "Confucian work dynamism" (eigenvalue = 1.28, alpha reliability = 0.60).

Five Underlying Factors

Factor 1, congenial job content, consists of five statements. They all deal with the environment or job context in which the job is performed (Schuler, 1998). This group of hotel Chinese restaurant managers valued the social and organizational working environment if their superiors could allow them to have considerable job freedom, decision-making participation, good superiors and peer cooperation, real contribution to company success, and little tension and stress. The hotel Chinese restaurant managers think that it is "very important" if the management could provide them with the aforementioned pleasant working environment.

Factor 2, desirable job content, attained the highest mean value (mean value = 3.95) among all the five identified factors. It consists of four statements, and they all share one common characteristic in that they all have direct relation with the physical aspects or job content of a job (Thomason, 1981). Hotel Chinese restaurant managers extremely valued having a job that can provide them with high job security, good physical working conditions, high earnings, and sufficient time left for personal or family life. One should not confuse the physical working conditions with the pleasant working environment of Factor 1, which is only concerned with the social and organizational working environment of a job. Physical working conditions were considered as an element job content, because it spells out the physical conditions of the job to be performed, e.g., temperature and location, etc.

Factor 3, job status and prospects, had a mean value of 3.63, which was ranked third among the five factors. These three statements divulge two job expectations of the hotel Chinese restaurant managers. Job variety and adventure will enrich the managers' skills, knowledge, and experience, so that they are more adapt in handling higher levels of jobs. Furthermore, with the enhanced skills, knowledge, and experience, these might facilitate the managers to acquire a better job in prestigious hotels and create a better personal profile in the industry.

TABLE 26.2. Factor analysis with Varimax rotation and reliability analysis of the work values of hotels' Chinese restaurant managers in Hong Kong (n = 152)

Attributes	Mean	Factor loading	Factor and overall mean	Cumulative variance
Have considerable freedom to adopt you own approach to the job?	3.75	0.73	*Factor 1:* Congenial job context 3.65	24.54
Be consulted by your direct superior in his/her decisions?	3.58	0.67		
Work with people who cooperate well with one another?	3.91	0.63		
Make a real contribution to the success of your company or organization	3.80	0.55		
Have little tension and stress on the job?	3.20	0.50		
Have sufficient time left for your personal or family life?	3.47	0.72	*Factor 2:* Desirable job content 3.95	31.79
Have security of employment?	4.30	0.67		
Have good physical working conditions (good ventilation and lighting, adequate workspace, etc.)?	4.04	0.66		
Have an opportunity for high earning?	3.97	0.50		
Have an element of variety and adventure in the job?	3.49	0.70	*Factor 3:* Job status and prospect 3.63	38.54
Have an opportunity for advancement to higher level jobs?	4.03	0.67		
Work in a prestigious, successful company or organization?	3.38	0.63		
Have challenging tasks to do, from which you can get a personal sense of accomplishment?	3.66	0.75	*Factor 4:* Self-fulfillment and accountability 3.60	44.92
Have an opportunity for helping other people?	3.51	0.62		
Have a sense of shame for falling in achieving the requirements of your job?	3.63	0.56		

Attributes	Mean	Factor loading	Factor and overall mean	Cumulative variance
Have an opportunity for protecting your "face"?	3.22	0.74	*Factor 5:* Confucian work dynamism 3.35	50.47
Have an element of non-competitiveness in the job?	3.09	0.69		
Live in an area desirable to you and your family?	3.74	0.50		

Notes: (1) The overall mean value of all 23 statements was 3.64, with standard deviation 0.38. (2) Statement: "Have a good working relationship with your direct superior" was originally loaded into Factor 2. This statement was not selected for Factor 2 because it has a factor loading of 0.39 which was lower than 0.50. (3) Statement: "Have a situation of ordering relationship by status and observing this order" was originally loaded into Factor 3. This statement was not selected for Factor 3 because it has a factor loading of 0.29 which was lower than 0.50. (4) Statement: "Serve your country" was loaded into Factor 6 alone. Although its factor loading was 0.86 with eigenvalue at 1.14 and holds 5.0 per cent of variance, it was not selected as an independent factor with only single item. (5) Statement: "Have loyalty to superiors:" was originally loaded into Factor 7. This statement was not selected for Factor 7 because it has a factor loading of 0.46 which was lower than 0.50. (6) Statement: "Work in a well-defined job situation where the requirements are clear" was loaded into Factor 7 alone. Although its factor loading was 0.83 with eigenvalue at 1.10 and holds 4.7 per cent of variance, it was not selected as an independent factor with single item. Statements derived from Chinese value survey.

Factor 4, self-fulfillment and accountability, had a mean value of 3.6. The similarity of these three statements is that they all exhibit the desire of the managers for self-development. This self-development has both intrinsic and extrinsic aspects. Two of the statements in Factor 4 were belonging to intrinsic attribute, that is, sense of achievement, and sense of shame, whereas the other statement concerns helping other people, and was an example of extrinsic attribute. It is commonly believed that Hong Kong people will prefer devoting more time to achieve their much desired economic rewards rather than spending time in augmenting their psychological health. Maslow (1954) states that people will opt out of the self-development until the lower level needs are fulfilled. Perhaps this is the reason why this factor attained a fairly low ranking compared to the previous three factors.

Finally, Factor 5, Confucian work dynamism, achieved the lowest mean value (mean value = 3.35) in comparison with the other four identified factors. The three positively loaded statements reflect Confucian work ethics that are germane to social hierarchy, protecting the status quo, and to personal virtue (Bond, 1987), for example, attaching importance to the family, respect for tradition with a strong desire to save "face," and noncompetitiveness, etc. It is not surprising to find that all hotel Chinese restaurant managers regarded the Confucian work dynamism as moderately important.

Hong Kong people's lives have been influenced by the former British government in many aspects, including traditional Chinese values, by virtue of education and business. Some traditional Chinese values were not perceived as important by the Hong Kong people, for instance, loyalty to superiors and serving one's country, etc. The impact of Western capitalism and colonialism explains the reason why this factor attained the lowest ranking among all of the five factors.

After analyzing the overall mean value of these five factors, all the hotel Chinese restaurant managers ranked Factor 2, desirable job content, as the most important factor among all of the five identified factors. The results of this study confirm those of Chau (1977), Mok and Finley (1986), and Mok et al. (1998), who discovered that Hong Kong workers in general, and hospitality workers in particular, put great emphasis on monetary rewards. By the time this research was launched, Hong Kong was confronting a serious economic downturn. Many hotels had to adopt a strategy of cutbacks and retrenchment in order to sustain their competitive advantage in the sluggish market. Many hotel employees were laid off by various hotels. These kinds of cutbacks and retrenchment strategies have created a threatening effect on the hotel employees.

The Impact of Demographic Factors on the Five Identified Dimensions

In order to gain a better understanding of the significance of these five identified factors germane to different demographic variables, independent t-test and ANOVA (analysis of variance) were conducted (see Table 26.3). Two significant findings were found in analyzing

TABLE 26.3. Summary of Hotels' Chinese Restaurant Managers' Demographic Impacts on Five Factors Identified by Independent T-Test and ANOVA Analysis

Demographic variable	Valid n	Factor 1 Congenial job context		Factor 2 Desirable job content		Factor 3 Job status and prospect		Factor 4 Self-fulfillment and accountability		Factor 5 Confucian work dynamism	
		Mean	F-value	Mean	F-value	Mean	F-value	Mean	F-value	Mean	F-value
Gender			0.18*		3.46		3.54		0.06		0.08
Male	133	3.69		3.98		3.64		3.61		3.37	
Female	19	3.36		3.74		3.56		3.49		3.23	
Age			1.58		1.17		0.48		0.93		0.48
Under 35	59	3.71		4.04		3.69		3.66		3.34	
35-39	41	3.70		3.89		3.59		3.63		3.43	
Above 39	52	3.55		3.88		3.60		3.51		3.30	
Number of years in attaining education			3.21		6.35**		8.27**		6.18**		0.72
11 years or fewer	41	3.48		3.70		3.44		3.35		3.25	
12-13 years	65	3.68		3.97		3.55		3.62		3.41	
14 years or more	46	3.75		4.13		3.92		3.78		3.36	
Length of service in present hotel			1.21		1.18		0.31		0.01		0.00
Fewer than 3 years	40	3.60		3.99		3.70		3.58		3.35	
3-5 years	50	3.59		3.84		3.61		3.60		3.35	
More than 5 years	62	3.73		4.00		3.61		3.60		3.35	

TABLE 26.3 *(continued)*

Demographic variable	Valid *n*	Factor 1 Congenial job context		Factor 2 Desirable job content		Factor 3 Job status and prospect		Factor 4 Self-fulfillment and accountability		Factor 5 Confucian work dynamism	
		Mean	F-value	Mean	F-value	Mean	F-value	Mean	F-value	Mean	F-value
Length of service in Chinese restaurant industry			2.01		0.27		1.01		2.40		0.88
Fewer than 6 years	54	3.60		3.94		3.63		3.62		3.39	
6-10 years	44	3.58		3.90		3.54		3.44		3.24	
More than 10 years	54	3.76		3.99		3.72		3.70		3.40	
Kind of work			0.47		7.77		7.07		2.74		9.38
Manager	105	3.70		4.00		3.62		3.63		3.37	
Manager of other managers	47	3.54		3.81		3.67		3.53		3.31	
Type of hotel			0.73		2.36		2.14		2.94		2.25
High tariff A	65	3.71		4.04		3.75		3.72		3.42	
High tariff B	58	3.60		3.81		3.52		3.47		3.21	
Medium tariff	29	3.63		4.00		3.60		3.57		3.47	

Notes: *denotes significance level < 0.05; **denotes significance level < 0.01

different demographic variables against the five identified factors. First of all, in the aspect of gender, female hotel Chinese restaurant managers scored significantly lower than male hotel Chinese restaurant managers in terms of Factor 1, congenial job context. Female hotel Chinese restaurant managers perceived that congenial job context has lesser importance compared with male ratings. Traditionally, the "Li" concept, which is defined as the rules of correct behavior entailing both rights and responsibilities for all Chinese people (Bond and Hwang, 1986), led to the development of a management style in China known as "rule by man" (Jacobs et al., 1995). Because of the long domination of Confucianism, rule by man has prevailed. Man plays a dominant role in both society and family, while woman should follow the instruction given by man. Thus, under this construction, women are endowed with the "communal" virtues of kindness and consideration, but also with the deficits of subjectivity, unpredictability, and weakness (Bond, 1991). This structure gradually developed into a tradition that still exists in China and Hong Kong. For the Chinese restaurant industry in Hong Kong, particularly in the hotel field, the majority of the managerial positions are still dominated by male managers. Female managers tend to adopt a rather passive attitude by accepting the adversity philosophically; hence, they seldom play an active role in striving for their own fate, such as job freedom, participation in decision making, and peer cooperation.

Moreover, this group of hotel Chinese restaurant managers believed that when they exerted more time in attaining education, the more important Factor 2, desirable job content; Factor 3, job status and prospect; and Factor 4, self-fulfillment and accountability, will become. In the Hong Kong situation, all people perceive that the more years of education they receive, the better job they can get in terms of salary, job status, and personal sense of achievement. Since most of them only attained secondary education (i.e., thirteen years of education) in Hong Kong, hotel Chinese restaurant managers think that if they could spend more time on attaining a higher education, this will help them obtain better job status and prospects in the future, particularly in the hotel environment in Hong Kong.

On the other hand, it is interesting to discover that no significant differences were found in the five identified factors in relation to other demographic variables, such as age, length of service in present hotel, length of service in Chinese restaurant industry, kind of work, and type of hotel. All the hotel Chinese restaurant managers possess the same view in rating all these five factors as of "moderate importance" to them. In the field of Chinese restaurant industry in Hong Kong, it is not uncommon that Chinese restaurant personnel have to work in a junior position for quite a long period of time to gain work experience before they can attain a managerial position in any type of Chinese restaurant. Perhaps this may explain the reason why all of these hotel Chinese restaurant managers hold a united perspective in relation to these factors.

CONCLUSIONS AND RECOMMENDATIONS

Pursuant to the results of this research are a few notable points that might be worth contemplation by the senior executives of the hospitality companies. In most Western cultures, for example, managerial individual initiative and achievement is rewarded and encouraged, whereas managers in many Asian organizations must seek consensus before acting, and team commitment and cooperation are foundation principles of management. As women will likely become the major labor workforce in the future (Hotel and Catering International Management Association, 1999), hotel senior management of multinational companies should consider providing targeted training, for example, assertiveness training, and management courses for woman awareness. Moreover, hotel senior management could also develop positive female role models to act as mentors for younger women. The purpose of these human resources strategic plans is to enhance the managerial competence of those female managers to cope with the practices of those multinational hotel companies as well as the challenge of the new millennium.

On the other hand, it is interesting to discover that no significant difference was found in hotel Chinese restaurant managers from different types of hotels in relation to the demographic variables. In other words, it is believed that the values of Chinese restaurant managers do not change, irrespective of the ranking of the hotel they work in.

Although this sample of managers perceived that a better education qualification would help them achieve a better job prospect, it seems that scarcely any formal vocational education and technical training system is established to meet the long-desired need of the Chinese restaurant personnel in the Chinese restaurant industry, especially in Hong Kong. Consequently, the Chinese restaurant managers may confront difficulties in enhancing their professional status in the Chinese food-service field even though they have such professional skills. There is an immediate need for relevant catering institutions to launch a systematic Chinese food service training course for the Chinese food service personnel to acquire the knowledge and skills of this profession. Overseas institutions could also collaborate with mainland China colleges to offer accredited Chinese food service courses for the overseas food-service personnel. The collaboration with overseas institutions will not only augment the professional status of Chinese food service in a broader perspective, but will also promote the Chinese cuisine worldwide. The recent establishment of the Chinese Cuisine Training Institute in Hong Kong indicates the determination of the Hong Kong Special Administrative Region in nurturing Chinese cuisine both locally and internationally.

Ultimately, this research revealed that Hong Kong Chinese managers may have a change in value system, with Factor 5, Confucian work dynamism, being the lowest among all five factors. It may be due to the special result of the Hong Kong "East Meets West" phenomenon: Hong Kong Chinese, born in Hong Kong, with traditional Chinese culture but educated in the British system. This longitudinal training makes the work value system changes.

This is only a first step in a much-needed series of steps that systematically explores the work values of Chinese restaurant managers in hotel environment. Further study is needed to test the positive results found here and to develop further understanding of the Chinese food service personnel's work values of other places, for instance, in China, Taiwan, and Macau.

REFERENCES

Bond, M.H. (1987). Chinese culture connection: Chinese values and the search for culture-free dimensions of culture. *Journal of Cross-Cultural Psychology, 18:* 143-164.

Bond, M.H. (1991). *Beyond the Chinese Face.* Hong Kong: Oxford University Press.

Bond, M.H. and Hwang, K.K. (1986). The social psychology of Chinese people. In Bond, M.H. (ed.), *The Psychology of the Chinese People* (pp. 195-200). Hong Kong: Oxford University Press.

Chau, T. (1977). Workers' attitudes in Hong Kong: A comparison with other countries. *The Hong Kong Manager,* September: 8-13.

Chinese food wins McDonald's food (2001). *Apple Daily,* November 13, p. A16.

Collins, G. and Williams, M. (2000). Racial diversity is rare for waiters in elite restaurants. *The New York Times,* May 30, p. B1.

Dillon, L.S. (1999). The occidental tourist. *Training & Development Journal,* 44(5): 72-80.

Dowling, P., Schuler, R. and Welch, D. (1994). *International Dimension's of Human Resource Management,* Belmont, CA: Wadsworth.

George, R.T. (2001). Dining Chinese: A consumer subgroup comparison. *Journal of Restaurant and Foodservice Marketing, 4*(2): 67-86.

Gliatis, N. and Guerrier, Y. (1993). Managing international career moves in international hotel companies. *Progress in Tourism, Recreation and Hospitality Management, 5:* 229-241.

Go, F. and Pine, R. (1995). *Globalization Strategy in the International Hotel Industry.* London, UK: Routledge.

Hair, J.F. Jr, Anderson, R.L., Tatham, R.E., and Black, W.C. (1995). *Multivariate Data Analysis with Readings,* 4th edition. New York: Prentice-Hall.

Hoecklin, L. (1995). *Managing Cultural Differences: Strategies for Competitive Advantage.* London, UK: Addison-Wesley.

Hofstede, G. (1980a). *Cultural Consequences: International Differences in Work-Related Values.* Newbury Park, CA: Sage.

Hofstede, G. (1980b). Motivation, leadership, and organization: Do American theories apply abroad? *Organizational Dynamics,* Summer: 42-63.

Hofstede, G. and Bond, M.H. (1984). Hofstede's culture dimensions: An independent validation using Rokeach's value survey. *Journal of Cross-Cultural Psychology, 15:* 417-433.

Hofstede, G. and Bond, M.H. (1988). The Confucius connection: From cultural roots to economic growth. *Organization Dynamics, 16*(4): 4-21.

Hotel and Catering International Management Association (1999). *Managing diversity: An age diverse workforce.* Management brief No. 6. Surrey, UK: HCIMA.

Hong Kong Tourist Association (1999). *Hotel Supply Situation,* No. 2. Hong Kong: HKTA.

Hsu, F.L.K. (1970). *American and Chinese: Passage to Differences,* 3rd edition. Honolulu, HI: University Press of Hawaii.

International foods: Indian cuisine takes no. 1 spot in the UK (2001). *Retail World,* August 6-17, p. 24.

Jacobs, L., Gao, G., and Herbig, P. (1995). Confucian roosts in China: A face for today's business. *Management Decision, 33*(10): 29-34.

Kalleberg, A.L. (1977). Work values and job rewards: A theory of job satisfaction. *American Sociological Review, 42*(1): 124-143.

Kanchier, C. and Wally, R.U. (1989). Factors influencing career change, *International Journal for the Achievement of Counseling, 12*(4): 309-321.

Kim, J.O. and Mueller, C. (1994). *Factor Analysis: Statistical Methods and Practical Issues.* In Michael, S.L. (ed.), *Factor Analysis and Related Techniques* (pp.). Newbury Park, CA: Sage.

Kindle, I. (1982). Chinese consumer behavior: Historical perspective plus an update on communication hypotheses. In Sheth, J. and Tan, C.T. (eds.), *Historical Perspectives of Consumer Behavior.* Singapore: National University of Singapore and Association for Consumer Behavior.

Lai, T. and Lam, Y. (1986). A study on work-related values of managers in the people's republic of china (Part 1). *The Hong Kong Manager,* January: 23-59.

Li, Y.Y. (2001). Foreword. In Wu, Y.H. and Tan, C.B. (eds.), *Changing Chinese Foodways in Asia* (pp. vii-xiii). Hong Kong: The Chinese University Press.

Littlejohn, D. (1997). Internationalization in hotels: Current aspects and developments. *International Journal of Contemporary Hospitality Management, 9*(5/6): 187-192.

Loscocco, K. (1989). The instrumentally oriented factory worker: Myth or reality? *Work and Occupations, 16*(1): 3-25.

Maslow, A. (1954). *Motivation and Personality.* New York: Harper & Row.

Meglino, B.M., Ravlin, E.C., and Adkins, C.L. (1989). A work values approach to corporate culture: A field test of the value congruence process and its relationship to individual outcomes, *Journal of Applied Psychology, 74*(3): 424-432.

Mok, C. and Finley, D. (1986). Job satisfaction and its relationship to demographics and turnover of hotel food-service workers in Hong Kong. *International Journal of Hospitality Management, 5*(2): 71-78.

Mok, C., Pine, R., and Pizam, A. (1998). Work values of Chinese hotel managers. *Journal of Hospitality & Tourism Research, 21*(3): 1-16.

Morgan, W. (1971). The sensitivity of managers to the attitudes of non-supervisory food service workers and its effect upon the attraction and retention of industry workers. Unpublished doctoral thesis, Cornell University, Ithaca, NY.

Mottaz, C. (1986). Gender differences in work satisfaction, work-related rewards and values, and the determinants of work satisfaction. *Human Relations, 39*(4): 359-77.

Mottaz, C. (1988). Determinants of organizational commitment. *Human Relations, 41*(6): 467-482.

Mullins, L. (1985). Management and managerial behavior. *International Journal of Hospitality Management, 4*(1): 39-41.

Norusis, M.J. (1994). *SPSS Professional Statistics 6.1.* Chicago, IL: SPSS Inc.

Overstall, O. (1997). Benchmarking expatriate policy? In *HR Director: The Arthur Andersen Guide to Human Capital* (Spring/Summer). London, UK: Profile Pursuit.

Pinfield, L.T. (1984). A comparison of pre- and post-employment work values. *Journal of Management, 10*(3): 363-370.

Pizam, A. (1993). Managing cross-cultural hospitality enterprises. In Jones, P. and Pizam, A. (eds.), *The International Hospitality Industry: Organizational and Operational Issues*. New York: John Wiley.

Powers, T.F. (1992). Managing international hospitality. *FIU Hospitality Journal, 1:* 25-34.

Ralston, D.A., Gustafson, D.J., David, J., Cheung, F. and Terpstra, R.H. (1999). Differences in managerial values: A study of the US, Hong Kong and the PRC managers. *Journal of International Business Studies, 3:* 249-275.

Ralston, D.A., Gustafson, D.J., Elsass, P.M., Cheung, F., and Terpstra, R.H. (1992). Eastern values: A comparison of managers in the United States, Hong Kong, and the people's republic of China. *Journal of Applied Psychology, 77*: 664-671.

Redding, G.S. (1984). Varieties of the iron rice bowl. *The Hong Kong Manager,* May: 11-15.

Rokeach, M. (1973). *The Nature of Human Values*. New York: Free Press.

Schuler, R.S. (1998). *Managing Human Resources*, 6th edition. Cincinatti, OH: South-Western College Publishing.

Shay, J. and Tracey, B. (1997). Expatriate managers: Reasons for failure and implications for training. *Cornell Hotel and Restaurant Administration Quarterly,* 38(1): 30.

Siu, V., Tsang, N., and Wong, S. (1997). What motivates Hong Kong's hotel employee? *Cornell Hotel and Restaurant Administration Quarterly, 38*(5): 44-49.

Spinale, J. (1980). How to stop supervisors from sabotaging your training efforts. *Training, 17*(3): 48-50.

Tanner, S. and Tucker, A. (1996). All of the best and none of the worst of Hong Kong. *Forbes (FYI Supplement), 23* (September): 174-182.

Thomas, D. (1999). Cultural diversity and work group effectiveness: An experimental study. *Journal of Cross-cultural Psychology,* March, pp. 242-263.

Thomason, G. (1981). *A Textbook of Personnel Management*, 4th edition. London, UK: Institute of Personnel Management.

Tung, R.L. and Miller, E.L. (1990). Managing in the twenty-first century: The need for global orientation. *Management International Review, 31:* 5-18.

Walker, J.E., Tausky, C., and Oliver, D. (1982). Men and women at work: Similarities and differences in work values within occupational grouping. *Journal of Vocational Behavior, 21:* 7-36.

Wood, J., Wallace, J., and Zeffanc, R.M. (2000). *Organizational behavior: A global perspective,* 2nd edition. Singapore: John Wiley & Sons.

Yu, W.Y. and Pine, R. (1994). Attitudes of Hong Kong hotel managers towards the use of expatriates. *International Journal of Hospitality Management, 13*(2): 183-187.

Index

Page numbers followed by the letter "b" indicate boxed exhibits; those followed by the letter "i" indicate illustrations; those followed by the letter "t" indicate tables.

Global Cases on Hospitality Industry
© 2008 by The Haworth Press, Taylor & Francis Group. All rights reserved.
doi:10.1300/5923_27